IoT, Smart Cities, and Big Data Symposium

Shensheng Tang	Missouri Western State U
Wee Peng Tay	Nanyang Technological U
Rong Yu	Guangdong University of Technology,

Security Symposium

Qing Yang	Montana State University, USA
Yi Qian	University of Nebraska Lincoln, USA
Jun Huang	Chongqing University of Posts and Telecommunications, China

Technical Program Committee

Rong Chai	Chongqing University of Posts and Telecommunications, China
Hongbin Chen	Guilin University of Electronic Technology, China
Zhi Chen	University of Electronic Science and Technology of China
Peter Chong	Nanyang Technological University, Singapore
Dezun Dong	National University of Defense Technology, China
Wei Dong	Zhejiang University, China
Jun Fang	University of Electronic Science and Technology of China
Zesong Fei	Beijing Institute of Technology, China
Feifei Gao	Tsinghua University, China
Ping Guo	Chongqing University, China
Guoqiang Hu	Nanyang Technological University, Singapore
Tao Huang	Beijing University of Posts and Telecommunications, China
Xiaoge Huang	Chongqing University of Posts and Telecommunications, China
Fan Li	Beijing Institute of Technology, China
Zhenyu Li	Institute of Computing Technology, Chinese Academy of Sciences, China
Hongbo Liu	Indiana University-Purdue University Indianapolis, USA
Hongqing Liu	Chongqing University of Posts and Telecommunications, China
Jiang Liu	Beijing University of Posts and Telecommunications, China
Qiang Liu	University of Electronic Science and Technology of China, China
Wenping Liu	Hubei University of Economic, China
Rongxing Lu	Nanyang Technological University, Singapore
Yilin Mo	Nanyang Technological University, Singapore
Jianquan Ouyang	Xiangtan University, China
Tian Pan	Beijing University of Posts and Telecommunications, China

Contents – Part II

Network Architecture and SDN

Signal Detection and Estimation (2)

Heterogeneous Networks

Internet of Things

Hardware Design and Implementation

Mobility Management

SDN and Clouds

Navigation, Tracking and Localization

FMN

Contents –Part I

System Performance Evaluation and Enhancement

Optical Systems and Networks

Signal Detection and Estimation (2)

Energy Harvesting Systems

Energy-Efficient Resource Allocation in Energy Harvesting Communication Systems: A Heuristic Algorithm

Yisheng Zhao[✉], Zhonghui Chen, Yiwen Xu, and Hongan Wei

College of Physics and Information Engineering, Fuzhou University,
Fuzhou, People's Republic of China
{zhaoys,czh,xu_yiwen,weihongan}@fzu.edu.cn

Abstract. Harvesting energy from the environment is a method to improve the energy utilization efficiency. However, most renewable energy has a poor stability due to the weather and the climate. The reliability of the communication systems will be influenced to a large extent. In this paper, an energy-efficient downlink resource allocation problem is investigated in the energy harvesting communication systems by exploiting wireless power transfer technology. The resource allocation problem is formulated as a mixed-integer nonlinear programming problem. The objective is to maximize the energy efficiency while satisfying the energy causality and the data rate requirement of each user. In order to reduce the computational complexity, a suboptimal solution to the optimization problem is obtained by employing a quantum-behaved particle swarm optimization (QPSO) algorithm. Simulation results show that the QPSO algorithm has a higher energy efficiency than the traditional particle swarm optimization (PSO) algorithm.

Keywords: Energy harvesting communication · Resource allocation · Heuristic algorithm

1 Introduction

Green communication is an attractive solution to improve the energy utilization efficiency of communication systems. Resource management strategies such as power control and resource allocation are effective measures to save energy, which can minimize the total transmission power and maximize the system throughput, respectively. In addition, energy harvesting communication is an emerging trend of green communication [1]. It can provide electrical energy for communication equipments by collecting renewable energy such as solar energy and wind energy from the surroundings, which can significantly reduce energy consumption.

Energy harvesting communication has recently attracted extensive research attention. The stochastic characteristic of energy harvesting was taken into account in [2]. An optimal power policy was proposed, which can maximize the average throughput under additive white Gaussian noise channel. The authors of

© ICST Institute for Computer Sciences, Social Informatics and Telecommunications Engineering 2018
Q. Chen et al. (Eds.): ChinaCom 2016, Part II, LNICST 210, pp. 3–12, 2018.
DOI: 10.1007/978-3-319-66628-0_1

[3] presented an optimum transmission policy under the constraints of the energy storage and the energy causality. It was shown that the proposed transmission policy could maximize the short-term throughput of an energy harvesting node. The optimal packet scheduling problem in a single-user communication scenario with an energy harvesting transmitter was investigated in [4]. The goal was minimize the transmission time by adaptively changing the transmission rate according to the traffic load and available energy. In [5], for single-user Gaussian channel and two-user Gaussian multiple access channel, two online algorithms for minimizing packet transmission time were developed, respectively. In two-hop communication systems with an energy harvesting source and a non-energy harvesting relay, the joint time scheduling and power allocation problem was discussed in [6]. The objectives of short-term throughput maximization and transmission time minimization were both taken into consideration. An optimal power allocation strategy was explored in energy harvesting and power grid coexisting wireless communication systems [7]. The optimization problem was formulated as minimizing the grid power consumption with random energy and data arrival. The optimal solution was obtained by the Lagrangian multiplier method.

However, there still exist a series of challenges for energy harvesting communication. Most renewable energy has a poor stability due to the weather and the climate, which will bring about serious effect on the communication system performance. Moreover, because the capacity of the existing energy storage device is limited, the restriction of limited energy should be taken into account. Wireless power transfer technology [8,9] can provide electrical power for communication equipments by harvesting energy from the electromagnetic wave. It is able to overcome the disadvantage of the renewable energy that is easily affected by the climate change, which is a promising solution to energy harvesting communication. Therefore, there is a strong motivation to investigate the resource allocation problem in the energy harvesting communication systems using wireless power transfer technology.

In this paper, we propose an energy-efficient resource allocation strategy in the energy harvesting communication systems. Specifically, an energy-efficient downlink resource allocation problem is investigated in the wireless power transfer systems. The objective is to maximize the energy efficiency under the constraints of the energy causality and the data rate requirement of each user. The formulated optimization problem is a mixed-integer nonlinear programming problem, which is difficult to derive the optimal solution. In order to degrade the computational complexity, a quantum-behaved particle swarm optimization (QPSO) algorithm is exploited to solve the optimization problem. A suboptimal solution is obtained with an acceptable complexity.

2   System Model and Problem Formulation

The network architecture of wireless power transfer systems is shown in Fig. 1. The scenario of one base station and multiple users are taken into account. The base station is provided with electrical energy by the traditional power grid.

Each user is equipped with an energy harvesting equipment, which can harvest energy from the eletromagnetic wave in the surrounding environment. When the base station sends data to an active user, other idle users can harvest energy from the received eletromagnetic wave. The collected energy is stored in the energy storage device, which is used to communicate with the base station at a certain time in the future.

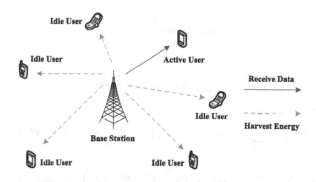

Fig. 1. Network architecture of wireless power transfer systems.

Energy-efficient downlink resource allocation problem is investigated in the above wireless power transfer systems. It is assumed that the base station sends data to K users by N sub-carriers during T time slots. Meanwhile, only one user can communicate with the base station at the t-th time slot, which is denoted by a binary variable $\delta_{t,k} \in \{0,1\}$. Moreover, $p_{t,n,k}$ indicates the transmission power for the k-th user on the n-th sub-carrier at the t-th time slot. The system capacity can be obtained by the following expression:

$$C_{total} = \sum_{t=1}^{T}\sum_{n=1}^{N}\sum_{k=1}^{K} \delta_{t,k} W \log_2 \left(1 + \frac{p_{t,n,k}h_{t,n,k}^2}{N_0 W}\right), \tag{1}$$

where W is the sub-carrier bandwidth, $h_{t,n,k}$ denotes the channel gain for the k-th user on the n-th sub-carrier at the t-th time slot, and N_0 represents the power spectral density of additive white Gaussian noise. At the same time, system energy consumption per second is shown as:

$$E_{total} = P_C + \sum_{t=1}^{T}\sum_{n=1}^{N}\sum_{k=1}^{K} \delta_{t,k} p_{t,n,k} - P_H, \tag{2}$$

where P_C denotes the circuit energy consumption per second and P_H indicates the energy harvested by idle users per second. The specific expression of P_H is denoted as:

$$P_H = \sum_{t=1}^{T}\sum_{n=1}^{N}\sum_{k=1}^{K} \delta_{t,k} p_{t,n,k} \left(\sum_{j \neq k} \eta h_{t,n,j}^2\right), \tag{3}$$

where η indicates the energy harvesting efficiency of the idle user. Here, for simplicity, we assume that each idle user has the equal energy harvesting efficiency. Moreover, $h_{t,n,j}$ represents the channel gain for the j-th idle user on the n-th sub-carrier at the t-th time slot.

The objective of resource allocation problem is to maximize the energy efficiency while satisfying several constraint conditions. This is an optimization problem, which can be formulated as follows:

$$\underset{\delta_{t,k}, p_{t,n,k}}{\text{maximize}} \frac{C_{total}}{E_{total}}, \tag{4a}$$

$$C1: \sum_{n=1}^{N}\sum_{k=1}^{K} \delta_{t,k} p_{t,n,k} \leq P_{\max}, \forall t, \tag{4b}$$

$$C2: \sum_{n=1}^{N}\sum_{j=1}^{K} \delta_{t,j} p_{t,n,j} \left(\eta h_{t,n,k}^2 \right) \geq (1 - \delta_{t,k}) P_k^{\min}, \forall t, k, \tag{4c}$$

$$C3: \sum_{t=1}^{T}\sum_{n=1}^{N} \delta_{t,k} W \log_2 \left(1 + \frac{p_{t,n,k} h_{t,n,k}^2}{N_0 W} \right) \geq R_k^{\min}, \forall k, \tag{4d}$$

$$C4: \delta_{t,k} \in \{0, 1\}, \forall t, k, \tag{4e}$$

$$C5: \sum_{k=1}^{K} \delta_{t,k} \leq 1, \forall t, \tag{4f}$$

$$C6: p_{t,n,k} \geq 0, \forall t, n, k, \tag{4g}$$

where the objective function is the energy efficiency and its unit is bits per Joule (bits/J). The first constraint indicates that the total transmission power in the base station is limited to the maximum power $P_{\max}$. The second constraint ensures that the energy harvested by the k-th idle user at the t-th time slot is no less than the minimum value $P_k^{\min}$, which is called the energy causality. The third constraint guarantees that the data rate of the k-th user is greater than or equal to the minimum value $R_k^{\min}$. The fourth and fifth constraints show that the base station only sends data to one user at the t-th time slot. The sixth constraint reveals that the transmission power in the base station is nonnegative. It is noted that the objective function is nonlinear. Besides, the values of $\delta_{t,k}$ and $p_{t,n,k}$ are discrete and continuous, respectively. As a consequence, the above optimization problem is a mixed-integer nonlinear programming problem.

3   Suboptimal Solution to Resource Allocation Optimization Problem

The optimization problem in (4) is quite difficult to obtain a globally optimal solution with a low computational complexity. Therefore, a heuristic algorithm is used to derive a suboptimal solution with an acceptable complexity.

The QPSO algorithm [10,11] is adopted to solve the optimization problem in (4). The QPSO algorithm is an improved version of the traditional PSO algorithm [12]. Compared with the PSO algorithm, it can achieve a globally suboptimal solution. The PSO algorithm is easy to fall into a locally optimal solution. The original constrained optimization problem needs to be transformed to an unconstrained form, which can be done by the penalty function method. Thus, a fitness function that consists of one objective function and one penalty function is constructed as follows:

$$F\left(\delta_{t,k}, p_{t,n,k}\right) = f\left(\delta_{t,k}, p_{t,n,k}\right) - \alpha P_f\left(\delta_{t,k}, p_{t,n,k}\right), \tag{5}$$

where $f\left(\delta_{t,k}, p_{t,n,k}\right)$ is the objective function, α denotes the penalty factor, and $P_f\left(\delta_{t,k}, p_{t,n,k}\right)$ indicates the penalty function that includes six items:

$$P_f\left(\delta_{t,k}, p_{t,n,k}\right) = P_f^1 + P_f^2 + P_f^3 + P_f^4 + P_f^5 + P_f^6. \tag{6}$$

They are corresponding to six constraints of the optimization problem in (4), which are shown as:

$$P_f^1 = \sum_{t=1}^{T}\left[\max\left(0, \sum_{n=1}^{N}\sum_{k=1}^{K}\delta_{t,k}p_{t,n,k} - P_{\max}\right)\right]^2, \tag{7a}$$

$$P_f^2 = \sum_{t=1}^{T}\sum_{k=1}^{K}\left[\max\left(0, A\right)\right]^2, \tag{7b}$$

$$P_f^3 = \sum_{k=1}^{K}\left[\max\left(0, B\right)\right]^2, \tag{7c}$$

$$P_f^4 = \sum_{t=1}^{T}\sum_{k=1}^{K}\left(\delta_{t,k}^2 - \delta_{t,k}\right)^2, \tag{7d}$$

$$P_f^5 = \sum_{t=1}^{T}\left[\max\left(0, \sum_{k=1}^{K}\delta_{t,k} - 1\right)\right]^2, \tag{7e}$$

$$P_f^6 = \sum_{t=1}^{T}\sum_{n=1}^{N}\sum_{k=1}^{K}\left[\max\left(0, -p_{t,n,k}\right)\right]^2, \tag{7f}$$

where $\max\left(\cdot, \cdot\right)$ returns a greater number between two numbers. Moreover, for the A and B in P_f^2 and P_f^3, their expressions are given as:

$$A = \left(1 - \delta_{t,k}\right)P_k^{\min} - \sum_{n=1}^{N}\sum_{j=1}^{K}\delta_{t,j}p_{t,n,j}\left(\eta h_{t,n,k}^2\right), \tag{8}$$

$$B = R_k^{\min} - \sum_{t=1}^{T}\sum_{n=1}^{N}\delta_{t,k}W\log_2\left(1 + \frac{p_{t,n,k}h_{t,n,k}^2}{N_0 W}\right). \tag{9}$$

In order to apply the QPSO algorithm to the formulated optimization problem, resource allocation results of K users are defined as the particle position. We assume that there are M particles in the multi-dimensional space. For the m-th particle, its position vector $\mathbf{X}_m$ can be expressed as:

$$\mathbf{X}_m = \left(\mathbf{X}_m^1, \mathbf{X}_m^2, ..., \mathbf{X}_m^k, ..., \mathbf{X}_m^K \right),$$ (10)

where $\mathbf{X}_m^k$ denotes the resource allocation result of the k-th user. The specific expression of $\mathbf{X}_m^k$ is shown as:

$$\mathbf{X}_m^k = \left(\delta_{1,k}, \delta_{2,k}, ..., \delta_{T,k}, p_{1,1,k}, p_{1,2,k}, ..., p_{T,N,k} \right).$$ (11)

It can be seen that $\mathbf{X}_m^k$ is a multi-dimensional vector. The first T elements indicate the time slot allocation result. The rest TN elements denote power allocation result on different sub-carriers at different time slots.

The position of each particle is updated according to the following iterative equation:

$$\begin{cases} \mathbf{X}_m(s+1) = \mathbf{P} + \beta \left| \mathbf{C}(s) - \mathbf{X}_m(s) \right| \cdot \ln\left(1/u \right), \ r \geq 0.5 \\ \mathbf{X}_m(s+1) = \mathbf{P} - \beta \left| \mathbf{C}(s) - \mathbf{X}_m(s) \right| \cdot \ln\left(1/u \right), \ r < 0.5 \end{cases},$$ (12)

where s denotes the iteration number and the maximum iteration number is S, β is the contraction-expansion coefficient, u and r are both random numbers between 0 and 1, and $\mathbf{C}(s)$ is the mean best position. The value of β in the s-th iteration can be calculated by:

$$\beta = 0.5 \frac{S-s}{S} + 0.5.$$ (13)

In addition, $\mathbf{C}(s)$ can be obtained by:

$$\mathbf{C}(s) = \frac{1}{M} \sum_{m=1}^{M} \mathbf{P}_m(s),$$ (14)

where $\mathbf{P}_m(s)$ is the best position of the m-th particle in the s-th iteration. Based on the fitness function in (5), $\mathbf{P}_m(s)$ can be derived by:

$$\mathbf{P}_m(s) = \begin{cases} \mathbf{X}_m(s), F\left[\mathbf{X}_m(s) \right] > F\left[\mathbf{P}_m(s-1) \right] \\ \mathbf{P}_m(s-1), F\left[\mathbf{X}_m(s) \right] \leq F\left[\mathbf{P}_m(s-1) \right] \end{cases}.$$ (15)

Moreover, the vector $\mathbf{P}$ in (12) is given by the following expression:

$$\mathbf{P} = \varphi \cdot \mathbf{P}_m(s) + (1 - \varphi) \cdot \mathbf{G}(s),$$ (16)

where φ is a random number between 0 and 1, and $\mathbf{G}(s)$ denotes the global best position of all the particles in the s-th iteration. $\mathbf{G}(s)$ can be obtained by:

$$\begin{cases} \xi = \arg \max_{1 \leq m \leq M} \left\{ F\left[\mathbf{P}_m(s) \right] \right\} \\ \mathbf{G}(s) = \mathbf{P}_\xi(s) \end{cases}.$$ (17)

4   Simulation Results and Analysis

In this section, the performance of the proposed resource allocation strategy is evaluated by simulation. The related parameters are set as $T = 5$, $N = 32$, $W = 15$ kHz, $N_0 = 2 \times 10^{-8}$ W/Hz, $P_C = 5$ W, $\alpha = 1.5$, and $S = 10$. Without loss of generality, we assume that the values of $P_k^{\min}$ and $R_k^{\min}$ are 0.1 W and 1 Mbps, respectively. Moreover, the values of different $h_{t,n,k}$ are generated by random numbers with uniform distribution between 0 and 1. In addition, an existing resource allocation algorithm based on particle swarm optimization (PSO) [12] is used for comparison.

Figure 2 presents the relationship between the energy efficiency and the number of particles for different numbers of users under QPSO and PSO algorithms. It can be observed that the energy efficiency increases gradually as the number of particles increases. The reason is that more accurate suboptimal solution can be obtained under more particles. Moreover, for the QPSO algorithm, the energy efficiency increases with the growth of the number of users. This is because more idle users can harvest the energy from the received electromagnetic wave. In addition, the QPSO algorithm has a higher energy efficiency than the PSO algorithm under the same number of users. It can be explained that the QPSO algorithm can obtain a globally suboptimal solution while the PSO algorithm is easy to fall into a locally optimal solution.

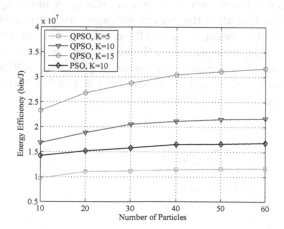

Fig. 2. Energy efficiency versus number of particles with $\eta = 0.1$ and $P_{\max} = 10$ W.

Figure 3 depicts the relationship between the energy efficiency and the number of particles for different energy harvesting efficiency under QPSO and PSO algorithms. For the QPSO algorithm, we can see that the energy efficiency grows with the increase of the energy harvesting efficiency from 0.1 to 0.5. That is because idle users can harvest more energy from the received eletromagnetic wave. Additionally, the QPSO algorithm with $\eta = 0.1$ outperforms the PSO algorithm with $\eta = 0.3$. The reason is that the QPSO algorithm can effectively avoid searching the solution in a local area to a great degree.

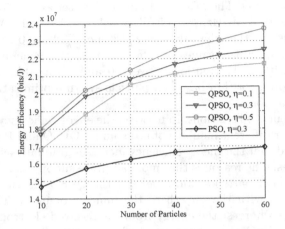

Fig. 3. Energy efficiency versus number of particles with $K = 10$ and $P_{\max} = 10$ W.

Figure 4 illustrates the relationship between the energy efficiency and the number of users for different energy harvesting efficiency under QPSO and PSO algorithms. We can find that the energy efficiency rises up as the number of users increases. That is because more idle users can harvest the energy from the received electromagnetic wave. Furthermore, although $\eta = 0.1$, the QPSO algorithm has a better performance in terms of the energy efficiency than the PSO algorithm with $\eta = 0.3$. The reason is that the PSO algorithm cannot obtain a globally suboptimal solution.

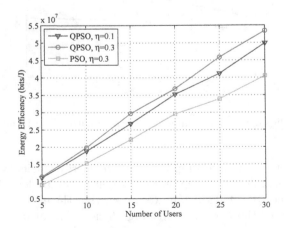

Fig. 4. Energy efficiency versus number of users with $M = 20$ and $P_{\max} = 10$ W.

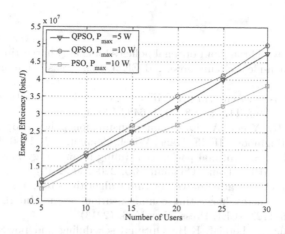

Fig. 5. Energy efficiency versus number of users with $\eta = 0.1$ and $M = 20$.

Figure 5 shows the relationship between the energy efficiency and the number of users for different the maximum power under QPSO and PSO algorithms. It can be seen that the energy efficiency increases with the growth of the maximum power under the QPSO algorithm. It can be explained that the active user can send signal with a higher power. Thus, a higher system capacity can be obtained. At the same time, all the idle users can harvest more energy. In addition, the QPSO algorithm with $P_{max} = 5$ W has a better performance than the PSO algorithm with $P_{max} = 10$ W. This is because the QPSO algorithm can overcome the disadvantage of the PSO algorithm to a large extent.

5   Conclusion

In this paper, an energy-efficient resource allocation problem based on QPSO algorithm was presented in the wireless power transfer systems. The resource allocation problem was formulated as a mixed-integer nonlinear programming problem. The objective was to maximize the energy efficiency under the constraints of the energy causality and the data rate requirement of each user. Moreover, the suboptimal solution to the formulated optimization problem was derived by introducing the QPSO algorithm. The proposed resource allocation strategy has a higher energy efficiency by the simulation evaluation. For simplicity, we assume that the base station only sends data to one user at one time slot. Multiple users can be provided service at the same time in the practical communication systems, which will be taken into account in future work.

Acknowledgments. This work is supported in part by the Science and Technology Development Foundation of Fuzhou University (Grant No. 2014-XY-30), the National Natural Science Foundation of China (Grant No. U1405251), the Natural Science Foundation of Fujian Province (Grant No. 2015J05122 and Grant No. 2015J01250), and the Scientific Research Starting Foundation of Fuzhou University (Grant No. 022572).

References

1. Xu, J., Zhang, R.: Throughput optimal policies for energy harvesting wireless transmitters with non-ideal circuit power. IEEE J. Sel. Areas Commun. **32**, 322–332 (2014)
2. Ozel, O., Ulukus, S.: Achieving AWGN capacity under stochastic energy harvesting. IEEE Trans. Inf. Theory **58**, 6471–6483 (2012)
3. Tutuncuoglu, K., Yener, A.: Optimum transmission policies for battery limited energy harvesting nodes. IEEE Trans. Wirel. Commun. **11**, 1180–1189 (2012)
4. Yang, J., Ulukus, S.: Optimal packet scheduling in an energy harvesting communication system. IEEE Trans. Commun. **60**, 220–230 (2012)
5. Vaze, R.: Competitive ratio analysis of online algorithms to minimize packet transmission time in energy harvesting communication system. In: IEEE INFOCOM 2013, pp. 1115–1123. IEEE Press, New York (2013)
6. Luo, Y., Zhang, J., Letaief, K.B.: Optimal scheduling and power allocation for two-hop energy harvesting communication systems. IEEE Trans. Wirel. Commun. **12**, 4729–4741 (2013)
7. Gong, J., Zhou, S., Niu, Z.: Optimal power allocation for energy harvesting and power grid coexisting wireless communication systems. IEEE Trans. Commun. **61**, 3040–3049 (2013)
8. Zhou, X., Zhang, R., Ho, C.K.: Wireless information and power transfer: architecture design and rate-energy tradeoff. IEEE Trans. Commun. **61**, 4754–4767 (2013)
9. Sun, Q., Li, L., Mao, J.: Simultaneous information and power transfer scheme for energy efficient MIMO systems. IEEE Commun. Lett. **18**, 600–603 (2014)
10. Sun, J., Xu, W., Bin, F.: A global search strategy of quantum-behaved particle swarm optimization. In: IEEE Conference on Cybernetics and Intelligent Systems, pp. 111–116. IEEE Press, New York (2004)
11. Zhao, Y., Li, X., Li, Y., Ji, H.: Resource allocation for high-speed railway downlink MIMO-OFDM system using quantum-behaved particle swarm optimization. In: IEEE International Conference on Communications, pp. 936–940. IEEE Press, New York (2013)
12. Gong, Y., Zhang, J., Chung, H., Chen, W., Zhan, Z.H., Li, Y., et al.: An efficient resource allocation scheme using particle swarm optimization. IEEE Trans. Evol. Comput. **16**, 801–816 (2012)

Relay Selection Scheme for Energy Harvesting Cooperative Networks

Mengqi Yang, Yonghong Kuo, and Jian Chen[✉]

Xidian University, Xi'an, Shaanxi Province, People's Republic of China
jianchen@mail.xidian.edu.cn

Abstract. Harvesting energy from the radio-frequency signal is an appealing approach to replenish energy in energy-constrained networks. In this paper, relay selection (RS) in a half-duplex decode-and-forwarding multi-relay network with an energy harvesting source is investigated. Without relying on dedicated wireless power transfer, in our system the source is powered by salvaging energy from the relaying signals. In this network, RS will affect both the current transmission quality and the source energy state in the following transmission block, which is not considered in the traditional RS schemes. Thus, a two-step distributed RS scheme is proposed to improve the system performance and is compared with the max-min signal-to-noise ratio strategy. In our proposed RS scheme, the system outage probability is derived in a closed form, and the diversity gain is shown to achieve the full diversity order. Finally, numerical results are given to evaluate the performance and verify the analysis.

Keywords: Cooperative communications · Energy harvesting · Relay selection · DF-relay · Distributed

1 Introduction

Harvesting energy from wireless radio frequency (RF) signals, which is a very promising technology to realize green communications, has recently drawn considerable attention [1]. Since RF signal carries information as well as energy, simultaneous wireless information and power transfer (SWIPT) was first introduced in [2,3], where the tradeoff between harvested energy and information was investigated. Considering practical limitations, two realizable circuit designs for SWIPT were proposed as time switching (TS) and power splitting (PS), respectively [4].

In several practical wireless networks, such as sensor networks and wireless body area networks, a sensor node as the information source is powered by batteries which are inconvenient or even impossible to be replaced. Therefore, energy harvesting (EH) is a meaningful technology for power supply in networks with an energy-constrained source node [5]. In [6], the authors considered a three-node cooperative network performing wireless power transfer (WPT) where the source is wireless-powered by the access point before the data transmission.

© ICST Institute for Computer Sciences, Social Informatics and Telecommunications Engineering 2018
Q. Chen et al. (Eds.): ChinaCom 2016, Part II, LNICST 210, pp. 13–22, 2018.
DOI: 10.1007/978-3-319-66628-0_2

In all the above works, additional time or power resources compared with traditional networks are consumed for power transfer. For the PS structure, the received signal is split into two streams for EH and information decoding separately, whereas for the TS and WPT structure, a part of transmission time is sacrificed for EH. In contrast, an appealing solution for half-duplex cooperative networks with an energy-constrained source is to salvage energy during the relaying interval and use the harvested energy for information transfer in the following transmission. Due to the broadcast nature of wireless medium, the relaying signals can be received and further converted to usable DC power by the source without additional time or power consumption. The transmission outage performance for such an EH cooperative network was analyzed in [7], and the optimal power allocation scheme to maximize the system throughput was proposed in [8]. However, both the works in [7,8] assume the single-relay scenario.

Considering the multi-relay scenario, optimal relay selection (RS) is an easy implemented and effective approach for developing system performance, and the max-min signal-to-noise ratio (SNR) criterion is the outage optimal RS scheme in the traditional cooperative networks [9]. However, in the scenario where source salvages energy from the relaying signals, RS affects both the current transmission quality and the source energy state in the next transmission block, which is not considered in existing RS schemes. For example, to select a relay merely minimizing the outage probability in the current transmission may cause a low transmit power of the source in the following transmission, and on the other hand, to select a relay which can maximize the harvested energy may lead to a high outage probability of the current transmission. The reason is that the data transmission is influenced by both the two hops channel qualities, while EH only depends on the channel gain of the first hop. Thus, RS in this considered system should take into account both the current performance and the future evolution of the network. Beyond that, since in practical networks the future channel coefficients can not be known in the current transmission, it is difficult to find the exact tradeoff of the system performance between the current and the future transmissions.

In this paper, we investigate the decode-and-forwarding (DF) multi-relay two-hop network where an energy-constrained source salvages energy from the relaying signals during the current transmission block and will utilize the harvested energy for information transfer in the following transmission. Motivated by above observations, we propose a two-step RS scheme to improve the system performance in this considered network, and the RS scheme is performed in the distributed mechanism to decrease the complexity and energy consumption of the energy-constrained source. The system performance achieved by our proposed RS scheme is evaluated in outage probability and is compared with the max-min SNR scheme. Furthermore, we derive the closed-form outage probability expressions for the proposed RS scheme and analyze the achievable diversity order in high-SNR regime. Analytical results show that the proposed scheme achieves the full diversity order.

2   System Model

Consider a half-duplex DF relay-assisted network which consists of an RF-EH source S, a destination D, and M DF-relays R_i $i = 1, 2, ..., M$, as shown in Fig. 1. There is no direct link between S and D. The transmission is performed with the help of one selected relay. We assume that all channels experience independent Rayleigh fading, and M relays are clustered relatively close together. Consequently, the coefficients of source-to-relay and relay-to-destination links, denoted as $\{h_1, h_2, ..., h_M\}$ and $\{g_1, g_2, ..., g_M\}$, are independent and identically distributed (i.i.d.) complex Gaussian random variables, i.e., $h_i \sim \mathcal{CN}(0, \Omega_h)$ and $g_i \sim \mathcal{CN}(0, \Omega_g)$. Moreover, the block-fading channel model is considered which means the channel coefficients remain constant during one transmission block but change independently from one block to another. In addition, let $h_i(k)$ and $g_i(k)$ denote the channel coefficients in the k-th block.

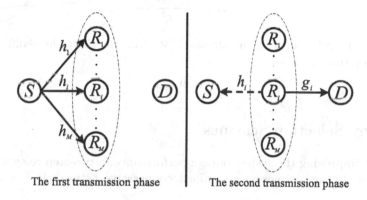

The first transmission phase   The second transmission phase

Fig. 1. System model with illustration of the two transmission phases in a transmission block.

Similar to the traditional relay-assisted communication, a transmission block is performed in two phases. In the first phase of $(k-1)$-th block, S broadcasts information with a transmit power $P_S(k-1)$, which depends on the harvested energy in the previous transmission. After that, a selected relay R_i decodes and forwards the information powered by a stabilized power source P_R in the second phase. Meanwhile, S harvests energy from the forwarding signal transmitted by R_i for further data transmission in the k-th block. Considering the channel reciprocity, the harvested energy at S in the $(k-1)$-th block is given by

$$E_S(k-1) = \eta P_R |h_i(k-1)|^2 T/2, \tag{1}$$

where η, $0 < \eta \leq 1$, denotes the conversion efficiency of EH and T denotes the time duration of a transmission block. In addition, we assume there is a dedicated power transfer from the relay to the source in order to guarantee the initial transmission. In k-th block, the received signal at R_i is expressed as

$$y_i^R(k) = \sqrt{\eta P_R |h_i(k-1)|^2} x(k) h_i(k) + n_i(k), \tag{2}$$

where $x(k)$ is the information signal with unity energy and $n_i(k)$ is baseband additive white Gaussian noise (AWGN) with zero mean and variance σ_i^2. The signal observation at D via relay R_i is given by

$$y_i^D(k) = \sqrt{P_R}x(k)g_i(k) + n_d(k), \tag{3}$$

where $n_d(k)$ is AWGN at D and $n_d(k) \sim \mathcal{CN}(0, \sigma_d^2)$. We assume both σ_i^2 and σ_d^2 are equal to σ_o^2 for simplicity.

From Eq. (2), the first-hop received SNR at relay R_i is expressed as

$$\gamma_i^R(k) = \frac{\eta P_R|h_i(k-1)|^2|h_i(k)|^2}{\sigma_o^2}. \tag{4}$$

According to Eq. (3), the SNR at D with the help of the i-th relay is given by

$$\gamma_i^D(k) = \frac{P_R|g_i(k)|^2}{\sigma_o^2}. \tag{5}$$

Setting the target transmission rate as $\mathbf{R}$ bps/Hz, the SNR threshold at each receiver is given by

$$\gamma_{\text{th}} = 2^{2\mathbf{R}} - 1. \tag{6}$$

3   Relay Selection Schemes

Aiming at improving the system outage performance, a two-step relay selection scheme for the source-energy-constrained cooperative network is described as follows:

- Construct a set, denoted by $\mathcal{R}(k)$, containing all the relays by which the signal transmitted can be successfully decoded at D in the k-th block, i.e., $\mathcal{R}(k) \triangleq \{R_i \mid \gamma_i^D(k) \geq \gamma_{\text{th}}, i = 1, 2, ..., M\}$.
- A relay in $\mathcal{R}(k)$ which will maximize the received SNR of the first hop will be selected, i.e., $R^*(k) = \arg \max_{R_i \in \mathcal{R}(k)} \{\gamma_i^R(k)\}$. In the case that $\mathcal{R}(k) = \varnothing$, all nodes will keep silence in the k-th block for saving energy due to an inevitable outage.

To simplify the notations, denote the channel gains of link $S - R^*(k)$ and link $R^*(k) - D$ as $|h^*(k)|^2$ and $|g^*(k)|^2$, respectively. By substituting Eq. (4), we have

$$R^*(k) = \arg \max_{R_i \in \mathcal{R}(k)} \left\{ \frac{\eta P_R|h^*(l)|^2|h_i(k)|^2}{\sigma_o^2} \right\}, \tag{7}$$

where l is the index of a recent block, in which $\mathcal{R}(l)$ is not a null set. Since the random variable $|h^*(l)|^2$ has produced a sample value in the k-th block, Eq. (7) can be simplified as

$$R^*(k) = \arg \max_{R_i \in \mathcal{R}(k)} \{|h_i(k)|^2\}. \tag{8}$$

Eqs. (7) and (8) indicate an important feature that the instantaneous energy state information of S is not demanded in the proposed RS scheme which leads to the lower system overhead compared with the max-min SNR scheme [9].

The above RS process can be performed in a distributed RS mechanism based on timing structure. At the beginning of a transmission block, relays estimate all the channel coefficients via pilot packets transmitted by S and D. Afterwards, each relay R_i sets the initial value of its countdown timer as $1/|h_i(k)|^2$. The relay which counts to zero first, will broadcast one bit signal to announce itself the best relay. Due to space limitations, more details about distributed RS mechanism can be seen in [10].

4   Performance Analysis

In this section, the performance of the proposed RS scheme is studied in terms of the outage probability.

For the proposed two-step RS scheme, the outage probability can be written as

$$P_{\text{out}}^{\text{Pro}} = \Pr\{|\mathcal{R}(k)| = 0\} + \underbrace{\Pr\{|\mathcal{R}(k)| > 0, |h^*(l)|^2|h^*(k)|^2 < \frac{\varepsilon}{\eta}\}}_{P_1}, \qquad (9)$$

where $\varepsilon = (2^{2\mathbf{R}} - 1)\sigma_o^2/P_R$ and $|\mathcal{R}(k)|$ denotes the cardinality of set $\mathcal{R}(k)$. Recall that $\{|h_i(k)|^2 \mid i = 1, 2, ..., M\}$ and $\{|g_i(k)|^2 \mid i = 1, 2, ..., M\}$ follow independent and identically exponential distribution with mean Ω_h and Ω_g, respectively. The corresponding cumulative distribution function (CDF) of $|h_i(k)|^2$ is given as $F_{|h_i(k)|^2}(x) = 1 - e^{-x/\Omega_h}$, and that of $|g_i(k)|^2$ is $F_{|g_i(k)|^2}(x) = 1 - e^{-x/\Omega_g}$. According to order statistics, the probability of $|\mathcal{R}(k)| = m$ is given as

$$\Pr\{|\mathcal{R}(k)| = m\} = \binom{M}{m} (\Pr\{|g_i(k)|^2 \geq \varepsilon\})^m (\Pr\{|g_i(k)|^2 < \varepsilon\})^{M-m}$$

$$= \frac{M!}{(M-m)!m!} e^{-m\varepsilon/\Omega_g} (1 - e^{-\varepsilon/\Omega_g})^{M-m}. \qquad (10)$$

On the other hand, by using the Total Probability Theorem, P_1 can be calculated as follows:

$$P_1 = \sum_{m=1}^{M} \Pr\{|\mathcal{R}(k)| = m\} \Pr\{|h^*(l)|^2|h^*(k)|^2 < \frac{\varepsilon}{\eta} \mid |\mathcal{R}(k)| = m\}$$

$$= \sum_{m=1}^{M} \sum_{n=1}^{M} \Pr\{|\mathcal{R}(k)| = m\} \frac{\Pr\{|\mathcal{R}(l)| = n\}}{1 - \Pr\{|\mathcal{R}(l)| = 0\}}$$

$$\times \underbrace{\Pr\{|h^*(l)|^2|h^*(k)|^2 < \frac{\varepsilon}{\eta} \mid |\mathcal{R}(k)| = m, |\mathcal{R}(l)| = n\}}_{P_2}, \qquad (11)$$

where the denominator is for probability normalization due to the fact that the transmission happens only when $\mathcal{R}(k)$ is not a null set. The factor P_2 can be calculated as

$$P_2 = \int_0^\infty \Pr\{|h^*(k)|^2 < \frac{\varepsilon}{\eta y} ||\mathcal{R}(k)| = m\} \Pr\{|h^*(l)|^2 = y ||\mathcal{R}(l)| = n\} dy. \quad (12)$$

The condition, $|\mathcal{R}(k)| = m$, has no effect on $|h_i(k)|^2$ which is still exponentially distributed. Thus, from Eq. (8), the conditional CDF of $|h^*(k)|^2$ and the probability distribution function (PDF) of $|h^*(l)|^2$ are given as

$$F_{|h^*(k)|^2 ||\mathcal{R}(k)|=m}(x) = (\Pr\{|h_i(k)|^2 < x\})^m = (1 - e^{-x/\Omega_h})^m, \quad (13)$$

$$\Pr\{|h^*(l)|^2 = y ||\mathcal{R}(l)| = n\} = \frac{n}{\Omega_h}(1 - e^{-y/\Omega_h})^{n-1} e^{-y/\Omega_h}. \quad (14)$$

Therefore, P_2 can be calculated as

$$\begin{aligned}
P_2 &= \int_0^\infty \frac{n}{\Omega_h}(1 - e^{-\varepsilon/(\Omega_h \eta y)})^m (1 - e^{-y/\Omega_h})^{n-1} e^{-y/\Omega_h} dy \\
&\stackrel{(e)}{=} \frac{n}{\Omega_h} \sum_{a=0}^m \sum_{b=0}^{n-1} \binom{m}{a} \binom{n-1}{b} (-1)^{a+b} \int_0^\infty e^{-a\varepsilon/(\Omega_h \eta y)-(b+1)y/\Omega_h} dy \\
&= n \sum_{a=1}^m \sum_{b=0}^{n-1} \binom{m}{a} \binom{n-1}{b} (-1)^{a+b} \frac{1}{b+1} \sqrt{\frac{4a(b+1)\varepsilon}{\Omega_h^2 \eta}} \mathbf{K}_1 \left(\sqrt{\frac{4a(b+1)\varepsilon}{\Omega_h^2 \eta}} \right) \\
&\quad + n \sum_{b=0}^{n-1} \binom{n-1}{b} (-1)^b \frac{1}{b+1}, \quad (15)
\end{aligned}$$

where $\mathbf{K}_1(x)$ is the first-order modified Bessel function of the second kind [11, Eq. (3.324.1)], and the equal sign (e) is obtained by binomial expansions. Furthermore, by changing the variable, we have

$$n \sum_{b=0}^{n-1} \binom{n-1}{b} (-1)^b \frac{1}{b+1} = -\sum_{b=1}^n \binom{n}{b} (-1)^b = 1. \quad (16)$$

Thus, P_2 can be expressed as

$$P_2 = 1 - \sum_{a=1}^m \sum_{b=1}^n \binom{m}{a} \binom{n}{b} (-1)^{a+b} \sqrt{\frac{4ab\varepsilon}{\Omega_h^2 \eta}} \mathbf{K}_1 \left(\sqrt{\frac{4ab\varepsilon}{\Omega_h^2 \eta}} \right). \quad (17)$$

By plugging Eqs. (10), (11) and (17) into Eq. (9), the analytical expression for the outage probability of the proposed RS scheme is given as

$$P_{\text{out}}^{\text{Pro}} = (1 - e^{-\varepsilon/\Omega_g})^M + \frac{1}{1 - (1 - e^{-\varepsilon/\Omega_g})^M}$$

$$\times \sum_{m=1}^{M} \sum_{n=1}^{M} \binom{M}{m}\binom{M}{n}(1 - e^{-\varepsilon/\Omega_h})^{2M-m-n} e^{-(m+n)\varepsilon/\Omega_h}$$

$$\times \left(1 - \sum_{a=1}^{m} \sum_{b=1}^{n} \binom{m}{a}\binom{n}{b}(-1)^{a+b}\sqrt{\frac{4ab\varepsilon}{\Omega_h^2 \eta}}\mathbf{K}_1\left(\sqrt{\frac{4ab\varepsilon}{\Omega_h^2 \eta}}\right)\right). \tag{18}$$

In addition, Eq. (18) can be used for the analysis of the diversity gain achieved by the proposed RS scheme. To clarify the analytical results, we set constant coefficients $\eta = \Omega_h = \Omega_g = 1$, which have no impact on diversity order obtained at high SNR. When $x \to 0$, the following approximations can be established: [6]

$$x\mathbf{K}_1(x) \approx 1 + \frac{x^2}{2}\ln\frac{x}{2}, \tag{19}$$

$$1 - e^{-x} \approx x. \tag{20}$$

Thus, in high SNR regime, i.e., $\varepsilon \to 0$, by applying (19), P_2 can be approximated as

$$P_2 \approx 1 - \sum_{a=1}^{m} \sum_{b=1}^{n} \binom{m}{a}\binom{n}{b}(-1)^{a+b}(1 + ab\varepsilon \ln(ab\varepsilon))$$

$$= \sum_{a=1}^{m} \binom{m}{a}(-1)^a a \sum_{b=1}^{n} \binom{n}{b}(-1)^b b\varepsilon\left(\ln\frac{1}{ab} + \ln\frac{1}{\varepsilon}\right)$$

$$\approx \varepsilon \ln\frac{1}{\varepsilon}\left(\sum_{a=1}^{m} \binom{m}{a}(-1)^a a\right)\left(\sum_{b=1}^{n} \binom{n}{b}(-1)^b b\right)$$

$$= \varepsilon \ln\frac{1}{\varepsilon}\left(\sum_{a=1}^{m} \binom{m}{a}(-1)^{a+1} a\right)\left(\sum_{b=1}^{n} \binom{n}{b}(-1)^{b+1} b\right). \tag{21}$$

Using (20) and (21), the outage probability in high SNR regime can be approximated as follow:

$$P_{\text{out}}^{\text{Pro}} \approx \varepsilon^M + \sum_{m=1}^{M} \sum_{n=1}^{M} \binom{M}{m}\binom{M}{n}\varepsilon^{2M-m-n+1}\ln\frac{1}{\varepsilon}$$

$$\times \left(\sum_{a=1}^{m} \binom{m}{a}(-1)^{a+1} a\right)\left(\sum_{b=1}^{n} \binom{n}{b}(-1)^{b+1} b\right), \tag{22}$$

Recall the following property about the sums of binomial coefficients: [11, Eq. (0.154.2)]

$$\sum_{k=1}^{K} \binom{K}{k}(-1)^{k+1} k = 0, \tag{23}$$

for $K \geq 2$. By applying (23), the approximated outage probability can be simplified as

$$P_{\text{out}}^{\text{Pro}} \approx \varepsilon^M + M^2 \varepsilon^{2M-1} \ln \frac{1}{\varepsilon} = \varepsilon^M + M^2 \varepsilon^M \left(\varepsilon^{M-1} \ln \frac{1}{\varepsilon} \right), \qquad (24)$$

where $\varepsilon^{M-1} \ln(1/\varepsilon) \to 0$ when $\varepsilon \to 0$ and $M \geq 2$. Therefore, we have $\frac{\log P_{\text{out}}^{\text{Pro}}}{\log \varepsilon} \to M$, which indicates that the proposed RS scheme achieves a full diversity gain.

5   Numerical Results

In this section, numerical results are presented to verify the analysis and evaluate the performance of our proposed RS scheme. And as a benchmark, the simulation results of the outage performance achieved by max-min SNR criterion are shown in Figs. 1 and 3. We set the noise variance as $\sigma_i^2 = \sigma_d^2 = \sigma_o^2 = 1$, and the average channel gain as $\Omega_h = \Omega_g = 1$. The energy conversion efficiency is assumed as $\eta = 1$. Throughout this section, the term "SNR" represents the transmitted SNR at relays i.e., $\text{SNR} = P_R/\sigma_o^2$.

Figure 2 shows the outage probabilities as a function of SNR where the target rate is $\mathbf{R} = 3$ bps/Hz and the number of relays is 3 or 6. The accuracy of our closed-form expressions of the outage probability is verified by simulation results. Moreover, it is demonstrated that the outage performance gains of our proposed scheme is advanced with the increase of SNR. The reason is that, for the proposed RS scheme, more relays are active due to high SNR. It means a better source-to-relay link can be selected, which improves the energy state of source in the following block.

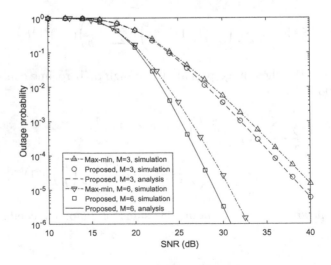

Fig. 2. Outage probability vs. SNR for $\mathbf{R} = 3$ bps/Hz.

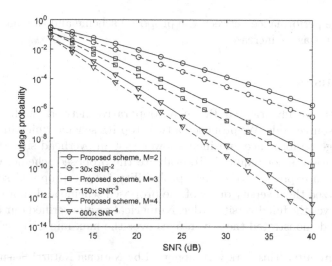

Fig. 3. Verification of the diversity order for the proposed RS scheme when $\mathbf{R} =$ 1 bps/Hz.

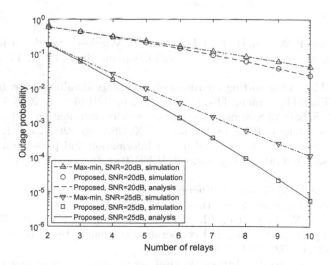

Fig. 4. Outage probability vs. number of relays for $\mathbf{R} = 3$ bps/Hz.

In Fig. 3, the analysis about the diversity gains is verified. The full curves are generated by analytical results, and the dot-dash lines are drawn as auxiliary lines with the diversity order of M. It can be seen that the full curves tend to straight lines and get parallel to the auxiliary lines with the increase of SNR. Therefore, our proposed scheme is verified to achieve the full diversity order, as is derived by the analytical results.

Figure 4 shows the performance gap versus the number of relays when the target rate is $\mathbf{R} = 3$ bps/Hz and SNR is 20 dB or 25 dB. It is obvious that the gap of outage performance between the proposed scheme and the max-min SNR scheme extends as M increases.

6 Conclusion

In this paper, we investigated RS in a cooperative network with an energy-constrained source node. We proposed a two-step RS scheme which improves the system outage performance and incurs lower system overhead since the energy state information is not required. To evaluate the proposed scheme, we derived the closed-form expression of outage probability for the proposed scheme. We further analyzed the diversity order of the proposed scheme and showed that the scheme achieves the full diversity order. Numerical results verified our theoretical analysis and demonstrated the advantages over the max-min SNR scheme.

Acknowledgments. This work was supported by National Natural Science Foundation of China (61540046) and the "111" project of China (B08038).

References

1. Lu, X., Wang, P., Niyato, D., Kim, D.I., Han, Z.: Wireless networks with RF energy harvesting: a contemporary survey. IEEE Commun. Surv. Tutor. **17**(2), 757–789 (2015)
2. Varshney, L.R.: Transporting information and energy simultaneously. In: Proceedings of IEEE ISIT, Toronto, ON, Canada, pp. 1612–1616, July 2008
3. Grover, P., Sahai, A.: Shannon meets Tesla: wireless information and power transfer. In: Proceedings of IEEE ISIT, Austin, TX, USA, pp. 2363–2367, January 2010
4. Zhou, X., Zhang, R., Ho, C.K.: Wireless information and power transfer: architecture design and rate-energy tradeoff. IEEE Trans. Commun. **61**(11), 4754–4767 (2013)
5. Sudevalayam, S., Kulkarni, P.: Energy harvesting sensor nodes: survey and implications. IEEE Commun. Surv. Tutor. **13**(3), 443–461 (2011)
6. Chen, H., Li, Y., Rebelatto, J.L., Uchoa-Filhoand, B.F., Vucetic, B.: Harvest-then-cooperate: wireless-powered cooperative communications. IEEE Trans. Sig. Process. **63**(7), 1700–1711 (2015)
7. Ishibashi, K., Ochiai, H., Tarokh, V.: Energy harvesting cooperative communications. In: Proceedings of IEEE PIMRC, Sydney, NSW, Austrilia, pp. 1819–1823, September 2012
8. Huang, X., Ansari, N.: Optimal cooperative power allocation for energy harvesting enabled relay networks. IEEE Trans. Veh. Commun. **65**(4), 2424–2434 (2016)
9. Krikidis, I., Thompson, J., McLaughlin, S., Goertz, N.: Max-min relay selection for legacy amplify-and-forward systems with interference. IEEE Trans. Wirel. Commun. **8**(6), 3016–3027 (2009)
10. Bletsas, A., Khisti, A., Reed, D.P., Lippman, A.: A simple cooperative diversity method based on network path selection. IEEE J. Sel. Areas Commun. **24**(3), 659–672 (2006)
11. Gradshteyn, I.S., Ryzhik, I.M.: Table of Integrals, Series and Products, 7th edn. Academic, New York (2007)

Dynamic Power Control for Throughput Maximization in Hybrid Energy Harvesting Node

Didi Liu[1,2(✉)], Jiming Lin[3], Junyi Wang[3], Hongbing Qiu[3],
and Yibin Chen[3]

[1] School of Telecommunication Engineering, Xidian University,
Xi'an 710071, China
ldd866@gxnu.edu.cn
[2] Guangxi Key Lab of Multi-source Information Mining and Security,
Guangxi Normal University, Guilin 541004, China
[3] Guangxi Experiment Center of Information Science,
Guilin University of Electronic Technology, Guilin 541004, China

Abstract. In this paper, we consider a wireless communication node with hybrid energy harvesting (EH) sources which results in great difficulty in obtaining the statistical knowledge of joint EH process. In addition, the wireless channel fluctuates randomly due to fading. Our goal is, under this condition, to develop a dynamic power control policy for the transmitter such that the time average throughput of the system is maximized over an infinite horizon, taking into account the circuit energy consumption and inefficiency of the rechargeable battery. Such a dynamic power control problem is formulated as a stochastic network optimization problem. The problem is solved by utilizing Lyapunov optimization and an efficient on-line algorithm with quite low complexity is obtained. Simulation results illustrate that the proposed algorithm has the same performance as the optimal one with giving statistical knowledge of the stochastic processes.

Keywords: Energy harvesting · Throughput maximization · Hybrid energy sources · Lyapunov optimization · Wireless communication

1 Introduction

In recent years, the energy harvesting (EH) technique has been advanced very rapidly, many communication devices are capable of harvesting energy from environments around us, such as solar, vibration, magnetic and thermoelectric energy sources, and so on. Due to several significant advantages over conventional grid-powered and non-rechargeable battery-powered wireless devices, such as reduction the usage of conventional energy and the accompanying carbon footprint, energy-sufficient operation with extent lifetime limited only by their hardware lifetime, and so on, the EH technology gains more and more applications in communications systems [1–3]. However, energy harvest brings new problem in the form of intermittency and randomness of

© ICST Institute for Computer Sciences, Social Informatics and Telecommunications Engineering 2018
Q. Chen et al. (Eds.): ChinaCom 2016, Part II, LNICST 210, pp. 23–32, 2018.
DOI: 10.1007/978-3-319-66628-0_3

available energy, which necessitates an efficiently utilization of the harvested energy in order to maximize the throughput of EH communication system.

Various power control and data scheduling schemes have been designed for EH communication systems with the aim of maximizing the throughput in the past few years [4–8]. These studies mainly divide into two categories based on EH model: deterministic model and statistics model. The Deterministic model refers to the availability of knowledge of events, such as energy arrival and channel fade level, prior to the start of data transmission; The statistics model refers to the availability of the statistics knowledge only causally over time, but not a priori. In [4], based on the deterministic model, optimal off-line broadcast scheduling polices for a single user EH communication system were presented to minimize the transmission completion time. Optimal offline and online power allocation algorithms for EH communication system in fading channels were proposed in [5] based on the above two models to minimize the outage probability. Similar as [5], the optimal power control time sequences were proposed in [6, 7] to maximize throughput by a deadline. Furthermore, EH relay was considered and both offline and online power allocation schemes were proposed to maximize the end-to-end throughput [8] based on the above two models.

In the aforementioned works [4–8] on EH communication systems, it is assumed that the EH transmitter was supplied solely by an energy harvester which collected energy from one specific type of renewable energy source. In practice, there is no actual model of the distributions of the stochastic energy arriving time and amount of arrived energy yet [9]. Especially, it is greatly difficult to know the statistical knowledge of the energy arrival generated jointly by multiple energy harvesters collecting energy from various renewable resources. Therefore, the results in the aforementioned literatures are not applicable to the EH communication systems supplied jointly by multiple EH energy sources with great difficulty in obtaining the statistical knowledge of the joint EH process.

In this paper, we address the above issues and focus on dynamic power allocation algorithm design for an EH communication node supplied jointly by multiple renewable energy sources under the condition of unknowing probability distributions of the joint EH process and channel state, such that the time average throughput of the wireless communication system is maximized. Such a problem can be formulated as a stochastic network optimization and solved by Lyapunov optimization developed in [10]. The early works [10, 11] used Lyapunov optimization technique show that the queuing naturally fits in the renewable supplier scheduling problem and present a simple dynamic algorithm that does not require prior statistical information. We apply the approach to EH transmitter with multiple energy harvesters in fading channel with additive Gaussian noise in this paper. At the same time, the efficiency of battery, the peak power of the transmitter and the special relationship between transmission rate and power is taken into account. The problem is now more complex and practical.

The contributions of this paper are summarized as follows: (1) we consider a wireless communication node powered together by multiple EH sources in fading channel without the statistical knowledge of the EH process and channel state, which has not been addressed before. (2) Under this case, we exploit an efficient online power control policy for the EH communication node, our proposed algorithm is universal and robust.

2 System Model and Problem Formulation

We consider a point-to-point wireless communication node where the transmitter (node) is equipped with multiple energy harvesters harvesting energy from various renewable energy sources as shown in Fig. 1, the wireless channel fluctuates randomly due to fading. The system has two queues, data queue and energy queue. The energy harvested jointly by multiple energy harvesters buffers in the rechargeable battery (energy queue) before it used to support the operation of wireless transmissions. We assume that the capacity of the energy storage buffer is infinite, so the harvested energy will not overflow. In practice the buffer is large enough (compared to energy consumed in a slot), this is a good approximation. Furthermore, it is assumed that the transmitter has an infinite backlog of data, so that there is always data to be sent.

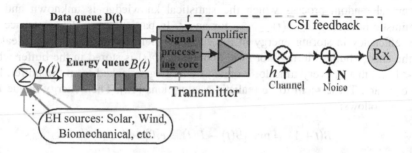

Fig. 1. The EH transmitter model with multiple energy-harvesters in fading channel

The system is slotted in time $t \in \{0, 1, 2, \cdots\}$ with fixed size Δt, where Δt is the time frame length. Without loss of generality, we assume the interval Δt is 1 s. The channel state fluctuates randomly due to fading and remains constant in the duration of each slot but may change at slot boundaries. Suppose that the channel state information (CSI) at the beginning of every timeslot is known at the transmitter via channel monitoring and feedback link [6]. The channel state in slot t (representing, for example, attenuation value and/or noise levels) is denoted by $h(t)$, and assume that it is independent and identically distributed (i.i.d.) over slots in a finite set H, i.e. $h(t) \in H$ for all t, but its probability distribution is not given. We further assume that the values of $h(t)$ is deterministically bounded by finite constants, $h_{\min} \leq h(t) \leq h_{\max}$.

The transmission rate μ_{ab} over the wireless link (a, b) depends on the channel state h_{ab} and transmission power $P_{tra}(t)$ with relationship, $\mu_{ab}(t) - g(P_{tra}(t), h_{ab}(t))$, where the rate-power function $g(\cdot)$ determines the number of bits in data queue that can be transferred over the wireless link (a, b). The function $g(\cdot)$ is assumed to be monotonically non-decreasing, such an important function is given by Shannon's capacity formula [6]:

$$\mu(t) = g(P_{tra}(t)) = \frac{1}{2}\log_2(1 + h(t)P_{tra}(t)) \quad \forall t \tag{1}$$

where $\mu(t)$ represents the transmission rate on timeslot t. The function $g(\cdot)$ is a non-decreasing concave function. At low values of $P_{tra}(t)$, $g(\cdot)$ becomes a linear function.

In practice, the power consumption of the transmitter during the timeslot t denoted by $P(t)$ consists of two parts:

$$P(t) = P_{con} + P_{tra}(t) \tag{2}$$

where P_{con} is a constant power required for signal processing at the transmitter in each timeslot, while $P_{tra}(t)$ represents the transmission power on timeslot t, which is our decision variable depended on the channel state and available energy in the battery. Further, the transmission power $P_{tra}(t)$ is limited by a continuous power constraint, i.e., $0 \le P_{tra}(t) \le P_{peak}$, where P_{peak} is the maximum transmission power of the transmitter.

Multiple energy harvesters harvest energy from various renewable resources simultaneously, and the sum of energy during timeslot t harvested jointly by multiple energy harvesters is denoted as $b(t)$ (that is, the input of the energy queue). The $\{b(t)\}$ is a general random process which the statistical knowledge is unknown and has deterministic boundary $0 \le b(t) \le b_{max}$ for any t. In particular, we take into account energy efficiency in storing energy in the energy buffer, a portion of energy leakage from the energy buffer, during slot t only energy $\beta \cdot b(t)$ is stored in the buffer where $0 < \beta < 1$ and that in every timeslot e units of energy gets leaked from the buffer, here e is a constant. These seem to be realistic assumptions [12]. Then energy queue $B(t)$ updates as follows:

$$B(t+1) = \max[B(t) - P(t) - e, 0] + \beta \cdot b(t) \tag{3}$$

Apart from the fixed peak power constraint, the energy consumption of the transmitter during current timeslot t must conform to the energy stored constraint: $P(t) \cdot \Delta t \le B(t)$, $\forall t$. Note that Δt is 1 s and does not influence the results. For convenience, we do not write the Δt in the following.

In the long run, the time average energy consumption of the transmitter must be less than or equal to the time average energy harvested, namely the system must satisfy the following constraint: $\bar{P} \le \beta \bar{b} - e$, where

$$\bar{P} = \lim_{t \to \infty} \frac{1}{t} \sum_{\tau=0}^{t-1} E\{P(\tau)\}$$

$$\bar{b} = \lim_{t \to \infty} \frac{1}{t} \sum_{\tau=0}^{t-1} E\{b(\tau)\}$$

Our goal is maximize the time average throughput over an infinite horizon based on the above system model, under energy causality constraint, power constraint and the data transmission constraint. The throughput maximization problem can be formulated as follows:

$$\max : \lim_{t \to \infty} \frac{1}{t} \sum_{\tau=0}^{t-1} E\{\mu(\tau)\} \tag{4}$$

$$\text{s.t.} : \bar{P} \le \beta \bar{b} - e \tag{5}$$

$$P(t) \le B(t) \, \forall t \tag{6}$$

$$0 \le P_{\text{tra}}(t) \le P_{\text{peak}} \, \forall t \tag{7}$$

Next, we establish a virtual queue $Q(t)$ as energy budget queue. Indeed, defining $Q(0) = 0$, we propagate the energy budget queue $Q(t)$ value according to the following equality:

$$Q(t+1) = \max[Q(t) - \beta \cdot b(t), 0] + P(t) + e \tag{8}$$

This virtual queue $Q(t)$ can ensure the inequality constraint (5) holds when it is mean rate stable, which follows the virtual queue stable theorem in [10]. Thus the constraint (5) can be transferred into that the virtual queue Q(t) is mean rate stable. Specifically, a discrete time queue $Q(t)$ is mean rate stable if

$$\lim \sup_{t \to \infty} \frac{1}{t} E\{Q(t)\} = 0$$

according to the definition in [10].

The problem can be formulated as a stochastic network optimization, the harvested energy and the channel state during every slot are random variables, and transmission power $P_{\text{tra}}(t)$ is our decision variable. We must decide for each timeslot whether or not to allocate power and how much power on the current time or wait for a more energy-efficient future channel state, taking into account currently available energy stored in the battery, such that the time average throughput is maximized over an infinite horizon.

3 Solution of the Optimization Problem

In this section, we utilize Lyapunov optimization to solve the above optimization problem and present a dynamic power control policy. First we define Lyapunov function: $L(t) \triangleq \frac{1}{2}Q(t)^2$, the conditional Lyapunov drift in one timeslot is given by the following definition:

$$\Delta(L(t)) \triangleq E\{L(t+1) - L(t) \mid Q(t)\} \tag{9}$$

Our dynamic algorithm is designed to observe the current queues backlog $Q(t)$, $B(t)$, the current channel state $h(t)$ and the incoming energy $b(t)$, then to make a decision $P_{\text{tra}}(t)$ to minimize a bound on the following expression every slot t:

$$\min : \Delta(L(t)) - V \cdot E\{\mu(t) | Q(t)\} \tag{10}$$

(10) is called drift-plus-penalty expression [10], and V is a positive parameter that is used to tune the tradeoff between performance and queue backlog. The objective is to minimize the weighted sum of drift and penalty, which can be proven bounded in the following:

$$\Delta(L(t)) - VE\{\mu(t)|Q(t)\}$$
$$\leq C - VE\{\mu(t)|Q(t)\} + Q(t)E\{P(t) + e - \beta b(t)|Q(t)\} \tag{11}$$

where

$$C = \frac{(P_{\text{peak}} + e)^2 + \beta^2 \cdot b_{\text{max}}^2}{2} \tag{12}$$

The proof uses the Lyapunov optimization technique, and is given in [10].

3.1 The Dynamic Algorithm

Due to the left-hand-side of (11) tightly bounded by the right-hand side of (11), minimizing the right-hand-side of the drift-plus-penalty bound (11) every slot t leads to the following dynamic optimization algorithm:

Every slot t, observing $B(t)$, $Q(t)$, $h(t)$ and $b(t)$, then we choose $P_{\text{tra}}(t)$ according to the following optimization:

$$\min : Q(t)[P(t) + e - \beta \cdot b(t)] - V \cdot \mu(t)$$
$$s.t : P(t) \leq B(t) \forall t \tag{13}$$
$$0 \leq P_{\text{tra}}(t) \leq P_{\text{peak}} \forall t$$

Then we update the actual and virtual queue $B(t)$ and $Q(t)$ by (3) and (8), respectively.

Substituting the rate-power formula (1) and energy consumption (2) into (13), then differentiating with respect to the transmission power P_{tra}, we obtain the optimal transmission power which maximize (13) in timeslot t and denote it as $P_{\text{tra}}^*(t)$,

$$P_{\text{tra}}^*(t) = \frac{V}{2 \ln 2 \cdot Q(t)} - \frac{1}{h(t)} \tag{14}$$

However, based on the power constraint (6) and (7), on slot t, the practical transmission power is given by:

$$P_{\text{tra}}(t) = \min\{B(t) - e - P_{\text{con}}, \min[P_{\text{peak}}, \max(P_{\text{tra}}^*(t), 0)]\} \tag{15}$$

The dynamic power control algorithm proposed is given in detail in Table 1.

Table 1. Dynamic power allocation algorithm.

Algorithm 1.   Dynamic power allocation algorithm
Initialization:
1: P_{con}, P_{peak}, β, e, V, T, $Q(1) = 0$, $B(1)$
Repeat:
2: for $t = 1 : 1 : T$
Observe $B(t)$, $Q(t)$, $h(t)$ and $b(t)$,
Solve $P_{tra}^*(t)$ according to $P_{tra}^*(t) = \frac{V}{2\ln 2 \cdot Q(t)} - \frac{1}{h(t)}$
3: Choose the practical transmission power according to
$P_{tra}(t) = \min\{B(t) - e - P_{con}, \min[P_{peak}, \max(P_{tra}^*(t), 0)]\}$
4: Update the queues $B(t)$ and $Q(t)$ by
$B(t+1) = \max[B(t) - P(t) - e, 0] + \beta \cdot b(t)$
$Q(t) = \max[Q(t) - \beta \cdot b(t), 0] + P(t) + e$
end

3.2   Analysis of Complexity of the Proposed Algorithm

The proposed on-line power control algorithm in this paper is simple to implement. As shown in Table 1, we just need to observe $B(t)$, $Q(t)$, $h(t)$ and $Q(t)$ every slot t and choose $P_{tra}(t)$ such that Eq. (13) is minimized. Besides, our algorithm based on Lyapunov optimization does not need a priori statistical knowledge of the EH process and the channel state, so the dynamic power control proposed in this paper is a universal policy and apply to any general EH communication node.

The performance analysis of the algorithm in theory cannot be showed for lack of space.

4   Simulation Results

To evaluate the performance of the proposed real-time power control algorithm, first of all, note that we adopt the following distributions just for exposition purpose. The analysis in the previous section does not depend on the distributions. The related simulation settings is summarized in Table 2.

To better evaluate the performance of our proposed algorithm, in following we compare Lyapunov optimization (L.O) algorithm used in our work against the throughput optimization (T.O) algorithm developed in [12], which requires the priori statistical knowledge of the incoming energy. The comparison about the normalized throughput and the accumulated throughput using two different algorithms is shown in Figs. 2 and 3. In Fig. 2, we assume that the rechargeable battery has initial energy of 200 J, we can see that the throughput exploited Lyapunov optimization algorithm is better than of the algorithm using in [12]. The reason is that the throughput optimization algorithm in [12] is designed for no initial energy stored in the battery at beginning of system operation.

Table 2. Simulation settings.

Parameters	Value
Bandwidth	B
Timeslot length	1 s
Channel fading	Gaussian
Average SNR	100 dB
Avg. harvesting rate	120 mJ/slot
EH process	i.i.d. poisson process
Max transmission power	400 mW
Constant power P_{con}	15 mW
Efficiency factor β	0.9
Energy leakage e	5 mJ/slot

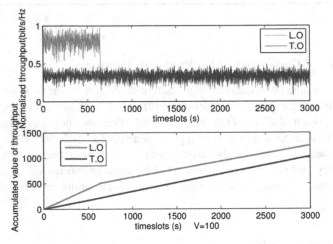

Fig. 2. Comparison between two different algorithms (Battery has initial energy of 200J)

Then we assume B(0) = 0, as shown in Fig. 3, the performance curve of two algorithm overlap. It means that our proposed algorithm has the same performance over the long time compared with the optimal throughput algorithm in [12], but our proposed algorithm has own advantage which does not require the priori statistical knowledge of the incoming energy, while the T.O algorithm developed in [12] requires the priori statistical knowledge of the incoming energy. Hence the algorithm proposed in this paper has universality.

In order to study the impact of parameter V on the performance, we have plotted Fig. 4 showing the relationship between the performance and the value of V. We can see that the performance reach saturation when V is larger than a certain value (V = 100 seen from Fig. 4).

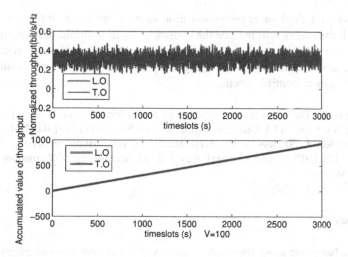

Fig. 3. Comparison between two different algorithms (Battery has no initial energy)

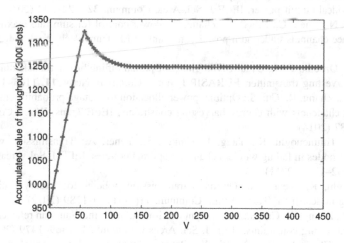

Fig. 4. Performance for different V value (Battery has initial energy of 200J)

5 Conclusion

The dynamic power control for a single-user wireless communication node with multiple renewable sources has been discussed. Under the condition that the EH process and channel state are time-varying with unknown statistics knowledge, we develop a universal power control policy which can be applied to any general EH communication node by utilizing Lyapunov optimization towards the goal of the time average throughput maximization. It was proved that the proposed algorithm is efficient and simple to implement due to its low complexity. Simulation results demonstrate that the proposed algorithm has the not worse performance with the optimal one which needs the statistical knowledge of the stochastic processes.

While we treat single-user communication case in this paper, it has only one data queue. The furture work will include the consideration of multiple-user communication case where multiple data queues are adopted for different customers with different deadlines, a new transmission scheduling will be developed between multiple users with the new power control scheme.

Acknowledgment. The research was supported by the National Natural Science Foundation of China (Grant No. 61261017,), Guangxi Natural Science Foundation (2014GXNSFAA118387), Foundation of Key Laboratory of Cognitive Radio and Information Processing, Ministry of Education (CRKL150206) and Guangxi Key Lab of Multi-source Information Mining & Security (MIMS14-06).

References

1. Ozel, O., Tutuncuoglu, K., Ulukus, S., Yener, A.: Fundamental limits of energy harvesting communications. IEEE Commun. Mag. **53**(4), 126–132 (2015)
2. Xu, J., Zhang, R.: Troughput optimal policies for energy harvesting wireless transmitters with non-ideal circuit power. IEEE J. Sel. Area. Commun. **32**, 322–332 (2014)
3. Hassanul, N., Yuen, C., Saeed, S., Zhang, Z.: Power control for sum rate maximization on interference channels under sum power constraint. IEEE Trans. Veh. Tech. **64**(2), 593–609 (2015)
4. Erkal, H., Ozcelik, F.M., Uysal-Biyikoglu, E.: Optimal offline broadcast scheduling with an energy harvesting transmitter. EURASIP J. Wirel. Commun. Netw. **11**, 1163–1175 (2013)
5. Huang, C., Zhang, R., Cui, S.: Optimal power allocation for outage probability minimization in fading chanenels with energy harvesting constraints. IEEE Trans. Wirel. Commun. **13**, 1075–1087 (2014)
6. Ozel, O., Tutuncuoglu, K., Yang, J., Ulukus, S., Yener, A.: Transmission with energy harvesting nodes in fading wireless channels: optimal policies. IEEE J. Sel. Areas Commun. **29**(8), 1732–1743 (2011)
7. Tutuncuoglu, K., Yener, A.: Optimum transmission policies for battery limited energy harvesting nodes. IEEE Trans. Wirel. Commun. **11**(3), 1180–1189 (2012)
8. Huang, C., Zhang, R., Cui, S.: Throughput maximization for the Gaussian relay channel with energy harvesting constraints. IEEE J. Sel. Areas Commun. **31**, 1469–1479 (2013)
9. Chen, H., Zhao, F., Yu, R., Li, X.: Power allocation and transmitter switching for broadcasting with multiple energy harvesting transmitters. EURASIP J. Wirel. Commun. Netw. **1**, 1–11 (2014)
10. Neely, M.J.: Stochastic Network Optimization with Application to Communication and Queueing Systems. Morgan & Claypool Publishers, San Rafael (2010)
11. Neely, M.J., Tehrani, A.S., Dimakis, A.G.: Efficient algorithms for renewable energy allocation to delay tolerant consumers. In: IEEE International Conference on Smart Grid Communications, pp. 549–554 (2010)
12. Sharma, V., Mukherji, U., Joseph, V., Gupta, S.: Optimal energy management policies for energy harvesting sensor nodes. IEEE Trans. Wirel. Commun. **9**, 1326–1335 (2010)

Power Allocation Algorithm for Heterogeneous Cellular Networks Based on Energy Harvesting

Xiaoyu Wan, Xiaolong Feng, Zhengqiang Wang[(⊠)], and Zifu Fan

Key Lab of Mobile Communications Technology,
Chongqing University of Posts and Telecommunications,
Chongqing 400065, People's Republic of China
{wanxy,wangzq,fanzf}@cqupt.edu.cn, fengxlcqupt@163.com

Abstract. Cellular network can use renewable energy through energy harvesting technology in green communication. In this paper, power allocation for heterogeneous cellular networks (HetNets) with energy harvesting is proposed to maximize the system energy efficiency. Considering the minimal transmit rate of the users and the battery capacity of the system, a low complexity power allocation algorithm based on fractional programming is proposed to maximize the energy efficiency of the system. Simulation results demonstrate the effectiveness of the proposed algorithm.

Keywords: Energy efficiency · Energy harvesting · Power allocation · Battery capacity

1 Introduction

The heterogeneous cellular networks (HetNets), which composed of macro base stations (MBS) with small cells (SCs), is a promising technique to increase the data rate compared with the conventional MBS. However, as the number of small cell increases, energy consumption of the HetNets also increases. Energy harvesting technique has become the important technique to save the energy consumption and improving the energy efficiency in HetNets. Energy harvesting technology is a promising approach to prolong the lifetime and improve the energy efficiency of networks [1]. Energy harvesting mode of the network can generally be divided into two types according to the specific sources of the harvested energy [2]. The first one is that the base stations (BSs) and users harvest renewable energy from the environment, such as solar energy or wind energy.

This work was partially supported by the National Natural Science Foundation of China (No. 11502039), Scientific and Technological Research Program of Chongqing Municipal Education Commission (No. KJ1600424), PhD research startup foundation of Chongqing University of Posts and Telecommunications (No. A2015-41), and the Science Research Project of Chongqing University of Posts and Telecommunications for Young Scholars (No. A2015-62).

© ICST Institute for Computer Sciences, Social Informatics and Telecommunications Engineering 2018
Q. Chen et al. (Eds.): ChinaCom 2016, Part II, LNICST 210, pp. 33–43, 2018.
DOI: 10.1007/978-3-319-66628-0_4

The second one is that BSs and users harvest energy from ambient radio signals. In this paper, we focus on power allocation in the HetNets with renewable energy supply.

Because the base station using energy harvesting has become increasingly prominent technology for green communication, a large number of researchers have made contributions in this field. Different energy efficient optimization algorithms [3–6] has been proposed. In [3], the authors consider a device-to-device (D2D) communication provided EH heterogeneous cellular network (D2D-EHHN), and propose an efficient and low-complex transmission mode selection strategy for the D2D-EHHN. In [4], a generalized Stackelberg game is proposed to investigate the optimal energy and resource allocation problem of an autonomous energy harvesting base station. In [5], the authors propose a user association algorithm in HetNets with BSs solely powered by renewable energy supply. In [6], energy efficiency optimization of downlink base station cooperation with energy harvesting is proposed. In [7], the authors consider a more complicated network scenarios compared to [6], and discuss the optimization of power efficiency in the two layer cellular network scenario without considering battery capacity constraints. In [8], energy efficient resource allocation algorithm is studied in an orthogonal frequency division multiple access (OFDMA) downlink network with hybrid energy harvesting base station. In [9], the authors study the effects of different energy arrival rates on the overall system rate for cellular system with energy harvesting, but the algorithm complexity is very high.

In this paper, aiming at the problem of high complexity, we consider a HetNets with energy harvesting and propose a low complexity energy efficient power allocation optimization algorithm to improve energy efficiency of the system. The remainder of this paper is organized as follows. The system model is presented in Sect. 2. Section 3 introduces the energy efficiency maximization problem. Solving algorithm, through the transformation of the problem, and finally through the two layer iteration to solve the initial optimization problem in Sect. 3, Simulation results are given in Sect. 4. Conclusions are stated in Sect. 5.

2   System Model

We focus on HetNets as shown in Fig. 1, consisting of one macrocell and multiple femtocells. Each base station of femtocell can be are powered by renewable energy harvesting unit or grid hybrid power supply. When the base station can not get enough energy to work well, it will switch to using power of the grid. In order to ensure the system coverage blind spots, stable power grid energy is used by the station of macrocell provide energy. Considering the actual deployment scenario, the system adopts centralized power control, which greatly reduces the computing power of the base station. The bandwidth of the system is B, and the frequency reuse factor is 1, that is, all the base stations use the same spectrum resource [6]. The channel model between the user and the base station is Rayleigh fading, and the channel gains of different time slots are independent and identically distributed. (i.i.d) [8].

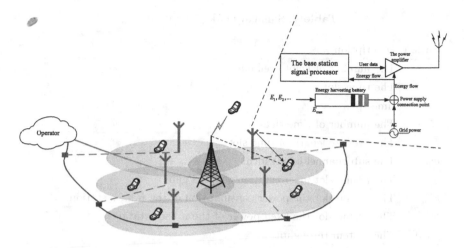

Fig. 1. System model

In renewable energy and grid hybrid power supply for the HotNets, each base stations with renewable energy harvesting devices has different energy rates. In order to provide a more general energy harvesting model for the system, we do not make specific assumption on the type of the energy collector. The arrival of energy in the energy collector is modeled as a poisson process with the arrival rata λ_E [10].

In order to facilitate the reader, the main parameters used in this paper are listed in Table 1. Assume that the energy efficiency maximization problem is considered in a fixed time interval of length T. We divide the continuous time T into K discrete time slot so as to design an power allocation.

Then, the total throughput $C(p)$ of the system and total energy consumption $P(p)$ can be expressed as follows.

$$C(p) = \sum_{n=1}^{N} \sum_{i=1}^{K} C_{i,n} \tag{1}$$

where $C_{i,n}$ is the rate of the n-th femtocell in time slot i which can be given as follows.

$$C_{i,n} = w_n \log_2 \left(1 + \frac{g_{i,n}\, p_{i,n}^R}{\sum\limits_{j=1, j \neq n}^{N} g_{i,j}\, p_{i,j}^R + \sigma^2} \right) \tag{2}$$

The total power $P(p)$ consumed by the system is given by

$$P(p) = \sum_{n=1}^{N} \sum_{i=1}^{K} \left(p_{i,n}^R + p_{i,n}^O \right) \tag{3}$$

Energy efficiency maximization problem of the system is as follows.

Table 1. Summary of key notations

Nation	Description
N	The number of Femto cellular
i	The time slot i
T	time span
K	The number of time slots
$\overline{L}_E$	The average length of time slot
w_n	The sub channel bandwidth
$g_{i,0}$	The i time slot macro station channel gain
$p_{i,n}^R$	The i time slot the power consumption of the n base station
$p_{i,n}^O$	The i time slot the fixed power of the n base station
$C(p)$	The system throughput
$p(p)$	Total energy consumption of the system
U	The utility function
$E_{i,n}$	The i time slot n base station the remaining energy of the battery
$E_{0,n}$	The n base station initial energy in the battery
$E_{n,\max}$	The n base station the maximum capacity of the battery
$p_{i,n}^{\max}$	The i time slot the n base station maximum transmitted power
$p_{i,0}^O$	The i time slotfixed power of macro station
$p_{i,n}^R$	The i time slot radio frequency (RF) power of macro station

$$\max_p \frac{\sum_{n=1}^N \sum_{i=1}^K w_n \log_2 \left(1 + \frac{g_{i,n} \, p_{i,n}^R}{\sum_{j=1, j \neq n}^N g_{i,j} \, p_{i,j}^R + \sigma^2} \right)}{\sum_{n=1}^N \sum_{i=1}^K \left(p_{i,n}^R + p_{i,n}^O \right)} \tag{4}$$

s.t.

$$C1 : \sum_{i=1}^j \overline{L_E} \left(p_{i,n}^R + p_{i,n}^O \right) \leq \sum_{i=0}^j E_{i,n}, \forall j, n;$$
$$C2 : \sum_{i=0}^j E_{i,n} - \sum_{i=1}^j \overline{L_E} \left(p_{i,n}^R + p_{i,n}^O \right) \leq E_{\max,n}, \forall j, n;$$
$$C3 : \sum_{i=1}^K \overline{L_E} \, C_{i,n} \geq R_{\min}$$
$$C4 : p_{i,n}^R, p_{i,n}^O \geq 0, \forall i, n;$$
$$C5 : p_{i,n}^R \leq p_{i,n}^{\max}, \forall i, n;$$

where $C1$ and $C2$ is energy use and storage condition. The derivation process is given in appendix A. $E_{i,n}$ is the energy arrival for femtocell i in time slot n, C3 is the lowest transmit rate constraint for the system, C4 means that transmission power of the n-th femtocell is nonnegative in time slot i, and C5 indicate the maximum total transmit power constraint for the n-th femtocell in time slot i, respectively.

3   Power Allocation Algorithm

Because of the limitation of causality of energy arrival, we need dynamic programming to solve (3). In order to simplify the resource allocation algorithm, we assume that the resource allocation policy in each time so as to design a low complexity algorithm. Therefore, we consider the efficiency maximization problem for a fixed time $i = 1, \cdots, K$ by sequential optimization method.

$$
\max_{p} \frac{\sum_{n=1}^{N} w_n \log_2 \left(1 + \dfrac{g_{i,n}\, p_{i,n}^{R}}{\sum\limits_{j=1,j\neq n}^{N} g_{i,j}\, p_{i,j}^{R} + \sigma^2} \right)}{\sum_{n=1}^{N} \left(p_{i,n}^{R} + p_{i,n}^{O} \right)}
\tag{5}
$$

s.t.

$$
\begin{aligned}
&C_1' : \sum_{k=1}^{i} \overline{LE} \left(p_{k,n}^{R} + p_{k,n}^{O} \right) \leq \sum_{k=0}^{i} E_{k,n}, \forall n; \\
&C_2' : \sum_{k=0}^{i} E_{k,n} - \sum_{k=1}^{i} \overline{LE} \left(p_{k,n}^{R} + p_{k,n}^{O} \right) \leq E_{\max,n}, \forall n; \\
&C_3' : \overline{LE}\, C_{i,n} \geq \tfrac{R_{\min}}{K}, \forall n; \\
&C_4' : p_{i,n}^{R}, p_{i,n}^{O} \geq 0, \forall n; \\
&C_5' : p_{i,n}^{R} \leq p_{i,n}^{\max}, \forall n;
\end{aligned}
$$

The objective function in (5) is non-concave function, therefore problem (5) is a non-convex optimization problem. In order to solve problem (5), we transform it into an equivalent problem based on fractional programming function [11]. Let

$$
C'(p) = \sum_{n=1}^{N} w_n \log_2 \left(1 + \frac{g_{i,n}\, p_{i,n}^{R}}{\sum\limits_{j=1,j\neq n}^{N} g_{i,j}\, p_{i,j}^{R} + \sigma^2} \right), \quad P'(p) = \sum_{n=1}^{N} \left(p_{i,n}^{R} + p_{i,n}^{O} \right)
$$

and $q = C'(p)/P'(p)$ represent the energy efficiency of the system for a given power allocation scheme, and $q* = C'(p*)/P'(p*)$ represent the optimal power allocation scheme such that the energy efficiency of the system is maximized, we have following theorem [12].

Theorem 1. *Consider $p*$ satisfies constraint $C_1' - C_5'$ and $q* = C'(p*)/P'(p*)$. Then, $p*$ is the solution of problem (5) if and only if*

$$
p^* = \arg \max_{p} C(p) - q^* P(p)
\tag{6}
$$

As a consequence of Theorem 1, solving problem (5) is equivalent to finding the unique zero of the auxiliary function $F(q)$, where $F(q)$ is given by

$$
F(q) = \max_{\{p_i\}_{i=1}^{N}} \sum_{n=1}^{N} w_n\, C_{i,n} - q \sum_{n=1}^{N} \left(p_{i,n}^{R} + p_{i,n}^{O} \right)
\tag{7}
$$

such that q satisfies constraints $C_1' - C_5'$.

Next, we use Lagrange dual method to solve problem (7). The Lagrange function of (7) is as follows.

$$
\begin{aligned}
L\left(p, \gamma, \beta, \mu, \upsilon\right) &= \sum_{n=1}^{N} w_n C_{i,n} - q \sum_{n=1}^{N} \left(p_{i,n}^{R} + p_{i,n}^{O}\right) \\
&- \sum_{n=1}^{N} \gamma_n \left(p_{i,n}^{R} - p_{i,n}^{\max}\right) - \sum_{n=1}^{N} \beta_n \left(\frac{R_{\min}}{K} - \overline{L_E} C_{i,n}\right) \\
&- \sum_{n=1}^{N} \mu_n \left(\sum_{k=1}^{i} \overline{L_E} \left(p_{k,n}^{R} + p_{k,n}^{O}\right) - \sum_{k=0}^{i} E_{k,n}\right) \\
&- \sum_{n=1}^{N} \upsilon_n \left(\left[\sum_{k=0}^{i} E_{k,n} - \sum_{k=1}^{i} \left(\overline{L_E} p_{k,n}^{R} + \overline{L_E} p_{k,n}^{O}\right)\right] - E_{\max,n}\right),
\end{aligned}
\tag{8}
$$

where $\gamma = (\gamma_1, \gamma_2, \ldots, \gamma_N)$, $\mu = (\mu_1, \mu_2, \ldots, \mu_N)$ and $\upsilon = (\upsilon_1, \upsilon_2, \ldots, \upsilon_N)$ are the multiplier of the constraints.

Therefore, the Lagrangian dual function can be expressed as follows:

$$
\min_{\gamma, \beta, \mu, \upsilon \geq 0} \max_{p \geq 0} L\left(p, \gamma, \mu, \upsilon\right).
$$

Application KKT (Karush-Kuhn-Tucker) conditions, we can get:

$$
p_{i,n}^{R} = \frac{w}{\ln 2(q + \gamma_n)} - \frac{\sum\limits_{j=1, j \neq n}^{N} g_{i,j}\, p_{i,j}^{R} + \sigma^2}{g_{i,n}}
\tag{9}
$$

For a given q, we can use the method of sub-gradient method to find $p_{i,n}^{R}$ by update the multipliers as follows [13].

$$
\begin{aligned}
\gamma_n^{(t+1)} &= \gamma_n^{(t)} + \nabla_\gamma^{(t+1)} \times \left(p_{i,n}^{R} - p_{i,n}^{\max}\right) \\
\mu_n^{(t+1)} &= \mu_n^{(t)} + \nabla_\mu^{(t+1)} \times \left(\sum_{k=1}^{i} \overline{L_E} \left(p_{k,n}^{R} + p_{k,n}^{O}\right) - \sum_{k=0}^{i} E_{k,n}\right) \\
\upsilon_n^{(t+1)} &= \upsilon_n^{(t)} + \nabla_\upsilon^{(t+1)} \\
&\times \left(\sum_{k=0}^{i} E_{k,n} - \sum_{k=1}^{i} \left(\overline{L_E} p_{k,n}^{R} + \overline{L_E} p_{k,n}^{O}\right) - E_{\max,n}\right) \\
\beta_n^{(t+1)} &= \beta_n^{(t)} + \nabla_\beta^{(t+1)} \left(\frac{R_{\min}}{K} - \overline{L_E} w_n \log_2 \left(1 + \frac{g_{i,n} p_{i,n}^{R}}{\sum\limits_{j=1, j \neq n}^{N} g_{i,j} p_{i,j}^{R} + \sigma^2}\right)\right)
\end{aligned}
\tag{10}
$$

Where $\nabla^{(t+1)} = \frac{1}{t}$ is update step size for each iteration, t is the number of iterations. Then, the optimal energy efficiency q^* can be obtained by solve equation $F(q) = 0$ by bisection method. The flow chart of the proposed algorithm is given in Fig. 2.

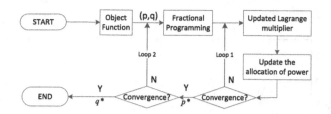

Fig. 2. Flow chart of algorithm

Table 2. Simulation parameter settings

Parameter	Value
Macro cellular/femto cellular radius	500 m/50 m
The minimum signal to noise ratio	1 dB
Femto cellular maximum transmitted power	100 mW
White noise levels	2*10e−9 W
The channel fading model	Rayleigh
The sub channel bandwidth	5 MHz
The average time slot width	2 s
Femto cellular static power consumption	2 W

4   Simulation Results and Discussion

In the simulation conditions, we set offline optimal power allocation algorithm is the inner loop around eleven times to realize iterative convergence, outer loop around six times the iterative convergence, This shows that the algorithm complexity is low (Table 2).

Figure 3 show the average energy efficiency versus number of iterations for different number of femtocell. The proposed power allocation algorithm will be convergence in 11 times. Thus, the complexity of the proposed algorithm is low.

As shown in Fig. 4, the average energy efficiency of the system will be increased as the energy arrival rate increases. This is because the system can harvest more power for each femtocell to maximize the energy efficiency.

Figure 5 shows the relationship of battery capacity and power grid average energy efficiency under different energy arrive rate. From the figure, we can see that the maximum system efficiency is no longer affected when battery capacity exceeds a certain value.

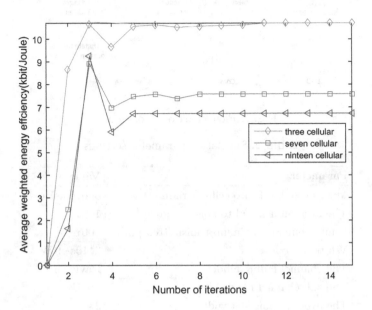

Fig. 3. Average energy efficiency versus number of iterations

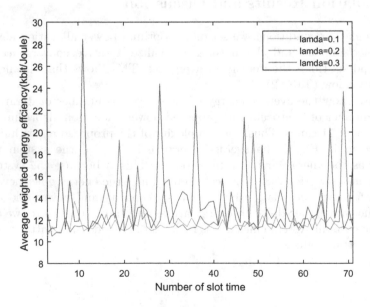

Fig. 4. Total energy efficiency versus energy arrival rate

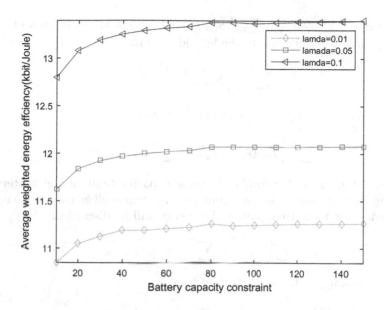

Fig. 5. Average energy efficiency versus battery capacity constraint

5   Conclusions

A low complexity energy efficient power allocation algorithm in HetNets based on energy harvesting is proposed using fractional programming. Through the simulation analysis, the algorithm can guarantee the quality of coverage and business on the basis of the lower area of the interference. The impact of energy arrival rate and battery capacity constraint on the energy efficiency of system. The next step of work is the study of hybrid energy supply, to improve the regional energy efficiency.

Appendix A

Energy use and storage conditions $C1$ and $C2$ can be derived as follows. Let $S_{i,n} = \overline{L_E}\left(p_{i,n}^R + p_{i,n}^O\right)$ be the energy used for femtocell n in time slot i. Then, for time slot 1 to K, we have following inequality constraints.

$$i = 1 : \overline{L_E}\left(p_{1,n}^R + p_{1,n}^O\right) \leq E_{0,n} + E_{1,n}, \forall n$$
$$i = 2 : \overline{L_E}\left(p_{2,n}^R + p_{2,n}^O\right) \leq E_{2,n} + (E_{0,n} + E_{1,n}) - S_{1,n}, \forall n$$
$$= E_{0,n} + E_{1,n} + E_{2,n} - S_{1,n}$$
$$\vdots$$
$$i = K : \overline{L_E}\left(p_{K,n}^R + p_{K,n}^O\right)$$
$$\leq E_{K,n} + (E_{0,n} + E_{1,n} + \cdots + E_{K-1,n}) - (S_{K-1,n} + \cdots + S_{1,n})$$
$$= \sum_{i=0}^{K} E_{i,n} - \sum_{i=1}^{K-1} S_{i,n}$$

therefore $S_{j,n} \le \sum_{i=0}^{j} E_{i,n} - \sum_{i=1}^{j-1} S_{i,n}$ is hold for $j = 1, \cdots, K$, move the item $\sum_{i=1}^{j-1} S_{i,n}$ from the right side to the left side, we have

$$\sum_{i=1,n}^{j} S_{i,n} \le \sum_{i=0}^{j} E_{i,n} \tag{11}$$

substitute $S_{i,n} = \overline{LE} \left(p_{i,n}^{R} + p_{i,n}^{O} \right)$ into (11), we have

$$\sum_{i=1}^{j} \overline{LE} \left(p_{i,n}^{R} + p_{i,n}^{O} \right) \le \sum_{i=0}^{j} E_{i,n}, \forall n;$$

Therefore $C1$ is hold. Meanwhile, because capacity limit of the battery, the remaining battery energy in each time slot for femtocell n cannot exceed the battery capacity, more than part of the energy will be discarded:

$$\sum_{i=0}^{j} E_{i,n} - \sum_{i=1}^{j} S_{i} \le E_{\max,n}$$

for each time slot $j = 1, \cdots, K$, then we have

$$\sum_{i=0}^{j} E_{i,n} - \sum_{i=1}^{j} \overline{LE} \left(p_{i,n}^{R} + p_{i,n}^{O} \right) \le E_{\max,n}$$

Therefore C2 is hold.

References

1. Hossain, E., Hasan, M.: 5G cellular: key enabling technologies and research challenges. IEEE Instrum. Meas. Mag. **18**(3), 11–21 (2015)
2. Liu, D.T., Wang, L.F., et al.: User association in 5G networks: a survey and an outlook. IEEE Commun. Surv. Tutor. **18**(2), 1018–1044 (2016)
3. Yang, H.H., Lee, J., Quek, T.Q.S.: Heterogeneous cellular network with energy harvesting-based D2D communication. IEEE Trans. Wirel. Commun. **15**(2), 1406–1419 (2016)
4. Diamantoulakis, P.D., Pappi, K.N., Karagiannidis, G.K., Poor, H.V.: Autonomous energy harvesting base stations with minimum storage requirements. IEEE Wirel. Commun. Lett. **4**(3), 265–268 (2015)
5. Zhang, T., Xu, H., Liu, D., Beaulieu, N.C., Zhu, Y.: User association for energy-load tradeoffs in Hetnets with renewable energy supply. IEEE Commun. Lett. **19**(12), 2214–2217 (2015)
6. Gong, J., Zho, S., Zhou, Z., Niu, Z.: Downlink base station cooperation with energy harvesting. In: 2014 IEEE International Conference on Communication Systems (ICCS), Macau, pp. 87–91 (2014)
7. Reyhanian, N., Maham, B., Shah-Mansouri, V., Yuen, C.: A matching-game-based energy trading for small cell networks with energy harvesting. In: 2015 IEEE 26th Annual International Symposium on Personal, Indoor, and Mobile Radio Communications (PIMRC), Hong Kong, pp. 1579–1583 (2015)
8. Ng, D.W.K., Lo, E.S., Schober, R.: Energy-efficient resource allocation in OFDMA systems with hybrid energy harvesting base station. IEEE Trans. Wirel. Commun. **12**(7), 3412–3427 (2013)

9. Mao, Y., Zhang, J., Letaief, K.B.: A lyapunov optimization approach for green cellular networks with hybrid energy supplies. IEEE J. Sel. Areas Commun. **33**(12), 2463–2477 (2015)
10. Gorlatova, M., Wallwater, A., Zussman, G.: Networking low-power energy harvesting devices: measurements and algorithms. In: Proceedings of IEEE International Conference on Computer Communications (INFOCOM), Shanghai (2011)
11. Dinkelbach, W.: On nonlinear fractional programming. Manag. Sci. **13**, 492–498 (1967)
12. Schaible, S., Ibaraki, T.: Fractional programming. Eur. J. Oper. Res. Int. J. **12**(4), 325–338 (1983)
13. Boyd, S., Mutapcic, A.: Subgradient Methods. Notes for EE364b, Stanford University (2007)

Price-Based Power Allocation in Energy Harvesting Wireless Cooperative Networks: A Stackelberg Game Approach

Chongyang Li[✉] and Xin Zhao

School of Electronics and Information Technology, Sun Yat-sen University,
Guangzhou 510006, China
{lizhy46,zhaox43}@mail2.sysu.edu.cn

Abstract. In this letter, a wireless cooperative network is considered, in which multiple source-destination pairs communicate with each other via an energy harvesting relay. We propose a price-based power allocation scheme to distribute the harvested energy among the multiple users. We model the interaction between the relay and the destinations as a Stackelberg game and then study the joint utility maximization of the relay and the destination. The Stackelberg equilibriums for the proposed game are characterized. Simulation results show the effectiveness of the proposed algorithm in comparison with the uniform pricing algorithm.

Keywords: Stackelberg game · Wireless power transfer · Price · Power allocation

1 Introduction

With rapid growth of wireless services in recent years, issues in energy consumption become increasingly critical for wireless communication systems. Therefor energy harvesting, a technique to collect energy from the environment, has recently received considerable attention as a sustainable solution to overcoming the bottleneck of energy constrained wireless networks [1]. Unlike conventional energy harvesting techniques rely on external energy sources such as solar and wind [2], ambient radio signal can also be a practicable source since radio signal carries energy as well as information at the same time, so that wireless signals can be used as a means for the delivery of information and power simultaneously [3]. The work [4] investigated the optimal information/energy beamforming strategy to achieve the maximum harvested energy for multi-user MISO SWIPT system with separated information/energy receivers. SWIPT for relay system and multiple access channel was consider in [5]. The problem in such energy harvesting networks is that practical circuits cannot realize energy harvesting and data detection from wireless signals at the same time. In [6], the authors introduced a general receive architecture, in which the circuits for energy harvesting and signal detection are operated in a time sharing or power splitting manner. The

© ICST Institute for Computer Sciences, Social Informatics and Telecommunications Engineering 2018
Q. Chen et al. (Eds.): ChinaCom 2016, Part II, LNICST 210, pp. 44–53, 2018.
DOI: 10.1007/978-3-319-66628-0_5

performance difference between power splitting and time sharing is studied in broadcasting scenarios in [7]. In a power splitting scheme, the received signal is split with an adjustable power splitting ratio to enable simultaneous energy harvesting and information decoding.

In this paper, we consider a general wireless cooperative network, where multiple source-destination pairs communicate with each other via an energy harvesting relay. Specifically, the cooperative transmission consists of two time slots of duration $\frac{T}{2}$. In the first slot, multiple sources deliver their information to the relay via orthogonal channels. At the end of the first phase, the relay splits the signals sent from the i-th source into two streams, one for detection and the other for energy harvesting. Then in the second phase, the relaying transmissions are power by the energy harvested at the relay. The relay's strategies to distribute the harvested energy among the multiple users are investigated in [8], e.g., the noncooperative individual transmission strategy and the equal allocation scheme. In this letter, we propose a new price-based power allocation scheme, where the relay price the destinations to control the transmission power under the total transmit power constraint. The relay will choose a suitable price to maximize its revenue from the destinations. The destination will choose an optimal power to maximize its utility after the relay set prices for them. A Stackelberg game is formulated to model the strategy between the relay and the destinations and we study the Stackelberg equilibriums for the proposed power allocation game.

Notations: Boldface capital and lowercase letters denote matrices and vectors, respectively. The inequalities for vectors are defined element-wise, i.e., $\boldsymbol{x} \preceq \boldsymbol{y}$ represents $x_i \leq y_i, \forall i$, where x_i and y_i are the i-th elements of the vector $\boldsymbol{x}$ and $\boldsymbol{y}$, respectively. The superscript T denotes the transpose operation of a vector.

2   System Model and Problem Formulation

Consider an energy harvesting communication scenario, where N source nodes (S_i, for $i = 1, ..., N$) intended to communicate with their respective destination nodes (D_i, for $i = 1, ..., N$) through an intermediate relay node (R). Each node is equipped with a single antenna. For simplicity, we assume that channel state information (CSI) of each link is perfectly known to the relay. Further, the relay nodes are operate in the half-duplex mode with two transmission phases. Among the various energy harvesting relaying models, we focus on power splitting. Let θ_i denote the power splitting coefficient for S_i at R. At the end of the first phase, R harvests the following amount of energy from S_i:

$$E_i = \eta P_{S_i} h_{i,j} \theta_i \frac{T}{2}, \tag{1}$$

where η denotes the energy harvesting efficiency factor, P_{S_i} denotes the transmission power at S_i, h_i denotes the channel power gain between S_i and R.

Then the total power reserved at the relay at the end of the first phase is:

$$P_R = \sum_{i=1}^{N} \frac{E_i}{\frac{T}{2}} = \sum_{i=1}^{N} \eta P_{S_i} h_i \theta_i \frac{T}{2}, \tag{2}$$

Assuming that the battery is sufficiently large, the relay can accumulate a significant amount of power for relaying transmission. We focus on the strategy to distribute the harvested energy among the multiple users. The strategy between the relay and the multiple users is modeled as a Stackelberg game. The relay is the leader in this game. It choose a price on per transmission power for each destination to maximize its own revenue. Then the destinations will decide the transmit power to maximize their utilities based on the assigned power price.

Let λ_i denotes the price paid to R on per transmission power for D_i. The total revenue of the relay can be expressed as:

$$U_R = \sum_{i=1}^{N} \lambda_i p_i, \tag{3}$$

where p_i denotes the transmission power allocated to D_i at the relay. Let $\boldsymbol{\lambda} = [\lambda_1, \lambda_2, \cdots, \lambda_N]^T$. The problem of the relay is formulated as:

$$\max_{\boldsymbol{\lambda} \succeq 0} \quad U_R = \sum_{i=1}^{N} \lambda_i p_i,$$

$$\text{s.t.} \quad \sum_{i=1}^{N} p_i \leq P_R,$$

$$p_i \geq 0. \tag{4}$$

The data rate D_i can achieve is $R_{D_i} = \frac{1}{2} \log_2(1 + \frac{p_i g_i}{\sigma_i^2})$, where p_i denotes the channel power gain between R and D_i, and σ_i^2 denotes the background noise at D_i. Without loss of generality, it is assumed for convenience that $\sigma_i^2 = \sigma^2, \forall i$. The utility for D_i can be defined as:

$$U_{D_i} = \frac{1}{2} \omega_i \log_2(1 + \frac{p_i g_i}{\sigma^2}) - \lambda_i p_i, \tag{5}$$

where ω_i denotes the equivalent utility per unit data valuation contributing to D_i's utility. Let $\mathbf{p} = [p_1, p_2, \cdots, p_N]^T$. The problem for D_i is formulated as:

$$\max_{p_i \geq 0} \quad U_{D_i} = \frac{1}{2} \omega_i \log_2(1 + \frac{p_i g_i}{\sigma^2}) - \lambda_i p_i. \tag{6}$$

The problem (4) and (6) together form a Stackelberg game in which R is the leader. The objective is to find the Stackelberg Equilibrium (SE) point(s).

3   Optimal Price-Based Power Allocation Algorithm

For the proposed Stackelberg game, the SE is defined as follows.

Definition 1: Let $\boldsymbol{\lambda}^*$ be a solution for problem (4) and p_i^* be a solution for problem (6) of $D_i(i = 1, ..., N)$. The point $(\boldsymbol{\lambda}^*, \mathbf{p}^*)$ is a SE for the addressed game if for any $(\boldsymbol{\lambda}, \mathbf{p})$ with $\boldsymbol{\lambda} \succeq 0$ and $\mathbf{p} \succeq 0$, the following conditions are satisfied:

$$U_R(\boldsymbol{\lambda}^*, \mathbf{p}^*) \geq U_R(\boldsymbol{\lambda}, \mathbf{p}^*), \tag{7}$$

$$U_{D_i}(p_i^*, \mathbf{p}_{-i}^*, \boldsymbol{\lambda}^*) \geq U_{D_i}(p_i, \mathbf{p}_{-i}^*, \boldsymbol{\lambda}^*), \forall i. \tag{8}$$

The SE can be obtained as follows: For a given $\boldsymbol{\lambda}$, problem (6) is solved first. Then, the optimal price of problem (4) can be obtained with the optimal power allocated strategy p_i^*.

Recall problem (6), it is observed that the objective function is a concave function with the allocated power p_i, and the constraint is affine. Thus, problem (6) is a convex optimization problem. Therefore, we can solve the problem by using the KKT conditions.

Lemma 1: For a given price λ_i, the optimal solution for problem (8) is given by:

$$p_i^* = \left(\frac{\frac{1}{2}\omega_i}{\lambda_i} - \frac{\sigma^2}{g_i}\right)^+, \forall i, \tag{9}$$

where $(\cdot)^+ \triangleq max(\cdot, 0)$.

From (9), the power allocated to D_i is zero if the price for D_i is too high, i.e., $\lambda_i \geq \frac{\frac{1}{2}\omega_i g_i}{\sigma^2}$. This means that D_i will be removed from the game. Substituting (9) into problem (4):

$$\max_{\boldsymbol{\lambda} \succeq 0} \quad \sum_{i=1}^{N} \left(\frac{1}{2}\omega_i - \frac{\lambda_i \sigma^2}{g_i}\right)^+,$$

$$\text{s.t.} \quad \sum_{i=1}^{N} \left(\frac{\frac{1}{2}\omega_i}{\lambda_i} - \frac{\sigma^2}{g_i}\right)^+ \leq P_R. \tag{10}$$

Assume P_R is large enough so that all the destinations are involved, i.e., $\lambda_i < \frac{\frac{1}{2}\omega_i g_i}{\sigma^2}, \forall i$. Then problem (10) can be transformed to the following form:

$$\min_{\boldsymbol{\lambda} \succeq 0} \quad \sum_{i=1}^{N} \frac{\lambda_i \sigma^2}{g_i},$$

$$\text{s.t.} \quad \sum_{i=1}^{N} \frac{\frac{1}{2}\omega_i}{\lambda_i} \leq P_R + \sum_{i=1}^{N} \frac{\sigma^2}{g_i}. \tag{11}$$

Obviously, this problem is convex. Next, we will give the optimal solution to problem (11).

It is observed that problem (11) is a convex optimization problem. Thus, there is no duality gap between this problem and its dual optimization problem. Therefor, problem (11) can be solved by its dual problem.

The Lagrangian function of problem (11) is given as:

$$L(\boldsymbol{\lambda}, \alpha, \boldsymbol{\beta}) = \sum_{i=1}^{N} \frac{\lambda_i \sigma^2}{g_i} + \alpha \left(\sum_{i=1}^{N} \frac{\frac{1}{2}\omega_i}{\lambda_i} - P_R - \sum_{i=1}^{N} \frac{\sigma^2}{g_i} \right)$$
$$- \sum_{i=1}^{N} \beta_i \lambda_i, \tag{12}$$

where α and β_i are non-negative dual variables associated with the constrains $\sum_{i=1}^{N} \frac{\frac{1}{2}\omega_i}{\lambda_i} \leq P_R + \sum_{i=1}^{N} \frac{\sigma^2}{g_i}$ and $\lambda_i \geq 0$.

The dual objective is then defined as $G(\boldsymbol{\lambda}, \alpha, \boldsymbol{\beta}) = \max_{\boldsymbol{\lambda} \succeq 0} L(\boldsymbol{\lambda}, \alpha, \boldsymbol{\beta})$, and the dual optimization problem is given by $\min_{\alpha \geq 0, \boldsymbol{\beta} \succeq 0} G(\boldsymbol{\lambda}, \alpha, \boldsymbol{\beta})$. Then, KKT conditions are given as follows:

$$\frac{\partial L(\boldsymbol{\lambda}, \alpha, \boldsymbol{\beta})}{\partial \lambda_i} = \frac{\sigma^2}{g_i} - \alpha \frac{\frac{1}{2}\omega_i}{\lambda_i^2} - \beta_i = 0, \forall i, \tag{13}$$

$$\alpha \left(\sum_{i=1}^{N} \frac{\frac{1}{2}\omega_i}{\lambda_i} - P_R - \sum_{i=1}^{N} \frac{\sigma^2}{g_i} \right) = 0, \tag{14}$$

$$\alpha \geq 0, \beta_i \geq 0, \lambda_i \geq 0, \beta_i \lambda_i = 0, \forall i, \tag{15}$$

$$\sum_{i=1}^{N} \frac{\frac{1}{2}\omega_i}{\lambda_i} - P_R - \sum_{i=1}^{N} \frac{\sigma^2}{g_i} \leq 0. \tag{16}$$

From (13), we have:

$$\lambda_i^2 = \alpha \frac{\frac{1}{2}\omega_i}{\frac{\sigma^2}{g_i} - \beta_i}, \forall i. \tag{17}$$

Lemma 2: $\beta_i = 0, \forall i$.

Proof: We prove it by contradiction. Assume that $\beta_i \neq 0$ for any arbitrary i. Then, from $\beta_i \lambda_i = 0$ in (15), we have $\lambda_i = 0$. Substituting it into (17), we have $\alpha = 0$ since $\omega_i > 0$. Then, from (17), it follows that $\lambda_i = 0, \forall i$, which contradicts (16), and thus we have $\beta_i = 0, \forall i$. ∎

Lemma 3: $\sum_{i=1}^{N} \frac{\frac{1}{2}\omega_i}{\lambda_i} - P_R - \sum_{i=1}^{N} \frac{\sigma^2}{g_i} = 0$.

Proof: We prove it by contradiction. Assume that $\sum_{i=1}^{N} \frac{\frac{1}{2}\omega_i}{\lambda_i} - P_R - \sum_{i=1}^{N} \frac{\sigma^2}{g_i} \neq 0$. Then from (14), we have $\alpha = 0$. Then, from (17), it follows that $\lambda_i = 0, \forall i$, which contradicts (16), and thus we have $\sum_{i=1}^{N} \frac{\frac{1}{2}\omega_i}{\lambda_i} - P_R - \sum_{i=1}^{N} \frac{\sigma^2}{g_i} = 0$. ∎

According to Lemma 2, (17) can be rewritten as $\lambda_i = \sqrt{\frac{\frac{1}{2}\omega_i g_i \alpha}{\sigma^2}}, \forall i$. Substituting it into (16) and according to Lemma 3, we have $\sqrt{\alpha} = \frac{\sum_{i=1}^{N} \sqrt{\frac{\frac{1}{2}\omega_i \sigma^2}{g_i}}}{P_R + \sum_{i=1}^{N} \frac{\sigma^2}{g_i}}$. Thus, we have:

$$\lambda_i = \sqrt{\frac{\frac{1}{2}\omega_i g_i}{\sigma^2}} \frac{\sum_{i=1}^{N} \sqrt{\frac{\frac{1}{2}\omega_i \sigma^2}{g_i}}}{P_R + \sum_{i=1}^{N} \frac{\sigma^2}{g_i}}, \forall i. \tag{18}$$

With the results obtained above, we give the optimal solution for problem (11) by the following proposition.

Proposition 3: The optimal solution to problem (11) is given by

$$\lambda_i^* = \sqrt{\frac{\frac{1}{2}\omega_i g_i}{\sigma^2}} \frac{\sum_{i=1}^{N} \sqrt{\frac{\frac{1}{2}\omega_i \sigma^2}{g_i}}}{P_R + \sum_{i=1}^{N} \frac{\sigma^2}{g_i}}, \forall i \in \{1, 2, \cdots, N\}. \tag{19}$$

Now, we relate the optimal solution of problem (11) to that of the original problem (10) in the following proposition.

Proposition 4: The power prices given by (19) are the optimal solutions of problem (10) if and only if $P_R > \frac{\sum_{i=1}^{N} \sqrt{\frac{\frac{1}{2}\omega_i \sigma^2}{g_i}}}{\min_i \sqrt{\frac{\frac{1}{2}\omega_i g_i}{\sigma^2}}} - \sum_{i=1}^{N} \frac{\sigma^2}{g_i}$.

Proof: Sufficiency Part: It is observed that the price vector $\boldsymbol{\lambda}^*$ given by (19) is the optimal solution of problem (10) if $\lambda_i < \frac{\frac{1}{2}\omega_i g_i}{\sigma^2}, \forall i \in \{1, 2, \cdots, N\}$. Substituting (19) into these inequalities yields $\sqrt{\frac{\frac{1}{2}\omega_i g_i}{\sigma^2}} \frac{\sum_{i=1}^{N} \sqrt{\frac{\frac{1}{2}\omega_i \sigma^2}{g_i}}}{P_R + \sum_{i=1}^{N} \frac{\sigma^2}{g_i}} < \frac{\frac{1}{2}\omega_i g_i}{\sigma^2}, \forall i \in \{1, 2, \cdots, N\}$. Thus, it follows that $P_R > \frac{\sum_{i=1}^{N} \sqrt{\frac{\frac{1}{2}\omega_i \sigma^2}{g_i}}}{\sqrt{\frac{\frac{1}{2}\omega_i g_i}{\sigma^2}}} - \sum_{i=1}^{N} \frac{\sigma^2}{g_i}, \forall i \in \{1, 2, \cdots, N\}$. Furthermore, the inequalities given above can be compactly written as:

$$P_R > \frac{\sum_{i=1}^{N} \sqrt{\frac{\frac{1}{2}\omega_i \sigma^2}{g_i}}}{\min_i \sqrt{\frac{\frac{1}{2}\omega_i g_i}{\sigma^2}}} - \sum_{i=1}^{N} \frac{\sigma^2}{g_i}. \tag{20}$$

Necessity Part: We prove it by contradiction. Assuming that destinations are sorted by the following order: $\frac{\frac{1}{2}\omega_1 g_1}{\sigma^2} > \cdots > \frac{\frac{1}{2}\omega_{N-1} g_{N-1}}{\sigma^2} > \frac{\frac{1}{2}\omega_N g_N}{\sigma^2}$. Then, in Proposition 4, the condition becomes:

$$P_R > T_N, T_N = \frac{\sum_{i=1}^{N} \sqrt{\frac{\frac{1}{2}\omega_i \sigma^2}{g_i}}}{\sqrt{\frac{\frac{1}{2}\omega_N g_N}{\sigma^2}}} - \sum_{i=1}^{N} \frac{\sigma^2}{g_i}. \tag{21}$$

Now, suppose $T_{N-1} < P_R \leq T_N$, where T_{N-1} is a threshold shown later in (24). Suppose that $\boldsymbol{\lambda}^*$ given by (19) is still optimal for Problem (10) with $T_{N-1} < P_R < T_N$. Then, since $P_R \leq T_N$, from (19) it follows that $\lambda_N^* \geq \frac{\frac{1}{2}\omega_N g_N}{\sigma^2}$ and thus $(\frac{\frac{1}{2}\omega_N}{\lambda_N} - \frac{\sigma^2}{g_N})^+ = 0$. From Problem (10) it then follows that $\lambda_1^*, \cdots, \lambda_{N-1}^*$ is the optimal solution of the following problem:

$$\max_{\boldsymbol{\lambda} \succeq 0} \sum_{i=1}^{N-1} (\frac{1}{2}\omega_i - \frac{\lambda_i \sigma^2}{g_i})^+,$$

$$\text{s.t.} \quad \sum_{i=1}^{N-1} (\frac{\frac{1}{2}\omega_i}{\lambda_i} - \frac{\sigma^2}{g_i})^+ \leq P_R. \tag{22}$$

This problem is similar to Problem (10). Thus, from the proof of the previous sufficiency part, we can show that the optimal solution for this problem is given by:

$$\lambda_i^* = \sqrt{\frac{\frac{1}{2}\omega_i g_i}{\sigma^2}} \frac{\sum_{i=1}^{N-1} \sqrt{\frac{\frac{1}{2}\omega_i \sigma^2}{g_i}}}{P_R + \sum_{i=1}^{N-1} \frac{\sigma^2}{g_i}}, \forall i \in \{1, 2, \cdots, N-1\}, \tag{23}$$

if $P_R > T_{N-1}$, where T_{N-1} is obtained as the threshold for P_R above which $\lambda_i^* < \frac{\frac{1}{2}\omega_i g_i}{\sigma^2}$ holds $\forall i \in \{1, 2, \cdots, N-1\}$, i.e.,

$$T_{N-1} = \frac{\sum_{i=1}^{N-1} \sqrt{\frac{\frac{1}{2}\omega_i \sigma^2}{g_i}}}{\sqrt{\frac{\frac{1}{2}\omega_{N-1} g_{N-1}}{\sigma^2}}} - \sum_{i=1}^{N-1} \frac{\sigma^2}{g_i}. \tag{24}$$

Obviously, the optimal power price solution in (23) for the above problem is different from that given by (19). Thus, this contradicts with our presumption that $\boldsymbol{\lambda}^*$ is optimal for Problem (10) with $T_{N-1} < P_R \leq T_N$. ∎

Therefore, the optimal solution of problem (10) can be given by the following theorem.

Theorem 1: Assuming that all the destinations are sorted in the order $\frac{\frac{1}{2}\omega_1 g_1}{\sigma^2} > \cdots > \frac{\frac{1}{2}\omega_{N-1} g_{N-1}}{\sigma^2} > \frac{\frac{1}{2}\omega_N g_N}{\sigma^2}$, the optimal solution for problem (10) is given by:

$$\boldsymbol{\lambda}^* = \begin{cases} q_N[\sqrt{\frac{\frac{1}{2}\omega_1 g_1}{\sigma^2}}, \sqrt{\frac{\frac{1}{2}\omega_2 g_2}{\sigma^2}}, \cdots, \sqrt{\frac{\frac{1}{2}\omega_N g_N}{\sigma^2}}]^T, \\ \qquad\qquad\qquad\qquad\qquad \text{if} \qquad P_R > T_N \\ q_{N-1}[\sqrt{\frac{\frac{1}{2}\omega_1 g_1}{\sigma^2}}, \cdots, \sqrt{\frac{\frac{1}{2}\omega_{N-1} g_{N-1}}{\sigma^2}}, \infty]^T, \\ \qquad\qquad\qquad\qquad\qquad \text{if} \ T_N \geq P_R > T_{N-1} \\ \qquad\qquad\qquad\qquad \vdots \\ q_1[\sqrt{\frac{\frac{1}{2}\omega_1 g_1}{\sigma^2}}, \infty, \cdots, \infty]^T, \\ \qquad\qquad\qquad\qquad\qquad \text{if} \qquad T_2 \geq P_R > T_1 \end{cases} \qquad (25)$$

where $q_K = \frac{\sum_{i=1}^{K}\sqrt{\frac{\frac{1}{2}\omega_i \sigma^2}{g_i}}}{P_R + \sum_{i=1}^{K}\frac{\sigma^2}{g_i}}$ and $T_K = \frac{\sum_{i=1}^{K}\sqrt{\frac{\frac{1}{2}\omega_i \sigma^2}{g_i}}}{\sqrt{\frac{\frac{1}{2}\omega_K g_K}{\sigma^2}}} - \sum_{i=1}^{K}\frac{\sigma^2}{g_i}, \forall K \in$

$\{1, 2, \cdots, N\}$.

Proof: If $P_R > T_N$, the optimal $\boldsymbol{\lambda}^*$ is readily obtained by Proposition 3. For other intervals of P_R, e.g., $T_{N-1} < P_R \leq T_N$, the proof of the optimality for the corresponding $\boldsymbol{\lambda}^*$ can be obtained similarly as Proposition 3. ∎

Now, the proposed Stackelberg game is completely solved. And the SE for this game is then given by the following proposition.

Proposition 5: The SE for the Stackelberg game formulated in problem (4) and (6) is $(\boldsymbol{\lambda}^*, \mathbf{p}^*)$, where $\boldsymbol{\lambda}^*$ is given by (25), and $\mathbf{p}^*$ is given by (9).

4 Simulation Results

In this section, computer simulations will be carried out to evaluate the performance of the proposed power allocation protocol described in the previous sections. For simplicity, we assume that the variance of the noise is 1, and the payoff factors $\omega_i, \forall i$ are all equal to 2.

An wireless cooperative network with one energy harvesting relay and three user pairs is considered. Without loss of generality, the channel power gains are chosen as follows: $g_1 = 10, g_2 = 1, g_3 = 0.1$.

Now, we compare the system performance obtained by the price-based power allocation algorithm with the uniform pricing algorithm proposed in [9]. In Fig. 1, we present the total income of the relay versus the total energy harvested at it. It is observed that the revenue of the relay increases as P_R increases in both tow algorithms. This is because that the pricing strategies for the relay increases as the available energy increases. And for the same available power P_R, the revenues of the relay under the price-based power allocation algorithm are more than the uniform pricing algorithm. In addition, when P_R is sufficiently small, the revenues of the relay under the tow pricing schemes are identical. It is because that when P_R is very small, there is only one destination active in this game, and thus the proposed price-based algorithm is same as the uniform pricing scheme.

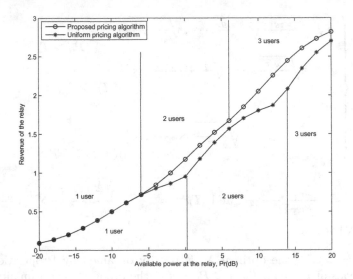

Fig. 1. Revenue of the relay vs. P_R

5   Conclusions

In this letter, we have studied a power allocation strategies for a cooperative network in which multiple user pairs communicate with each other via an energy harvesting relay. And we propose a price-based power allocation scheme to distribute the harvested energy among the multiple users. The Stackelberg game model is adopted to investigate the joint utility maximization of the relay and the destination, closed-form solutions are obtained for the strategy proposed. Compared with the uniform pricing algorithm, simulation results show that the proposed price-based algorithm improves the revenue of the relay for all the available power P_R.

References

1. Raghunathan, V., Ganeriwal, S., Srivastava, M.: Emerging techniques for long lived wireless sensor networks. IEEE Commun. Mag. **44**(4), 108–114 (2006)
2. Paradiso, J., Starner, T.: Energy scavenging for mobile and wireless electronics. IEEE Pervasive Comput. **4**(1), 18–27 (2005)
3. Grover, P., Sahai, A.: Shannon meets Tesla: wireless information and power transfer. In: Proceedings of IEEE International Symposium on Information Theory (2010)
4. Xu, J., Liu, L., Zhang, R.: Multiuser MISO beamforming for simultaneous wireless information and power transfer. In: Proceedings of IEEE International Conference on Acoustics, Speech and Signal Processing (ICASSP), pp. 4754–4758 (2013)
5. Chalise, B.K., Zhang, Y.D., Amin, M.G.: Energy harvesting in an OSTBC based amplify-and-forward MIMO relay system. In: Proceedings of IEEE International Conference on Acoustics, Speech and Signal Processing (ICASSP), pp. 3201–3204, March 2012

6. Zhou, X., Zhang, R., Ho, C.K.: Wireless information and power transfer: architecture design and rate-energy tradeoff. IEEE Trans. Commun. (submitted). http://arxiv.org/abs/1205.0618
7. Zhang, R., Ho, C.K.: MIMO broadcasting for simultaneous wireless information and power transfer. IEEE Trans. Wirel. Commun. **12**(5), 1989–2001 (2013)
8. Ding, Z., Perlaza, S.M., Poor, H.V.: Power allocation strategies in energy harvesting wireless cooperative networks. IEEE Trans. Wirel. Commun. **13**(12), 846–860 (2014)
9. Kang, X., Zhang, R., Motani, M.: Price-based resource allocation for spectrum-sharing femtocell networks: a stackelberg game approach. IEEE J. Sel. Areas Commun. **30**(3), 538–549 (2012)

Resource Allocation Schemes (1)

Coverage and Capacity Optimization Based on Tabu Search in Ultra-Dense Network

Xin Su, Xiaofeng Lin, Jie Zeng[✉], and Chiyang Xiao

Tsinghua National Laboratory for Information Science and Technology,
Research Institute of Information Technology, Tsinghua University, Beijing, China
zengjie@tsinghua.edu.cn

Abstract. To meet the requirements of high system capacity and coverage of 5G network, ultra-dense network is viewed as the key technology for networking evolution. And for densely deployed small cell network, self-optimization is crucial in the aspect of reducing the cost of network management while optimizing the network performance. This paper focuses on the coverage and capacity optimization, proposing a mathematical combined optimization function to balance the conflicting key performance indicators. And under this model, we propose the tabu search algorithm for generating new antenna transmit power to optimize the performance. Simulation results show that our proposed algorithm gets significant improvement in network performance and outperforms the adaptive simulated annealing in convergence speed while optimizing.

Keywords: Ultra-dense network · Coverage and capacity optimization · Tabu search · Small cell

1 Introduction

The explosive growth of mobile data traffic these years puts forward high requirements for the bandwidth and performance of coverage and capacity of the 5th generation (5G) networks, such as ultra-high traffic volume density and ultra-high peak data rate [1]. This makes the traditional way of covering just by macro base station (MBS) difficult to meet the users' needs nowadays. Besides, large amount of data traffic occurs in some hot-spot areas, such as the office building, dense residential area, subway and other apartment, meanwhile, the data traffic is also unevenly distributed, thus causing not ideal signals and congestion in part of the network. Therefore, the ultra-dense deployment of short-distance, low-power small cell base stations become an effective solution for the challenges. Ultra-dense network (UDN) is viewed as one of the key technologies for 5G [2]. The densely deployed small cells can bring hundreds of times capacity improvement in extreme cases [1], as well as enhancement in coverage, thereby increasing the capacity of the entire network. In particular, for both indoor and outdoor high-density services requiring areas, the dense deployment of small cell base stations can effectively improve the quality of service (QoS) and provide more efficient services [3]. However, the expected large number of small

© ICST Institute for Computer Sciences, Social Informatics and Telecommunications Engineering 2018
Q. Chen et al. (Eds.): ChinaCom 2016, Part II, LNICST 210, pp. 57–66, 2018.
DOI: 10.1007/978-3-319-66628-0_6

cells as well as their much more dynamic unplanned deployment raises a variety of challenges in the area of network management [4]. To improve the network performance, automate the optimization of the network, simplify the network designing and reduce operation cost of the network, the network should be more intelligent to improve itself when needing. As one of the self-organized functions, self-optimization of the network can replace manually operations, thus reducing the cost of network management while optimizing the network performance. Through monitoring changes of performance indexes and fault events during the network operation, self-optimization can automatically select certain optimization algorithm to adjust corresponding parameters of the network, so as to achieve optimal system performance.

The coverage and capacity optimization (CCO) is based on the identification of the coverage and capacity issues and select an optimization algorithm to automatically modify parameters, to repair and improve the coverage and capacity problems. Most of the contributions consider the antenna downtilt as the parameter to be modified in LTE networks [5], while in ultra-dense network, the small cell base stations' antennas are omnidirectional and isotropic, hence we choose other parameters like transmit power to modify. Most of the existing work concentrates on combined optimization. [6] constructed an objective function to jointly maximize throughput and coverage, using a probability distribution function (PDF) for throughput measurements and an estimate of the number of covered and uncovered users of each considered cell. [7] proposed a general concept for the self-organization of multiple KPIs rather than only an algorithm for tilt-based CCO. And they proposed an effective tilt-based algorithm which combined to optimize coverage and capacity in downlink (DL) and uplink (UL) jointly. What's more, it used a real-world urban LTE deployment scenario in practice and outperformed well. [8] used the concept of effective capacity as the optimization objective, which involved the index of coverage in function, thus achieving joint optimization. When facing high complexity optimizing scenario, [9] introduced a low-complexity interference approximation model and formulated the optimization problem as a mixed-integer linear program. They proposed a traffic-light-related approach to consider multi-parameter optimization. [10] only modified a limited set of basic beams combined with an overall beam, to reduce complexity caused by 2-dimensional antenna arrays, while achieving adequate performance gains by Nelder-Mead and Q-learning approach. However, that paper mainly optimized coverage in its cost function instead of its so-called CCO. In this paper, we focus on optimize coverage and capacity in UDN, and propose a tabu search (TS) algorithm for adjusting parameters and reduce complexity under our proposed combined mathematical model.

The remainder of the paper is organized as follows. In Sect. 2, the system model and our defined mathematical model for combined optimization is introduced. In Sect. 3, we present our proposed TS algorithm and describe details applying in our ultra-dense small cell network. Simulation environment and results of CCO performance are presented and contrast with the Simulated Annealing (SA) approach in Sect. 4, and Sect. 5 concludes this paper.

2   System Model

We consider a scenario case based on a hexagonal 19-site network deployment, which has original one site deployed in the middle and other six ones wrap-around it symmetrically, also with other twelve ones attached to these six ones' sides. These are 19 macro base stations, each with three sectors deployed as hexagon. The path loss between users and their serving base stations is defined by the distance between them, including propagation loss, shadow fading and antenna gain. It can be affected by many configuration parameters, including transmit power. In our work, we adjust the transmit power of the small cells with other parameters fixed, to optimize coverage and capacity in the network.

Consider a 19-site network consisting of K MBSs, M SBSs and N deployed UEs. MBSs are indexed as l, $l = 1, 2, \cdots, K$, SBSs are indexed as j, $j = 1, 2, \cdots, M$, while UEs are indexed as i, $i = 1, 2, \cdots, N$. The transmit power of all the SBSs is denoted by the vector $\mathbf{p}$, $\mathbf{p} = \{p_1, p_2, \cdots, p_M\}$. In the downlink, the transmission channel gain between SBS j and the UE i is expressed as g_{ij}, thus the received signal strength at UE i from SBS j is defined as follows:

$$P_{rx}(i, j) = p_j g_{ij} \tag{1}$$

Assume that the system noise is σ^2, hence the downlink SINR of UE i associated with SBS j is calculated as:

$$SINR_i = \frac{g_{ij} p_j}{\sigma^2 + \sum_{k \neq j} g_{ik} p_k} \tag{2}$$

Then we use a function to map each user's $SINR$ to its spectal efficiency, shown in the form of a step function with each step a linear function.

$$SE_i = Map(SINR_i) \tag{3}$$

The performance of coverage and capacity can be judged by a measurement of spectral efficiency, that is, using average spectral efficiency to represent coverage and edge spectral efficiency for capacity. Hence, we use a combined optimization function to judge the performance of coverage and capacity of the overall system. The function can balance coverage and capacity optimization objectives, by using a compromise coefficient γ, $0 < \gamma < 1$. The combined optimization function is defined as follows:

$$F(\mathbf{p}) = (1 - \gamma)SE_{ave} + \gamma SE_{edge} \tag{4}$$

where SE_{ave} is the average spectral efficiency which can be obtained by calculating the mean of all UEs' spectral efficiency, while SE_{edge} stands for the edge spectral efficiency which can be obtained by calculating the 5% -tile of the UEs' spectral efficiency. The typical value γ can take is 0.5, and a bigger value means we choose to pay more attention to improving the coverage performance, otherwise, to improving the capacity performance.

3   Optimization Schemes Based on Tabu Search

In order to optimize the combined function shown in 4, we use the improved tabu search algorithm to iteratively update the transmit power of SBSs. Tabu search are more used to solve combinatorial optimization problems, especially when the dimension of the problem is really high and with large amount of data. It can reduce the complexity when finding the optimal solution. The main idea of TS is to mark some local optimal solutions and try to avoid (but not completely prohibit) them, so as to avoid falling into local optima.

The TS algorithm begins with an initial solution vector, which in our work is the initial transmit power of all SBSs. However, in our work, the number of SBSs comes to 152, which means each macro cell has two small cell clusters and four SBSs in each cluster. What's more, to find a more optimal solution vector, TS defines a neighborhood around its last iteration's solution vector. In view of the transmit power of each SBS is in the range of $[-10\,\text{dBm}, 24\,\text{dBm}]$, we may have a large amount of neighborhood vectors to deal with. In order to avoid high complexity caused by the two aspects described above when calculating, instead of dealing with all the transmit power in one small iteration, we choose to view the SBSs in the same macro cell as a group. And in each inner iteration we just change one group's transmit power, to make the power vector move to the best vector among this group's neighboring vectors. The inner iteration continued until all the 19 groups' transmit power vectors have been changed to a best solution in their neighboring vectors. After finished one outer iteration, which means all SBSs' transmit power has moved to a best solution in their neighboring vectors, TS algorithm continues next outer iteration. As for the specific method to choose the best vector among neighboring vectors, definitions of related concepts should be given first. Firstly, the "neighboring vector" are the vectors that only have one element different from all the elements of the given vector. The difference aforementioned is constrained by "neighbor range", which means that the difference between the changed element and the one in the given vector must be no more than neighbor range. The TS algorithm attempts to avoid local optima by marking the newly gotten solution vectors of the past few iterations as "tabu". The number of the past few iterations is called "tabu period", set as P, which means if a solution vector is marked as tabu in an iteration, it will remain as tabu in tabu matrix for P outer iterations. The marking "tabu" is stored in "tabu matrix", whose entries corresponding to certain solution vectors are non-negative integers. These integers are updated in each outer iteration, that is, usually begin with P and minus one in each later iteration until come to zero. After making the definition clear, the steps of TS algorithm are explained in Algorithm 1.

In this paper, to begin with, TS algorithm gets initial SBSs' transmit power vector $\mathbf{p}$, marked as BSF, which means the vector chosen is best so far and will change during the iterations. Set initial algorithm parameters. All entries of the tabu matrix are set to 0, the tabu period is set to P. The neighbor range is set to r, the change of transmit power is 1 dBm per unit, so that the difference between the changed element and the one in the given vector must be no more than r dBm.

Algorithm 1. CCO based on tabu search algorithm.

Initialization:
1: $BSF = \mathbf{p}$
2: $FBest = F(\mathbf{p})$
3: **Tmtx** $= zeros;$
4: **for** m_iter iterations **do**
5:    $found = 0$
6:    $l = 1$
7:    **for** lth MBS **do**
8:       find neighborhood vectors of BSF, only change elements corresponding to the lth MBS
9:       calculate F of these neighborhood vectors
10:       **for** all F of the neighborhood vectors **do**
11:          find the best F of these neighborhood vectors
12:          **if** the best $F > FBest$, or the best $F < FBest$ but "non-tabu" **then**
13:             update $FBest$ with the best F
14:             update BSF with the best neighborhood vector
15:             mark BSF "tabu" and update corresponding entries in tabu matrix with P
16:             $found = 1$
17:             Break
18:          **end if**
19:          exclude the best vector from the neighborhood vectors
20:       **end for**
21:       **if** $found = 0$ **then**
22:          update $FBest$ with the oldest best F
23:          update BSF with the oldest best neighborhood vector
24:          mark BSF "tabu" and update corresponding entries in tabu matrix with P
25:       **end if**
26:    **end for**
27:    update entries of tabu matrix as: **Tmtx** $= max\{\textbf{Tmtx} - 1, 0\}$
28: **end for**
29: **return** BSF and $FBest$

Set the maximum number of iterations to m_iter. Calculate initial value of the combined function $F(\mathbf{p})$ according to 4, marked as $FBest$ which reveals the best optimization function when iterating. Also, set a bool flag, $found$, which is initialized to be 0 and denotes whether the best vector among neighboring vectors has been found or not.

The search algorithm described above is terminated if the maximum number of iterations m_iter is reached. And our final solution vector BSF has been found before the iteration was stopped. The SBSs transmit power can be updated according to the gotten BSF. Thus, the coverage and capacity optimization has been optimized in the ultra-dense small cell network by using the improved TS algorithm.

4   Simulation Results

In this section, we apply the TS algorithm proposed in system-level simulation and evaluate the combined function to judge the performance, in contrasting with SA approach. In the following, we first introduce our simulation scenario, and then compare the TS and the SA algorithm upon the combined performance, the coverage performance and the capacity performance.

4.1   Scenario

Consider a hot-spot area, for example the area around office building, with MBSs deployed outdoor and SBSs indoor. The indoor clusters are uniformly random within 2 sectors of macro geographical area. And the SBSs are uniformly random

Table 1. Scenario configuration

Parameters	Value
MBS layout	Hexagonal grid/19 sites/3 sectors
SBS layout	Clusters and SBS are indoor
System bandwidth per carrier	10 MHz downlink
MBS carrier frequency	2.0 GHz
SBS carrier frequency	3.5 GHz
MBS maximum transmit power	46 dBm
SBS maximum transmit power	24 dBm
Path loss model	Free space, wall penetration, omnidirectional
MBS penetration loss	20 dB
SBS penetration loss	Outdoor: 23 dB, Indoor: 46 dB
Thermal noise density	−174 dBm/Hz
Number of clusters per macro cell	2
Number of small cell per cluster	4
Active UEs per macro cell	60
Proportion of indoor hot-spot UEs	1/3
Inter-site distance	500 m
Radius of cluster	50 m
Minimum MBS-UE distance	35 m
Minimum SBS-UE distance	5 m
Minimum MBS-center of cluster distance	105 m
Minimum center of cluster-cluster distance	130 m
Minimum SBS-SBS distance	20 m
MBS shadowing standard deviation	4 dB
SBS shadowing standard deviation	3 dB
Shadowing correlation distance	50 m
Traffic model	Full buffer
Scheduling algorithm	Round-robin

dropping within the cluster areas. In our system-level simulation, we build the topology of our ultra-dense network, the channel model, resource allocation and the coverage and capacity self-optimization of the SBSs. The abstract topology of the network and its enlarged display with hot-spot areas and UEs are shown in Fig. 1. In the part of resource allocation, we calculate each UE's (including hot users and others) $SINR$, and assigned to certain BS to access to according to $SINR$. Then we apply our proposed TS algorithm to optimize and evaluate the performance. Some crucial parameters in simulation are presented in Table 1. The channel model is set based on requirements of 3GPP TR36.842 (V12.0.0).

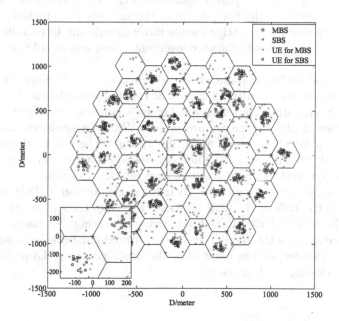

Fig. 1. Scenario of ultra-dense network with densely deployed small cells (Color figure online)

4.2 Analysis

SA is used in simulation in contrast with our proposed TS algorithm. To contrast in the same computational and space complexity, instead of randomly modifying one elements of the last accepted vector, we use a policy similar to TS algorithm for modifying part of vectors in SA. The policy is, finding the best among its neighboring vectors as the modified vector. For fair, the neighbor range comes to be 4, the same as one of neighbor ranges of the TS algorithm simulation.

The parameters concerning the SA are: the initial temperature $T = 3e - 3$, and the parameter T decreases by a scale factor $\eta = 0.998$ over iterations. If the new value of the combined function $F(\mathbf{p})$ is worse than the best so far, calculate the relative difference between the two as the probability pr, and then receive the new vector and the new value with a probability of pr. The parameters concerning the TS are: the initial tabu period $P = 5$, the neighbor range

$r \in \{4, 6, 8, 12\}$. Both algorithm begin with the solution vector with all SBSs' power $24\,\text{dBm}$, and the maximum iteration is 30.

As different parameter settings have different influence on the performance of TS algorithm, especially the neighbor range, in addition to contrast with SA, we also compare the performance of different neighbor range. Figure 2 shows that, for the same neighbor range of $r = 4$, our proposed TS algorithm has a significantly faster convergence in iteration than SA, while finally reach almost the same near global optimum as the contrast approach with a gain of about 32%. And the final optima of both algorithms aren't locked into local. On the other hand, we can notice the fact that TS algorithm converges faster under different parameter settings from the perspective of the number of iterations. Nevertheless, higher neighbor range setting means more calculating in each iteration, so the condition of $r = 4$ has the most convergent speed among all the simulation conditions.

Our optimization function is a combined function of CCO. Figure 3 shows the overall throughput of the ultra-dense small cell network. As can be seen from the figure, TS algorithm converges quickly to a constant during the iteration, achieving a gain of 21% capacity improvement. While SA approach only achieves a gain of 15%, lower than the TS algorithm's result. There is an obvious decline in the curve of TS with $r = 12$. That is because that TS can accept a worse solution than the best so far to avoid locking into local optima.

Figure 4 shows the Cumulative Distribution Function (CDF) of the UE throughput in the cells of the final solution. The edge throughput is defined by the one of the 5-tile% UEs' throughput sequence sorting. As can be seen from the figure, the average throughput and edge throughput both improve after the optimization. Besides, on the point of 5-tile%, our proposed TS algorithm also has better performance than the SA.

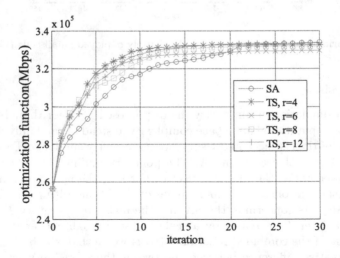

Fig. 2. Combined optimization performance for the TS and SA (Color figure online)

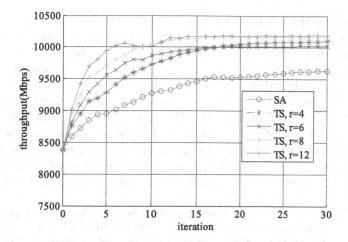

Fig. 3. Overall throughput performance for the TS and SA (Color figure online)

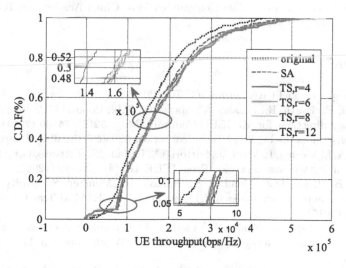

Fig. 4. CDF for UE throughput before and after optimization via the TS and SA (Color figure online)

5 Conclusions

This paper aims to optimize coverage and capacity in ultra-dense network. In order to solve combinational optimization problem, especially when the dimension of the problem is really high and with large amount of data, we introduced the TS algorithm for adjusting parameters under our proposed combined optimization mathematical model. The TS algorithm begins with an initial solution vector and searching for the next solution in its neighborhood, particularly, the algorithm marks some local optima as tabu and try to avoid but not completely prohibit them in later iterative searches. Simulation results show that our proposed optimization model can represent the performance of coverage and capacity well and balance the two conflicting key performance indicators in optimization. More importantly, our proposed TS algorithm improves the coverage and capacity performance significantly with low computational complexity, which means the algorithm can be used for real-time optimization and realize self-optimization for UDN. Besides, from the results obtained in simulation, we can draw the conclusion that the TS algorithm outperforms the adaptive SA approach in terms of convergence speed while achieving near global optimum. Additionally, the TS algorithm proposed in this paper is applied under fixed parameters. Therefore, modifying some parameters adaptive in optimizing process may bring better solution while lowing the computational complexity.

Acknowledgments. This work was supported by the China's 973 project (No. 2012CB31600), the China's 863 Project (No. 2014AA01A706), the National S&T Major Project (No. 2014ZX03004003), Science and Technology Program of Beijing (No. D161100001016002), S&T Cooperation Projects (No. 2015DFT10160B), and by State Key Laboratory of Wireless Mobile Communications, China Academy of Telecommunications Technology (CATT).

References

1. 5G Whitepaper, FuTURE Forum 5G SIG (2015)
2. Boccardi, F., Heath, R., Lozano, A., Marzetta, T.L., Popovski, P.: Five disruptive technology directions for 5G. IEEE Commun. Mag. **52**(2), 74–80 (2014)
3. Small cells-whats the big idea? Technical report 6295097, Small Cell Forum (2012)
4. Fehske, A.J., Viering, I., Voigt, J., Sartori, C., Redana, S., Fettweis, G.P.: Small-cell self-organizing wireless networks. Proc. IEEE **102**(3), 334–350 (2014)
5. Partov, B., Leith, D.J., Member, S., Razavi, R., Member, S.: Utility fair optimization of antenna tilt angles in LTE networks. IEEE/ACM Trans. Netw. **23**(1), 175–185 (2015)
6. Berger, S., Fehske, A., Zanier, P., Viering, I., Fettweis, G.: Online antenna tilt-based capacity and coverage optimization. IEEE Wirel. Commun. Lett. **3**(4), 437–440 (2014b)
7. Berger, S., Simsek, M., Fehske, A., Zanier, P., Viering, I., Fettweis, G.: Joint downlink and uplink tilt-based self-organization of coverage and capacity under sparse system knowledge. IEEE Trans. Veh. Technol. **65**(4), 2259–2273 (2015)
8. Wang, X., Teng, Y., Song, M., Wang, X., Xing, A.: Joint optimization of coverage and capacity in heterogeneous cellular networks. In: IEEE PIMRC, pp. 1788–1792 (2015)
9. Engels, A., Reyer, M., Xu, X., Mathar, R., Zhang, J., Zhuang, H.: Autonomous self-optimization of coverage and capacity in LTE cellular networks. IEEE Trans. Veh. Technol. **62**(5), 1989–2004 (2013)
10. Soszka, M., Berger, S., Fehske, A., Simsek, M., Butkiewicz, B., Fettweis, G.: Coverage and capacity optimization in cellular radio networks with advanced antennas. In: 19th International ITG Workshop on Smart Antennas, pp. 1–6. IEEE WSA, Ilmenau (2015)

Dynamic APs Grouping Scheme Base on Energy Efficiency in UUDN

Shanshan Yu, Xi Li[✉], Hong Ji, and Yiming Liu

Key Laboratory of Universal Wireless Communications, Ministry of Education,
Beijing University of Posts and Telecommunications,
Beijing, People's Republic of China
{yushanshan, lixi, jihong, liuyiming}@bupt.edu.cn

Abstract. Ultra dense Network (UDN) is considered as a promising technology for 5G. With dense access points (APs), one user can be served by several APs cooperatively. Hence, how to choose APs and group them is a big challenge. In this paper, a dynamic APs grouping scheme is proposed for the downlink of User-centric UDN (UUDN). This scheme takes terrain and network topology into consideration to divide the APs into several available candidate sets (ACSs). The APs can be chosen from the ACS as the group member for UE's APs group (APG). Once the service requirement changes or user moves, the group should be changed accordingly. The optimal objective is maximum energy efficiency under the constraints of transmission power and user's data rate requirements. This scheme solves the problem of AP selection and power allocation. It is modeled as a discrete mixed combinational optimization problem, and a quantum-behaved particle swarm optimization (QPSO) algorithm is adopted to solve it efficiently. In addition, simulation results have also proved the effectiveness and flexibility of the proposed scheme.

Keywords: UDN · User-centric · Dynamic APs grouping · Energy efficiency

1 Introduction

With the rapid development of wireless technologies, the research of the fifth generation mobile communication (5G) for the future mobile communication started to emerge. 5G has several distinct characteristics, such as high rate, high capacity, and low delay. Since Ultra Dense Network (UDN) is considered as a promising technology for 5G, each user can be served by more than one access points (AP) [1]. Therefore, how to serve users with multiple APs cooperatively is a big challenge.

The previous works mainly research cooperation in cellular systems to improve the performance of cell edge users. The authors in [2] proposed an adaptive mode switch scheme and power allocation method to achieve a joint optimization for performance of edge users and center users. Nevertheless, the considered distributed framework would result in large signaling overhead. In order to reduce power consumption and data overhead in downlink coordinated multipoint (CoMP) transmission, the authors in [3, 4] proposed a cooperative set selection method. A semi-dynamic cooperative cluster selection scheme was proposed in [3] and the authors in [4] confined the number of APs.

© ICST Institute for Computer Sciences, Social Informatics and Telecommunications Engineering 2018
Q. Chen et al. (Eds.): ChinaCom 2016, Part II, LNICST 210, pp. 67–77, 2018.
DOI: 10.1007/978-3-319-66628-0_7

Some cooperative distributed radio resource management algorithms for time synchronization, carrier selection, and power control were discussed in [5]. The authors in [6] proposed a joint planning methodology. Although the simulation showed its advantage, the scenario and AP type still could be improved. Energy efficiency was an important factor which has to be considered [7]. Energy saving with small cell on/off was proposed in [8]. The proposed method considered four clusters to simplify calculation. While the cluster was fixed, this would result to limitation. The authors in [9] proposed a radio access network coordination framework toward 5G network. Its coordination procedure employed the concept of cluster, but cluster partition was vague which would result to congestion and cost. In the UDN, the authors in [10] proposed a APs cooperation method with dynamical clustering in super dense Cloud-RAN. This approach put forth a downlink cellular model. In order to analyze the performance of the proposed approach, a deterministic rectangular grid model was used to compare with it, which is based on stochastic geometry. This approach mainly considered the SIR, and the result was relevant to the size of the cluster. The concept of device-centric is proposed in [11]. It introduced virtualized device-centric radio access architecture for 5G, its advantage was to meet the stringent quality of service (QoS) requirements of users. Some researchers also proposed a concept of user-centric for UDN (UUDN), they noted that AP's group (APG) would be a challenge.

In this paper, we aim at the problem of how to serve users with multiple APs cooperatively in UUDN. A dynamic APs grouping scheme for downlink is proposed. Grouping procedure can be concluded as initiating, creating group and recreating process dynamically. Initiating adopts a concept of available candidate sets (ACSs). When UE accesses to the network, the local control unit can choose the APs from the ACS to create a group. By dynamically recreating group when the requirement of the UE changed, this process can guarantee UE's real time data rate demand. Grouping criterion is to maximize the energy efficiency. It subjects to the constraints of transmission power for different AP types and user's data rate requirements. This is a discrete mixed combinational optimization problem, and the sub-optimal solution can be obtained by adopting a quantum-behaved particle swarm optimization (QPSO) algorithm [12]. Simulation results show the performance of the proposed scheme.

The remainder of this paper is organized as follows. Section 2 describes the system model. Section 3 shows the access scheme in detail. Problem formulation and the solution are provided in Sect. 4. Section 5 shows the simulation results and discussions. The conclusion and future work are given in Sect. 6.

2 System Model

2.1 UUDN System Architecture

In the UUDN scenario, we uniformly name low power nodes as APs. The nodes include Micro, Pico, Femto, Relay and so on. User Equipment (UE) itself also can act as APs in UUDN. UUDN is a User-Centric system which focuses on the experience and requirements of UE [13]. There are some core features of UUDN as following:

(1) Intelligent network: The network can intelligently and dynamically detect UE, and record user's requirement and radio link environment.
(2) Transparent network: For UE, the network changes with the UE's mobility, but UE will not realize the handover process.
(3) Dynamical network: By focusing on UE experience, it can provide service adaptively, jointly and cooperatively.

The system architecture is shown as Fig. 1. It is a control plane and user plane detached structure. This architecture can reduce the signaling overhead and switch AP's status into active or sleep mode in a concentrated control manner.

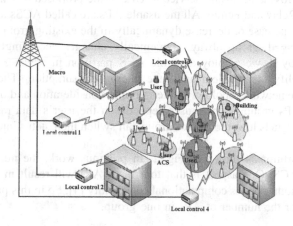

Fig. 1. The architecture of UUDN

2.2 Channel Model

In this paper, multiple APs serve to each UE cooperatively in downlink multiple-input multiple-output (MIMO) system. AP and UE are equipped with transmitting antennas and receiving antennas, respectively. The received signal is described as:

$$y = \mathbf{H}x + \mathbf{n} \tag{1}$$

where x denotes N_t-dimensional transmitted signal vector, H is $N_r \times N_t$ channel matrix, y and n indicates N_r-dimensional received signal vector and noise vector.

We suppose that the rank of H is denoted by $R = rank(\mathbf{H})$. Based on singular value decomposition (SVD) theorem, channel matrix H can be decomposed as:

$$\mathbf{H} = \mathbf{U} \begin{bmatrix} \mathbf{D} & \mathbf{0} \\ \mathbf{0} & \mathbf{0} \end{bmatrix} \mathbf{V}^H \tag{2}$$

where U is a $N_r \times N_R$ unitary matrix, D is a diagonal matrix whose diagonal values are the singular values of H. D is a $N_R \times N_R$ matrix and is described as $\mathbf{D} = diag$ $(\lambda_1, \lambda_2, \cdots \lambda_R)$. V indicates $N_R \times N_t$ unitary matrix, and superscript H is conjugate transpose.

Through formula derivation, we can transform a MIMO channel into R parallel single-input single-output (SISO) channels. It can decrease or eliminate interference among channels. Moreover, the channel gain of each SISO channel is $\lambda_i (i = 1, 2, \cdots, R)$.

3 Dynamic APs Grouping Scheme

In hotspot area where a large number of APs are distributed, how to serve users with multiple APs cooperatively is a big challenge. We propose a method to group APs dynamically to provide accessing service to UE. In the proposed scheme, APs are not limited to Pico, Relay and Femto. All the usable APs are called ACSs and divided into groups. APs can increase or decrease dynamically in the existing groups. With the UE requirement changed, group always dynamically changes accordingly. As APs are ultra-dense deployed, we employ dynamic ACS partition in advance. This way can help us to simplify the problem and save energy consumption. The way of ACS partition will take network topology and terrain into consideration and the ACSs do not overlap. Then APs grouping for a user depends on the user's data rate requirement. When the traffic data is low, the APs of group can switch their status into sleep mode to save energy.

The ACS partition is shown as Fig. 2. In previous work, the number of APs is limited in one ACS. One aspect is that too much APs will result in large signaling overhead, and another one is computational complexity [4]. So in this paper, we design an upper limit for the number of APs in one group.

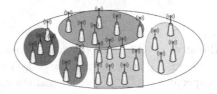

Fig. 2. ACSs partition

The APs in the group will be adjusted by the change of UE's requirements or channel link conditions. Figures 3 and 4 are shown to explain the procedure of dynamic grouping.

Figure 3 shows the situation when UE enters, local control unit will activate all of the APs. After the calculation according to the optimal objective, several APs will be chosen to create a group, while others will be tuned to sleep mode. Once UE's requirement has changed, its group will be changed as Fig. 4 shows. The proposed scheme can be concluded as three steps:

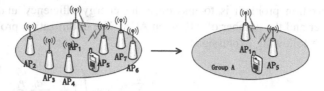

Fig. 3. Dynamic grouping according to UE's requirement

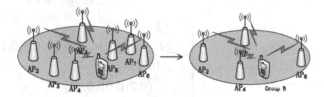

Fig. 4. Grouping changes when UE's requirement changes

Step 1. By combining the network topology and terrain, the dense APs are divided into several ACSs. In one ACS, there are three kinds of Aps: Relay, Pico and Femto. The number and types of APs are unfixed and random.

Step 2. When the UE requires accessing an ACS, local control unit activates APs belonging to the ACS. According to the UE's requirement, the AP group is setup.

Step 3. As UE's requirement and channel link condition may be changed; existing group would not fulfill UE's demand. For this situation, the proposed scheme can change the group with UE's requirement accordingly. Grouping criterion is to maximize energy efficiency under the constraint of UE's requirement and power limit.

4 Problem Formulation and Optimal Solution

In this section, an optimization problem about dynamic APs grouping in UUDN is formulated firstly. Then the solutions are given by adopting QPSO algorithm.

4.1 Problem Formulation

In one ACS, APs will be selected to create a group depending on UE's data rate requirement. When the requirement has changed, the APs in the group can change accordingly. The number of APs in the group will increase or decrease, and then the member's resource will be reallocated. We suppose that perfect channel state information (CSI) is known at the transmitter by dedicated backhaul links and feedback channels, and regardless of the latency. Therefore, the instantaneous channel gain can be available. In addition, a binary variable is used to represent the power allocation, indicating whether the i-th AP is chosen to provide service or not.

The optimization problem is to maximize the energy efficiency under the constraints of power and the number of APs in an ACS. The optimization problem can be presented as the following expressions:

$$\max_{\{I_1,I_2,...I_n,P_1,P_2\cdots P_n\}} \frac{C}{P} = \max_{\{I_1,I_2,...I_n,P_1,P_2\cdots P_n\}} \frac{\sum\limits_{i=1}^{n} W \log_2\left(1 + \frac{I_i\lambda_i^2 P_i}{\sigma_n^2 + \sum\limits_{k\neq i} I_k P_k}\right)}{\sum\limits_{i=1}^{n}(I_i P_i + I_i P_{c_i})}$$

$$s.t: \begin{cases} C \geq R \\ 0 \leq P_i \leq P_{imax}, P_{imax} \in \{1, 0.5, 0.1\} \\ I_i \in \{0,1\} \\ P_{c_i} \in \{0.2, 0.01, 0.02\} \\ n = 5 \end{cases} \tag{3}$$

where I_i represents AP's status, W represents the bandwidth, $\sum\limits_{k\neq i} I_k P_k$ is interference among APs, P_i indicates the transmission power of the i-th AP, λ_i is channel gain, n indicates the number of AP, σ_n^2 is Additive White Gaussian Noise (AWGN) which can express as $\sigma_n^2 = n_0 W$ and P_{c_i} indicates the power consumption of link. In the first constraint, R is the requirement of UE and C represents the rate that can be provided by the group. Then P_{imax} indicates the different power upper limit.

4.2 Optimal Solution

Because the optimization problem is a discrete mixed combinational optimization problem, we intend to employ a heuristic algorithm QPSO to resolve it. In terms of QPSO, we have to transform the constraint into unconstrained form, so the penalty function is introduced in the paper. Then the fitness function includes the optimization objective function and one penalty function. The fitness can be expressed as follows:

$$F = f(I_i, P_i) + \alpha G(I_i, P_i) \tag{4}$$

where the objective function is $f(I_i, P_i)$, α is penalty factor, $G(I_i, P_i)$ represents penalty function and its expression form as follows:

$$G = [\max(0, C - R)]^2 + [\max(0, -P_{imax})]^2 + [\max(0, P_i - P_{imax})]^2 + (I_i^2, -I_i)^2 \tag{5}$$

where $C = \sum\limits_{i=1}^{n} W \log_2\left(1 + \frac{I_i\lambda_i^2 P_i}{\sigma_n^2}\right)$ and $\max(\cdot, \cdot)$ returns the larger number of the two values.

We can define the particle as a vector and each of the vectors is consist of two variables. So it is a two-dimension vector and the expression can be defined as:

$$\mathbf{X}_i = (I_1, \cdots, I_i, P_1, \cdots, P_i) \tag{6}$$

where I_i denotes the status of the i-th AP and its value is 0 or 1. 0 represents that this AP's status is in sleep mode and 1 is active mode, P_i means the power of this AP.

Every particle updates their positions and calculates respective local, global best position and mean best position. Through limitation iterations, we can calculate a sub-optimal solution. It is worth noting that we adopt three types of APs in the group, so we need to judge the AP's type to confirm its upper limit of power to satisfy its penalty function. The procedure of the algorithm can be described as follows:

Step 1. Initialize the particle's position and choose the maximum iteration value.
Step 2. Based on the fitness function (4), calculate a best position as the global best position, a mean best position and update particle's position. It's an iteration process.
Step 3. Calculate each particle's current position by fitness function (4) and then output the current optimal solution.

5   Simulation Results and Discussions

In this section, the proposed scheme was evaluated by simulations. We assume each ACS has 5 APs and the types of APs, including the Pico, Relay and Femto. Simulation has two cases, with the group including three types of AP or only one kind of AP. The user's requirement is 5×10^8 bps and channel gain is assumed to be a random number between 0 and 1. The simulation parameters are shown in Table 1.

Table 1. Parameters of simulation.

Parameter	Value
α	1.5
W	30 M
n_0	2×10^{-7} W/Hz
P_{imax_relay}	30 dbm/1 W
P_{imax_pico}	27 dbm/0.5 W

Case 1 shows the group with 5 APs. There are three types: relay, pico and femto. Their power upper limits are shown in Table 1, 1 W, 0.5 W and 0.1 W, respectively. Set 1 shows AP power distribution and status, it can be expressed as follows:

$$X_{11} = \{0, 1, 1, 1, 1, 0.91, 0.29, 0.05, 0.06, 0.03\} \tag{7}$$

$$X_{12} = \{1, 1, 1, 0, 1, 0.7, 0.2, 0.03, 0.08, 0.04\} \tag{8}$$

$$X_{13} = \{1, 1, 1, 1, 1, 0.5, 0.11, 0.03, 0.06, 0.02\} \tag{9}$$

$$X_{14} = \{1, 1, 1, 1, 0, 0.3, 0.01, 0.06, 0.04, 0.06\} \tag{10}$$

$$X_{15} = \{1, 1, 1, 1, 0, 0.6, 0.08, 0.01, 0.01, 0.09\} \tag{11}$$

$$X_{16} = \{0, 1, 1, 1, 1, 0.8, 0.3, 0.04, 0.01, 0.07\} \tag{12}$$

The energy efficiency diagram is shown in Fig. 5. In the setting of the simulation scenario, the transmission rate can reach their peak rates for gigabit per second, therefore, in the power allocation, the service rate is far higher than the required rate. It can be seen from the curves in the following figure that the gradual increase of the emission power is a downward trend, which is consistent with the trend of the energy efficiency curve. According to the above six sets of values, the horizontal coordinate value will be limited to the maximum transmission power of the data. Because of the limitation of the AP number and AP type for an ACS, the total emission power of the mechanism will be a limited set, but this does not affect the trend of the curve.

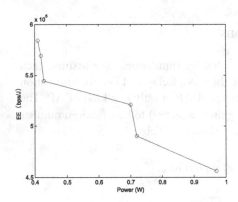

Fig. 5. Hybrid AP energy efficiency

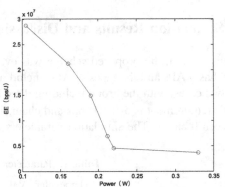

Fig. 6. Single type AP energy efficiency

Case 2 is a single AP type as Femto and the maximum transmission power limit is 0.1 w. In this scenario, the power allocation and the AP are selected as shown below:

$$X_{21} = \{1, 1, 1, 1, 1, 0.07, 0.08, 0.05, 0.02, 0.08\} \tag{13}$$

$$X_{22} = \{1, 0, 1, 1, 1, 0.08, 0.09, 0.03, 0.05, 0.03\} \tag{14}$$

$$X_{23} = \{1, 1, 1, 1, 1, 0.002, 0.07, 0.08, 0.01, 0.05\} \tag{15}$$

$$X_{24} = \{1, 1, 1, 1, 0, 0.03, 0.05, 0.03, 0.05, 0.06\} \tag{16}$$

$$X_{25} = \{1, 1, 1, 1, 1, 0.01, 0.003, 0.02, 0.07, 0.002\} \tag{17}$$

$$X_{26} = \{0, 1, 1, 1, 1, 0.08, 0.07, 0.073, 0.05, 0.03\} \tag{18}$$

As shown in Fig. 6 for case 2, this case and the case 1 can provide the similar user's rate. Meanwhile, the energy efficiency is improved to a maximum of three times of case 1. The main reason for this phenomenon is that the circuit loss of Femto is low. According to the above six sets of values plotted curve chart, the horizontal coordinates are the limited, this is because of the limited number of APs in the group.

In order to show the feasibility of the proposed mechanism, the fixed power AP hybrid cooperative algorithm is used to compare with the proposed method. The AP type selection and the maximum transmission power are the same as the above values. In this group, all the APs are cooperating to provide service to the user, and the maximum transmission power of AP in the group is 1.8 W. The power setting and energy efficiency of the multiple hybrid APs are shown in the Tables 2 and 3:

Table 2. Multiple APs fixed power allocation type table.

Relay	Pico	Femto	Femto	Femto	EE (10^6)
1	0.5	0.1	0.1	0.1	2.27
0.8	0.4	0.08	0.08	0.08	3.47
0.5	0.25	0.05	0.05	0.05	3.6
0.2	0.1	0.02	0.02	0.02	4.7

Compared with the dynamic energy distribution of this mechanism, dynamic allocation makes energy efficiency improved. According to the UE's rate requirement, the power allocation of each AP can be adjusted dynamically, rather than the overall operation, so that power allocation and AP selection are more flexible. From the comparison of are more flexible. From the comparison of Figs. 6 and 8, the proposed dynamic power allocation can improve the efficiency of at least 1.2 times.

Compared with the dynamic power allocation proposed by this mechanism, the energy efficiency value is also very close to the results obtained by the fixed power allocation value, which proves the reliability of the mechanism. And from Figs. 7 and 8, the allocation strategy adopted by the mechanism has been improved.

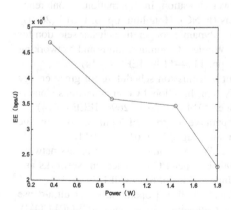

Fig. 7. Fixed power for hypbrid APs

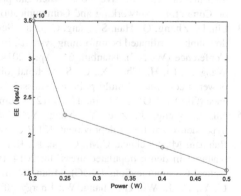

Fig. 8. Fixed power for single type AP

Table 3. Fixed power allocation table for femto

Femto	Femto	Femto	Femto	Femto	EE (10^6)
0.1	0.1	0.1	0.1	0.1	1.55
0.08	0.08	0.08	0.08	0.08	1.85
0.05	0.05	0.05	0.05	0.05	2.27
0.04	0.04	0.04	0.04	0.04	3.50

6 Conclusions

This paper proposes a dynamic APs grouping scheme in UUDN. According to the topology of network and terrain, the dense APs are divided into several ACSs. When UE accesses to the network, the APs of the ACS corresponding to the UE will be activated. Then we adjust the cooperative APs to create a group and switch the inactive APs into sleep mode. When the UE's data rate requirement has changed, the group can dynamically adjust its members accordingly. The adjustment and grouping criterion is to maximize the energy efficiency under the constraints of transmission power and UE's demand. Since this problem is a discrete mixed combinational optimization, we employ QPSO algorithm to solve it. Simulation results demonstrate the proposed scheme can save power consumption and is flexible in use. Future work will consider the scenario that backhaul link routing selection base on the AP's group.

Acknowledgements. This work is supported by National Natural Science Foundation of China under Grant 61302080 and 61271182.

References

1. Xu, J., et al.: Cooperative distributed optimization for the hyper-dense small cell deployment. IEEE Commun. Mag. **52**(5), 61–67 (2014)
2. Zong, Z., Feng, H., et al.: Distributed framework of downlink CoMP MU-MIMO transmission with adaptive mode switch and power allocation. In: International Conference on Computing, Networking and Communications (ICNC), Honolulu, pp. 611–615 (2014)
3. Liu, D., Zhang, Q., Han, S., Yang, C., et al.: Semi-dynamic cooperative cluster selection for downlink coordinated beamforming systems. In: Wireless Communications and Networking Conference (WCNC), Istanbul, 6–9 April 2014, pp. 1194–1199. IEEE (2014)
4. Wang, Z., Li, H., Chen, X., Ci, S.: Optimal joint transmission scheduling for green energy powered coordinated multi-point transmission system. In: Global Communications Conference (GLOBECOM), Austin, TX, 8–12 December 2014, pp. 2690–2696. IEEE (2014)
5. Xu, J., Wang, J., Zhu, Y., Yang, Y.: Cooperative distributed optimization for the hyper-dense small cell deployment. IEEE Commun. Mag. **52**(5), 61–67 (2014)
6. Rahman, M., Machuca, C.M., Grobe, K., Kellere, W.: Advantages of joint access network planning in dense populated areas. In: 2014 19th European Conference on Networks and Optical Communications (NOC), Milano, 4–6 June 2014, pp. 67–73. IEEE (2014)
7. Li, Y., Li, J., Wu, H., Zhang, W.: Energy efficient small cell operation under ultra-dense cloud radio access networks. In: Global Communications Conference (GLOBECOM), Austin, TX, 8–12 December 2014, pp. 1120–1125. IEEE (2014)

8. Dao, N., Zhang, H., Li, X., Leroux, P.: Radio access network coordination framework toward 5G mobile wireless networks. In: 2015 International Conference on Computing, Networking and Communications (ICNC), Garden Grove, 16–19 February 2015, pp. 1039–1043 (2015)

9. Lee, N., Heath, R.W., Morales Jimenez, D., Lozano, A.: Base station cooperation with dynamic clustering in super-dense cloud-RAN. In: Global Communications Conference (GLOBECOM), Atlanta, GA, 9–13 December 2013, pp. 784–788. IEEE (2013)

10. Maaref, A., Ma, J., Salem, M., Baligh, H., Zarifi, K.: Device-centric radio access virtualization for 5G networks. In: IEEE 2014 Global Communications Conference (GLOBECOM 2014), Austin, TX, 8–12 December 2014, pp. 887–893. IEEE (2014)

11. Olsson, M., Cavdar, C., Frenger, P., Tombaz, S., Sabella, D., Jantti, R.: 5GrEEn: towards green 5G mobile networks. In: Wireless and Mobile Computing, Networking and Communications (WiMob), Lyon, 7–9 October 2013, pp. 212–216. IEEE (2013)

12. Liu, Y., Li, X., Ji, H., et al.: Joint APs selection and resource allocation for self-healing in ultra dense network. In: 2016 International Conference on Computer, Information and Telecommunication Systems (CITS), Kunming, China, 6–8 July 2016. IEEE (2016)

13. Chen, S., Qin, F., Hu, B., Li, X., et al.: User-centric ultra-dense networks (UUDN) for 5G: challenges, methodologies and directions. IEEE Wirel. Commun. Mag. 23(2), 78–85 (2016)

Virtual Small Cell Selection Schemes Based on Sum Rate Analysis in Ultra-Dense Network

Qi Zhang[1], Jie Zeng[2(✉)], Xin Su[2], Liping Rong[2], and Xibin Xu[2]

[1] Broadband Wireless Access Laboratory,
Chongqing University of Posts and Telecommunications, Chongqing, China
[2] Tsinghua National Laboratory for Information Science and Technology,
Research Institute of Information Technology,
Tsinghua University, Beijing, China
zengjie@tsinghua.edu.cn

Abstract. Ultra-Dense Network (UDN) is regarded as a major development trend in the evolution of future networks, due to its ability to provide larger sum rate to the whole system and meet higher users' Quality of Service (QoS). Different from the existing heterogeneous network, UDN has a smaller cell radius and a new network structure. The core concept of UDN is to deploy the low power Base Stations (BSs), i.e. Virtual Small Cells (VSCs). First, we derive an ergodic sum rate expression. To acquire the maximum ergodic sum rate of all the users, then we adopt the selection mode based on minimum distance. Due to the consideration of the computation complexity of the above VSC selection scheme, we finally propose a novel VSC selection scheme based on pattern search. The simulation results demonstrate the correctness of the ergodic sum rate expression and show the lower computation complexity of the proposed VSC selection scheme comparing with the above reference scheme.

Keywords: Ultra-dense network · Virtual small cell · Sum rate · Pattern search

1 Introduction

Current heterogeneous network is consisted of macro-cells and small cells. This network structure could not be able to meet the traffic demand which is increasing rapidly in the future 5th Generation (5G). In [1], it is predicted that the traffic demand would increase at least a 1000x network capacity in 2020. To meet the more traffic demand, enhanced technologies are essential. So far, there are some potential candidates in [2], such as UDN, massive Multiple-Input Multiple-Output (MIMO), and Non-Orthogonal Multiple Access (NOMA). This paper focuses on UDN which is seen as a major development trend in the evolution of future networks, due to its ability to provide larger sum rate to the whole system and meet higher users' QoS. In recent years, UDN attracts many researchers in colleges and workers in industries. Both the industry and academia are working together, e.g. Mobile and wireless communications Enablers for the 2020 Information Society (METIS) and 5th Generation Non-Orthogonal Waveforms (5GNOW), to meet the capacity demand of the 5G mobile communication systems [3, 4].

© ICST Institute for Computer Sciences, Social Informatics and Telecommunications Engineering 2018
Q. Chen et al. (Eds.): ChinaCom 2016, Part II, LNICST 210, pp. 78–87, 2018.
DOI: 10.1007/978-3-319-66628-0_8

Different from the existing heterogeneous network, UDN has a smaller cell radius and a new network structure. In urban areas, there exist many potential hot spots, such as conference halls, hospitals, and schools. In these areas, users are more easily to aggregate in a small place. At the same time, many users require high data transmission rate to support kinds of multimedia business. To meet the demand, VSC is presented in [5]. The core concept of UDN is to deploy the low power Base Stations (BSs) in the network, and the number of BSs is even larger than the number of Mobile Stations (MSs) [6]. We regard each low-power BS as a VSC.

There have been some researches of the VSC in UDN. Recently, [7] analyzes radius of VSC based large-scale distributed antenna system, and proves that the number of BSs and MSs has an impact on the downlink rate. [8] proposes a novel Resource Allocation (RA) scheme which is based on the sectoring of VSC. Its main idea is to reuse the Physical Resource Blocks (PRBs) of sectoring and improve the system capacity. [9] draws attention to the sum-rate maximization, and they develop a new formulation of the beamforming problem for sum-rate maximization in VSC and analyze the structure of its optimal solutions. Different from the existing single cell serving mode, [10, 11] present the concept of VSC clustering in UDN. [10] utilizes VSC clustering technique to maximize energy saving gain. [11] studies orthogonal training resource allocation problem for VSC cooperative network through a graph-theoretic approach aiming at minimizing the overall training overhead and then demonstrates that the proposed low complexity algorithm performs closely to the optimal solution.

This paper aims to maximize ergodic sum rate of all the users in UDN with low computation complexity. In this paper, the following tasks are completed: we first derive an ergodic sum rate expression. Second, due to the consideration of the computation complexity of the VSC selection scheme based on minimum distance, we propose a novel VSC selection scheme based on pattern search. Also, the two schemes can acquire almost the same maximum ergodic sum rate of all the users. The simulation results demonstrate the correctness of the ergodic sum rate expression and show the lower computation complexity of the proposed VSC selection scheme comparing with the reference scheme.

The remainder of this paper is organized as follows: In Sect. 2, we present the system model of VSC with multi-user environment. Section 3 derives an ergodic sum rate expression. In Sect. 4, we propose VSCs selection schemes based on maximum sum rate analysis. We provide simulation results in Sect. 5. Finally, conclusions are provided in Sect. 6.

2 System Model

We consider the downlink transmission in UDN with K MSs and N VSCs. Both of them are equipped with a single antenna. As shown in Fig. 1, nine VSCs and four MSs uniformly and randomly are distributed in the area, and the number of VSCs is larger than the number of MSs ($K < N$). In our analysis, the total available power of VSCs is P. We assume each VSC has the same power constraint, i.e. the j_{th} VSC transmitted power is $P_j = P/N$, $(j = 1, 2, 3 \ldots N)$. The transmitted signal to noise power ratio for all VSCs is $\gamma_0 = \frac{P}{N\sigma_n^2}$. If the j_{th} VSC is turned off, $P_j = 0$. A principal goal of this paper is to determine the pairings of N VSCs and their supporting MSs which maximize the ergodic sum rate. Let us denote the transmission mode

$$X = [u_1, u_2, \ldots, u_N] \tag{1}$$

as the MS index of N VSCs where $u_n \in \{0, 1, \ldots, K\}$, $(n = 1, 2, \ldots N)$ represents the MS index supported by the n_{th} VSC. If n_{th} VSC turns off, we define $u_n = 0$. From (1), let us define $G_{i,S}(x) = \{n | u_n = i, n \in \{1, 2, \ldots, N\}\}$ as the set of VSC indices supporting the i_{th} MS, and $G_{i,I}(x) = \{n | u_n \neq i, u_n \neq 0, n \in \{1, 2, \ldots, N\}\}$ as the set of VSC indices supporting other MSs except i_{th} MS. For MS i, the signal from VSCs in $G_{i,S}$ is regarded as the useful signal, while the signal transmitted from VSCs in $G_{i,I}$ is treated as interference. In Fig. 1, the transmission mode $X = [1, 1, 3, 2, 1, 3, 2, 4, 0]$. For 1_{th} MS, the useful signal is from $G_{1,S}$, i.e. 1_{th} VSC, 2_{th} VSC and 5_{th} VSC, and the interference information is from 3_{th} VSC, 4_{th} VSC, 6_{th} VSC, 7_{th} VSC and 8_{th} VSC.

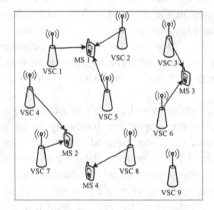

Fig. 1. Structure of UDN with four MSs and nine VSCs ($K = 4$, $N = 9$).

The received signal of i_{th} MS is

$$y_i = \sum_{j=1}^{N} \sqrt{P_j} g_{i,j} x_j + n_i, (i = 1, 2, \ldots, K) \tag{2}$$

where $x_j (j = 1, 2, \ldots, N)$ is the transmitted symbol from the VSC j with the average power $E[|x_j|^2] = 1$, P_j is the power allocated to VSC j, $g_{i,j}$ denotes the channel gain from i_{th} MS to j_{th} VSC, and n_i represents the additive white Gaussian noise with variance σ_n^2 for the i_{th} MS. The channel gain is $g_{i,j} = \sqrt{Cd_{i,j}^{-\alpha} s_{i,j}} h_{i,j}$, where C is a constant, $d_{i,j}$ is the distance from i_{th} MS to j_{th} VSC, α is the path loss factor, $s_{i,j}$ denotes shadow fading, and $h_{i,j}$ is the independent and identically distributed complex Gaussian random variable. Let $10 \lg s_{i,j}$ represent zero mean Gaussian random variable, and its standard deviation equals 1. Also the mean value of $h_{i,j}$ is 0, and standard deviation of $h_{i,j}$ is 1.

3 Ergodic Sum Rate Analysis

In this paper, inter-MS interference is regarded as the Gaussian noise since it can be interpreted as the worst effect that the measurement noise can have [12]. We use $\Omega_{i,j}$ to represent $Cd_{i,j}^{-\alpha}s_{i,j}$, i.e. $\Omega_{i,j} = Cd_{i,j}^{-\alpha}s_{i,j}$. Then we can do the following theoretical derivations. And the Signal to Interference plus Noise power Ratio (SINR) of the i_{th} MS is generally represented as

$$\rho_i = \frac{\sum\limits_{l \in G_{i,S}} (\frac{P}{N})\Omega_{i,l}|h_{i,l}|^2}{\sum\limits_{k \in G_{i,I}} (\frac{P}{N})\Omega_{i,k}|h_{i,k}|^2 + \sigma_n^2} = \frac{\sum\limits_{l \in G_{i,S}} (\frac{d_{i,l}}{R})^{-\alpha}s_{i,l}|h_{i,l}|^2}{\sum\limits_{k \in G_{i,I}} (\frac{d_{i,k}}{R})^{-\alpha}s_{i,k}|h_{i,k}|^2 + \frac{NR^\alpha}{CP/\sigma_n^2}}$$

$$= \frac{\sum\limits_{l \in G_{i,S}} \gamma_{i,l}}{\sum\limits_{k \in G_{i,I}} \gamma_{i,k} + \beta} = \frac{\gamma_{i,S}}{\gamma_{i,I} + \beta} \tag{3}$$

where $\gamma_{i,l} = (\frac{d_{i,l}}{R})^{-\alpha}s_{i,l}|h_{i,l}|^2$ is the logarithmic normal distributed random variable, β represents $\frac{NR^\alpha}{CP/\sigma_n^2}$, and R is the normalized distance.

In the following, we consider the Probability Density Function (PDF) of ρ_i to derive a closed form of the ergodic sum rate. The corresponding PDF of ρ_i can be expressed as [13]

$$f_{\gamma_{i,l}}(x) = \int_0^\infty \frac{1}{\omega}\exp(-\frac{x}{\omega})\frac{\xi}{\sqrt{2\pi}\sigma_{i,l}\omega}\exp[-\frac{(10\lg\omega - \mu_{i,l})^2}{2\sigma_{i,l}^2}]d\omega \tag{4}$$

where $\mu_{i,l} = 10\lg[(d_{i,l}/R)^{-\alpha}]$, $\sigma_{i,l}$ is the standard deviation of $10\lg s_{i,l}$, and $\xi = 10/\ln 10$ is a constant. The moment-generating function of $\gamma_{i,l}$ can be expressed as follows [13]

$$\Psi_{\gamma_{i,l}}(s) \approx \frac{1}{\sqrt{\pi}}\sum_{p=1}^M W_p[1 - 10^{0.1(\sqrt{2}\sigma_{i,l}Z_p + \mu_{i,l})}s]^{-1} \tag{5}$$

where Z_p and W_p are the p_{th} root of M order Hermite polynomial and the corresponding integral weighted coefficient respectively.

Let us regard $\gamma_{i,S} = \sum \gamma_{i,l}$ as the sum of several independent random variable. Its moment-generating function is

$$\Psi_{\gamma_{i,S}}(s) = \prod_{l \in G_{i,S}} \Psi_{\gamma_{i,l}}(s). \tag{6}$$

$\gamma_{i,S}$ can approximatively be expressed by a logarithmic normal distributed random variable, so the PDF of $\gamma_{i,S}$ is denoted as [14]

$$f_{\gamma_{i,S}}(x) = \frac{\xi}{\sqrt{2\pi}\sigma_{i,S}x} \exp[-\frac{(10\lg x - \mu_{i,S})^2}{2\sigma_{i,S}^2}](x \geq 0). \tag{7}$$

The corresponding moment-generating function of $\gamma_{i,S}$ is [13]

$$\Psi_{\gamma_{i,S}}(s) \approx \frac{1}{\sqrt{\pi}} \sum_{p=1}^{M} W_p \exp[10^{0.1(\sqrt{2}\sigma_{i,S}Z_p + \mu_{i,S})}s]. \tag{8}$$

Here, the Eq. (6) is equal to the Eq. (8), i.e.

$$\prod_{l\in G_{i,S}} \Psi_{\gamma_{i,l}}(s) = \frac{1}{\sqrt{\pi}} \sum_{p=1}^{M} W_p \exp[10^{0.1(\sqrt{2}\sigma_{i,S}Z_p + \mu_{i,S})}s]. \tag{9}$$

When there are two different values for variable s, we can get binary equation groups of $\mu_{i,S}$ and $\sigma_{i,S}$. The equation groups can be solved by numerical method. So $\gamma_{i,S}$ can be approximatively expressed as a logarithmic normal distributed random variable through the parameter $(\mu_{i,S}, \sigma_{i,S})$.

In the same way, $\gamma_{i,I} + \beta$ can be approximatively expressed as a logarithmic normal distributed random variable, and its PDF is

$$f_{\gamma_{i,I}+\beta}(y) = \frac{\xi}{\sqrt{2\pi}\sigma_{i,I}(y - \beta)} \exp[-\frac{(10\lg(y - \beta) - \mu_{i,I})^2}{2\sigma_{i,I}^2}](y \geq \beta). \tag{10}$$

From (3), SINR of the i_{th} MS ρ_i is the radio between $\gamma_{i,S}$ and $\gamma_{i,I} + \beta$, so the PDF of ρ_i is denoted as

$$f_{\rho_i}(\rho) = \int_\beta^\infty y f_{\gamma_{i,S}}(\rho y) f_{\gamma_{i,I}+\beta}(y) dy = \frac{\xi^2}{2\pi\sigma_{i,S}\sigma_{i,I}\rho} \cdot$$
$$\int_0^\infty \frac{1}{x} \exp - \frac{\{10\lg[\rho(x+\beta)] - \mu_{i,S}\}^2}{2\sigma_{i,S}^2} \cdot \exp[-\frac{(10\lg x - \mu_{i,I})^2}{2\sigma_{i,I}^2}]dx(y - \beta \rightarrow x). \tag{11}$$

From the above, we can denote ergodic rate of i_{th} MS as

$$E[R_i] = \int_0^\infty \log_2(1 + \rho) f_{\rho_i}(\rho) d\rho$$
$$= \frac{\xi^2}{2\pi\sigma_{i,S}\sigma_{i,I}\rho} \cdot \int_0^\infty \frac{1}{x} \exp(-\frac{(10\lg x - \mu_{i,I})^2}{2\sigma_{i,I}^2}) \int_0^\infty \frac{\log_2(1 + \rho)}{\rho} \cdot$$
$$\exp(-\frac{\{10\lg[\rho(x+\beta)] - \mu_{i,S}\}^2}{2\sigma_{i,S}^2})d\rho dx. \tag{12}$$

We can get the following equation through the Gauss-Hermite integration

$$E[R_i] = \frac{1}{\pi} \sum_{q=1}^{M} W_q \cdot [\sum_{p=1}^{M} W_p \log_2(1 + \frac{10^{0.1(\sqrt{2}\sigma_{i,S}Z_p + \mu_{i,S})}}{10^{0.1(\sqrt{2}\sigma_{i,I}Z_p + \mu_{i,I})} + \beta})] \tag{13}$$

where Z_p and W_p are the p_{th} root of M order Hermite polynomial and the corresponding integral weighted coefficient respectively. So the ergodic sum rate of K MSs is

$$R_{sum} = \sum_{i=1}^{K} E[R_i]. \qquad (14)$$

4 Analysis on VSC Selection Schemes

In this section, we study the VSC selection scheme based on minimum distance and propose a novel VSC selection scheme for the ergodic sum rate maximization using the derived expression in the previous section.

4.1 VSC Selection Scheme Based on Minimum Distance

We introduce a VSC selection scheme based on the minimum distance where the number of mode candidates increases dramatically for large N. For N VSCs and K MSs, we can define all mode candidates as $\mathcal{X}$. The size of the set of mode candidates $\mathcal{X}$ is given as $2^N - N$ [15].

In this scheme, we first set $X_0 = [u_1, u_2, \ldots, u_N]$ as the mode where each VSC serves its nearest MS with turning on all the VSCs. Then, we turn off VSCs in this transmission mode one by one with $2^N - 1$ distinct combinations, and generate a mode candidate by replacing the corresponding user indices to 0. Then, all these $2^N - 1$ candidates are added to the mode candidate set $\mathcal{X}$. Finally, after evaluating the ergodic sum rate for each candidate mode in $\mathcal{X}$ using the expressions derived in Sect. 3, we select the best mode which exhibits the maximum rate.

4.2 VSC Selection Scheme Based on Pattern Search

In this subsection, we propose a novel transmission mode selection scheme which reduces the computation complexity comparing with VSC selection scheme based on minimum distance. This scheme is based on pattern search. The objective function is

$$f_{obj}(X) = R_{sum}. \qquad (15)$$

Our objection is searching the $X_{opt} = \arg\max_{X \in \mathcal{X}} R_{sum}$. The mode selection procedure is described in Table 1, where $I_N(i, *)$ means the i row of the N order identity matrix.

5 Simulation Results and Analysis

In this section, we demonstrate the correctness of the ergodic sum rate expression. And we also evaluate computation complexity of the proposed VSC selection scheme comparing with the selection mode based on minimum distance by a system level

Table 1. VSC selection sheme based on pattern search.

Step 1. Initialization

Set $X_0 = [u_1, u_2, ..., u_N]$ as the mode where each VSC serves its nearest MS

initial step size $T = 1$

$$\Delta X_i = \begin{cases} I_N(i,*), 1 \le i \le N \\ -I_N(i-N,*), N+1 \le i \le 2N \end{cases}$$

Step 2. While $T > 0.5$

$\qquad X_i = X_{opt} + T \cdot \Delta X_i$ for $i = 1, 2, ..., 2N$

$\qquad$ if $\max f_{obj}(X_i) > f_{obj}(X_{opt})$

$\qquad\qquad \{X_{opt} \leftarrow \arg\max_{X_i} f_{obj}(X_i), T \leftarrow 2T\}$

$\qquad$ else $T \leftarrow 0.5T$

$\qquad$ end If

$\qquad$ end while

Step 3. For $i = 1 : K$

$\qquad X_i = [i, i, ..., i]$

$\qquad$ if $\max f_{obj}(X_i) > f_{obj}(X_{opt})$

$\qquad\qquad \{X_{opt} \leftarrow \arg\max_{X_i} f_{obj}(X_i)\}$

$\qquad$ end if

$\qquad$ end for

---

simulator. The results of simulation with the method of Monte Carlo are given. In this simulation, we use wrap-around to have reliable interference calculation. The number of generated channel realizations is equivalent to 5000. More specific parameter is shown in Table 2 in detail.

In Fig. 2, each VSC chooses the nearest MS to serve with all VSCs turned on, and the two pairing lines are almost overlap with different K. So it can demonstrate the correctness of the ergodic sum rate expression. With the increasing of K or the transmitted signal to noise power ratio γ_0, the ergodic sum rate is increasing.

In Fig. 3, the ergodic sum rate by VSC selection scheme based on pattern search is similar to the result of VSC selection scheme based on minimum distance. However,

Table 2. Basic parameters of simulation scenario.

Parameter	Value
Carrier frequency	2 GHz
(Inter Site Distance) ISD	35 m
$\sigma_{i,j}$	6 dB
α	4
The order of Hermite polynomial M	20

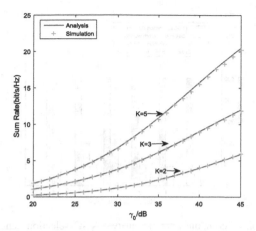

Fig. 2. Ergodic sum rate with different K.

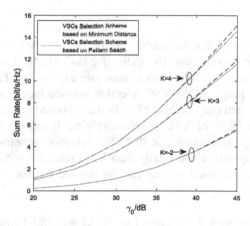

Fig. 3. The ergodic sum rate comparison between VSC selection scheme based on minimum distance and VSC selection scheme based on pattern search.

the proposed scheme has lower computation complexity than VSC selection scheme based on minimum distance. From Fig. 4, the computation complexity of VSC selection scheme based on minimum distance is a constant value with different number of MSs K. Because the computation complexity of VSC selection scheme based on minimum distance is only related to the number of VSCs N. However, the computation complexity of VSC selection scheme based on pattern search is much lower than the computation complexity of VSC selection scheme based on minimum distance with different $K(K<N)$. When N is given, the computation complexity of VSC selection scheme based on pattern search increases with K and then start to change little. This is because when K is closed to N, there are almost the same number of times the objective function is called.

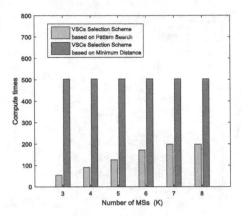

Fig. 4. The comparison of compute times about two VSC selection scheme with different K $(K < N, N = 9)$.

6   Conclusions

In this paper, we have studied the multi-MSs downlink VSC and have derived an ergodic sum rate expression using the PDF of MSs' SINR. The simulation result demonstrates the correctness of the ergodic sum rate expression. Through the derived expressions, we have proposed the VSC selection scheme based on pattern search to maximize the ergodic sum rate of whole MSs. In the proposed scheme, the ergodic sum rate is similar to the result of VSC selection scheme based on minimum distance. However, simulation results show that the VSC selection scheme based on pattern search has lower computation complexity than VSC selection scheme based on minimum distance. So the proposed scheme can get desired ergodic sum rate with lower computation complexity.

Acknowledgments. This work was supported by the China's 863 Project (No. 2014AA01A 706), the National S&T Major Project (No. 2014ZX03004003), Science and Technology Program of Beijing (No. D161100001016002), and by State Key Laboratory of Wireless Mobile Communications, China Academy of Telecommunications Technology (CATT).

References

1. Lopez-Perez, D., Ding, M., Claussen, H., Jafari, A.H.: Towards 1 Gbps/UE in cellular systems: understanding ultra-dense small cell deployments. IEEE Commun. Surv. Tutor. **17**, 2078–2101 (2015)
2. Boccardi, F., Heath, R.W., Lozano, A., Marzetta, T.L., Popovski, P.: Five disruptive technology directions for 5G. IEEE Commun. Mag. **52**(2), 74–80 (2014)
3. Gaspar, S., Wunder, G.: 5G Cellular communications scenarios and system requirements. https://www.5gnow.eu
4. Popovski, P., Braun, Y., Mayer, H.-P'., Fertl, P.: Requirements and KPIs for 5G mobile and wireless system. Technical report (2014). https://www.metis2020.com

5. Ana, G., Sofia, M.L., Alberto, D.R., Azeddine, G.: Virtual small cells using large antenna arrays as an alternative to classical HetNets. In: 2015 IEEE 81st Vehicular Technology Conference (VTC Spring), pp. 1–6 (2015)
6. Gelabert, X., Legg, P., Qvarfordt, C.: Small cell densification requirements in high capacity future cellular networks. In: IEEE International Conference on Communications Workshops, pp. 1112–1116 (2013)
7. Wang, J., Dai, L.: Downlink rate analysis for virtual-cell based large-scale distributed antenna systems. J. IEEE Trans. Wirel. Commun. 15(3), 1998–2011 (2016)
8. Sattiraju, R., Klein, A., Ji, L.: Virtual cell sectoring for enhancing resource allocation and reuse in network controlled D2D communication. In: 81st IEEE Vehicular Technology Conference (VTC Spring), Glasgow, pp. 1–6 (2015)
9. Kim, J., Lee, H.W., Song, C.: Virtual cell beamforming in cooperative networks. IEEE J. Sel. Areas Commun. 32(6), 1126–1138 (2014)
10. Feng, C., Xiao, Q.: Cooperative virtual cell clustering for green cellular networks. In: IEEE 75th Vehicular Technology Conference (VTC Spring), pp. 1–5 (2012)
11. Chen, Z., Hou, X., Yang, C.: Training resource allocation for user-centric base-station cooperation networks. J. IEEE Trans. Veh. Technol. 65(4), 2729–2735 (2015)
12. Cover, T.M., Thomas, J.A.: Elements of Information Theory. Wiley, Hoboken (2006)
13. Simon, M.K., Alouini, M.S.: Digital Communication Over Fading Channels, 2nd edn, pp. 32–34. Wiley, Hoboken (2005)
14. Metha, N.B., Wu, J., Molisch, A.F.: Approximating a sum of random variables with a lognormal. J. IEEE Trans. Wirel. Commun. 6(7), 2690–2699 (2007)
15. Kim, H., Lee, S.R., Lee, K.J.: Transmission schemes based on sum rate analysis in distributed antenna systems. J. IEEE Trans. Wirel. Commun. 11(3), 1201–1209 (2012)

System Level Performance Evaluation
for Ultra-Dense Networks

Qianbin Chen$^{(\boxtimes)}$, Ya Zhang, and Lun Tang

Chongqing Key Lab of Mobile Communications Technology,
Chongqing University of Posts and Telecommunications,
Chongqing 400065, China
{chenqb, tangl}@cqupt.edu.cn, zhangya122333@sina.cn

Abstract. The ultra-dense network (UND) has been considered as an effective scheme to satisfy the growing demands on data rate in the wireless network. And it can easily improve the throughput by increasing the number of base stations. In this paper, the performance of UDN with various small cell densities is evaluated. And the throughput, spectrum efficiency and energy efficiency are taken into consideration to evaluate the performance of the deployment strategies. As can be seen from the simulation results, the throughput and area spectrum efficiency are obviously improved with the increasingly dense cells. However, as the network densification the positive influence on throughput and spectrum efficiency would be decreased.

Keywords: Ultra dense networks · Throughput · Spectrum efficiency · Energy efficiency

1 Introduction

The popularization of smart devices and rapid development of internet services lead to a prophecy that the traffic flow of mobile data traffic will increase a 1000-fold till the year of 2020 [1]. In order to meet future mobile communication systems under the conditions of the traffic demand, from the spectral efficiency and energy efficiency, the heterogeneous networks (HetNets) is a practical approach to maximize the spectral efficiency and minimize the energy consumption [2]. Moreover, the 5th generation mobile networks (5G) will provide support for a new kind of network deployment such as ultra-dense network [3]. And advanced small cell technology will be adopted in 5G systems to bring highly quality of experience of users.

The small cells, which including picocells, femtocells and microcells, have been attracting more and more attention to improve service coverage and system capacity. In order to make the best of spectrum, small cells usually adopt the same frequency as the macro cells. And they often have lower transmit power than macro cells to reduce co-channel interference. Currently, small cells are widely deployed in small commercial areas or at home. Indeed, small cells already have a larger number than macro cells. Meanwhile, green communication has been paid more attention in global scale. And the energy efficiency is one of the most importance parts of the performance. However, what problems the UDN will bring to spectrum and energy consumption have not been

© ICST Institute for Computer Sciences, Social Informatics and Telecommunications Engineering 2018
Q. Chen et al. (Eds.): ChinaCom 2016, Part II, LNICST 210, pp. 88–96, 2018.
DOI: 10.1007/978-3-319-66628-0_9

well known. This paper has evaluated the network performance in UND using several parallel metrics likes SINR distribution and throughput. Particularly, varieties of spectrum efficiencies and energy efficiencies are also considered for assessing the network performance in different dense network scenarios.

The organization of the paper is as follows. Section 2 provides an overview of system model. In Sect. 3 the main simulation results of performance evaluation in UND are discussed. Following that, some problems and challenges in UND are discussed in Sect. 4. Finally, in Sect. 5 the conclusions are presented.

2   System Model

2.1   Scenario and Parameter

In this paper the traditional 7 Macro layout of hexagonal deployment has been used as the base scenario for the simulation. And as shown in Fig. 1, in the center cell (Cell 0) a lot of Pico eNodeBs (PeNBs) are randomly deployed, but there are no PeNBs in the Macro cells locating around the center cell. The function of surrounding Macro eNodeBs (MeNBs) is providing interference, so that the scenario is realistic. And the number of Pico is increased from 20 to 120 with an interval of 20, which results in 97, 190, 282, 375, 468 or 560 cells per square km deployed in the scenario, respectively. It's worth noticing that all eNBs i.e. MeNBs and PeNBs are transmitting in the same frequency. And the specific simulation parameters can be found in Table 1.

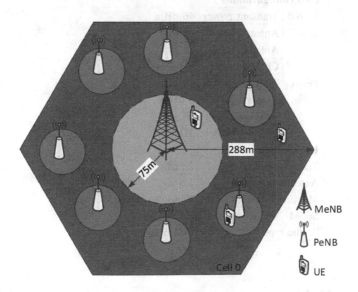

Fig. 1. Simulation scenario.

Table 1. Simulation parameters.

Parameters	Value
System configurations	
Frequency	2 GHz
Bandwidth	10 MHz (50RBs)
Duplex	FDD
Antenna configuration	DL: 2×2
ISD	500 m
Frequency reuse factor	1
Minimum distance between eNB and UE	35 m (MeNB)/10 m (PeNB)
Minimum distance between MeNB and PeNB	75 m
Minimum distance between PeNB and PeNB	40 m
Noise	−174 dBm/Hz
Fast fading	Jakes model
Number of UEs	30 (Macro)/5 (Pico)
Number of Picos	20/40/60/80/100/120
Scheduler	PF
eNB configurations	
MeNB	Transmit power	46 dBm
	Antenna gain	17 dBi
	Antenna height	25 m
	Channel model	3D-UMa
PeNB	Transmit power	30 dBm
	Antenna gain	5 dBi
	Antenna height	10 m
	Channel model	3D-UMi
UE configurations	
Transmit power	23 dB
Antenna height	1.5 m
Mobility type	Random walk
Speed	3 km/h
Traffic type	Full buffer

2.2 Channel Model

The channel model of the simulation handles packet transmission and models the propagation loss taking into account four different fields as suggested in [4]: (i) the penetration loss, (ii) the path loss, (iii) the fast fading, and (iv) the shadowing fading

[5]. And the propagation loss can be divided into two kinds of channel parameters. The first one is the large scale parameters including the path loss and shadow fading. The second one is the small scale parameters, like fast fading. And to meet the complex simulation scenarios in UND there are variety channel models can be chosen such as 3D channel, WINNER II and traditional channel models.

2.3 Antenna Model

A 3D antenna model is adopted for this simulation. The horizontal radiation pattern (1) and vertical radiation pattern (2) are both considered as well as the electrical down tilt [6]. The horizontal radiation pattern is given by:

$$A_{E,H}(\varphi) = -\min\left[12\left(\frac{\varphi}{\varphi_{3dB}}\right)^2, A_m\right] \, |[dB]$$ (1)

where $A_{E,H}(\varphi)$ is the antenna attenuation in the horizontal direction φ, the value of φ is from $-180°$ to $180°$, φ_{3dB} is the horizontal 3 dB beam width and the default is $65°$, and $A_m = 30$ dB is the maximum gain, and min [,] denotes the minimum function. The vertical radiation pattern is similar as the horizontal antenna pattern and it is given by:

$$A_{E,V}(\theta) = -\min\left[12\left(\frac{\theta - \phi_{tilt}}{\theta_{3dB}}\right)^2, SLA_V\right] \, |[dB]$$ (2)

where $A_{E,V}(\theta)$ is the relative antenna attenuation in the vertical direction θ, $-90° \leq \theta \leq 90°$, and θ_{3dB} is the vertical 3 dB beam width corresponding to $\theta_{3dB} = 65°$. $SLA_V = 30$ dB, ϕ_{tilt} is electrical down tilt, and it may be assumed to be $90°$. And the combined antenna radiation pattern is computed as:

$$A(\theta, \varphi) = -\min\{-[A_{E,V}(\theta) + A_{E,H}(\varphi)], A_m\} \, |[dB]$$ (3)

2.4 Protocol Stack

The protocol stack has been set up as a container of Radio Resource Control (RRC), Radio Link Control (RLC), MAC and PHY entities. Generally speaking, the RRC contains a lot functions including broadcasting the relevant system information, operating the RRC connection between the UE and the E-UTRAN, managing the mobility and allocating the wireless resources etc.

The RLC entity provides interactions between the radio bearer and the MAC entity [7]. Besides, it models the unacknowledged data transmission at the RLC layer [8]. The most important functionalities of RLC are the segmentation and the concatenation of service data units. And the RLC entity comprises three different types of RLC: Acknowledged Mode (AM), Unacknowledge Mode (UM) and Transparent Mode (TM).

While the MAC entity provides all the most important procedures for the radio interface, such as scheduling requests and radio resource allocation [9]. Moreover, in this entity the Adaptive Modulation Coding (AMC) module is further defined.

Moreover, PHY provides reliable environment for the data transmission between transmission media and interconnection equipment. And it is directly facing the actual data transmission physical media to provide a transport raw bit stream over a physical media layer to the MAC.

3 Simulation Evaluation

As known the throughput and spectrum efficiency are two key performance indicators for evaluating the capacity in the 4G network. And the energy efficiency attracts more and more people's attention for the communication industry towards green development. In the following, all the performances are evaluated as well the SINR.

3.1 SINR

The performance of a cellular system in a certain environment is highly dependent on the radio propagation conditions. The quality of the radio propagation is determined by the transmission power of the eNB and the interference which set a limit on the maximum throughput, as defined by Shannon capacity bound.

Figures 2 and 3 respectively show the CDF of UE SINR and the SINR spatial distribution corresponding to 20, 40, 60, 80, 100 and 120 small cells deployments. It is evident that, the UE SINR is deteriorated as the density of Pico developments. And the reason can be easily owe to interferences from the other co-frequency eNBs except the serving eNB. As shown in Fig. 3, the coverage is becoming larger with the Pico cell density, and on the other side the percent of high UE SINR is becoming lower. That is because, with more and more Pico cells deployments, more areas are occupied by Pico cells. At the same time that leads to a problem, as mentioned earlier, the interference will be stronger.

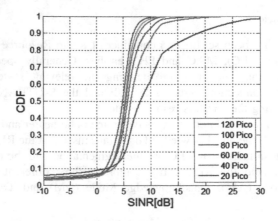

Fig. 2. CDF of UE SINR for different Pico densities.

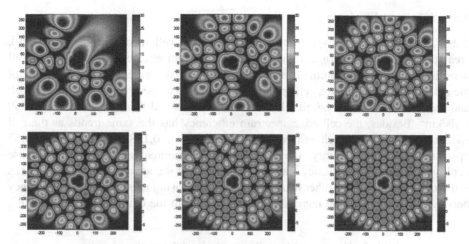

Fig. 3. SINR spatial distribution for different Pico densities.

3.2 Throughput

Network densification has the potential to linearly increase the throughput of the network with the number of deployed cells through spectrum reuse, and it is deemed to be the key technology to provide most of the throughput gains in future networks [10]. As shown in Fig. 4(a), increasing the number of Pico development will increase the throughput of the entire cellular networks. But the pace of increasing in throughput becomes slower. Moreover, Fig. 4(b) shows that the maximum rate is gradually decreased due to the increasing density of cells. As spectrum resources can be fully utilized in the same frequency network development, the same frequency is adopted in both Macro and Pico. Nevertheless, the interference will grow with the increasing of network nodes in the same frequency. That is the reason why the increasing of the throughput becomes slow.

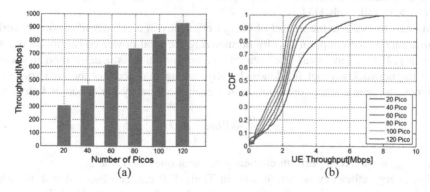

Fig. 4. The network throughput (a) and the CDF of UE throughput (b) for different Pico densities.

3.3   Spectrum Efficiency

Table 2 provides relevant spectrum efficiency such as cell spectrum efficiency (η_{cell}), area spectrum efficiency (η_{area}) and cell edge spectrum efficiency (η_{edge}) versus cell densities. As for cell spectrum efficiency, it is shown to decrease with the increasing of the cell density. Initially, the cell spectrum efficiency is at the level of 1.47 bps/Hz/cell and reduces to 0.77 bps/Hz/cell when network is densified from 97 cells/km^2 to 560 cells/km^2. Besides, the cell edge spectrum efficiency has the same trends as the cell spectrum efficiency, which reduces from the level of 0.158 bps/Hz/cell to 0.067 bps/Hz/cell. On the contrary, the high degree of resource reuse because of dense deployments with co-frequency leads to an increase of the area spectrum efficiency as shown in Table 2. On the other hand, the pace of increasing in area spectrum efficiency becomes slower due to the increasing interference from the other co-frequency eNBs.

Table 2. Various spectrum efficiencies for different Pico densities.

Pico number	ρ_{cell} [cells/km^2]	η_{cell} [bps/Hz/cell]	η_{edge} [bps/Hz/cell]	η_{area} [bps/Hz/km^2]
20	97	1.47	0.158	142.23
40	190	1.12	0.127	211.62
60	282	1.01	0.107	285.82
80	375	0.92	0.092	342.99
100	468	0.84	0.078	392.73
120	560	0.77	0.067	431.85

3.4   Energy Efficiency

The energy to bit ratio (λ_I) is one of the most common metric used for evaluating the energy efficiency of the performance in a network, especially in urban environments. And it is defined by the amount of power consumed in providing an aggregate network capacity. From other side, it also can be described as energy consumed for transmitting per bit information. This metric is appropriate for assessing the energy efficiency of a network with full loads [11].

In order to evaluate the impact of energy efficiency in a cell densification network, the area energy consumption (λ_A) by normalizing the total power consumption is also given in [12] to 1 km^2 area. The area energy consumption is usually used in a case where the network without full loads. Finally, taking into account the area spectrum efficiency and area energy consumption, the energy-efficiency is defined as following:

$$E_{eff} = \frac{\eta_{area}}{\lambda_A} \| [bps / Hz / w] \tag{4}$$

where η_{area} is the area spectrum efficiency as mentioned in Table 2.

The energy efficiency is summarized in Table 3. It can be observed that, the area energy consumption is increasing as the network deployment densified. It increases from 276.898 w/km^2 to 739.861 w/km^2 when the network is densified from 97

Table 3. Various energy efficiencies for different Pico densities.

Pico number	ρ_{cell} [cells/km^2]	λ_I [w/bps] * 10e−6	λ_A [w/km^2]	E_{eff} [bps/Hz/w]
20	97	0.194	276.898	0.514
40	190	0.174	369.491	0.573
60	282	0.161	462.083	0.619
80	375	0.161	554.676	0.618
100	468	0.164	647.269	0.607
120	560	0.171	739.861	0.584

cells/km^2 to 560 cells/km^2. That is because the network coverage is constant, more and more power will be consumed with the increasing in the eNB density. From another aspect, increasing the eNB density will first increase the energy-efficiency E_{eff} and then decrease. The reason can be deduced from the growth trend of the area spectrum efficiency and the cell density. It can be observed that, the increment of the cell density is a constant i.e. the acceleration of the area energy consumption is a constant. However, due to the increasing interference with the increasing cell density the acceleration of the area spectrum efficiency is becoming smaller. That can lead to the E_{eff} increases from 0.514 bps/Hz/w to 0.619 bps/Hz/w when the network is densified from 97 cells/km^2 to 282 cells/km^2 and then decreases to 0.584 bps/Hz/w.

4 Challenges in Ultra Dense Networks

Although UDN is a promising technology to improve the throughput and meet the demand of the increasing traffic, there are also some issues in UDN like the intense co-frequency interference as mentioned before. Some researches consider the enhanced inter-cell interference coordination (eICIC) and the coordinated multi-point (CoMP) as feasible ways to overcome the interference. But how effectively they would perform in UDN is indeterminate so far. And as more and more small cell stations deployed the energy consumption is another hotspot in UDN. Moreover, the reduced Inter Site Distances (ISD) in UDN will raise the handover frequency and handover failure rate of mobile users. And UDN would bring some problems to the mobility management. Some new schemes of mobility management for example dual connectivity should be further explored. Also challenges of this network architecture could be the flexible connection to the core networks, dynamic on-off and the random deployment of small cells, and the flat system architecture of system.

5 Conclusions

In this paper, the network performance in different dense network scenarios has been evaluated. From the SINR distribution point of view, the SINR of the overall network deteriorates as the density of Pico deployments. From the throughput point of view, network densification can increase the throughput. But the acceleration of throughput is becoming smaller as the network densification. From the point of spectrum efficiency, the area spectrum efficiency is raised just like the throughput. However, for the cell spectrum efficiency and cell edge spectrum efficiency, they will decrease with the increasing of cell density. As for energy consumption, the area energy consumption is improved as the network deployment densified. On the other side, it can be found that the energy-efficiency defined above rises at first and then falls. And it could be also found that the UDN will cause some problems such as the intense inter-cell interference and more frequent handover.

Acknowledgments. This work is supported by National Science and Technology Major Project (No. 2014ZX03003010-004) and National High Technology Research and Development Program of China 863 Program (No. 2014AA01A701), as well as Chongqing Natural Science Foundation (No. CSTC2012jjA40049).

References

1. Wang, Y., Xu, J., Jiang, L.: Challenges of system-level simulations and performance evaluation for 5G wireless networks. IEEE Access **2**, 1553–1561 (2014)
2. Zhang, N., Cheng, N., Gamage, A.T., Zhang, K., Mark, J.W., Shen, X.: Cloud assisted HetNets toward 5G wireless networks. IEEE Commun. Mag. **53**(6), 59–65 (2015)
3. Gao, Z., Dai, L., Mi, D., Wang, Z., Imran, M.A., Shakir, M.Z.: MmWave massive-MIMO-based wireless backhaul for the 5G ultra-dense network. IEEE Wirel. Commun. **22**(5), 13–21 (2015)
4. Access, Evolved Universal Terrestrial Radio: Further Advancements for E-UTRA Physical Layer Aspects (Vol. 9.0.0). 3GPP TR 36.814 (2010)
5. Capozzi, F., Piro, G., Grieco, L.A., Boggia, G., Camarda, P.: On accurate simulations of LTE femtocells using an open source simulator. EURASIP J. Wirel. Commun. Netw. **2012** (1), 1–13 (2012)
6. Access, Evolved Universal Terrestrial Radio: Study on 3D Channel Model for LTE (Vol. 12.1.0). 3GPP TR36.873 (2015)
7. Access, Evolved Universal Terrestrial Radio: Radio Link Control (RLC) Protocol Specification (Vol. 12.1.0.). 3GPP TS 36.322 (2014)
8. Piro, G., Grieco, L.A., Boggia, G., Capozzi, F., Camarda, P.: Simulating LTE cellular systems: an open-source framework. IEEE Trans. Veh. Technol. **60**(2), 498–513 (2011)
9. Access, Evolved Universal Terrestrial Radio: Medium Access Control (MAC) Protocol Specification (Vol. 12.1.0). 3GPP TS 36.321 (2014)
10. López-Pérez, D., Ding, M., Claussen, H., Jafari, A.H.: Towards 1 Gbps/UE in cellular systems: understanding ultra-dense small cell deployments. IEEE Commun. Surv. Tutor. **17** (4), 2078–2101 (2015)
11. Correia, L.M., Zeller, D., Blume, O., Ferling, D., Jading, Y., Gódor, I., Van Der Perre, L.: Challenges and enabling technologies for energy aware mobile radio networks. IEEE Commun. Mag. **48**(11), 66–72 (2010)
12. Yunas, S.F., Isotalo, T., Niemelä, J., Valkama, M.: Impact of macrocellular network densification on the capacity, energy and cost efficiency in dense urban environment. Int. J. Wirel. Mob. Netw. **5**(5), 99 (2013)

Green Distributed Power Control Algorithm for Multi-user Cognitive Radio Networks

Yinmeng Wang, Jian Chen$^{(\boxtimes)}$, Chao Ren, and Huiya Chang

Xidian University, Xi'an, Shannxi Province, People's Republic of China
jianchen@mail.xidian.edu.cn

Abstract. Considering both system energy efficiency (EE) and the implementation of distributed power control algorithm in multi-user cognitive radio networks (CRNs), a multi-leader Stackelberg power control game algorithm is proposed to achieve continuous Pareto improvements in non-cooperative power control game (NPG) in this paper. By combining the advantages of cooperative and non-cooperative games with consideration of secondary users' quality of service (QoS) requirements, the problems of low system EE of non-cooperative game and limited Pareto improvement of single leader Stackelberg game are solved. Simple utility function and time back-off are utilized to facilitate the implementation of distributed algorithm. Simulations show that the proposed algorithm improves the system EE as Pareto improvement is reached. Meanwhile, primary user's QoS is guaranteed as secondary users transmit with lower power.

Keywords: Energy efficiency · Cognitive radio networks · Stackelberg game theory · Pareto improvement

1 Introduction

With the increasing energy consumption in wireless networks, green wireless communications arouse great attention, which aim at improving energy efficiency (EE). Power control [1] is an efficient radio management method to reduce mutual interference and improve the EE.

Power control schemes based on game theory are investigated. In [2], a non-cooperative power control game (NPG) was investigated to solve the power control issues in multi-secondary-user underlay cognitive radio networks (CRNs). The utility function was designed based on EE, which was easy to realize distributed computation and reduced the power consumption of the base stations [2]. In [3], the authors modified the utility function designed in [2] with a novel pricing function to pursue higher EE. However, Nash equilibrium (NE) in the non-cooperative game is inefficient since the users act selfishly [4]. In [5], hierarchy-based cooperative Stackelberg game was introduced to deal with the inefficient NE problem. In [6], Stackelberg game was used to pursue high EE for single user while total EE of multiple secondary users (SUs) was ignored. In [7], the

© ICST Institute for Computer Sciences, Social Informatics and Telecommunications Engineering 2018
Q. Chen et al. (Eds.): ChinaCom 2016, Part II, LNICST 210, pp. 97–106, 2018.
DOI: 10.1007/978-3-319-66628-0_10

authors focused on maximizing multiple SUs' total EE with Stackelberg game. However, only one-shot Pareto improvement was obtained in [7]. Thus, the EE can be further improved by continuous Pareto improvements.

In this paper, we focus on achieving high total EE of multiple users by continuous Pareto improvements in underlay CRNs. We proposed a distributed power control algorithm based on Stackelberg game to improve EE. In the proposed algorithm, the utility function is simply defined based on EE and time back-off [8] is used to implement the distributed algorithm. Continuous Pareto improvements are achieved with multiple leaders implementing power-decreasing strategy. Thus, high total EE of multiple users is achieved in the green communications. We also prove the existence of Stackelberg Equilibrium (SE) and investigate the computational complexity of the proposed algorithm.

2   System Model and Problem Formulation

In underlay CRNs, N pairs of SUs simultaneously share the same band with a pair of primary users (PUs). To make the figure simple and clear, in Fig. 1, only three pairs of SU transceivers (SU-TXi and SU-RXi, $i = \{1, 2, 3\}$ and a pair of PU transceiver (PU-T and PU-R) are shown and the interference links between SUs are not shown. Log-normal channel model is considered. The channel gains of links SUs−PU and secondary transmitter (ST) j−secondary receiver (SR) j are denoted by g_j and h_j, respectively. h_{ij} denotes channel gain between ST i and SR j. Local knowledge between two direct links about channel information can be acquired by each SU. In underlay CRNs, three constraints should be satisfied. First, the interference to PUs caused by SUs should not exceed the interference threshold I_{th}. Second, the maximum power budget of SU j, e.g. p_j, is $p_j^{\max}$. Last, each pair of SUs (e.g. the j th) needs to meet a target signal-to-noise plus interference ratio (SINR) γ_j^{tar} to guarantee the quality of service (QoS). In this paper, we aim to maximize the total EE of the system. For each SU, the utility u_j is defined as [2,3,5]

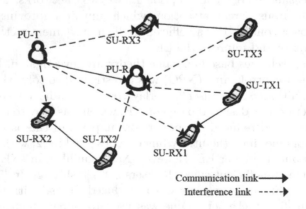

Fig. 1. System model

$$u_j\left(p_j, P_{-j}\right) = \frac{LR}{Mp_j} f_j(\gamma_j), \tag{1}$$

where R, M and L represent transmit rate, data length and information length of each packet, respectively. P_{-j} is a set $\{p_1, \ldots, p_{j-1}, p_{j+1}, \ldots, p_N\}$. $f_j(\gamma_j)$ is a monotonic deceasing function to measure the probability of correct reception:

$$f_j(\gamma_j) = (1 - 2P_{ej})^M. \tag{2}$$

Here, $P_{ej} = 0.5 \exp(\frac{-\gamma_j}{2})$, which represents the binary error rate of a noncoherent frequency shift keying modem. The utility function can be interpreted as the number of information bits received per Joule of energy expended.

The optimization problem in this paper is written as:

$$\max \quad w = \sum_{j \in N} u_j$$

$$s.t. \quad \sum_{j \in N} p_j |g_j|^2 \le I_{th},$$

$$p_j \in (0, p_j^{\max}], \tag{3}$$

$$\gamma_j = \frac{p_j |h_j|^2}{\sum\limits_{i=1,\, i \ne j}^{N} p_i |h_{ij}|^2 + \delta_j^2} \ge \gamma_j^{\text{tar}}.$$

Here, w is social welfare [5] as defined in [7]. δ_j^2 contains the interference to SU j caused by primary transmitter and additive white Gaussian noise.

3 Review of NPG and Stackelberg Game

3.1 NPG Algorithm and NE

An appropriate model for power control problem is given by NPG [4]. In [4], the optimization problem is written as

$$\max \quad u_j(p_j, P_{-j}), j \in \{1, \ldots, N\}. \tag{4}$$

We denote the utility function alternatively as $u_j(p_j, P_{-j})$, where u_j is the same as (1) and P_{-j} represents the power of players excluding j.p_j represents the power of user j. Non-cooperative game is described as $G = [N, \{p_j\}, \{u_j\}]$, where $N = \{1, \ldots, N\}$ is the SU player set. $\{p_j\}$ is the policy set and $\{u_j\}$ is the utility function set.

The works [4,9] on NPG algorithm show that the unique NE exists when users choose their policies selfishly and rationally. The NE can be described as $p^{\text{NE}} = (p_1^{\text{NE}}, \ldots, p_N^{\text{NE}})$, where $p_j^{\text{NE}} = \min(p_j^{\max}, p_j^{\sim})$ and $p_j^{\sim}$ is

$$p_j^{\sim} = \frac{\gamma_j^{\sim}\left(\sum\limits_{k \ne j} h_{kj} p_k^{\text{NE}} + \delta_j^2\right)}{h_j}, \tag{5}$$

which represents the transmit power of SU j. The $\gamma_j^{\sim}$ is the SINR, which is the solution to (6)

$$f'(\gamma_j)\gamma_j - f(\gamma_j) = 0. \tag{6}$$

At the NE, the corresponding SINR of $p_j^{\sim}$ depends on the function $f_j(\gamma_j)$ in (2). $\gamma_j^{\sim}$ is defined as 'the best SINR at the NE' and each SU transmits with the corresponding power of the best SINR. NPG algorithm provides a solution for power control when NE is achieved. However, the NE is inefficient from the sense of two perspectives: (1) if some users continue to decrease power to break the NE, the utility of each user will increase; (2) the SUs selfishly maximize their own utilities without considering the interference to PU and other SUs.

3.2 The Single-Leader Stackelberg Game for Power Control

Stackelberg game for power control is introduced to deal with the inefficient NE in NPG. In the game, one user is the leader while the other users are followers. If the leader chooses the power to maximize its utility, an equilibrium will be achieved among users, namely Stackelberg Equilibrium (SE).

In single-leader Stackelberg power game [5], both the leader and followers improve their EE with respect to non-cooperative setting. Two kinds of SUs exist when the followers reach a NE [4,9]. The first kind of SUs satisfies the equation $p_j^{\mathrm{NE}} = p_j^{\sim}$ and transmits with the corresponding 'best SINR at the NE' power. The second kind of SUs satisfies the equation $p_j^{\mathrm{NE}} = p_j^{\max}$ transmitting with maximum power. When leader decreases power, its interference to other SUs decreases. Then a new equilibrium is reached. The first kind of SUs keeps in the 'best SINR'. However, their power decreases and their EE increases according to (1). The power of the second kind of SUs is kept in $p_j^{\max}$. But the interference to them decreases as the leader and the first kind of SUs decrease their power. Hence, the SINR of the second kind of SUs increases and their EE increases according to (1). Last, if the leader continues to decrease power, the second kind of SUs will transform into the first kind of SUs. That means all the SUs transmit with the corresponding 'best SINR' power and their EE increases. No matter what power the leader chooses, followers enable to achieve a NE. With the decrease in leader's power, the EE of the two kinds of SUs increases. Thus, the new NE, namely SE, is a Pareto improvement.

However, in Stackelberg power control game, only one-shot Pareto improvement is achieved. What's more, some prerequisites are needed. Leader needs to acquire more knowledge than followers [6]. Followers are cognitive SUs able to know the leader's strategy [7]. However, in [6], distributed management was ignored. In underlay CRNs, SUs are unable to sense as [7].

4   Distributed Multi-leader Stackelberg Power Control Game

To achieve higher EE, a distributed multi-leader Stackelberg power control game algorithm (DMSPG) is proposed in this section. In DMSPG, firstly, single-leader game achieves SE and one-shot Pareto improvement is reached. Then, multiple leaders implement power-decreasing strategy to achieve continuous Pareto improvements. Since SUs interfere with each other, the change of the leader's power can affect followers. Hence, followers adjust their power according to their SINR to react to the leader. Finally, continuous Pareto improvements are achieved to improve the total EE.

4.1 The Criterion of Choosing Leader in DMSPG Algorithm

In DMSPG algorithm, SU i^* is chosen as leader from the followers. The criterion is

$$i^* = \arg\min\left\{Q_i\right\}, \gamma_i > \gamma_i^{\text{tar}}, \tag{7}$$

where Q_i is

$$Q_i = \frac{u_i\left(p_i, \mathbf{P}_{-i}\right)}{p_i|g_i|^2 + \sum_{j \neq i} p_i\,|h_{ij}|^2}. \tag{8}$$

In (8), the numerator includes the EE of SU i while the denominator consists of the interference to PU and other SUs caused by SU i. A SU is chosen as leader considering two aspects: (1) the SU induces more negative effects to the others; (2) the SU makes less contribution to the whole system. Leader implements Variable-step power-decreasing strategy to break the original NE. Then a SE is reached.

4.2 The Proposed DMSPG Algorithm

The DMSPG algorithm is described with four steps.

- Step 1: the initialization of NPG
  1. Execute NPG algorithm and the SUs reach a NE.
  2. Once SUs achieve the equilibrium, they broadcast flag information INIT-FINISHED + ID. INIT-FINISHED means initialization is finished and ID represents the identification.
  3. When those SUs succeed to hear the $N-1$ INIT-FINISHED and equipment ID, they broadcast flag LEADER-START. It means the process of choosing leader starts.
- Step 2: choosing leader based on the criterion in (8)
  1. All SUs calculate their own Q values. Then, Q values are set as the start time of time back-off. SUs start to listen to the flag STOP-LEADER by virtual timer fashion.
  2. The SU whose timer is the first to become zero will broadcast flag STOP-LEADER.
  3. Once the other SUs listen to STOP-LEADER flag, the leader-choosing process will stop.

- Step 3: single leader performs power-decreasing game
  1. The leader decreases power level with an initial step size Δp. The SINR of the other SUs changes and the NE is broken. Then all the followers have to play non-cooperative game to achieve a SE.
  2. All SUs calculate their EE e.g. u_j. Then all SUs except the leader set their time back-off with u_j as start time. These SUs start to listen to the flag STOP-EE by a time back-off fashion.
  3. Each SU sends a flag STOP-EE when the countdown finishes. The leader calculates u_j based on the time all the STOP-EE heard. The total social welfare w of the system is calculated according to (2). If w is lower, it means the step size Δp in (1) is big. SUs change to the original power and leader shortens step size to $0.5 * \Delta p$. Then go back to (1). This process keeps taking half the step size until w increases and the QoS of SUs is satisfied. Then the transmit power of each SU remain unchanged. The step size of the leader is retained.
  4. Leader keeps repeating (3) with the step size retained in (3) till prescribed accuracy requirement is satisfied. It means no more utility could be attained even to decrease the leader's power and the SE is achieved.
- Step 4: multiple leaders perform power-decreasing game
  1. The leader chosen in Step 3 is put in leader set and does not take participate in leader-choosing any more. Then according to Step 2, another appropriate leader is chosen from followers.
  2. The new leader takes power-decreasing strategy in Step 3. Other leaders keep their original power.
  3. Estimate whether the algorithm is convergent according to practical application, for example, given terminal time. If it is not convergent, the process goes back to (1) until it is.

4.3 Analysis of Multi-leader Game and Continuous Pareto Improvements in DMSPG

The Uniqueness and Existence of SE. According to the analysis of single-leader game, no matter what power lever the leader sets, the followers will achieve a NE by non-cooperative game. If the leader chooses the power which maximizes its utility, the leader and the followers will achieve a SE. In this paper, the SE of multi-leader game exists as the single-leader Stackelberg game is played once more after a new leader is chosen. According to [5], the uniqueness of a SE is proved in single-leader Stackelberg game, the uniqueness of the SE in multi-leader Stackelberg game in this paper can be proved as [5].

The Efficiency of DMSPG Analysis. According to the analysis of single-leader game, the power of both leader and followers does not increase. In Step 4, the other leaders endure less interference and their SINR improves. Their EE increases according to (1). What's more, followers achieve one-shot Pareto improvement and their EE increases. The other leaders' power in leader set is invariable and followers' power does not increase. The partial derivative of $u_j(\cdot)$ with respect to p_j is

$$\frac{\partial u_j(p_j, P_{-j})}{\partial p_j} = \frac{LR}{Mp_j^2}(f'(\gamma_j)\gamma_j - f(\gamma_j)). \tag{9}$$

The $u_j(\cdot)$ monotonously increases with respect to p_j if γ_j is no more than the solution $\tilde{\gamma_j}$ to (6). When leader1 in Step 3 decreases power, its utility decreases. According to Step 3, when the leader1 chooses the step, it should ensure that its EE doesn't decrease. If its SINR increases, its EE (utility) won't decrease. Thus, according to (9), this leader's power decreases and its interference caused by the other leaders and followers decreases much more. Hence, its SINR increases and its QoS is satisfied.

Based on the above analysis, the EE of both other leaders and followers increases while the leader1's EE doesn't decrease. Hence, the total EE improves and a Pareto improvement is achieved. In Step 4, multiple leaders continue to decrease power and continuous Pareto improvements are achieved. Given the convergent conditions according to practical conditions, the algorithm ends.

Computational Complexity of DMSPG. The DMSPG algorithm ends in finite time. In the first step of proposed algorithm, the initialization of NPG results in a computation of $O(N^2)$. In the second step, every SU calculate its own utility and the computational complexity is $O(N)$. In the third step, the SUs play NPG after the leader decreases its power, resulting a computation of $O(N^2)$. In the fourth step, since another leader is chosen from the followers and the Stackelberg game is played once more, the computational complexity is $O(N^3)$. Thus, the overall computational complexity of proposed algorithm is $O(N^3)$. On the other hand, for followers, the computational complexity is mainly decided by the NPG, thus, the computational complexity of each follower is $O(N^2)$. For each leader, the computational complexity is decided by the forth step, since there are N SUs in total, the computational complexity is $O(N)$.

5   Numerical Results

In underlay CRNs, nine SUs in set $SU_i, i \in [1, 9]$ are sorted based on communication distance. SU_1's communication distance is the nearest while SU_9 is the furthest. The comparison of the ESIA algorithm [3], the OL algorithm [6] and the DMSPG algorithm is given. The ESIA algorithm is based on non-cooperative game while the OL algorithm is based on single-leader game. The total bits M is 80 and information bits L is 64. The bits rate R is 10 kbps. What's more, the SINR threshold of SU γ^{tar} is 6 dB and SINR threshold of PU $\gamma_{\text{pu}}^{\text{tar}}$ is 8 dB. The noise power δ^2 is 5×10^{-15} and PU power P_{pu} is 0.03 W. In addition, the precision is 5 and original step size is 0.001 W. The path loss A is 0.097.

Figure 2 shows the average SINR of PU. With the increase in the number of SUs, SINR of PU decreases. However, the SINR of PU in DMSPG algorithm is

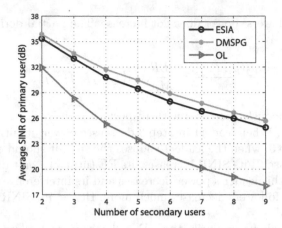

Fig. 2. Average SINR of PU of three algorithms (Color figure online)

higher than that in ESIA algorithm and OL algorithm. This can be explained as follows. In DMSPG, with the decrease in leader's power, the other SUs' power decreases. Hence, the interference to PU decreases and the SINR of PU improves. The ESIA is based on non-cooperative game and SUs cause more interference to PU. In the OL algorithm, only one leader is chosen and SUs cause more interference to PU.

Figure 3 shows the total power of SUs. With the increase in number of SUs, the total power of SUs increases. However, SUs' power in DMSPG is lower than that in ESIA and OL. This is because SUs' power is non-increasing in DMSPG. ESIA is based on non-cooperative game and SUs' power decreases less. In OL, only one-shot Pareto improvement is achieved.

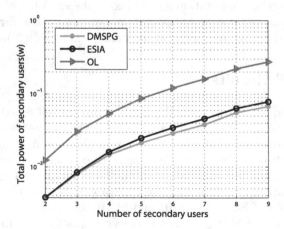

Fig. 3. Transmit power of SUs of three algorithms (Color figure online)

Figure 4 shows the total utilities of SUs. With the increase in number of SUs, the total utilities of SUs increase. The utilities of DMSPG are higher than ESIA and OL. The reason is that DMSPG is based on multi-leader Stackelberg game and enables to achieve continuous Pareto improvements. Thus, the proposed algorithm achieves higher total EE of multiple SUs.

The transmit power of the SUs (use SU_3, SU_5, SU_8 and SU_9 as example) with iteration times is shown in Fig. 5. We can see that the transmit power converges to the equilibrium within 30 iterations, which proves the convergence of proposed algorithm. The power of SU_3 is lowest while the power of SU_9 is the highest. The reason is that the power of SU increases With the distance of SU transceiver and the SUs are sorted based on communication distance as mentioned above.

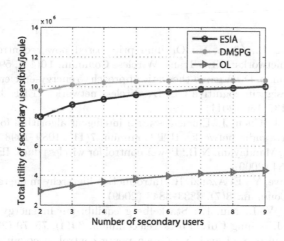

Fig. 4. Utilities of SUs of three algorithms (Color figure online)

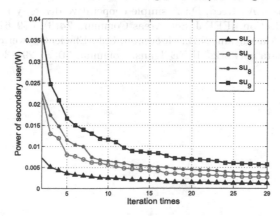

Fig. 5. Transmit power of SUs with iteration times (Color figure online)

6   Conclusion

In this paper, we aim at improving total EE of multiple users in green wireless communications. Considering distributed power control, we propose a distributed Stackelberg game power control algorithm to decrease SUs' power. Meanwhile, continuous Pareto improvements are achieved with multiple leaders implementing power-decreasing strategies. Simulations testify that the proposed DMSPG algorithm reduces SU's power and improves the total EE of the system.

Acknowledgments. This work was supported by the National Natural Science Foundation of China (Grant No. 61540046) and the 111 Project of China (Grant No. B08038).

References

1. Wang, Z., Jiang, L., Chen, H.: Optimal price-based power control algorithm in cognitive radio networks. IEEE Trans. Wireless Commun. **16**(11), 5909–5920 (2014)
2. Buzzi, S., Saturnino, D.: A game-theoretic approach to energy-efficient power control and receiver design in cognitive CDMA wireless networks. IEEE J. Sel. Top. Sig. Process. **5**(1), 137–150 (2011)
3. Kuo, Y., Yang, J., Chen, J.: Efficient swarm intelligent algorithm for power control game in cognitive radio networks. IET Commun. **7**(11), 1089–1098 (2013)
4. Goodman, D.J., Mandayam, N.B.: Power control for wireless data. IEEE Pers. Commun. **7**(2), 48–54 (2000)
5. Lasaulce, S., Haye, Y., El Azouzi, R.: Introduction hierarchy in energy games. IEEE Trans. Wirel. Commun. **8**(7), 3833–3843 (2009)
6. Wang, L., Xu, W.-J., Niu, K.: Stackelberg equilibrium in energy-efficient power control games. J. Beijing Univ. Posts Telecommun. **34**(4), 75–79 (2011)
7. Le, T.-M., Lasaulce, S., Hayel, Y.: Green power control in cognitive wireless networks. IEEE Trans. Veh. Technol. **62**(4), 1741–1754 (2013)
8. Bletsas, A., Khisti, A., Reed, D.: A simple cooperative diversity method based on network path selection. IEEE J. Sel. Areas Commun. **24**(3), 659–672 (2006)
9. Saraydar, C.U., Mandayam, N.B., Goodman, D.J.: Efficient power control via pricing in wireless data networks. IEEE Trans. Commun. **50**(2), 291–303 (2002)

Optimal Channel Selection and Power Control over D2D Communications Based Cognitive Radio Networks

Ya Gao$^{(\boxtimes)}$, Wenchi Cheng, Zhiyuan Ren, and Hailin Zhang

State Key Laboratory of Integrated Services Networks,
Xidian University, Xi'an 710071, China
gaoya@stu.xidian.edu.cn, {wccheng,zyren,hlzhang}@xidian.edu.cn

Abstract. We develop the joint optimal channel selection and power control scheme for video streaming with D2D communications in cognitive radio networks. In particular, we build the virtual queue model to evaluate the delays experienced by various streaming, which reflects the video distortion. To minimize the video distortion, we formulate an optimization problem, which is proved to be a quasi-convex optimization problem. Using the hypo-graph form, we convert the original problem into an equivalent convex optimization problem, solving which we can derive the joint channel selection and power control scheme in D2D communications based cognitive radio networks. The extensive simulation results obtained validate our developed joint channel selection and power control scheme. We also show that our developed scheme can significantly increase the average peak signal-to-noise ratio (PSNR) as compared with the existing research works.

Keywords: Cognitive radio networks · D2D communication · Channel selection · Power control · Video distortion · Convex optimization

1 Introduction

The evolving fifth generation (5G) wireless networks are envisioned to provide higher data rates, reduce end-to-end delay, improve the quality of experience (QoE) of mobile users, and mitigate the interference. This motivates the innovation of new communication paradigms. *Cognitive radio networks*, allowing secondary users (SUs) to spectrum share or time share the idle licensed spectrum with primary users (PUs), can efficiently increase the spectrum efficiency in frequency-domain and time-domain [1]. *D2D communications*, which enable data exchange directly between two mobile users (called *D2D pair*) in

This work was supported in part by the National Natural Science Foundation of China (No. 61401330), the 111 Project of China (B08038), and the Natural Science Foundation of Shaanxi Province (No. 2016JQ6027).

© ICST Institute for Computer Sciences, Social Informatics and Telecommunications Engineering 2018
Q. Chen et al. (Eds.): ChinaCom 2016, Part II, LNICST 210, pp. 107–117, 2018.
DOI: 10.1007/978-3-319-66628-0_11

proximity bypassing base station (BS) or core network, can increase the spectrum efficiency in space-domain [2]. As a result, employing D2D communications in cognitive radio networks can significantly increase the spectrum efficiency in frequency/time/space-domain. Therefore, cognitive radio network coexisting with D2D communications, as a promising, but challenging, technical approach, has been paid much research attention.

The authors of [3] analyzed the engineering insights useful for system design in the D2D communications with cognitive radio assistance. The authors of [4] proposed a cognitive spectrum access in D2D-enabled cellular networks. Most of these works concentrate on how to improve the network performance by employing D2D communication in cognitive radio networks. However, for realtime video streams, the delay-sensitive traffic imposes new challenges for D2D communications based cognitive radio networks. To guarantee realtime transmission for delay-sensitive traffic, it is necessary to take the video distortion into account for D2D communications based cognitive radio networks.

To remedy the above deficiencies, in this paper we propose the joint optimal channel selection and power control scheme for video streaming over D2D communications based cognitive radio networks. Applying the "M/G/1 queues with vacations" theory, we build the virtual queue model to evaluate the delays experienced by various streaming. Then, we formulate the distortion minimization problem subject to the required capacity constraints and power constraints, which is proved to be a quasi-convex problem. Adopting the hypo-graph form, we convert the original problem into an equivalent convex problem. We develop the Lagrange-dual method to derive the joint optimal channel selection and power control scheme. The extensive simulation results obtained validate our proposed joint channel selection and power control scheme and show the better performance than the existing research works.

The rest of this paper is organized as follows. Section 2 shows the system model for the considered D2D communications based cognitive radio networks. Section 3 formulates the video distortion minimization, converts the original optimization problem into a strict convex optimization problem and solves the problem by developing primal-dual method. Section 4 simulates and evaluates our proposed channel selection and power allocation scheme. The paper concludes with Sect. 5.

2   The System Model

2.1   Network Model

We consider the D2D communications based cognitive radio network model as shown in Fig. 1, which consists of a number of important components described as follows. PUs, the traditional cognitive primary nodes, communicate with other terminals through the BS. SUs implement D2D communications with each other, forming D2D pairs. Both PUs and SUs share the same bandwidth B which is licenced to PUs. There are M channels in the cognitive radio networks. The PUs can only occupy their assigned channels. From the perspective of SUs, there is

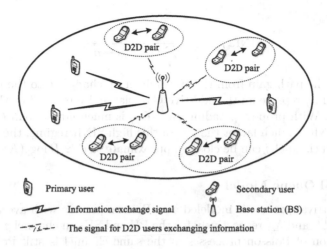

Fig. 1. The network model.

no need to differentiate different PUs on one channel. Therefore, we reduce the PUs on one channel into one aggregate PU. As a result, there are two sets of users on each channel: one aggregate PU and several SUs.

As transmitters, SUs take their actions of channel selection and power allocation for each packet. We denote the channel selection strategy of SU_i, $(1 \leq i \leq N)$ as $\boldsymbol{\alpha}_i = [\alpha_{i1}, \alpha_{i2}, \dots, \alpha_{iM}]$, where $\alpha_{ij} \in [0,1]$ represents the probability of SU_i to choose channel j for transmission. Hence, we have $\sum_{j=1}^{M} \alpha_{ij} = 1$.

Let $\boldsymbol{P}_i = [P_{i1}, P_{i2}, \dots, P_{iM}]$ denote by the power allocation of SU_i on each channel j $(1 \leq j \leq M)$. Due to D2D nodes' power-consumption constraints [2], each secondary user needs to satisfy an individual power constraint $\sum_{j=1}^{M} P_{ij} \leq P_i^{\max}$, where $P_i^{\max}$ is the maximum power constraint for SU_i.

2.2 Channel Model

Let x_i denote by the stream bit rate of SU_i, and $\mathcal{C}_{ij}$ denote by the "capacity". According to the channel selection strategy, the stream bit rate of SU_i over channel j is $\alpha_{ij}x_i$. Clearly, for each channel j, the stream bit rate of SU_i cannot exceed the channel capacity

$$\alpha_{ij}x_i \leq \mathcal{C}_{ij}. \tag{1}$$

The interference-limited network model is adopted. Hence, the channel capacity of channel j selected by SU_i can be written as the global and nonlinear functions of the transmit power $\boldsymbol{P}$ and channel conditions, which is given as follows:

$$\mathcal{C}(\boldsymbol{P}) = B \log_2 [1 + K \cdot \text{SINR}(\boldsymbol{P})]. \tag{2}$$

Here, the parameter $K = (-1.5/\ln \text{BER})$, where BER represents the required bit-error rate. The signal-to-interference-plus-noise ratio (SINR) from SU_i to the receiving node using channel j can be expressed as follows:

$$\text{SINR}_{ij} = \frac{G_{jj}P_{ij}}{\sum\limits_{k\neq j}\sum\limits_{h\neq i} G_{kj}P_{hk} + n_j},\tag{3}$$

where G_{kj} is the path gain from the transmitter on channel k to the receiver on channel j and n_j represents the additive Gaussian noise power (for the receiver of channel j). With proper spreading gain, G_{jj} is much larger than G_{jk}, $k \neq j$. Hence, $K \cdot \text{SINR}$ is much larger than 1. In this high SINR regime, the attainable rate of SU_i on channel j can be closely approximate to $\mathcal{C} \simeq B \log_2(K \cdot \text{SINR})$ [5].

2.3   Virtual Queue Model

The packet arrival process is modeled as a Poisson process with average packet arrival rate λ_j^{PU} and λ_{ij} respectively for the PU and SU_i on channel j. Note that the aggregation of Poisson processes in the same channel is still Poisson. The packets of the competing users are physically waiting in their buffer locally. For each channel j, Fig. 2 depicts N physical queues Q_{ij} for SU_i with the arrival rate λ_{ij}, a physical queue for PU_j with the arrival rate λ_j^{PU}, and a virtual queue $\tilde{Q}_j$ of channel j with the arrival rate of $\sum_{k=1}^{N} \lambda_{kj} + \lambda_j^{\text{PU}}$. Since $\alpha_{ij}x_i$ represents the stream bit rate of SU_i over channel j, the arrival rate of SU_i can be determined by $\lambda_{ij} = \alpha_{ij}x_i/L_i$, where L_i is the average packet length of SU_i. The ARQ protocol is considered to decrease packet errors. The service time of the physical queue users can be modeled as a geometric distribution. We adopt the M/G/1 model for the traffic description of physical queues. Based on, the well-known P-K formula [6], the first and second moments of the service time of SU_i using channel j can be derived as follows:

$$\begin{cases} \mathbb{E}[X_{ij}] = \frac{L_i}{\mathcal{C}_{ij}(1-P_{ij}^{\text{err}})}; \\ \mathbb{E}[X_{ij}^2] = \frac{L_i^2(1+P_{ij}^{\text{err}})}{\mathcal{C}_{ij}^2(1-P_{ij}^{\text{err}})^2}, \end{cases}\tag{4}$$

where P_{ij}^{err} is the packet error rate of SU_i over channel j.

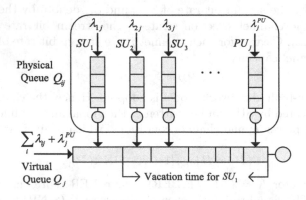

Fig. 2. The queuing process and the virtual queue.

For channel j, one SU can be allowed to transmit data on it at the same time. All the packets from different SUs on channel j form the virtual queue $\tilde{Q}_j$, as shown in Fig. 2. Given that the service time of SUs $\mathbb{E}[X_{ij}]$ are identically distributed (i.i.d), the virtual queue $\tilde{Q}_j$ is modeled as "M/G/1 queues with Vacations [7]". From the perspective of SU_i, at the end of its service time, the transmitter goes on a "vacation". In this "vacation" time, another user can send its traffic. In physical queues, we assume that a packet will join into the virtual queue once it arrives. Hence, the total delay is the service time in physical queue. Note that the total delay in physical queue becomes the service time in virtual queue. The service time in virtual queue is thus the service time in physical queue. Consequently, the end-to-end delay in virtual queue is the service time in physical queue plus the waiting time in virtual queue. The expectation of the vacation time $\mathbb{E}[V_{ij}]$, waiting time $\mathbb{E}[W_{ij}]$, and end-to-end delay $\mathbb{E}[D_{ij}]$ of SU_i using channel j can be derived as follows:

$$
\begin{cases}
\mathbb{E}[V_{ij}] &= \sum\limits_{k=1, k\neq i}^{N} \dfrac{\mathbb{E}[X_{kj}^2]}{2\mathbb{E}[X_{kj}]} + \dfrac{\mathbb{E}[X_j^{PU\,2}]}{2\mathbb{E}[X_j^{PU}]}; \\
\mathbb{E}[W_{ij}] &= \dfrac{\lambda_{ii}\mathbb{E}[X_{ij}^2]}{2(1-\lambda_{ii}\mathbb{E}[X_{ij}])} + \mathbb{E}[V_{ij}]; \\
\mathbb{E}[D_{ij}] &= \mathbb{E}[X_{ij}] + \mathbb{E}[W_{ij}].
\end{cases}
\tag{5}
$$

Let P_{ij}^{loss} represent the probability of packet loss for SU_i sending packets through channel j. For video streaming, P_{ij}^{loss} can be determined by the probability that the video session violated its play-out deadline d_0, i.e., $P_{ij}^{\text{loss}} = \Pr(\mathbb{E}[D_{ij}] > d_0)$. Based on the work of [8], we have:

$$
\Pr(\mathbb{E}[D_{ij}] > d_0) = \rho_{ij} \exp\left(-\frac{\rho_{ij}d_0}{\mathbb{E}[D_{ij}]}\right), \quad \rho_{ij} < 1,
\tag{6}
$$

where ρ_{ij} represents the normalized loading of SU_i using channel j, which is confirmed as $\rho_{ij} = \lambda_{ij}\mathbb{E}[X_{ij}]$. Since the normalized loading $\rho_{ij} < 1$ leads to a bounded delay $\mathbb{E}[D_{ij}]$ [6], which is expected for the video streaming, we can obtain:

$$
\alpha_{ij}x_i < \mathcal{C}_{ij}(1 - P_{ij}^{\text{err}}),
\tag{7}
$$

where $\mathcal{C}_{ij}(1 - P_{ij}^{\text{err}})$ can be regarded as the achievable capacity under $\rho_{ij} < 1$. By contrast, Eq. (1) is a more relaxed constraint. Hence, we use Eq. (7) as the rate constraint.

2.4   Video Distortion Model

As a measurement of wireless video quality, an additive model to capture video distortion is used [9]. The overall Mean-Squared-Error (MSE) distortion consists of two types of distortions: the distortion caused by signal compression D_{com} and the distortion caused by transmission errors D_{err}. We can calculate the overall MSE as follows:

$$
D_{\text{all}} = D_{\text{com}} + D_{\text{err}}.
\tag{8}
$$

The distortion D_{com} is determined by the compressed method, which can be approximated by:

$$D_{\text{com}} = \frac{\theta}{R - R_0} + D_0, \tag{9}$$

where R is the video stream bit rate, which is equivalent to $\alpha_{ij}x_i$. The parameters θ, R_0 and D_0 depend on the encoded sequence as well as the encoded structure. Note that θ, R_0 and D_0 can be estimated by nonlinear regression. Hence, they are assumed constants in this paper. Likewise, D_{err} can be modeled by a linear function with respect to packet error rate P^{err} and probability of packet loss P^{loss} as follows:

$$D_{\text{err}} = \sigma[P^{\text{err}} + (1 - P^{\text{err}})P^{\text{loss}}], \tag{10}$$

where σ is a constant.

3   Video Distortion Minimization

To minimize the total distortion of SUs, in this section we first formulate the video distortion minimization problem. Then, we develop the primal-dual method to solve the video distortion minimization problem.

3.1   Problem Formulation

Let $\boldsymbol{\alpha} = [\boldsymbol{\alpha}_1, \boldsymbol{\alpha}_2, \ldots, \boldsymbol{\alpha}_N]^T$ and $\boldsymbol{P} = [\boldsymbol{P}_1, \boldsymbol{P}_2, \ldots, \boldsymbol{P}_N]^T$ denote by the total channel selection and power control strategies across all the SUs. The video distortion minimization problem can be formulated as follows:

$$\boldsymbol{P1} : \min_{(\boldsymbol{\alpha}, \boldsymbol{P})} \sum_{i=1}^{N} \sum_{j=1}^{M} \boldsymbol{\alpha}^T D_{\text{all}} \tag{11}$$

subject to:

$$\alpha_{ij}x_i < \mathcal{C}_{ij}(1 - P_{ij}^{\text{err}}), \forall i, j; \tag{12}$$

$$\sum_{j=1}^{M} \alpha_{ij} = 1, \alpha_{ij} \in [0, 1], \forall i; \tag{13}$$

$$\sum_{j=1}^{M} P_{ij} \leq P_i^{\text{max}}, P_{ij} \geq 0, \forall i; \tag{14}$$

$$\mathcal{C}(\boldsymbol{P}) = B \log_2 [1 + K \cdot \text{SINR}(\boldsymbol{P})], \forall i, j. \tag{15}$$

The objective function in Eq. (11) is set to minimize the total weighted video distortion for all SUs. The weight is channel selection probability $\boldsymbol{\alpha}$. The decision variables are $\boldsymbol{\alpha}$ and $\boldsymbol{P}$. The constraint Eq. (12) makes sure that the stream bit rate for SU_i using channel j cannot exceed the achievable capacity of channel j.

The constraints Eqs. (13) and (14) ensure the feasibility of channel selection and power control. The constraint Eq. (15) indicates the calculation of the capacity of channel j.

It is clear the constraints Eqs. (12)–(14) are convex functions. Because the $K \cdot \text{SINR}$ is much larger than 1, the constraint Eq. (15) can be approximated to $\mathcal{C}(\boldsymbol{P}) = B \log_2 [K \cdot \text{SINR}(\boldsymbol{P})]$, which can be further converted into a nonlinear concave function through a log transformation, leading to a critical convexity property [5]. Next, we prove the convexity of the objective function Eq. (11). We first rewrite the objective function Eq. (11) as follows:

$$\min_{(\boldsymbol{\alpha},\boldsymbol{P})} \sum_{i=1}^{N} \sum_{j=1}^{M} \alpha_{ij}(D_0 + \sigma P_{ij}^{\text{err}}) + \frac{\theta \alpha_{ij}}{\alpha_{ij} x_i - R_0} + \sigma(1 - P_{ij}^{\text{err}})\alpha_{ij}\rho_{ij} \exp\left(-\frac{\rho_{ij} d_0}{\mathbb{E}[D_{ij}]}\right).$$

Theorem 1. *The objective function of this Video Distortion Minimization problem is a quasi-convex problem.*

Proof. It is easy to prove that the first term $\alpha_{ij}(D_0 + \sigma P_{ij}^{\text{err}})$, the second term $\frac{\theta \alpha_{ij}}{\alpha_{ij} x_i - R_0}$ and the multiplication $\alpha_{ij}\rho_{ij} = \frac{\alpha_{ij}^2 x_i}{\mathcal{C}_{ij}(1 - P_{ij}^{\text{err}})}$ of the third term in the objective function are all convex. We denote $f = \rho_{ij} d_0 = \frac{\alpha_{ij} x_i d_0}{\mathcal{C}_{ij}(1 - P_{ij}^{\text{err}})}$, checking its Hessian matrix, we can obtain:

$$\frac{\partial^2 f}{\partial \alpha_{ij}^2} \cdot \frac{\partial^2 f}{\partial P_{ij}^2} - \left[\frac{\partial^2 f}{\partial \alpha_{ij} P_{ij}}\right]^2 = -\left[\frac{x_i d_0 B}{\mathcal{C}_{ij}^2 P_{ij}(1 - P_{ij}^{\text{err}})\ln 2}\right]^2 \leq 0. \qquad (16)$$

Therefore, the numerator of the exponent is concave. For the denominator of the exponent $\mathbb{E}[D_{ij}]$, the first derivative with respect to $\mathcal{C}_{ij}$ and the Hessian matrix are shown as follows:

$$\frac{\partial \mathbb{E}[D_{ij}]}{\partial \mathcal{C}_{ij}} = \frac{-L_i \left[\alpha_{ij}^2 x_i^2 + 2\mathcal{C}_{ij}(1 - P_{ij}^{\text{err}})(\mathcal{C}_{ij} - \alpha_{ij} x_i)\right]}{2\mathcal{C}_{ij}^2[\mathcal{C}_{ij}(1 - P_{ij}^{\text{err}}) - \alpha_{ij} x_i]^2} \leq 0, \qquad (17)$$

$$\frac{\partial^2 \mathbb{E}[D_{ij}]}{\partial \alpha_{ij}^2} \cdot \frac{\partial^2 \mathbb{E}[D_{ij}]}{\partial \mathcal{C}_{ij}^2} - \left[\frac{\partial^2 \mathbb{E}[D_{ij}]}{\partial \alpha_{ij} \partial \mathcal{C}_{ij}}\right]^2 = \frac{L_i^2 x_i^2(1 + P_{ij}^{\text{err}})}{\mathcal{C}_{ij}^3} \geq 0. \qquad (18)$$

The Hessian matrix of $\mathbb{E}[D_{ij}]$ is semipositive. Hence $\mathbb{E}[D_{ij}]$ is convex with respect to α_{ij} and $\mathcal{C}_{ij}$. Note that $\mathbb{E}[D_{ij}]$ is nonincreasing of $\mathcal{C}_{ij}$. Meanwhile, $\mathcal{C}_{ij}$ is concave. As a result, $\mathbb{E}[D_{ij}]$ is convex with respect to α_{ij} and P_{ij}. Since the numerator $\rho_{ij} d_0$ is concave, and the denominator $\mathbb{E}[D_{ij}]$ is convex, the function $\exp(-\frac{\rho_{ij} d_0}{\mathbb{E}[D_{ij}]})$ is quasi-convex. Consequently, the objective function is quasi-convex. ∎

In the objective function, the first term, second term and the multiplication of the third term are all convex. To make the primal objective function strictly convex, we just need to make the exponent part convex. For this reason, auxiliary variable t is introduced. We apply the hypo-graph form to replace the quasi-convex function as follows:

$$tE[D_{ij}] - \rho_{ij} \leq 0, \ t \geq 0. \tag{19}$$

The Eq. (19) is strictly convex. Consequently, the optimization problem $P1$ can be equivalently converted to the optimization problem $P2$ as follows:

$$P2: \min_{(\boldsymbol{\alpha},\boldsymbol{P},t)} \sum_{i=1}^{N} \sum_{j=1}^{M} \alpha_{ij}(D_0 + \sigma P_{ij}^{\text{err}}) + \frac{\theta \alpha_{ij}}{\alpha_{ij}x_i - R_0} + \sigma(1 - P_{ij}^{\text{err}})\alpha_{ij}\rho_{ij}\exp(-d_0 t)$$

subject to the constraints Eqs. (12)–(15) and (19).

It is clear that $P2$ is a strict convex optimization problem because the objective function and the constraints are all convex.

3.2 Lagrange-Dual Method

We utilize the Lagrange-dual method to develop a solution algorithm for the video distortion minimization problem. We first define the Lagrangian function for the video distortion minimization problem $P2$ in Eq. (20), where κ_1, κ_2, and κ_3 are the Lagrange multipliers associated with the problem's constraints.

$$
\begin{aligned}
L = \sum_{i=1}^{N}\sum_{j=1}^{M} &\left[\alpha_{ij}(D_0 + \sigma P_{ij}^{\text{err}}) + \frac{\theta \alpha_{ij}}{\alpha_{ij}x_i - R_0} + \sigma(1 - P_{ij}^{\text{err}})\alpha_{ij}\rho_{ij}\exp(-d_0 t) \right] \\
&+ \sum_{j=1}^{M} \kappa_1 \left(\alpha_{ij}x_i - C_{ij}(1 - P_{ij}^{\text{err}}) \right) + \sum_{i=1}^{N} \kappa_2 \left(\sum_{j=1}^{M} P_{ij} - P_i^{\max} \right) \\
&+ \sum_{i=1}^{N}\sum_{j=1}^{M} \kappa_3 \left(tE[D_{ij}] - \rho_{ij} \right). \tag{20}
\end{aligned}
$$

Since the optimization problem $P2$ is strictly convex, the duality gap is zero. We use gradient projection method to solve the Lagrange problem. In order to expand the Lagrange function, we replace ρ_{ij} and $E[D_{ij}]$ in L with their expressions in Sect. 2. As the Lagrange function is differentiable, the gradients of L with respect to the Lagrange multipliers are obtained as

$$
\begin{cases}
\frac{\partial L}{\partial \kappa_1} = \alpha_{ij}x_i - C_{ij}(1 - P_{ij}^{\text{err}}); \\
\frac{\partial L}{\partial \kappa_2} = \sum_{j=1}^{M} P_{ij} - P_i^{\max}; \\
\frac{\partial L}{\partial \kappa_3} = \sum_{i=1}^{N}\sum_{j=1}^{M} \left[t\left(\frac{L_i(2C_{ij} - \alpha_{ij}x_i)}{2C_{ij}[C_{ij}(1 - P_{ij}^{\text{err}}) - \alpha_{ij}x_i]} + E[V_{ij}] \right) - \frac{\alpha_{ij}x_i}{C_{ij}(1 - P_{ij}^{\text{err}})} \right].
\end{cases} \tag{21}
$$

By applying the gradient projection method, the Lagrange multipliers are calculated iteratively as follows:

$$\kappa_1(s+1) = \left[\kappa_1(s) + \nu\frac{\partial L}{\partial \kappa_1} \right]^+, \tag{22}$$

where $\nu > 0$ is the gradient step size, s represents the gradient numbers, and $[\cdot]^+$ denotes $\max(0, \cdot)$. The remaining Lagrange multipliers κ_2 and κ_3 are obtained iteratively using similar equations.

Taking the derivation of L with respect to α_{ij}, P_{ij} and t, setting the results to zero, respectively, we can obtain Eq. (23), where α_{ij} and P_{ij} can be numerically solved in the next section.

$$
\begin{cases}
\frac{\partial L}{\partial \alpha_{ij}} = \sum_{i=1}^{N} \sum_{j=1}^{M} \left\{ D_0 + \sigma P_{ij}^{\mathrm{err}} - \frac{\theta R_0}{(\alpha_{ij} x_i - R_0)^2} + \frac{2\alpha_{ij} x_i \exp(-d_0 t)}{\mathcal{C}_{ij}(1-P_{ij}^{\mathrm{err}})} + \kappa_1 x_i - \frac{\kappa_3 x_i}{\mathcal{C}_{ij}(1-P_{ij}^{\mathrm{err}})} \right. \\
\qquad \left. + \frac{\kappa_3 t x_i L_i (1+P_{ij}^{\mathrm{err}})}{2[\mathcal{C}_{ij}(1-P_{ij}^{\mathrm{err}})-\alpha_{ij} x_i]^2} \right\} = 0, \\[2ex]
\frac{\partial L}{\partial P_{ij}} = \sum_{i=1}^{N} \sum_{j=1}^{M} \frac{B}{P_{ij} \ln 2} \left\{ -\frac{\sigma \alpha_{ij}^2 x_i}{\mathcal{C}_{ij}^2} \exp(-d_0 t) - \kappa_1(1-P_{ij}^{\mathrm{err}}) + \frac{\kappa_3 \alpha_{ij} x_i}{\mathcal{C}_{ij}^2(1-P_{ij}^{\mathrm{err}})} \right. \\
\qquad \left. + \kappa_3 t L_i \frac{2\mathcal{C}_{ij}(1-P_{ij}^{\mathrm{err}})\alpha_{ij} x_i - 2\mathcal{C}_{ij}^2(1-P_{ij}^{\mathrm{err}})-\alpha_{ij}^2 x_i^2}{2\mathcal{C}_{ij}^2[\mathcal{C}_{ij}(1-P_{ij}^{\mathrm{err}})-\alpha_{ij} x_i]^2} \right\} + \kappa_2 = 0, \\[2ex]
t^* = -\frac{1}{d_0} \log \left\{ \frac{\kappa_3}{d_0 \sigma \pi_i \alpha_{ij}^2} \left[\frac{L_i(2\mathcal{C}_{ij}-\alpha_{ij} x_i)}{2[\mathcal{C}_{ij}(1-P_{ij}^{\mathrm{err}})-\alpha_{ij} x_i]} + \mathbb{E}[V_{ij}]\mathcal{C}_{ij} \right] \right\}.
\end{cases}
$$
$$\tag{23}$$

4 Numerical Results

In this section, we evaluate the performance of our proposed joint optimal channel selection and power allocation scheme. We set the bandwidth $B = 10\,\mathrm{MHz}$, the packet length $L_i = 1\,\mathrm{Kbits}$, delay deadline $d_0 = 0.5\,\mathrm{s}$, the transmit power constraint $P_i^{\max} = 0.1\,\mathrm{W}$, the bit-error-rate BER $= 10^{-3}$, the noise power $n_j = -104\,\mathrm{dB}$, and the parameters for distortion model $D_0 = 0.38$, $\theta = 2.53\,\mathrm{kbps}$ and $R_0 = 18.3\,\mathrm{kbps}$, respectively. The path gain G_{kj} is determined by the relative physical distance d_{kj} from the transmitter of channel k to the receiver of the channel j, i.e., $G_{kj} = d_{kj}^{-\beta}$, where β is the path loss. In our simulation, we set $d_{jj} = 10\,\mathrm{m}$, $d_{jk} = 100\,\mathrm{m}$ $(j \neq k)$ and $\beta = 4$.

First, we simulate the network with two SUs (a D2D pair) and three channels (i.e., $N = 2$ and $M = 3$), to show the results using simple network such that our model can be clearly understood. The initial channel selection and power control are set to be $\alpha_{ij} = 1/3$ and $P_{ij} = 30\,\mathrm{mW}$ ($1 \leq i \leq 2$ and $1 \leq j \leq 3$), respectively. The packet error rate for SUs across all the channels are $P_{11}^{\mathrm{err}} = 0.11$, $P_{12}^{\mathrm{err}} = 0.08$, $P_{13}^{\mathrm{err}} = 0.15$, $P_{21}^{\mathrm{err}} = 0.05$, $P_{22}^{\mathrm{err}} = 0.12$ and $P_{23}^{\mathrm{err}} = 0.01$. We set the required stream bit rates of SU_i $x_1 = 840\,\mathrm{kbps}$ and $x_2 = 960\,\mathrm{kbps}$, respectively. The normalized loadings of PU_j are set to be $\rho_1 = 0.25$, $\rho_2 = 0.35$ and $\rho_3 = 0.15$ respectively, and the second moment normalized loadings are set to be $\rho_j^2 = 1 \times 10^{-4}$.

Figures 3 and 4 depict the optimal channel selection and power allocation scheme for SU_1 and SU_2 across all the channels. As shown in Figs. 3 and 4, the probability for SU_1 choosing channel 2 is $\alpha_{12} = 0.83$, which is bigger than choosing the other channels. The probability for SU_2 choosing channel 2 is $\alpha_{22} = 0.07$, which is smaller than choosing the other channels. Meanwhile, the power allocation of SU_1 for channel 2 is $P_{12} = 53.63\,\mathrm{mW}$, which is bigger than the other channels. The power allocation of SU_2 for channel 2 is $P_{22} = 4.98\,\mathrm{mW}$,

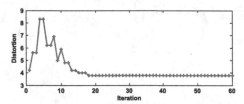

Fig. 3. Optimal channel selection.

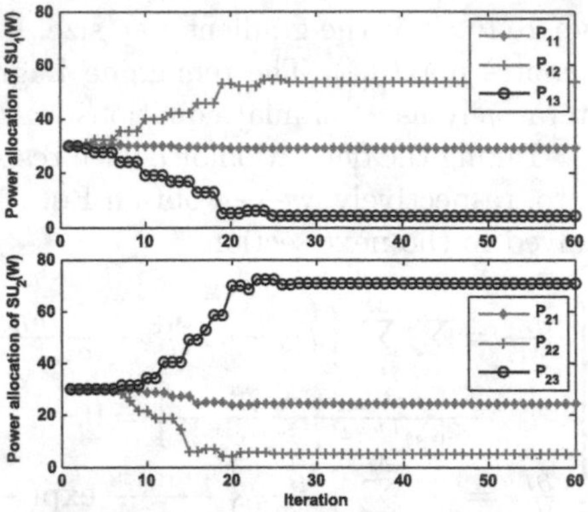

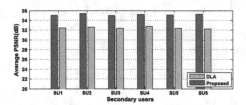

Fig. 4. Optimal power allocation.

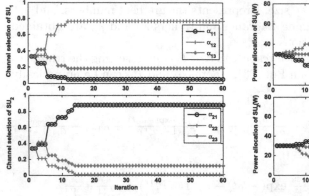

Fig. 5. Video distortion versus iterations.

Fig. 6. Comparison with DLA.

which is smaller than the other channels. This is due to the reason that channel capacity is limited, thus channels with smaller packet error rate and lighter traffic loadings are assigned more data traffic and transmit power. Figure 5 plots the overall video distortion of all the applications. The overall video distortion (MSE) converges to 3.80, which is equivalent to the peak signal-to-noise ratio of 42.33 dB. As compared with DLA algorithm in [10] whose utility function cannot converge to a steady state, our algorithm can achieve a better performance.

Next, we consider the network with six SUs and ten channels. We set the bandwidth $B = 1$ MHz and simulate 100 times with different channel states (i.e. packet error rate) as well as the normalized loadings and calculate the average PSNR for the traffics from six SUs. We compare our proposed scheme with DLA algorithm. The comparison results depicted in Fig. 6 show that our joint scheme can achieve a better performance than the DLA algorithm.

5   Conclusion

In this paper, we studied the video distortion minimization problem in D2D communications based cognitive radio network by jointly optimize the channel selection and power control scheme. We first evaluated the delays experienced by various streaming. Then, we formulated the video distortion minimization problem. Using the hypo-graph form, we equivalently converted the original quasi-convex problem into a strict convex optimization problem, solving which, we derived the joint channel selection and power control scheme. The extensive simulation results obtained showed the better performance than the existing research works.

References

1. Cheng, W., Zhang, X., Zhang, H.: Full-duplex spectrum-sensing and MAC-protocol for multichannel nontime-slotted cognitive radio networks. IEEE J. Sel. Areas Commun. **33**(5), 820–831 (2015)
2. Cheng, W., Zhang, X., Zhang, H.: Optimal power allocation with statistical QoS provisioning for D2D and cellular communications over underlaying wireless networks. IEEE J. Sel. Areas Commun. **34**, 1–12 (2015)
3. Mohammad, G.K., Yan, Z., Kwang, C.C.: Connectivity of cognitive device-to-device communications underlying cellular networks. IEEE J. Sel. Areas Commun. **33**(1), 81–99 (2015)
4. Sakr, A.H., Tabassum, H., Hossain, E., Kim, D.I.: Cognitive spectrum access in device-to-device-enabled cellular networks. IEEE Commun. Mag. **53**(7), 126–133 (2015)
5. Chiang, M.: Balancing transport and physical layers in wireless multihop networks: jointly optimal congestion control and power control. IEEE J. Sel. Areas Commun. **23**(1), 104–116 (2005)
6. Kleinrock, L.: Queuing Systems, Volume I: Theory. Wiley-Interscience, New York (1975)
7. Bertsekas, D., Gallager, R.: Data Networks. Prentice Hall Inc, Upper Saddle River (1987)
8. Jiang, T., Tham, C.K., Ko, C.C.: An approximation for waiting time tail probabilities in multiclass systems. IEEE Commun. Lett. **5**(4), 175–177 (2001)
9. Stuhlmuller, K., Frber, N., Link, M., Girod, B.: Analysis of video transmission over lossy channels. IEEE J. Sel. Areas Commun. **18**(6), 1012–1032 (2000)
10. Shiang, H.P., Schaar, M.: Queuing-based dynamic channel selection for heterogeneous multimedia applications over cognitive radio networks. IEEE Trans. Multimedia **10**(5), 896–909 (2008)

Network Architecture and SDN

Research on Load Balancing for Software Defined Cloud-Fog Network in Real-Time Mobile Face Recognition

Chenhua Shi, Zhiyuan Ren[✉], and Xiuli He

The State Key Laboratory of ISN in School of Telecommunications Engineering,
Xidian University, Xi'an, Shaanxi, China
{chshi,zyren,xlhe}@s-an.org

Abstract. The real-time camera-equipped mobile devices have been widely researched recently. And cloud computing has been used to support those applications. However, the high communication latency and unstable connections between cloud and users influence the Quality of Service (QoS). To address the problem, we integrate fog computing and Software Defined Network (SDN) to the current architecture. Fog computing pushes the computation and storage resources to the network edge, which can efficiently reduce the latency and enable mobility support. While SDN offers flexible centralized control and global knowledge to the network. For applying the software defined cloud-fog network (SDC-FN) architecture in the real-time mobile face recognition scenario effectively, we propose leveraging the SDN centralized control and fireworks algorithm (FWA) to solve the load balancing problem in the SDC-FN. The simulation results demonstrate that the SDN-based FWA could decrease the latency remarkably and improve the QoS in the SDC-FN architecture.

Keywords: Mobile face recognition · Cloud computing · Fog computing · Cloud-fog network · Software Defined Network · Load balancing

1 Introduction

With the rapid popularization of mobile terminals, it is useful and convenient to detect and recognize face on smart phones, tablets or laptops, which causes numerous novel applications based on face recognition on mobile devices, such as pay-with-your-face, photo tagging, face login and etc.

The face recognition applications on mobile devices require real-time response time and mobility support. However, lots of face information needs to be processed during the course of recognition. Thus, it is difficult for the resource constrained mobile devices to process computationally intensive real-time recognition tasks. Offloading the real-time face recognition tasks to the cloud computing platform is naturally regarded as a competitive method to tackle such limitation.

In the cloud-based network architecture, cloud servers provide powerful computation and storage capacity for the face recognition applications. But there still remains several challenges. It takes a relatively long time for users to send images to the cloud since the cloud is far from end users. Furthermore, as more and more intelligent

© ICST Institute for Computer Sciences, Social Informatics and Telecommunications Engineering 2018
Q. Chen et al. (Eds.): ChinaCom 2016, Part II, LNICST 210, pp. 121–131, 2018.
DOI: 10.1007/978-3-319-66628-0_12

services are supported by cloud computing, the load of the cloud is heavier, which leads to a poor robustness. Therefore, the cloud-based network architecture would not satisfy the latency requirement of real-time face recognition well.

To overcome the above problem, in this paper we propose a novel software defined cloud-fog network architecture which integrates fog computing and Software Defined Network (SDN) to the cloud-based architecture. The employment of SDN can ease the control of the network, increase network scalability and provide global knowledge to the network [1]. To support the real-time mobile face recognition service, we introduce fog computing. Fog is considered as a cloud close to the end users, which offers computation and data resources at the network edge, and thus enables a new breed of services that require low latency, mobility support and geo-distribution [2]. However, the fog network usually consists of a large number of distributed resource-poor devices, and a single fog device can't efficiently process numerous tasks. Therefore, it's necessary to execute distributed computing in fog network.

Load balancing is one of the key technologies of the distributed computing. Balancing the load according to an effective load balancing strategy can reduce the response time remarkably. As the load on the cloud increases tremendously, lots of works have been researched to balance the load of cloud computing [3, 4]. Although fog is usually considered as a local cloud, the load balancing strategies of the cloud computing can't be applied to the fog network directly since the fog network is heterogeneous and dynamic. Moreover, very few literatures concern about the load balancing of task processing in the fog network. Most existing researches mainly focus on the applications, resource allocation and energy management [5–7]. Therefore, we investigate the efficient load balancing policy in the software defined cloud-fog network (SDC-FN) to decrease the latency.

The main contributions of this paper are summarized as follows:

(1) We integrate fog computing and SDN to the cloud-based mobile face recognition architecture to solve the latency problem.
(2) We formulate the load balancing in SDC-FN as an optimization problem.
(3) We propose applying fireworks algorithm (FWA) based on SDN centralized control to solve the load balancing problem.

The rest of the paper is structured as follows. In Sect. 2, we introduce the SDC-FN architecture; In Sect. 3, we formulate a theoretical model of the load balancing problem in the SDC-FN and propose applying fireworks algorithm (FWA) based on SDN centralized control to solve the load balancing problem; Our simulation results are described in Sect. 4. Finally, we conclude our work in Sect. 5.

2   SDC-FN Architecture

When users use the face recognition applications, they take face photos with mobile terminals, and then the applications send the photo information to the processing center to perform the following steps: face detection, projection and a database search for getting the recognition results. In SDC-FN, in order to decrease the response time, we introduce fog network to perform the preprocess operations including face

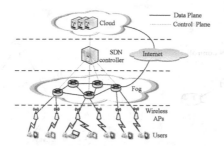

Fig. 1. SDC-FN architecture

detection and projection. Meanwhile, SDN is necessary for its centralized control. The overall architecture is shown in Fig. 1.

The architecture comprises of infrastructure layer, fog computing layer, control layer, and cloud computing layer.

The infrastructure layer consists of mobile terminals and wireless Access Points (Aps). Mobile terminals connect to the APs through one hop wireless link. APs are located on the network edge, which can be deployed in high density. Meanwhile, APs run the OpenFlow protocol, which are responsible for forwarding the received data. And the forwarding rules are formulated by SDN controller.

The fog computing layer is composed of edge network devices (e.g., routers, switches) whose computing and storage capability are limited. Fog devices are OpenFlow-enabled, which not only interact with SDN controller, but also collaborate with APs to forward data rapidly. Moreover, the face recognition task can be pre-processed by fog devices, such as face detection and projection, thereby decrease the communication latency and alleviate the burden on the cloud. Since the preprocessing operations are computationally-intensive operations, it will lead to long latency that numerous preprocessing tasks are handled by a single fog device. Therefore, it is essential to execute distributed computing to balance the load.

The control layer includes SDN controller. OpenFlow-enabled SDN controller controls the SDC-FN in a centralized way and it can collect the global knowledge of the topology by interacting with fog devices and APs. Moreover, we run the load balancing algorithm on the controller to develop an optimal load balancing strategy.

The cloud computing layer consists of cloud servers. Cloud servers utilize their huge storage capacity to store a large quantity of facial information and set up a face database. The facial feature information extracted by fog devices is delivered to the cloud to match with the known faces in the database.

3 FWA-Based Load Balancing Algorithm in SDC-FN

3.1 Theoretical Model

We consider the fog network with k fog devices. The network topology is illustrated in Fig. 2.

We can abstract the above topology as a weighted undirected graph $G = (V, E)$ with vertex set V and edge set E, as shown in Fig. 3.

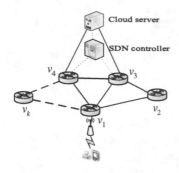

Fig. 2. SDC-FN topology

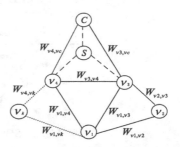

Fig. 3. The weighted undirected graph

In Fig. 3, $V = \{v_1, v_2, \cdots, v_k, S, C\}$, where vertex v_i denotes the fog device, S and C represent the SDN controller and the cloud respectively. We denote the computing capacity of fog device v_i as c_{vi}, and the computing capacity of the cloud sever is c_c. In edge set $E = \{e_{v_1 v_2}, \cdots, e_{v_i v_j}, \cdots, e_{v_{k-1} v_k}, e_{v_3 v_c}, e_{v_4 v_c}\}$, each edge represents a communication links between nodes, and the weight of each edge $e_{vi,vj}$, i.e., $w_{vi vj}$ represents the communication latency between nodes v_i and v_j. During the course of face recognition, the recognition tasks, i.e., $Task$ received by fog device v_i can be divided into many small subtasks $Task_i$ firstly, which satisfies the condition $Task_i = \delta_i Task$, where δ_i is the portion of the subtask in the total task. Secondly, the subtasks are allocated to appropriate fog devices to perform preprocessing operations. Finally, the results of preprocessing $Task_{pre}$ will be transmitted to the cloud for the final recognition results and the results will be sent back to end users. Therefore, the total processing time t of the task in SDC-FN can be expressed as:

$$t = \max\left\{\frac{\delta_i Task}{c_{v_i}} + w_{v_i,v_j}\, m_{v_i,v_j}\right\} + \frac{Task_{pre}}{c_c} + w_{v_i,c} \qquad (1)$$

where $\delta_i Task / c_{vi}$ denotes the computation time of the subtask $Task_i$ on fog device v_i, $w_{vi,vj}$ is the communication latency between fog devices v_i and v_j, $m_{vi,vj}$ denotes whether there is a subtask allocation relationship between fog devices v_i and v_j. When $m_{vi,vj} = 1$, there exists the relationship; when $m_{vi,vj} = 0$, the relationship doesn't exist. The $Task_{pre}/c_c$ part is the computation time of the task $Task_{pre}$ on the cloud, and $w_{vi,c}$ represents the communication latency between fog device v_i and cloud.

For achieving the minimum task processing latency t, we must find a group of optimal δ_i. In summary, the problem can be formulated as:

$$\min\left\{\max\left[\frac{\delta_i Task}{c_{v_i}} + w_{v_i,v_j} m_{v_i,v_j}\right] + \frac{Task_{pre}}{c_c} + w_{v_i,c}\right\} \quad i,j = 1, 2, \cdots, k. \qquad (2)$$

$$s.t. \, m_{v_i,v_j} = \begin{cases} 1, & \delta_i \neq 0 \\ 0, & \delta_i = 0 \end{cases}. \tag{3}$$

$$\sum_{i=1}^{k} \delta_i = 1$$

3.2 SDN-Based FWA Algorithm

In the model of the load balancing problem in Sect. 3.1, it is necessary to find a set of optimal load distribution coefficients δi to obtain the minimum latency. In SDC-FN, the subtask processed on each fog device is $Task_i = \delta_i Task$. Accordingly, the subtasks on k fog devices form a k dimension vector $TA = (Task_1, Task_2, \ldots, Task_k)^T$. Assuming the tasks are received by fog device v_I, from Eq. (1), the total latency t can be expressed as:

$$t(TA) = \max \left\{ \frac{Task_1}{c_{v_1}} + w_{v_1,v_1} m_{v_1,v_1}, \cdots, \frac{Task_k}{c_{v_k}} + w_{v_1,v_k} m_{v_1,v_k} \right\} + \frac{Task_{pre}}{c_c} + w_{v_1,v_c} m_{v_1,v_c}. \tag{4}$$

The resolution of δ_i can be converted into the resolution of vector TA, which could be formulated as the following optimization problem:

$$\min\{t(TA)\}, TA \in I. \tag{5}$$

$$s.t. \, TA(i) \geq 0$$
$$\sum_{i=1}^{k} TA(i) = Task. \tag{6}$$

And the solution space I is:

$$I = \prod_{i=1}^{k} [Task_{i\,\min}, Task_{i\,\max}] = \prod_{i=1}^{k} [0, Task]. \tag{7}$$

In this paper, we introduce fireworks algorithm (FWA) to solve the load balancing problem, namely the above optimization problem. FWA is one of the latest swarm intelligence optimization problem proposed by Tan and Zhu [8]. Although there has been few works about the FWA's implementation, the results show that it has exhibited promising performance in dealing with various optimization problems [9, 10].

The steps of leveraging FWA to resolve the load balancing problem, i.e., Eq. (5), are shown as follows:

(1) The fireworks $\{TA_i\}_{i=1}^{N}$ should be randomly initialized in the solution space, where N denotes the number of fireworks. The position of each firework is $TA_i = (Task_1(i), Task_2(i), \cdots, Task_k(i))^T$.

(2) Computing the fitness value of each firework according to the optimization objective function $t(TA)$. The explosion amplitude A_l and the number S_i of explosion sparks for each fireworks TA_i can be defined as: [8]

$$A_i = A \times \frac{t(TA_i) - t_{\min} + \varepsilon}{\sum_{i=1}^{N} (t(TA_i) - t_{\min}) + \varepsilon} . \tag{8}$$

$$S_i = M \times \frac{t_{\max} - t(TA_i) + \varepsilon}{\sum_{i=1}^{N} (t_{\max} - t(TA_i)) + \varepsilon} . \tag{9}$$

where A and M are two constants for controlling the maximum value of the explosion amplitude and the number of explosion sparks, $t_{max} = max(t(TA_i))$ and $t_{min} = min((t(TA_i))$ ($i = 1,2,...,N$) represent the maximum and minimum fitness value in the current fireworks population respectively, and ε is the machine epsilon to avoid zero-division-error. In order to avoid the overwhelming effects of the better fireworks, it's necessary to limit the number of sparks S_i: [8]

$$\hat{S}_1 = \begin{cases} round(a * M), S_i < aM \\ round(b * M), S_i > bM, a < b < 1 \\ round(S_i), \text{otherwise} \end{cases} \tag{10}$$

where a, b are two constants.

(3) Generating explosion sparks according to the calculated number of the sparks S_i and the explosion amplitude A_i. When an explosion occurs, there exists a random offset value in $[-A_i, A_i]$, which is added to z dimensions randomly chosen from TA_i. The chosen z dimensions are calculated as: [8]

$$z = round(d \times U(0, 1)) \tag{11}$$

where d represents the dimension of TA_i, $U(0,1)$ is a random number uniformly distributed between 0 and 1. Each dimension $k \in \{1,2...,z\}$ of the generated explosion sparks $T\hat{A}_i$ can be expressed as: [8]

$$T\hat{A}_{ik} = TA_{ik} + A_i \times U(-1, 1) \tag{12}$$

where $U(-1,1)$ is a random number uniformly distributed between -1 and 1
If $T\hat{A}_i$ is out of the bound of the solution space on the dimension k, it will be mapped to a new location according to the equal: [8]

$$T\hat{A}_{ik} = TA_{LB,k} + |T\hat{A}_i| \% (TA_{UB,k} - TA_{LB,k}) \tag{13}$$

where $TA_{UB,k}$ and $TA_{LB,k}$ denote the upper and lower boundary of the solution space on the dimension k, respectively.

(4) Generating Gaussian mutation sparks to maintain the diversity of sparks. FWA randomly selects Mg fireworks in the fireworks population and chooses z dimensions randomly according to Eq. (11) in each firework of these Mg fireworks to perform Gaussian mutation. (Mg is a constant to control the number of Gaussian sparks). Each dimension $k \in \{1,2...,z\}$ of the generated Gaussian sparks $T\hat{A}_i$ can be calculated as: [8]

$$T\hat{A}_{ik} = TA_{ik} \times N(1,1). \tag{14}$$

where $N(1,1)$ represents the Gauss distribution with mean 1, variance 1. Similarly, if $T\hat{A}_i$ is out of the bound of the solution space on the dimension k, it will be mapped to a new location according to Eq. (13).

5) Selecting N individuals as a new fireworks population from the current generation of fireworks, explosion sparks and Gaussian sparks to enter into the next generation. The individual with minimum fitness value is deterministically transmitted to the next generation. In order to maintain the diversity, the remaining $N-1$ individuals are selected based on Roulette Wheel Selection. For individual TA_i, the selection probability $P(TA_i)$ is calculated as: [8]

$$P(TA_i) = \frac{R(TA_i)}{\sum\limits_{TA_j \in K} TA_j} \tag{15}$$

$$R(TA_i) = \sum\limits_{TA_j \in K} d(TA_i - TA_j) = \sum\limits_{TA_j \in K} \|TA_i - TA_j\| \tag{16}$$

where K is the set of all current individuals including both fireworks and sparks, $R(TA_i)$ is the distance between individual TA_i and other individuals.

(6) Repeating step 2–5 until the end termination condition is reached.

In the above analysis of the FWA-based load balancing strategy, SDN controller collects the information of all nodes, formulates an optimal load balancing strategy by running the FWA and sends flow tables including the strategy to fog devices.

4 Simulation Results

We consider the scenario with 10 fog devices. In the real network circumstance, the communication latency $w_{vi,vj}$ between the nodes mainly includes uplink transmission latency, downlink transmission latency and other latency. Other latency includes propagation latency and queuing latency. Some important parameters of SDC-FN and FWA in the simulation are summarized in Tables 1 and 2 respectively, referring to [9, 11]. The task loads in the experiment are simulation setting. All the simulating results are obtained by MATLAB and they are the means of many repeated experiments.

Table 1. The related parameters of SDC-FN

Parameter	SDC-FN devices										
Type	C	v_1	v_2	v_3	v_4	v_5	v_6	v_7	v_8	v_9	v_{10}
c_c/c_{vi} (Gbps)	10	1	2	3	0.4	0.5	0.6	0.6	0.7	0.5	1
Uplink bandwith (Mbps)	2	84	86	71	80	83	90	86	89	87	79
Downlink bandwidth (Mbps)	1.8	99	100	98	101	96	104	99	105	102	97
Other latency (ms)	10	1	1	1.2	1.1	1.2	1	1.3	1	1.3	1

Table 2. The related parameters of FWA algorithm

Parameters	Values
Number of fireworks N	20
Maximum value of the explosion amplitude A	30
Number of sparks M	64
Constant parameter a	0.04
Constant parameter b	0.8
Number of Gaussian sparks Mg	20

4.1 Latency Performance Comparison Between the Cloud-Based Architecture and SDC-FN

In the simulation, we compare the SDC-FN based on FWA load balancing algorithm with the cloud-based architecture to evaluate the latency performance of the SDC-FN.

The comparison result is shown in Fig. 4. When the workload is lower than 1 Gb, the recognition task processing latency in SDC-FN is lower than in the cloud-based architecture, but their latency values have little difference. This is because in the cloud-based architecture, the computing capacity of the cloud severs is more powerful, and transmitting a small amount of tasks to the cloud will not generate high communication latency. However, with the increase of task, the latency

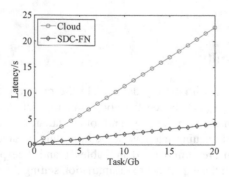

Fig. 4. Latency performance comparison between the cloud-based architecture and SDC-FN

in the cloud-based architecture is dramatically higher than that in SDC-FN because of the increasing transmission latency. Compared with the cloud-based architecture, the reason why SDC-FN shows good latency performance is that the cloud is far from the users and there is limited bandwidth while the fog is proximity to end users and the communication bandwidth is higher. Therefore, the SDC-FN architecture can efficiently reduce the latency to improve the QoS.

4.2   Latency Performance Comparison of Multiple Load Balancing Algorithms

To validate the high efficiency of the FWA-based load balancing algorithm in reducing latency in SDC-FN, we compare it with the PSO-CO [12], Weighted Round Robin (WRR) [13] and Pick-KX load balancing algorithm [14].

Figure 5 shows the simulation results of four load balancing algorithms in SDC-FN. With the increase of the task quantity, the FWA-based algorithm obtained lower latency than other three algorithms. On one hand, in FWA, the fireworks with low fitness generate more sparks in a small range, which has a strong local search capability for the location of the fireworks. Conversely, the high fitness fireworks create less sparks in a large scale, which has a certain global search capability. Thus, the FWA based algorithm can achieve a better global load balancing strategy. On the other hand, the WRR and Pick-KX algorithm don't consider the communication latency when balancing the load, and the PSO-CO may fall into the local optimum, thereby they can't formulate a good load balancing strategy to reduce latency. When the task quantity is 20 Gb, the delay performance of FWA-based algorithm improved by 66.7%, 58.3%, 13.1% compared with WRR, Pick-KX and PSO-CO, respectively. Accordingly, applying the FWA-based load balancing algorithm in SDC-FN can reduce the task processing latency efficiently of the real-time mobile face recognition.

4.3   Influence of the Uplink Bandwidth for the Latency of SDC-FN

Since the bandwidth has a great impact on the transmission latency and can affect the total task processing time, we are motivated to investigate the influence of the band-width on the latency performance in SDC-FN in this section. We vary the uplink bandwidth of the cloud from 2 to 30 Mbps to evaluate how it affects the latency in SDC-FN by comparing it with the cloud-based architecture, and the task quantity is fixed to 20 Gb.The result is shown in Fig. 6. The figure illustrates that, the latency of cloud-based architecture decreases dramatically with the increase of the up-link bandwidth, but it stays steady when the up-link bandwidth is higher than 10 Mbps. While there are relatively little latency reduction in SDC-FN. Since in SDC-FN, a small amount of facial feature information after preprocessing is transmitted to the cloud, thus, the transmission latency would not decrease significantly when the uplink bandwidth of the cloud increases. And the latency in SDC-FN always keeps a low level, which indicates SDC-FN is more appropriate for real-time face recognition.

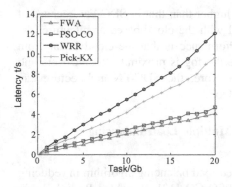 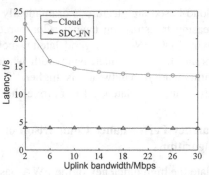

Fig. 5. Latency performance comparison among multiple load balancing algorithms in SDC-FN

Fig. 6. Influence of the up-link bandwidth for the latency of SDC-FN

5 Conclusions

In this paper, we have introduced a novel network architecture which integrates fog computing and SDN to the cloud-based architecture in the real-time mobile face recognition to decrease the latency of the recognition service. Then, we set up a theoretical model of the load balancing problem in the software defined cloud-fog network (SDC-FN). On this basis, we proposed a SDN-based FWA centralized load balancing algorithm to balance the load for reducing latency efficiently. Simulation results reveal that: (1) The algorithm has good performance in reducing latency. (2) Applying the SDC-FN architecture in the real-time mobile face recognition scenario can meet the users' requirement of fast response time and improve the QoS. Our focus of the next step is to improve the performance of the FWA-based load balancing algorithm in the SDC-FN and implement the algorithm in the real SDC-FN platform.

Acknowledgments. This work was supported in part by National Natural Science Foundation of China (No. 61401331, No. 61401328), 111 Project in Xidian University of China (B08038), Hong Kong, Macao and Taiwan Science and Technology Cooperation Special Project (2014DFT10320, 2015DFT10160), The National Science and Technology Major Project of the Ministry of Science and Technology of China (2015zx03002006-003) and Fundamental Research Funds for the Central Universities (20101155739).

References

1. Truong, N.B., Lee, G.M., Ghamri-Doudane, Y.: Software defined networking-based vehicular adhoc network with fog computing. In: IEEE International Symposium on Integrated Network Management, Ottawa, pp. 1202–1207. IEEE Press (2015)
2. Bonomi, F., Milito, R., Zhu, J., Addepalli, S.: Fog computing and its role in the internet of things. In: Proceedings of the First Edition of the MCC Workshop on Mobile Cloud Computing, MCC 2012, New York, pp. 13–16 (2012)

3. Aslam, S., Shah, M.A.: Load balancing algorithms in cloud computing: a survey of modern techniques. In: National Software Engineering Conference, pp. 30–35 (2015)
4. Panwar, R., Mallick, B.: Load balancing in cloud computing using dynamic load management algorithm. In: 2015 International Conference on Green Computing and Internet of Things (ICGCIoT), pp. 773–778. IEEE Computer Society (2015)
5. Yi, S., Hao, Z., Qin, Z., Li, Q.: Fog computing: platform and applications. In: Third IEEE Workshop on Hot Topics in Web Systems and Technologies, pp. 73–78. IEEE Computer Society (2015)
6. Aazam, M., St-Hilaire, M., Lung, C.H., Lambadaris, I.: PRE-fog: IoT trace based probabilistic resource estimation at fog. In: 2016 13th IEEE Annual Consumer Communications & Networking Conference (CCNC), pp. 12–17 (2016)
7. Al Faruque, M., Vatanparvar, K.: Energy management-as-a-service over fog computing platform. IEEE Internet Things J. **3**, 161–169 (2016)
8. Tan, Y., Zhu, Y.: Fireworks algorithm for optimization. In: Tan, Y., Shi, Y., Tan, K.C. (eds.) ICSI 2010. LNCS, vol. 6145, pp. 355–364. Springer, Heidelberg (2010). doi:10.1007/978-3-642-13495-1_44
9. Bacanin, N., Tuba, M.: Fireworks algorithm applied to constrained portfolio optimization problem. In: 2015 IEEE Congress on Evolutionary Computation (CEC), pp. 1242–1249 (2015)
10. Imran, A.M., Kowsalya, M.: A new power system reconfiguration scheme for power loss minimization and voltage profile enhancement using fireworks algorithm. Int. J. Electr. Power Energy Syst. **62**, 312–322 (2014)
11. Hassan, M.A., Xiao, M., Wei, Q., Chen, S.: Help your mobile applications with fog computing. In: 2015 12th Annual IEEE International Conference on Sensing, Communication, and Networking-Workshops (SECON Workshops), pp. 1–6 (2015)
12. Li, X.Y., Tian, P., Kong, M.: A new particle swarm optimization for solving constrained optimization problems (in Chinese). J. Syst. Manag. **16**, 120–129 (2007)
13. Radojevi, B., Žagar, M.: Analysis of issues with load balancing algorithms in hosted (cloud) environments. In: 2011 Proceedings of the 34th International Convention, pp. 416–420 (2011)
14. Zhang, H., Liao, J.X., Zhu, X.M.: Advanced dynamic feedback and random dispatch load-balance algorithm (in Chinese). Comput. Eng. **33**, 97–99 (2007)

Applying TOPSIS Method for Software Defined Networking (SDN) Controllers Comparison and Selection

Firas Fawzy Zobary[1,2](✉)

[1] Research Center of Network and Computing,
Chongqing University of Posts and Telecommunications,
Chongqing, People's Republic of China
firas_zobary@hotmail.com
[2] Faculty of Information Engineering, Damascus University,
Damascus, Syrian Arab Republic

Abstract. Current traditional IP networks start to be complex as the demands of the users is ever-growing. Software Defined Network (SDN) is a new paradigm to ease the management of the network and make the network programmable by decoupling the control plane and forwarding plane (such as switch and router). A centralized controller is used to manage the control plane, and it interacts with forwarding plane using a standardized OpenFlow protocol. However, many controllers are used recently such as POX, Ryu, ONOS, and OpenDaylight. The important question is which is the best controller to use in our network and fits our network's goals? To answer this question, a decision making method is proposed in this paper. First, four SDN controllers are selected, and five criteria are analyzed to collect these controllers' properties. Then a Multi-Criteria Decision Making method named TOPSIS is used to rank the controllers and choose the best one. By applying this method, a comparative study is done to evaluate the four controllers in an environment of LAN topology, and "Ryu" controller is selected as the best one based on our criteria.

Keywords: Software defined networking · POX · Ryu · ODL · ONOS · MCDM

1 Introduction

Try to imagine the Internet as an old man who was living in the 50 s and moved to our life as it is now. That man will be shocked to find a lot of strange things like airplanes, mobile phones, and everything looks unfamiliar and very complex for his understanding. He will not be able to survive in our lifetime unless he starts to learn about these new things and adapt himself to use it. That's exactly how the internet is working now since its origin. When the internet was created it was very simple, not architected to use mobile or high-speed data transferring, and not secured well. It was designed for only exchanging information between end-nodes.

© ICST Institute for Computer Sciences, Social Informatics and Telecommunications Engineering 2018
Q. Chen et al. (Eds.): ChinaCom 2016, Part II, LNICST 210, pp. 132–141, 2018.
DOI: 10.1007/978-3-319-66628-0_13

Networks now are becoming a critical component of all the fields, and the goal now is to interconnect everything, through cloud computing, mobility or new concepts, like the internet of things.

However, in spite of its common adoption, traditional IP networking is still complex, very hard to manage. The switches, routers, and other devices implement a huge number of standardized protocols and proprietary interfaces that are still keep increasing.

Software Defined Network (SDN) is a new paradigm in which the network control is decoupled from the forwarding functions and both are communicating using a standardized OpenFlow protocol which enables the control plan to become directly programmable and the underlying infrastructure to be totally abstracted, so that makes this architecture ideal for today's applications which have a dynamic nature and demand high bandwidth.

The network will be programmable through software applications that run on the network operating system and interact with the devices from the data plane that becomes simple forwarding elements [1]. The architecture of SDN consists of two main planes, control plane and forward plane. The control plane is handled separately inside a controller which is one of the most important pieces of this technology's architecture. However, when we want to design our network using the concept of SDN, we must choose a suitable controller for our requirements. This decision problem is troublesome for many designers as it is difficult to define the right metrics, and the number of controllers keeps increasing. To solve this problem, we searched about the existing SDN controllers that are being used nowadays. We used websites, surveys, literature and any available resource providing this information. In the end, four controllers have been selected for our comparison to select the best one depending on properties we have already chosen. These controllers are: POX [2], Ryu [3], OpenDaylight [4], and ONOS [5].

As SDN controllers have different properties means that selecting a controller is a Multi-Criteria Decision Making (MCDM) problem [6]. Many MCDM methods are used for solving this kind of problems like Multiple Attribute Utility (MAUT), the Technique for Order of Preference by Similarity to Ideal Solution (TOPSIS), ELEC-TRE, AHP, etc. Recently researchers focus on AHP/ANP [13] based methods. Although these methods use experts' judgments and pairwise comparisons, but experts' intuitions and opinions conflict in uncertainty, and pairwise comparisons might be inconsistent with each other. SDN controllers comparison using AHP is tedious and time consuming. We used TOPSIS to select the best controller as it's more effective and quick for comparing and selecting the best alternative. In this paper, we proposed TOPSIS method to be combined with entropy to identify the criteria importance for SDN controller selection. Entropy is employed to get the weights of the criteria, and then TOPSIS method is used to rank the controllers and select the best controller that adjusts the decision maker's needs.

The outline of the paper is as follows: in Subsect. 2.1, we describe how the investigation about the controllers is done and which controllers' properties we'll focus on during the comparison. Subsect. 2.2 analyzes the candidate controllers based on these properties. In Sect. 3 we describe the comparison method that have been chosen and its steps. Section 4 describes the experimental work and the results of the method. Finally, a conclusion and future work is described in Sect. 5.

2 SDN Controllers Investigation

2.1 Methodology for the Investigation

To collect the properties of our selected SDN controllers, we have searched the white papers, surveys, and conferences that have described those controllers. Then we tried to search the official websites of each controller and other websites talking about them. We choose the following properties to use during the comparison between controllers.

- **Interfaces**: the controlling applications interact with the controller using northbound (NB) API and the controllers interact with the data plane using southbound (SB) API as shown in Fig. 1. NB uses many kinds of technologies such as REST [7]. SB APIs are divided into two categories: management and control. The management technologies are like OpenvSwitch Database Management Protocol (OVSDB) [8] and Simple Network Management Protocol (SNMP) [9]. The most famous SB control protocol is OpenFlow [10]. In forwarding plane, both physical and virtual switches can be used.

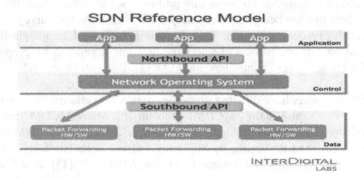

Fig. 1. SDN architecture

- The available documentation of each controller.
- **The OpenFlow version** that each controller uses. OpenFlow was developed during last years from version 1.0, and now we are in version 1.5, but still not all controllers support the same versions.
- **Programming language** by which each controller is used to develop applications. When we want to write our SDN application, we should use the programming language which is supported by the controller we choose for our network. In this paper, the priority for a programming language is its simplicity and how it's easy to learn when we want to develop our applications. Thus, we considered that the simpler programming language, the better the controller is.

- **Performance**: a comparison between controllers by their RTT delays time in switching mode was made. To do that, a tree topology was created using *mininet* tool [11]. Also, 16 hosts were created. Then ten ICMP packets were generated between the hosts 1&16, and the average RTT was calculated. These results were monitored during simple L2 learning switch phase where the controller links the source MAC address with the switch port from which the packet arrived and updates the flow table inside the switch by adding an entry to be used for forwarding any future packets holding that MAC address as a destination. The topology is illustrated in Fig. 2.

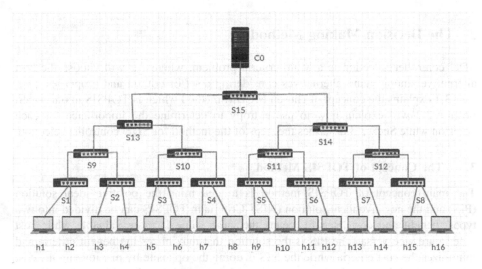

Fig. 2. SDN topology

2.2 SDN Controllers Overview

Four SDN controllers have been analyzed here: POX, Ryu, OpenDayLight, and ONOS.

A Python-based SDN controller, POX is a networking software platform. "POX is NOX's younger siblings" [2]. This controller is intended for faster development and is used to explore network virtualization, controller design, programming models, and to prototype new network applications. POX supports OpenFlow v1.0 as a southbound interface.

Ryu (the Japanese word for "flow") is a component-based SDN framework written in Python. It provides software components with well-defined API that make it easy for developers to create new network management and control applications. Ryu supports OpenFlow 1.0 to 1.4 and OVSDB as a southbound interface, and REST as a northbound interface.

OpenDaylight (ODL) is a modular Open SDN platform for networks of any size and scale. It's an open source controller, written in Java, and provides production-level performance and support. The goal of OpenDaylight project is to create robust code that covers most of the major components of the SDN architecture. The main drawback is the complexity and the fact that it takes time for learning to develop applications. It supports OpenFlow versions 1.0 & 1.3, and OVSDB in the southbound interface, and REST and OSGI as a northbound interface.

Another SDN controller is Open Network Operating System (ONOS). It is a software defined networking (SDN) OS for service providers that have scalability, high availability, and abstractions to make it easy to create apps and services. It's written in Java. Thus, it requires more time to learn, unlike POX or Ryu that were written in Python. ONOS supports OpenFlow version 1.0 and 1.3 and NetConf as a southbound interface.

3   The Decision Making Method

SDN controller selection is a Multi-criteria problem, where we will choose the best alternative among many alternatives considering a set of criteria and properties. Section 3.1 explains the concept of chosen MCDM method which is TOPSIS in our paper. Section 3.2 will explain how to use entropy to determine the importance for each criterion while Sect. 3.3 describes the steps of the method for SDN controller selection.

3.1   The Concept of TOPSIS Method

The main concept of TOPSIS method is to determine the positive ideal solution (PIS) and the negative ideal solution (NIS). Criteria in TOPSIS can be divided into two types: benefit and cost. Benefit means the large value is more valuable while cost criteria are vice versa. The PIS is the solution that maximizes the benefit criteria and minimizes the cost criteria while the NIS is doing the opposite by maximizing the cost criteria and minimizing the benefit criteria. After determining the PIS and the NIS, the technique will be to choose the alternative that has the shortest distance to the PIS and the farthest distance to the NIS. In general, any MCDM problem should have m alternatives and n criteria. The problem can be expressed in nxm matrix as follows:z

$$
\begin{array}{c}
\quad C_1, \quad C_2, \quad \cdots \quad C_n \\
D = \begin{array}{c} A_1 \\ A_2 \\ \vdots \\ A_m \end{array}
\begin{bmatrix}
x_{11} & x_{12} & \cdots & x_{1n} \\
x_{21} & x_{22} & \cdots & x_{2n} \\
\cdots & \cdots & \ddots & \cdots \\
x_{m1} & x_{m2} & \vdots & x_{mn}
\end{bmatrix}
\end{array}
$$

$$
W = (w_1, w_w, \cdots, w_n)
$$

where $A_1, A_2, \ldots, A_m$ are alternatives, $C_1, C_2, \ldots, C_n$ are the criteria that we use, x_{ij} is the performance of alternative A_i under criterion C_j and w_j is the weight of criterion C_j, where $\sum_{j=1}^{n} w_j = 1$.

To perform the comparison across the criteria, matrix D should be transformed into dimensionless units by using the following equation:

$$P_{ij} = \frac{x_{ij}}{\sum_{i=1}^{m} x_{ij}}, j \in [1 \ldots n] \tag{1}$$

3.2 Determination of Criteria Weights

When we want to compare SDN controllers and select the best one to use in our network, we'll face a problem that each criterion has a different importance. So it's necessary to determine the importance for each criterion which it's called "criterion's weight." There are many techniques to do that such as eigenvector method, entropy method, etc. Here, we will use entropy method to determine the weights for criteria.

In information theory, the entropy by Shannon [12] can be used to determine the disorder degree of the system is. Entropy weights method is based on the amount of information to determine the index's weight. Entropy value e_j can be calculated as:

$$e_j = \frac{- \sum_{i=1}^{m} P_{ij} ln(P_{ij})}{ln(m)}, i \in [1..m], j \in [1 \ldots n] \tag{2}$$

Each criterion has different information, and the degree of that variation is calculated as:

$$d_j = 1 - e_j, j \in [1 \ldots n] \tag{3}$$

Now we can calculate the weight for each criterion as:

$$w_j = \frac{d_j}{\sum_{j=1}^{n} d_j}, j \in [1 \ldots n] \tag{4}$$

3.3 Selecting the Best Alternative

To do that we should first determine the PIS and the NIS. We labeled them as (A^+) and (A^-), respectively as:

$$A^+ = \left(P_1^+, P_2^+, \cdots, P_m^+\right) \tag{5}$$

$$A^- = \left(P_1^-, P_2^-, \cdots, P_m^-\right) \tag{6}$$

where:

$$P_j^+ = \left\{maxP_{ij}, j \in J^+; minP_{ij}, j \in J^-\right\} \tag{7}$$

$$P_j^- = \left\{minP_{ij}, j \in J^+; maxP_{ij}, j \in J^-\right\} \tag{8}$$

As J^+ and J^- are the sets of benefit and cost criteria respectively. Next step is to calculate the distance between each alternative and the PIS (A^+) and NIS (A^-) as follows:

$$d_i^+ = \sqrt{\sum_{j=1}^n w_j(P_j^+ - P_{ij})^2} \tag{9}$$

$$d_i^- = \sqrt{\sum_{j=1}^n w_j(P_j^- - P_{ij})^2} \tag{10}$$

The last step is to calculate the relative degree of closeness of each alternative to the ideal solution. The relative degree of closeness for each alternative is defined as

$$\mu_i = \frac{d_i^-}{d_i^+ + d_i^-}, i \in [1, m] \tag{11}$$

The evaluation object is ranked according to the value of the relative degree of closeness. The best alternative is the one who has the highest μ.

4   The Best SDN Controller Selection (Experimental Results)

In this section, we'll apply previous MCDM method (TOPSIS) to select the best SDN controller among four controllers we choose for our comparison. Those controllers are: POX, Ryu, ODL, and ONOS, and the criteria for evaluating the alternatives are described as follows:

- Interfaces the controller uses to interact with applications and data plane (C1).
- Documentation for each controller (C2).
- OpenFlow version supported by a controller (C3).
- The programming language used by developers to develop applications (C4).
- Performance as the average RTT delays time for ICMP packets in milliseconds (C5).

The last criterion was studied in [14]. From the investigation that was done in Sect. 2.2, the results about each controller can be summarized in Table 1 shown below:

Table 1. Controllers' properties comparison

	Interfaces	Documentation	OpenFlow Version	Programming language	Average RTT (ms)
POX	OVSDB + OF	Poor	1.0	Python	20.76
Ryu	OVSDB + REST + OF	Medium	1.0 to 1.4	Python	11.86
ODL	REST + OSGI + OF + OVSDB	Good	1.3	Java	21.71
ONOS	REST + OSGI + OF + Netconf	Medium	1.0 & 1.3	Java	22.65

It's clear that the first four criteria are benefits as the higher value means the better controller, whereas the fifth one is cost criterion as the higher value of delay means the less performance from the controller.

The goal now is to convert the information in Table 1 into quantitative items that can be processed mathematically. To do that a range scale $[1 \rightarrow 4]$ will be used to refer to each qualitative item in the first four criteria, whereas the last criterion is already quantitative as we used the average RTT delay in milliseconds. We'll take into consideration that the high value in the scale $[1 \rightarrow 4]$ refers to a better performance according to what we have read in the available resources and what is the reputation about each candidate controller. After that, we'll have the decision matrix in Table 2.

Table 2. Decision matrix

	C_1	C_2	C_3	C_4	C_5
POX	1	1	1	3	20.76
RYU	2	2	4	3	11.86
ODL	3	3	1	4	21.71
ONOS	3	2	2	4	22.65

In Table 3. The normalized dimensionless matrix, PIS (A^+), NIS (A^-), entropy and the weights are shown. The last step is shown in Table 4, where we calculated the distances d_i^+ and d_i^-, then the relative degree of closeness μ_i. Based on μ_i values the alternatives are ranked and according to our method and criteria the best SDN controller is Ryu.

Table 3. Normalized matrix, entropy (e), weights (w), PIS, and NIS

	C_1	C_2	C_3	C_4	C_5
POX	0.111	0.125	0.125	0.214	0.27
RYU	0.222	0.25	0.5	0.214	0.154
ODL	0.333	0.375	0.125	0.286	0.282
ONOS	0.333	0.25	0.25	0.286	0.294
e	0.945	0.953	0.875	0.992	0.98
w	0.216	0.184	0.49	0.031	0.078
A^+	0.333	0.375	0.5	0.286	0.154
A^-	0.111	0.125	0.125	0.214	0.294

In the end, Fig. (3) shows the chart of alternatives and their distances to the PIS (d+) and NIS (d−) and the relative degree of closeness (μ).

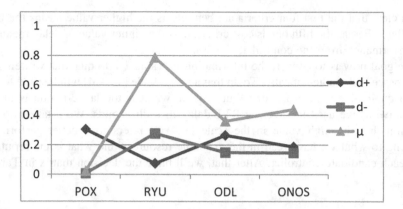

Fig. 3. Final results

Table 4. Distances and relative closeness

	d^+	d^-	μ
POX	0.304	0.007	0.023
Ryu	0.075	0.276	0.786
ODL	0.265	0.149	0.36
ONOS	0.187	0.146	0.438

5   Conclusion and Future Work

In this paper, we proposed TOPSIS method with entropy weights to compare and select the best controller among four chosen SDN controllers based on five criteria in an environment of LAN topology. The result showed that the proposed method is simple and flexible. In the end, our alternatives were ranked as Ryu, ONOS, ODL, and POX which means that Ryu controller is the best controller according to the criteria we studied as it had the shortest distance to the PIS and the farthest distance to the NIS. In the future works, more criteria can be added such as hardware system requirements of each controller. Also, a larger network scale such as datacenter with much more network devices can be added to the topology and the same comparative study would be applied to check if the results will stay the same or a different controller will be chosen, and also we can apply another MCDM methods to see if Ryu controller will stay the best alternative or using pairwise comparisons will affect the selection results.

References

1. Kreutz, D., Ramos, F.M.V., Esteves Verissimo, P., Esteve Rothenberg, C., Azodolmolky, S., Uhlig, S.: Software-defined networking: a comprehensive survey. Proc. IEEE **103**(1), 14–76 (2015)

2. About POX | NOXRepo. http://www.noxrepo.org/pox/about-pox/. Accessed 26 Apr 2016 ·
3. Ryu SDN Framework. http://osrg.github.io/ryu/. Accessed 26 Apr 2016
4. The OpenDaylight Platform | OpenDaylight. https://www.opendaylight.org/. Accessed 26 Apr 2016
5. ONOS - A new carrier-grade SDN network operating system designed for high availability, performance, scale-out. http://onosproject.org/. Accessed 26 Apr 2016
6. Ehrgott, M., Gandibleux, X.: Multiple Criteria Optimization: State of the Art Annotated Bibliographic Surveys. Kluwer Academic Publishers, Boston (2002)
7. Fielding, R.T.: Architectural styles and the design of network-based software architectures, University of California, Irvine (2000)
8. Pfaff, B., Davie, B.: The Open vSwitch Database Management Protocol (2013)
9. hjp: doc: RFC 1157: Simple Network Management Protocol (SNMP). http://www.hjp.at/doc/rfc/rfc1157.html. Accessed 26 Apr 2016
10. McKeown, N., Anderson, T., Balakrishnan, H., Parulkar, G., Peterson, L., Rexford, J., Shenker, S., Turner, J.: OpenFlow: enabling innovation in campus networks. ACM SIGCOMM Comput. Commun. Rev. 38(2), 69–74 (2008)
11. Mininet Overview - Mininet. http://mininet.org/overview/. Accessed 26 Apr 2016
12. Shannon, C.E.: A mathematical theory of communication. ACM SIGMOBILE Mob. Comput. Commun. Rev. 5(1), 3–55 (2001)
13. Wei, C.C., Chien, C.F., Wang, M.J.J.: An AHP-based approach to ERP system selection. Int. J. Prod. Econ. 96(1), 47–62 (2005)
14. Huang, J.: Combining entropy weight and TOPSIS method for information system selection. In: 2008 IEEE Conference on Cybernetics and Intelligent Systems, pp. 1281–1284. IEEE, September 2008

Robust Congestion Control in NFVs and WSDNs with Propagation Delay and External Interference

Xi Hu$^{(\boxtimes)}$ and Wei Guo

National Key Laboratory of Science and Technology on Communications,
University of Electronic Science and Technology of China, Chengdu 611731, China
huxi027@163.com, guowei@uestc.edu.cn

Abstract. In today's networks, two new concepts have emerged aiming at cost reduction and control network congestion, namely Network Functions Virtualization (NFV) and Software Defined Networking (SDN). NFV proposes to run the network functions as software instances on datacenters (DC), while SDN presents a new network architecture where the control plane is shifted to a centralized controller. Wireless Software Defined Networking (WSDN) is considered based on the wireless environments, such as propagation delay and external interference. It is critical to keep the network stable at the ideal stable state during congestion control. However, stability control is insufficient to achieve these aims in the presence of propagation delay and external interference.

In this paper, we propose robust congestion control to tackle these problems. Firstly, the traditional WNCS model is introduced to present a basic control model with delay. Then, a robust congestion control model in NFVs and WSDNs is presented, which is extended the traditional WNCS model by utilizing Lyapunov-Krasovskii functionals. Next, Lyapunov-Krasovskii functionals and linear matrix inequalities (LMIs) are adopted to analyze system stabilization with external disturbance. The sufficient conditions are formulated by Linear Matrix Inequalities (LMIs). Finally, a numerical simulation is conducted to indicate the effectiveness of the proposed scheme.

Keywords: Linear Matrix Inequality (LMI) · Lyapunov-Krasovskii functionals · Network Functions Virtualization (NFV) · Robust congestion control · Wireless Software Defined Networking (WSDN)

1 Introduction

With the rapid growth of user data, network services, and the persistent necessity of reducing costs and control network congestion, today's wireless network is facing various challenges [1]. As a key challenge, virtualization of all aspects of our daily life has been resulted in wireless network environments. It turns out that wireless network itself has to be virtualized. New standards and technologies have been developed for network virtualization.

© ICST Institute for Computer Sciences, Social Informatics and Telecommunications Engineering 2018
Q. Chen et al. (Eds.): ChinaCom 2016, Part II, LNICST 210, pp. 142–151, 2018.
DOI: 10.1007/978-3-319-66628-0_14

We have seen growing interest in the operation of the network functions as software - a trend known as Network Functions Virtualization (NFV) [2]. NFV has arisen as an operator-promoted initiative with the objective of increasing the flexibility of network services control and management within the operators' networks [3]. The network functions through software that run on several hardware can be achieved to allocate the network resources. The concept of NFV involves implementing network functions in software which could be located in kinds of infrastructures, including data centres, network nodes and so on. The NFV group of the European Telecommunications Standards Institute (ETSI) is working on developing standards to promote the NFV approach [3].

In parallel, Software Defined Networking (SDN) is being used to steer flows through proper network functions to enforce control policies and jointly manage network [2,4]. Wireless SDN (WSDN) presents a new architecture where the control plane is shifted to a centralized controller [5].

"NFV and WSDN" is able to achieve three important goals: (i) satisfying Quality of Service (QoS) requirement on VNF performance or availability; (ii) accurately monitoring and manipulating network traffic, and controlling network congestion; (iii) minimizing VNF network costs and maximizing global throughput. However, simultaneously achieving all three goals is not possible today, and fundamentally requires more control than NFV and WSDN can offer [2].

It is essential to effectively control network congestion and manage sorts of QoS in current WSDNs to keep network stability in these VNFs [7–9]. Moreover, the stabilized WSDN adopted the stability control may become unstable again due to propagation delay and external interference. Propagation delays increase network cost and reduce network reliability [10]. The external interference in WSDNs leads to network instability [11]. Thus the paper re-stabilizes the network parameters at the ideal states, and a novel concept of robust congestion control is proposed in the network of "NFV and WSDN" architecture. Robust congestion control means that the network parameters are convergent for congestion control in the presence of external interference.

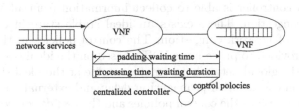

Fig. 1. The padding waiting time for robust control in NFVs and WSDNs.

The padding waiting time is considered as a key parameter for robust congestion control in NFVs and WSDNs. As shown in Fig. 1, the processing time is the duration consumed to process a VNF. A waiting duration may also be introduced by a ideal state to slow down the data plane, and further processing of VNFs is postponed for this waiting duration. The padding waiting time is defined as the sum of the processing time and the waiting duration. When all VNFs have the same processing speeds and the sum of the padding waiting time is minimized, the total service time of all VNFs may be shortened and the WSDN throughput may be maximized.

Excessively limited padding waiting time at source-side may reduce the network throughput and link utilization, and prevent the network from working at the ideal state. Meanwhile, the padding waiting time at source-side may fluctuate unstably around the ideal state under the influence of the external interferences. The instability of all VNFs may cause the instability of the whole network. All VNFs unify their states to achieve the robust congestion control from the centralized controller, so as to minimize the overload of each VNF and keep maximizing the throughput of global WSDN.

Robust control have attracted particular interest in the literature for the traditional network control system [10,12], however, these studies have three crucial limitations. The control policies are firstly not implemented in VNFs. Then, propagation delay is seldom considered in the path of VNF-to-controller during congestion control. And the last limitation is that the traditional theories of the Wireless Network Control Systems (WNCSs) model for robust congestion control do not work well in WSDNs.

Therefore, we focus on modeling the robust congestion control problem and designing the control policies through sufficient conditions of robust congestion control by means of Lyapunov-Krasovskii functionals. A new robust congestion control model is proposed by using Lyapunov-Krasovskii functionals [13,14]. The centralized controller generates control polices and feeds control instructions to the VNFs. Thus, the VNFs could follow these instructions as software to make proper adjustments of the padding waiting time.

2   Model and Analysis

Figure 2 shows a typical scenario of VNFs in WSDNs with propagation delay. The centralized controller is able to collect information from all VNFs to deal with network congestion. There exists an ideal stable state in each VNF for stability control of network congestion. The control policies in the centralized controller are provided to process the VNFs based on the ideal stable state. Our goal is to keep the global network parameters stable at the ideal stable state by robust congestion control with propagation delay and external interference.

The controller designs the control policies and then sends control instructions to adjust the padding waiting time in each VNF. There exists a set of network services, where each network service is composed of a set of VNFs. Each VNF must be processed by means of QoS requirement, satisfying the QoS constraints between the difficult VNFs that compose the corresponding network services.

With propagation delay and external interference, the current state $\bar{S}_i(k)$ in each VNF is considered to constantly approach to the ideal state $\bar{S}_1(k) \rightarrow S_1(k), \cdots, \bar{S}_i(k) \rightarrow S_i(k), \cdots, \bar{S}_N(k) \rightarrow S_N(k)$ by robust congestion control,

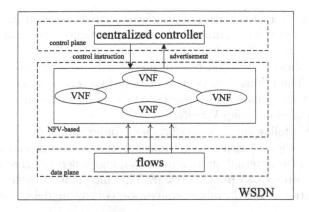

Fig. 2. A typical scenario of NFV with propagation delay in WSDNs.

where k is the discrete count number. $x_i(k) = \bar{S}_i(k) - S_i(k)$ is defined as the error state of the padding waiting time and $\lim_{k \to \infty} ||\bar{S}_i(k) - S_i(k)|| = 0$ for $i = 1, \ldots, N$.

According to analyzing the propagation delay in the closed-loop WSDN, the propagation delay from the VNF to the centralized controller (VC) and from the centralized controller to the VNF (CV) are defined as d_{vc} and d_{cv}, respectively. Suppose that the VC delay d_{vc} and CV delay d_{cv} are constants in WSDNs. The VNF receives the feedback message from the controller with the CV delay d_{cv} in Fig. 2. Denote the constant $d = d_{vc} + d_{cv}$.

The VNFs constantly adjust their padding waiting times following the control instructions. Initially, each VNF advertises the error state of the padding waiting time $x(k) = (x_i(k))$ to the controller. With the packet-in message, the controller calculates $x(k)$, and the controller classifies the global information of the error state and generates a control policy $u(k)$ to keep the padding waiting time stable. The control policy needs to stabilize the padding waiting time in the presence of propagation delay and external interference. The controller makes proper adjustments of the weighted matrix $B_u \in \mathbb{R}^{n \times n}$. Finally, the controller sends a packet-out message, which indicates that the flow originated the packet-in message has been implemented. The closed-loop WSDN is accomplished and modeled with propagation delay as $x(k + 1) = Ax(k) + B_u u(k)$, where A is the parameters represented the network features that are non-negative constant matrices with appropriate dimensions.

The control instruction $u(k) = Kx(k)$, $K \in \mathbb{R}^{n \times n}$ denotes robust congestion control strength, and the control policies are considered as

$$x(k + 1) = Ax(k) + B_u Kx(k - d) \tag{1}$$

Considering external interference, the closed-loop network model can be formulated into a robust $H\infty$ control model. Simultaneously, the closed-loop WSDN (1) with the external interference part add as in (2)

$$x(k + 1) = Ax(k) + B_u Kx(k - d) + B_w w(k), \tag{2}$$

where B_w is the weight of external interference that is non-negative constant matrices with appropriate dimensions. For convenience, we assume that the external interference is limited energy and duration.

Thus, the robust congestion control model is converted into a robust $H\infty$ control model. The robust $H\infty$ control model of the error state of the padding waiting time in the presence of propagation delay and external interference is formulated in the closed-loop WSDN.

Consider the following $H\infty$ performance index $J = \sum_{k=0}^{\infty}\{z^T(k)z(k) - \gamma^2 w^T(k)w(k)\}$, where J denotes the relation of the energy of the controlled output $z(k)$ and the external interference $w(k)$, and γ denotes $H\infty$ performance index that is a prescribed positive scalar. This inequality denotes robust $H\infty$ control in traditional WNCS robust congestion control model.

3   Problem Formulations of Robust $H\infty$ Control

According to (1), the robust $H\infty$ control model of the error state of the padding waiting time in the presence of propagation delay and external interference in the closed-loop WSDN is described by

$$\begin{cases} x(k+1) = Ax(k) + B_u u(k) + B_w w(k) \\ \quad u(k) = Kx(k-d) \\ \quad z(k) = Ix(k), \end{cases} \tag{3}$$

where $x(k) = [x_1(k), \ldots, x_n(k)]^T \in \mathbb{R}^n$ is the error state which denotes the varying value of the padding waiting time between the current state and the ideal state, $u(k) = [u_1(k), \ldots, u_n(k)]^T \in \mathbb{R}^n$ is the control instruction, $w(k) = [w_1(k), \ldots, w_n(k)]^T \in \mathbb{R}^n$ is the external interference of limited energy and duration with convariance matrix w and has expectation zero, $z(k) = [z_1(k), \ldots, z_n(k)]^T$ as a measurement is the output of the robust congestion control, k is the discrete count number. Define $A = (a_{ij})_{n \times n} = \begin{cases} a_{ij} = 0, \ if \ i < j \\ 0 \le a_{ij} \le 1, \ if \ i \ge j \end{cases}$, $B_u = (b_{ij})_{n \times n}$, $B_w = diag\{\widehat{b}_1, \widehat{b}_2, \ldots, \widehat{b}_n\}$, and the constant matrix $I \in \mathbb{R}^{n \times n}$.

Definition 1. *For the sake of the simplicity, the closed-loop WSDN (3) is stable with constant propagation delay $d = d_{vc} + d_{cv}$ in NFVs and WSDNs.*

Definition 2. *The closed-loop WSDN (3) is said to be stable, if there exists a state feedback control instruction $u(k) = Kx(k-d)$, $K \in \mathbb{R}^{n \times n}$. Thus, $u(k)$ is said to the robust congestion control policies.*

Lemma 1 *(Schur Complement). Given constant matrices P, Q, R, where $P^T = P$, $Q^T = Q$, then the LMI $\begin{bmatrix} P & R \\ R^T & -Q \end{bmatrix} < 0$ is equivalent to the following condition: $Q > 0$, $P + RQ^{-1}R^T < 0$.*

4   Criteria of Robust $H\infty$ Control

In the following, let $\bar{A} = A - I$, $\bar{B} = B_u K$. Rewrite closed-loop WSDN of the error state (3) into a more compact form as

$$\begin{cases} y(k) = \bar{A}x(k) + \bar{B}x(k-d) + B_w w(k) \\ z(k) = Ix(k), \end{cases} \tag{4}$$

where $y(k) = x(k+1) - x(k)$ is the difference state, and $y(k) = [x_1(k+1) - x_1(k), x_2(k+1) - x_2(k), \ldots, x_n(k+1) - x_n(k)]^T$.

Theorem 1. *Consider the robust $H\infty$ control model of the error state with propagation delay and external interference in the closed-loop WSDN (4). Given the external interference attenuation level γ and positive integers d. If there exist appropriate dimension symmetric positive definite matrices $P > 0$, $Q > 0$ and $R > 0$, $X = \begin{bmatrix} X_{11} & X_{12} \\ * & X_{22} \end{bmatrix} \geq 0$, and appropriate dimension matrices N_1, N_2, so that the following conditions (5) and (6) hold:*

$$\Xi = \begin{bmatrix} X_{11} & X_{12} & N_1 \\ * & X_{22} & N_2 \\ * & * & R \end{bmatrix} > 0, \tag{5}$$

$$\Omega = \begin{bmatrix} \omega_{11} & \omega_{12} & PB_w & \bar{A}^T & d\bar{A}^T & I \\ * & \omega_{22} & 0 & \bar{B}^T & d\bar{B}^T & 0 \\ * & * & -\gamma^2 I & B_w^T & dB_w^T & 0 \\ * & * & * & -P^{-1} & 0 & 0 \\ * & * & * & * & -dR^{-1} & 0 \\ * & * & * & * & * & -I \end{bmatrix} < 0, \tag{6}$$

where $\omega_{11} = P\bar{A} + \bar{A}^T P + Q + N_1 + N_1^T + dX_{11}, \omega_{12} = P\bar{B} - N_1 + N_2^T + dX_{12}, \omega_{22} = -Q - N_2 - N_2^T + dX_{22}$. Thus, the WSDN achieve robust $H\infty$ control.

Proof. We firstly define $y(l) = x(l+1) - x(l)$. Then, we obtain $x(k+1) = x(k) + y(k)$, and $x(k) - x(k-d) - \sum_{l=k-d}^{k-1} y(l) = 0$.

In the closed-loop WSDN, the Lyapunov-Krasovskii functionals can be expressed by

$$V(k) = x^T(k)Px(k) + \sum_{j=k-d}^{k-1} x^T(j)Qx(j) + \sum_{\theta=-d+1}^{0} \sum_{j=k-1+\theta}^{k-1} y^T(j)Ry(j).$$

where $P = P^T > 0$, $Q = Q^T > 0$ and $R = R^T > 0$ are positive definite symmetric matrices. Define $\Delta V(k) = V(k+1) - V(k)$, thus

$$\begin{aligned} \Delta V(k) \leq & 2x^T(k)Py(k) + y^T(k)Py(k) + x^T(k)Qx(k) \\ & - x^T(k-d)Qx(k-d) + dy^T(k)Ry(k) - \sum_{l=k-d}^{k-1} y^T(l)Ry(l). \end{aligned} \tag{7}$$

For any appropriate dimension matrix $N_i(i = 1, 2)$, we have

$$0 = 2[x^T(k)N_1 + x^T(k-d)N_2] \times [x(k) - x(k-d) - \sum_{l=k-d}^{k-1} y(l)]. \quad (8)$$

And for an appropriate dimension matrix $X = \begin{bmatrix} X_{11} & X_{12} \\ * & X_{22} \end{bmatrix} \geq 0$, we get

$$0 \leq \sum_{l=k-d}^{k-1} \zeta_1^T(k)X\zeta_1(k) - \sum_{l=k-d}^{k-1} \zeta_1^T(k)X\zeta_1(k) = d\zeta_1^T(k)X\zeta_1(k) - \sum_{l=k-d}^{k-1} \zeta_1^T(k)X\zeta_1(k). \quad (9)$$

Thus, from (7) to (9), we have

$$\Delta V(k) \leq \zeta_2^T(k)\{\Lambda + \Pi_1^T(P+dR)\Pi_1\}\zeta_2(k) - \sum_{l=k-d}^{k-1} \zeta_3^T(k,l)\Xi\zeta_3(k,l) + \gamma^2 w^T(k)w(k). \quad (10)$$

with $\zeta_1(k) = [x^T(k)\ x^T(k-d)]^T, \zeta_2(k) = [x^T(k)\ x^T(k-d)\ w^T(k)]^T, \zeta_3(k,l) = [x^T(k)\ x^T(k-d)\ y^T(l)]^T, \Lambda = \begin{bmatrix} \varphi_{11} & \varphi_{12} & PB_w \\ * & \varphi_{22} & 0 \\ * & * & -\gamma^2 I \end{bmatrix}, \Pi_1 = [\bar{A}\ \bar{B}\ B_w]^T, \Pi_2 = [I\ 0\ 0]$.

Defining $\Theta = \Lambda + \Pi^T P\Pi + d\Pi^T R\Pi$ and using Schur Complement Lemma (Lemma 1), the LMIs in (10) can make inequalities $\Theta < 0$ true. Then there exists a positive scalar $\varepsilon > 0$ such that $\Theta < \varepsilon I < 0$. Therefore, it follows that $\Delta V(k) \leq -\varepsilon \|x(k)\|^2 < 0\ \forall x(k) \neq 0$.

Considering $w(k) \neq 0$ and Schur Complement Lemma, following the inequalities (5) and (6), we have

$$\Delta V(k) + z^T(k)z(k) - \gamma^2 w^T(k)w(k) \leq \xi^T(k)\Omega\xi(k) < 0.$$

Sum k from 0 to ∞ with the initialization of $V(0) = 0$, we can obtain

$$\sum_{k=0}^{\infty} \{z^T(k)z(k) - \gamma^2 w^T(k)w(k)\} < 0.$$

Based on the Lyapunov-Krasovskii theory, the robust $H\infty$ control model of the error state of the padding waiting time with propagation delay and external interference in the closed-loop WSDN can achieve robust $H\infty$ control $J < 0$ with desired $H\infty$ performance index $\|T_{wz}(z)\|_\infty < \gamma$ following (5) and (6).

The proof is completed.

5   Simulation Results

In this section, a numerical example is designed to verify the effectiveness of our stabilization criteria given in Theorem 1. Following (5) and (6), in real WSDN with QoS requirement (shown in Fig. 2), there are eight priority levels, denoted from 0 to 7 with 0 being the highest, which are assigned to differentiated flows with different characteristics. Consider the closed-loop WSDN (3) with different parameters in order to clearly demonstrate control policies with different QoS priorities in the centralized controller:

$B_w = diag\{0.2, 0.1, 0.31, 0.51, 0.11, 0.21, 0.31, 0.41\}$ and

$$A = \begin{bmatrix} 0.5 & 0 & 0 & 0 & 0 & 0 & 0 & 0 \\ 0.76 & 0.15 & 0 & 0 & 0 & 0 & 0 & 0 \\ 0.65 & 0 & 0.3 & 0 & 0 & 0 & 0 & 0 \\ 0.31 & 0 & 0.51 & 0.22 & 0 & 0 & 0 & 0 \\ 0.63 & 0.14 & 0 & 0.25 & 0.33 & 0 & 0 & 0 \\ 0.36 & 0 & 0.25 & 0 & 0 & 0.47 & 0 & 0 \\ 0.36 & 0.94 & 0.74 & 0.51 & 0 & 0.65 & 0.45 & 0 \\ 0.31 & 0.26 & 0 & 0.59 & 0 & 0.3 & 0.1 & 0.14 \end{bmatrix}.$$

where A denotes the relationship between $x(k+1)$ and $x(k)$, and we define $A = (a_{ij}) = \begin{cases} a_{ij} = 0, & if\ i < j \\ 0 \le a_{ij} \le 1, & if\ i \ge j \end{cases}$, that means the QoS requirement. The QoS requirement is applied in VNFs to guarantee flows with different priorities controlled. Before starting its execution, the flow with lower priority needs to wait for the completions of all flow queues with non-lower priorities in the VNF k. Additionally, the waiting time consists of the probability weight of every non-lower priority.

5.1   Effectiveness Verification of the Proposed Scheme

According to Theorem 1, there exists a feasible solution to LMIs (5) and (6). We use the zero initial state $x(0) = [0\ 0\ 0\ 0\ 0\ 0\ 0\ 0]$ to reflect the stability of error state at the initial moment. Suppose the control strength $K = -0.1I$, the control policy $B_u = A$. The scenario of the error state $x_i(k), i = 0, 1, \ldots, 7$ with the different priorities are considered to make a comparison. Suppose that a function with constant value and limited count number represents the external interference with limited energy and duration to make the simulation tractable.

Notably, the error states $x(k)$ may increase and then make convergence in the presence of propagation delay and external inferences, as shown in Fig. 3. The result represents that all error states $x(k)$ reach an agreement by the centralized controlling. Thus, this simulation can be conducted to indicate the effectiveness of the proposed scheme in NFVs and WSDNs.

5.2   Design of Control Policy on Robust $H\infty$ Control

This section introduces the design of the control policy based on the proposed scheme in NFVs and WSDNs. We select the intermediate priority $i = 4$ in the simulation. Figure 4 shows the variations of the error state under the different control strength K. The initial state is $y_4(0) = 0$. Compared with the control strength K, it is notable that a tighter control results in the smaller width.

Therefore, the appropriate adjustments of QoS control policy can easily be designed in the controller. The control policy can be designed to control the width measurement.

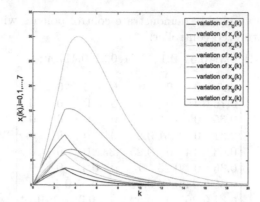

Fig. 3. The variations of error state $x_i(k), i = 1, 2, \ldots, 7$ with eight QoS priorities to represent its variation in the presence of propagation delay and external interference.

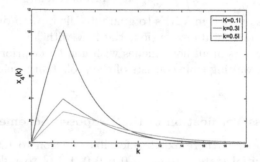

Fig. 4. The variations of error state $x_4(k)$ (at QoS priority levels $i = 4$) with different control strength K in the presence of propagation delay and external interference.

6 Conclusion

This paper have adopted robust control to tackle the problems of keeping the network stable during congestion control in NFVs and WSDNs. A robust control model with propagation delay and external interference is presented by using Lyapunov-Krasovskii functionals. The sufficient conditions have been formulated by LMIs. The numerical simulation has conducted to indicate the effectiveness of the proposed scheme. The approach that we have presented can possibly be extended to model and analyze more complex robust control approaches in WSDNs. For future studies, more complex control algorithms modeled in WSDNs would be discussed.

Acknowledgment. This work is supported by the 863 project (Grant Nos. 2014AA01A701); The National Natural Science Foundation of China (Grant Nos. 61271168, 61471104).

References

1. Basta, A., Kellerer, W., Hoffmann, M., Morper, H.J., Hoffmann, K.: Applying NFV and SDN to LTE mobile core gateways, the functions placement problem. In: Proceedings of the 4th Workshop on all Things Cellular: Operations, Applications, Challenges, pp. 33–38. ACM (2014)
2. Gember-Jacobson, A., Viswanathan, R., Prakash, C., Grandl, R., Khalid, J., Das, S., Akella, A.: OpenNF: enabling innovation in network function control. ACM SIGCOMM Comput. Commun. Rev. **44**(4), 163–174 (2015)
3. Ferrer Riera, J., Escalona, E., Batalle, J., Grasa, E., Garcia-Espin, J.A.: Virtual network function scheduling: Concept and challenges. In: International Conference on Smart Communications in Network Technologies (SaCoNeT), pp. 1–5. IEEE (2014)
4. Anwer, B., Benson, T., Feamster, N., Levin, D., Rexford, J.: A slick control plane for network middleboxes. In: Proceedings of the Second ACM SIGCOMM Workshop on Hot Topics in Software Defined Networking, pp. 147–148. ACM (2013)
5. Agarwal, S., Kodialam, M., Lakshman, T.V.: Traffic engineering in software defined networks. In: INFOCOM, 2013 Proceedings IEEE, pp. 2211–2219. IEEE (2013)
6. McKeown, N., Anderson, T., Balakrishnan, H., Parulkar, G., Peterson, L., Rexford, J., Turner, J.: OpenFlow: enabling innovation in campus networks. ACM SIGCOMM Comput. Commun. Rev. **38**(2), 69–74 (2008)
7. Tomovic, S., Prasad, N., Radusinovic, I.: SDN control framework for QoS provisioning. In: Telecommun. Forum Telfor (TELFOR), pp. 111–114. IEEE (2014)
8. Nam, H., Calin, D., Schulzrinne, H.: Intelligent content delivery over wireless via SDN. In: 2015 IEEE Wireless Communications and Networking Conference (WCNC), pp. 2185–2190. IEEE (2015)
9. Caria, M., Jukan, A., Hoffmann, M.: A performance study of network migration to SDN-enabled traffic engineering. In: 2013 IEEE Global Communications Conference (GLOBECOM), pp. 1391–1396. IEEE (2013)
10. Yu, X., Tomsovic, K.: Application of linear matrix inequalities for load frequency control with communication delays. IEEE Trans. Power Syst. **19**(3), 1508–1515 (2004)
11. Yang, L., Guan, X.P., Long, C.N., Luo, X.Y.: Feedback stabilization over wireless network using adaptive coded modulation. Int. J. Autom. Comput. **5**(4), 381–388 (2008)
12. Lpez-Rodrguez, F., Campelo, D.R.: A robust SDN network architecture for service providers. In: IEEE Global Communications Conference, pp. 1903–1908. IEEE (2014)
13. Moon, Y.S., Park, P., Kwon, W.H., Lee, Y.S.: Delay-dependent robust stabilization of uncertain state-delayed systems. Int. J. Control **74**(14), 1447–1455 (2001)
14. Yue, D., Han, Q.L., Lam, J.: Network-based robust H∞ control of systems with uncertainty. Automatica **41**(6), 999–1007 (2005)
15. Liu, X., Hong, L., Jingyu, R.: Research on predictive control of stochastic network-induced delay for network control systems. In: 2011 Chinese Control and Decision Conference (CCDC), pp. 929–932. IEEE (2011)

Latency-Aware Reliable Controller Placements in SDNs

Yuqi Fan[1(✉)], Yongfeng Xia[1], Weifa Liang[2], and Xiaomin Zhang[1]

[1] School of Computer and Information, Hefei University of Technology,
Hefei 230009, Anhui, China
yuqi.fan@hfut.edu.cn
[2] Research School of Computer Science, The Australian National University,
Canberra, ACT 0200, Australia

Abstract. Most existing research on controller placement in Software-Defined Networking (SDN) investigated controller placements without jointly taking into account both the communication reliability and the communication latency between controllers and switches if any link in the network fails. In this paper, we first introduce a new latency metric that considers the communication delay between the switches and the controllers with and without the single-link-failure. We then formulate a novel SDN controller placement problem with the aim to minimize the communication delay, for which we propose an efficient algorithm. We also show that there is a non-trivial trade-off between a primary path and its backup path in terms of communication delay. We finally conduct experiments through simulations. Experimental results demonstrate that the proposed algorithm is very promising.

Keywords: SDN · Multiple controller placements · A single link failure · The latency · Placement algorithms

1 Introduction

Software-Defined Networking (SDN) is a new networking paradigm that decouples the control plane from the data plane, making the network management much simpler and flexible [1]. Multiple SDN controllers [2–4] can improve the system performance in terms of scalability, delay, etc. through intelligent controller placements.

Lots of effort on controller placements has been taken in recent years, which focuses mainly on which locations the controllers should be placed, and how to map each switch to one of the placed controllers to minimize the accumulated communication latency between switches and their controllers. For example, Heller et al. [5] tackled the controller placement problem with the aim to minimize the node-to-controller propagation latency, and reduced the problem to the facility location problem. Yao et al. [6] minimized the total cost of flow set-up requests from switches to controllers, where each switch was assigned a

© ICST Institute for Computer Sciences, Social Informatics and Telecommunications Engineering 2018
Q. Chen et al. (Eds.): ChinaCom 2016, Part II, LNICST 210, pp. 152–162, 2018.
DOI: 10.1007/978-3-319-66628-0_15

weight that is defined as the product of numbers of flow requests and the delay from each switch to the controller. Yao et al. [7] placed the controllers to the network to minimize the maximum latency under the constraints on controller capacities.

The communication reliability is another important concern in controller placements in SDNs [8]. Hock et al. [9] introduced a resilience framework to cope with the resilience of link outages by proposing a Pareto-based optimal controller placement method. Müller et al. [10] proposed a controller placement strategy to maximize the number of node-disjoint paths between each switch and its controller. Hu et al. [11] introduced a new metric, referred as the expected percentage of control path loss, to maximize the reliability of control networks. Ros and Ruiz [12] proposed a strategy that connects each switch to a subset of controllers instead of a single one to ensure the required reliability.

Notice that a high latency in the backup paths between controllers and switches will degrade the entire network performance. To the best of our knowledge, very little attention in literature has ever been paid on the latency between the failure-free and a single-link-failure cases in SDNs. In this paper, we will deal with the multiple controller placements in an SDN with an objective to minimize the total latency of both primary and backup paths.

The main contributions of this paper are as follows. We investigate the controller placement problem to reduce the latency with and without a single-link-failure. We define a novel metric integrating the latency in both primary and backup paths, and propose an efficient algorithm for multiple controller placements based on the proposed placement metric. We also conduct experiments through simulations to evaluate the performance of the proposed algorithm. Experimental results demonstrate the proposed algorithm is very promising.

The rest of the paper is organized as follows. The network model is introduced, and the problem is precisely defined in Sect. 2. The proposed algorithm is presented in Sect. 3. The performance evaluation of the proposed algorithm is given in Sect. 4, and the conclusions are detailed in Sect. 5.

2   Problem Formulation

We model an SDN network as an undirected graph $G = (V, E)$, where V is the set of switches (or nodes) and E is the set of links. Each controller will be co-located with a switch [9], and each switch is controlled by only one controller. We assume that there is at most one link failure in the network [13]. The notations used in the paper are listed in Table 1.

A primary path $p_{i,k}$ needs to be set up between a switch s_i and its corresponding controller c_k. In case a link in path $p_{i,k}$ fails, a backup path needs to be built to replace the failed primary path. In this paper we aim to find a proper location for each controller, and determine the exact mapping between the controllers and the switches, with the objective to minimize the average accumulated latency between switches and controllers. In other words, our optimization objective is to

Table 1. Table of notations

Notation	Definition
s_i	Node/switch i
(i, j)	The link between nodes i and j
c_k	Controller c_k
C	Controller set
u_k	The processing capacity of controller c_k
$r_{i,k}$	The number of requests from switch s_i to the mapped controller c_k
$x_{i,k}$	Indicate whether switch s_i is mapped to controller c_k $(= 1)$ or not $(= 0)$
$y_{i,k}$	Denotes whether controller c_k is placed onto switch s_i $(= 1)$ or not $(= 0)$
$p_{i,k}$	The link set of the primary path between switch s_i and controller c_k
$l^p_{i,k}$	The latency in the primary path between switch s_i and controller c_k
$l^b_{i,k,i',j'}$	The latency in the backup path between switch s_i and controller c_k under link (i', j') failure
$l_{i,k}$	The accumulated latency in the primary path and backup paths between switch s_i and controller c_k

Minimize:

$$\frac{\sum\limits_{i=1}^{|V|}\sum\limits_{k=1}^{|C|} l_{i,k}}{|S|}. \tag{1}$$

Subject to:

$$l_{i,k} = \lambda_1 l^p_{i,k} + \lambda_2 \frac{\sum\limits_{(i',j') \in p_{i,k}} l^b_{i,k,i',j'}}{|p_{i,k}|}, \tag{2}$$

$$\sum_{k=1}^{|C|} x_{i,k} = 1, \quad \forall s_i \in V, \tag{3}$$

$$\sum_{i=1}^{|V|} y_{i,k} = 1, \quad \forall c_k \in C, \tag{4}$$

$$y_{i,k} \le x_{i,k}, \quad \forall s_i \in V, \forall c_k \in C, \tag{5}$$

$$\sum_{i=1}^{|V|} x_{i,k} \cdot r_{i,k} \le u_k, \quad \forall c_k \in C. \tag{6}$$

Equation (2) defines the accumulated latency in the primary path and backup path between a switch s_i and its controller c_k, where parameters λ_1 and $\lambda_2(\lambda_1 + \lambda_2 = 1)$ are constant weights used for weighting between the two latency sources. The latency of the backup path takes into account all possible failures of links in the primary path. Equation (3) ensures that each switch is mapped to exactly one controller. Equation (4) mandates that each controller is placed onto exactly one switch. Equation (5) dictates that switch s_i is mapped to controller c_k if controller c_k is placed onto switch s_i. Equation (6) signifies that the number of requests from its switches to a controller cannot exceed the computing capacity of the controller.

3   Algorithm for Controller Placements

It is known that the controller placement problem with the aim to minimize the accumulated latency of all primary paths is a $\mathcal{NP}$-hard problem [5]. Clearly, the controller placement problem in this paper is $\mathcal{NP}$-hard too, as the former is a special case of our problem where the accumulated latency of backup paths has not been incorporated into the optimization objective.

In this section, we propose a Latency-Aware Reliable Controller placement algorithm (LARC) for the problem. A switch is mapped to a controller by the shortest path, and the path cost is the total weight of all the links that the path traverses. We create an auxiliary graph with each link cost incorporating both primary path latency and average path latency upon the link failure. We place each new controller on the auxiliary graph by searching the location that incurs the least total path cost between the switches and the controllers. Algorithm LARC consists of two stages.

Stage one: A weighted auxiliary graph, $G' = (V', E')$, is constructed from the SDN G which will be used for the controller placements. Each edge in E' is assigned a weight that is the accumulated latency on both primary and backup paths.

Stage two: Determine the location of each to-be-placed controller and map each switch to one of the controllers, by utilizing the auxiliary graph and the proposed metric for controller placements.

3.1   The Construction of the Auxiliary Graph

The weighted auxiliary graph $G' = (V', E')$ is constructed from the SDN $G = (V, E)$ as follows, where $V' = V$ and $E' = E$. Denote by $w_{i,j}$ the weight of link (i, j). For the failure of link (i, j), we calculate the average path latency $w_{i,j}^f$ between all pairs of nodes. The new weight of link (i, j) in G', $w_{i,j}'$, is calculated by Eq. (7), where weights λ_1 and λ_2 are constants with $\lambda_1 + \lambda_2 = 1$.

$$w_{i,j}' = \lambda_1 w_{i,j} + \lambda_2 w_{i,j}^f. \tag{7}$$

3.2   Controller Placement

The detailed algorithm is given in Algorithm 1, which places the controllers on the network based on the auxiliary graph, and maps each switch to one of the controllers. Specifically, the algorithm proceeds iteratively using the greedy strategy. Within each iteration, a single controller is placed. This procedure continues until all K controllers are placed. For each controller c_k, Algorithm 1 computes the cost of placing it at a location v, which is the total cost of the shortest paths between all unassigned switches and controller c_k located at v (see steps 3–7 of the algorithm). It then chooses a location v with the minimum cost, and map those unassigned switches to controller c_k one by one until the computing capacity u_k of controller c_k is reached (see steps 8–11 of the algorithm). Once controller c_k has been placed at location v, the path cost of mapping a switch to pre-placed controller may be reduced by mapping the switch to controller c_k. Therefore, we perform a procedure Remap, to change the mapping relationship between all placed controllers and the switches assigned to them.

Algorithm 1. *Controller Placement*

Input: Auxiliary graph $G' = (V', E')$
Input: Set of switches S
Input: Number of controllers K
Output: Set of locations placed with controllers C_p
Output: Mapping relationship between switches and controllers
1: $V_p = V', C_p = \varnothing, S' = S$;
2: **for** $k = 1...K$ **do**
3:   **for** each location $v \in V_p$ **do**
4:     Assume controller c_k is placed at location v;
5:     Find the shortest path between each switch $s_i \in S'$ and a controller c_k at location v in G', and assume the cost of the path is $c^p_{i,v}$;
6:     Evaluate $c^c_v = \sum_{i \in S'} c^p_{i,v}$ the total cost of the paths from all the switches in S' to controller c_k at location v;
7:   **end for**
8:   Choose the location v with the least cost c^c_v to place controller c_k;
9:   Sort the switches in S' in the non-descending order of path cost $c^p_{i,v}$;
10:   Map the switches to controller c_k iteratively provided that the mapping does not exceed the computing capacity u_k of the controller, assuming that S^m is the mapped switch set;
11:   $C_p = C_p \bigcup \{v\}, S' = S' - S^m, V_p = V_p \setminus v$;
12:   Remap;
13:   Relocate;
14: **end for**

Procedure Remap proceeds iteratively. Within each iteration, for a given switch s_i that has been mapped to a controller, the procedure will calculate the accumulated delay of mapping switch s_i to each controller, and find the controller c_k that incurs the least accumulated delay. Switch s_i is then mapped to controller c_k if this mapping will not exceed the computing capacity of controller c_k.

Changing the location of a placed controller may also reduce the delay between the controllers and switches. Algorithm 1 performs Relocate to further reduce the mapping cost. For each controller c_k that has been placed at a location, Relocate evaluates whether deploying each controller c_k onto an assigned switch location v will reduce the total delay between the switches and the controllers. The total delay is the cost sum of the minimum cost paths between all assigned switches to controller c_k at location v.

Assume K, N and L are the numbers of controllers, switches and links, respectively. In the first stage of algorithm LARC, to construct the auxiliary graph G' from the network G, we iteratively delete a link in G and calculate the shortest path between all pairs of nodes, using Dijkstra's algorithm, where Dijkstra's algorithm runs in time $O(N^2)$, and hence the calculation of the paths of all pairs of nodes can be performed in $O(N^3)$ time. The construction of the auxiliary graph construction takes $O(L \cdot N^3)$ time.

The second stage of algorithm LARC places the controllers one by one. As the shortest paths has been figured out already in the first stage, the localization of a controller can be determined within $O(N)$ time. Algorithm 1 performs procedures Remap and Relocate after placing a new controller. In the worst case, procedure Remap has to change the mapping relationship between all the K controllers and N switches. The worst case time complexity of procedure Remap is $O(KN)$. For all the placed controllers, procedure Relocate checks all potential locations that can accommodate the controllers, and hence procedure Relocate runs in time $O(KN)$. Algorithm 1 thus takes $O(K^2N)$ time. Consequently, the time complexity of algorithm LARC is $O(L \cdot N^3) + O(K^2N) = O(N^3L + K^2N) = O(N^3L)$ since $N \geq K$.

4 Performance Evaluation

In this section, we evaluate the performance of the proposed controller placement algorithm. We also investigate the impact of important parameters on the performance of the proposed algorithm.

4.1 Simulation Setup

We evaluate the proposed algorithm LARC against the state-of-the-arts: SVVR [10] and CPP [5], where algorithm SVVR maximizes the connectivity between switches and controllers, by exploring the path diversity, while algorithm CPP places the controllers in such a way that the average latency from the switches to the controllers is minimized. The network topologies used in the simulation are ATT (ATT North America) and Internet2 [5,14]. The capacities of controllers and the request rates of switches are set as the same as those used by algorithm SVVR. All controllers have identical computing capacity of 1800 kilorequests/s, and each switch generates the requests with the rate of 200 kilorequests/s. We use the geographical distance between two locations as an approximation of latency [5].

4.2 Performance Evaluation of the Proposed Algorithm

4.2.1 Weighting Impact of Backup Paths

We first evaluate the performance of different algorithms LARC, SVVR and CPP by varying the latency weights of primary and backup paths λ_1 and $\lambda_2(\lambda_1 + \lambda_2 = 1)$ in Eq. (7), assuming that the number of controllers K is 5.

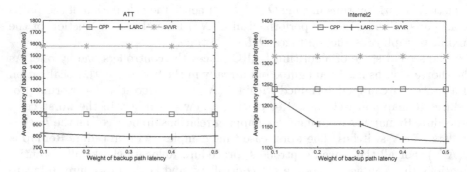

Fig. 1. The average latency of backup paths under different weighting

Figure 1 shows the average latency of backup paths by varying the value of λ_2 after single link failure. Algorithm LARC outperforms algorithm CPP by 24% and 11% for two different networks ATT and Internet2, respectively. Algorithm LARC places the controllers by jointly considering the latencies of both primary and backup paths, while algorithm CPP deploys the controllers with the objective of optimizing the primary path latency only. Algorithm SVVR is the worst one among the three mentioned algorithms. Algorithm SVVR aims to maximize the number of disjoint paths between switches and controllers. However, the latency is not considered in controller placements.

Figure 2 depicts the average latency of primary paths by varying the value of λ_2. Algorithm SVVR has the worst performance, as it focused on finding the maximum number of disjoint paths between switches and controllers for communication reliability without taking into account the communication latency. Algorithm CPP performs better than algorithm LARC on different networks. The average latency of primary paths delivered by algorithm LARC increases from 0.3% to 14% for ATT, and from 0.1% to 17% for Internet2. In general, when the weight λ_2 is no greater than 0.3, algorithm LARC is only slightly worse than CPP, as algorithm LARC considers the latencies of both primary and backup paths, while algorithm CPP places controllers without any consideration of backup path latency.

Figure 3 demonstrates the average accumulated latency of primary and backup paths. The performance of algorithm SVVR is the worst, since it does not consider the latency when deploying the controllers. Algorithm LARC outperforms algorithm CPP by 9% on ATT and 4% on Internet2, respectively.

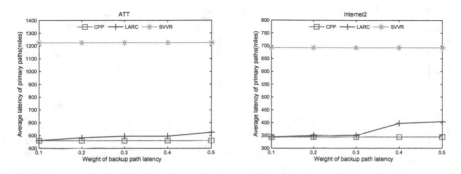

Fig. 2. The average latency of primary paths by varying the latency weight of backup paths

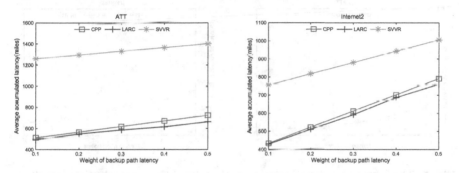

Fig. 3. The average accumulated latency by varying the latency weight of backup paths

4.2.2   Impact of the Number of Controllers

We then study the impact of number of controllers on the performance of different algorithms, assuming the weight λ_2 of backup path latency is set at 0.2. Figure 4 plots the average latency curves of backup paths with different number of controllers. Algorithm LARC outperforms both algorithms SVVR and CPP, since algorithm LARC considers the latencies of both primary and backup paths at the same time. Specifically, with 9 controller placements, algorithm LARC outperforms algorithm CPP in terms of the average delay of backup paths by 27% on ATT and 10% on Internet2, respectively, and the performance improvement diminishes with the growth of the number of controllers.

Figure 5 demonstrates the average latency of primary paths with different number of controllers. Similar to the one shown in Fig. 2, algorithm CPP performs slightly better than algorithm LARC, since algorithm CPP places the controllers with the aim to minimize the latency of primary paths, while algorithm LARC strives for the fine tradeoff of the delays between the primary and backup paths. For both ATT and Internet2, the average latency of primary paths delivered by algorithm CPP is 10% better than that of algorithm LARC, while algorithm SVVR is the worst one.

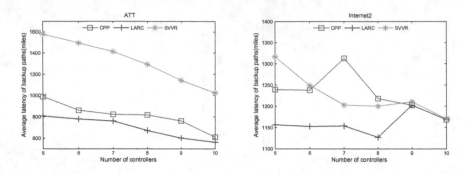

Fig. 4. The average latency of backup paths with different number of controllers

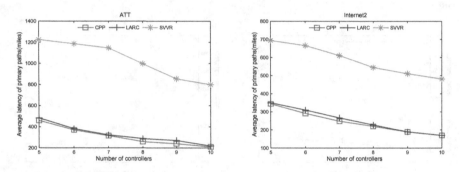

Fig. 5. The average latency of primary paths with different number of controllers

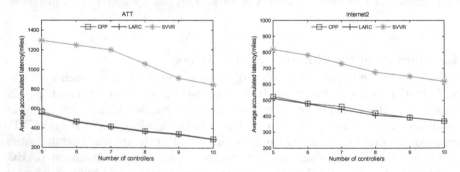

Fig. 6. The average accumulated latency with different number of controllers

Figure 6 illustrates the average accumulated latency by varying the number of controllers. As shown in Fig. 3, algorithm LARC achieves the best performance among the three algorithms, and algorithm LARC outperforms algorithm CPP by 3% on ATT and 4% on Internet2, respectively. Figures 4 and 5 imply that the decrease on the average latency of backup paths can compensate the increase on the average latency of primary paths.

5 Conclusions

Controller placements in Software-Defined Networking (SDN) are crucial in the SDN performance. Most existing studies placed the controllers without jointly considering the communication reliability and the communication latency between controllers and switches if any link in the network fails. In this paper, we introduced a novel latency metric that incorporates the communication delay between the switches and the controllers due to a single link failure. We formulated an SDN controller placement problem with the aim to minimize the average accumulated delay of primary and backup paths between all the switches and their corresponding controllers due to a single link failure, and proposed an efficient algorithm for the problem. We also conducted experiments through simulations. Experimental results demonstrate that the proposed algorithm is very promising.

Acknowledgments. This work was partially supported by Anhui Provincial Natural Science Foundation [1608085MF142].

References

1. Nunes, B.A.A., Mendonca, M., Nguyen, X.N., Obraczka, K., Turletti, T.: A survey of software-defined networking: past, present, and future of programmable networks. IEEE Commun. Surv. Tut. **16**, 1617–1634 (2014)
2. Hassas Yeganeh, S., Ganjali, Y.: Kandoo: a framework for efficient and scalable offloading of control applications. In: ACM SIGCOMM Workshop on Hot Topics in Software Defined Networking, pp. 19–24 (2012)
3. Koponen, T., Casado, M., Gude, N., Stribling, J., Poutievski, L., Zhu, M., Ramanathan, R., Iwata, Y., Inoue, H., Hama, T., et al.: Onix: a distributed control platform for large-scale production networks. In: USENIX Symposium on Operating Systems Design and Implementation, vol. 10, pp. 1–6 (2010)
4. Tootoonchian, A., Ganjali, Y.: HyperFlow: a distributed control plane for Open-Flow. In: 2010 Internet Network Management Conference on Research on Enterprise Networking (2010)
5. Heller, B., Sherwood, R., McKeown, N.: The controller placement problem. In: ACM SIGCOMM Workshop on Hot Topics in Software Defined Networking, pp. 7–12 (2012)
6. Yao, L., Hong, P., Zhang, W., Li, J., Ni, D.: Controller placement and flow based dynamic management problem towards SDN. In: 2015 IEEE International Conference on Communication Workshop, pp. 363–368 (2015)
7. Yao, G., Bi, J., Li, Y., Guo, L.: On the capacitated controller placement problem in software defined networks. IEEE Commun. Lett. **18**, 1339–1342 (2014)
8. Zhang, Y., Beheshti, N., Tatipamula, M.: On resilience of split-architecture networks. In: 2011 IEEE Global Telecommunications Conference, pp. 1–6 (2011)
9. Hock, D., Hartmann, M., Gebert, S., Jarschel, M., Zinner, T., Tran-Gia, P.: Pareto-optimal resilient controller placement in SDN-based core networks. In: International Teletraffic Congress, pp. 1–9 (2013)
10. Müller, L.F., Oliveira, R.R., Luizelli, M.C., Gaspary, L.P., Barcellos, M.P.: Survivor: an enhanced controller placement strategy for improving SDN survivability. In: 2014 IEEE Global Communications Conference, pp. 1909–1915 (2014)

11. Hu, Y., Wendong, W., Gong, X., Que, X., Shiduan, C.: Reliability-aware controller placement for software-defined networks. In: 2013 IFIP/IEEE International Symposium on Integrated Network Management, pp. 672–675 (2013)
12. Ros, F.J., Ruiz, P.M.: On reliable controller placements in software-defined networks. Comput. Commun. **77**, 41–51 (2016)
13. Markopoulou, A., Iannaccone, G., Bhattacharyya, S., Chuah, C.N., Diot, C.: Characterization of failures in an IP backbone. In: 2004 IEEE International Conference on Computer Communications, vol. 4, pp. 2307–2317 (2004)
14. The Internet Topology Zoo. http://www.topology-zoo.org

Signal Detection and Estimation (2)

Multiantenna Based Blind Spectrum Sensing via Nonparametric Test

Guangyue Lu[1], Cai Xu[1(✉)], and Yinghui Ye[2]

[1] National Engineering Laboratory for Wireless Security,
Xi'an University of Posts and Telecommunications, Xi'an, China
tonylugy@163.com, houstonxc@163.com
[2] State Key Laboratory of Integrated Services Networks, Xidian University,
Xi'an, China
connectyyh@126.com

Abstract. Multiantenna based spectrum sensing algorithms are widely used in cognitive radio networks on account of improving the system reliability. Utilizing the difference between the received signal and the noise statistical covariances, two kinds of novel spectrum sensing algorithms, binomial distribution based detection (DD) and wilcoxon signed rank test based detection (WSD), are proposed based on the sample covariance matrix calculated from a limited number of received signal samples. BD and WSD algorithms do not need any priori information of the primary signal and the noise. In addition, their thresholds are found via the statistical theory. Compared with energy detection (ED), maximum-minimum eigenvalue (MME) and covariance absolute value (CAV), those two algorithms can obtain better performance. Finally, the performance of the proposal is verified by simulations.

Keywords: Cognitive radio · Spectrum sensing · Multiantenna · Covariance matrix · Binomial distribution · Wilcoxon signed rank test

1 Introduction

High-rate wide-band wireless communication will bring a huge demand of spectrum. Limited available spectrum resources and inefficient static spectrum allocation policy result that the lack of spectrum resources become increasingly serious. On the one hand, the rapid growth of radio communication service and the appearance of new system, protocol and network result in further competition of wireless spectrum. On the other hand, most of the available spectrum have been assigned to the licensed users. Therefore, unlicensed users can only use the a little spectrum which is nearly saturation.

The statically spectrum allocation way, which is widely used in the current spectrum management system, causes that a large amount of idle spectrum are not applied, and then leads to low spectrum efficiency. To solve the problem of the shortage of spectrum resources, regulators consider using dynamic allocation for spectrum management.

© ICST Institute for Computer Sciences, Social Informatics and Telecommunications Engineering 2018
Q. Chen et al. (Eds.): ChinaCom 2016, Part II, LNICST 210, pp. 165–174, 2018.
DOI: 10.1007/978-3-319-66628-0_16

Cognitive Radio (CR) [1], which achieves the dynamic allocation of spectrum resources, can improve the spectrum utilization. As the fundamental task for CR network, spectrum sensing [2] allows secondary users to use the licensed spectrum to primary users when they are not active.

It has been shown that multiantenna based blind spectrum sensing algorithms are not affected by noise uncertainty to which the classical energy detection (ED) [3,4] is known to be sensitive. Those algorithms are mainly divided into two categories, the eigenvalue based algorithms [5,6] and the covariance based algorithms [7,8]. The eigenvalue based algorithms, such as the maximum minimum eigenvalue (MME) [5] and the maximum eigenvalue trace (MET) [6] algorithms, exploit the difference between the eigenvalue of sample covariance matrices of the primary signals and noises. Nevertheless, it is difficult to obtain the accurate decision threshold. Meanwhile, high computational intensity is required for those detectors.

The covariance absolute value (CAV) [7] algorithm is proposed in order to overcome the above defects. The test statistic is set according to the ratio of the sum of all elements in the absolute value of covariance matrix and the sum of the absolute value of diagonal elements. The accurate decision threshold can be obtained and the computational complexity is low because it does not need eigen-decomposition. However, their performance is worse than ED.

In this paper, we present two kinds of novel nonparametric tests based spectrum sensing algorithms, which utilize the upper triangular elements of sample covariance matrix. The proposed BD and WSD algorithms require no prior information of noise and primary signal. In other words, they are robust to noise uncertainty. To compare with BD, WSD gets better performance but needs higher computational complexity. It is revealed in the simulation that the performance of proposed detectors is superior to traditional multiantenna based blind spectrum sensing algorithms and ED algorithm.

The rest of this paper is organized as follows. System model is given in Sects. 2 and 3 gives the proposed algorithm. Computational complexity of various algorithms are compared in Sect. 4. Simulation results are presented in Sect. 5 and concluding remarks are made in Sect. 6.

2   System Model

2.1   Signal Model

Consider a multiantenna cognitive radio system with one primary user with single antenna and one secondary user with M antennas. As shown in Fig. 1, the essential problem of spectrum sensing is to detect the primary user in the noise environment. Generally, the spectrum sensing can be expressed as a binary hypothesis test problem. H_0 denotes the null hypothesis (absence of the primary user) and H_1 stands for the alternative hypothesis (presence of the primary user). The signal model of spectrum sensing in array antenna receiver is formulated as follows:

$$x_m(n) = \begin{cases} w_m(n), & H_0 \\ hs(n) + w_m(n), & H_1 \end{cases}, n = 1, 2, \cdots, N \qquad (1)$$

where $x_m(n)$ and $w_m(n)$ represent the received signal and additive white Gaussian noise (AWGN) from the mth$(1 \leq m \leq M)$ antenna, $w_m(n)$ $N(0, \sigma^2)$. $s(n)$ denotes the primary signal. h represents channel gain. Without loss of generality, we assume $h = 1$ in array antennas system. N is the number of samples. It is assumed that the primary signal is independent of the noise. Let us express the receive signals as a $M \times N$ matrix.

$$X = \begin{bmatrix} x_1(1) & x_1(2) & \cdots & x_1(N) \\ x_2(1) & x_2(2) & \cdots & x_2(N) \\ \vdots & \vdots & \ddots & \vdots \\ x_M(1) & x_M(2) & \cdots & x_M(N) \end{bmatrix} \qquad (2)$$

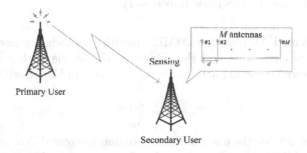

Fig. 1. System model for cognitive radio network with multiple antennas

The sample covariance matrix is defined as

$$R = \frac{1}{N} XX^H \qquad (3)$$

$r_{i,j}$ is the $(i,j)_{th}$ element of $\mathbf{R}$.

$$r_{i,j} = \frac{1}{N} \sum_{n=1}^{N} x_i(n) x_j(n) \qquad (4)$$

There are two probabilities can measure the performance of different algorithms in spectrum sensing:

- probability of detection P_d, which defines the probability of the algorithm deciding the presence of primary signal exist under H_1.
- probability of false alarm P_{fa}, which defines the probability of the algorithm claiming the presence of the primary signal under H_0.

2.2   Previous Works

Energy Detection: multi-antenna assisted ED algorithm is a classical sensing method, which does not need any information of the primary signal. The total energy of received signal is regarded as the test statistic, namely

$$T_{ED} = \sum_{n=1}^{N} \sum_{m=1}^{M} |x_m(n)|^2 \underset{H_0}{\overset{H_1}{\underset{<}{\geq}}} \gamma_{ED} \tag{5}$$

Nevertheless, to calculate the decision threshold, the noise power is required. In practice, it is not easy to obtain accurate noise power so that the performance will decrease. The SNR wall, which means a minimum SNR below that a signal cannot be reliably detected, is also cased by noise uncertainty. This indicates that ED is influenced by the noise uncertainty.

Eigenvalue Based Detection: MME algorithm, which compares the ratio of the maximum eigenvalue and the minimum eigenvalue with a threshold, is proposed to overcome the impact of noise uncertainty in ED algorithm. The test statistic is given by

$$T_{MME} = \frac{\lambda_{\max}}{\lambda_{\min}} \tag{6}$$

where λ_{max} and min are the maximum and minimum eigenvalue of sample covariance matrix $\mathbf{R}$. MME algorithm is popular due to the fact that it does not need of any prior knowledge and is free of noise uncertainty. The drawback is its complexity caused by eigen-decomposition.

Covariance Based Detection: In order to reduce the complexity of MME algorithm, the difference of statistics covariance matrix between H_0 and H_1 is employed to detect whether PU exits or not. The test statistic is

$$T_{CAV} = \frac{\frac{1}{M} \sum_{i=1}^{M} \sum_{j=1}^{M} |r_{i,j}|}{\frac{1}{M} \sum_{i=1}^{M} |r_{i,i}|} \tag{7}$$

CAV algorithm avoids calculating the eigenvalue, therefore, the computational complexity decreased.

3   Nonparametric Test Based Detection

Although MME and CAV is robust to noise uncertainty, the performance is worse than ED. Two kinds of blind spectrum-sensing algorithms, which do not need any prior information of the primary signal and the noise, are proposed in this paper.

We consider the upper triangular elements of $\mathbf{R}(r_{i,j}, ij)$ to design test statistics. The total number of $r_{i,j}(i < j)$ in $\mathbf{R}$ is $M(M-1)/2$, which is been signed as L. Try to seek the difference of $r_{i,j}$s symcenter under H_0 and under H_1.

Under H_0, the mean value is given by

$$E\left[r_{i,j}\right] = E\left[\frac{1}{N}\sum_{n=1}^{N} x_i(n)x_j(n)\right]$$
$$= \frac{1}{N}\sum_{n=1}^{N} E\left[w_i(n)\right] E\left[w_j(n)\right] = 0 \tag{8}$$

and under H_1, we have

$$E\left[r_{i,j}\right] = E\left[\frac{1}{N}\sum_{n=1}^{N} x_i(n)x_j(n)\right]$$
$$= \frac{1}{N}\sum_{n=1}^{N} E\left[s(n)^2\right] \tag{9}$$

Comparing (5) and (6), we obtain that $r_{i,j}$s symcenter is zero under H0 but not equals to zero under H_1. We can realize spectrum sensing via evaluating the distributional difference of the data greater than zero and less than zero.

As the symcenter of the whole data, there are two points to consider.

- The data volume on both sides of the symcenter is equal.
- The distribution of data on both sides of the symcenter is identical.

3.1   Binomial Distribution Based Detection

BD algorithm only takes advantage of the first point to realize spectrum sensing. When H_0, the symcenter of $r_{i,j}$ is zero, so there is approximate one half data volume in both sides of zero. The number of the data greater than zero is half of the total data in theory, which equals to $L/2$.

When H_1, the symcenter of $r_{i,j}$ is larger than zero, so the number of the data greater than zero exceeds $L/2$ in theory. Based on the above analysis, we can determine the state of primary user by the means of whether the number of $r_{i,j}$ greater than zero equals to $L/2$. The test statistic for BD method is given as

$$T_{BD} = \sum_{i=1}^{M} \sum_{j=1,j>i}^{M} u(r_{i,j}) \tag{10}$$

where $u(\bullet)$ represents step function. It is obvious that spectrum sensing can be transformed to a hypothesis test problem.

$$\begin{cases} T_{BD} = L/2, H_0 \\ T_{BD} > L/2, H_1 \end{cases} \tag{11}$$

Once the T_B is computed, it will be compared to a predefined threshold λ_B. The statistical test problem transforms into

$$H_0 : T_{BD} \leq \lambda_B$$
$$H_1 : T_{BD} > \lambda_B \tag{12}$$

To derive the false alarm probabilities for the BD detector, the cumulative distribution function (CDF) of the test statistic T_{BD} should be derived under hypotheses H_0. $u(r_{i,j})$ can be seen as a Bernoulli experiment. Therefore, T_B can be seen as $M(M-1)/2$ Bernoulli experiment.

$$T_B \sim B(L, p) \tag{13}$$

where B denotes binomial distribution. p represents the probability of $r_{i,j}$ greater than zero, and then according to the above analysis, $p = 0.5$ under H_0. Hence, the cumulative distribution function (CDF) [9] of T_{BD} is defined as

$$F_B(t) = \sum_{l=0}^{t} C_L^l 0.5^L \tag{14}$$

For the given P_{fa}, the threshold can be obtained as

$$\gamma_B = F_B^{-1}(1 - P_{fa}) \tag{15}$$

- From the received signal matrix $\mathbf{X}$, calculate the sample covariance matrix $\mathbf{R}$ according to (3).
- Count the elements larger than zero from the upper triangle of $\mathbf{R}$ as T_{BD}.
- Find the threshold λ_B for a given probability of false alarm according to (12).
- Accept the null hypothesis H_0 if $T_{BD} > \lambda_B$. Otherwise, reject H_0 in favor of the presence of the primary user signal.

It is worth mentioning that the BD only need count the element larger than zero from $\mathbf{R}$ and does not make full use of $\mathbf{R}$. In other words, BD can get low computational complexity and suboptimum performance.

3.2   Wilcoxon Signed Rank Test Based Detection

In the following, we describe the wilcoxon signed rand test, which is a nonparametric statistical test, based spectrum sensing detector. The WSD algorithm compares the distribution of the measures on the different sides of symcenter. When H_0, the distribution of the measures on the different sides of zero are the same. Nevertheless, when H_1, the two distributions are different.

First of all, obtain the absolute value $|r_{i,j}|$ $(i < j)$, whose total number is L. Renumber those value: $|r_l|$ $(l = 1, 2, , L)$. Then, rank $|r_l|$ and get order statistic $|r|_{(l)}$. Specifically, α_l represents the rank of $|r_l|$, in other words, $|r_l| = |r|_{(\alpha l)}$. If the symcenter of data is zero, the density should be approximately the same on both sides of the data. It further means that the original positive data and negative data should be staggered after taking absolute value. Therefore, the sum of rank of positive data is nearly equal to the sum of rank of negative data in the absolute value.

The test statistic of the WSD algorithm is given by

$$T_W = \sum_{l=1}^{L} \alpha_l u(r_l) \tag{16}$$

Under null hypothesis, the mean and variance of T_W can be expressed as

$$E(T_W) = E(\sum_{l=1}^{L} \alpha_l u(r_l))$$
$$= \tfrac{1}{2} \sum_{l=1}^{L} E(\alpha_l) = \tfrac{1}{4}L(L+1) \tag{17}$$

$$\mathrm{var}(T_W) = \mathrm{var}(\sum_{l=1}^{L} \alpha_l u(r_l))$$
$$= \tfrac{1}{4} \sum_{l=1}^{L} \mathrm{var}(\alpha_l) = \tfrac{1}{24}L(L+1)(2L+1) \tag{18}$$

A large sample modificatory test statistic of the WSD algorithm [10] is given by

$$T_{WSD} = \frac{T_W - \tfrac{1}{4}L(L+1)}{\sqrt{\tfrac{1}{24}L(L+1)(2L+1)}} \tag{19}$$

which under H_0 has a standard normal distribution. Given the required P_{fa}, the decision threshold is determined by

$$\gamma_W = F_W^{-1}(1 - P_{fa}) \tag{20}$$

where $F_W^{-1}(\bullet)$ is the inverse function of $F(\bullet)$ with $F(\bullet)$ being the CDF of T_W.

4   Implementation and Complexity Comparison

Figure 2 shows the procedures of WSD algorithm, BD algorithm, ED algorithm, MME algorithm and CAV algorithm. The computational complexity of calculateing sample covariance matrix is $O(NM^2)$. WSD algorithm need to rank the upper triangle elements of $\mathbf{R}$, whose total number is $L = M(M-1)/2$. The rank complexity is $O(Llog_2(L))$. The complexity of BD algorithms after calculate $\mathbf{R}$ is $O(L)$. In the MME algorithm, a complexity of $O(M^3)$ is required in the calculation of the eigen-decomposition. The complexity of MME algorithm is higher than the proposed algorithms. Although the procedure of ED algorithm is simple, it needs noise power as prior information and is influenced by noise uncertainty. The comparison of computational complexity is given in Table 1.

5   Simulation Results

To evaluate the performance of the proposed BD and WSD sensing algorithm, we have make simulations in MATLAB along with the ED, MME and CAV sensing methods. In the following simulations, $M = 4$, $N = 50$ and false alarm probability $P_{fa} = 0.1$ are assumed. When there is noise uncertainty α, the range of noise variance can be set as $[B^{-1}\sigma^2, B\sigma^2]$, where $B = 10^{0.1\alpha}$.

Figure 3 presents the performance comparison of those algorithms. The performance of ED descends dramatically with the increase of noise uncertainty,

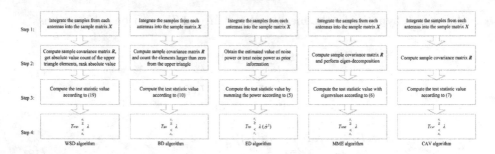

Fig. 2. Procedures of WSD algorithm, BD algorithm, ED algorithm, MME algorithm and CAV algorithm. Note that the knowledge of noise power is required in the ED algorithm.

Table 1. Computational complexity comparison

Algorithm	Computational complexity
WSD	$O(NM^2 + Llog_2(L))$
BD	$O(NM^2)$
ED	$O(NM)$
MME	$O(NM^2 + M^3)$
CAV	$O(NM^2)$

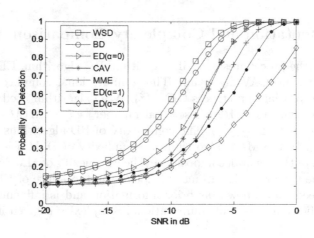

Fig. 3. P_d vs SNR with $P_{fa} = 0.1$ and $M = 4$, $N = 50$

however, other algorithms remains high performance no matter what the noise uncertainty is. It is clear that WSD and BD algorithms perform better than the ED, MME and CAV sensing methods. The WSD algorithm gets optimal performance compared with BD algorithm, which is consistent with theoretical analysis. Figure 4 shows the ROC performance comparison with the WSD, BD, ED, CAV, MME algorithms. There are four antennas and 40 sample points in

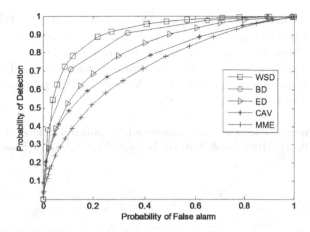

Fig. 4. ROC curves with SNR $= -8\,$dB

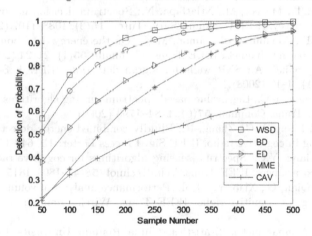

Fig. 5. Detection performances versus sample number with SNR $= -10\,$dB

each antenna. The signal noise ratio(SNR) is $-8\,$dB. It is clear that the WSD and BD algorithms perform better. In order to further compare several kinds algorithms, Fig. 5 gives the simulation performance for P_d at different sample size. The SNR is set as $-10\,$dB. Compared with other algorithm, the performance of CAV algorithm improves slowly with the increase of sample number. In summary, the simulation result shows that the proposed algorithms can reach better performance than traditional algorithms.

6   Conclusion

In this paper, two sensing algorithms based on nonparametric test theory have been proposed for multi-antenna CR system. The upper triangular elements of sample covariance matrix are utilized to calculate test statistics and the threshold is set according to given probability of false alarm. It is worth noting that the proposed algorithms do not need any knowledge of signal and noise. In addition, the computational complexity of BD algorithm is just higher than ED algorithm. Simulation analysis have shown that the performance of the proposed algorithms is much better than ED, MME and CAV.

Acknowledgement. This work was supported by Natural Science Foundation of China (61271276, 61301091), and Natural Science Foundation of Shaanxi Province (2014JM8299).

References

1. Haykin, S.: Cognitive radio brain-empowered wireless communications. IEEE J. Sel. Areas Commun. **23**(2), 201–220 (2005)
2. Masonta, M.T., Mzyece, M., Ntlatlapa, N.: Spectrum decision in cognitive radio networks: a survey. IEEE Commun. Surv. Tutor. **15**(3), 1088–1107 (2013)
3. Digham, F.F., Alouini, M.-S., Simon, M.K.: On the energy detection of unknown signals over fading channels. IEEE Trans. Commun. **55**(1), 21–24 (2007)
4. Tandra, R., Sahai, A.: SNR walls for signal detection. IEEE J. Sel. Top. Sig. Process. **2**(1), 4–17 (2008)
5. Zeng, Y., Liang, Y.C.: Eigenvalue based spectrum sensing algorithms for cognitive radio. IEEE Trans. Commun. **57**(6), 1784–1793 (2009)
6. Zeng, Y.H., Liang, Y.C., Zhang, R.: Blindly combined energy detection for spectrum sensing in cognitive radio. IEEE Sig. Process Letter. **15**, 649–652 (2008)
7. Zeng, Y., Liang, Y.C.: Spectrum-sensing algorithms for cognitive radio based on statistical covariances. IEEE Trans. Veh. Technol. **58**(4), 1804–1815 (2009)
8. Huang, L., Qian, C., Xiao, Y., et al.: Performance analysis of volume-based spectrum sensing for cognitive radio. IEEE Trans. Wirel. Commun. **14**(1), 317–330 (2015)
9. Wang, X.: Nonparametric Statistics. China Renmin University Press, Beijing (2005)
10. Oyeka, I.C.A., Ebuh, G.U.: Modified wilcoxon signed-rank test. Open J. Stat. **02**(2), 172–176 (2012)

Blind Spectrum Sensing in Cognitive Radio Using Right Anderson Darling Test

Yuxin Li[1], Yinghui Ye[2(✉)], Guangyue Lu[1], and Cai Xu[1]

[1] National Engineering Laboratory for Wireless Security,
Xi'an University of Posts and Telecommunications, Xi'an, China
513292504@qq.com, tonylugy@163.com, houstonxc@163.com
[2] State Key Laboratory of Integrated Services Networks,
Xidian University, Xi'an, China
connectyyh@126.com

Abstract. Goodness of Fit tests have been used to find available spectrum with excellent detection performance in Cognitive Radio System. To extend those works, in this paper, we reformulate the spectrum sensing as a unilateral Goodness of Fit testing problem. With difference to previous available works, a random variable that obeys central F distribution with presence of primary user (PU) signal and a non-F distribution with absence of PU signal, which provides technical support for achieving blind spectrum sensing; furthermore, inspired by the thought of unilateral hypothesis test, we apply Right Anderson Darling (RAD) test to achieve bind spectrum sensing and derive a blind spectrum sensing called RAD sensing. Finally, the validness of proposed algorithm is proved by enormous Monte Carlo simulations.

Keywords: Cognitive radio · Blind spectrum sensing · F distribution · Right-Anderson Darling test

1 Introduction

Cognitive radio (CR) is a dynamic spectrum management technology by means of finding "spectrum holes" and making full use of idle spectrum, which is designed to solve spectrum shortage. Spectrum sensing, as a prerequisite and basis technology for CR, is to monitor spectrum state and detect "spectrum holes" in order to avoid interference to the primary user (PU) [1].

To this end, the common spectrum sensing algorithms consist of Cyclostationary Feature Detection (CFD) algorithm, Matched-Filter detection (MF), Energy Detection (ED), eigenvalue based spectrum sensing and Goodness of Fit (GoF) based spectrum sensing [2]. For examples, the PU signal (i.e., signal waveform, modulation, etc.) must be as a prior information, in addition, MF has relatively high requirement for synchronization [3]; ED algorithm is the most common method because of its low complexity, however it is sensitive to noise uncertainty, which results in low robustness and difficulty in setting threshold [4].

© ICST Institute for Computer Sciences, Social Informatics and Telecommunications Engineering 2018
Q. Chen et al. (Eds.): ChinaCom 2016, Part II, LNICST 210, pp. 175–182, 2018.
DOI: 10.1007/978-3-319-66628-0_17

To overcome this difficulty, algorithms based on eigenvalue are proposed such as Maximum Minimum Eigenvalue (MME) [5] and generalized likelihood ratio test (GLRT) [6] based spectrum sensing. The proposed algorithms are free of noise uncertainty but at the cost of high computational complexity.

Recently, Goodness of Fit (GoF) test, as a nonparametric hypothesis test, has been widely used in cognitive radio system via testing whether the received signal comes from the assumed distribution [7–13]. In this case, the spectrum sensing problem is transformed into a GoF testing problem and GoF test (i.e., AD criterion) is used to examine it. To be more explicit, we firstly assume the received signal obeys a particular distribution with the absence of PU signal and deviates from the distribution with the presence of PU signal, and then exploit the GoF test to solve the above problem. For instance, Wang assumes that the PU signals remain the same during the sampling period due to the fact that PU signals are often narrowband signal whose envelope changes very slowly after down-conversion, low pass filtering and sampling at CR system, in such hypothesis, the author first presents Anderson Darling (AD) sensing, where the spectrum sensing is converted into check whether the received signal obeys the normal distribution or not [7]. In addition, the performance of AD sensing is evaluated through enormous Monte Carlo simulations and prove that AD sensing outperforms ED. However, the noise power is needed for AD sensing [8]. To achieve blind spectrum sensing, a new random variable is constructed and the spectrum sensing problem is reformulated as a Students testing problem; then the AD test is used to achieve spectrum sensing [9]. Similarly, the characteristic function is also exploited into spectrum sensing; then a blind spectrum sensing based on characteristic function and AD test (CAD) is proposed [9]. Afterwards, Shen extended it into MISO [10] and MIMO CR system [11]. However, the spectrum sensing algorithms based on characteristic function have heavy complexity compared to AD sensing [7] and Students distribution based spectrum sensing [9].

In this paper, from another perspective to view the spectrum sensing based on GoF test, we extend the above works [7–11] and reformulate the spectrum sensing as a unilateral F distribution testing problem. In addition, we construct a random variable and prove that it obeys a central F distribution when the PU signal is not transmitted and a non-F distribution when the PU signal is transmitted. The constructed random variable provides technical support for achieving blind spectrum sensing since it is free of noise power. Inspired by [14], the AD criterion is suited to two-sided hypothesis test problem due to the fact that the AD criterion gives equal weight to differences between empirical and theoretical distribution functions corresponding to all the observation and the spectrum sensing problem is transformed as a unilateral F distribution testing problem in this paper. Therefore, we apply the Right AD (RAD) criterion [14], which addresses the difference between the empirical distribution and assumed distribution in right tail, to check whether the constructed random variable comes from central F distribution or not and present a blind spectrum dubbed RAD sensing. Finally, the validness of proposed algorithm is proved by the enormous Monte Carlo simulations.

2 System Model

Without loss of generality, spectrum sensing is transmitted as a binary hypothesis testing problem: H_0 denotes the null hypothesis (absence of the primary user) and H_1 stands for the alternative hypothesis (presence of the primary user). To be more explicit, the spectrum sensing mathematical model can be described as

$$\begin{cases} x_i = w_i, & H_0 \\ x_i = \sqrt{\rho}u + w_i, & H_1 \end{cases} \tag{1}$$

Where x_i is the received signal at time i ($i = 1, 2, ..., N$); w_i represents additive white Gaussian noise (AWGN) with mean zero and variance σ^2, that is, $w_i \sim N(0, \sigma^2)$; u is the signals transmitted by PU, ρ meets SNR $= 10 \lg (\rho u^2/\sigma^2)$ and SNR is signal-to-noise ratio (SNR). We adopt the PU signal model in [7–12] and assume that $u = 1$. Therefore, when SNR remains unchanged, x_i obeys Gaussian distribution, that is,

$$x_i \sim \begin{cases} N(0, \sigma^2), & H_0 \\ N(k\sigma, \sigma^2), & H_1 \end{cases} \tag{2}$$

where $k = \sqrt{\rho}/\sigma = \sqrt{10^{0.1 SNR}}$.

3 Spectrum Sensing as Goodness of Fit Testing

Generically, achieving blind spectrum sensing based on GoF test has two steps. The first step is to construct a random variable, which is free of noise variance and has obvious difference between H_1 and H_0, so as to formulate the spectrum sensing as GoF testing problem. The second step is to find a powerful GoF criterion to verify the above problem. In the following, we will obtain a random variable with irrelevance of noise variance and formulate spectrum sensing as GoF testing problem.

First, we divide the received signals $x_1, x_2, ..., x_N$ into $L(L < N)$ parts, each part has $M = N/L$ data. Thus, the mean and variance of l_{th} ($l = 1, 2, ..., L$) sample can be expressed as, respectively

$$\bar{x}_l \overset{\Delta}{=} \frac{1}{M} \sum_{i=1+M(l-1)}^{Ml} x_i \tag{3}$$

$$s_l^2 \overset{\Delta}{=} \frac{1}{M-1} \sum_{i=1+M(l-1)}^{Ml} (x_i - \bar{x}_l)^2 \tag{4}$$

Lemma 1. *Let's denote a new random variable* $T_l \overset{\Delta}{=} \frac{M\bar{x}_l^2}{s_l^2}$, *if* $x_i \sim N(0, \sigma^2)$, *the variable* T_l *obeys the central F distribution with 1 and $M - 1$ degrees of freedom respectively.*

Proof. If $\bar{x}_l \sim N(0, \sigma^2/M)$, it is obvious that $M\bar{x}_l/\sigma^2 \sim \chi_1^2$ after normalization and square. Note that χ_1^2 is central chi-square distribution with 1 degree of freedom and noncentral parameter k^2M. In addition, the random variable $(M-1)s_l^2/\sigma^2$ obeys central chi-square distribution with $M-1$ degrees of freedom according to Cochran Theorem [15]. Based on the above analysis, it is easily obtained that $M\bar{x}_l^2/s_l^2$ has central F distribution with 1 and $M-1$ degrees of freedom respectively, that is, $T_l \sim F_{1,M-1}$.

Lemma 2. *If $x_i \sim N(k\sigma, \sigma^2)$, the variable T_l obeys the noncentral F distribution with 1, $M-1$ degrees of freedom and noncentral parameter k^2M respectively, that is, $T_l \sim F_{1,M-1,k^2M}$.*

Proof. If $\bar{x}_l \sim N(k\sigma, \sigma^2/M)$, it is easily to find that $M\bar{x}_l/\sigma^2 \sim \chi_{1,k^2M}^2$ after normalization and square. Note that χ_{1,k^2M}^2 is non-central chi-square distribution with 1 degree of freedom and noncentral parameter k^2M. Similarly, according to Cochran Theorem [15], the random variable $(M-1)s_l^2/\sigma^2$ obeys chi-square distribution with $M-1$ degrees of freedom. Therefore, it is easily obtained that $M\bar{x}_l^2/s_l^2$ has noncentral F distribution with 1, $M-1$ degrees of freedom and noncentral parameter k^2M respectively, that is, $T_l \sim F_{1,M-1,k^2M}$.

From the Lemmas 1 and 2, when there is no PU signal within the desired frequency band, the random variable T_l comes from the central F distribution with 1 and $M-1$ degrees of freedom; when the PU signal is transmitted within the desired frequency, the random variable T_l obeys the noncentral F distribution with 1, $M-1$ degrees of freedom and noncentral parameter k^2M. Note that the probability density function (PDF) of the noncentral F distribution deviates rightward from the central F distribution.

To sum up, the spectrum sensing can be described as the following GoF testing problem,

$$\begin{cases} T_l \, obeys \, F_{1,M-1}, & H_0 \\ T_l \, deviates \, rightward \, from \, F_{1,M-1}, \, H_1 \end{cases} \tag{5}$$

4   Right-Anderson Darling Sensing

In this section, in order to find "spectrum holes", GoF test is used to examine the above problem that is described in (5) via measuring the distance between empirical Cumulative Distribution Function (CDF) and assumed CDF. Most previous works utilize AD criterion to achieve spectrum sensing due to effectiveness for two-sided hypothesis testing problem. The AD criterion can be written as

$$A_L^2 = L \int_{-\infty}^{+\infty} [G_L(T) - G_0(T)]^2 \frac{dG_0(T)}{G_0(T)(1 - G_0(T))} \tag{6}$$

where L is the number of constructed random variable T_l; $(G_0(T)(1-G_0(T))^{-1}$ is nonnegative weight function. $G_0(T)$ is the assumed CDF; $G_L(T)$ is the empirical CDF and can be calculated by

$$G_L(T) = |\{i : T_i \leq T, 1 \leq i \leq L\}| \tag{7}$$

where $|\bullet|$ is indicates cardinality. From (6) and [14], AD criterion is obviously not the best choice for unilateral hypothesis test since it gives equal weight to both tails of distributions and not utilizes all of unilateral hypothesiss feature(i.e., $G_L(T) - G_0(T)$ is always less than zero in theory when there has transmitted PU signal, in this case, the absolute of $G_L(T) - G_0(T)$ is bound to lead to performance loss). To surmount this problem, based on the AD criterion, Jin et al. [13] proposes a unilateral AD (UAD) criterion using $G_L(T) - G_0(T)$ rather than the absolute of $G_L(T) - G_0(T)$ in (6); furthermore, the author verify that the UAD criterion is more powerful for unilateral hypothesis via Monte Carlo simulation compared to AD criterion. However, the theoretical detection threshold only is gotten via Monte Carlo simulation, which hinder the field of application.

Subsequently, sinclair proposed a more power GoF test dubbed as RAD criterion for unilateral hypothesis via modifying the nonnegative weight function and giving large weight to the right tail [14]. Moreover and fortunately, the author gives the way to calculate accurate theoretical detection threshold and prove that RAD test is more powerful for unilateral hypothesis compared to AD criterion.

In this paper, we select RAD criterion to test unilateral hypothesis due to its effectiveness for testing (5), and apply it to spectrum sensing, yielding a blind spectrum sensing dubbed RAD sensing. The RAD test statistic is given by

$$R_L^2 = L \int_{-\infty}^{+\infty} [G_L(T) - G_0(T)]^2 \frac{dG_0(T)}{(1 - G_0(T))} \tag{8}$$

By breaking the whole integral in (8) into L parts, it is easy to show that it can be rewritten as

$$R_L^2 = \frac{L}{2} - 2 \sum_{n=1}^{L} Z_n - \frac{1}{L} \sum_{n=1}^{L} (2n - 1) \ln(1 - Z_{L+1-n}) \tag{9}$$

where $Z_n = G_0(T_l)$. Once the R_L^2 is acquired, it will be compared with a threshold λ_{RAD} using the following detection criterion

$$\begin{cases} R_L^2 \geq \lambda_{RAD}, H_1 \\ R_L^2 < \lambda_{RAD}, H_0 \end{cases} \tag{10}$$

According to [14], we can find a function to describe the relationship between threshold and false alarm probability (P_f) for RAD criterion. The functions is described as,

$$P_f = 0.889(1.835\lambda_{RAD})^{-1/2} \exp(-1.835\lambda_{RAD}) \tag{11}$$

where the λ_{RAD} is the detection threshold. For a given P_f, we can approximately calculate the λ_{UAD} using formula (11). For examples, when $P_f = 0.05$, $\lambda_{UAD} = 1.303$; when $P_f = 0.1$, $\lambda_{UAD} = 2.060$.

In summary, RAD sensing algorithm can be concluded as follows

Step 1: For a given false alarm probability, calculate decision threshold λ_{RAD}. via formula (11);
Step 2: Compute via formula (9);
Step 3: Make a conclusion according to formula (10).

5   Simulation Results

In this section, simulation is implemented using Matlab and detailed analysis is given in order to compare the performance of five algorithms (i.e., AD sensing, ED method, CAD sensing and RAD sensing, AD-F sensing). Note that AD-F sensing presents that AD criterion is used to test (5). The performance is assessed via the maximum of detection probability in accord with a certain false alarm probability. Note that noise variance is not needed for RAD, AD-F, CAD sensing.

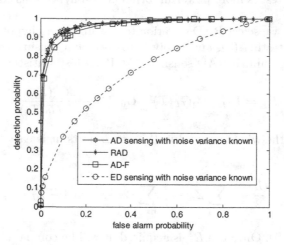

Fig. 1. ROC curves for four methods over AWGN channel with SNR $= -8$ dB, $L = 64$

For assessing the performance of RAD sensing, Fig. 1 gives receiver operating curves (ROC) of four algorithms with SNR $= -8$ dB and $N = 64$ over Additive White Gaussian Noise (AWGN) Channels. As is shown in Fig. 1, AD sensing has the best detection performance among four algorithms. For example, when $P_f = 0.1$, the detection probabilities of AD sensing, RAD sensing, AD-F sensing and AD are about 0.92, 0.91, 0.84 and 0.39 respectively. It is worth noting that RAD sensing outperforms AD-F sensing since the RAD criterion is more powerful than AD criterion for unilateral alternative hypothesis, which is corresponding to a practical case. Note that the noise variance is not needed for RAD sensing and AD-F sensing.

Figure 2 presents the detection probabilities of AD sensing, CAD sensing, RAD sensing with respect to different SNRs for $N = 64$ and $P_f = 0.05$ in the case of quasi static fading channel. In the quasi static fading channel, the channel gain is assumed to obey the standard normal distribution in this simulation. From Fig. 2, on one hand, the performance of AD sensing is also great than RAD and CAD because the noise variance is needed for AD sensing; on the other hand, it is not hard to find that RAD sensing has best detection probability when $L = 1$. Note that with the absence of noise variance, in this case, RAD algorithm has a marginal performance loss compared to AD sensing with the noise known and slightly outperforms the CAD sensing. Note that CAD sensing dose not need noise variance.

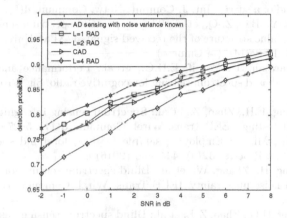

Fig. 2. Detection probability against SNRs for three methods over a quasi static fading channel with $P_f = 0.05$, $L = 64$

6 Conclusion

In this paper, we construct a variable random and formulate the spectrum sensing as a unilateral GoF testing problem. Then a powerful GoF test called RAD criterion is applied to examine it and a blind spectrum sensing dubbed RAD sensing is proposed. Both simulation and analysis demonstrate that the RAD sensing has excellent performance without the need of noise uncertainty. For instance, RAD sensing is better than CAD sensing and has a ignorable performance loss compared to AD sensing. Note that the noise variance is needed for AD sensing but is not needed for CAD sensing. In further, we are interested to extend our work into MISO CR system and MIMO CR system.

Acknowledgement. This work was supported by Natural Science Foundation of China (61271276, 61301091), and Natural Science Foundation of Shaanxi Province (2014JM8299).

References

1. Yinghui, Y., Guangyue, L.: Blind spectrum sensing based on the ratio of mean square to variance. J. China Univ. Posts Telecommun. **23**(1), 42–48 (2016)
2. Yucek, T., Arslan, H.: A survey of spectrum sensing algorithms for cognitive radio applications. IEEE Commun. Surv. Tutor. **11**(1), 116–130 (2015)
3. Bhargavi, D., Murthy, C.R.: Performance comparison of energy, matched-filter and cyclostationarity-based spectrum sensing. In: 2010 IEEE Eleventh International Workshop on Signal Processing Advances in Wireless Communications (SPAWC), pp. 1–5. IEEE (2010)
4. Abdulsattar, M.A., Hussein, Z.A.: Energy detection technique for spectrum sensing in cognitive radio: a survey. Int. J. Comput. Netw. Commun. **4**(5), 223–242 (2012)
5. Lu, G.-Y., Mi, Y., Bao, Z.-Q., et al.: The cooperative spectrum sensing algorithms based on eigenvalue structure of the received signal. J. Xi'an Univ. Posts Telecommun. **19**(2), 1–12 (2014). (in Chinese)
6. He, Y., Ratnarajah, T., Yousif, E.H.G., et al.: Performance analysis of multi-antenna GLRT-based spectrum sensing for cognitive radio. Sig. Process. **120**, 580–593 (2016)
7. Wang, H., Yang, E.H., Zhao, Z., et al.: Spectrum sensing in cognitive radio using goodness of fit testing. IEEE Trans. Wirel. Commun. **8**(11), 5427–5430 (2009)
8. Ye, Y., Lu, G., Mi, Y.: Employing sample features for blind spectrum sensing algorithm. J. Sig. Process. **32**(4), 444–450 (2016)
9. Shen, L., Wang, H., Zhang, W., et al.: Blind spectrum sensing for cognitive radio channels with noise uncertainty. IEEE Trans. Wirel. Commun. **10**(6), 1721–1724 (2011)
10. Shen, L., Wang, H.Q., Zhao, Z.J., et al.: Blind spectrum sensing based on goodness of fit test for cognitive radio in noise of uncertain power. J. Commun. **32**(11), 27–34 (2011)
11. Shen, L., Wang, H., Zhang, W., et al.: Multiple antennas assisted blind spectrum sensing in cognitive radio channels. IEEE Commun. Lett. **16**(1), 92–94 (2012)
12. Shen, L., Chen, P., Wang, H., et al.: Bind spectrum sensing in MIMO cognitive radio channels. Chin. J. Radio Sci. **28**(6), 1110–1115 (2013)
13. Jin, M., Guo, Q., Xi, J., et al.: Spectrum sensing based on goodness of fit test with unilateral alternative hypothesis. Electron. Lett. **50**(22), 1645–1646 (2014)
14. Sinclair, C.D., Spurr, B.D., Ahmad, M.I.: Modified anderson darling test. Commun. Stat.- Theory Methods **19**(10), 3677–3686 (1990)
15. Cochran, W.G.: The distribution of quadratic forms in a normal system, with applications to the analysis of covariance. Math. Proc. Cambridge Philos. Soc. **30**(02), 178–191 (1934)

A Computationally Efficient 2-D DOA Estimation Approach for Non-uniform Co-prime Arrays

Fenggang Sun[1,2(✉)], Lei Zhao[3], Xiaozhi Li[4], Peng Lan[2], and Yanbo Zi[2]

[1] College of Communications Engineering, PLA University of Science and Technology, Nanjing 210007, China
sunfg@sdau.edu.cn
[2] College of Information Science and Engineering, Shandong Agricultural University, Tai'an 271018, China
lanpeng@sdau.edu.cn
[3] Ji'nan Wenwang Center, Jinan 250100, China
[4] Shandong Medicine Technician College, Tai'an 271000, China
lfr1972@sina.com

Abstract. This paper investigates the problem of two dimensional (2-D) directions-of-arrival (DOA) estimation of multiple signals in co-prime planar arrays. The array consists of two uniform planar arrays with their respective inter-element spacing being both larger than half wavelength, which can enhance the resolution but at the cost of phase ambiguity. The phase ambiguity problem can be addressed by combining the results of two subarrays. Specifically, we apply the multiple signal classification (MUSIC) algorithm to each subarray to acquire their respective spectrum; then we obtain the joint spatial spectrum, which is defined as the product of the respective spatial spectrums; Finally, according to co-prime property, we search over the angular field for the spectral peaks to estimate the DOA uniquely. Finally, we verify the effectiveness of the proposed method via simulations.

Keywords: Directions-of-arrival estimation · Two dimensional (2-D) · Co-prime planar array · Phase ambiguity · Joint spatial spectrum

1 Introduction

Over several decades, direction of arrival (DOA) estimation has become a crucial problem in array signal processing and has been widely used in various fields such as radar, sonar, and wireless communications [1–4]. Among various DOA estimation methods, two dimensional (2-D) DOA estimation has drawn a remarkable amount of attention [5–8], because their array models are more practical in actual applications. Traditionally, the most commonly used array is mainly uniform array geometry; however, an appropriate non-uniform array geometry can provide higher estimation accuracy than the uniform geometry [9].

© ICST Institute for Computer Sciences, Social Informatics and Telecommunications Engineering 2018
Q. Chen et al. (Eds.): ChinaCom 2016, Part II, LNICST 210, pp. 183–192, 2018.
DOI: 10.1007/978-3-319-66628-0_18

The history of research on non-uniform array geometry can date back to minimum-redundancy arrays [10]. The introduction of co-prime linear arrays in [11] has created renewed interest in such geometries. A co-prime linear array is composed of two uniform subarrays, which have co-prime integers M and N sensors, respectively and the corresponding inter-element spacings are N and M of half wavelength. It is proved that a co-prime array consisting of $M + N - 1$ sensors can provide $\mathcal{O}(MN)$ degrees of freedom and therefore enhance the estimation performance [11]. Thereby, the co-prime array structure can reduce the cost of array design and motivates the study of DOA estimation with non-uniform co-prime arrays [12–17]. In [12], Zhou $et~al.$ proposed to search over the total angular field for each subarray and uniquely determine the true DOAs by finding the common peaks. To reduce the computational complexity, Weng and Djuric in [13] proposed a projection-like approach to avoid spectral search. In [14], the authors generalized the co-prime arrays from the viewpoint of difference co-array equivalence and verify the performance. In [15], Tan $et~al.$ proposed a super resolution DOA estimation approach for co-prime arrays. Recently, a partial search based method is proposed in [16] to reduce the complexity.

To the best of our knowledge, most of the works on co-prime arrays focus on 1-D DOA estimation and cannot be directly extended to estimate 2-D DOAs. Among various 2-D DOA methods, the classical multiple signal classification (MUSIC) method for 2-D case as [6] can provide a reasonable resolution and is regarded as one of the most popular techniques. In this paper, we study the 2-D DOA estimation method for co-prime planar arrays to enhance estimation performance with reduced complexity.

In this paper, we first formulate the co-prime planar array for the 2-D case, which includes two uniform planar subarrays of sizes $M \times M$ and $N \times N$, and the inter-element spacings for each subarray are N and M times of half wavelength, respectively. Similar to [12], there exist multiple ambiguous peaks for each real DOA in MUSIC spectrum. However, due to the co-prime property, the common peaks correspond to the real DOAs and there are no other common peaks except for the real DOAs. Therefore, we introduce the notation of joint spatial spectrum, which is defined as the product of spatial spectrum of the two subarrays. Accordingly, the joint spatial spectrum generates peaks only at the positions of real DOAs. Consequently, by searching for the peaks of the joint spectrum, the real DOAs can be uniquely estimated with phase ambiguity being removed successfully. We list the main novelty of this paper as follows:

- We formulate a special array geometry of 2-D co-prime planar array, which consists of two uniform subarrays. The non-uniform structure provides higher resolution than the uniform structure.
- We introduce the notation of the joint spectrum, by searching the peaks of which, the DOAs can be uniquely estimated. The proposed method can achieve a better performance-complexity tradeoff.
- We conduct extensive simulations to verify the effectiveness of the proposed method.

The rest of this paper is organized as follows. Section 2 gives the model of 2-D co-prime planar array. In Sect. 3, the proposed 2-D DOA estimation method is presented. Simulation results are provided in Sects. 4 and 5 concludes this paper.

2 System Model

Consider a co-prime planar array geometry that includes two uniform subarrays with size of $M_{s,i} = M_i \times M_i$ $(i = 1, 2)$ sensors, where M_i denotes the sensor number along the x and y-axis of the ith subarray, the integers M_1 and M_2 are mutually co-prime. The spacing of the ith subarray is denoted as $d_i = M_{\widetilde{i}}\lambda/2$, where λ is wavelength and $\widetilde{i} = 1, 2, \widetilde{i} + i = 3$. The sensor elements of the ith subarray are located in the set $L_i = \{(md_i, nd_i), 0 \leq m, n \leq M_i - 1\}$. Therefore, the sensor elements of the entire array are located in $L = L_1 \cup L_2$. Figure 1 shows a specific co-prime planar array geometry with $M_1 = 4$ and $M_2 = 3$. The elements of two subarrays only overlap at the location $(0, 0)$, therefore, the total number of sensor elements is $M_c = \sum\limits_{i=1}^{2} M_i^2 - 1$.

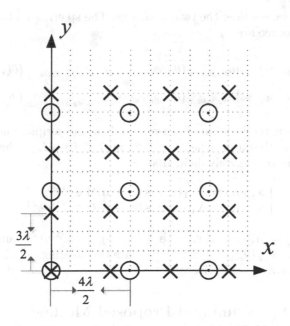

Fig. 1. An example of the co-prime planar array model with $M_1 = 3$ and $M_2 = 4$.

Assume K far-field narrowband sources imping on the array from different directions simultaneously. Specifically, the kth source is from angle $(\theta_k \phi_k)$, where the azimuth angle $\theta_k \in [0, \pi]$ is measured counterclockwise from the x-axis, and the elevation angle $\phi_k \in \left[0, \frac{\pi}{2}\right]$ is the angle between the incident direction and the z-axis.

The signal received by the entire array at time t $(t = 1, 2, \ldots, T)$ is denoted as

$$\mathbf{x}(t) = \mathbf{A}(\theta, \varphi)\mathbf{s}(t) + \mathbf{n}(t) = \sum_{k=1}^{K} \mathbf{a}(\theta_k, \phi_k)s_k(t) + \mathbf{n}(t) \in \mathcal{C}^{M_c \times 1} \qquad (1)$$

where the $M_c \times K$ steering matrix $\mathbf{A}(\theta, \phi)$ is given as

$$\mathbf{A}(\theta, \phi) = [\mathbf{a}(\theta_1, \phi_1), \ldots, \mathbf{a}(\theta_K, \phi_K)] \qquad (2)$$

Here the vector $\mathbf{s}(t) = [s_1(t), s_2(t), \ldots, s_K(t)]^T$ is the corresponding transmit signal vector, and $s_k(t)$ denotes the complex-valued transmit signal for source k; $\mathbf{n}(t) \in \mathcal{C}^{M_c \times 1}$ denotes the additive white Gaussian noise (AWGN) vector with zero means and variance σ_n^2. The steering vector $\mathbf{a}(\theta_k, \phi_k) \in \mathcal{C}^{M_c \times 1}$ is the response with respect to the angles θ_k and ϕ_k. For the sensor at the location (x, y), the corresponding response can be denoted as $a_{x,y}(\theta_k, \phi_k) = \exp(i \sin \phi_k [x \cos \theta_k + y \sin \theta_k])$. Therefore $\mathbf{a}(\theta_k, \phi_k)$ is given as

$$\mathbf{a}(\theta_k, \phi_k) = \left[a_{x_1, y_1}(\theta_k, \phi_k), \cdots, a_{x_{M_c}, y_{M_c}}(\theta_k, \phi_k)\right]^T \qquad (3)$$

As in Fig. 1, we consider the two subarrays. The steering vectors corresponding to the kth source are

$$\begin{cases} \mathbf{a}_{s,1}(\theta_k, \phi_k) = \left[a_{x_{1,1}, y_{1,1}}(\theta_k, \phi_k), \cdots, a_{x_{1,M_{s,1}}, y_{1,M_{s,1}}}(\theta_k, \phi_k)\right]^T, \\ \mathbf{a}_{s,2}(\theta_k, \phi_k) = \left[a_{x_{2,1}, y_{2,1}}(\theta_k, \phi_k), \cdots, a_{x_{2,M_{s,2}}, y_{2,M_{s,2}}}(\theta_k, \phi_k)\right]^T \end{cases} \qquad (4)$$

where $(x_{i,j}, y_{i,j})$ is the location of sensors, and the subscript i and j denote the ith subarray and jth sensor, where $i = 1, 2$ and $1 \leq j \leq M_{s,i}$. Then the received signal vectors are respectively defined as

$$\begin{cases} \mathbf{x}_{s,1}(t) = \mathbf{A}_{s,1}(\theta, \varphi)\mathbf{s}(t) + \mathbf{n}(t) \in \mathcal{C}^{M_{s,1} \times 1} \\ \mathbf{x}_{s,2}(t) = \mathbf{A}_{s,2}(\theta, \varphi)\mathbf{s}(t) + \mathbf{n}(t) \in \mathcal{C}^{M_{s,2} \times 1} \end{cases} \qquad (5)$$

where $\mathbf{A}_{s,1}(\theta, \phi) = [\mathbf{a}_{s,1}(\theta_1, \phi_1), \ldots, \mathbf{a}_{s,1}(\theta_K, \phi_K)] \in \mathcal{C}^{M_{s,1} \times K}$ and $\mathbf{A}_{s,2}(\theta, \phi) = [\mathbf{a}_{s,2}(\theta_1, \phi_1), \ldots, \mathbf{a}_{s,2}(\theta_K, \phi_K)] \in \mathcal{C}^{M_{s,2} \times K}$ are the steering matrices for the first and second subarrays, respectively.

3   MUSIC Spectrum and Proposed Method

To estimate 2-D DOAs, in this section, we first use the classic 2-D MUSIC approach for the two subarrays, where phase ambiguity problem arises due to the larger inter-element spacing. According to the co-prime property, the two spatial spectrums have common peaks only at the positions of real DOAs. Therefore, we can uniquely estimate the DOAs by finding the peaks of joint spatial spectrum, which is defined as the product of the spectrums of the two subarrays.

3.1   MUSIC Spectrum

The covariance matrices of data vector (5) are obtained as

$$\begin{cases} \mathbf{R}_1 = E\left[\mathbf{x}_{s,1}(t)\mathbf{x}_{s,1}^H(t)\right] = \mathbf{A}_{s,1}(\theta,\phi)\mathbf{R}_{ss}\mathbf{A}_{s,1}^H(\theta,\phi) + \sigma_n^2\mathbf{I}_{M_{s,1}} \\ \mathbf{R}_2 = E\left[\mathbf{x}_{s,2}(t)\mathbf{x}_{s,2}^H(t)\right] = \mathbf{A}_{s,2}(\theta,\phi)\mathbf{R}_{ss}\mathbf{A}_{s,2}^H(\theta,\phi) + \sigma_n^2\mathbf{I}_{M_{s,2}} \end{cases} \quad (6)$$

where $\mathbf{R}_{ss} \triangleq E\left\{\mathbf{s}(t)\mathbf{s}^H(t)\right\}$ is the source covariance matrix. In practice, the theoretical array covariance matrix $\mathbf{R}_i$ given in Eq. (6) is unavailable and it is usually estimated by

$$\begin{cases} \widehat{\mathbf{R}}_1 = \frac{1}{T}\sum\limits_{t=1}^{T}\mathbf{x}_{s,1}(t)\mathbf{x}_{s,1}^H(t) \\ \widehat{\mathbf{R}}_2 = \frac{1}{T}\sum\limits_{t=1}^{T}\mathbf{x}_{s,2}(t)\mathbf{x}_{s,2}^H(t) \end{cases} \quad (7)$$

where T is the number of snapshots. The eigenvalue decomposition (EVD) of (7) can be expressed as

$$\begin{cases} \widehat{\mathbf{R}}_1 = \widehat{\mathbf{S}}_1\widehat{\mathbf{\Lambda}}_{1,s}\widehat{\mathbf{S}}_1^H + \widehat{\mathbf{G}}_1\widehat{\mathbf{\Lambda}}_{1,n}\widehat{\mathbf{G}}_1^H \\ \widehat{\mathbf{R}}_2 = \widehat{\mathbf{S}}_2\widehat{\mathbf{\Lambda}}_{2,s}\widehat{\mathbf{S}}_2^H + \widehat{\mathbf{G}}_2\widehat{\mathbf{\Lambda}}_{2,n}\widehat{\mathbf{G}}_2^H \end{cases} \quad (8)$$

where $\widehat{\mathbf{S}}_i$ and $\widehat{\mathbf{G}}_i$ are the estimated signal- and noise-subspace matrices, respectively. The MUSIC [6] spatial spectrum are obtained as

$$\begin{cases} P_{MUSIC,1}(\theta,\phi) = \dfrac{1}{\mathbf{a}_{s,1}^H(\theta,\phi)\widehat{\mathbf{G}}_1\widehat{\mathbf{G}}_1^H\mathbf{a}_{s,1}(\theta,\phi)} \\ P_{MUSIC,2}(\theta,\phi) = \dfrac{1}{\mathbf{a}_{s,2}^H(\theta,\phi)\widehat{\mathbf{G}}_2\widehat{\mathbf{G}}_2^H\mathbf{a}_{s,2}(\theta,\phi)} \end{cases} \quad (9)$$

We plot the MUSIC spectrum of each subarray in Fig. 2. In the next section, we analyze the problem of phase ambiguity, which is caused by the larger distance between adjacent elements.

3.2   Joint Spectrum and Proposed Method

In the two decomposed subarrays, due to the large distance between adjacent sensors, there exists the problem of phase ambiguity [12]. Figure 2(a) and (b) shows the MUSIC spectrum for each decomposed subarray. As can be seen, there exist multiple peaks for each source. The DOA cannot be uniquely estimated by a single subarray. Then we consider combining the results of the two subarrays. For each source, it must generate a peak at the position of real DOA, i.e., there exists at least one common peak for the two subarrays. However, due to the special property of the co-prime structure, there are no common peaks except for the real DOAs. Therefore, we define the joint spectrum as

$$P_{MUSIC}(\theta,\phi) = P_{MUSIC,1}(\theta,\phi) \times P_{MUSIC,2}(\theta,\phi) \quad (10)$$

In the joint spectrum $P_{MUSIC}(\theta,\phi)$, the peaks are only generated at the positions of real DOAs. We plot the joint spectrum $P_{MUSIC}(\theta,\phi)$ as shown

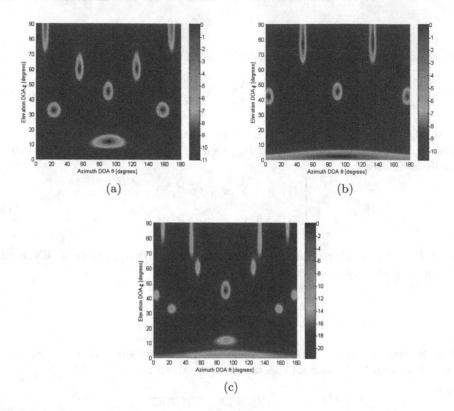

Fig. 2. The normalized spatial MUSIC spectrum with $M_1 = 3$ and $M_2 = 4$: (a) the spectrum of the first subarray, (b) the spectrum of the second subarray, and (c) the joint spectrum. The true DOA of the source is $(\theta, \phi) = (90°, 45°)$.

in Fig. 2(c). It is quite clearly that although there exists the problem of phase ambiguity in each subarray, we can eliminate it by combing the results of each subarray. Consequently, by searching for the peaks of the joint spectrum, the real DOAs can be uniquely estimated.

In 2-D MUSIC based DOA estimation methods, since they all involve a tremendous 2-D spectral search step, the complexity of which is much heavier than that of EVD [18]. Therefore, we approximately compute the complexity in terms of spectral search. The complexity of 2-D MUSIC is roughly denoted as $\mathcal{O}\left(J\left(M_1^2 + M_2^2\right)^2\right)$, where J denotes the number of spectral points over the total angular field. The complexity of the proposed method is about $\mathcal{O}\left(J\left(M_1^4 + M_2^4\right)\right)$. Hence, the computational complexity of proposed method is reduced, as compared to the 2-D MUSIC method.

4   Numerical Results

We validate the estimation performance of the proposed method via simulations in this section. We exhibits numerical results to compare the proposed method for co-prime planar arrays with that of 2-D MUSIC method for uniform planar arrays. The two decomposed uniform arrays of the co-prime planar arrays are of the size $M_1 \times M_1$ and $M_2 \times M_2$, with $M_1 = 3$ and $M_2 = 4$. For fair comparison, the traditional uniform planar array is set with the size of 4×6. The searching interval is set as $0.1°$ for all methods. The root mean square error (RMSE), defined as

$$RMSE = \sqrt{\frac{1}{QK} \sum_{q=1}^{Q} \sum_{k=1}^{K} \left(\left(\theta_k - \widehat{\theta}_k^{(q)} \right)^2 + \left(\phi_k - \widehat{\phi}_k^{(q)} \right)^2 \right)} \qquad (11)$$

is used as the performance metric. Here Q is the total number of Monte-Carlo trials. $\left(\widehat{\theta}_k^{(q)}, \widehat{\phi}_k^{(q)} \right)$ is the estimate result of the kth true DOA at the qth trial, $q = 1, 2, \ldots, Q$. In the section, $Q = 400$ rounds of Monte-Carlo runs are conducted.

First, we consider the case that there exists only one source at the DOA $(20°, 30°)$. Figure 3 shows the RMSE performance of different methods versus SNR when the snapshot number $T = 100$ and $T = 400$, respectively. Figure 4 plots he RMSE performance different methods versus the snapshot number when $SNR = 0\,\mathrm{dB}$ and $SNR = 5\,\mathrm{dB}$, respectively. As is shown, with the increase of SNR and the snapshot number, the RMSE performance of the two methods improves gradually. As compared with 2-D MUSIC, the proposed method

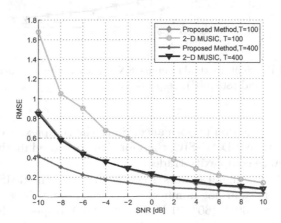

Fig. 3. RMSEs of different methods versus SNR with a single source at the DOA $(20°, 30°)$.

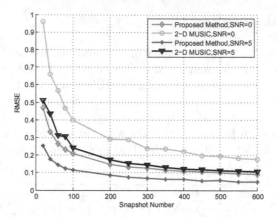

Fig. 4. RMSEs of different methods versus the snapshot number with a single source at the DOA $(20°, 30°)$.

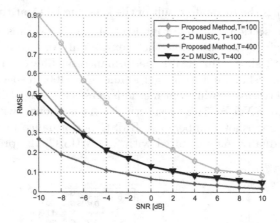

Fig. 5. RMSEs of different methods versus SNR with a single source at the DOAs $(20°, 30°)$, $(60°, 40°)$, and $(80°, 60°)$, respectively.

provides superior estimation performance. Since the complexity of the proposed method is smaller than 2-D MUSIC, therefore, the proposed method can achieve a better performance-complexity tradeoff.

For the case of three signal sources, Figs. 5 and 6 show the RMSE performance versus SNR and the snapshot number, respectively. The three desired sources are at the DOAs $(20°, 30°)$, $(60°, 40°)$, and $(80°, 60°)$, respectively. All the other simulation parameters are the same as the case of one signal source. As can be seen, the proposed method is always better than the 2-D MUSIC method across the whole SNR range and snapshot parameter range.

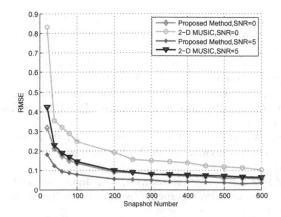

Fig. 6. RMSEs of different methods versus the snapshot number with three sources at the DOAs $(20°, 30°)$, $(60°, 40°)$, and $(80°, 60°)$, respectively.

5 Conclusion

In this paper, we have constructed a special array geometry of 2-D co-prime planar arrays, which can be decomposed into two uniform planar subarrays with the distance between adjacent sensors larger than the half-wavelength. For a single source, there exist multiple ambiguous DOAs in each subarray. To eliminate ambiguity, we introduced the notion of joint spectrum which is defined as the product of the 2-D MUSIC spectrum of the two subarrays. By utilizing the co-prime property, the real DOA can be uniquely estimated by searching for the peak of the joint spectrum. Extensive simulations have been conducted to verify the effectiveness of the proposed method and results are compared with that from the classic 2-D MUSIC method.

Acknowledgment. This work is supported by Key Projects in the National Science and Technology Pillar Program during the Twelfth Fiveyear Plan Period (2011BAD32B02). Shandong Provincial Natural Foundation, China (ZR2017PF007 and ZR2016FB19).

References

1. Krim, H., Viberg, M.: Two decades of array signal processing research: the parametric approach. IEEE Sig. Process. Mag. **13**(4), 67–94 (1996)
2. Wu, Q., Ding, G., Wang, J., Yao, Y.-D.: Spatial-temporal opportunity detection for spectrum-heterogeneous cognitive radio networks: two-dimensional sensing. IEEE Trans. Wirel. Commun. **12**(2), 516–526 (2013)
3. Ding, G., Wu, Q., Yao, Y.-D., Wang, J., Chen, Y.: Kernel-based learning for statistical signal processing in cognitive radio networks: theoretical foundations, example applications, and future directions. IEEE Sig. Process. Mag. **30**(4), 126–136 (2013)

4. Wu, Q., Ding, G., Xu, Y., Feng, S., Du, Z., Wang, J., Long, K.: Cognitive internet of things: a new paradigm beyond connection. IEEE Internet Things J. **1**(12), 129–143 (2014)
5. Liang, J., Liu, D.: Joint elevation and azimuth direction finding using L-shaped array. IEEE Trans. Antennas Propag. **58**(6), 2136–2141 (2010)
6. Chen, Y.M., Lee, J.H., Yeh, C.C.: Two-dimensional angle-of-arrival estimation for uniform planar arrays with sensor position errors. IEE Proc. F Radar Sig. Process. **140**(1), 37–42 (1993)
7. Zhang, W., Liu, W., Wang, J., Wu, S.: Computationally efficient 2-D DOA estimation for uniform rectangular arrays. Multidimension. Syst. Sig. Process. **25**(4), 847–857 (2013)
8. Heidenreich, P., Zoubir, A.M., Rubsamen, M.: Joint 2-D DOA estimation and phase calibration for uniform rectangular arrays. IEEE Trans. Sig. Process. **60**(9), 4683–4693 (2012)
9. Chen, H., Wang, Y., Wan, S.: Performance improvement of estimation direction-of-arrival via array geometry arrangement. In: IEEE International Symposium Antennas and Propagation Society, vol. 3, pp. 1600–1603. IEEE (1999)
10. Moffet, A.: Minimum-redundancy linear arrays. IEEE Trans. Antennas and Propag. **16**(2), 172–175 (1968)
11. Vaidyanathan, P.P., Pal, P.: Sparse sensing with co-prime samplers and arrays. IEEE Trans. Sig. Process. **59**(2), 573–586 (2011)
12. Zhou, C., Shi, Z., Gu, Y., Shen, X.: DECOM: DOA estimation with combined MUSIC for coprime array. In: Proceedings of IEEE International Conference on Wireless Communications and Signal Process (WCSP), Hangzhou, pp. 1–5 (2013)
13. Weng, Z., Djuric, P.: A search-free DOA estimation algorithm for coprime arrays. Digit. Sig. Process. **24**, 27–33 (2014)
14. Qin, S., Zhang, Y., Amin, M.G.: Generalized coprime array configurations for direction-of-arrival estimation. IEEE Trans. Sig. Process. **63**(6), 1377–1390 (2015)
15. Tan, Z., Eldar, Y.C., Nehorai, A.: Direction of arrival estimation using co-prime arrays: a super resolution viewpoint. IEEE Trans. Sig. Process. **62**(21), 5565–5576 (2014)
16. Sun, F., Lan, P., Gao, B.: Partial spectral search-based DOA estimation method for co-prime linear arrays. Electron. Lett. **51**(24), 2053–2055 (2015)
17. Sun, F., Wu, Q., Sun, Y., Ding, G., Lan, P.: An iterative approach for sparse direction-of-arrival estimation in co-prime arrays with off-grid targets. Digit. Sig. Process. **61**, 35–42 (2016). http://dx.doi.org/10.1016/j.dsp.2016.06.007
18. Rubsamen, M., Gershman, A.B.: Direction-of-arrival estimation for nonuniform sensor arrays: from manifold separation to Fourier domain MUSIC methods. IEEE Trans. Sig. Process. **57**, 588–599 (2009)

Low-Complexity MMSE Signal Detection Based on WSSOR Method for Massive MIMO Systems

Hua Quan$^{(\boxtimes)}$, Silviu Ciocan, Wang Qian, and Shen Bin

Chongqing Key Lab of Mobile Communications, Chongqing University of Posts and
Telecommunications, Chongqing 400065, People's Republic of China
huashiquan123@outlook.com

Abstract. Signal detection algorithm based on the linear minimum mean square error (LMMSE) criteria can achieve quasi-optimal performance in uplink of massive MIMO systems where the base stations are equipped with hundreds of antennas. However, it introduces complicated matrix inversion operations, thus making it prohibitively difficult to implement rapidly and effectively. In this paper, we first propose a low complexity signal detection approach by exploiting the weighting symmetric successive over-relaxation (WSSOR) iterative method to circumvent the computations in the matrix inversion. We then present a proper initial solution, relaxation parameter, and scope of the weighting factor to accelerate the convergence speed. Simulation results prove that the proposed simplified method can reach its performance quite close to that of the LMMSE algorithm with no more than three iterations.

Keywords: Massive MIMO detection · Minimum mean square error · Weighting symmetric successive over-relaxation

1 Introduction

In traditional MIMO system, a base station is usually mounted with multiple antennas and simultaneously serves multiple users. This kind of system has been widely utilized in mobile communication to enhance data throughput and link range without demanding additional bandwidth or transmit power [1,2]. Beneficial from this advantage, MIMO technology plays a significant role in the majority of up-to-date wireless communication standards, such as 4G LTE and LTE-Advanced [3]. However, due to the constantly increasing demands for higher data rates, these systems are already approaching their throughout limits. In order to utilize resources more efficiently, reduce interference, improve the transmission rate and robustness, an emerging technique referred to as massive MIMO which employs antenna arrays with a few hundred of antennas at base station is proposed in recent years [4,5]. It has been regarded as an enabler for the development of future broadband wireless networks and the next generation mobile communication systems [6,7].

It is not trivial to establish a practical system to gain the extremely attractive advantages of massive MIMO technology and low-complexity signal detection

© ICST Institute for Computer Sciences, Social Informatics and Telecommunications Engineering 2018
Q. Chen et al. (Eds.): ChinaCom 2016, Part II, LNICST 210, pp. 193–202, 2018.
DOI: 10.1007/978-3-319-66628-0_19

algorithms are of an actual interest in system uplink when the number of single-antenna users is getting tremendously large [4]. Many signal detection algorithms that work very efficiently in conventional MIMO systems fail in massive MIMO systems because of computational complexity or performance. For examples, the complexity of the maximum likelihood (ML) detector, which is optimal among the hard decision methods, grows exponentially with the modulation order and the number of transmit antennas. The fix-complexity sphere decoding (FSD) [8] and tabu search(TS) [9] algorithms are put forward to obtain quasi-optimal performance, but their complexity is not affordable when the configuration of MIMO system is large or the modulation order is high [10]. One has no choice but to turn to linear detection algorithms such as zero-forcing (ZF) and MMSE due to their relatively low complexity and good bit error(BER) performance for multiuser massive MIMO systems [4], but such algorithms still require complexity of $O(K^3)$ for calculating a matrix inversion, where K is the number of single antennas user. Therefore, many efforts have been dedicated to relieving the burdensome high complexity problem for practical detector design.

In [11], Neumann series expansion was proposed to approximate the matrix inversion in LMMSE detection, the performance and computational complexity of which scaled with the number of selected terms of Neumann series. However, when the number of selected terms was larger than two, the complexity of Neumann series expansion method was the same as that of the exact matrix inversion based detection method. In [12], Richardson iteration was proposed to avoid complicated matrix inversion, but the tradeoff between the signal detection performance and computational complexity did not meet expectations. In this paper, we first propose the WSSOR method to avoid direct matrix inversion on the premise of LMMSE filtering matrix is symmetric positive definite in massive MIMO systems and maintain good performance at same time. Then we present a proper initial solution, relaxation parameter and scope of the weighting factor to speed up the convergence rate.

The rest of paper is organized as follows: Sect. 2 introduces the general massive MIMO system model. Section 3 proposes the WSSOR-based signal detector. Simulation results are given in Sect. 4. Section 5 provides a summary of our findings and concludes the paper.

Notations: Lower-case and upper-case boldface symbols are used to represent column vectors and matrices, respectively. The superscripts T, H and -1 respectively denote the transpose, conjugate-transpose and inverse of a matrix. $\mathbf{Tr}(.)$ denotes the trace and $\mathbf{I}_K$ is the $K \times K$ identity matrix.

2   Massive MIMO System Model

Suppose an uplink multiuser massive MIMO system is composed of N receive antennas at the base station and K single-antenna user equipments ($K \leq N$). Let $\mathbf{x}_c = [x_1, x_2, \ldots, x_K]^T$ stand for the vector containing the symbols simultaneously transmitted by all the users, where $x_k \in \mathbb{B}$ is the symbol transmitted from the k-th user and $\mathbb{B}$ is the modulation alphabet. Let $\mathbf{H}_c \in \mathbb{C}^{N \times K}$ represent the channel coefficient matrix, whose entries are assumed to be independently and identically distributed. Therefore, the received signal vector $\mathbf{y}_c$ at the base station can be denoted as

$$\mathbf{y}_c = \mathbf{H}_c\mathbf{x}_c + \mathbf{z}_c. \tag{1}$$

where $\mathbf{z}_c$ is the additive white Gaussian noise vector with its entries follow the Gaussian distribution $\mathbb{CN}(0, \sigma^2)$.

Focusing on the uplink signal detection, when the subscript is dropped for convenience, the complex-valued system model (1) can be written in the real domain as

$$\mathbf{y} = \mathbf{Hx} + \mathbf{z}, \tag{2}$$

where $\mathbf{H} \in \mathbb{R}^{2N \times 2K}$, $\mathbf{y} \in \mathbb{R}^{2N}$ and $\mathbf{z} \in \mathbb{R}^{2N}$.

The task of massive MIMO signal detection at the base station is to detect the transmitted signal vector $\mathbf{x}$ on the basis of the received signal vector $\mathbf{y}$. It is worth mentioning that the channel coefficient matrix $\mathbf{H}$ can be obtained by time or frequency domain training pilots without loss of generality [13,14]. It has been testified that LMMSE detection algorithm is quasi-optimal for recovering the transmitted signal vector $\hat{\mathbf{x}}$ from all the K single-antenna users

$$\hat{\mathbf{x}} = (\mathbf{H}^H\mathbf{H} + \sigma^2\mathbf{I}_{2K})^{-1}\mathbf{H}^H\mathbf{y} = \mathbf{W}^{-1}\mathbf{y}_{\mathrm{MF}}. \tag{3}$$

where $\mathbf{y}_{\mathrm{MF}} = \mathbf{H}^H\mathbf{y}$ is regarded as the matched-filter output of $\mathbf{y}$, and LMMSE filtering matrix $\mathbf{W}$ is described as

$$\mathbf{W} = \mathbf{G} + \sigma^2\mathbf{I}_{2K}. \tag{4}$$

where $\mathbf{G} = \mathbf{H}^H\mathbf{H}$ stands for the Gram matrix. It is worth noting that the exact computation of matrix inversion $\mathbf{W}^{-1}$ needs unbearable complexity of $O(K^3)$.

3   Near-Optimal Massive MIMO Signal Detector with Low Complexity

In this section, first of all, we propose a low complexity signal detection algorithm employing WSSOR without exact matrix inversion. Then we present the proper initial solution, relaxation parameter, and scope of the weighting factor for the WSSOR method, which are able to enhance the convergence rate in the case of high-order modulation. In addition, we analyze the computational complexity of the proposed algorithm in detail.

3.1   Signal Detection Based on WSSOR Method

Inspired by the special characteristics that the LMMSE filtering matrix $\mathbf{W}$ has the property of being symmetric positive definite in massive MIMO systems uplink [15], we can utilize the WSSOR method to efficiently solve Eq. (3) with low complexity. Unlike that the LMMSE signal detector straightforwardly computes

$\mathbf{W}^{-1}\mathbf{y}_{\mathrm{MF}}$, the WSSOR method converts the matrix inversion problem into the one of solving linear equation

$$\mathbf{A}\mathbf{s} = \mathbf{b}, \tag{5}$$

where $\mathbf{A}$ denotes the symmetric positive definite matrix, $\mathbf{s}$ the $N \times 1$ solution vector, and $\mathbf{b}$ the $N \times 1$ measurement vector. The successive over-relaxation (SOR) method [15] can solve the linear equation efficiently in an iterative way. It greatly helps one avoid the complicated matrix inversion calculation and it is entirely different from the conventional method that directly computes $\mathbf{A}^{-1}\mathbf{b}$ to estimate $\mathbf{s}$. Due to the fact that matrix $\mathbf{A}$ is symmetric positive definite, we can decompose it into a diagonal matrix $\mathbf{D_A}$, a strictly lower triangular matrix $\mathbf{L_A}$, and a strictly upper triangular matrix $\mathbf{L_A^H}$. Hence, the iterations of SOR can be represented as

$$\mathbf{s}^{(t+1)} = (\mathbf{A_A} + \frac{1}{\omega}\mathbf{D_A})^{-1}\left[((\frac{1}{\omega} - 1)\mathbf{D_A} - \mathbf{L_A^H})\mathbf{s}^{(t)} + \mathbf{b}\right], \tag{6}$$

where the superscript t represents the number of iterations, and ω indicates the relaxation parameter, which imposes an strong impact on the convergence rate.

Observing that LMMSE filtering matrix $\mathbf{W}$ has the property of being symmetric positive definite in massive MIMO systems uplink, we may decompose $\mathbf{W}$ in another manner as

$$\mathbf{W} = \mathbf{D} + \mathbf{L} + \mathbf{L}^H, \tag{7}$$

where $\mathbf{D}$, $\mathbf{L}$ and $\mathbf{L}^H$ represent the diagonal matrix, the strictly lower triangular matrix, and the strictly upper triangular matrix of the LMMSE filtering matrix $\mathbf{W}$, respectively. By using the SOR method, the transmitted signal vector $\mathbf{x}$ can be expressed as

$$\mathbf{x}^{(t+1)} = (\mathbf{L} + \frac{1}{\omega}\mathbf{D})^{-1}\left[((\frac{1}{\omega} - 1)\mathbf{D} - \mathbf{L}^H)\mathbf{x}^{(t)} + \mathbf{y}_{\mathrm{MF}}\right], \tag{8}$$

where $\mathbf{x}^{(0)}$ is the initial solution of SOR and it is set as a $2K \times 1$ zero vector in general [16]. Consequently, the signal detection problem in Eq. (3) can be solved by SOR method in accordance with

$$(\mathbf{D} + \omega\mathbf{L})\mathbf{x}^{(t+1)} = (1 - \omega)\mathbf{D}\mathbf{x}^{(t)} - \omega\mathbf{L}^H\mathbf{x}^{(t)} + \omega\mathbf{y}_{\mathrm{MF}}. \tag{9}$$

As $\mathbf{D} + \omega\mathbf{L}$ is a lower triangular matrix, we can solve Eq. (9) to obtain $\mathbf{s}^{(t+1)}$ with low complexity and set relaxation parameter ω within value scope $0 < \omega < 2$.

However, when we encounter the more complex problems, very complicated eigenvalue needs to be analyzed. Thus, [17] proposed Chebyshev acceleration and symmetric successive over-relaxation (SSOR). SSOR is the improved method of symmetry of the SOR, whose basic idea is to combine SOR iterative method and backward SOR. The iterations of SSOR can be carried out in the following two steps:

Step 1: Compute the previous half iteration which is identical with the SOR iteration [16] by

$$(\mathbf{D} + \omega\mathbf{L})\overline{\mathbf{x}}^{(t+1/2)} = (1 - \omega)\mathbf{D}\overline{\mathbf{x}}^{(t)} - \omega\mathbf{L}^H\overline{\mathbf{x}}^{(t)} + \omega\mathbf{y}_{\mathrm{MF}}, \tag{10}$$

Step 2: Compute the latter half iteration which is the SOR method with the equations taken in reverse order by

$$(\mathbf{D} + \omega\mathbf{L}^H)\overline{\mathbf{x}}^{(t+1)} = (1 - \omega)\mathbf{D}\overline{\mathbf{x}}^{(t+1/2)} - \omega\mathbf{L}^H\overline{\mathbf{s}}^{(t+1/2)} + \omega\mathbf{y}_{\mathrm{MF}}. \tag{11}$$

where $\overline{\mathbf{x}}$ represents the vector that needs to be estimated in SSOR for the propose of weighting the solution of SOR and SSOR, and $\overline{\mathbf{x}}^{(0)}$ indicates the initial solution of SSOR, which is chosen as a $2K \times 1$ zero vector in particular.

Compared with the SOR method, the SSOR method has two advantages. Firstly, the structure of SSOR method is symmetric, which implies that the convergence rate of SSOR can be improved by using Chebyshev acceleration. Secondly, a simple and quantified relaxation parameter can be employed to approximate a precise relaxation parameter with negligible performance loss, considering the convergence rate of SSOR method is not very sensitive to the relaxation parameter ω. A detailed description of the relaxation parameters is given in the next subsection.

Based on the basic idea of the SOR and the SSOR iterative method, we employ the averaging weight to deal with the vector derived by the iteration of Eq. (9) and the vector derived by iteration of Eq. (11). The WSSOR method can be described as

$$\hat{\mathbf{x}} = \theta\mathbf{x}^{(t+1)} + (1 - \theta)\overline{\mathbf{x}}^{(t+1)}, \tag{12}$$

where superscript t represents the number of iterations, and θ indicates the weighting factor, $\theta \in [0, 1]$. When $\theta = 0$, the WSSOR iteration will degenerate into SSOR iteration; as for $\theta = 1$, it just boils down to the SOR iteration.

Applying the WSSOR method mentioned above to solve the equation. In consequence, we obtain the estimated signal vector in the tth iteration is

$$\hat{\mathbf{x}}^{(t+1)} = \mathbf{B}\hat{\mathbf{x}}^{(t)} + \mathbf{C}, \tag{13}$$

where $\mathbf{B} = \theta(1 - \omega)((\mathbf{D} + \omega\mathbf{L})^{-1} - (\mathbf{D} + \omega\mathbf{L}^H)^{-1})\mathbf{D} + \theta\omega((\mathbf{D} + \omega\mathbf{L})^{-1}\mathbf{L}^H - (\mathbf{D} + \omega\mathbf{L}^H)^{-1}\mathbf{L}) + (1-\omega)(\mathbf{D}+\omega\mathbf{L}^H)^{-1}\mathbf{D}+\omega(\mathbf{D}+\omega\mathbf{L}^H)^{-1}\mathbf{L}$. $\mathbf{C} = \omega(\mathbf{D}+\omega\mathbf{L})\mathbf{y}_{\mathrm{MF}}$, the weighting factor $\theta \in [0, 1]$. Proper relaxation parameter and initial solution will be given in subsection B.

3.2 Proper Relaxation and Parameter and Initial Solution

From Eqs. (9), (11), and (13), it is clear that the setting of relaxation parameter may result in some effects on the convergence rate of the WSSOR method. In [18], the optimal relaxation parameter ω^{opt} has been proposed as

$$\omega^{opt} = \frac{2}{1 + \sqrt{2(1 - \rho(\mathbf{B}_J))}}, \tag{14}$$

where $\rho(\mathbf{B}_J)$ denotes the spectral radius of Jacobi iteration matrix $\mathbf{B}_J$, which can be represented by

$$\mathbf{B}_J = \mathbf{D}^{-1}\mathbf{W} - \mathbf{I}_{2K}. \tag{15}$$

Each element of the diagonal matrix $\mathbf{D}$ will tend towards a fixed value N in massive MIMO systems [4], which indicates that we have

$$\mathbf{D}^{-1} \approx \frac{1}{N}\mathbf{I}_{2K}. \tag{16}$$

Furthermore, as $\mathbf{W}$ is a central Wishart matrix, when N and K are large enough and the system configuration ratio $\beta = K/N$ remains fixed, the largest eigenvalue λ_{max} of $\mathbf{W}$ can be well approached by [4]

$$\lambda_{max} = N(1+\beta)^2. \tag{17}$$

Therefore, we can exploit a simple proper relaxation parameter $\overline{\omega}$ to replace ω^{opt} (14) with insignificant error as

$$\overline{\omega} = \frac{2}{1+\sqrt{2(1-c)}}, \quad c = (1+\beta)^2 - 1. \tag{18}$$

which signifies that the relaxation parameter $\overline{\omega}$ only depends on the system configuration ratio β. The relaxation parameter $\overline{\omega}$ will be a constant in case that the configuration of massive MIMO system is kept as a fixed value.

For convenience, the initial vectors of tradition iterative algorithms are often selected as zero vectors. However, better performance can be achieved by choosing a proper initial solution than zero vectors under the same number of iterations. As $\mathbf{D}^{-1}$ is a very good approximation for $\mathbf{W}^{-1}$ when K/N is large enough, and $\mathbf{G} \approx N\mathbf{I}_{2K}$ according to the channel hardening phenomenon, we can obtain $\mathbf{W}^{-1} \approx \mathbf{D}^{-1} \approx (N + \sigma^2/E_x)\mathbf{I}_{2K}^{-1} \approx N^{-1}\mathbf{I}_{2K}$, where E_x represents the transmission power. Then, the proper initial solution of (12), (13) and (14) can be selected as [19]

$$\mathbf{x}^{(0)} = \frac{1}{N}\mathbf{I}_{2K}\mathbf{y}_{\mathrm{MF}}. \tag{19}$$

3.3   Computational Complexity Analysis

Owing to that fact that number of multiplication is dominant in computational complexity, in this subsection, we evaluate the complexity with respect to the required number of multiplications in each iteration. The whole complexity is mainly composed of two parts. The first part originates from the calculation of Eq. (9), for which the solution can be expressed by

$$\overline{x}_m^{(t+1/2)} = (1-\omega)\overline{x}_m^{(t)} + \frac{\omega}{W_{m,m}}\left(y_{\mathrm{MF}}^m - \sum_{k<m} W_{m,k}\overline{x}_k^{(t+1/2)} - \sum_{k>m} W_{m,k}\overline{x}_k^{(t)}\right), \tag{20}$$

where $\overline{x}_m^{(t+1/2)}$, $\overline{x}_m^{(t)}$, and y_{MF}^m indicate the m-th element of $\overline{\mathbf{x}}^{(t+1/2)}$, $\overline{\mathbf{x}}^{(t)}$ and $\mathbf{y}_{\mathrm{MF}}$ in Eq. (13), respectively. The entry $W_{m,k}$ indicates the mth row and kth column of the matrix $\mathbf{W}$. It is easy to know that the required number of multiplications in the computation of each element of $\mathbf{s}^{(t+1/2)}$ is $K+1$. Due to the K elements in $\overline{\mathbf{s}}^{(t+1/2)}$, the overall number of multiplications needed for this part is $K^2 + K$.

The second part is from the computation of (11). Same as (20), the solution to (11) can be written as

$$\overline{x}_m^{(t+1)} = (1 - \omega)\overline{x}_m^{t+1/2} + \frac{\omega}{W_{m,m}}(y_{\mathrm{MF}}^m - \sum_{k<m} W_{m,k}\overline{x}_k^{(t+1/2)} - \sum_{k>m} W_{m,k}\overline{x}_k^{(t+1)}),$$

(21)

where $\overline{x}_m^{(t+1)}$ indicates the mth element of $\overline{\mathbf{x}}^{(t+1)}$ in (11). According to (11), we can conclude that this part also requires $K^2 + K$ times of multiplications.

In a word, the entire complexity of the proposed WSSOR based signal detector is $t(2K^2 + 2K)$. Compared with MMSE algorithm, the complexity has been reduced from $O(K^3)$ to $O(K^2)$. A comparison between Neumann series expansion and WSSOR about computational complexity is shown in Fig. 1. It is clear that the complexity of proposed WSSOR method is significantly lower than that of the Neumann series expansion after two iterations. When the number of iteration is larger than two, Neumann series expansion based signal detector loses the advantage in computational complexity.

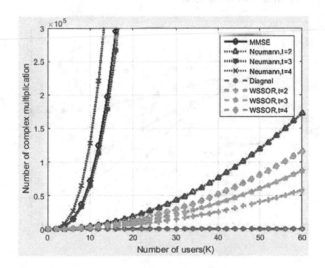

Fig. 1. Complexity comparison against the number of users K

4   Simulation Result

To verify the performance of the proposed WSSOR signal detection algorithm compared with the Neumann series expansion one, we provide the BER simulation results in this section. The BER performance of the MMSE algorithm with exact matrix inversion and just inversion of its diagonal elements are included as the benchmark for comparison. We consider massive MIMO systems with $N \times K = 128 \times 16$. The modulation scheme of 16QAM is adopted and weighting factor θ is chosen as 0.75. In the following simulation diagrams, t will denote the

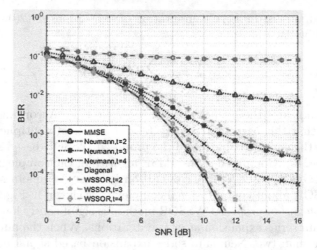

Fig. 2. BER performance comparison between Neumann and WSSOR without proper relaxation parameter and initial solution

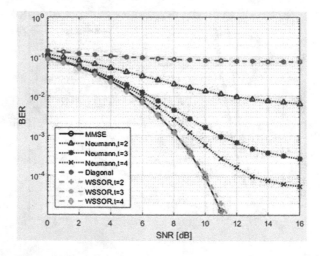

Fig. 3. BER performance comparison between Neumann and WSSOR with proper relaxation parameter and initial solution

number of iterations for the algorithm based on WSSOR method, but the first terms of the algorithm based on Neumann series expansion.

Figure 2 shows the BER performance comparison between Neumann-based signal detector and WSSOR-based signal detector without proper relaxation parameter and initial solution. We can observed from Fig. 2, the BER performance of both Neumann-based signal detector and WSSOR-based signal detector improves when increasing of the number of iterations. However, the proposed algorithm outperforms the Neumann-based one with the same number of iterations t. For example, when $t = 4$, to achieve the BER performance of 10^{-4}, the required SNR by WSSOR-based signal detector just requires 10 dB, while the Neumann-based one is about 14 dB. Furthermore, we can conclude that WSSOR-based signal detector obtains quasi-optimal BER performance of LMMSE signal detector though fewer iterations.

Instead of choosing zero vector as the initial solution and $0 < \omega < 2$, we find a proper initial solution and relaxation parameter in Fig. 3. When the BER performances in Figs. 2 and 3 are compared, it is clear that proper initial solution and relaxation parameter are helpful for accelerating the convergence rate evidently. For instance, the algorithm with proper initial solution and relaxation parameter outperforms the conventional one, especially in cases where the number of iteration t is small. When $t = 2$, the BER performance of the WSSOR method with proper initial solution and relaxation parameter is nearly similar to the one without them when $t = 4$, which implies we can be close to the optimal BER performance of LMMSE signal detector through only a smaller number of iterations.

5 Conclusion

In this paper, in accordance with the special characteristics of massive MIMO systems, we propose a low complexity detection method based on the WSSOR method, which exploits an iterative strategy to detect the transmitted signal vectors without demanding complicated matrix inversion. The complexity has been reduced from $O(K^3)$ to $O(K^2)$. Meanwhile, we present proper initial solution and relaxation parameter, which improve the detection performance and convergence rate. Simulation results illustrate that the proposed algorithm outperforms the Neumann expansion-based signal detector, and achieves near-optimal detection performance via only a small number of iterations.

Acknowlegement. This work was supported by the National Science and Technology Major Project of the Ministry of Science and Technology of China (Grant No. 2015ZX03001033-002).

References

1. Boccardi, F., Heath, R.W., Lozano, A., et al.: Five disruptive technology directions for 5G. Commun. Mag. IEEE **52**(2), 74–80 (2013)
2. Gesbert, D., Kountouris, M., Heath, R.W., et al.: Shifting the MIMO paradigm. IEEE Sig. Process. Mag. **24**(5), 36–46 (2007)
3. 3rd Generation Partnership Project; Technical Specification GroupRadio Access Network; Evolved Universal Terrestrial Radio Access (E-UTRA) Multiplexing and channel coding (Release 9), TS 36. 212Rev. 8.3.0, 3GPP Organizational Partners, May 2008
4. Rusek, F., Persson, D., Lau, B.K., et al.: Scaling up MIMO: opportunities and challenges with very large arrays. IEEE Sig. Process. Mag. **3**(1), 40–60 (2012)

5. Jose, J., Ashikhmin, A., Marzetta, T.L., et al.: Pilot contamination and precoding in multi-cell TDD systems. IEEE Trans. Wirel. Commun. **10**(8), 2640–2651 (2009)
6. Larsson, E.G., Edfors, O., Tufvesson, F., et al.: Massive MIMO for next generation wireless systems. IEEE Commun. Mag. **52**(2), 186–195 (2014)
7. Qian, M., Wang, Y., Zhou, Y., et al.: A super base station based centralized network architecture for 5G mobile communication systems. Digit. Commun. Netw. **1**(2), 152–159 (2015)
8. Barbero, L.G., Thompson, J.S.: Fixing the complexity of the sphere decoder for MIMO detection. IEEE Trans. Wirel. Commun. **6**(6), 2131–2142 (2008)
9. Srinidhi, N., Datta, T., Chockalingam, A., et al.: Layered tabu search algorithm for large-MIMO detection and a lower bound on ML performance. IEEE Trans. Commun. **59**(11), 1–5 (2010)
10. Goldberger, J., Leshem, A.: MIMO detection for high-order QAM based on a Gaussian tree approximation. IEEE Trans. Inf. Theory **57**(8), 4973–4982 (2011)
11. Wu, M., Yin, B., Wang, G., et al.: Large-scale MIMO detection for 3GPP LTE: algorithms and FPGA implementations. IEEE J. Sel. Top. Sig. Process. **8**(5), 916–929 (2014)
12. Gao, X., Dai, L., Yuen, C., et al.: Low-complexity MMSE signal detection based on Richardson method for large-scale MIMO systems. In: Vehicular Technology Conference, pp. 1–5. IEEE (2014)
13. Dai, L., Wang, Z., Yang, Z.: Spectrally efficient time-frequency training OFDM for mobile large-scale MIMO systems. IEEE J. Sel. Areas Commun. **31**(2), 251–263 (2013)
14. Fernandes, F., Ashikhmin, A., Marzetta, T.L.: Inter-cell interference in noncooperative TDD large scale antenna systems. IEEE J. Sel. Areas Commun. **31**(2), 192–201 (2013)
15. Gao, X., Dai, L., Hu, Y., et al.: Matrix inversion-less signal detection using SOR method for uplink large-scale MIMO systems. In: Global Communications Conference (GLOBECOM), 2014 IEEE, pp. 3291–3295 (2015)
16. Bjorck, A.: Numerical Methods for Least Squares Problems. Society for Industrial and Applied Mathematics (SIAM), Philadelphia (1996)
17. Ning, J., Lu, Z., Xie, T., et al.: Low complexity signal detector based on SSOR method for massive MIMO systems. In: IEEE International Symposium on Broadband Multimedia Systems and Broadcasting. IEEE (2015)
18. Bjorck, A.: Numerical Methods in Matrix Computations. Texts in Applied Mathematics. Springer, Cham (2015)
19. Guo, R., Li, X., Fu, W., et al.: Low-complexity signal detection based on relaxation iteration method in massive MIMO systems. Commun. China **12**(Supplement), 1–8 (2015)

Channel Characteristics and User QoS-Aware Handoff Target Spectrum Selection in Cognitive Radio Networks

Hadjor David and Rong Chai[✉]

Key Lab of Mobile Communication Technology,
Chongqing University of Posts and Telecommunications,
Chongqing 400065, People's Republic of China
chairong@cqupt.edu.cn

Abstract. In cognitive radio networks (CRNs), in the case that primary users (PUs) reclaim their channels, the secondary users occupying the spectrum of PUs may have to stop their transmission, waiting at current channel or perform spectrum handoff, i.e., switch to other channels. For handoff SUs, designing target spectrum selection schemes is of particular importance for it may affect the transmission performance and user quality of service (QoS) significantly. In this paper, we study spectrum handoff scheme design for a CRN deployed multiple channels. Jointly taking into account the characteristics of handoff candidate channels and user QoS requirements, we propose a channel characteristics and user QoS aware handoff target spectrum selection scheme for handoff SUs. Simulation results demonstrate the effectiveness of the proposed scheme.

1 Introduction

Static spectrum allocation (SSA) policy, in which fixed spectrum is allocated to licensed users, has been employed for a few decades and has served well in the past when the transmission requirement of wireless applications is relatively low [1]. With wireless and radio communications becoming far more widely used, the efficiency and effectiveness of traditional SSA policy have become highly undesired. The consequential effect is that, whereas, the licensed spectrum bands are substantially underutilized, portions of the unlicensed spectrum are becoming overcrowded, leading to the so-called spectrum scarcity problem.

Cognitive radio networks (CRNs) [2,3] have been identified as the key technology to stress the trade-off between spectrum demand growth and spectrum underutilization by enabling the development of dynamic spectrum access (DSA) mechanisms. In CRNs, unlicensed users, referred to as secondary users (SUs) are equipped with the capability of monitoring spectrum bands occupied by licensed users, i.e., primary users (PUs) and detecting the unused potions or idle periods between successive accesses of PUs, and are allowed to exploit the idle spectrum for data transmission. Through supporting the access of SUs on available spectrum in an opportunistic and dynamic manner, spectrum utilization can be improved significantly.

© ICST Institute for Computer Sciences, Social Informatics and Telecommunications Engineering 2018
Q. Chen et al. (Eds.): ChinaCom 2016, Part II, LNICST 210, pp. 203–213, 2018.
DOI: 10.1007/978-3-319-66628-0_20

As PUs have preemptive right over SUs in the licensed band, in the case that the PUs reclaim their channels, the SUs occupying the spectrum of PUs may have to stop their transmission, waiting at current channel or perform spectrum handoff, i.e., switch to other channels. For handoff SUs, designing target spectrum selection schemes is of particular importance for it may affect the transmission performance and user quality of service (QoS) significantly.

Several research works have addressed spectrum handoff problem or handoff target channel selection problem in CRNs. An M/G/1 queuing network model with preemptive resume priority (PRP) is proposed for CRNs, the waiting delay of SUs at the queue is analyzed and the spectrum with the minimum waiting delay is selected as the handoff channel in [4]. The authors in [5] formulate an optimization problem to proactively determine target channel with the objective of minimizing the cumulative delay per connection for new arriving SU while taking into account the channel switching time and the waiting time resulted from the channel obsolescence. Channel handoff agility is considered in [6], where SUs are only allowed to switch to their neighboring channels, a continuous-time Markov model is derived to analyze the forced termination and blocking probabilities of SUs. In [7], the authors propose a probabilistic approach in determining the initial and target channels for a handoff SU in a CRN, and the optimal channel offering the minimum transmission time is chosen as the handoff target channel. In [8] a dynamic channel selection approach is proposed to reduce connection disruption rate in CRNs.

In this paper, we study spectrum handoff scheme design for a CRN deployed multiple channels and consider the handoff performance of the network over a given time period. Jointly taking into account the characteristics of handoff candidate channels including SUs' waiting time for accessing the channel and channels' available transmission time, and user QoS requirements in terms of interrupting delay and transmission data rate, we propose a channel characteristics and user QoS-aware handoff target spectrum selection scheme for handoff SUs.

2 System Model

In this paper, we consider a CRN consisting of one primary base station (PBS), one cognitive base station (CBS), multiple PUs and SUs. We assume that each PU is allocated one of N licensed channel for accessing the PBS while each SU is allowed to access the licensed channel of PUs in an opportunistic manner.

In this paper, a M/G/1 queuing network model is proposed to characterize the spectrum usage between PUs and SUs [4]. To support the higher priority of PUs over SUs, the queue model is partitioned into two sub-queues, i.e., the high priority sub-queue for the PUs and the lower priority sub-queue for the SUs. The key features of the M/G/1 queuing model are described as follows.

- PUs and SUs may arrive at various channels with different rates. In the case that the channels are busy, users will wait in their corresponding sub-queues, i.e., PUs wait in the high priority sub-queues, and SUs wait in the low priority sub-queues till the channels become available.

- Users waiting in the same sub-queue are allowed to access the channels on the basis of first come first served (FCFS) scheduling scheme.
- To reduce the possibility of call drop, higher priority is given to interrupted SUs over new SUs, i.e., SUs with initial service requirement, thus interrupted SUs will be put before new SUs in the low priority sub-queues.

We assume the arrival process of the kth PU follows Poisson process with the arrival rate being $\lambda_k^{(p)}$ and the service time of the kth PU is exponentially distributed with mean $\mu_k^{(p)}$, $k = 1, 2, \cdots, N$. In this paper, it is assumed that a cognitive management entity, the cooperative centralized network controller (CCNC) is applied to collect user and network information and conduct spectrum selection scheme for SUs (Fig. 1).

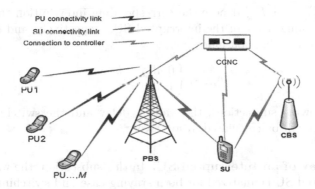

Fig. 1. System model

3   Interruption Delay Constraint and Transmission Time Constraint Formulation

The service of an interrupted SU may pose different QoS requirements on the transmission spectrum. In this paper, we assume each interrupted SU may have different interruption delay and transmission time requirements, which impose constraints on handoff target spectrum. In this section, we formulate the interruption delay constraint and the transmission time constraint of an interrupted SU during a handoff situation.

3.1   Interruption Delay Constraint

In the case that one PU reclaims its allocated channel, the SU occupying the channel should interrupt its transmission, stay at current channel or switch to another channel. For both cases, the interrupted SU cannot resume its data communications until the PUs have completed their transmission, thus resulting in waiting delay. If the interrupted SU chooses to switch to another channel, additional switching delay may occur due to spectrum handoff procedure.

The transmission interruption of an SU resulted from waiting in the channel queue or performing spectrum handoff might be unacceptable for delay sensitive services. Hence, for an interrupted SU, handoff target spectrum should meet certain interruption delay constraint. Denoting $T^{\max}$ as the maximum acceptable interruption delay of the interrupted SU, the kth channel can be selected as the handoff target spectrum of the SU only if it meets the following delay constraint:

$$T_{j,k}^{(\mathrm{I})} \leq T^{\max}, \; 1 \leq k \leq K. \tag{1}$$

Assume that an interrupted SU with initial source channel j chooses the kth channel as its target channel, the corresponding interruption time can be calculated as:

$$T_{j,k}^{(\mathrm{I})} = T_k^{(\mathrm{w})} + \delta_{j,k} T_{j,k}^{(\mathrm{s})} \tag{2}$$

where $T_{j,k}^{(\mathrm{I})}$, $T_{j,k}^{(\mathrm{w})}$ and $T_{j,k}^{(\mathrm{s})}$ denote the corresponding interruption time, waiting delay and switching delay of the interrupted SU, respectively, and $\delta_{j,k}$ denotes the binary spectrum handoff index, i.e.,

$$\delta_{j,k} = \begin{cases} 0, \text{ if } j = k; \\ 1, \text{ if } j \neq k. \end{cases} \tag{3}$$

In the following subsections, the waiting delay and the switching delay of interrupted SU will be calculated, respectively.

Waiting Delay of an Interrupted SU. In this subsection, the waiting delay of an interrupted SU is analyzed for both staying case and switching case.

a. Staying Case
In the case that an interrupted SU chooses to stay on its current channel, it will be put at the beginning of the sub-queue of the SUs and wait until the PUs in the channel complete their transmissions. Hence, the waiting delay can be expressed as the channel busy time due to the transmission of the PUs. Assuming the kth channel is originally allocated to the kth PU, the waiting delay of the interrupted SU can be calculated as:

$$T_k^{(\mathrm{w})} = \mathrm{E}[T_k^{(\mathrm{p})}], \tag{4}$$

where $T_k^{(\mathrm{p})}$ denotes the busy time of the kth channel due to the transmission of the originally allocated PU, $\mathrm{E}[z]$ denotes the expectation value of z, $\mathrm{E}[T_k^{(\mathrm{p})}]$ can be derived as follows.

Denoting $I_k^{(\mathrm{p})}$ as the idle period of the kth channel due to the transmission of the PU, we obtain:

$$\mathrm{E}[I_k^{(\mathrm{p})}] = \frac{1}{\lambda_k^{(\mathrm{p})}}. \tag{5}$$

The utilization factor of the kth channel, denoted by $\rho_k^{(\mathrm{p})}$ can be expressed as:

$$\rho_k^{(\mathrm{p})} = \frac{\mathrm{E}[T_k^{(\mathrm{p})}]}{\mathrm{E}[T_k^{(\mathrm{p})}] + \mathrm{E}[I_k^{(\mathrm{p})}]} = \frac{\lambda_k^{(\mathrm{p})}}{\mu_k^{(\mathrm{p})}}. \tag{6}$$

Combining (4) and (5), we can obtain:

$$T_k^{(w)} = \frac{1}{\mu_k^{(p)} - \lambda_k^{(p)}}. \tag{7}$$

b. Switching Case

In the case that an interrupted SU chooses to switch to another channel, it will be put into the low-priority sub-queue in the target channel and has to wait for the PU or the SU transmitting on the channel to complete its transmission. Furthermore, the interrupted SU also needs to wait for the PUs and the previously interrupted SUs waiting in sub-queues to complete their transmission. Hence, the waiting delay of the interrupted SU can be calculated as the sum of the busy time of the channel due to the transmission of PUs or SUs, and the remaining service time of the channel, i.e.,

$$T_k^{(w)} = \frac{1}{2}E[T_k^{(p)}] + \frac{1}{2}E[T_k^{(s)}] + E[T_k^{(r)}], \tag{8}$$

where $T_k^{(s)}$ denotes the transmission time of an existing SU on the kth channel, and $T_k^{(r)}$ denotes the remaining service time of users on the kth channel. $E[T_k^{(s)}]$ can be calculated as:

$$E[T_k^{(s)}] = \frac{1}{\mu_k^{(s)} - \lambda_k^{(s)}}. \tag{9}$$

$E[T_k^{(r)}]$ in (7) can be calculated as:

$$E[T_k^{(r)}] = \frac{\lambda_n^{(p)}}{\left(\mu_n^{(p)}\right)^2} + \frac{\lambda_k^{(s)}}{\left(\mu_k^{(s)}\right)^2}. \tag{10}$$

Switching Delay of an Interrupted SU. In the case that an interrupted SU decides to switch from the jth channel to the kth channel, intra-system or inter-system handoff may occur as the jth channel and the kth channel may belong to the same CRN or different CRNs. For both cases, the SU may conduct the handoff procedure proactively or reactively, resulting in four types of handoff. The corresponding switching delay can be examined, respectively.

a. Proactive and Intra-system Handoff:

Denoting $T^{(s,1)}$ as the switching delay of proactive and intra-system handoff, we obtain:

$$T^{(s,1)} = t_{syn}^{sen} + t_{sen} + t_{dec} + t_{switch} + t_{syn}^{tx}, \tag{11}$$

where t_{syn}^{sen} denotes the synchronization time for spectrum sensing, t_{sen} denotes the time period for sensing spectrum resource, t_{dec} denotes the time period for determining a target handoff spectrum, t_{switch} denotes the time required for switching from current channel to the target channel, and t_{syn}^{tx} denotes the time required for synchronizing to the transmission slots in the target channel.

b. Proactive and Inter-system Handoff: In the case that a proactive handoff is performed between two heterogeneous CRNs, the reconfiguration of radio frequency (RF) front end is required. Denoting the time required for reconfiguration as t_{recfg}, the resulted switching delay denoted by $T^{(s,2)}$ can be expressed as:

$$T^{(s,2)} = t_{\text{recfg}} + T^{(s,1)}. \tag{12}$$

c. Reactive and Intra-system Handoff: In the case that a reactive handoff is performed inside one CRN, a handoff preparation time, denoted by t_{prep} is required to collect measurement information and determine the handoff spectrum, thus, the resulted switching delay denoted by $T^{(s,3)}$ can be expressed as:

$$T^{(s,3)} = t_{\text{prep}} + T^{(s,1)}. \tag{13}$$

d. Reactive and Inter-system Handoff: In the case that a reactive handoff is performed between two heterogeneous CRNs, both handoff preparation and reconfiguration of RF front end are required. As a result, the switching delay denoted by $T^{(s,4)}$ can be expressed as:

$$T^{(s,4)} = t_{\text{recfg}} + T^{(s,3)}. \tag{14}$$

3.2   Remaining Transmission Time Examination

In the case that the available transmission time on the current channel does not meet the requirement of the SU, there is a possibility of future interruptions. To reduce the number of subsequent spectrum switches, the remaining transmission time, i.e., the transmission time required for the SU to complete its transmission and the available transmission time of candidate spectrum are examined and compared in transmission time constraint.

Denoting L^0 and L^t as the length of original data packets and that of transmitted packets before interruption, respectively, and L as the length of un-transmitted data packets of the interrupted SU. i.e.,

$$L = L^0 - L^t \tag{15}$$

The expected length of time required by the interrupted SU to complete its remaining transmission on the kth candidate channel, denoted by $T_k^{(t)}$ can be calculated as:

$$T_k^{(t)} = \frac{L}{R_k} \tag{16}$$

where R_k is the data rate on the kth channel and can be expressed as:

$$R_k = B_k \log_2\left(1 + \frac{P|h_k|^2}{\sigma^2}\right) \tag{17}$$

where B_k is the bandwidth of the kth channel, P denotes the transmit power of the interrupted SU, h_k and σ^2 denote respectively the transmission gain and the noise power of the link from the interrupted SU to its CBS on the kth channel.

Denoting T_k^{av} as the available transmission time useable by the SU on the kth channel, the transmission time constraint can be expressed as:

$$T_k^{(\mathrm{t})} \leq T_k^{(\mathrm{av})}. \tag{18}$$

4   Proposed Handoff Spectrum Selection Scheme

The proposed handoff spectrum selection scheme consists of two functional levels, i.e., interruption delay constraint-based spectrum selection, and available transmission time constraint-based spectrum selection. The detail description of the proposed scheme will be presented in the following subsections.

4.1   Staying on Current Channel

Given that channel switching upon interruption can be costly, we propose a scheme in which, an interrupted SU first considers the possibility of staying on its default channel so as to resume its transmission after the holding time of the interrupting PU provided its current channel meets interruption delay constraint and transmission time constraint. For an interrupted SU with the original channel being j, the interruption delay constraint can be expressed as:

$$T_{j,j}^{(\mathrm{I})} \leq T^{\mathrm{max}} \tag{19}$$

In the case that above constraint meets, we further examine the transmission time constraint on current channel, i.e.,

$$T_j^{(\mathrm{t})} \leq T_j^{\mathrm{av}}. \tag{20}$$

If (20) also holds, the interrupted SU will choose to stay on current channel and resume its transmission after the PU has completed its transmission on current channel.

In the case that constraint in (19) fails to meet, the interrupted SU will examine the characteristics of other channels and consider performing spectrum handoff, as discussed in following subsection. In the case that constraint in (19) meets while constraint in (20) fails to meet, the interrupted SU will jointly examine the characteristics of current channel and other channels, based on which a spectrum selection strategy can be made.

4.2   Interruption Delay Constraint Based Spectrum Selection

In a situation where the current operating channel fails to meet the constraints of the SU, the need to consider switching to a new channel other than the current channel may arise. For the kth channel, the interrupted SU needs to examine interruption delay constraint, i.e., check whether (1) holds. We let M denote the set of candidate channels that meet the interruption delay constraint in (1). According to the value of M, following three cases should be considered.

Case 1: $M = 0$, meaning no channel meets the interruption delay constraint of the interrupted SU, hence, the handoff fails.

Case 2: $M = 1$, indicating only one candidate channel meets the interruption delay constraint of the interrupted SU, hence, this channel is selected as the handoff channel of the SU.

Case 3: $M > 0$, i.e., more than one candidate channel meets the interruption delay constraint of the interrupted SU, the SU will further examine the transmission time constraint of these candidate channels and then select the optimal channel.

4.3   Transmission Time Constraint Based Spectrum Selection

Assume the kth channel meets the interruption delay constraint of the interrupted SU, the SU can then examine the transmission time constraint of the channel according to (18). We let Z denote the number of candidate channels that jointly satisfy user service constraints in (1) and (18), depending on the value of Z, three cases may arise:

Case 1: $Z = 0$, i.e., no single candidate channel jointly meets the constraints in (1) and (18), thus, the SU will have to perform further spectrum handoff. In this case, we propose a maximum transmission amount based spectrum selection strategy in which the SU selects a channel that can transmit the highest amount of bits within the available transmission time. Therefore, the channel k* is selected as the target channel which meets:

$$k^* = \arg\ \max(T_k^{\mathrm{av}} R_k),\ \ k = 1, 2 \ldots, N. \tag{21}$$

Case 2: $Z = 1$, indicating only one candidate channel jointly satisfies the constraints in (1) and (18), therefore, the user simply chooses it as handoff target channel.

Case 3: $Z > 1$, indicating multiple candidate channels jointly satisfy the interruption delay constraint and the transmission time constraint. In this case, we propose a maximum data rate based spectrum selection strategy, i.e., selecting the channel with the best transmission rate as target channel for handoff. Hence the k* channel is chosen if:

$$k^* = \arg\ \max(R^k),\ \ k = 1, 2 \ldots, N. \tag{22}$$

5   Simulation Results

In this section, we examine the performance of the proposed spectrum selection scheme. The simulation experiments are carried out through MATLAB software. In our simulation, we assume 2 to 10 ($M = 2 - 10$) channels each assigned to a licensed user. The simulation time is chosen as a number of time slots with the duration of each time slot being 5.77×10^{-4} s. $\lambda_k^{(\mathrm{p})}$ and $\mu_k^{(\mathrm{p})}$ are chosen as 0.5 and 4, respectively. Table 1 shows other parameters used in our simulation.

Table 1. Simulation parameters

Parameter	Value
Transmission power of SU	0.6 W
Interruption delay threshold of SU	$9 \cdot 232 \times 10^{-3}$ s
Radius of coverage Network	50 m
Network Bandwidth	2 MHz
Number of slots per channel	512
Packet length of SU	18×10^5 bits
Power of noise	−60 dBm

Averaging over 1000 simulations, the results of our proposed channel selection scheme are shown in the figures below.

Figure 2 shows the average number of handoff versus the packet length of SU. It can be observed that the number of handoff increases as the packet length grows. The reason is that longer transmission time is required for larger number of packets, thus may need multiple handoff. It can also be seen that the rate of handoff reduces with the increase in the number of available channels. This is because when the number of available channel increases, the probability of finding a channel that meets SU constraints becomes high.

Figure 3 shows the transmission time and the mean interruption of SU versus the number of channels. It can be seen that the two performance metrics behave in a similar way, i.e., both decline with the increase in the number of available channels. As the number of candidate channels increases, the probability that a user will find a channel that meets its transmission constraint is relatively high leading to less subsequent interruptions, hence the decline in the interruption delay, which is also reflected in the decreasing of total transmission time.

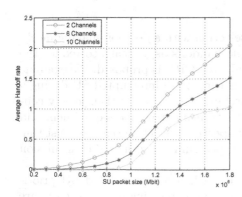

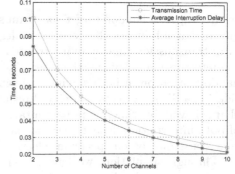

Fig. 2. Average number of handoff versus the packet size of SU

Fig. 3. Transmission time and average waiting delay versus number of channels

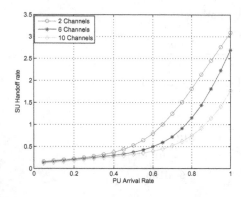
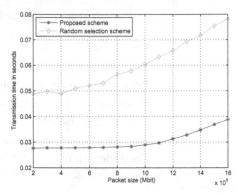

Fig. 4. Average number of handoff versus the arrival rate of PU

Fig. 5. Transmission time versus the arrival rate of PU

Figure 4 shows the average number of handoff versus the arrival rate of PUs. It can be observed that the average number of handoff increases with the increase in the arrival rate of PUs and the handoff rate reduces with the increase in the number of available channels, this is because when there are multiple channels available, SU can suitably find a target channel that meets its constraints such that the need for further interruptions and switching becomes relatively low, thus keeping handoff rate relatively small.

In Fig. 5, we compare the total transmission time in the proposed scheme and a random choice channel selection. Both transmission times decline with increase in the number of available channels, however, it can be seen from that the proposed scheme offers smaller total transmission time in comparison with a random choice channel selection.

6   Conclusions

In this paper, a handoff target spectrum selection with a decision-making mechanism that minimizes the need for multiple handoffs as a means to reduce the total transmission time of an interrupted SU in a CRN is proposed. We examine the interruption delay and the transmission time of an interrupted SU during a handoff situation in both staying and switching scenarios and then jointly considering a SU's interruption delay threshold, transmission time requirement and channel available time, we present a target spectrum selection scheme consisting of both interruption delay constraint-based spectrum selection and transmission time constraint-based spectrum selection.

Through simulation, we have shown that when an interrupted SU prioritizes staying on the default channel, switching and signaling overhead costs are eliminated thereby reducing the total service time. We have also shown that, when handoff is possible, if the SU considers only channels with relatively minimal interruption delay and, therefore, selects only candidate channels that offer desired transmission time as target channels, by jointly considering the SU's remaining transmission time and the transmission time available on the candidate channel: the number of future spectrum handoffs is considerably reduced thereby enhancing the performance of the SU.

Acknowledgement. This work is supported by the National Science and Technology Specific Project of China (2016ZX03001010-004) and the 863 project (2014AA01A701).

References

1. Federal Communications Commission: ET Docket No. 03–322, December 2003
2. Mitola, J., Maguire, J.G.Q.: Cognitive radio: making software radios more personal. IEEE Pers. Commun. **6**, 13–18 (1999)
3. Mitola, J.: Cognitive radio: an integrated agent architecture for software defined radio. Ph.D. thesis, Royal Institute of Technology (KTH), Sweden (2000)
4. Wang, L.C., Wang, C.W., Chang, C.J.: Modeling and analysis for spectrum handoffs in cognitive radio networks. IEEE Trans. Mob. Comput. **11**, 1499–1513 (2012)
5. Wang, L.C., Wang, C.W., Chang, C.J.: Optimal target channel sequence design for multiple spectrum handoffs in cognitive radio networks. IEEE Trans. Commun. **60**(9), 2444–2455 (2012)
6. NoroozOliaee, M., Hamdaoui, B., Cheng, X., Znati, T., Guizani, M.: Analyzing cognitive network access efficiency under limited spectrum handoff agility. IEEE Trans. Veh. Technol. **63**, 1402–1407 (2014)
7. Sheikholeslami, F., Nasiri-Kenari, M., Ashtiani, F.: Optimal probabilistic initial and target channel selection for spectrum handoff in cognitive radio networks. IEEE Trans. Wirel. Commun. **14**, 570–584 (2015)
8. Kahvand, M., Soleimani, M.T., Dabiranzohouri, M.: Channel selection in cognitive radio networks: a new dynamic approach. In: 2013 IEEE Malaysia International Conference in Communications (MICC), pp. 407–411 (2013)

Heterogeneous Networks

A Tractable Traffic-Aware User Association Scheme in Heterogeneous Networks

Xiaobing Lin, Kun Yang, and Xing Zhang[✉]

Wireless Signal Processing and Network Laboratory,
Key Lab of Universal Wireless Communications, Ministry of Education,
Beijing University of Posts and Telecommunications, Beijing, China
hszhang@bupt.edu.cn

Abstract. In Heterogeneous networks (HetNets), the power difference between macro base stations (MBSs) and small base stations (SBSs) causes severe load unbalance. Therefore, cell range expansion (CRE) is proposed as an effective method to extend the coverage of SBSs and achieve balanced utilization of BSs. However, the downlink (DL) quality for offloaded user equipment (UE) cannot be guaranteed. In this paper, a traffic aware user association scheme is proposed in HetNets. Distinct association biases are applied to different UEs according to their requirements. System performance of the proposed scheme is analyzed using the tool of stochastic geometry. The results show that the proposed scheme can improve DL throughput by enhancing the rate coverage of UEs, meanwhile signal-to-interference-plus-noise ratio (SINR) requirement with low data rate demand UEs is ensured. Moreover, the optimal association bias, which maximizes DL throughput, can be derived through particle swarm optimization (PSO), and it changes with different densities of BSs and UEs.

Keywords: Traffic demand · User association · Cell range expansion · System capacity · Heterogeneous networks

1 Introduction

With the rapid development of smart terminals, cellular networks face an overwhelming growth in data traffic [1,2]. To satisfy the extremely high data demand, HetNets are proposed to improve the coverage and throughput of wireless communication systems [3,4]. The SBSs in HetNets can provide network access for closer users and offload the data traffic from MBSs to earn traffic offloading gains. However, the transmit power of MBSs is always larger than that of SBSs, the conventional association policy of reference signal receiving power (RSRP) [5] leads to unbalanced load. Hence, CRE, which allows a UE to access in SBSs with lower DL SINR, was proposed as an effective method to extend the coverage of SBSs and achieve load balance.

Several studies have addressed the application of CRE. In [6], the authors focused on the joint transmission of DL and uplink (UL), and derived the transmission success probability and energy efficiency (EE) using stochastic geometry.

© ICST Institute for Computer Sciences, Social Informatics and Telecommunications Engineering 2018
Q. Chen et al. (Eds.): ChinaCom 2016, Part II, LNICST 210, pp. 217–226, 2018.
DOI: 10.1007/978-3-319-66628-0_21

Authors of [7] concerned with the cell edge users and presented an adaptive CRE algorithm to improve the cell edge user throughput in HetNets. A scheme with rate-based CRE offset was proposed in [8], which adjusts the CRE offset according to the ratio of a user's UL and DL data demands. In [9], a Pico-specific upper bound CRE bias estimation algorithm for HetNets was proposed. However, these papers neglect the fact that the types and needs of UEs grow rapidly in fifth generation (5G) scenario, traffic demand for UEs should be considered.

In this paper, a tractable traffic-aware user association (TUA) scheme is proposed in HetNets, where distinct association biases are applied to UEs according to different user traffic demands. The main contributions are as follows:

- Proposed scheme is able to balance system loads by offloading some high traffic demand UEs from MBSs to SBSs for better rate coverage, while ensuring the SINR coverage of low traffic demand UEs. Furthermore, proposed scheme can improve rate performance of UEs and enhance system DL throughput compared to traditional RSRP association.
- The expression of SINR coverage, rate coverage, and system DL throughput are derived theoretically using the tool of stochastic geometry.
- The optimal association bias factor θ^*_{S,u_H}, which can maximize DL throughput, can be derived through particle swarm optimization (PSO). Numerical results show that either UE density or BS density has an effect on θ^*_{S,u_H}.

2   System Model

In this paper, a 2-tier HetNet consisting MBSs and SBSs is considered. The position of BSs are modeled according to an independent homogeneous Poisson Point Processes (PPP) Φ_v with intensity λ_v, where $v = M$ for MBS, and $v = S$ for SBS. UEs are divided into high data rate UEs and low data rate UEs according to different traffic types. For example, UEs with voice demand are low data rate UEs, and UEs with video demand are high data rate UEs. It is also assumed that all kinds of UEs are located as independent PPP Φ_u with intensity λ_u, where $u = u_H$ for high data rate UEs, and $u = u_L$ for low data rate UEs.

BSs in the same tier have the same transmit power P_v over bandwidth W. Assumed that downlink signals experience path loss with a path loss exponent α, where $\alpha > 2$. The fading between a BS and a UE is assumed to be Rayleigh fading with unit average power, i.e. $h \sim \exp(1)$. Interference signals arise from all other BSs except the serving BS, and there is no intra-cell interference, e.g. orthogonal multiple access is applied within a BS area [5].

2.1   Traffic-Aware User Association Scheme

In traditional RSRP association method [5], all UEs are associated with the serving BSs offering the maximum received power. However, in RSRP mode, MBSs have bigger coverage area than SBSs because of much higher transmit power, which causes unbalanced loads of BSs. Besides, different UEs have characteristic requirements. For u_L, it is easy to achieve user demand, it is also important to ensure high signal-to-interference-plus-noise (SINR) quality and make data traffic reliable. For u_H, high data rate transmission is a key requirement. In proposed TUA scheme, different UEs use diverse association biases. Specifically, the SBS coverage area for u_L remains unchanged, while the SBS coverage area for u_H is expanded. That means u_L are connected to the serving BSs offering maximum DL received power for best SINR quality, while u_H are associated with BSs based on biased received power to have a probability of offloading from MBS to SBS. The TUA scheme can be expressed respectively as follows

$$\begin{cases} if \ P_M\theta_{M,u}\|x_M\|^{-\alpha} > P_S\theta_{S,u}\|x_S\|^{-\alpha} \ \ then \ to \ MBS \\ if \ P_M\theta_{M,u}\|x_M\|^{-\alpha} < P_S\theta_{S,u}\|x_S\|^{-\alpha} \ \ then \ to \ SBS \end{cases}, \qquad (1)$$

where $\|x_v\|$ is the distance between a UE to its nearest BS in vth tier, and $\theta_{v,u}$ is the association bias factor of different UEs u in vth tier. In TUA scheme, we have

$$\theta_{M,u_L} = \theta_{S,u_L} = 1, \ and \ \ \frac{\theta_{S,u_H}}{\theta_{M,u_H}} > 1. \qquad (2)$$

Figure 1 illustrates the DL UE association with TUA scheme in HetNets. The biggest solid circle presents the MBS coverage area for higher transmit power of MBS. According to the association rule of TUA scheme, the SBS coverage area for UEs with different data rate demands differs. The smallest solid circle is the SBS coverage area for u_L, while the dotted circle is the expanded SBS coverage area for u_H. As shown in Fig. 1, some u_H, e.g. UE1, are offloaded from MBS to SBS for high achieved rate and also system balance.

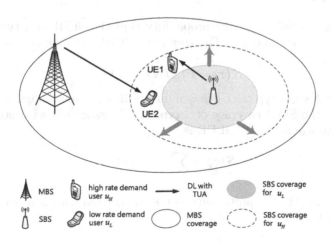

Fig. 1. An illustration of UE association with TUA scheme in HetNets.

2.2 SINR Model

According to Slivnyak's theorem [10], a typical UE located at origin is analyzed. Because all BSs are assumed to use the same bandwidth, the DL interference comes from all BSs except the serving BS, which can be modeled as a PPP Φ_I with a density of $\lambda_I = \sum_v \lambda_v$. Hence, the SINR of a typical UE connected with vth tier is written as

$$SINR_v = \frac{P_v h_{x_v} \|x_v\|^{-\alpha}}{\sum\limits_{y_i \in \Phi_I} P_i h_{y_i} \|y_i\|^{-\alpha} + \sigma^2}, \tag{3}$$

where $\|y_i\|$ is the distance from interference BSs of ith tier to the typical UE, and σ^2 is the constant additive noise power.

3 System Performance Analysis

In this section, we mainly analyze the SINR coverage, rate coverage, and DL throughput. Especially, DL throughput can be given as

$$DL\,Throughput = \sum_{u \in \Phi_u} R_u, \tag{4}$$

where R_u is the achievable traffic rate of UEs.

3.1 SINR Coverage

SINR coverage is defined as the probability that the SINR of a typical UE is larger than SINR threshold τ. Therefore, the SINR coverage can be expressed by definition as

$$S\left(\tau\right) = \mathbb{P}\left(SINR > \tau\right). \tag{5}$$

In the HetNets, a typical UE has multiple BSs to connect with. Hence, let $S_v\left(\tau\right)$ defines the SINR coverage of a typical UE associated with vth tier, and the SINR coverage for a typical UE is

$$S\left(\tau\right) = \sum_v A_v S_v\left(\tau\right). \tag{6}$$

According to [11], the probability of UEs associated with vth tier in DL can be derived as bellows

$$A_v^u = \frac{\lambda_v}{\sum\limits_{i \in \{M,S\}} \lambda_i \left(\frac{P_i}{P_v} \hat{\theta}_{i,u}\right)^{2/\alpha}}, \tag{7}$$

where $\hat{\theta}_{i,u} = \frac{\theta_{i,u}}{\theta_{v,u}}$.

Let D_v^u denotes the distance from a typical UE u to its DL serving BS in vth tier, and the probability distribution function (PDF) of D_v^u can be written as [11]

$$f_{D_v^u}(r) = \frac{2\pi\lambda_v}{A_v^u} r \exp\left\{-\pi r^2 \sum_{i\in\{M,S\}} \lambda_i \left(\frac{P_k}{P_v}\hat{\theta}_{k,u}\right)^{2/\alpha}\right\}. \tag{8}$$

Theorem 1. *The DL SINR coverage of a typical UE $u \in \{u_L, u_H\}$ can be given as*

$$\mathcal{S}^u(\tau) = \sum_v 2\pi\lambda_v \int_{r>0} r \exp\left\{-r^\alpha P_v^{-1}\tau\sigma^2\right.$$
$$\left.-\pi r^2\left(\sum_{i\in\{M,S\}} \lambda_i\left(\frac{P_i}{P_v}\right)^{\frac{2}{\alpha}}\left(\hat{\theta}_{i,u}^{2/\alpha} + \tau^{\frac{2}{\alpha}}\int_{\left(\frac{\hat{\theta}_{i,u}}{\tau}\right)}^\infty {}^{2/\alpha}\frac{1}{1+u^{\frac{\alpha}{2}}}du\right)\right)\right\} dr. \tag{9}$$

Proof. Using (8) into the definition of SINR coverage in (5), and we can get the SINR coverage of a typical UE which is associated with vth tier BS as follows

$$\mathcal{S}_v(\tau) = \mathbb{E}_r\left[\mathbb{P}(SINR_v > \tau)|r\right]$$
$$= \int_{r>0} \mathbb{P}\left(\frac{P_v h r^{-\alpha}}{I+\sigma^2} > \tau\right) f_{D_v^u}(r)dr$$
$$= \int_{r>0} \mathbb{P}\left(h > r^\alpha P_v^{-1}\tau\left(I+\sigma^2\right)\right) f_{D_v^u}(r)dr \tag{10}$$
$$= \int_{r>0} \mathbb{E}_{I_r}\left(\exp\left(-r^\alpha P_v^{-1}\tau\left(I+\sigma^2\right)\right)\right) f_{D_v^u}(r)dr$$
$$= \int_{r>0} \exp(-r^\alpha P_v^{-1}\tau\sigma^2) \prod_{i\in\{M,S\}} \mathcal{L}_{I_i}(r^\alpha P_v^{-1}\tau) f_{D_v^u}(r)dr,$$

where I is the interference, and $\mathcal{L}_{I_i}(r^\alpha P_v^{-1}\tau)$ is the Laplace transform of the interference from BSs in ith tier derived as

$$\mathcal{L}_{I_i}\left(r^\alpha P_v^{-1}\tau\right)$$
$$= \mathbb{E}_{I_i}\left(\exp\left(-r^\alpha P_v^{-1}\tau I_i\right)\right)$$
$$= \mathbb{E}_{\Phi_i}\left(\exp\left(-r^\alpha P_v^{-1}\tau \sum_{y\in\Phi_i} P_i h_y\|y\|^{-\alpha}\right)\right) \tag{11}$$
$$= \exp\left(-2\pi\lambda_i \int_{z_i}^\infty \left(1 - \frac{1}{1+r^\alpha P_v^{-1}P_i\tau y^{-\alpha}}\right) y dy\right)$$
$$= \exp\left(-\pi r^2\lambda_i\left(\frac{P_i}{P_v}\tau\right)^{\frac{2}{\alpha}} \int_{\left(\frac{\hat{\theta}_i}{\tau}\right)}^\infty {}^{2/\alpha}\frac{1}{1+u^{\frac{\alpha}{2}}}du\right),$$

where z_i is the distance of the nearest interference of ith tier expressed as

$$z_i = \left(\frac{P_i}{P_v}\hat{\theta}_k\right)^{1/\alpha} r.$$

Hence, $\mathcal{S}_v(\tau)$ can be got by applying (10) and (11) in (5), and the SINR coverage of Theorem 1 can be easily derived from (7).

Corollary 1. *When $\sigma^2 = 0$ and $\alpha = 4$, the expression of SINR coverage is*

$$S(\tau) = \sum_{v\in\{M,S\}} \frac{\lambda_v}{\sum_{i\in\{M,S\}} \lambda_i\left(\sqrt{\frac{P_i}{P_v}\hat{\theta}_i} + \sqrt{\frac{P_i}{P_v}\tau}\arctan\sqrt{\tau/\hat{\theta}_i}\right)}. \tag{12}$$

3.2   Rate Coverage

According to Shannon theorem, the rate R of a typical UE is

$$R = \frac{W}{N} \log \left(1 + SINR\right), \tag{13}$$

where W denotes the bandwidth of the system, and N is the total number of UEs in coverage area of the serving BS.

The rate coverage is defined as the probability that the rate of a typical UE is larger than rate threshold ρ. Therefore, the rate coverage can be expressed by definition as

$$\mathcal{R}\left(\rho\right) = \mathbb{P}\left(R > \rho\right). \tag{14}$$

Denote demands of u as ρ_u. It is noticeable that $\rho_{u_H} > \rho_{u_L}$ as definition. Similar to SINR coverage in last part, the rate coverage in HetNets is

$$\mathcal{R}\left(\rho\right) = \sum_v A_v \mathcal{R}_v\left(\rho\right). \tag{15}$$

Theorem 2. *The rate coverage of a typical UE $u \in \{u_L, u_H\}$ is*

$$\mathcal{R}^u\left(\rho_u\right) = \sum_v 2\pi\lambda_v \times \int_{r>0} r \exp\left\{-r^\alpha P_v^{-1}\left(2^{\frac{\rho_u \tilde{N}_v}{W}} - 1\right)\sigma^2\right.$$
$$\left.-\pi r^2\left(\sum_{i\in\{M,S\}} \lambda_i \left(\frac{P_i}{P_v}\right)^{2/\alpha}\left(\hat{\theta}_i^{2/\alpha} + \left(2^{\frac{\rho_u \tilde{N}_v}{W}}-1\right)^{\frac{2}{\alpha}}\int_{\left(\frac{\hat{\theta}_i}{2^{\frac{\rho_u \tilde{N}_v}{W}}-1}\right)}^{\infty}\left(\frac{1}{\cdots}\right)^{2/\alpha}\frac{1}{1+u^{\frac{\alpha}{2}}}du\right)\right)\right\} dr, \tag{16}$$

where $\tilde{N}_v$ is the average number of UEs connected to the serving BS in vth tier given as

$$\tilde{N}_v = 1 + 1.28\frac{\sum\limits_{k\in\{u_H,u_L\}} \lambda_k A_v^k}{\lambda_v}.$$

Proof. According to the definition of rate coverage in (14), the rate coverage of a typical UE u connected with vth tier with a rate coverage threshold ρ_u is

$$\mathcal{R}_v^u\left(\rho_u\right) = \mathbb{P}\left(R^u > \rho_u\right)$$
$$= \mathbb{E}_{N_v}\left[\mathbb{P}\left(\frac{W}{N_v}\log\left(1 + SINR^u\right) > \rho_u\right)|N_v\right]$$
$$\approx \mathbb{P}\left(SINR^u > 2^{\frac{\rho_u \tilde{N}_v}{W}} - 1\right) \tag{17}$$
$$= \mathcal{S}^u\left(2^{\frac{\rho_u \tilde{N}_v}{W}} - 1\right).$$

In this paper, different UE clusters are deployed independently according to PPP in the system. Therefore, the average load of tagged serving BS in v tier can derived referring to [11] as follows:

$$\tilde{N}_v = 1 + 1.28\frac{\lambda_{u_H} A_v^{u_H}}{\lambda_v} + 1.28\frac{\lambda_{u_L} A_v^{u_L}}{\lambda_v}$$
$$= 1 + 1.28\frac{\sum\limits_{k\in\{u_H,u_L\}} \lambda_k A_v^k}{\lambda_v}. \tag{18}$$

Hence, Theorem 2 can be derived by applying (7), (17) and (18) into (15).

Corollary 2. *When $\sigma^2 = 0$ and $\alpha = 4$, the rate coverage can be expressed as*

$$\mathcal{R}^u\left(\rho_u\right) = \sum_{v \in \{M,S\}} \frac{\lambda_v}{\sum_{i \in \{M,S\}} \lambda_i \sqrt{\frac{P_i}{P_v}}\left(\sqrt{\hat{\theta}_{i,u}} + \sqrt{2^{\frac{\rho_u \tilde{N}_v}{W}} - 1}\arctan\sqrt{\frac{2^{\frac{\rho_u \tilde{N}_v}{W}} - 1}{\hat{\theta}_{i,u}}}\right)}. \tag{19}$$

3.3 DL Throughput

In this paper, two kinds of UEs classified by different data rate demands are served by HetNets. As definition of DL throughput in (4) previously, the total system DL throughput should consider achievable throughput of all UEs as below

$$DL \; Throughput = \sum_{k \in \{u_H, u_L\}} \lambda_k \rho_k \mathcal{R}^k\left(\rho_k\right) \quad (Kbps/m^2). \tag{20}$$

4   Numerical Results

In this section, series of numerical results are presented to verify the accuracy of system model and analysis. Especially, the DL throughput in the HetNets is evaluated in detail. For clarity, the analysis in this section is limited to an interference-limited 2-tier HetNet. Table 1 shows the key simulation parameters of the system.

Table 1. Simulation parameters

Parameter	Value
MBS density (m^{-2}), λ_M	1×10^{-6}
SBSs density (m^{-2}), λ_S	1×10^{-5}
MBS transmit power (W), P_M	20
SBS transmit power (W), P_S	0.13
SINR coverage threshold (dB), τ	-10
Rate coverage threshold of u_H (Kbps), ρ_{u_H}	1024
Rate coverage threshold of u_L (Kbps), ρ_{u_L}	12
System bandwidth (MHz), W	20
Path loss, α	4

In Fig. 2, the SINR coverage and rate coverage under different association bias factor θ_{S,u_H} are shown in (a) and (b), respectively. As shown in Fig. 2(a), it is noticeable that u_L remains the same SINR coverage, while u_H has a decreasing trend. This is because different association biases are applied to u_L and u_H. For u_L, the association bias factor always has $\theta_{u_L} = 1$, which means that the association for u_L is based on maximum received power, hence u_L can always get reliable SINR quality resulting from high SINR coverage. Moreover, for u_H, the bigger the association bias factor θ_{S,u_H} is, the wider SBS coverage area is. Hence, more u_H are offloaded from MBSs to SBSs through expanding SBS coverage area, which causes declining SINR coverage performance due to both deterioration of the received signal power and enhanced interference.

Figure 2(b) presents the rate coverage of different UEs compared to traditional RSRP mode. Because u_H have higher data rate demands than u_L, the rate coverage of u_H is clearly interior to that of u_L. Moreover, proposed TUA scheme can obviously improve the rate coverage of u_H, and slightly enhance the rate coverage of u_L. That is due to the fact that some u_H are offloaded from MBSs to SBSs, which relieves the congestion of MBSs and balances the BSs load.

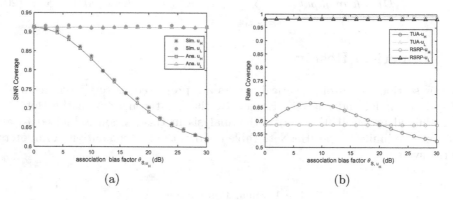

(a)   (b)

Fig. 2. Coverage performance of classified UEs under different association bias factor θ_{S,u_H} ($\lambda_{u_H} = 2e^{-5}m^{-2}$, $\lambda_{u_L} = 4e^{-5}m^{-2}$): (a) SINR coverage with TUA scheme, (b) comparison of rate coverage with TUA and RSRP schemes.

System DL throughput is demonstrated in Fig. 3. An optimal association bias factor θ^*_{S,u_H}, which maximizes the DL throughput, is obtained using PSO. It is shown that θ^*_{S,u_H} changes with different ratios of MBS density and SBS density. Compared to traditional RSRP mode, TUA scheme can enhance DL throughput by 16%, which mainly benefits from the improvement of rate performance. Furthermore, increasing density of SBSs can also yield significant DL throughput enhancement, because UEs are prone to be connected to SBSs as increase of SBSs, which also contributes to load balance in HetNets.

In Fig. 4, the relations between optimal association bias factor θ^*_{S,u_H} and distributions of both UEs and BSs are presented. When the density of u_L is increasing, the θ^*_{S,u_H} is on the rise. Moreover, as the decrease of SBS density, the θ^*_{S,u_H} also has a remarkable growth. It is obvious that both more UEs and less SBSs can cause more serious congestion of MBSs. Therefore, larger association bias factor θ_{S,u_H} contributes to system load balance, which is beneficial to enhance DL throughput.

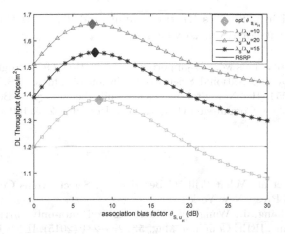

Fig. 3. Comparison of DL throughput performance under different association bias factor and SBSs deployments ($\lambda_M = 1e^{-6}m^{-2}$, $\lambda_{u_H} = 2e^{-5}m^{-2}$, $\lambda_{u_L} = 4e^{-5}m^{-2}$).

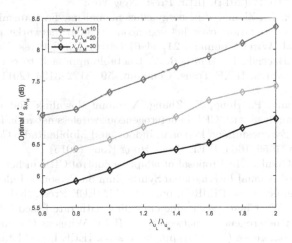

Fig. 4. The relations between optimal association bias and both UEs and BSs densities ($\lambda_{u_H} = 2e^{-5}m^{-2}$, $\lambda_M = 1e^{-6}m^{-2}$).

5 Conclusion

In this paper, a tractable TUA scheme in HetNets is proposed, where different association biases are applied to satisfy various UEs traffic demands. The expression of SINR coverage, rate coverage, and DL throughput are derived theoretically. Specifically, TUA scheme is able to balance loads by offloading some high traffic demand UEs u_H from MBSs to SBSs in DL. Numerical results illustrate that TUA scheme can improve rate coverage of UEs and enhance system DL throughput by 16% compared to traditional RSRP association method, while the SINR quality of u_L is ensured. Moreover, there is an optimal association bias factor θ^*_{S,u_H} which maximizes DL throughput, and it reveals that θ^*_{S,u_H} differs as either UE density or BS density changes.

Acknowledgment. This work is supported by the National 973 Program under grant 2012CB316005, by the National Science Foundation of China (NSFC) under grant 61372114, 61571054, the New Star in Science and Technology of Beijing Municipal Science & Technology Commission (Beijing Nova Program: Z151100000315077).

References

1. Andrews, J., et al.: What Will 5G Be? IEEE J. Select. Areas Commun. 136–144 (2013). IEEE Press, New York
2. Zhang, X., Zhang, J., Wang, W.: Macro-assisted data-only carrier for 5G green cellular systems. IEEE Commun. Mag. **53**, 223–231 (2015). IEEE Press, New York
3. Zhang, X., Zhang, Y., Yu, R.: Enhancing spectral-energy efficiency for LTE-advanced heterogeneous networks: a users social pattern perspective. IEEE Wirel. Commun. **21**, 10–17 (2014). IEEE Press, New York
4. Zhang, X., Yu, R., Zhang, Y.: Energy-efficient multimedia transmissions through base station cooperation over heterogeneous cellular networks exploiting user behavior. IEEE Wirel. Commun. **21**, 54–61 (2014). IEEE Press, New York
5. Andrews, J., Baccelli, F., Ganti, R.: A tractable approach to coverage and rate in cellular networks. IEEE Trans. Commun. **59**, 3122–3134 (2011). IEEE Press, New York
6. Yang, K., Wang, P., Hong, X., Zhang, X.: Joint downlink and uplink network performance analysis with CRE in heterogeneous wireless network. In: 26th Annual International Symposium on Personal, Indoor, and Mobile Radio Communications (PIMRC), pp. 1659–1663. IEEE Press, Hong Kong (2015)
7. Kikuchi, K., Otsuka, H.: Proposal of adaptive control CRE in heterogeneous networks. In: 23rd Annual International Symposium on Personal, Indoor, and Mobile Radio Communications (PIMRC), pp. 910–914. IEEE Press, Sydney (2012)
8. Sun, S., Liao, W., Chen, W.: Traffic offloading with rate-based cell range expansion offsets in heterogeneous networks. In: IEEE Wireless Communications and Networking Conference (WCNC), pp. 2833–2838. IEEE Press, Istanbul (2014)
9. Sun, Y., Deng, T., Fang, Y., et al.: A method for pico-specific upper bound CRE bias setting in HetNet. In: IEEE Wireless Communications and Networking Conference Workshops (WCNCW), pp. 80–84. IEEE Press, Shanghai (2013)
10. Chiu, S., Stoyan, D., Kendall, W., et al.: Stochastic Geometry and Its Applications. Wiley, Hoboken (2013)
11. Singh, S., Dhillon, H., Andrews, J.: Offloading in heterogeneous networks: modeling, analysis, and design insights. IEEE Trans. Wirel. Commun. **12**, 2484–2497 (2013). IEEE Press, New York

An Optimal Joint User Association and Power Allocation Algorithm for Secrecy Information Transmission in Heterogeneous Integrated Networks

Mingxue Chen[✉], Yuanpeng Gao, Rong Chai, and Qianbin Chen

School of Communication and Information Engineering,
Chongqing University of Posts and Telecommunications, Chongqing, China
mingxuechen@outlook.com, gyp2342623@126.com, chairong@cqupt.edu.cn

Abstract. In recent years, radio access technologies have experienced rapid development and gradually achieved effective coordination and integration, resulting in heterogeneous networks (HetNets). User equipments (UEs) located in the overlapping area of various networks of Het-Nets are capable of selecting the base station (BS) of one network for association and conduct information interaction. In this paper, we study user association and power allocation problem for HetNets with eavesdroppers. To achieve secrecy data transmission in a secret and energy-efficient manner, the concept of joint secrecy energy efficiency of the network is introduced and is defined as the ratio of secrecy transmission rate and the power consumption of the BSs. An optimization problem is formulated which maximizes the joint secrecy energy efficiency under the constraints of maximum power of the BSs and the minimum data rate requirement of the UEs, and the optimal user association and transmit power strategy is obtained through applying iterative algorithm and Lagrange dual method. Numerical results demonstrate the efficiency of the proposed algorithm.

Keywords: HetNets · User association · Power allocation · Secrecy information transmission · Secrecy energy efficiency

1 Introduction

In recent years, radio access technologies have experienced rapid development and gradually achieved effective coordination and integration, resulting in HetNets [1], in which user equipments (UEs) located in the overlapping area of various networks are capable of selecting the base station (BS) of one network for association and information interaction. User association scheme design in HetNets is of particular importance for it may affect user quality of service (QoS) and network performance significantly.

Some research works have considered user association or cell association problem in HetNets. In [2], the authors addresses the cell association problem of a

© ICST Institute for Computer Sciences, Social Informatics and Telecommunications Engineering 2018
Q. Chen et al. (Eds.): ChinaCom 2016, Part II, LNICST 210, pp. 227–236, 2018.
DOI: 10.1007/978-3-319-66628-0_22

multi-tier HetNet and propose a unified distributed cell association and resource allocation algorithm to maximize the sum utility of long term rate with long term rate QoS constraints and maximize global outage probability with outage QoS constraints. The authors in [3] examine the impact of mobile backhaul networks on LTE-A HetNets, and propose a backhaul-aware user association algorithm to achieve network load balancing and the performance enhancement in terms of transmission delay and service block probability. In [4], user association problem in HetNets is studied and a distributed optimization method is proposed to maximize the utilization of the BSs.

References in [5,6] jointly consider user association and power allocation in HetNets. The authors in [5] study the joint BS association and power allocation problem for the downlink transmission in HetNets, and propose a two-stage algorithm to maximize the minimum data rate of the UEs. In [6], the authors consider the joint optimization of BS association and power allocation in a wireless downlink HetNet under the proportional fairness criterion and propose a utility function maximization based BS association and power allocation strategy.

It should be noted that compared to traditional cellular networks, the network architecture of HetNets becomes more open and diverse, which makes the information exchange more susceptible to eavesdropping, hence, the problem of secure transmission becomes extremely important in HetNets. In [7], the authors consider the network scenario in which eavesdroppers exist in HetNets and propose a joint resource allocation algorithm which jointly considers physical layer security, cross-tier interference and joint optimal allocation of power and subcarrier to maximize the achievable secrecy sum rate of the network. The authors in [8] investigate secure communications in a two-tier downlink HetNets, which comprises one macrocell and multiple femtocells with each cell having multiple users and an eavesdropper which attempts to wiretap the intended macrocell UEs. The authors consider an orthogonal spectrum allocation strategy to eliminate co-channel interference and propose the secrecy transmit beamforming scheme operating in the macrocell to maximize the secrecy rate of users.

In this paper, we study user association and power allocation problem for HetNets with eavesdroppers. To achieve data transmission in a secret and energy-efficient manner, the concept of joint secrecy energy efficiency of the network is introduced and is defined as the ratio of secrecy transmission rate and the power consumption of the BSs. An optimization problem is formulated which maximizes the joint secrecy energy efficiency under the constraints of maximum power of the BSs and the minimum data rate requirement of the UEs, and the optimal user association and transmit power strategy is obtained through applying iterative algorithm and Lagrange dual method.

The rest of the paper is organized as follows. Section 2 describes the system model considered in this paper. We jointly design user association and power allocation strategy for the heterogeneous integrated network described in Sect. 3. The solution of the optimization problem is discussed in Sect. 4. Simulation results are presented in Sect. 5. Finally, we conclude this paper in Sect. 6.

2   System Model

In this paper, we study the downlink transmission in a HetNet, which consisting of multiple overlapping access networks and a number of users, which may associate to one of the networks and conduct information interaction. We assume that each network is assigned a portion of spectrum and no spectrum sharing is allowed among networks and within each network, thus no transmission interference exists. Further assume that inside each network, there exists an eavesdropper which may eavesdrop the information of the UEs associated with the network.

We denote the number of networks and UEs by M and N, respectively. We assume each network only has one BS, for convenience, the BS of the ith network is referred to as BS_i, $1 \le i \le M$. We further assume that each UE can only associated with one BS and each BS can only serve one UE on given time-frequency resource block. Figure 1 shows the HetNet model we considered in this paper.

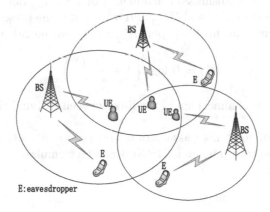

Fig. 1. System model

3   Secrecy Energy Efficiency Optimization Problem Formulation

In this section, the joint secrecy energy efficiency optimization is formulated.

$$\eta = \sum_{i=1}^{M} \sum_{j=1}^{N} x_{i,j} \eta_{i,j} \tag{1}$$

where $x_{i,j}$ denotes the association variable between BS_i and the jth UE(UE_j), and $\eta_{i,j}$ represents the secrecy energy efficiency of BS_i when associating with UE_j and can be expressed as:

$$\eta_{i,j} = \frac{R_{i,j}^{\text{sec}}}{P_{i,j} + P^{\text{cir}}} \tag{2}$$

where $R_{i,j}^{\text{sec}}$ denotes the secrecy data transmission rate of the link between BS_i and UE_j, $P_{i,j}$ and P^{cir} denote the transmit power and the circuit consumption power of BS_i when transmitting to UE_j respectively. We assume that the circuit consumption power of the BSs is constant in this paper.

$R_{i,j}^{\text{sec}}$ in (2) can be expressed as:

$$R_{i,j}^{\text{sec}} = R_{i,j}^{\text{u}} - R_{i,j}^{\text{e}} \tag{3}$$

where $R_{i,j}^{\text{u}}$ denotes the data rate of the link between BS_i and UE_j, $R_{i,j}^{\text{e}}$ denotes the data rate of the eavesdropper when eavesdropping UE_j in the ith network. $R_{i,j}^{\text{u}}$ in (3) can be expressed as:

$$R_{i,j}^{\text{u}} = B_i \log\left(1 + \frac{P_{i,j}h_{i,j}}{\sigma^2}\right) \tag{4}$$

where B_i denotes the transmission bandwidth of BS_i, $h_{i,j}$ denotes the channel gain of the link between BS_i and UE_j, and σ^2 denotes the noise power, which is assumed to be a constant in this paper. $R_{i,j}^{\text{e}}$ in (3) can be calculated as:

$$R_{i,j}^{\text{e}} = B_i \log_2\left(1 + \frac{P_{i,j}h_i^{\text{e}}}{\sigma^2}\right) \tag{5}$$

where h_i^{e} denotes the channel gain of the link between BS_i and the eavesdropper of the ith network

The problem of joint user association and power allocation algorithm for secrecy information transmission in HetNets can be formulated as following optimization problem:

$$\max_{x_{i,j},P_{i,j}} \quad \eta \tag{6}$$

$$\text{s.t.} \quad \text{C1}: \ P_{i,j} \geq 0,$$

$$\text{C2}: \ P_{i,j} \leq P_i^{\max},$$

$$\text{C3}: \ \sum_{i=1}^{M} R_{i,j}^{\text{sec}} \geq R_j^{\min},$$

$$\text{C4}: \ x_{i,j} \in \{0,1\},$$

$$\text{C5}: \ \sum_{j=1}^{N} x_{i,j} \leq 1,$$

$$\text{C6}: \ \sum_{i=1}^{M} x_{i,j} \leq 1.$$

In (6), $P_i^{\max}$ denotes the maximum permissible power of BS_i, the constraint C2 represents that the transmit power of BS_i should be less than its maximum permissible power, $R_j^{\min}$ denotes the minimal secrecy data rate required from UE_j, apparently, the constraint C3 characterizes the data rate requirement of UE_j.

4 Solution of the Optimization Problem

The optimization problem formulated in (6) is a nonlinear mixed-integer optimization problem the solution which is difficult to obtain directly. Indeed, as it is assumed that each UE can only access one network and each network can only serve one UE for given resource block, and there is no cross interference between various networks, the power allocation for a particular UE-BS pair can be conducted independently to obtain the locally optimal transmit power, based on which user association can be performed. Hence, we can equivalently transform the original optimization problem into two subproblems, i.e., the subproblem of optimal power allocation, and the subproblem of user association. Through solving the two subproblems successively, the optimal joint power allocation and user association strategy can be obtained.

4.1 Optimal Power Allocation Subproblem

Assuming UE_j associates with the BS_i, i.e., $x_{i,j} = 1$, the optimal power allocation subproblem for BS_i can be formulated as follows:

$$\max_{P_{i,j}} \quad \eta_{i,j} \tag{7}$$

$$\text{s.t.} \quad C1 - C3 \text{ in } (6).$$

The optimization problem formulated in (7) is a nonconvex nonlinear fractional program, which can be transformed into a convex problem. Without loss of generality, we denote $q_{i,j}^*$ as the maximum secrecy energy efficiency of BS_i when associating to UE_j, which can be expressed as:

$$q_{i,j}^* = \frac{R_{i,j}^{\text{sec}}(P_{i,j}^*)}{P_{i,j}^* + P^{\text{cir}}}, \tag{8}$$

where $P_{i,j}^*$ denotes the optimal transmit power of BS_i when associating to UE_j. It can be proved that the maximum secrecy energy efficiency $q_{i,j}^*$ is achieved if and only if

$$\max_{P_{i,j}} R_{i,j}^{\text{sec}}(P_{i,j}) - q_{i,j}^*(P_{i,j} + P_{cir})$$
$$= R_{i,j}^{(\text{sec},*)}(P_{i,j}^*) - q_{i,j}^* P_{i,j}^* = 0. \tag{9}$$

Hence, the optimization problem expressed in (7) can be rewritten as:

$$\max_{q_{i,j}, P_{i,j}} R_{i,j}^{\text{sec}}(P_{i,j}) - q_{i,j}(P_{i,j} + P_{cir}) \tag{10}$$

$$\text{s.t.} C1 - C3 \text{ in } (6).$$

To obtain the optimal secrecy energy efficiency and transmit power strategy of (9), we apply an iterative algorithm. The proposed algorithm is summarized in Algorithm 1 and the convergence to the optimal secrecy energy efficiency can be guaranteed in [9] (Table 1).

Table 1. Algorithm 1. Solving secrecy energy efficiency maximization problem

1. Initialize the maximal iteration number $L_{\max}$ and the tolerate value ω
2. Set $q_{i,j}=0$ and the iterative index $l=0$
3. Repeat main loop
4. For a given $q_{i,j}$, solving power allocation subproblem to obtain the locally optimal power allocation strategy $P'_{i,j}$
5. If $R^{\text{sec}}_{i,j}(P'_{i,j}) - q_{i,j}(P'_{i,j} + P^{\text{cir}}) \leq \omega$ then
6. Convergence=true
7. Return $q^*_{i,j} = \frac{R^{\text{sec}}_{i,j}(P'_{i,j})}{P'_{i,j} + P^{\text{cir}}}$
8. else,set $q_{i,j} = \frac{R^{\text{sec}}_{i,j}(P_{i,j}')}{P_{i,j}' + P^{\text{cir}}}$ and let $l = l + 1$
9. end if
10. Until the algorithm is converged or $l = L_{\max}$

For a given $q_{i,j}$, the optimization problem formulated in (10) can be transformed into following problem:

$$\max_{P_{i,j}} R^{\text{sec}}_{i,j} - q_{i,j}(P_{i,j} + P^{\text{cir}}) \tag{11}$$

$$\text{s.t.C1} - \text{C3 in (6)}$$

We apply Lagrange dual method to solve above optimization problem. The Lagrangian of the problem can be expressed as:

$$L(\alpha, \beta, P_{i,j}) = R^{\text{u}}_{i,j} - q_{i,j}(P_{i,j} + P^{\text{cir}}) \\ -\alpha(P_{i,j} - P^{\max}_j) - \beta(R^{\min}_i - R^{\text{sec}}_{i,j}), \tag{12}$$

where α and β are Lagrange multipliers, the Lagrange dual problem of (12) can be formulated as follows:

$$\min_{\alpha, \beta} \max_{P_{i,j}} L(\alpha, \beta, P_{i,j}) \\ \text{s.t.} \ \alpha \geq 0, \beta \geq 0 \tag{13}$$

For a given set of Lagrange multipliers $\{\alpha, \beta\}$ using standard optimization techniques, the optimal power allocation policy $P_{i,j}$ can be obtained as:

$$P_{i,j} = \left[\frac{(h_{i,j} + h^e_i)\sigma^2 + ((h_{i,j} - h^e_i)\sigma^4 + 4h_{i,j}h^e_i t)^{1/2}}{2h_{i,j}h^e_i} \right]^+ \tag{14}$$

where $t = \left[\frac{(1+\beta)B_j(h_{i,j}-h_i^e)\sigma^2}{(\alpha+q_{i,j})\ln 2}\right]^+$, $[z]^+ = \max\{0, z\}$.

The dual function is differentiable, the iterative algorithm can be used to solve the optimal Lagrange multipliers which leads to

$$\alpha(t+1) = [\alpha(t) - \varepsilon_1(P_i^{\max} - P_{i,j})]^+, \tag{15}$$

$$\beta(t+1) = [\beta(t) - \varepsilon_2(\sum_{i=1}^{M} R_{i,j}^{\text{sec}} - R_j^{\min})]^+. \tag{16}$$

where the iteration index $\varepsilon_i(i = 1, 2)$ is the positive step size.

4.2   User Association Subproblem

Through assuming $x_{i,j} = 1$, we can obtain the locally optimal power allocation strategy, denoted as $P_{i,j}^*$ and $q_{i,j}^*$. Substituting $P_{i,j}$ by $P_{i,j}^*$ in (1), we obtain:

$$\eta - \sum_{i=1}^{M}\sum_{j=1}^{N} x_{i,j}\frac{R_{i,j}^{\text{sec},*}}{(P_{i,j}^* + P^{\text{cir}})}, \tag{17}$$

where $R_{i,j}^* = B_i\log_2\left(1 + \frac{P_{i,j}^* h_{i,j}^2}{\sigma^2}\right)$. For given $P_{i,j}^*$, $\frac{R_{i,j}^{\text{sec},*}}{(P_{i,j}^* + P^{\text{cir}})}$ is a constant, therefore, the problem of maximizing (17) is equivalent to selecting the optimal $x_{i,j}$ subject to user association constraints, which can be expressed as the following optimal user association subproblem:

$$\max_{x_{i,j}} \sum_{i=1}^{M}\sum_{j=1}^{N} x_{i,j}\frac{R_{i,j}^{\text{sec},*}}{(P_{i,j}^* + P^{\text{cir}})} \tag{18}$$
$$\text{s.t.} \quad \text{C4} - \text{C6 in (6)}$$

The optimization model formulated in (18) is a nonlinear integer optimization problem, which is in general very difficult to be solved. However, it can be observed that given the constraints on user association, the optimization problem can be described by a bipartite graph and the problem of optimal user association can be regarded as an optimal matching problem in the bipartite graph, which can then be solved based on the typical algorithm such as modified Kuhn-Munkres algorithm in [10].

A weighted bipartite graph G with bipartite division $G^0 = (V_1, V_2, E)$ is constructed, where the set of vertices V_1 represents the collection of the interrupted users, i.e., $V_1 = [\text{SU}_1, \text{SU}_2, \dots, \text{SU}_M]$, SU_m represents the mth interrupted SU, $1 \le m \le M$, and the set of vertices V_2 represents the collection of subchannels, i.e., $V_2 = [C_1, C_2, \dots, C_N]$, the weight of the edge, i.e., $E\{V_1, V_2\}$ is defined as:

The steps for solving the optimal user association subproblem based on the K-M algorithm can be described as follows.

1. Find an initial feasible vertex labeling and determine G_l^0 from G^0.
2. A distribution of H is selected in G_l^0.

3. If H is perfect, then the optimization problem is solved. Otherwise, the label having not being allocated by the distribution H is selected in G_l^0. Set $S = V_1$, and $\mathrm{T} = \Psi$, which denotes the empty set.
4. $N_{G_l^0}(S)$ denotes the collection of points which connect with S in G_l^0. If $N_{G_l^0}(S) \neq T$, go to step (2). Otherwise, $N_{G_l^0}(S) = T$. Find

$$\Delta = \min(l(u) + l(v) \geq w(u,v)|u \in S, v \in V_2 - T) \tag{19}$$

and replace existing labeling l with l' by

$$l'(u) = \begin{cases} l(u) - \Delta, & u \in S \\ l(u) + \Delta, & u \in T \\ l(u), & \text{others.} \end{cases}$$

The process continues until an equal subgraph consisting a complete match is obtained.

5   Simulation Results

In the simulation, we consider a HetNet scenario consisting of multiple overlapping access networks. Assuming the numbers of UEs and BSs are both chosen from 3 to 5, respectively. We assume that all users are randomly located in a rectangular region with the size being 100×100. The minimum rate requirements of UEs when associating to BS are 0.99 Mbps, 0.97 Mbps, 0.90 Mbps, 0.89 Mbps, 0.95 Mbps, 0.88 bps respectively, the noise power is -47 dBm, the bandwidth is 1 MHz. The simulation results are averaged over 1000 independent adaptation processes where each adaptation process involves different positions of UEs and eavesdroppers.

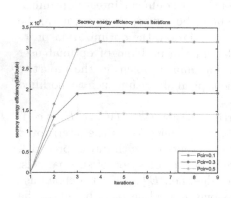
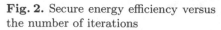
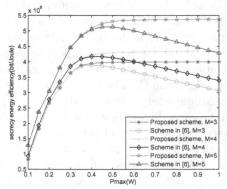

Fig. 2. Secure energy efficiency versus the number of iterations

Fig. 3. The secrecy energy efficiency versus maximum transmit power (different number of BS)

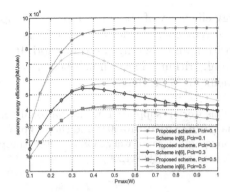

Fig. 4. Secrecy energy efficiency versus maximum transmit power (different circuit power)

Figure 2 shows the secrecy energy efficiency versus the number of iterations for different of circuit power. P^{max} is chosen as 0.8 W in plotting the figure. It can be observed that the iterative algorithm converges within a small number of iterations.

Figure 3 shows the secrecy energy efficiency versus the maximum transmit power for different numbers of BSs, and the results are obtained from the proposed scheme and the scheme proposed in [6]. P^{cir} is chosen as 0.5 W in plotting the figure. As the maximum transmit power increases, the proposed scheme performs better than the scheme proposed in [6]. This is because the scheme proposed in [6] failed to allocate the optimal power to the UEs, resulting in a undesired transmission performance. It also can be seen from the figure that for a small P^{max}, the secrecy energy efficiency increases with the increasing of P^{max}, indicating a larger power threshold is desired for achieving the maximum secrecy energy efficiency. However, as P^{max} reaches to a certain value, the secrecy energy efficiency becomes a fixed value for the transmit power being less than P^{max} has resulted in the optimal secrecy energy efficiency, which will no longer vary with P^{max}.

The secrecy energy efficiency versus the maximum transmit power for different circuit power consumption is shown in Fig. 4. It can be seen from the figure that the total secrecy energy efficiency decreases with the increase of the circuit power consumption. Compared to the scheme proposed in [6], our proposed scheme offers larger secrecy energy efficiency.

6 Conclusion

In this paper, an optimal user association and power allocation scheme is proposed in HetNets. The factors, including channel characteristics and eavesdroppers are taken into account jointly in optimal UE association and allocating the transmit power of UEs, we formulate the problem of joint user association and resource allocation as an optimization problem with the objective function being the total secrecy energy efficiency of UEs in HetNets. The optimization problem which maximizes the secrecy energy efficiency for UEs is formulated and solved through iterative algorithm and Lagrange dual method. It is verified by simulation that the proposed algorithm achieves much better secrecy energy efficiency than the proposed scheme in [6] in HetNets.

Acknowledgement. This work is supported by the National Science and Technology Specific Project of China (2016ZX03001010-004) and the 863 project (2014AA01A701), the special fund of Chongqing key laboratory (CSTC) and the project of Chongqing Municipal Education Commission (Kjzh11206).

References

1. Jo, M., Maksymyuk, T., Batista, R.L., Maciel, T.F., de Almeida, A.L.F., Klymash, M.: A survey of converging solutions for heterogeneous mobile networks. IEEE Wirel. Commun. **21**(6), 54–62 (2014)
2. Boostanimehr, H., Bhargava, V.K.: Unified and distributed QoS-driven cell association algorithms in heterogeneous networks. IEEE Trans. Wireless Commun. **14**(3), 1650–1662 (2015)
3. Beyranvand, H., Lim, W., Maier, M., Verikoukis, C., Salehi, J.A.: Backhaul-aware user association in FiWi enhanced LTE-A heterogeneous networks. IEEE Trans. Wirel. Commun. **14**(6), 2992–3003 (2015)
4. Wang, L., Chen, W., Li, J.: Congestion aware dynamic user association in heterogeneous cellular network: a stochastic decision approach. In: 2014 IEEE International Conference on Communications (ICC), Sydney, NSW, pp. 2636–2640 (2014)
5. Sun, R., Hong, M., Luo, Z.Q.: Joint downlink base station association and power control for max-min fairness: computation and complexity. IEEE J. Select. Areas Commun. **33**(6), 1040–1054 (2015)
6. Shen, K., Yu, W.: Distributed pricing-based user association for downlink heterogeneous cellular networks. IEEE J. Select. Areas Commun. **32**(6), 1100–1113 (2014)
7. Shiqi, G., Chengwen, X., Zesong, F., Jingming, K.: Resource allocation for physical layer security in heterogeneous network with hidden eavesdropper. China Commun. **13**(3), 82–95 (2016)
8. Lv, T., Gao, H., Yang, S.: Secrecy transmit beamforming for heterogeneous networks. IEEE J. Select. Areas Commun. **33**(6), 1154–1170 (2015)
9. Khakurel, S., Musavian, L., Le-Ngoc, T.: Energy-efficient resource and power allocation for uplink multi-user OFDM systems. In: Proceedings of IEEE PIMRC 2012, Sydney, Australia, pp. 357–361, September 2012
10. Zhou, X., Yang, L., Yuan, D.: Bipartite matching based user grouping for grouped OFDM-IDMA. IEEE Trans. Wirel. Commun. **12**(10), 5248–5257 (2013)

Energy-Efficient Femtocells Active/Idle Control and Load Balancing in Heterogeneous Networks

Xiaoge Huang[✉], Zhifang Zhang, Weipeng Dai, Qiong Huang,
and Qianbin Chen

School of Communication and Information Engineering,
Chongqing University of Posts and Telecommunications, Chongqing, China
{Huangxg,Huangqiong,Chenqb}@cqupt.edu.cn, zhang-zhi-fang@hotmail.com

Abstract. In this paper, we present a network energy-efficient resource-
allocation scheme for dense small cell heterogeneous networks by jointly
controlling femtocell base stations active/idle strategies and load balancing with SINR constraints among users. The optimization problem is NP-
hard, thus obtaining the optimal solution is extremely computationally
complex. Therefore, we formulate the optimization problem to two sub
optimization problems: the load balancing design and the femtocell base
stations active/idle switch strategies control. In load balancing design
scheme, we optimize the load balancing of the small cell heterogeneous
networks under the fixed femtocell base stations active/idle strategies.
In femtocell base stations active/idle switch strategies scheme, we optimize the network energy efficiency while achieving the minimum service
requirement among users. Combined with the optimal load balancing
design, we solve the femtocell base stations active/idle switch strategies
scheme by observation that the network energy efficiency is an increasing
function of both user number and femtocell number. Simulation results
show that the proposed algorithm could achieve a considerable performance improvement in terms of network energy efficiency compared with
the traditional algorithms.

Keywords: Energy efficient · Femtocell · Load balancing · Stations
active/idle switch

1 Introduction

Recently, the amount of mobile data traffic widespread has been increasing explo-
sively. On the one hand, to meet surging traffic need, one of the promising
solutions is to increase heterogeneity for cellular networks, particularly through
development of small cell base stations (SBSs). e.g., picocell base stations (PBSs)

Q. Chen—This work is supported by the National Natural Science Foundation
of China (NSFC) (61401053, 61201205), the 863 project No. 2014AA01A701, and
Changjiang Scholars and Innovative Research Team in University (IRT1299), Special
Fund of Chongqing Key Laboratory (CSTC).

© ICST Institute for Computer Sciences, Social Informatics and Telecommunications Engineering 2018
Q. Chen et al. (Eds.): ChinaCom 2016, Part II, LNICST 210, pp. 237–247, 2018.
DOI: 10.1007/978-3-319-66628-0_23

and femtocell base stations (FBSs), which differ primarily in terms of maximum transmit power, easy-of-deployment, physical size, and cost [1]. Because the difference between the power and the number of access node, the traditional cell association scheme is no longer applicable, so the cell association issue should be reconsidered. Existing works have dealt with various issues related to small cells (SCs) problems, such as coverage improvement, traffic offload, load balancing (LB) and others. In [2], the authors proposed the offloading based on LB, which studied the offloading process performance from the macrocell layer to the small cell layer and exploited LB in the small cell layer with Voronoi diagrams. In order to maximize the network utility, the authors in [3] deployed the edge SBSs to serve users far from marco base stations (MBSs). A general quality of service (QoS) cell association scheme is provided in [4], which maximize the user's transmission rate as the target function and model the cell association to NP-hard problem.

On the other hand, seeking for high network energy efficiency (NEE) is a trend for the next generation wireless communication [5]. Recently, there are many existing research works such as [6–8] focus on NEE. In [6], the authors proposed an optimization scheme based on heuristic algorithm to minimize network energy consumption. The work issues in [7] aim to maximize the NEE under the rate fairness constraints among users. In [8], authors developed the optimization problem of long-term BS turning off scheme, which jointly optimizes the developed BS-user association and subcarrier allocation to maximize the NEE or minimize total power consumption by taking the constraints of rate proportion and average sum rate into consideration. Nevertheless, none of these existing works consider the impact of the BSs active/idle operation with the corresponding LB design on the network performance.

In this paper, we study the problem of NEE in dense small cell heterogeneous networks (HetNets), the work aims to maximize the NEE under the constraints of network outage probability and user's QoS requirements by jointly considering optimal FBSs strategies and LB design. Apparently, due to the interference coupling between FBSs and LB constraints involving various variables, the optimization problem is non-convex, thus the optimal solution is extremely computationally complicated. By exploiting the properties of the optimization problem, we transform original problem into two sub-optimization problems and solve them iteratively, which optimize the LB and FBSs active/idle strategies separately.

The rest of the paper is organized as follows. Section 2 describes the system model and problem formulation. Section 3.1 introduces the proposed LB algorithm. Based on the above LB algorithm, the FBSs active/idle switch strategies algorithm is proposed in Sect. 3.2. Simulation results with various parameters are presented in Sect. 4. Finally, Sect. 5 concludes the paper.

2   System Model

In this section, we present the system model. As shown in Fig. 1, we consider downlink communication scenarios in a spectrum sharing small cell HetNets with 3-tiers of BSs, each tier models a particular type of BS: tier 1 consist of

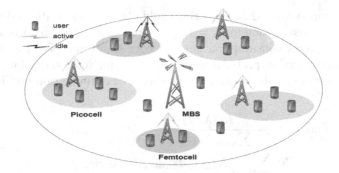

Fig. 1. Small cell heterogeneous networks

traditional MBSs, tier 2 and tier 3 are comprised of PBSs and FBSs respectively. In the scenario, users are randomly distributed in the coverage of the MBS.

We denote the sets of BSs and users by $\mathcal{B}$ and $\mathcal{U}$ with size $|N_\beta|$ and $|N_u|$, respectively. The transmission power of BS $n \in \mathcal{B}$ is P_n, Denote λ_n, $n \in \mathcal{B}$, as the indicators corresponding to the BS state, i.e., when BS n is active, $\lambda_n = 1$, and otherwise $\lambda_n = 0$, and let $\lambda = [\lambda_1, \ldots, \lambda_{|N_\beta|}]$. Thus the received SINR at user k association with BS n is given by:

$$SINR_{kn}(\lambda) = \frac{P_n \cdot L(d_{k,n}) \cdot \lambda_n}{\sum_{i \in I_k} P_i \cdot L(d_{k,i}) \cdot \lambda_i + N_0} \tag{1}$$

where N_0 is the noise power, and I_k denotes the BSs set containing all BSs interfering user k, $L(\cdot)$ is the pathloss function, $d_{k,i}$ and $d_{k,n}$ is the distance from user k to BS i and BS n, respectively. In the network, we use the path loss models from [3]. The pathloss is calculated by:

MBS to user	$L_I(d) = 34 + 40 \log_{10}(d) dB$
PBS to user	$L_I(d) = 34 + 40 \log_{10}(d) dB$
FBS to user	$L_{II}(d) = 37 + 30 \log_{10}(d) dB$

The achievable data rate of user k when associated with BS n is $r_{kn}(\lambda) = \log(1 + SINR_{kn}(\lambda))$. Let X_{kn} denote the network selection parameter of user k at BS n, i.e., $X_{kn} = 1$ means that user k is associated with BS n, otherwise, $X_{kn} = 0$. In this paper, we assume that users can be associated with only one BS at a time. The rate of user k is given by $R_k(\lambda, X) = \sum_{n \in \mathcal{B}} X_{kn} r_{kn}(\lambda)$. Because the FBSs will switch between active/idle state, two categories of power consumption need to be taken into account, i.e., basic power and transmit power consumption. The power consumption model described in [8] is used in our scenario.

$$E_n(\lambda) = \sigma P_n \lambda_n + (1 - \delta) P_n^0 \lambda_n + \delta P_n^0 \tag{2}$$

where $E_n(\lambda)$ is the power consumption of BS n, P_n^0 denotes the baseline power consumption when there is no user in the cell, (i.e., $\sum_{k \in \mathcal{U}} X_{kn} = 0$). However, in order to improve the NEE, the FBSs could choose their state to decrease the baseline power consumption to $P_s = \delta P_n^0$, where $0 < \delta < 1$. Here, σ represent the portion of the power consumption due to feeder losses and power amplifier. We address an optimization problem in dense small HetNets, and jointly optimize the FBSs operation strategies and LB designs. The optimization problem can be expressed as P1:

$$\max_{\lambda, X} \quad \frac{\sum_{k \in \mathcal{U}} R_k(\lambda, X) \cdot \theta_k^n}{\sum_{n \in \mathcal{B}} E_n(\lambda)} \tag{P1}$$

$$\text{s.t.} \quad C_1: \sum_{k \in \mathcal{U}} X_{k,n} \leq L_{n\_max}, \forall n \in \mathcal{B}$$

$$C_2: \sum_{n \in \mathcal{B}} X_{k,n} \leq 1, \forall k \in \mathcal{U}$$

$$C_3: \sum_{n \in \mathcal{B}} X_{k,n} SINR_k^n \geq SINR_k^{target}, \forall k \in \mathcal{U}$$

$$C_4: P_{net} < \varrho$$

$$C_5: X_{k,n} \in (0,1), \forall n, k$$

$$C_6: \lambda_n \in (0,1), \forall n$$

The constraint C_1 ensure that the number of users associated with BS n is no more than its maximum load, where L_{n_max} denotes the maximum load of BS n. The constraint C_2 mean that users could be associated with only one BS at a time. In addition, the constraint C_3 ensure the received SINR of user k associated with BS n to meet the minimum requirement of user k, where $SINR_k^{target}$ is the SINR threshold of user k. The constraint C_4 guarantee the network outage probability (i.e., ϱ). P_{net} is defined as the number of outage users divided by the total users. θ_k^n denotes access factor to control the probability of users association with BS n.

3 LB and FBSs Active/Idle Switch Strategies Algorithm

Notice that the optimization is difficult to obtain the optimal solution, due to the following reasons. Firstly, the problem is a discrete optimization problem involving the FBSs state control and users assignment. Secondly, the issue is influenced by not only the LB but also the FBSs operation strategies, which is complicated by the potential interference coupling among FBSs due to optimizing variables λ. In order to reduce the computation complexity, we decompose the optimization into two sub-optimization problems. i.e., namely LB design under the fixed FBSs active/idle strategies, and then select the optimal FBSs active/idle strategies that lead to the maximum NEE among all possible choices of λ.

3.1 Load Balancing Design Under Fixed FBSs Active/Idle Strategies

For a given FBSs operation strategy, we focus on maximizing the NEE, while take into account the requirement of the user's target-SINR and LB. We propose optimal cell association LB (CALB) algorithm consisting of cell selection step and cell association step. In CALB, firstly, we choose a candidate cell list which could meet the SINR requirement. Then, we choose the optimal cell from their candidate cell list of each user to maximize the utility function. Considered both LB and the SINR requirements of users, we first define an utility function, which composes of access factor and the user's energy efficiency. The access factor is related to the available resources and the scheduling method of the BS, and it represents the probability of user successfully access to a certain cell. The utility function is defined as:

$$\omega_k^n(\lambda) = \theta_k^n(\lambda) \cdot EE_k^n(\lambda) \tag{3}$$

where ω_k^n is the integrated utility value, θ_k^n is the access factor, EE_k^n is the energy efficiency of user k associated with BS n. We define the effective load of BS n as the number of users associated with it, L_n is the current load of BS n, and L_{n_max} is maximum acceptable load (the maximum number of users could be serviced by BS n). Generally, L_{n_max} is related with the maximum resources of the BS n could be provided as well as the scheduling scheme. Let L_{n_sim} denote the maximum number of users of BS n could be served in each Transmission Time Interval (TTI). If $L_n > L_{n\_sim}$, the BS n is not considered as an overloaded BS, since in the following TTI, some users may be served by other BSs due to the dynamic LB schedule. In this paper, we adapt the Rounding Robin Scheduling (i.e., $L_{n\_max} = 2L_{n\_sim}$), and update θ_k^n by the following process:

$$\theta_k^n = \begin{cases} \frac{L_{n\_max}-L_n}{L_{n\_max}} & \text{if } L_n < L_{n\_sim} \\ \frac{L_{n\_max}-L_n}{L_{n\_max}} \cdot \frac{L_{n\_sim}}{L_n} & \text{if } L_n \geq L_{n\_sim} \end{cases} \tag{4}$$

During the updating process, the BSs with smaller load will get lager access factor, thus the cells with smaller load are more likely to be selected. When a BS is full-loaded, the access factor reduce to zero, therefore, the user can not access the over-loaded cells. EE_k^n in (3) represents the energy efficiency of user k, which is given by

$$EE_k^n(\lambda) = \frac{\alpha \log_2(1 + SINR_k^n(\lambda))}{P_n} \tag{5}$$

Thus, the energy efficiency of BS n can be calculated by

$$EE_n(\lambda) = \frac{\sum r_{k,n}(\lambda)}{P_n}, \ k \in \{k|X_{k,n} = 1\} \tag{6}$$

where $\alpha = 0.6$ represents the Shannon fading loss. Let $\Psi(k)$ denote the degree of freedom of user k, which is the number of BSs could be selected by user k under the SINR target constraint. For user k, we conclude the LB design algorithm to the following steps:

- Step 1: User k obtain its respective candidate cell list C_k, in which all cells could meet its SINR target requirement, and calculate the degree of freedom $\Psi(k)$ of user k.

- Step 2: Repeat step 1 until every user in the network obtain its candidate set, then the users exchange their candidate list to the nearby BSs.
- Step 3: Let the users with smaller degree of freedom to select the cell preferentially. During the cell selection, the BS circularly send the feedback information to the users, and the feedback information contains the current load, maximum load and downlink transmission power of the BS.
- Step 4: When the user k obtained all the feedback information from its candidate cells, the $\omega_k^n(\lambda)(\forall n \in C_k)$ can be calculated.
- Step 5: The BS n^* with the largest $\omega_k^n(\lambda)$ will be selected for user k. Once a user makes the choice, it sends an access request signal to the BS n^* before access it.

The proposed optimal cell association LB algorithm is summarized in Algorithm 1.

Algorithm 1. Optimal Cell Association LB Algorithm (CALB)

1: **Initialization** :
2: $L = \mathbf{0}_{|\mathbf{N}_\beta| \times \mathbf{1}}$; $X = \mathbf{0}_{|\mathbf{N}_\mu| \times |\mathbf{N}_\beta|}$; $\Psi = \mathbf{0}_{|\mathbf{U_k}| \times \mathbf{1}}$;
3: Cell Selection Step
4: **for all** $k \in \mathbf{U}$ **do**
5:    $\mathbf{C_k} = \{n \in B | SINR_k^n \geq SINR_k^{target}\}$
6:    **for all** $k \in \mathbf{C_k}$ **do**
7:       $TRAN(n, C_k)$: transfer C_k to BS
8:    **end for**
9: **end for**
10: Cell Association Step
11: **for all** $n \in B$ **do**
12:    $U_n = \{k \in U | n \in C_k\}$;
13:    **for all** $k \in U_n$ **do**
14:       Calculate $\Psi(k) = |C_k|$;
15:    **end for**
16:    $SU_n = SORT(D, U_n)$; % $SORT$ array users in ascending order according to their degree of freedom.
17:    **for all** $k \in SU_n$ **do**
18:       Calculate $\omega_k^n, \forall n \in C_k$;
19:       $n^* = arg_n\{max(\omega_k^n)\}$;
20:       $X_k^{n^*} = 1$;
21:       $L_n^* = L_n^* + 1$;
22:       **if** $L_n^* = L_{n^*\_max}$;
23:       **BS** n^* notifies the users $\in U_n$ to delete the BS n^* in its cell list.
24:       Update degree of freedom of users$\in U_n$.
25:       $SU_n = SORT(D, U_n)$;
26:       **end if**
27:    **end for**
28: **end for**

Notably, the CALB algorithm is a low-complexity distributed algorithm and not need to search the entire network for each user.

3.2   FBSs Active/Idle Switch Strategies Control

Based on the LB design from the previous steps. We determine the optimal FBSs active/idle strategies to maximize the NEE. Since a large of portion power consumption is assumed by the circuits of active BSs. Our main concern is how to save energy by switching off unnecessary FBSs. Problem (P1) is a discrete optimization problem, and the optimal FBSs active/idle operation strategies can be found by exhaustive search over $2^{|B_s|}$ possible cases, where the B_s denotes the number of FBSs. However, it is difficult to get a closed-form solution on optimal operation strategies, which results in high complexity and time-consumed by exhaustive search. To deal with problem mentioned above, we optimize the FBSs active/idle operation strategies that maximize the NEE under the network outage constraint. The optimal FBSs active/idle switch strategies control algorithm (FAIS) combined with the optimal solution from CALB algorithm to maximize the NEE is composed of two steps.

Algorithm 2. Optimal FBSs Active/Idle Switch Strategies Control Algorithm (FAIS)

1: **Initialization** :
2: All BSs are active, i.e., $N_p = 0$ and $\lambda_0 = I_{1 \times |B|}$
3: **repeat**
4: Calculate the NEE $\zeta'(N_p)$ by CALB Algorithm with a given SCS operation strategy λ_{N_p}
5: Calculate EE_n for all active BSs based on equation (6)
6: Find femtocell n^* such that $n^* = argmin EE_{n_{(\lambda_n=1)}}$
7: Update λ_{N_p} with $\lambda_{n^*} = 0$, and $N_p = N_p + 1$
8: **until** $\zeta'(N_p - 2) > \zeta'(N_p - 1)$
9: **return** $\lambda' = \lambda_{(N_p-1)}$

- Step 1: Based on a given FBSs active/idle operation strategy, we can obtain the optimal cell selection by CALB algorithm and a NEE value.
- Step 2: Denote the number of idle FBSs is N_p, there are $C_{B_s}^{N_p}$ numbers of NEE corresponding to the associated FBSs active/idle operation strategies. Among these NEE, we can obtain the optimal FBSs operation strategies with the maximum NEE. which is denoted as $\zeta(N_p)$.

To avoid the exhaustive search for getting the optimal N_p, we can switch FBSs in turns, when increasing the idle FBSs number N_p can not improve the NEE the algorithm stop. The proposed optimal FBSs active/idle switch strategies control algorithm (FAIS) is summarized in Algorithm 2. Notice that the proposed algorithm combined with the optimal LB design provides a sub-optimal solution for problem (P1). Moreover, the idle FBSs could be periodically active and broadcast beacon messages. Therefore, we can periodically process FAIS algorithm to adapt the variation of the system traffic.

4   Simulation Results

In this section, we provide simulation results to evaluate the performance of the proposed scheme described in the previous section. The analytical results show a better communication service and a larger performance gain by the proposed CALB algorithm and the maximum NEE could be achieved by FAIS algorithm. In the simulation, we only switch off the FBSs. The main simulation parameters used in the simulation are summarized in Table 1. Parameter σ refers to literature [9], and $\delta = 0.1$ when FBS is idle. We consider the following conventional algorithms for comparison with the proposed algorithm:

- Baseline algorithm (Max-SINR): user association based on max-SINR scheme, and FBSs are not switch off.
- No association off algorithm (NAO) [8]: user association based on max-SINR scheme, and the FBSs initially without associated users will be switched off.
- Lowest association off algorithm (LAO) [10]: user association based on max-SINR scheme, and half of the FBSs with the smallest number of associated users will be switched off.

Table 1. Simulation parameter

Parameter name	Value
Macro cell radius	200 m
MBS transmission power	46 dBm
PBS transmission power	35 dBm
FAP transmission power	20 dBm
MBS load ($L_{sim}^{macro}, L_{max}^{macro}$)	40,80
PBS load ($L_{sim}^{pico}, L_{max}^{pico}$)	8,16
FAP load ($L_{sim}^{femto}, L_{max}^{femto}$)	4,8
Bias-SINR offset	3 dB
Shadow fading	Log-normal
N_0 noise power	-174 dB/Hz

In Fig. 2, we show the normalized load (defined as the current load divided by the maximum load of BS) per BS with different algorithms for $|N_\beta| = 10$ and $|N_\mu| = 150$. It is observed that the Max-SINR and the Bias-SINR algorithm could be overloaded. BS No. 7, 8, 9 are over-load by Max-SINR algorithm, whereas BS No. 6, 7, 8, 9 are over-load by Bias-SINR algorithm. Compared with the tradition LB algorithm, the proposed CALB/FAIS algorithm could achieve the load balancing (the normalized load of each BS is less or equal 1).

In Fig. 3, the outage probability of network (defined as the number of outage users divided by the total users)is illustrated with respect to the number of users. With the increasing number of users, compared with the proposed CALB/FAIS algorithm, the Max-SINR and the Bias-SINR algorithm have higher outage probability, which could reached 14% and 17% when the number of users increased

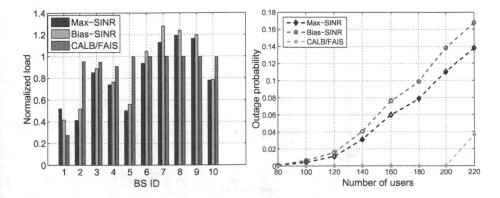

Fig. 2. Normalized load of different algorithms

Fig. 3. Outage probability of different algorithms v.s. the number of users

to 220. For the proposed algorithm, when the number of users is less than 200, the outage probability is zero. Moreover, even the number of users increase to 220, the outage probability is less than 4% due to the limited resources.

In Fig. 4, the performance gains of various algorithms compared to the baseline algorithm is depicted respectively. It is observed that the proposed algorithm could achieved the largest NEE and EC improvement. Apparently, it can obtain the highest energy saving gain at the cost of the network throughput.

Figure 5 shows NEE gain of various algorithms compared to the baseline algorithm v.s. the number of FBSs $|\beta_S|$. It is shown that the NEE gains of all algorithms are increasing in $|\beta_S|$. Because with the number of FBSs increasing, the network load becomes lower. Therefore, larger percentage of FBSs can be switched off to save energy, so as to improve NEE.

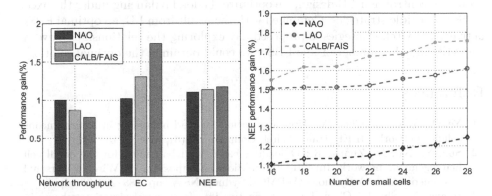

Fig. 4. Performance gain of different algorithms

Fig. 5. NEE gain of different algorithms v.s. $|\beta_s|$

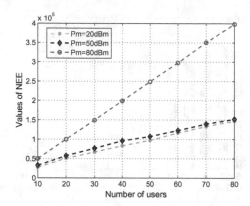

Fig. 6. NEE with different P_m v.s. number of users

To investigate the impact of transmission power of MBS in HetNet, we compare the NEE of the proposed CALB/FAIS algorithm with different P_m in Fig. 6. Particularly, when the network become dense, there will be more users association from FBSs to MBSs. This is because the MBSs can provide greater NEE with higher P_m. In this case, the larger number of FBSs can be switched off to improve NEE.

5 Conclusion

We investigate the joint LB design and FBSs active/idle strategies for maximizing the NEE in dense HetNets. The optimization problem is NP-hard. In order to reduce the complexity of algorithm, we decomposed the optimization problem into two sub-optimization problems. i.e., LB design and FBSs active/idle switch strategies control. For LB design, we optimize the load balancing under the fixed FBSs active/idle strategies. Combined with the result from LB, an optimal FBSs active/idle switch strategies is proposed. By exploring the relationship between the NEE and the number of idle FBSs, we could obtained the optimal solution.

References

1. Ye, Q., Rong, B., Chen, Y.: User association for load balancing in heterogeneous cellular networks. IEEE Trans. Wirel. Commun. **12**(6), 2706–2716 (2013)
2. Sun, Y., Xu, X., Zhang, R.: Offloading based load balancing for the small cell heterogeneous network. In: 2014 International Symposium on Wireless Personal Multimedia Communications (WPMC), Sydney, NSW, pp. 288–293 (2014)
3. Huang, X., Shi, L., Chen, L.: Cost-effective interference coordination scheme in high dense small cell heterogeneous network. In: China Communications (2015)
4. Boostanimehr, H., Bhargava, V.K.: Unified and distributed QoS-driven cell association algorithms in heterogeneous networks. IEEE Trans. Wirel. Commun. **14**(3), 1650–1662 (2014)

5. Li, A., Liao, X., Yang, Y.: A distributed energy-efficient algorithm for resource allocation in downlink femtocell networks. In: 2014 IEEE 25th Annual International Symposium on Personal, Indoor, and Mobile Radio Communication (PIMRC), Washington, DC, pp. 1169–1174 (2014)
6. Mesodiakaki, A., Adelantado, F., Alonso, L.: Energy-efficient context-aware user association for outdoor small cell heterogeneous networks. In: 2014 IEEE International Conference on Communications (ICC), Sydney, NSW, pp. 1614–1619 (2014)
7. Jin, Y., Qiu, L., Liang, X.: Small cells on/off control and load balancing for green dense heterogeneous networks. In: 2015 IEEE Wireless Communications and Networking Conference (WCNC), New Orleans, LA, pp. 1530–1535 (2015)
8. Sun, L., Yang, C., Xu, Z.: Energy-efficient downlink transmission with base station closing in small cell networks. In: 2013 IEEE International Conference on Acoustics, Speech and Signal Processing (ICASSP), Vancouver, BC, pp. 4784–4788 (2013)
9. Imran, M.: Energy efficiency analysis of the reference systems areas of improvements and target breakdown. INFSO-ICT-247733 EARTH, Deliverable D2.3.2012 (2012)
10. Intel Corporation: Performance Evaluation of Small Cell On/Off (R1132933), 3GPP TSG RAN WG1 Meeting-74.2013 (2013)

Energy Efficiency of Heterogeneous Air-Ground Cellular Networks

Jie Xin[✉], Liqiang Zhao, and Guogang Zhao

State Key Laboratory of ISN, Xidian University, Xi'an 710071, Shaanxi, China
xidianxj@163.com, lqzhao@mail.xidian.edu.cn,
ggzhao@s-an.org

Abstract. With the development of aerial platforms, it becomes possible for aerial platform-based base stations to coordinate with terrestrial cellular networks and provide services for terrestrial users immediately and effectually. Hence, in the paper, a heterogeneous air-ground cellular network is proposed which can provide high data rate for local users while enhancing energy efficiency of the heterogeneous network. Different from regular topology of terrestrial cellular networks, performance of heterogeneous air-ground networks are analyzed with a random topology of aerial and terrestrial base stations using Poisson point process with different densities respectively. And the relationship between energy efficiency of heterogeneous networks and densities of aerial and terrestrial base stations is given in an explicit form. Simulations are carried out and show that energy efficiency of the heterogeneous network can be significantly improved with appropriate densities of terrestrial and aerial base stations.

Keywords: Aerial platforms · Heterogeneous air-ground cellular network · Poisson point process · Energy efficiency

1 Introduction

With aerial platforms developing quickly, a potential solution to satisfy the growing wireless business requirement lies in aerial platforms, which carry communications relay payloads [1, 2]. A payload can be a complete base station, or simply a transparent transponder [3]. Akin to the majority of satellites communications, line-of-sight propagation paths can be provided to most users, with a modest free-space path loss [4, 5], thus enabling services to take advantage of the best features of both terrestrial and aerial communications. A single aerial platform can replace a large number of terrestrial base stations, along with their associated costs, environmental impact and backhaul constraints.

Although aerial platforms provide a way to solve the communication business expansion, there are still some problems need to be overcome. On the one hand, aerial platforms cannot be deployed widely due to the high cost of installation and maintenance; on the other hand, energy efficiency has been the problem worthy of concern as green communication emerging. In paper [6], system energy efficiency was improved by reducing the number and size of active macro cells following traffic load conditions in both heterogeneous and homogeneous networks. And in paper [7], by analyzing the

© ICST Institute for Computer Sciences, Social Informatics and Telecommunications Engineering 2018
Q. Chen et al. (Eds.): ChinaCom 2016, Part II, LNICST 210, pp. 248–257, 2018.
DOI: 10.1007/978-3-319-66628-0_24

relationship between the optimal partial spectrum reuse factor and active probability ratio, energy consumption minimization in heterogeneous networks can be addressed. When set up aerial platforms, the density of base stations should not only be planned to reinforce the user throughput and system capacity, but also guarantee the improved energy efficiency (EE) with user's transmission rate constraint [8].

In this paper, we build a model of heterogeneous networks with terrestrial base stations and aerial platform-based base stations, where the distributions of aerial and terrestrial base stations are modeled as independent homogeneous Poisson point processes (PPPs) with different densities λ [9–11]. We further derive the more compact closed-form EE and find that with the respect of densities of terrestrial and aerial base stations changing into different values, the maximum EE of heterogeneous network will be obtained with exact values of λ. The theoretical framework is verified by simulations.

The rest of this paper is organized as follows. In Sect. 2, the hierarchy architecture and system model are described. Section 3 formulates and derives the EE model of the heterogeneous air-ground cellular networks. In Sect. 4, simulations are carried out to show and analyze numerical results. Finally, the conclusions are summarized in Sect. 5.

2 System Model

2.1 Hierarchy Architecture

We consider ground-ground and air-ground communications coexisting in the heterogeneous networks. A hierarchical architecture is proposed in Fig. 1, which includes both aerial and terrestrial base stations Poisson-point distributed in the heterogeneous air-ground networks. And user equipment (UE) makes connection with aerial or terrestrial base stations according to the channel state information (CSI). In general, the coverage of aerial base stations is much larger compared with terrestrial base stations.

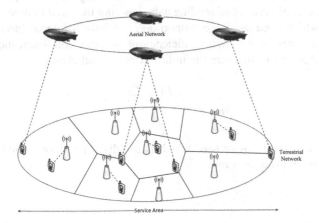

Fig. 1. Hierarchy architecture for air-ground heterogeneous networks

2.2 System Energy Efficiency

The cellular network model consists of terrestrial base stations arranged according to homogeneous Poisson point process (PPP) Ψ_b^m of intensity λ_m in the Euclidean plane. Consider an independent collection of aerial base station projections on the ground, located according to Poisson point process Ψ_b^s of intensity λ_s, and the attitudes of all the aerial base stations are assumed to be consistent in this paper. So the set of all base stations can be expressed as $\{\cup_i \Psi_b^i : i \in m, s\}$. Use $b_j^{(i)} \in \Psi_b^i$ to denote the jth base station belong to $i \in \{m, s\}$ layer. Furthermore, the distributions of system users are also assumed to be independent Poisson point distributed with density of λ_u. Let α_1, α_2 denote the pass loss coefficient of ground-ground link and ground-air link, which satisfy to $\alpha_1 > \alpha_2 \geq 2$ as a condition through this model.

In an arbitrary cell, the whole users can be denoted as Ψ_b^u, where $|\Psi_b^u| = N \in N^+$. The total bandwidth of base station $b_j^{(i)}$ for downlink is BHZ, and it is equally divided into N sub-bands (i.e. each user belonging to base station $b_j^{(i)}$ has $B_0 = B/N \, HZ$). In the kth sub-band, the associated user requires a specific service rate $R_{k,\min}$. We assume both terrestrial and aerial stations have the adaptive power control ability according to zero-delay channel state information. Therefore, the BS transmission power $P_{j,k}$ for $R_{j,k}$ on its sub-band is allocated to ensure the required service rate $R_{k,\min}$, and the total transmission power of base station $b_j^{(i)}$ can be obtained:

$$R_{j,k} = B_0 \log_2 \left(1 + \frac{P_{j,k} g_{j,k}}{I_{j,k} + \sigma^2} \right) \geq R_{k,\min}.$$
$$P_{total}^j = \sum_k P_{j,k} \quad s.t. P_{total}^j \leq P_M. \tag{1}$$

where σ^2 denotes power spectral density of Gaussian noise. $I_{j,k}$ is inter-layer interference plus cross-layer interference, $g_{j,k}$ is the power channel gains between user and its associated base stations.

When calculating the maximum transmission rate, many literatures just consider the transmission power of network of sending data, ignoring the circuit power consumption of equipment which occupies large proportion especially for aerial base stations. To comprehensively analyse the energy efficiency of wireless communication, we adopt the formula as follows to measure the utility of energy efficiency.

$$\eta_{EE} = \frac{\log_2 \left(1 + \frac{P_{j,k} g_{j,k}}{I_{j,k} + \sigma^2} \right)}{P_{total}^j + P_c}. \tag{2}$$

where P_c denotes circuit power loss, which is usually a fixed value and has no relationship with the transmission rate.

3   EE Analysis for Heterogeneous Networks

3.1   Interference Analysis and EE Formulation

For the users belonging to terrestrial base stations, unless otherwise noted, we assume that the tagged user and its associated base station experience only Rayleigh fading with mean 1. Employ a constant transmit power of $P_{j,k}^{(m)}$ and in this case, the received power of a typical user at distance $r_{j,k}$ from the home base station is $P_{j,k}^{(m)} h_{j,k}^m r_{j,k}^{-\alpha_1}$, where the random variable $h_{j,k}^m$ follows an exponential distribution with mean 1, denoted as $h_{j,k}^{(m)} \sim \exp(1)$. The transmission rate can be represented as follows:

$$R_{j,k}^{(m)} = B_0 \log_2 \left(1 + \frac{P_{j,k}^{(m)} h_{j,k}^m r_{j,k}^{-\alpha_1}}{(I_{10} + I_{11}) + \sigma^2} \right). \tag{3}$$

where I_{10} and I_{11} are the interferences of inter-layer and cross-layer. Since the total interference at a user is greatly higher than the noise power, i.e. $\sigma^2 \ll I_{10} + I_{11}$, we will not consider the effects of noise in this paper. The corresponding transmission power needed by user $u_{j,k}^{(m)}$ is

$$P_{j,k}^{(m)} = \left(2^{R_{j,k}^{(m)}/B_0} - 1 \right) (I_{10} + I_{11}) r_{j,k}^{\alpha_1}. \tag{4}$$

The interference power at the receiver is the sum of the received powers from all other base stations other than the home base station. For users connected with terrestrial base station $b_j^{(m)}$, the inter-layer interferences can be formulated as:

$$I_{10}^{\lambda_m} = \sum_{n \neq j} P_n h_{n,k}^{(m)} \left\| u_{j,k}^{(m)} - b_j^{(m)} \right\|^{-\alpha_1}. \tag{5}$$

where P_n is transmission power of interferential base stations.

Hence, for the users that belong to terrestrial stations, the moment generation function of I_{10} can be calculated as:

$$F_{I_{10}} = \exp \left(2\pi\lambda_m \int_{r_{j,k}^{(m)}}^{+\infty} \left(1 - \exp\left(-t \frac{P_m}{Nr^{\alpha_1}} \right) \right) r dr \right). \tag{6}$$

where P_m represents the maximum transmission power of terrestrial base stations.

According to the property of moment generation function, we have

$$I_{10} = E\left(I_{10}^{\lambda_m} \right) = -\frac{\partial}{\partial t} \ln F_{I_{10}}(t)|_{t=0} = \frac{2\pi\lambda_m P_m}{(\alpha_1 - 2)N} r_{j,k}^{(m)2-\alpha_1}. \tag{7}$$

In this paper, we assume that overages of aerial base stations do not overlap with each other, so the users connected with terrestrial base stations just receive interferences from their closest aerial base station, i.e.

$$I_{11} = E(I_{11}^{\lambda_s}) = \frac{P_s}{N} \left\{ \sqrt{\left(E(r_{n,k}^{(s)})\right)^2 + h^2} \right\}^{-\alpha_2} = \frac{P_s}{N} \left\{ \sqrt{\frac{[\Gamma(\frac{3}{2})]^2}{\pi \lambda_s} + h^2} \right\}^{-\alpha_2}. \tag{8}$$

where P_s is the transmission power of aerial base station with attitude h, and $\Gamma(x) = \int_0^{+\infty} r^{x-1} e^{-r} dr$.

According to Eqs. (7) and (8), the average transmission power needed by $u_{j,k}^{(m)}$ can be obtained as follows:

$$E\left[P_{j,k}^{(m)}\right] = \int_{r_{j,k}>0} \left(2^{R_{j,k}^{(m)}/B_0} - 1\right)(I_{10} + I_{11}) r_{j,k}^{\alpha_1} \cdot 2\pi \lambda_m r_{j,k} e^{-\pi \lambda_m r_{j,k}^2} = \frac{\left(2^{NR_{j,k}^{(m)}/B} - 1\right) X_1}{N}.$$

$$\tag{9}$$

$$X_1 = \frac{2P_m}{\alpha_1 - 2} + P_s \left[\sqrt{\frac{[\Gamma(\frac{3}{2})]^2}{\pi \lambda_s} + h^2} \right]^{-\alpha_2} \frac{\Gamma(\frac{\alpha_1}{2} + 1)}{(\pi \lambda_m)^{\frac{\alpha_1}{2}}}. \tag{10}$$

Assume that the coverage area of base station $b_j^{(m)}$ is S_m and all of terrestrial base stations have same transmission rate, i.e. $R_{j,k}^{(m)} = R_m$. With $\lambda_u S_m$ denoting the number of users belonging to $b_j^{(m)}$, total transmission power of terrestrial base station $b_j^{(m)}$ can be expressed as:

$$P_m^{S_m} = X_1 \left[\left(2^{NR_m/B} - 1\right) \lambda_u S_m \right]. \tag{11}$$

Because the overages of aerial base stations do not overlap with others, for the users served by aerial base stations, they just suffer from interference of cross-layer. In a similar way, the average transmission power of an aerial station with coverage of S_s can be represented as:

$$P_s^{S_s} = X_2 \left[\left(2^{NR_s/B} - 1\right) \lambda_u S_s \right]. \tag{12}$$

when assuming the following substitutions:

$$X_2 = \frac{2\pi \lambda_m P_m}{\alpha_1 - 2} \beta^{\frac{2-\alpha_1}{\alpha_1}} \frac{\Gamma\left(\frac{\alpha_2}{\alpha_1} + 1, h\right)}{(\pi \lambda_s)^{\frac{\alpha_2}{\alpha_1}}}. \tag{13}$$

where $\beta = P_m/P_s$, and $\Gamma(x, y)$ is half-baked gamma function which can be expressed as:

$$\Gamma(x,y) = \int_y^{+\infty} r^{x-1}e^{-r}dr. \tag{14}$$

The energy efficiency formula of heterogeneous network can be obtained from the derivation above:

$$\eta_{EE} = \frac{\lambda_u(R_m + R_s)}{B\left[\lambda_m\left(P_m^{S_m} + P_{OM}^{(m)}\right) + \lambda_s\left(P_s^{S_s} + P_{OM}^{(s)}\right)\right]}. \tag{15}$$

In formula (16), $P_{OM}^{(m)}, P_{OM}^{(s)}$ separately represent the circuit power consumption of terrestrial and aerial base stations.

3.2 Proof of Existence of the Optimal Solution

It can be discovered that the energy efficiency formula contains of λ_m and λ_s, then it will be verified how λ_m and λ_s influence the energy efficiency in system.

$$\frac{\partial\eta_{EE}}{\partial\lambda_m} = \frac{-\lambda_u(R_m + R_s)}{B^2\left[\lambda_m\left(P_m^{S_m} + P_{OM}^{(m)}\right) + \lambda_s\left(P_s^{S_s} + P_{OM}^{(s)}\right)\right]^2}$$
$$\cdot \frac{\partial\left\{B\left[\lambda_m\left(P_m^{S_m} + P_{OM}^{(m)}\right) + \lambda_s\left(P_s^{S_s} + P_{OM}^{(s)}\right)\right]\right\}}{\partial\lambda_m}. \tag{16}$$

$$\frac{\partial\left\{B\left[\lambda_m\left(P_m^{S_m} + P_{OM}^{(m)}\right) + \lambda_s\left(P_s^{S_s} + P_{OM}^{(s)}\right)\right]\right\}}{\partial\lambda_m} = B\left[P_{OM}^{(m)} + \frac{\partial(\lambda_m P_m^{S_m})}{\partial\lambda_m}\right] + \theta. \tag{17}$$

where $\theta = \frac{2\pi P_m}{\alpha_1 - 2}\beta^{\frac{2-\alpha_1}{\alpha_1}}\frac{\Gamma\left(\frac{\alpha_2}{\alpha_1} + 1, h\right)}{(\pi\lambda_s)^{\frac{\alpha_2}{\alpha_1}}}$.

Let $P_s\left[\sqrt{\frac{[\Gamma(\frac{3}{2})]^2}{\pi\lambda_s} + h^2}\right]^{-\alpha_2} \cdot \frac{\Gamma(\frac{\alpha_2}{2}+1)}{\pi^{\frac{\alpha_2}{2}}} = C$, we have $\frac{\partial(\lambda_m P_m^{S_m})}{\partial\lambda_m} = \mu \cdot \left[\frac{P_m}{\alpha_1 - 2} + C\left(1 - \frac{\alpha_1}{2}\right)\right]$

$\frac{1}{\lambda_m^{\frac{\alpha_1}{2}}}$], where $\mu = \left(2^{NR_m/B} - 1\right)\lambda_u S_m$, it is obvious that $\gamma = P_{OM}^{(m)} + \mu \cdot \frac{P_m}{\alpha_1 - 2} > 0$, hence

$$\frac{\partial\eta_{EE}}{\partial\lambda_m} = \frac{-\lambda_u(R_m + R_s)}{B^2\left[\lambda_m\left(P_m^{S_m} + P_{OM}^{(m)}\right) + \lambda_s\left(P_s^{S_s} + P_{OM}^{(s)}\right)\right]^2} \cdot \left\{B\left[\gamma + \mu C\left(1 - \frac{\alpha_1}{2}\right)\frac{1}{\lambda_m^{\frac{\alpha_1}{2}}}\right] + \theta\right\}. \tag{18}$$

In the formula above,

$$\frac{-\lambda_u(R_m + R_s)}{B^2\left[\lambda_m\left(P_m^{s_m} + P_{OM}^{(m)}\right) + \lambda_s\left(P_s^{s_s} + P_{OM}^{(s)}\right)\right]^2} < 0. \tag{19}$$

Because $\alpha_1 \geq 2$ and $C > 0$, by the extremity theory:

$$\lim_{\lambda_m \to 0} B\left[\gamma + \mu C\left(1 - \frac{\alpha_1}{2}\right)\frac{1}{\lambda_m^{\frac{\alpha_1}{2}}}\right] + \theta < 0, \ i.e. \frac{\partial \eta_{EE}}{\partial \lambda_m} > 0. \tag{20}$$

$$\lim_{\lambda_m \to +\infty} B\left[\gamma + \mu C\left(1 - \frac{\alpha_1}{2}\right)\frac{1}{\lambda_m^{\frac{\alpha_1}{2}}}\right] + \theta > 0, \ i.e. \frac{\partial \eta_{EE}}{\partial \lambda_m} < 0. \tag{21}$$

Due to the continuity of η_{EE}, there must be a constant λ_m^* making $\frac{\partial \eta_{EE}}{\partial \lambda_m} = 0$. Namely when given in the density of aerial base stations, the energy efficiency of heterogeneous network will achieve a maximum value with a suitable density of terrestrial base stations, and more detailed influences are shown in the following simulations.

By the same token, for the density of aerial stations we can draw the same conclusion, the proof in detail will not be given here.

4 Simulation Results

We consider an area of 10 km × 10 km on the ground serviced by terrestrial and aerial stations. The free path loss model is adopted for the air-ground radio link. Table 1. gives some of the main system-level simulation parameters.

Table 1. Simulation parameters

Parameter	Value
Radius of aerial and terrestrial cell	2000 m, 500 m
Maximum transmission power of aerial base stations	46 dBm
Maximum transmission power of terrestrial base stations	20 dBm
System bandwidth	20 MHz

We firstly simulate the relationship of energy efficiency and densities of terrestrial and aerial base stations to illustrate energy efficiency model conducted in the paper. Then we adjust the density of the users to observe the change in transmission power of terrestrial and aerial base stations. Finally, we simulate the change of system energy efficiency with varying densities of users.

Figure 2 shows that the variation of energy efficiency with varying densities of aerial base stations λ_s and terrestrial base stations λ_m under the condition of $R_s = R_m = 0.2$ Mbit/s and $\lambda_u = 1000/\text{km}^2$, we note that given in a certain λ_s, with λ_m increasing, energy efficiency of network is improved firstly and lowers then and there is

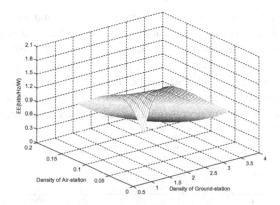

Fig. 2. Energy efficiency of integrated air-ground heterogeneous networks with different densities of terrestrial and aerial base stations

a certain value of λ_m which maximize the energy efficiency; and likewise when λ_m is given, there is an optimal value of λ_s. When terrestrial and aerial base stations are planned in small densities, throughput of the network is deficient and transmission power of terrestrial or aerial base stations need to be improved to satisfy the demand of users, which results in the reduction of energy efficiency. With increasing densities of terrestrial or aerial base stations, higher traffic rate can make the network throughput increase quickly, which leads to the improvement of energy efficiency.

In Fig. 3, we note that higher user density leads to the increase of transmission power of terrestrial and aerial base stations, and obviously higher rate needed by users means increasing transmission power, which results in the rise of power consumption. In addition, transmission power of aerial base stations is larger than which of terrestrial base stations with same density of users.

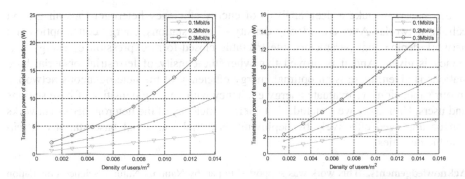

Fig. 3. Transmission power of aerial and terrestrial base stations with different densities of user

As illustrated in Fig. 4, the performance of energy efficiency over the heterogeneous network in varying $R_{k,\min}$ from 0.20, 0.25 to 0.30 Mbit/s is compared when λ_m and λ_s are given in a medium value. We note that with the density of network user increasing, energy efficiency of network is improved firstly and lowers then and there exists an optimal λ_u to maximize the energy efficiency. With small density of users, higher transmission rate needed by users leads to high energy efficiency. However, when the number of system user increases, power consumption increases rapidly to satisfy users' service request and leads to the increase of interferences, which restrict the increase of system throughput. As a result, although the higher traffic rate is needed with increasing users, high power consumption and serious interferences lead to lower energy efficiency.

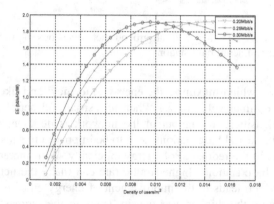

Fig. 4. Energy efficiency with various densities of users in different service rate ($\lambda_s = 0.14/\mathrm{km}^2$; $\lambda_m = 3.54/\mathrm{km}^2$; $B = 20\,\mathrm{MHz}$)

5   Conclusion

In this paper, we take a deep analysis of energy efficiency heterogeneous air-ground cellular networks. After considering density of base stations, energy consumption and network deployment parameters, the tractable closed-form expression of energy efficiency is given. And it is proved that when the density of terrestrial or aerial base stations is given, there is an optimal energy efficiency of the heterogeneous networks. In our simulation, we evaluate energy efficiency with varying densities of base stations and users. Ultimately we conclude that energy efficiency of the heterogeneous networks can be improved effectively by deploying terrestrial and aerial base stations in reasonable densities.

Acknowledgements. This work was supported in part by National Natural Science Foundation of China (61372070), Natural Science Basic Research Plan in Shaanxi Province of China (2015JM6324), Ningbo Natural Science Foundation (2015A610117), National High-tech R&D Program of China (863 Program-2015AA015701), and the 111 Project (B08038).

References

1. Oispuu, M., Nickel, U.: Array-based direction finding and localization for small aerial platforms. In: Antennas and Propagation in Wireless Communications, pp. 241–244. IEEE Press, Palm Beach (2014)
2. Rudnick, G., Clauß, S., Schulte, A.: Flight testing of agent supervisory control on heterogeneous unmanned aerial system platforms. In: IEEE/AIAA 33rd Digital Avionics Systems Conference, pp. 4B2-1–4B2-10. IEEE Press, Colorado Springs (2014)
3. Sagduyu, Y., Shi, Y., Ponnaluri, S., Soltani, S.: Optimal transmission decisions for airborne relay communications. In: Military Communications Conference, pp. 1685–1690. IEEE Press, Tampa (2015)
4. Chang, D., Lee, J., Lin, T.H.: A new perspective on satellite communications via incompatible signal polarization features and wavefront multiplexing techniques. In: Computing, Networking and Communications, pp. 390–394. IEEE Press, Garden Grove (2015)
5. Chang, D., Lee, J.: Satellite communications service provision via incompatible polarization diversity and orthogonal beams. In: 2015 IEEE Wireless Communications and Networking Conference, pp. 2256–2261. IEEE Press, New Orleans (2015)
6. Khirallah, C., Thompson, J.S., Vukobratovic, D.: Energy efficiency of heterogeneous networks in LTE-advanced. In: Wireless Communications and Networking Conference Workshops, pp. 53–58. IEEE Press, Paris (2012)
7. Chai, X., Zhang, Z., Long, K.: Joint spectrum-sharing and base station sleep model for improving energy efficiency of heterogeneous networks. IEEE Syst. J. **PP**, 1–11 (2015)
8. Xiao, X., Tao, X., Lu, J.: Energy-efficient resource allocation in LTE-based MIMO-OFDMA systems with user rate constraints. IEEE Trans. Veh. Technol. **64**, 185–197 (2015)
9. Jo, H.S., Sang, Y.J., Xia, P., Andrews, J.G.: Heterogeneous cellular networks with flexible cell association: a comprehensive downlink SINR analysis. IEEE Trans. Wirel. Commun. **11**, 3484–3495 (2012)
10. Andrews, J.G., Baccelli, F., Ganti, R.K.: A tractable approach to coverage and rate in cellular networks. IEEE Trans. Wirel. Commun. **59**, 3122–3134 (2011)
11. Mirahsan, M., Schoenen, R., Yanikomeroglu, H.: HetHetNets: heterogeneous traffic distribution in heterogeneous wireless cellular networks. IEEE J. Sel. Areas Commun. **33**, 2252–2265 (2015)

Capacity Analysis in the Cognitive Heterogeneous Cellular Networks with Stochastic Methods

Yinglei Teng, Mengting Liu[✉], and Mei Song

Electronic Engineering, Beijing University of Posts and Telecommunications,
Beijing 100876, China
lilytengtt@gmail.com, {liumengting, songm}@bupt.edu.cn

Abstract. Small cells are widely being deployed to enhance the performance of cellular networks, which results in a random distribution of base stations as well as a complex interference problem. Therefore, it becomes considerably challenging to derive a closed-form expression for the capacity of small cell enhanced heterogeneous cellular network especially when the cognitive radio (CR) technology is utilized to mitigate the possible interference. In this paper, we first use the discrete time Markov chain (DTMC) to achieve the spectrum mobility of macro base station (MBS) users, i.e. primary users (PUs) in the cognitive heterogeneous cellular networks (CHCNs). Meanwhile, by modeling MBSs and small base stations (SBSs) as two independent homogeneous Poisson point processes (HPPPs), we propose an integral way based on stochastic geometry (SG) to get the calculation of the interference. Simulation results show that our capacity analysis method of CHCNs serves well in approximating the network capacity by conquering the complex interference and the uncertainty of spectrum mobility, which turns out to be an efficient and promising approach.

Keywords: Cognitive heterogeneous cellular networks (CHCNs) · Markov chain · Stochastic geometry · Homogeneous Poisson point process (HPPP)

1 Introduction

The last few years have witnessed the proliferated deployment of small cells in the cellular network, e.g., pico cell, femto cell. The small cells can bring a high network capacity by providing heterogeneous access for indoor and outdoor hotspots. However, they also arouse a considerably complex problem, i.e., the cross-tier interference as well as co-tier interference. Meanwhile, the emerging of the small cells also aggravates the irregularity of network coverage. Therefore, the traditional regular hexagon network is not enough to provide the diverse rate requirement of different coverage.

Fortunately, by enabling cognitive radio (CR) technology on small cells to be aware of and adapt to communication environments, the interference issue can be tackled [1, 2]. The CR-enabled small base stations (SBSs) can actively acquire the information about the channel by spectrum sensing mechanism, which conduces to avoid the possible co-channel interferences and enhance the entire network performance. However, due to the irregular coverage of base stations and the troublesome interference problem,

© ICST Institute for Computer Sciences, Social Informatics and Telecommunications Engineering 2018
Q. Chen et al. (Eds.): ChinaCom 2016, Part II, LNICST 210, pp. 258–267, 2018.
DOI: 10.1007/978-3-319-66628-0_25

few works can give out a closed-form expression for the capacity of cognitive heterogeneous cellular networks (CHCNs). In addition, it becomes even more complicated
when spectrum mobility is involved. Therefore, it's far from easy to weigh the contribution of CR technology to the improvement of network capacity mathematically.

Recently, stochastic geometry (SG) wins its popularity through capturing the
topological randomness as well as acquiring tractable numerical results in the
increasingly complex networks [3–6]. Motivated by the favorable conclusions in
previous works, SG tends to be used in CHCNs. In [7], Hesham et al. utilize the SG to
model and analyze heterogeneous cellular networks from two aspects. They first exploit
SG to evaluate the load of each network tier, and then obtain the maximal frequency
reuse efficiency with spectrum sensing design for channel access by the assumption of
hard core point process (HCPP). But they only focus on the performance of cognitive
small cell network and get the outage probability for a small cell user. In [8], the
authors provide a performance analysis of two-tier HetNets with cognitive small cells
under the SG model with respect to the outage probability. They obtain the opportunistic spectrum access probability for small cell access points conditioned by the
spectrum sensing threshold. However, there are three weaknesses in the work. First, the
contribution of [8] is elaborated in the underlay fashion where the outage event of
primary users (PUs) is mainly caused by the aggregated interference from secondary
users (SUs) and noise environment. Second, only one PU is assumed in the derivation.
Third, the close-form derivation of interference from SUs to PU is obtained only in the
large-scale environment. [9] summarizes the previous work related to SG in the literatures for single-tier, multi-tier, as well as cognitive cellular wireless networks. The
author points out that only few results in the context of multi-tier cellular networks are
available to CHCNs and indicates that there are opportunities for innovating techniques
which facilitate the SG modeling.

After analyzing these, we can clarify some facts and difficulties in obtaining the
capacity derivation of cognitive multi-tier cellular networks. (i) The objective of CHCNs is
different from the conventional cognitive radio networks (CRNs) (i.e., cognitive networks
with licensed and unlicensed users). That is, we need to focus on the capacity aggregation
of both MBSs (similar to PUs in the conventional CRNs) and cognitive small cell base
stations (similar to SUs in the conventional CRNs) rather than an opportunistically utilization of SUs on the unlicensed band subject to a tolerable performance degradation for
the PUs. (ii) The spectrum access is sensitive to its mobility model which affects the
capacity derivation significantly. (iii) The calculation of interference becomes even more
difficult in the CHCNs. For one thing, the small cell infrastructure confuses traditional
regular deployment, also the spectrum reuse policy, and the interference becomes complicated to be observed. For another, it is never too easy to get the channel state information
(CSI) in the multi-cell system, especially in the multi-tier networks.

In this paper, we focus on a closed-form expression for the capacity of CHCNs,
which including two parts, i.e., deriving the distribution of time slots by the discrete
time Markov chain (DTMC) and approximating the co-tier and cross-tier interference
by an integral method. In order to get the interference of the whole coverage, the
integral method takes the integral of the probability of the interference according to the
distribution of the distance from the user to its serving base station. Further, under the
adopted homogeneous Poisson point process (HPPP) model, a series of simulations

illustrate that our proposed approach shows its superiority of weighing the network capacity accurately and efficiently, which also takes the spectrum mobility of macro base stations (MBSs) users into account.

The remaining sections of this paper are organized as follows. In Sect. 2, our model with SG modeling techniques is presented. Section 3 describes the DTMC for the purpose of analyzing the distribution of time slots and captures the capacity of CHCN by giving a closed-form expression. In Sect. 4, we provide numerical results and finally, Sect. 5 concludes the paper.

2 System Model

In this paper, we focus on a downlink two-tier CHCN where the users associate with the BS (MBS or SBS) which provides the highest reference signal receiving power (RSRP). Meanwhile, we assume that MBSs and their users use the licensed spectrum band, while SBSs and their users act as the unlicensed users that access the channels if sensing the vacant spectrum. Thereby, they work in an overlay fashion composing a typical cognitive radio system apparently, i.e., MBS and their users work as PUs while SBS and their users are SUs. To note that, they both serve as the cellular network, thus, both the capacity of MBSs and SBSs need to be taken into consideration in the CHCNs. Each time slot T_{slot} is divided into two periods, i.e., sensing period T_s, where SBSs and their users scan throughout the spectrum band and data transmission period, where SBSs access the channel if finding vacancy for MBSs. The structure of the frame is illustrated in Fig. 1. The time for merging the sensing results and their feedback to the serving SBSs is ignored. Here, we assume that only one user is allowed to access the channel during the time slot within each macro cell or small cell and there is no free time slot.

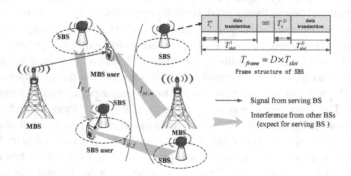

Fig. 1. Illustration of a two-tier heterogeneous network.

Instead of assuming the MBSs and SBSs are placed deterministically in a grid model, we adopt a HPPP model in this paper, where MBSs and SBSs accord to two independent HPPPs with density λ_M and λ_F respectively. Also, users located in the CHCNs accords to another HPPP with density λ_U, which includes X MBS users and Y SBS users. The idea of HPPP derives from SG which aims at weighing the network topologies from an average perspective rather than one single base station or user. It has been shown by [9] as an equally accurate model to capture the performance of the network compared with conventional grid model, whereas, the former is more preferable for its tractability to describe the increasing opportunistic placed base stations in the future.

As is shown in Fig. 1, since the overlay fashion is applied in this paper, there is no interference between two tiers, thus only co-tier interference remains. We assume that all the MBSs and SBSs simultaneously transmit to their associated users with the same power P_M and P_F. g_M denotes the transmission gain of MBS user from its serving MBS. Similarly, g_F is the transmission gain of SBS user from its serving SBS. Note that we only consider the large-scale fading for simplicity. The noise is assumed to be zero-mean complex additive white Gaussian random variables with power P_{Noise}. Then the signal to interference plus noise ratio (SINR) of MBS and SBS users are given respectively by (1) and (2).

$$SINR_m = \frac{P_M g_M}{I_{M,m} + P_{Noise}} \tag{1}$$

$$SINR_f = \frac{P_F g_F}{I_{F,f} + P_{Noise}} \tag{2}$$

where $I_{M,m}$ is the interference for MBS user m from other MBSs. Likewise, $I_{F,f}$ is the interference caused by other SBSs to SBS user f.

3 Capacity Derivation of Cognitive Heterogeneous Networks

In the CHCN model, it is hard to derive the capacity due to the uncertainty of spectrum mobility and the complex interference between users and the heterogeneous base stations. As the DTMC advantages in analyzing the reliability and performance of service portfolio, we consult to Markov chain to acquire the distribution of time slots. Meanwhile, the interference is captured with HPPP assumption in a SG way.

3.1 Markov Chain Model for the Spectrum Mobility

The method of DTMC to capture the spectrum mobility is defined by its state, transfer probability and steady probability. In what follows, we assume that MBS users arrive in the channel with a probability of λ_a and depart with a probability of λ_d.

(1) State

Let M time slots be occupied by MBS users on the channel, and use $\psi = \{\psi(u) = 0 \, or \, 1, u = 1, 2, \ldots, M\}$ to represent the occupancy state of all MBS users, in which $\psi(u) = 0$ means that the MBS user is on the channel while $\psi(u) = 1$ means it is absent. Then, $\phi(i) = \sum_{u=1}^{M} \psi(u) = i, 0 \leq i \leq D$ denotes that there are i MBS users in the frame and D is the number of time slots.

(2) Transfer probability
Here, the MBS users arrive and depart in a Poisson way, and once one MBS user arrives, a single time slot of consecutive frames will be occupied for an exponentially distributed time period until it leaves. The probability of k $(0 \leq k \leq i)$ MBS users' arrival during the frame is given by

$$P_A(k) = \mathbb{P}\{N_A = k\} = \frac{(\lambda_a T_{frame})^k}{k!} e^{-\lambda_a T_{frame}}. \tag{3}$$

where N_A is the number of MBS users who arrive at the channel during the frame and $T_{frame} = D \times T_{slot}$ means the total time of the frame.
Similarly, the probability of l $(0 \leq l \leq i+k)$ MBS users' departure during the frame is given by

$$P_D(l) = \mathbb{P}\{N_D = l\} = \frac{(\lambda_d T_{frame})^l}{l!} e^{-\lambda_d T_{frame}}. \tag{4}$$

where N_D is the number of MBS users leaving the channel during the frame.
Therefore, in the state $\phi(i)$, the probability of k MBS users' arrival is expressed by

$$A(i, k, l) = \begin{cases} P_A(k) & i-l+k<D \\ 1 - \sum\limits_{d=0}^{k-1} P_A(d) & i-l+k = D \end{cases}. \tag{5}$$

Correspondingly, the probability of l departures in state $\phi(i)$ is

$$D(i, k, l) = \begin{cases} P_D(l) & i-l+k > 0 \\ 1 - \sum\limits_{q=0}^{l} P_D(q) & i-l+k = 0 \end{cases}. \tag{6}$$

The transition probability matrix $\mathbf{P}$ can be derived by calculating all the state transforms probability P_{ij} from $\phi(i)$ to $\phi(i+H)$. The elements of the matrix P_{ij} is

$$P_{ij} = P_{i+H,i} = P((i+H)|i) = \sum\limits_{k=\max(-H,0)}^{i} A(i, H+k, k) D(i, H+k, k), 0 \leq i \leq D, -i \leq H \leq D-i \tag{7}$$

(3) Steady probability $\pi(i)$
Constructing the steady state probability $\pi(i)$, $i = 1, \ldots, D$ as the elements of matrix $\Pi = [\pi(0), \pi(1), \ldots, \pi(D)]$, we are able to obtain $\pi(i)$ by finding the solution with respect to the following condition equation.

$$\Pi = \Pi \bullet \mathbf{P} \tag{8}$$

(4) The number of MBS and SBS users
The average number of MBS users during the frame can be calculated by accumulating all the possible state.

$$N_p = \sum_{i=0}^{D} i \times \pi(i) \tag{9}$$

Therefore, the average number of SBS users is given by (10).

$$N_s = D - N_p \tag{10}$$

3.2 The Approximating Capacity of CHCN with HPPP Assumption

In this paper, assuming that interference is captured by the density of base stations, we consult to an integral way to derive the interference. The idea derives from "fluid model" in [10] where the integral of the density of BSs in the whole network is used to calculate the capacity. In the HPPP model, the probability density function (PDF) of the distance between the serving BS and the user (denoted as r) can be given by

$$f(r) = \lambda 2\pi r e^{-\lambda \pi r^2} \tag{11}$$

where $\lambda = \lambda_M \, or \, \lambda_F$.

As to the channel model, we only consider the power loss propagation for short. Hence, the transmission gain in (1) and (2) can be express as $g_M, g_F = r^{-\alpha}$ where α denotes the path loss exponent. Taking the integral in the coverage of interfering base stations, we can get the interference for MBS users and SBS users.

According to our assumption, only co-tier interference is considered. Therefore, there are two kinds of interference categorized by different tiers.

(1) When the channel is occupied by MBS users, for a specific MBS user, the interference from other MBSs is given by

$$I_{M,m} = \int_{0}^{2\pi} \int_{r}^{\infty} p_M \lambda_M 2\pi r e^{-\lambda_M \pi r^2} \times r^{-\alpha} dr d\theta = 2\pi p_M (\pi \lambda_M)^{\frac{\alpha}{2}} \left[\Gamma\left(1 - \frac{\alpha}{2}\right) - \Gamma\left(1 - \frac{\alpha}{2}, r\right) \right] \tag{12}$$

where $\Gamma(x) = \int_{0}^{\infty} t^{x-1} e^{-t} dt$ and $\Gamma(x,r) = \int_{0}^{r} t^{x-1} e^{-t} dt$ are standard gamma function and incomplete gamma function respectively.

(2) Similarly, when the channel is occupied by SBS users, thus, the interference from other SBSs is as follows

$$I_{F,f} = \int_{0}^{2\pi} \int_{r}^{\infty} p_F \lambda_F 2\pi r e^{-\lambda_F \pi r^2} \times r^{-\alpha} dr d\theta = 2\pi p_F (\pi \lambda_F)^{\frac{\alpha}{2}} \left[\Gamma\left(1 - \frac{\alpha}{2}\right) - \Gamma\left(1 - \frac{\alpha}{2}, r\right) \right] \tag{13}$$

Therefore, the whole network capacity can be expressed as

$$C = C_M + C_F = \frac{W\eta}{D} [N_p \sum_{m=1}^{X} \log_2(1 + SINR_m) + N_s \sum_{f=1}^{Y} \log_2(1 + SINR_f)] \tag{14}$$

where W is the bandwidth of the channel, $\eta = 1 - T_s/T_{slot}$ is the sensing efficient. C_M and C_F stand for the capacity of macro cells and small cells respectively.

4   Simulation Results and Analysis

To testify the proposed capacity expressions, we present several numerical metrics and give relative analysis in this section. In the two-tier CHCN, MBSs, SBSs and users are distributed in a HPPP way with density $4 \times 10^{-5}/m^2$, $8 \times 10^{-4}/m^2$ and $1.6 \times 10^{-4}/m^2$ respectively in a circular coverage with radius 500 m. The rest of the simulation parameters are listed in Table 1.

Table 1. Simulation parameters.

Symbol	Definition	Default value
P_M	The transmit power of MBS	20 W
P_F	The transmit power of SBS	0.1 W
P_{Noise}	The power of noise	−174 dBm/Hz
W	The physical bandwidth	1 Hz
α	The path loss exponent	3
D	The number of time slots in a frame	20
T_{slot}	The lasting time of each time slot	0.577 ms
T_s	The lasting time of sensing time	25 μs
λ_a	The arrival probability of the MBS users	0.8
λ_d	The departure probability of the MBS users	0.5

4.1   Comparison Between Theoretical Analysis and Simulation Result

We simulate the capacity of the network derived by integral method (theoretical analysis) and sum method (simulation) in HPPP model in Fig. 2. It can be figured out that the integral method has a lower capacity than that of the sum method. This is because the BSs and users modeled by HPPPs are located in a more random way, which brings a more conservative result by theoretical analysis compared with the simulation. Thereby, integral method aggregates a higher interference resulting in the lower capacity. Also, with the increase of SBSs density, the gap between the two

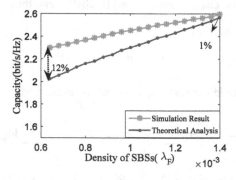

Fig. 2. Comparison between simulation result and theoretical analysis of network capacity.

methods gets smaller (when the density of SBSs increases from 0.00063 to 0.0014/m², the gap decreases from 12% to 1%). This reveals that the theoretical results approach the simulation at high density of SBSs.

4.2   Effect of the Spectrum Mobility of MBS Users

Figure 3 illustrates the network capacity under different departure probabilities with the increase of arrival probability of MBS users. It can be observed that the network capacity keeps growing with the increase of arrival probability of MBS users when the departure probability is 0.2, 0.5 and 0.9. Whereas, when the departure probability is 0.1, the network capacity exhibits a slight decline. Actually, at low departure probability values, high arrival probability of MBS users impacts the capacity by aggregating the interference, which results in a lower capacity (when the arrival probability goes from 0 to 1, the capacity decreases 5%). Conversely, in the case of high departure probability, there are more time slots occupied by MBS users with the increase of arrival probability of MBS users, which brings a higher capacity.

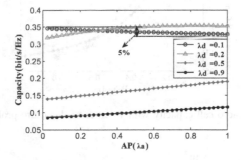

Fig. 3. Capacity comparison with variance of arrival probability (AP)

The capacity under different arrival probabilities with variance of departure probability of MBS users is shown in Fig. 4, in which we can see there is an optimal departure probability for each curve and it can be inferred from (4). Moreover, as is illustrated in Fig. 4, the curves flare up at low departure probability, but show a decline when the departure probability over certain values. The reason is that the whole capacity includes macro cell capacity and small cell capacity and both of the two parts have similar tendency with the whole capacity, as is depicted in Figs. 5 and 6. It can be observed that the macro cell capacity curve has the same tendency with the whole capacity curve while the small cell capacity curve acts conversely. In fact, in the case of low departure probability, more users can connect to MBSs rather than SBSs with the increasing departure probability, which leads to a higher macro cell capacity. Whereas, when the departure probability goes higher, the total number of the MBS users in the network becomes less, which results in a lower macro cell capacity. Opposite results can be derived for the SBS network since that they share the same frequency during each frame in the overlay fashion.

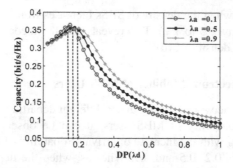

Fig. 4. Capacity comparison with variance of departure probability (DP).

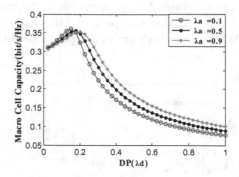

Fig. 5. Macro cell capacity with variance of departure probability.

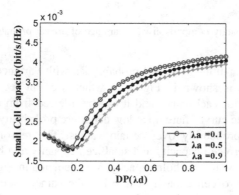

Fig. 6. Small cell capacity with variance of departure probability.

5   Conclusions

In this paper, we derive the network capacity by a stochastic method in a two-tier CHCN. A DTMC is employed to capture the spectrum mobility while an integral method is proposed to approximate the interference. Simulation is made in a HPPP network model, and results show that the proposed method turns out to be an efficient way to calculate the network capacity in CHCNs. Moreover, we also analyze the effect of the spectrum mobility of MBS users on the network capacity. It has shown that the arrival probability conduces to the network capacity at high departure probability and there is an optimal departure probability for each arrival probability.

Acknowledgments. This work was supported in part by the National Natural Science Foundation of China under Grant No. 61302081.

References

1. Cheng, S.M., Lien, S.Y., Chu, F.S.: On exploiting cognitive radio to mitigate interference in macro/femto heterogeneous networks. J. IEEE Wirel. Commun. **18**, 40–47 (2011)
2. ElSawy, H., Hossain, E.: Two-tier hetnets with cognitive femtocells: downlink performance modeling and analysis in a multichannel environment. J. IEEE Trans. Mob. Comput. **13**, 649–663 (2014)
3. Haenggi, M., Andrews, J.G., Baccelli, F.: Stochastic geometry and random graphs for the analysis and design of wireless networks. IEEE J. Sel. Areas Commun. **27**, 1029–1046 (2006)
4. Andrews, J.G., Baccelli, F., Ganti, R.K.: A tractable approach to coverage and rate in cellular networks. J. IEEE Trans. Commun. **59**, 3122–3134 (2011)
5. Dhillon, H.S., Ganti, R.K., Baccelli, F.: Modeling and analysis of K-tier downlink heterogeneous cellular networks. IEEE J. Sel. Areas Commun. **30**, 550–560 (2012)
6. Harpreet, S.D., Thomas, D. N., Andrews, J.G.: Coverage probability of uplink cellular networks. In: IEEE Global Communications Conference (Globecom 2012), pp. 2179–2184. IEEE Press, California (2012)
7. Hesham, E., Ekram, H., Dong, I.K.: HetNets with cognitive small cells: user offloading and distributed channel access techniques. J. IEEE Commun. Mag. **51**, 28–36 (2013)
8. Mohammad, G.K., Keivan, N., Halim, Y.: Outage performance of the primary service in spectrum sharing networks. J. IEEE Trans. Mob. Comput. **12**, 1955–1971 (2013)
9. Hesham, E., Ekram, H., Martin, H.: Stochastic geometry for modeling, analysis, and design of multi-tier and cognitive cellular wireless networks: a survey. J. IEEE Commun. Surv. Tutor. **15**, 996–1019 (2013)
10. Kelif, J.M., Eitan, A.: Downlink fluid model of CDMA networks. In: IEEE 61st Vehicular Technology Conference, pp. 2264–2268. IEEE Press, Stockholm (2005)

A Joint Bandwidth and Power Allocation Scheme for Heterogeneous Networks

Yujiao Chen$^{(\boxtimes)}$, Hong Chen, and Rong Chai

Key Lab of Mobile Communication Technology,
Chongqing University of Posts and Telecommunications, Chongqing, China
chenyujiao716@hotmail.com, 425996310@qq.com, chairong@cqupt.edu.cn

Abstract. Heterogeneous networks (HetNets) composed of macrocells and small cells are expected to improve the transmission performance of users significantly. In this paper, a joint bandwidth and power allocation scheme is proposed for femto base stations (FBSs) in HetNets. By taking into account bandwidth requirements of femto user equipments and bandwidth resource characteristics of the network, a bankruptcy game based bandwidth resource scheme is proposed for the FBSs, based on which a multi-objective optimization based power allocation scheme is proposed in which the energy efficiency optimization problem of each FBS is formulated respectively and is solved via ideal point method and genetic algorithm. Simulation results demonstrate the efficiency of the proposed scheme.

Keywords: Heterogeneous networks · Bandwidth allocation · Power allocation · Bankruptcy game · Multi-objective optimization

1 Introduction

The rapidly growing demand for mobile Internet applications poses great challenges on traditional cellular networks. Cellular heterogeneous networks (HetNets) which consist of both macrocells and small cells such as femtocells, picocells and relay nodes, etc., are proposed and expected to improve user quality of service (QoS) and network performance [1].

Macrocells and small cells in HetNets may share the same bandwidth of telecom operators, therefore bandwidth allocation scheme should be carefully designed to achieve efficient resource utilization and transmission performance enhancement. Two types of bandwidth allocation schemes have been proposed for HetNets, i.e., orthogonal and co-channel bandwidth allocation scheme, where, co-channel bandwidth allocation scheme is capable of achieving higher bandwidth usage compared to orthogonal spectrum allocation [2]. However, bandwidth sharing among cells may cause severe inter-cell interference, which highly limits the transmission performance of both cells. To achieve efficient interference management and network performance enhancement, reasonable bandwidth allocation and power allocation schemes should be designed.

© ICST Institute for Computer Sciences, Social Informatics and Telecommunications Engineering 2018
Q. Chen et al. (Eds.): ChinaCom 2016, Part II, LNICST 210, pp. 268–278, 2018.
DOI: 10.1007/978-3-319-66628-0_26

Several bandwidth allocation schemes and power allocation schemes have been proposed for HetNets in recent years. In [3], a semi-static hybrid spectrum allocation scheme is proposed which achieves the maximum capacity of macro user equipments (MUEs) and femto UEs (FUEs). The authors in [4] study joint bandwidth allocation and call admission control problem for a cellular HetNet, which minimizes the handover rate of UEs. In [5], the transmit power of macro base station (MBS) is determined through maximizing the minimum data rate of MUEs. Reference [6] considers power allocation problem for uplink transmission in HetNets, a sum-rate optimization problem is formulated under the constraints of cross-tier interference between HetNets and user QoS requirements.

Some research works jointly consider the impacts of allocated bandwidth and transmit power in HetNets. In [7], the authors design a subchannel allocation and BS selection scheme to achieve the maximal network throughput. Reference [8] proposes a joint user transmit power and BS association scheme to maximize the utility function of user data rate. However, this may result in large power consumption and low energy efficiency. In [9], the authors aim to maximize the energy efficiency of UEs to obtain the optimal joint bandwidth and power allocation policy. However, the authors assume that the UEs may compete over the shared bandwidth, which may result in lower energy efficiency. In addition, it is assumed that the bandwidth resource is sufficient in most of the previous research works, this may not be the case for the bandwidth requirement from small cells is highly dynamic, hence, designing bandwidth and power allocation scheme according to bandwidth resource characteristics is of great importance.

In this paper, we consider the joint bandwidth allocation and power allocation for HetNets, proposing a two-step resource allocation algorithm, which first allocates bandwidth to various FBSs according to different bandwidth requirements and bandwidth resource characteristics, then an energy efficiency based power allocation algorithm is designed for FBSs.

The rest of this paper is organized as follows. Section 2 introduces the system model considered in this paper. Sections 3 and 4 propose bandwidth and power allocation scheme, respectively. The performance evaluation and simulation results are presented in Sect. 5. Section 6 concludes this paper.

2 System Model

In this paper, we consider a HetNet consisting of one MBS and multiple femto BSs (FBSs) as shown in Fig. 1. Assuming that the MBS covers whole area while each FBS covers a small region of the area. Downlink transmission from BSs to UEs is considered in this paper, particularly, we assume that at interested time duration, the MBS transmits to one MUE, and each FBS transmits to one FUE, for convenience, the ith FBS and the ith FUE are denoted as FBS_i and FUE_i, respectively, $1 \leq i \leq N$, N denotes the number of FBSs.

To achieve efficient spectrum utilization, we assume that full spectrum sharing between MBS and FBSs is allowed, i.e., all the FBSs are allowed to use the whole spectrum of the MBS. To avoid transmission interference among FBSs, we assume various FBSs are assigned different portion of the spectrum of the MBS.

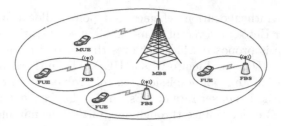

Fig. 1. System scenario

In this paper, we assume the total amount of the bandwidth and the transmit power of the MBS are given constants and study the bandwidth allocation and transmit power allocation problem of the FBSs under the constraints of the transmission interference between the MBS and the FBSs and the QoS requirement of both the MUE and the FUEs. We propose a two-step joint bandwidth allocation and transmit power allocation algorithm for the FBSs. In the following sections, the bandwidth allocation and power allocation algorithms are discussed respectively.

3   Bankruptcy Game Based Bandwidth Allocation Scheme for FBSs

In this paper, we assume that network bandwidth resource is limited compared to the bandwidth requirement of the FUEs, the maximal bandwidth requirement of the FUEs can not be reached. Under the condition that the FBSs may cooperate in sharing the bandwidth resource of the MBS, the bandwidth allocation problem can be modeled as a Bankruptcy cooperative game problem and solved via Shapley value method [10]. As the transmit power constraints of the FBS and the data rate requirement of the FUEs and the MUE may jointly affect the bandwidth requirement of the FBSs and the bandwidth allocation strategy in turn, we first examine the bandwidth allocation constraints.

3.1   Bandwidth Allocation Constraints of FBSs

Bandwidth allocation constraints of the FBSs consists of both lower bound and upper bound constraints of the allocated bandwidth of FBSs.

Lower Bound Constraint of Allocated Bandwidth: To guarantee signal receiving successfully, the signal-to-interference plus noise ratio (SINR) of the MUE should be greater than certain threshold, which may pose constraint on the transmit power of the FBSs in turn. Assume that the MBS and FBS_i share a portion of spectrum with the bandwidth being B_i, the SINR of the MUE on the spectrum can be calculated as

$$\text{SINR}_{\text{m},i} = \frac{P_{\text{m}}h_{\text{m}}}{P_i g_{i,\text{m}} + \sigma^2} \tag{1}$$

where P_{m} and P_i denote the transmit power of the MBS and FBS$_i$, respectively, h_{m} denotes the link gain from the MBS to the MUE, $g_{i,\text{m}}$ denotes the link gain from FBS$_i$ to the MUE, and σ^2 denotes the noise power of the link, which is assumed to be a constant for all the links in this paper. The SINR should meet certain constraint, i.e.,

$$\text{SINR}_{\text{m},i} \geq \text{SINR}_{\text{m}}^{\text{th}} \tag{2}$$

where $\text{SINR}_{\text{m}}^{\text{th}}$ denotes the SINR threshold of the MUE. Combining (1) and (2), we can obtain that

$$P_i \leq \frac{P_{\text{m}}h_{\text{m}}}{\text{SINR}_{\text{m}}^{\text{th}} g_{i,\text{m}}} - \frac{\sigma^2}{g_{i,\text{m}}}. \tag{3}$$

For convenience, we denote

$$P_i^{\text{max},1} = \frac{P_{\text{m}}h_{\text{m}}}{\text{SINR}_{\text{m}}^{\text{th}} g_{i,\text{m}}} - \frac{\sigma^2}{g_{i,\text{m}}}. \tag{4}$$

(3) can be rewritten as:

$$P_i \leq P_i^{\text{max},1}. \tag{5}$$

In addition, due to hardware limitation, the transmit power of FBSs should meet certain maximum power constraint, i.e.,

$$P_i \leq P_i^{\text{max},2} \tag{6}$$

where $P_i^{\text{max},2}$ denotes the maximum allowable transmit power of FBS$_i$. Denote

$$P_i^{\text{max}} = \min\{P_i^{\text{max},1}, P_i^{\text{max},2}\}. \tag{7}$$

Combining (5) and (6), we can express the upper bound constraint of FBS$_i$ as

$$P_i \leq P_i^{\text{max}}. \tag{8}$$

Denote R_i as the data rate of FBS$_i$ when transmitting to FUE$_i$, it can be expressed as

$$R_i = B_i \log_2\left(1 + \frac{P_i h_i}{P_{\text{m}} g_{\text{m},i} + \sigma^2}\right) \tag{9}$$

where h_i denotes the link gain from FBS$_i$ to FUE$_i$, $g_{\text{m},i}$ denotes the link gain from the MBS to FUE$_i$. Denoting R_i^{min} as the minimum data rate requirement of FBS$_i$, the data rate of FBS$_i$ should meet the data rate constraint

$$R_i \geq R_i^{\text{min}}. \tag{10}$$

Combining (8)–(10), we obtain

$$B_i \geq \frac{R_i^{\text{min}}}{\log_2(1 + \frac{P_i^{\text{max}} h_i}{P_{\text{m}} g_{\text{m},i} + \sigma^2})}. \tag{11}$$

Denote

$$B_i^{\min} = \frac{R_i^{\min}}{\log_2(1 + \frac{P_i^{\max} h_i}{P_m g_{m,i} + \sigma^2})}, \tag{12}$$

we obtain the lower bound constraint of the allocated bandwidth of FBS$_i$, i.e.,

$$B_i \geq B_i^{\min}. \tag{13}$$

Upper Bound Constraint of Allocated Bandwidth: To guarantee successful information transmission, the SINR of FUE$_i$ should meet certain constraint, i.e.,

$$\mathrm{SINR}_i = \frac{P_i h_i}{P_m g_{m,i} + \sigma^2} \geq \mathrm{SINR}_i^{\mathrm{th}} \tag{14}$$

where $\mathrm{SINR}_i^{\mathrm{th}}$ denotes the SINR threshold of FUE$_i$. From (14), we can obtain that

$$P_i \geq \frac{\mathrm{SINR}_i^{\mathrm{th}}(P_m g_{m,i} + \sigma^2)}{h_i}. \tag{15}$$

Set

$$P_i^{\min} = \frac{\mathrm{SINR}_i^{\mathrm{th}}(P_m g_{m,i} + \sigma^2)}{h_i}, \tag{16}$$

we obtain the lower bound constraint of P_i

$$P_i \geq P_i^{\min}. \tag{17}$$

We further assume that the service of FUEs has a maximum data rate requirement, which is resulted from the network architecture or resource management schemes. Denoting the maximum data rate of FUE$_i$ as $R_i^{\max}$, the maximum data rate requirement of FUE$_i$ can be expressed as

$$R_i \leq R_i^{\max}. \tag{18}$$

Combining (16)-(18), we obtain the upper bound constraint of the allocated bandwidth of FBS$_i$

$$B_i \leq \frac{R_i^{\max}}{\log_2(1 + \frac{P_i^{\min} h_i}{P_m g_{m,i} + \sigma^2})}. \tag{19}$$

Denote

$$B_i^{\max} = \frac{R_i^{\max}}{\log_2(1 + \frac{P_i^{\min} h_i}{P_m g_{m,i} + \sigma^2})}, \tag{20}$$

the upper bound constraint of B_i can be rewritten as:

$$B_i \leq B_i^{\max}. \tag{21}$$

The bandwidth requirement of FUE$_i$ can be considered in (13) and (21). Assuming the network bandwidth resource is limited compared to the bandwidth requirement of the FUEs. A brief introduction of bankruptcy game theory is presented, then the game model for FBSs bandwidth allocation is established and the optimal solution is presented.

3.2 Bankruptcy Game Formulation

The theory of bankruptcy game can be dated back to an estate allocation problem of a bankruptcy company. Assume that a company with estate E becomes bankrupt, it owes money to creditors, and the amount of the money claimed for all the creditors is D. Hence, the money E is needed to be divided among N creditors, as the estate of the bankrupt company is less than the sum of the claims from the creditors, i.e., $E < D$. This conflicting situation leads an N-person cooperative game, where the optimal solution for dividing the money can be obtained through solving the game model.

In order to design a fair and efficient bandwidth allocation scheme for FBSs, the problem of bandwidth allocation of can be modeled as a bankruptcy game of N persons. Assuming that $\sum_{i=1}^{N} B_i = B$, B denotes the total amount of bandwidth of the MBS. From discussion in previous subsection, we can obtain

$$B_i^{\min} \leq B_i \leq B_i^{\max}. \tag{22}$$

3.3 Shapley Value Based Solution

Shapley value method is commonly applied for solving bankruptcy game problem. According to the Shapley value method, assuming that the alliance formed by the FBSs constitutes a finite set N, with S denoting a subset of N, i.e., $S \subset N$, the characteristic function $v(S)$ of the union S can be calculated as

$$v(S) = \max(0, B - \sum_{i \notin S} B_i^{\max}), \tag{23}$$

$v(S)$ holds the largest number of the allocated bandwidth for the union S, then the Shapley value of the bankruptcy game model can be defined as

$$B_i = \sum_{S \subset N} \frac{(|S| - 1)!(N - |S|)!}{N!} [v(S) - v(S - \{i\})] \tag{24}$$

where $|S|$ denotes the number of elements in the set S. Assuming that FBS_i is in the coalition S, $v(S) - v(S - \{i\})$ represents the contribution that FBS_i makes to the coalition and $\frac{(|S|-1)!(N-|S|)!}{N!}$ represents the weight of the contribution that FBS_i makes to the coalition, which is dependent on the size of the S and the total number of the game players. From above formula, the Shapley value B_i, which corresponds to the bandwidth allocation scheme for FBS_i can be obtained.

4 Power Allocation Scheme for FBSs

Given the allocated bandwidth of the FBSs, we further design the power allocation scheme for the FBSs. The power allocation problem is formulated as an multi-objective optimization problem which is then solved via ideal point method and genetic algorithm (GA).

4.1 Proposed Optimization Scheme

In this subsection, the multi-objective power allocation optimization problem is formulated. From (9), it is apparent that the transmit power of FBS_i, the characteristics of the channel, including the bandwidth, the channel gain and the noise power jointly determine the transmission performance of the FBS. Particularly, given the channel characteristics, to maximize the data rate of FBS_i, the maximum transmit power should be applied. However, this may result in large power consumption and low energy efficiency, which are highly undesired. To jointly consider the transmission performance and the power consumption, we formulate the energy efficiency of the FBSs and design transmit power allocation strategy to achieve the maximum energy efficiency of each FBS in this paper.

The energy efficiency of FBS_i is defined as the ratio of the data rate and the power consumption of FBS_i, i.e.,

$$\eta_i = \frac{R_i}{P_i + P_{\text{cir}}}, \ 1 \leq i \leq N \tag{25}$$

where P_{cir} denotes the circuit power of FBS_i, which is assumed to be a constant for all FBSs in this paper.

In order to maximize the energy efficiency of all the FBSs, the multi-objective optimization problem can be formulated as

$$\max_{P_i} \ \eta_i, \ 1 \leq i \leq N \tag{26}$$

$$\text{s.t.} \quad \text{C1} : R_i \geq R_i^{\min},$$
$$\text{C2} : R_i \leq R_i^{\max},$$
$$\text{C3} : P_i \geq P_i^{\min},$$
$$\text{C4} : P_i \leq P_i^{\max},$$
$$\text{C5} : R_{\text{m}} \geq R_{\text{m}}^{\min}.$$

4.2 Solution to the Optimization Problem

The problem formulated in (26) is a multi-object optimization problem, the optimal solution of which is in general difficult to obtain. In this section, the ideal point method [11] is applied to solve the optimization problem.

The basic idea of the ideal point method is that for each objective function, the locally optimal solution, referred to as ideal result can be obtained independently without considering the joint constraints and the feasibility of the solutions, then a single objective optimization problem which minimizes the distance between the feasible solutions and the ideal solutions is formulated and solved based on GA.

Ideal Solution to Individual Optimization Objective: For the ith FBS, $1 \leq i \leq N$, the energy efficiency optimization problem can be expressed as

$$\max_{P_i} \ \eta_i \tag{27}$$

$$\text{s.t.} \quad C1 - C4 \text{ in } (26).$$

For convenience, we denote the maximum energy efficiency of FBS_i as

$$\eta_i^* = \frac{R_i(P_i^*)}{P_i^* + P_{\text{cir}}} = \max_{P_i} \ \{\frac{R_i(P_i)}{P_i + P_{\text{cir}}}\} \tag{28}$$

where P_i^* denotes the optimal transmit power of the ith FBS. According to [12], the maximum energy efficiency η_i^* is achieved if and only if

$$\max_{P_i} \ \{R_i(P_i) - \eta_i^{\max}(P_i + P_{\text{cir}})\} = R_i(P_i^*) - \eta_i(P_i^* + P_{\text{cir}}) = 0. \tag{29}$$

Hence, the optimization problem formulated in (27) can be equivalently transformed into following problem, i.e.,

$$\max_{\eta_i, P_i} \ R_i - \eta_i(P_i + P_{\text{cir}}) \tag{30}$$

$$\text{s.t.} \quad C1 - C4 \text{ in } (26).$$

To obtain the optimal energy efficiency η_i^*, we apply an iterative algorithm and the convergence to optimal energy efficiency can be guaranteed.

Single Objective Optimization Problem Formulation: The locally optimal η_i^*, $1 \leq i \leq N$ may not be feasible for the formulated multi-objective optimization problem. According to the ideal point method, we examine the distance between the feasible solutions and the locally optimal solution, denoted by Q,

$$Q = \sum_{i=1}^{N}(\eta_i - \eta_i^*)^2, \tag{31}$$

then the original multi-objective optimization problem can be converted into a single object optimization problem as follows,

$$\min_{P_i} \ Q \tag{32}$$

$$\text{s.t.} \quad C1\text{-}C5 \text{ in } (26).$$

The formulated single objective optimization problem can be solved based on GA.

5   Simulation Results

In the simulation, we consider a HetNet consisting of one MBS and five FBSs. Assuming all UEs are randomly located in a rectangular region with the size being 500×500, the MBS is located in the position with the coordinate being (255,200), the positions of the FBSs are listed in Table 1. In the simulation, the

Table 1. Simulation parameters

FBS$_1$	FBS$_2$	FBS$_3$	FBS$_4$	FBS$_5$
(97,350)	(40,60)	(417,100)	(250,405)	(460,460)

Table 2. Simulation parameters

Parameters	Value
The minimum rate requirement of FBS$_i$	400 kbps
The minimum rate requirement of MBS	100 kbps
The maximum power of MBS	0.5 W
Noise power	−200 dBm

transmission gain of the link between BS and UE is modeled as $h = (c/4\pi f d)^2$, where d denotes the distance between the source node and the destination node of the link, c denotes the speed of light, f denotes the carrier frequency of the transmit signal. Other simulation parameters are summarized in Table 2.

Assuming that the bandwidth offered by MBS is 1.2MHz, and the maximum bandwidth requirement of each FBS are 244, 297, 288, 298, and 299KHz, respectively. Comparing the bandwidth requirement and the total amount of the bandwidth of the MBS, the bankruptcy game can be modeled and the allocated bandwidth for each FBS can be calculated according to the Shapley value method. In Fig. 2, the allocated bandwidth for FBSs is plotted and compared with the maximum bandwidth requirement of the FBSs. It can be seen from Fig. 2 that the allocated bandwidth of all the FBSs meets the minimum bandwidth requirement and a relatively fair bandwidth allocation with respect to bandwidth requirement can be achieved. Fig. 3 shows the allocated transmit power of FBS$_1$ to FBS$_5$ versus the number of generations of GA. It can be seen from the figure that the transmit power curves of FBSs converge to constants, demonstrating the effectiveness of the applied GA.

Figures 4 and 5 show the total energy efficiency versus the maximum transmit power of the FBSs ($P_i^{\max}$), and the results are obtained from the proposed scheme and the scheme proposed in [8]. In Fig. 4, we examine the total energy efficiency for different circuit power consumption of the FBSs. Comparing the results obtained from the proposed scheme and the scheme proposed in [8], we can see that for small $P_i^{\max}$, the energy efficiency increases with the increase of $P_i^{\max}$ for both schemes, indicating a larger power threshold is desired for achieving the maximum energy efficiency. However, as $P_i^{\max}$ reaches to a certain value, the energy efficiency obtained from our proposed algorithm becomes a fixed value for the transmit power being less than $P_i^{\max}$ has resulted in the optimal energy efficiency, which will no longer vary with $P_i^{\max}$, whereas the energy efficiency obtained from the other scheme decreases with the increase of $P_i^{\max}$. This is because the scheme proposed in [8] aims to achieve the maximum data rate, thus may require higher power consumption, resulting in undesired

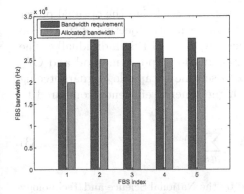

Fig. 2. Comparison of the maximum required bandwidth and allocated bandwidth of FBSs.

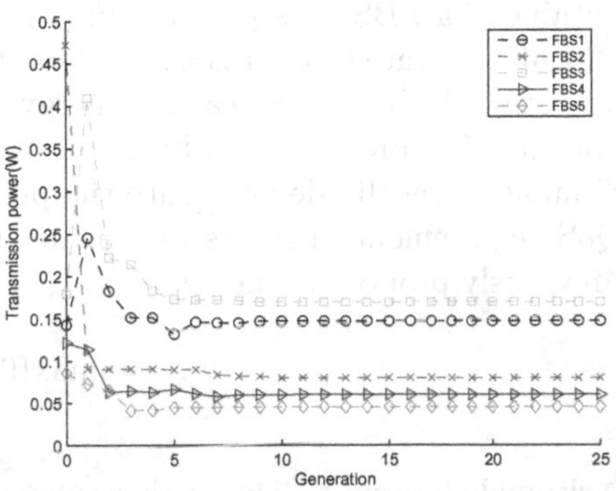

Fig. 3. Transmission power versus generations for FBSs

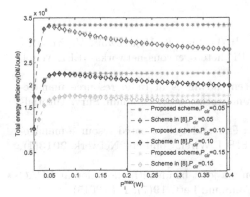

Fig. 4. Energy efficiency versus maximum transmit power (different circuit power)

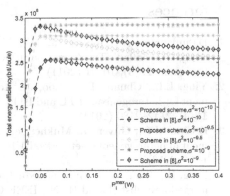

Fig. 5. Energy efficiency versus maximum transmit power (different noise power)

energy efficiency. Comparing the two curves in the figure, we can see that the proposed scheme outperforms the scheme proposed in [8].

In Fig. 5, we examine the total energy efficiency for different noise power of the links between BSs and UEs, i.e., σ^2. We can see from the figure as the value of σ^2 increases, the total energy efficiency decreases. This is because larger noise power results in worse transmission performance of the FBSs. Comparing the results obtained from the proposed scheme and the scheme proposed in [8], we can see that our proposed scheme outperforms previously proposed scheme.

6   Conclusion

In this paper, we study joint bandwidth and power allocation problem for Het-Nets. A bankruptcy game model is formulated and the amount of bandwidth is obtained for FBSs based on Shapley value method. To design the optimal power allocation strategy for FBSs, we then formulate a multi-objective optimization problem which maximizes the energy efficiency of the FBSs individually. The optimization problem is solved through applying ideal point method and GA. Simulation results demonstrate the proposed scheme is capable of guaranteeing QoS requirement of FUEs and achieving higher energy efficiency compared to previously proposed scheme.

$$v(S) = \max(0, E - \sum_{i \notin S} d_i^{\max}) \tag{33}$$

Acknowledgement. This work is supported by the National Science and Technology Specific Project of China (2016ZX03001010-004) and the 863 project (2014AA01A701), the special fund of Chongqing key laboratory (CSTC) and the project of Chongqing Municipal Education Commission (Kjzh11206).

References

1. Damnjanovic, A., Montojo, J., Wei, Y., Ji, T., Luo, T., Vajapeyam, M., Yoo, T., Song, O., Malladi, D.: A survey on 3GPP heterogeneous networks. IEEE Wirel. Commun. **18**(3), 10–21 (2011)
2. Ying, L.L., Chuah, T.C., Loo, J.: Recent advances in radio resource management for heterogeneous LTE and LTE-A networks. IEEE Commun. Surv. Tutorials **16**(4), 2142–2180 (2014)
3. Ertürk, M.C., Güven, I., Mukherjee, S.: Fair and QoS-oriented resource management in heterogeneous networks. EURASIP J. Wirel. Commun. Network. **2013**(1), 1–14 (2013)
4. Fang, B., Zhou, W.: Handover reduction via joint bandwidth allocation and CAC in randomly distributed HCNs. IEEE Commun. Lett. **19**(7), 1–1 (2015)
5. Jung, H.B., Kim, D.K.: Power control of femtocells based on max-min fairness in heterogeneous networks. IEEE Commun. Lett. **17**(7), 1372–1375 (2013)
6. Tai, M.H., Tran, N.H., Do, C.T.: Power control for interference management and QoS guarantee in heterogeneous networks. IEEE Commun. Lett. **19**, 1–1 (2015)
7. Estrada, R., Jarray, A., Otrok, H.: Energy-efficient resource allocation model for OFDMA macro-femtocell networks. IEEE Trans. Veh. Technol. **62**(7), 3429–3437 (2013)
8. Shen, K., Yu, W.: Distributed pricing-based user association for downlink heterogeneous cellular networks. IEEE J. Sel. Areas Commun. **32**(6), 1100–1113 (2014)
9. Ismail, M., Gamage, A.T., Zhuang, W.: Uplink decentralized joint bandwidth and power allocation for energy-efficient operation in a heterogeneous wireless medium. IEEE Trans. Commun. **63**(4), 1483–1495 (2015)
10. Shapley., L.S.: A value for N-person games. In: Kuhn, H.W., Tucker, A.W. (eds.) Annals of Mathematics Studies, pp. 307–317. Princeton University Press (1953)
11. Eichfelder, G.: Adaptive Scalarization Methods in Multiobjective Optimization. Springer, Heidelberg (2008)
12. Ng, D., Lo, E., Schober, R.: Energy-efficient resource allocation in OFDMA systems with large numbers of base station antennas. IEEE Trans. Wirel. Commun. **11**, 3292–3304 (2012)

Internet of Things

A Novel Power-Saving Scheduling
Scheme in Large Scale Smart-Grid Networks

Chen Chen[1](✉), Lei Liu[1], Mingcheng Hu[1], Qingqi Pei[1], Li Cong[2],
and Shengda Wang[2]

[1] State Key Laboratory of Integrated Services Networks,
Xidian University, Xi'an 710071, China
cc2000@mail.xidian.edu.cn
[2] Information and Communication Company,
Jilin Electric Power Company Limited, Changchun 130021, China

Abstract. The IEEE 802.11ah Task Group is going to specify a global WLAN standard. However, .ah drafts still employs the carrier sense multiple access with collision avoidance (CSMA/CA) medium access protocol, which is an energy-consuming protocol and not suitable for networks where STAs are generally battery supplied. Besides, since .ah could support up to 6000 stations at most to be scheduled within one BSS, the introduced overhead and corresponding processing delay are non-trivial. In this paper, a power saving scheduling scheme is proposed which could greatly reduce the introduced overhead while successfully scheduling the uplink/downlink traffic of meters. Our model could also save the station's battery with best efforts thus making our protocol specifically suitable for Smart-Grid networks where battery changing for stations is difficult. Numerical results show that our scheme outperforms the PSM (Power Saving Mechanism) and PSMP (Power Save Multi-Poll) protocols in terms of overheads, throughput and energy consumptions.

Keywords: Next generation WLAN · Smart grid · Power saving · Scheduling scheme

1 Introduction

Along with the popularity of the easy deployment, simple use, and high penetration of WI-FI interfaces in mobile communication devices, a fast growth is occurring for the outdoor deployment for ubiquitous wireless access. Smart Grid, which is proposed as a typical outdoor use-case [1] in IEEE 802.11ah (abbreviated as .ah later) draft, also require a fast and simple deployment of long-range wireless communication networks for meters and sensor devices in rural areas.

In .ah draft, a wireless coverage range up to 1 km is assumed. Sensors, such as power, gas, or water meter will require at least 100 kbps bit rate. The suggested infrastructure of smart grid meters application is plotted in Fig. 1. The typical discussed scenario involves just one BSS (Basic Service Set) with at most 6000 STAs [2]. Because the special characteristics of .ah networks such as low data rate, short payload, high coverage, large scale and long idle period, specialized MAC layer improvement is

© ICST Institute for Computer Sciences, Social Informatics and Telecommunications Engineering 2018
Q. Chen et al. (Eds.): ChinaCom 2016, Part II, LNICST 210, pp. 281–291, 2018.
DOI: 10.1007/978-3-319-66628-0_27

necessary. Notice that the usages of .ah determine that many small devices are expected to be battery powered. With respect to battery requirements, .ah needs long battery life, short data transmissions and power saving strategies.

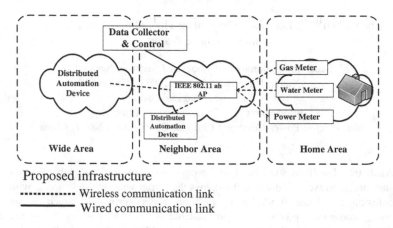

Proposed infrastructure

------------ Wireless communication link

—————— Wired communication link

Fig. 1. Our discussed smart grid usecase in IEEE 802.11ah

Particularly, an efficient power saving scheme is mandatory for the following reasons. First, STAs in .ah networks are generally battery supplied and often designed with power sleep functionality. Second, in view of the short payload, a large overhead incurred in power saving polling protocols, such as Power Save Mode (PSM) in IEEE 802.11b [3], Automatic Power Saving Delivery (APSD) in IEEE 802.11e [4] and Power Save Mode Poll (PSMP) in IEEE 802.11n [5], is not permitted. Third, considering the large scale property that there may be at most 6000 STAs contending for the shared medium in the worst case, a well-designed scheduling scheme is needed to further reduce the energy consumption from collisions. Finally, multiple years of battery life might be achieved by lowering the sleep state power consumption with an efficient power saving polling scheme considering energy efficiency and .ah use case with large numbers of STAs. In view of above problems, in this paper, we proposed an efficient power saving scheduling scheme in Smart-Grid Networks based on .ah drafts to reduce the polling overhead and at the same time improve the energy efficiency.

The rest of the paper is organized as follows. Section 2 describes the mechanism of our scheduling scheme in detail. Numerical results and corresponding performance evaluations are shown in Sect. 3. Our paper is concluded in Sect. 4.

2   Proposed Power Saving Polling Scheme

In this section, in view of the three kinds of traffics for a typical .ah network, i.e. down-link data transmitted by AP, up-link data that AP is expected and burst data, we proposed a scheduled multiple access mechanism using our presented Scheduling Indication Message (SIM) field that can unify the scheduling time and reduce the overhead to a great extent. Especially, when AIDs of the STAs which have packets to transmit or be received are successive or partially successive, our proposed scheme could greatly reduce the overhead. The introduced frame structures for scheduling are depicted in Fig. 2. Table 1 shows the corresponding usage of the control field in our proposed frame. Since we attempt to schedule the STAs within one community or one cell, we correspondingly name our proposed frame as Cell Polling Frame (CPF). Next, we will explain the configuration considerations to use our scheme.

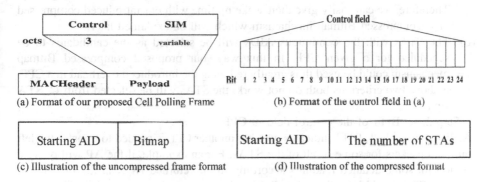

(a) Format of our proposed Cell Polling Frame   (b) Format of the control field in (a)

(c) Illustration of the uncompressed frame format   (d) Illustration of the compressed format

Fig. 2. The proposed frame formats

Table 1. Usage of control field in CPF frame

Bit	Value	Description
1	1	The current PSMP sequence will be followed by another PSMP
	0	There will be no PSMP sequence following the current PSMP sequence
2	1	SIM field is compressed
	0	SIM field is not compressed
3–7	–	The time used by scheduling a single STA
8	1	PSMP-Recovery frame
	0	The normal PSMP frame
9–15	–	Reserved
16–24	–	The length of SIM field

First, we suppose that there are several STAs which have downlink traffics on AP or wait for the opportunities to transmit uplink data to AP. We next divide these data exchanges procedure into multiple steps to demonstrate the usage of our scheme.

Step 1: determine the STAs set for scheduling
First of all, we must determine the set of STAs needed to be scheduled. Let **C_STA** denotes the set of STAs who have buffered downlink data on AP. Since the scale of the number of STAs associated with a single AP could reach or over 6000, an upper limit N_{max} should be configured to confine the number of STAs to be scheduled during one CPF. The determination of N_{max} may consider the configuration of duty cycles for STAs, services requirement, query frequency etc. After N_{max} is given, the

set of STAs to be scheduled during current CPF, i.e. **S_STA**, should be selected from **C_STA**. Two selection criterions are designed as follows:

(a) The STAs with the same service type will be selected as the candidates to be scheduled for a given CPF. In this way, we can calculate a wake up time for each scheduled station in a CPF and make the STAs in **C_STA** doze for a long time before or after they were scheduled. For instance, if all the STAs in a **C_STA** are waiting for the meter reading query and then responding the query with a short ACK, their average service duration could be estimated and may not vary greatly. Therefore, we can easily give their wake up time with our introduced compressed or uncompressed Bitmap mechanism which will be explained later.

(b) The STAs with the continuous AIDs will be selected as the candidates to be scheduled for a given CPF. In this way, our proposed compressed Bitmap mechanism could be used thus greatly reducing the introduced overhead in a CPF.

If the above two criterions both do not work, the STAs will be selected from **C_STA** randomly.

Step 2: set BIT1 of the control field in CPF

As listed in Table 1, BIT1 indicates whether another CPF is needed to transfer the left buffered packets for some or all of the STAs. For an example, if the AP will query a station for some detailed readings according to the returned ACK in the first query, another CPF should be followed to finish this transaction.

Step 3: set the SIM field in CPF

According to whether the AIDs for scheduled STAs are continuous, there maybe exist two different cases for setting the SIM field. Let AID_{min} denote the minimum AID in **S_AID**. For all the STAs in **S_AID**, if exists

$$AID_i = AID_{min} + i, i = 1, 2, \ldots, M - 1, \tag{1}$$

where AID_i is a member of **S_AID** and $M \leq N_{max}$ is the number of STAs schedule in this CPF, then it can be known that the AIDs in **S_AID** are continuous. If so, the compressed Bitmap mechanism could be used as step (a) describes. Otherwise, the uncompressed Bitmap mechanism will be enabled as step (b) indicates.

Fig. 3. SIM field for compressed Bitmap

Fig. 4. SIM field for uncompressed Bitmap

(a) If AIDs in current CPF are continuous, the SIM field will only include two subfield as shown in Fig. 3, i.e. AID_{start} and the number of scheduled STAs M, where AID_{start} denotes the AID of the first scheduled station in current CPF. In this way, for the ith scheduled station i, its AID could be derived as $AID_i = AID_{start} + i$. It is worth noting that the introduced overhead using this compressed Bitmap may be greatly reduced compared to the traditional method based on TIM frame.

(b) If AIDs involved in current CPF are not continuous, then the SIM field will has the following structure as shown in Fig. 4. Here, if Bit j in Bitmap is 1, it means that the corresponding station j has buffered data on AP. j's AID could also be derived as $AID_j = AID_{start} + j$. Correspondingly, if Bit j in Bitmap is 0, it means that station j will not be scheduled during this CPF.

Step 4: compute the unit service duration
We define the Unit service Duration (USD) as

$$T = \max\{\langle L_i/MCS_i\rangle\} + T_0, i = 1, 2, \ldots, M, \tag{2}$$

where L_i denotes the average packet length for station i and MCS_i indicates the sending rate for i using specific Modulation and Coding Scheme. Symbol $\langle x \rangle$ means adding the MAC and PHY header to payload x. T_0 equals to the needed duration for the transmission of a typical ACK frame whose payload length could be only few Bytes. This ACK frame may act as the querying response or a buffered report packet. The exact length for an ACK frame can be configured for specific applications and here we fix it to 32 Bytes. The introducing of USD into our work has two fold usages:

(a) Giving USD for all STAs to be scheduled, they can easily obtain their wake up time by step (8). In this way, all STAs can doze as long as possible to save energy.
(b) By introducing MCS for each scheduled station, the duration for downlink transmissions of all STAs could be intentionally kept almost the same. In this way, our definition of USD could be made full use thus accurately estimating the wake up time for STAs and saving energy.

Step 5: set the other BITS of the control field in CPF
To indicate whether compressed Bitmap mechanism is enabled, BIT2 needs to be set as listed in Table 1. Besides, according to the configuration of BIT2, BIT16–BIT24 will be set to denote the length of SIM field in Bytes. In other words, our scheme could support $(2^9 - 1) \times 8 = 4088$ STAs. However, since 2 Bytes have been used for AID_{start}, the maximum number of STAs is $(2^9 - 1 - 2) \times 8 = 4072$. We can expand the length of the field by introducing one more Byte, say, using BIT16–BIT32 to express the SIM field to support $(2^{17} - 1 - 2) \times 8 = 1048552$ STAs. But generally speaking, this case will never occur within one BSS.

Step 6: AP broadcasts the filled CPF
After configurations of the CPF frame, AP then broadcasts it to STAs. Next, STAs in S_STA will do corresponding actions according to the values of received fields.

Step 7: STAs receive CPF and do corresponding actions
Receiving the CPF, a station will first extract the value of BIT2 and decide whether this CPF has used the compressed Bitmap. If true, the range of AID to be scheduled can be determined as $[AID_{start}, AID_{start} + M - 1]$. One station i could know whether it will be scheduled during current CPF by judging $AID_i \in [AID_{start}, AID_{start} + M - 1]$ or not. If yes, the station needs to be awake for an USD from $T_{start}(i)$ which will be given in step 8. Otherwise, this station could keep sleeping during this CPF. If BIT2 is set to 0 which means uncompressed Bitmap has been used, a station should first check whether its AID equals to AID_{start}. If true, this station will be scheduled in current

CPF; If not, this station needs to check the corresponding BIT in received Bitmap. If the BIT is 1, this station will be schedule. Otherwise it could keep sleeping.

Step 8: compute the wake up time for a specific station

For a scheduled station, its wake up time $T_{start}(i)$ during a polling can be gotten:

$$T_{start}(i) = N_{before}(i) \times T, \tag{3}$$

where $N_{before}(i)$ is the number of STAs scheduled before i during current polling stage. T is the calculated USD during current CPF. Here, $N_{before}(i)$ could be determined as follows depending on the used Bitmap mechanism.

(a) If uncompressed Bitmap has been used, then

$$N_{before}(i) = \sum_{p=0}^{AID_i-AID_{start}-1} I_p\{\omega_p : \omega_p \in \mathbf{S\_AID}\}, \tag{4}$$

where I is a indicative function defined as follows:

$$I_p\{\omega_p : \omega_p \in \mathbf{S\_AID}\} = \begin{cases} 0, \omega_p \notin \mathbf{S\_AID} \\ 1, \omega_p \in \mathbf{S\_AID} \end{cases}. \tag{5}$$

(b) If compressed Bitmap has been used, then it is easy to obtain $N_{before}(i)$ as

$$N_{before} = AID_i - AID_{start}. \tag{6}$$

Step 9: payload transmission

After each station scheduled has known its own schedule, data exchange could be initiated between AP and STAs. For a scheduled station i, it will keep sleeping till $T_{start}(i)$. During $[T_{start}(i), T_{start}(i) + T]$, i will first receive the downlink traffic from AP. If there is still time left and i also has traffics to be uploaded to AP, it will keep awake and send the uplink payload. The setting of USD by Eq. (2) has reserved uplink duration for each scheduled station. Indeed, it is possible that some STAs have only uplink traffics. For instance, STAs or meters may trigger an alarm report whenever the predefined peak load threshold is surpassed. For this case, compared to the passive uplink traffics after a downlink query, the active uplink traffics could be uploaded at any time when STAs are awake according to their DTIM settings.

Step 10: AP sends Block ACK

After all the STAs in $\mathbf{S\_STA}$ have been scheduled, they will be awaken again to receive the block ACK sent by AP. This block ACK aims to confirm the uploaded traffics sent by specific STAs.

Next, we explain the CPF scheme in detail with a typical case as shown in Fig. 5. First AP sets the CPF according to the buffered traffics, AIDs of STAs and some related parameters. Then AP broadcasts the configured CPF to STAs in $\mathbf{S\_STA}$. We assume that STA1, STA2, STA3, STA4 and STA5 form the set $\mathbf{S\_STA}$. Receiving the CPF, each station orderly extracts the control fields in CPF. Here, STA1 to STA5 all have

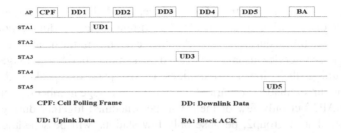

Fig. 5. The interaction mechanism when AP using the proposed scheme

buffered traffics on AP and require 5 USDs. Every station knows its wake up time and keeps sleeping before or after it. Specially, STA1, STA3 and STA5 have also uplink traffics, uploading their uplink packets following downlinks respectively. When the data service is finished, AP responses to the STAs by Block ACK(BA) [6].

3   Numerical Results

To evaluate the performance of our proposed scheme, we implement it in MATLAB with the typical parameters listed in Table 2. Our simulations are divided into two groups. In group 1, the overheads and throughput are compared among our scheme, PSM and PSMP with the number of scheduled stations changing. In group 2, the throughput and energy consumption are inspected with the data or burst size of each station varying. Since BlockACK has been adopted as an option in IEEE 802.11n draft, its impact on our model is also assessed.

Table 2. The important parameters in simulation

Description	Value	Description	Value
BER threshold	$10^{(-6)}$	Awaking power	1 W
Channel capacity	400 kbps	Sleeping power	0 W
Time slot length	20 μs	CW_{min}	32
Transmitting power	2 W	CW_{max}	1024
Receiving power	1.5 W	Size of data frame	100 bytes

The simulation topology is illustrated in Fig. 6, where Fig. 6(a) and (b) correspond to the test scenario for group 1 and group 2, respectively. For group 1, only one service is considered. In this way, since the traffic characteristics of stations for the same service are similar, the scheduling table for those stations will be arranged together. That is, most of the stations under AP1 in Fig. 6(a) will be scheduled in a CPF together whatever their AIDs are continuous or discontinuous. Unlike group 1, there are multiple services existent in group 2 such as current meter reading, daily usage checking, transmission fault checking and peak-load checking etc. Since different services employ different report frequency, a large number of stations may not be scheduled together during a specific duration. For instance, the daily usage checking might be invoked only once during a day while the current meter reading report may be requested several times during a day. Another example is the peak-load checking, which is a special service usually scheduled in summer but few arranged in other seasons regarding their lower possibilities to overpass the peak-load threshold. Therefore, for our simulation scenario 2, there are also a huge number of stations under the cover of AP2 but only few of them will be scheduled together during a specific duration. Note that in group2, because only few stations will be scheduled during a CPF, there will be many "zeroes" in our proposed bitmap. Thereupon, the performance between continuous or discontinuous AIDs cases for group 2 will be of great differences.

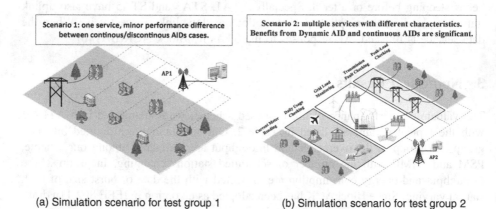

(a) Simulation scenario for test group 1   (b) Simulation scenario for test group 2

Fig. 6. Simulation topology

The performance evaluation indexes are defined as follows:

- Overhead: the difference between data rate and throughput;
- Average awaken time: the arithmetic average of the total awaken time for all stations;
- Average Energy consumption: the arithmetic average of the total consumed energy for all stations;
- Normalized throughput: the fraction of time the channel is used to successfully transmit payload bits.

The performance comparisons of overheads suppression among ours, PSM and PSMP have been plotted in Fig. 7 with the number of stations varying. Note that in Fig. 7, the AIDs of stations are not continuous. This case corresponds to the situation such as readings report for stations whose load is over the average load or reaching the peak load. The case with successive AIDs is also inspected with results shown in Fig. 9. The continuous AIDs are usually configured for the meters in a community or company where devices are sequentially installed. It can be concluded that our scheme has the best performance on overheads reduction. If Block ACK is enabled during a

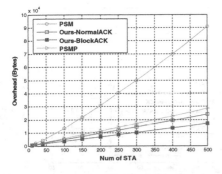

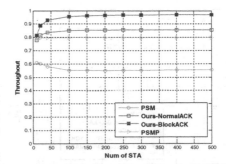

Fig. 7. The overheads comparisons with of the number of stations varying

Fig. 8. The normalized throughput comparisons with the number of stations varying

CPF, the overheads will be further decreased. It is worth noting that the superiority of our protocol over the other two is increasing with the number of stations grows. Actually, due to contentions among upload stations and the overheads from notifications sent by the control unit to notify stations to report their readings, PSM needs the most overheads to work. As for PSMP, although centralized scheduling is used to coordinate stations from competing, its larger scheduling overhead, i.e., 8 Bytes for each station, make it unsuitable for mass uplink traffics. In addition, due to the length limitation, only 31 stations can be scheduled at most during a PSMP scheduling frame [7]. In this way, PSMP needs several frames to finish the batch reports from a large number of stations. On the other hand, since our scheme introduces the bitmap mechanism and adopts centralized scheduling, the contention between stations is eliminated and the number of stations schedulable in a CPF is greatly increased thus making the final overheads very few.

Figure 8 shows the normalized throughput of three schemes with the number of stations changing. The normalized throughput is defined as the Bytes successfully received every unit time to the channel capacity. Since PSM uses competition-based multiple access for uplink traffics, part of the channel bandwidth is wasted for backoff and retransmissions. As a result, PSM shows the worst performance. When the number of stations is over 31, PSMP needs multiple scheduling frames to receive the uploaded traffics, thus outputting a worse throughput compared to ours. Another reason is the larger scheduling frame size than ours, which makes PSMP waste many time for overheads transmission thus decreasing the normalized throughput. Our scheduler could arrange up to 4072 stations once and uses a smaller scheduling frame thus resulting in a higher throughput. When BlockACK is enabled, the throughput could be further increased by eliminating the time cost by multiple handshakes.

The normalized throughput comparisons are shown in Fig. 9 with the data size varying. Note that in this simulation scenario, the case for continuous (abbreviated as "Con") and discontinuous (abbreviated as "Discon") AID have been investigated for our scheduler. Due to PSM and PSMP do not care the sequence of station's AID, this "Con" or "Discon" setting will not influence their results. Since PSM is a contention based protocol, its performance is the worst due to channel competing and data

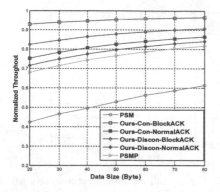

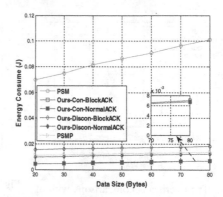

Fig. 9. The throughput comparisons with the data size varying

Fig. 10. The energy consumption comparisons with the data size varying

retransmission. Our scheme with four different configurations show a better performance than PSMP and PSM. As stated before, due to smaller scheduling frame and only one CPF needed, ours output superior normalized throughput over others. Especially when the AIDs are continuous, the normalized throughput is further increased considering the reduction of CPF size and generated overheads. It is worth noting that with the growing of data size, the normalized throughput increases for all protocols due to more sent Bytes during a unit time. In addition, the difference of different cases reduces when the data size increase. But as we have known, the data size in Smart-Grid networks is usually small, such as 76 Bytes for MPDU (MAC Protocol Data Unit) of PMU (Power Management Unit) [8], 480 Bytes for interval data read of meter [9], etc. Therefore, we can reasonable consider that our proposed scheme has a significant superiority on stations scheduling in Smart-Grid networks.

The performance for energy consumption is also compared among three protocols with the data size varying as shown in Fig. 10. Since the meters are battery powered, the energy efficiency is a very important factors in practice in Smart-Grid networks. It is worth noting that PSM still shows the worst performance consistent with the results in Figs. 7 and 8. As for PSMP, its energy efficiency is better than our scheme with discontinuous AIDs and BlockACK but worse than ours with normal ACK mechanism. This is because that a group of discontinuous AIDs will need a very long time to finish all active stations' uploading considering many "0" in the bitmap. When BlockACK is enabled, an extra awaking time is needed for all active stations to fetch their ACK from the BlockACK frame. As for the energy consumption for continuous AIDs case, since the bitmap has been greatly compressed, the time used for scheduling all the active nodes is much smaller than the discontinuous AIDs case thus saving the battery life to a great extent.

4   Conclusion

In this paper, a power saving scheduling scheme is proposed which could greatly reduce the introduced overhead while successfully scheduling the uplink/downlink traffic of meters. Our proposed model could also save the station's battery with best efforts thus making the scheme specifically suitable for Smart-Grid networks. Numerical results show that our scheme outperforms PSM and PSMP in terms of overheads, throughput and energy consumptions. Our future work will investigate the possibility to merge the IEEE 802.11ah based network with the public cellular network and extend the scalability of our model to make it suitable for the upcoming 5G mobile communication networks.

Acknowledgement. This work was supported by the National Natural Science Foundation of China (61201133, 61571338), the National Science and Technology Major Project of the Ministry of Science and Technology of China (2015zx03002006-003), the Natural Science Foundation of Shaanxi Province (2014JM2-6089), the National High-tech R&D Program of China (863 Program-2015AA015701), the Research collaboration innovation program of Xi'an (BD31015010001), the Hong Kong, Macao and Taiwan Science and Technology Cooperation Special Project (2014DFT10320, 2015DFT10160) and the "111 Project" of China (B08038).

References

1. Sun, W., Choi, M., Choi, S.: IEEE 802.11ah: a long range 802.11 WLAN at sub 1 GHz. J. ICT Stand. **1**, 83–108 (2013)
2. Khorov, E., Lyakhov, A., Krotov, A., Guschin, A.: A survey on IEEE 802.11ah: an enabling networking technology for smart cities. Comput. Commun. **58**, 53–69 (2015)
3. Tauber, M., Bhatti, S.N.: The effect of the 802.11 power save mechanism (PSM) on energy efficiency and performance during system activity. In: 2012 IEEE International Conference on Green Computing and Communications (GreenCom), pp. 573–580 (2012)
4. Gonzalez, F.V., Lundqvist, H., Leppanen, K.: Seamless handover in 802.11 with automatic power save delivery. In: 2014 IEEE 19th International Workshop on Computer Aided Modeling and Design of Communication Links and Networks (CAMAD), pp. 380–384 (2014)
5. Ma, C., He, S., Li, Y., Xu, Q., Yang, L.: Enhanced power-save multi-poll mechanism for multi-user downlink transmission in WLAN. In: 2015 IEEE China Summit and International Conference on Signal and Information Processing (ChinaSIP), pp. 881–885 (2015)
6. Chen, H.: Throughput analysis of block-ACK in IEEE 802.11n. In: The 2nd International Conference on Computer Application and System Modeling, ICCASM, pp. 956–959 (2012)
7. Xiao, Y.: IEEE 802.11n: enhancements for higher throughput in wireless LANs. IEEE Wirel. Commun. **12**, 82–91 (2005)
8. Khan, R.H., Khan, J.Y.: A comprehensive review of the application characteristics and traffic requirements of a smart grid communications network. Comput. Netw. **57**, 825–845 (2013)
9. Luan, W., Sharp, D., Lancashire, S.: Smart grid communication network capacity planning for power utilities. In: Transmission and Distribution Conference and Exposition, 2010 IEEE PES, pp. 1–4 (2010)

Preamble Design for Collision Detection and Channel Estimation in Machine-Type Communication

Shilei Zheng[✉], Fanggang Wang, and Xia Chen

Beijing Jiaotong University, Beijing, China
14120188@bjtu.edu.cn

Abstract. Preamble is widely used for initial synchronization, channel estimation, user identification, and collision detection in communication systems. For machine-type communication (MTC), there are massive machines within one cell. Contention-based random access could be a candidate protocol in this scenario. However, simultaneous transmission of multiple users can lead to signal aliasing. This paper designs a novel structure of preamble. Collisions of multiple users can be detected based on well-designed structure of the preamble. Furthermore, channel state information (CSI) can be estimated as a byproduct in the process of collision detection. We claim that the proposed preambles applies in flat-fading channel, multipath channel and asynchronous scenario. The simulation results validate the accuracy and robustness of the proposed scheme.

Keywords: Asynchronization · Contention-based random access · Collision detection · Channel estimation · Preamble

1 Introduction

In wireless systems, synchronization and channel estimation are generally accomplished by a particular signal, which is usually composed of two parts, i.e., a short training sequence for synchronization followed by a long training sequence mainly for channel estimation [1–3]. Optimal preamble sequences lead to high access probability and enhance the system performance [4]. Previous research of preamble design focused on scheduling-based communications. In this paper, we investigate preamble design for contention-based communications, which can detect collision as well in addition to synchronization acquisition and channel estimation.

Contention-based communications attract much interest due to its potential to serve a large number of wireless access terminals in machine-type communication (MTC) in 5G. So far, the cellular network is mainly based on scheduling, in which each user is assigned to a time/frequency/space unit orthogonal to other

---

F. Wang—This work was supported in part by the National Natural Science Foundation under Grant 61571034 and under Grant U1334202, the Fundamental Research Funds for the Central Universities under Grant 2015JBM112, and the State Key Laboratory of Rail Traffic Control and Safety under Grant RCS2016ZT013.

© ICST Institute for Computer Sciences, Social Informatics and Telecommunications Engineering 2018
Q. Chen et al. (Eds.): ChinaCom 2016, Part II, LNICST 210, pp. 292–301, 2018.
DOI: 10.1007/978-3-319-66628-0_28

users. In future, machines and/or things will be also connected into the network rather than human only. With massive terminals which generally requires random sparse traffic, contention-based communication becomes a good candidate. However, traditional contention-based protocol allows no collision. In [5], it employed a fully-distributed random access protocol for collision avoidance mechanism and in [6] it proposed using a novel medium access protocol Carrier Sense Multiple Access/Collision Detection with Reservation (CSMA/CDR) to resolve collision. In addition, adopting orthogonal spreading sequences having a high autocorrelation to detect the collision is another choice, such as using Zadoff-Chu (ZC) sequence [7,8]. For example, in the random access process of LTE, the network access point detects the collision by a bank of correlators, each of which is matched to a particular ZC sequence in the set [9].

However, the method of ZC sequence requires the correlation of different sequences to be zero and thus it is very sensitive to asynchronization. In this paper, we proposed a novel structure of preamble, with which we can detect collision and estimate CSI regardless of correlation issue at the receiver. Specifically, a Discrete Fourier Transformation (DFT) matrix is used to design the preamble, preamble matrices of different users can be obtained by alternating rows of a basis DFT matrix. Accordingly, a method of collision detection is provided which applies in practical channel conditions and channel state information can be estimated as a byproduct. The receivers can utilize the structure of the preamble to detect collision. And a collision detection algorithm which aims at asynchronous and multipath scenarios in practical communication is proposed. With the results of the algorithm, CSI can be estimated.

The rest of the paper is organized as follow. Section 2 introduces the system model. Sections 3 and 4 we propose method for collision detection, channel estimation in practical channel conditions. In Sect. 5 simulation results are provided. Finally, Sect. 6 concludes this paper.

2 System Model and Preamble Structure

Consider a multiple access channel with one access point and M users. The transmission of the users are contention-based, in which collision occurs with a large probability when there are massive users, which is a typical scenario in 5G communication.

Then, we introduce the structure of our proposed preamble by using a Discrete Fourier Transformation (DFT) matrix

$$G = \begin{bmatrix} 1 & 1 & 1 & \cdots & 1 \\ 1 & w & w^2 & \cdots & w^{L-1} \\ 1 & w^2 & w^4 & \cdots & w^{2(L-1)} \\ \vdots & \vdots & \vdots & \ddots & \vdots \\ 1 & w^M & w^{2M} & \cdots & w^{M(L-1)} \end{bmatrix} \tag{1}$$

where $w = e^{j\frac{2\pi}{L}}$, and $M, L \in \mathbb{Z}^+$. For illustration brevity, we define a vector as

$$g_i = \begin{bmatrix} 1, w^i, w^{2i}, \cdots, w^{i(L-1)} \end{bmatrix}^T, \quad i \in \mathcal{I}_M \tag{2}$$

where $\mathcal{I}_M = \{0, 1, \cdots, M\}$. In this paper, we propose to use G as a basis matrix. The number of rows is equal to maximum users which can be detected in a collision, and the number of columns is related to the diversity order which is further elaborated later. Accordingly, the basis matrix is rewritten by

$$G = \left[g_0, g_1, g_2, \cdots, g_M \right]^T. \tag{3}$$

The preamble matrix G_k for the kth user is obtained by alternating the first row and the $(k+1)$th row of the basis matrix G, which is written by

$$G_k = \left[g_k, g_2, \cdots, g_0, \cdots, g_M \right]^T \tag{4}$$

Note that the preamble matrix is sent column by column in practice. It is stacked up into an equal dimension matrix at the access point for detecting collision and estimating channels[1].

3 Collision Detection and Channel Estimation

3.1 Toy Model of Collision Detection

In this toy model, we assume that, in a noiseless channel the ith user and the kth user send their preambles in exactly the same slot. The overlapped preamble signal $Y_t = G_i + G_k$ at the access point can be expressed as

$$Y_t = \left[g_i + g_k, 2g_1, \cdots, g_0 + g_i, \cdots, g_k + g_0, \cdots, 2g_M \right]^T. \tag{5}$$

From the definition of the preamble matrix in (1) and (4), each element of the first column of Y_t is 2 currently, which is equal to the number of collision users. In practice, the preamble is contaminated by noises. Then, we average over all elements in the first column to determine the number of collisions. We further notice that the number of collisions can also be estimated by the sum of all elements of Y_t divided by that of G, which is straightforward since Y_t is obtained by alternating different rows of G only. After that, we can further determine which users collide from a decision matrix Y_t' calculated by

$$
\begin{aligned}
Y_t' &= Y_t - KG = G_i + G_k - 2G \\
&= \begin{bmatrix}
0 & w^i + w^k - 2 & \cdots & w^{i(L-1)} + w^{k(L-1)} - 2 \\
\vdots & \vdots & \ddots & \vdots \\
0 & 1 - w^i & \cdots & 1 - w^{i(L-1)} \\
\vdots & \vdots & \ddots & \vdots \\
0 & 1 - w^k & \cdots & 1 - w^{k(L-1)} \\
\vdots & \vdots & \ddots & \vdots \\
0 & 0 & \cdots & 0
\end{bmatrix}.
\end{aligned} \tag{6}
$$

---

[1] There could be misalignment among multiple users, which induces extra elements for reconstructing the preamble matrix. The extra elements can be simply ignored. Details are provided in Sect. 3.3.

The collision users are determined by the indices of nonzero rows in Y'_t except for the first row.

3.2 Collision Detection in Flat-Fading Channel

Consider a noiseless flat fading channel, and the ith user and the kth user still transmit in the same slot. The channel responses of the ith user and the kth user are h_i and h_k, respectively. Then the received preamble matrix Y_f can be expressed as

$$
Y_f = h_i G_i + h_k G_k
$$
$$
= \left[h_i g_i + h_k g_k , \cdots , h_i g_0 + h_k g_i , \cdots , h_i g_k + h_k g_0 , \cdots , (h_i + h_k) g_M \right]^T . \tag{7}
$$

Similarly to the previous toy model, we can average over the first column to get the sum of the channel fading of the two users, i.e., $h_i + h_k$. An alternative method is to sum up over all element divided by the sum of all element of G. Then the detection matrix Y'_f is calculated by

$$
Y'_f = Y_f - (h_i + h_k) G = h_i G_i + h_k G_k - (h_i + h_k) G
$$

$$
= \begin{bmatrix}
0 & h_i w^i + h_k w^k - (h_i + h_k) & \cdots & h_i w^{i(L-1)} + h_k w^{k(L-1)} - (h_i + h_k) \\
\vdots & \vdots & \ddots & \vdots \\
0 & h_i(1 - w^i) & \cdots & h_i(1 - w^{i(L-1)}) \\
\vdots & \vdots & \ddots & \vdots \\
0 & h_k(1 - w^k) & \cdots & h_k(1 - w^{k(L-1)}) \\
\vdots & \vdots & \ddots & \vdots \\
0 & 0 & \cdots & 0
\end{bmatrix} .
\tag{8}
$$

Similarly, we determine the collision users by finding nonzero rows in Y'_f except for the first row. Furthermore, channel fading of the users can be estimated (by averaging method) as

$$
\hat{h}_j = \frac{1}{L-1} \cdot \sum_{\ell=1}^{L-1} \frac{h_j(1 - w^{j\ell})}{1 - w^{j\ell}}, \quad j = i, k
\tag{9}
$$

where $\hat{h}_j$ is the estimated channel fading of user j, and $j = i, k$.

3.3 Collision Detection in Asynchronous Scenario

In this section, we consider two users collides in an asynchronous manner. First, we denote the received matrix by a delay sum operation, which is expressed as $C = \text{sum}(A, B; d)$, where the matrix A is summed up with a d-element-delay version of B, and the elementary delay occurs column by column from the first

elementary of the matrix signal is sent column by column. With the definition of the delay sum, the received signal matrix is expressed as

$$Y_a = \text{sum}(h_i G_i, h_k G_k; d) \tag{10}$$

where h_i and h_k are the channel state information of the ith user and the k user respectively, and here in this example d is the number of symbols between the two users. From the structure obtained by the delay sum, it can be seen that the previous preamble cannot be applied to detect the two collided users directly. Next, we proposed an enhanced structure of preamble. Define $f = e^{\frac{j2\pi}{N}}$, where N is the number of signal sampling points $(N > M + 1)$, matrix E can be expressed as

$$E = \text{diag}\left[f, f^2, \cdots, f^{M+1}\right]. \tag{11}$$

The preamble matrix F_i of the ith user can be designed by

$$F_i = EG_i = \left[fg_i, f^2 g_1, \cdots, f^{i+1} g_0, \cdots, f^{M+1} g_M\right]^T \tag{12}$$

The fundamental interpretation of this procedure is to modulate the symbols in each row to a different carrier, which can be realized by fast Fourier transform (FFT). Then, the received signal Y_a is expressed as

$$Y_a = \text{sum}(h_i F_i, h_k F_k; d)$$

$$
= \begin{bmatrix}
fh_i & fh_i w^i + f^{M-d+2} w^k & \cdots \\
\vdots & \vdots & \cdots \\
f^{d+1} h_i + fh_k & f^{d+1} h_i w^d + fh_k w^k & \cdots \\
\vdots & \vdots & \cdots \\
f^{M+1} h_i + f^{M-d+1} h_k & f^{M+1} h_i w^M + f^{M-d+1} h_k w^{M-d} & \cdots
\end{bmatrix}
$$

$$
\begin{bmatrix}
fh_i w^{i(L-1)} + f^{M-d+2} h_k w^{(M-d+1)(L-2)} & f^{M-d+2} h_k w^{(M-d+1)(L-1)} \\
\vdots & \vdots \\
f^{d+1} h_i w^{d(L-1)} + fh_k w^{k(L-1)} & 0 \\
\vdots & \vdots \\
f^{M+1} h_i w^{M(L-1)} + f^{M-d+1} h_k w^{(M-d)(L-1)} & 0
\end{bmatrix} \tag{13}
$$

The access point needs to demodulate each row of the received matrix Y_a with corresponding frequency. Then, the matrix after demodulation goes through low-pass filtering (LPF), the receiver gets a new matrix that eliminates the interference of other users. Collision detection and channel estimation can be proceeded as the previous scheme in flat-fading channel. Due to the fact that

$$\frac{1}{N} \sum_{q=0}^{N-1} e^{\frac{j2\pi qm}{N}} e^{-\frac{j2\pi qn}{N}} = \delta(m-n) \tag{14}$$

where $m, n = 1, 2, \cdots, M+1$, and $q = 0, 1, \cdots, N-1$. For example,

$$\frac{1}{N} \sum_{q=0}^{N-1} (w^{m-1} e^{\frac{j2\pi qm}{N}} + w^{n-1} e^{\frac{j2\pi qn}{N}}) e^{-\frac{j2\pi qn}{N}} = \begin{cases} w^{n-1} & , \ m \neq n \\ w^{m-1} + w^{n-1} & , \ m = n \end{cases}. \quad (15)$$

For two elements on the same frequency, both of them are not eliminated. For two elements on different frequency, only one will remains. So the demodulation and low-pass filtering can be substituted for the above process in this paper. Here we express the process as $\frac{1}{T} \int_t \boldsymbol{E}^H \boldsymbol{Y}_a$.

3.4   Influence of Multipath Effect and Noise

In a communication system, multipath and noise should be considered in practice. For the receiver, multipath can be interpreted as a signal with multiple copies with different attenuations and delays. The received signal is a delay sum of multiple components with different delays. The access point only regards these copies as some other collision users. This phenomenon shows clearly that the multipath does not affect the collision detection of the proposed preamble.

Because of the noise, the access point can not use nonzero rows to detect collision directly any more. Therefore, we should set a threshold based on the noise. In general, it is set to twice or three times the noise power. In the collision detection, if the average power of a row is greater than the threshold, this row will be regarded as nonzero row. So the problem of noise is solved.

4   Collision Detection Algorithm

Figure 1 is a flow-chart showing the process of collision detection. Where $\boldsymbol{Y}$ is a matrix that stacked up by the received signal, and symbols $m, \boldsymbol{Y}', \boldsymbol{Y}'', \boldsymbol{Y}''', H, h$ are defined to save the intermediate results. Ignore the influence of noise temporarily, and d_i represents the delay between the ith user and the $(i+1)$th user. The process of detection is as follow

Step 1: Every single row of matrix $\boldsymbol{Y}$ needs down-conversion (DC) and LPF. Then the receivers can get the matrix $\boldsymbol{Y}' = \frac{1}{T} \int_t \boldsymbol{E}^H \boldsymbol{Y}$.

Step 2: Testing $\boldsymbol{Y} - \boldsymbol{E}\boldsymbol{Y}' = 0$. If it is correct, that means every d_i is integral multiple of $M+1$. Then execute step 3. If it is false, jump to step 4.

Step 3: Here we define a new variable named m, and $m = 0$. Calculating $H = \frac{\text{sum}(\boldsymbol{Y}')}{\text{sum}(\boldsymbol{F})}$, where $\text{sum}(\cdot)$ denotes the sum of all elements of matrix $(\cdot)$. $h = \text{mean}(\boldsymbol{y}'_{m+1})$, where $\text{mean}(\boldsymbol{y}'_{m+1})$ denotes the mean value of $(m+1)$th column of matrix $\boldsymbol{Y}'$. If $H = h$, it means the rest of users after DC and LPF are synchronical completely, then execute step 3.1. If $H \neq h$, execute step 3.3.

Step 3.1: Calculating detection matrix $\boldsymbol{Y}''$ as follow

$$\boldsymbol{Y}'' = [\boldsymbol{y}'_{m+1}, \boldsymbol{y}'_{m+2}, \cdots, \boldsymbol{y}'_{m+L}] - H\boldsymbol{F} \quad (16)$$

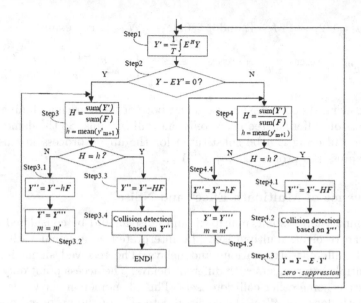

Fig. 1. Collision detection algorithm in asynchronous scenario.

where $[\boldsymbol{y}'_{m+1}, \boldsymbol{y}'_{m+2}, \cdots, \boldsymbol{y}'_{m+L}]$ means the $(m+1)$th column to $(m+L)$th column of matrix $\boldsymbol{Y}'$. Then continue to execute step 3.2.

<u>Step 3.2:</u> The access point determines the collision users and estimate the CSI by the nonzero rows in $\boldsymbol{Y}''$ except for the first row. And the algorithm ends.

Step 3.3: Calculating matrix $\boldsymbol{Y}'''$ as follow

$$\boldsymbol{Y}''' = [\boldsymbol{y}'_{m+1}, \boldsymbol{y}'_{m+2}, \cdots, \boldsymbol{y}'_{m+L}] - h\boldsymbol{F} \tag{17}$$

Then continue to execute the step 3.4.

<u>Step 3.4:</u> Checking how many columns with zero mean are there in matrix $\boldsymbol{Y}'''$, and assign the number to the variable m'; Then back to step 3, and reassign $\boldsymbol{Y}' = \boldsymbol{Y}'''$ and $m = m'$.

<u>Step 4:</u> Steps 3 and 4 are just the same, only when $H = h$, there are quite a few differences. If $H = h$, step 4 calculates the matris $\boldsymbol{Y}''$ as follow

$$\boldsymbol{Y}'' = [\boldsymbol{y}'_{m+1}, \boldsymbol{y}'_{m+2}, \cdots, \boldsymbol{y}'_{m+L}] - H\boldsymbol{F}. \tag{18}$$

Then access point determines the collision users and estimate the CSI by the nonzero rows in matrix $\boldsymbol{Y}''$ except for the first row. However, the algorithm does not end. The matrix $\boldsymbol{Y} - E\boldsymbol{Y}'$ in step 2 needs to be expanded into a row vector by columns. After removing all the zero elements at the head and tail of the row vector (Zero-Suppression/ZS), start with the first element, and convert it into a new matrix $[\boldsymbol{Y} - E\boldsymbol{Y}']_{ZS}$ by every $M + 1$ elements as one column. Then return to step 1, reassign the matrix $\boldsymbol{Y} = [\boldsymbol{Y} - E\boldsymbol{Y}']_{ZS}$ and start next loop.

5   Simulation Results and Analysis

In this section, the numerical results are presented to validate the performance of collision detection and channel estimation. In the simulation, we evaluated the proposed scheme in a flat Rayleigh fading channel both in synchronous and asynchronous scenarios. Considered 10 candidate users with a single access point, the size of the preamble matrix is $11 \times L$. We also investigate the effect of variable L on the performance of collision detection. The detection veracity rate (DVR) represents the error probability of detection. For Channel Estimation, the mean square error (MSE) is used to show its performance. Besides, this paper also simulates the performance of ZC-sequence as a comparison, where L' (must be a prime number) is the length of ZC-sequence, so L' is 11 at least in theory.

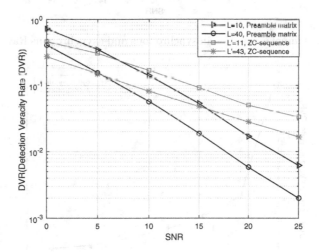

Fig. 2. Detection veracity rate of the proposed scheme and ZC-sequence of different lengths in asynchronous Rayleigh channel.

Figure 2 shows the DVR in asynchronous scenario. With the increase of SNR, the performance of preamble matrix becomes better and better, and exceeds ZC-sequence gradually. In fact, both ZC-sequence and preamble matrix are very sensitive to the synchronization problem. However, we optimize the preamble matrix by adding phase, so it performs better than ZC-sequence in the Asynchronous scenario. Figure 3 shows the Mean Square Error (MSE) of channel estimation in the Rayleigh channel when the communication is synchronous and asynchronous. In this figure, we can find the performance of channel estimation in an synchronous condition is worse. This is mainly because when the communication is asynchronous and the d_i is not integral multiple of $M + 1$, access point can separate the signals mixing together completely. If ignore the noise temporarily, the access point can get the original preamble matrix which carries the channel information, and CSI can be estimated with the whole matrix.

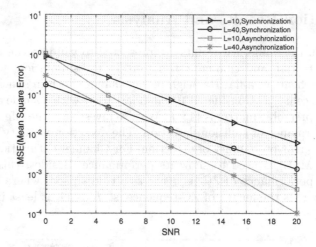

Fig. 3. MSE of channel estimation in synchronous and asynchronous Rayleigh channel.

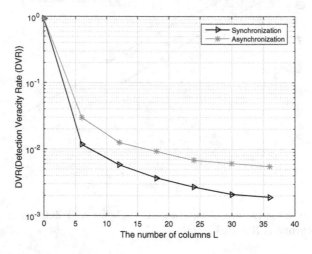

Fig. 4. Effects of L on DVR in synchronous and asynchronous Rayleigh channel (SNR = 20 dB).

However, if the communication is synchronous, the access point can only use the nonzero rows to estimate channel. So the performance in an asynchronous condition is better after SNR > 8 dB. Here we can see asynchronous scenario also has some advantages.

In Figs. 2 and 3, the performance of collision detection and channel estimation is affected by L, the number of columns of preamble matrix. As shown in Fig. 4, the simulation environment is in Rayleigh channel with SNR = 20 dB, we can see the synchronous performance is better than asynchronous performance as a whole. With the increase of L, the performance of collision detection overall is becoming better and better, but when the variable L grows to a certain degree, the performance does not change any more. The reason is the method of averaging or weighted average to suppress the noise is limited. Increasing the dimension of the preamble matrix can reduce the interference of noise. However, this trend will stop changing and keep smooth when L is large enough.

6 Conclusion

We proposed a new structure of preamble for contention-based communications. With the well-designed preamble structure, we can detect the number of collided users, which users are in the collision, and the channel state information of each user in both synchronous and asynchronous scenarios. In addition, it involves low amount of storage, which is the size of DFT matrix, and low computational complexity. The numerical results show that the proposed scheme exhibits better performance than using ZC-sequence as preamble.

References

1. Liang, T.-J., Fettweis, G.: MIMO preamble design with a subset of subcarriers in OFDM-based WLAN. In: Vehicular Technology Conference, vol. 2, pp. 1032–1036 (2005)
2. Hao, B., Wang, J., Wang, Z.: Low-complexity signaling-embedded preamble design based on relative subcarrier position. IEEE Commun. Lett. 18(9), 1657–1660 (2014)
3. Mavrokefalidis, C., Kofidis, E., Rontogiannis, A., Theodoridis, S.: Preamble design for channel estimation in OFDM/OQAM cooperative systems. In: Proceedings of the Tenth International Symposium on Wireless Communication Systems, Ilmenau, Germany, pp. 1–5 (2013)
4. Liu, J., Kang, G., Lu, S., Zhang, P.: Preamble design based on complete complementary sets for random access in MIMO-OFDM systems. In: Wireless Communications and Networking Conference, Kowloon, pp. 858–862 (2007)
5. Zihan, E., Choi, K.W., Kim, D.I.: Distributed random access scheme for collision avoidance in cellular device-to-device communication. IEEE Trans. Wirel. Commun. 14(7), 3571–3585 (2015)
6. Kim, D.-H., Park, C.-K.: CSMA/CD with reservations in wireless communication: a novel approach to resolve collisions. In: International Conference on Control, Automation and Systems, Seoul, pp. 2858–2864 (2007)
7. Piret, P.: A stochastic model for burst-correcting convolutional decoders. IEEE Trans. Inf. Theory 18(4), 532–535 (1972)
8. Kim, T., Choudhury, S., Jin, Z.Y., Doppler, K., Ghosh, C.: Simultaneous polling mechanism for low power sensor networks using ZC sequences. In: 2012 IEEE 23rd International Symposium on Personal Indoor and Mobile Radio Communications (PIMRC), Sydney, NSW, pp. 2024–2029 (2012)
9. Hua, M., Wang, M., Yang, K.W., Zou, K.J.: Analysis of the frequency offset effect on Zadoff-Chu sequence timing performance. IEEE Trans. Commun. 62(11), 4024–4039 (2014)

A Data Dissemination Strategy in SDN Enabled Vehicular Networks

Chen Chen$^{(\boxtimes)}$, Na Li, Yansong Li, Ronghui Hou, and Zhiyuan Ren

State Key Laboratory of Integrated Service Networks,
Xidian University, Xi'an 710071, China
cc2000@mail.xidian.edu.cn

Abstract. In a vehicular network, the vehicles generally need to handoff among RSUs (Road Side Units) frequently on highways due to their rapid mobility and the limit of RSU's radio coverage. This issue may cause a series of problems such as data transmission interruption or increasing of the transmission delay. In this paper, we took advantages of the emerging idea of SDN to improve the performance of the vehicular networks. Specifically, we proposed a SDN-based framework for the vehicular networks. In this framework, we developed three function modules over the SDN application layer. And then by installing appropriate rules on OpenFlow enabled RSUs, the controller can execute a wise scheduling of RSUs' downlink streams. In addition, based on this framework, we proposed a data dissemination strategy when a vehicle handoff among the RSUs to reduce the latency especially for bulk traffic. Simulation results demonstrate that our solution can significantly reduce the latency and the retransmission rate. In the paper, we adopted classical DCF mechanism in the IEEE 802.11p standard to implement our protocol, which makes our solution practical and compatible with previous drafts.

Keywords: SDN · OpenFlow · Vehicular network · DCF · RSU handoff

1 Introduction

Nowadays, vehicular networks have attracted more and more attentions, which is regarded as the key technology to improve the road safety and the construction of intelligent transportation system [1]. In a vehicular network, the communication between vehicles is known as V2V (vehicle-to-vehicle), and the vehicle and the infrastructure such as the RSU (roadside unit) is called V2I (vehicle-to-infrastructure). The V2V communication usually has strong randomness due to high dynamic of vehicles, therefore V2I communication is supposed to play an important role to improve the performance of the network especially in high mobility scenarios. In RSU-aided networks, vehicles traveling along the road can establish stable connections to RSUs deployed on the roadsides, which is able to provide high-bandwidth communication capability for data transmissions [2].

However, in traditional vehicular networks, the server always puts all the content in one RSU, while the coverage of existing RSU is still limited. As a result, the vehicle in the high-speed mobile scenarios such as highways will access another RSU even it

© ICST Institute for Computer Sciences, Social Informatics and Telecommunications Engineering 2018
Q. Chen et al. (Eds.): ChinaCom 2016, Part II, LNICST 210, pp. 302–313, 2018.
DOI: 10.1007/978-3-319-66628-0_29

doesn't take off all the contents from the previous attached RSU. When the vehicle successfully access the new RSU, it has to send the content requirement again [3]. As we can see, this process above causes much unnecessary communication overhead, especially transferring the bulk data and needing to switch RSUs frequently.

To solve the problems above, in this paper we propose a novel SDN based VANETs architecture and a kind of data dissemination strategy during the RSU handoff. The core idea of SDN [4, 5] is to realize the flexible controlling of the network traffic by decoupling the control plane and the data plane of the network equipment. SDN changes the original network with hardware configuration as the core to a software based network, which can greatly improve the performance in centralized controlling, programmability and other aspects of the existing architecture. In this paper, we first construct the SDN based VENETs architecture and explain the functions of every part in detail. Then through derivation we cut the bulk data the vehicle requested into different sizes and allocate to the corresponding RSU. Furthermore, we propose the pre-cache mechanism so that can reduce the kinds of communication overhead at utmost. At the end of the paper, we simulate the architecture and dissemination strategy we proposed in OPENET to verify the effectiveness of our solution.

2 Background and Related Work

2.1 Distributed Channel Access Mechanism in 802.11

So far the WLAN based 802.11p/wave protocol [6] is an important part of vehicle networks. The Federal Communications Commission (FCC) appoints 75 MHz band for vehicle networks communication based 802.11p. Among them, the first 1 MHz band is reserved as a security vacuum boundary, the rest is divided into seven adjacent 10 MHz band. As shown in Fig. 1, the channel is sequentially numbered Ch172, Ch174,..., Ch184, in which Ch178 is controlling channel CCH for controlling and managing the other six bands, the Ch172 is using as emergency message transmission channel, and the Ch184 is suitable for transmitting long-distance public safety information, at the same time, Ch174, Ch176, Ch180, Ch182 are common traffic channels using to transfer the traditional network data through RSUs [7].

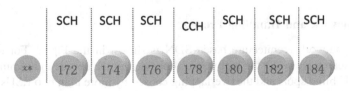

Fig. 1. Channel allocation of IEEE 802.11p Mac Layer

As known, common traffic channels have characteristics of traffic burst, low delay requirement and high throughput requirement which coincide with the CSMA/DCF protocol. Therefore, we consider using CSMA/DCF technology to compete ordinary

SCH channel slot in this paper. The vehicle passes messages occupying this slot to the RSU by one or two hops. Through the OpenFlow switches the messages in RSU are transferred to SDN controller, and then injected into the Internet. In the downlink, the messages from the Internet are sent to the RSU through the SDN controller, then the RSU completes the downlink slot forwarding to the vehicle by one hop or two hops at most.

2.2 Related Work

With the developing of SDN, the domestic and foreign scholars have conducted a lot of works about applying SDN in different fields. The network architecture based SDN proposed in a REF. [8] which has explained the function of each part in detail. More importantly, the practicability of the architecture is illustrated by the example of lane change prediction and traffic flow distribution at the last part of this paper. REF. [9] leveraged the emerging idea of SDN and OpenFlow technology to reorganize the architecture of enterprise WLAN to mitigate the impact of interference, which cannot be handled very well in conventional architecture. They proposed a downlink packets scheduling algorithm to mitigate the impact of interference among APs and clients, as well as conducted fine-grained downlink packets scheduling by installing appropriate rules in corresponding APs.

However, the solution about reducing kinds of communication overhead during the vehicle handoff process is still approaching the traditional method. The server will put all the data that the vehicle requested in RSUs along the way the vehicle passing. This solution will cause storage wasting and connection delay. So far few scholars propose a directive solution, yet their researches on other aspects have provided important references for us. REF. [10] proposed a hybrid Vehicle networks architecture aimed to improve the protocol extensibility which is similar with mesh network. The paper studied how to deploy RSU based vehicle traffic conditions and urban road structures. However its research scene is only in one simple high-way, leading the deployment issue is simplified as determining the access point distance according to the vehicle density. Liu [11] have analyzed the RSU flow of uplink and downlink, as well as put forward to take vehicles on the road as relay nodes for data transmission.

3 Data Dissemination During Handoffs Among RSUs

3.1 Framework and Handling Process

The vehicle network architecture based SDN is shown in the Fig. 2. For the convenience of research we select the highway no considering the export and turning, besides that, the RSU blind spots and the overlapping caused by more than two RSUs are out of consideration. Among them, RUS is a roadside unit with the function that can collect information including the road length, road conditions, the number of vehicles and location and state of nearby RSUs etc. At the same time, RSU can also communicate with the OBU in vehicle, collecting and storing the vehicle information including vehicle ID, speed, route and the requirement etc. Finally RSU as a relay device is responsible to forward the information above and information from the controller [12].

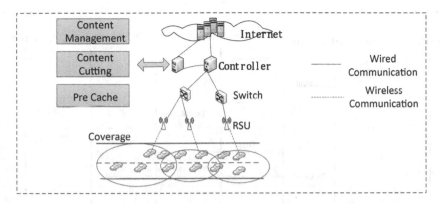

Fig. 2. The vehicle networks architecture based SDN

Each OpenFlow switch [13] in architecture is composed of three parts: security channels, OpenFlow protocols and flow tables. Security channel is for the communication between the switch and the controller transmitting the protocol commands and data packets. The OpenFlow protocol is the standard interface for communication between the controller and the OpenFlow switch. Each flow table contains a number of flow table entries, each of which contains a matching field and an action set, according which the switch processes the flow.

We select Floodlight as the controller that is responsible for the development and management of the forwarding strategy. Floodlight [14] uses a modular architecture to achieve the corresponding functions, which has a good extensibility. In this paper, through the controller north interface (API) we develop three modules respectively: Content Management, Content Cutting and Pre Cache. The Content Management module includes data management and user management. Data management is mainly used to manage the server IP, the location of RSUs, the current network topology and the data has been cached. User management records vehicle ID, speed, route, as well as the requirement. The Content Cutting module divides the data into different segments according to the information in Content Management module. Pre Cache module sends the packets to the corresponding RSU through the appropriate transmission path.

The top layer is Internet, which contains a large number of original servers, which is the terminal of data upload and download. The V2I communication adopts 802.11p protocol, while the connection of other parts adopts wired connection to ensure the reliability of transmission.

The System operation is shown in Fig. 3.

(1) The vehicle sends the vehicle information and request content to RSU through the OBU in vehicle.
(2) RSU as a relay device sends the information above to the SDN controller through the switches.
(3) Content Management module is triggered to update user information and data information.

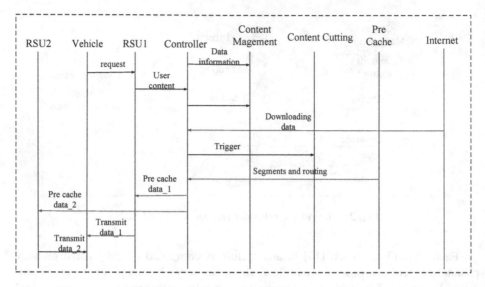

Fig. 3. System operation process

(4) The SDN controller interacts with the Internet interaction uploading or downloading the data.

(5) Content Cutting module divides the data received from Internet into different segments and packs them in unified form.

(6) Pre Cache module sends the packets to the corresponding RSU through the appropriate route.

(7) When the vehicle enters the corresponding RSU, the RSU authenticates the vehicle and transmits the packets pre cached in it.

3.2 Content Management

Since the SDN controller needs to make the routing strategies of global information, it is necessary to keep track of all the information and topology of the current network. In this paper, we use the Content Management module to store the data content and user information. The data content includes RSU management and data management.

The RSU manages packets as form in Table 1. The RSUs along the road are numbered as RSU_A, RSU_B, RSU_C, etc. The Location is just the location of the RSU. Name represents the name of the data that has been cached in the RSU. The throughput in the Table 1 is given when the vehicle is in the overlapping of two RSUs and they all have the content requested, then we will select the larger throughput of RSU for transmission (Here we ignore the RSU overlapping situation due to space limitations, and it is another research point). Data management includes the size of the packet, the update time, and the original server. Its format is shown in Table 2. User information packets include the user's ID, location, vehicle speed, travel path, and the requirement. The frame format is shown in Table 3.

Table 1. RSU management packet

Identity	Location	Name	Throughput
RSU_A	{31.7811, 230.0018}	Data1	320 Mb
RSU_B	{31.1368, 230.9945}	Data2	512 Mb
RSU_C	{31.0025, 230.8597}	Data3	128 Mb

Table 2. Data management packet

Identity	Size	Update time	Owner
Data1	1024	201601220530	{A, C}
Data2	800	201502243122	{B}

Table 3. User management packet

Identity	Location	Speed	Travel path	Requirement
Vehicle_1	{31.2564, 230.1269}	20 m/s	{D, E, G}	Data 1
Vehicle_2	{24.2356, 230.5612}	15 m/s	{D, E, F}	Data 3

3.3 Content Cutting

IEEE 802.11p protocol currently supports the maximum transmission distance within 1000 m, which can meet the communication requirement between the vehicles driving at 33 m/s (about 120 km/h) and between the vehicles and RSUs. Considering the constraints of antenna transmitting power, we suppose that the RSU transmission radius is Rr = 1000 m, and the vehicle density in the RSU is ρ, thus the number of vehicles is $\lambda = \rho 2R_r$. As known, the number of vehicles obeys Poisson distribution [15] so that the expectation and variance are λ. The probability function of the number of vehicles in one RSU is:

$$\rho(n) = \frac{\lambda^n e^{-\lambda}}{n!} = \frac{\left(\rho 2R_r\right)^n e^{-\rho 2R_r}}{n!}. \tag{1}$$

In the coverage range of the RSU, assuming the probability of a vehicle sending a data frame in a random time slot is τ, then the probability of collision between this data frame and other data frame sending from another node is. When the value of n is given, η will remain dependent and constant. The relationship is as following:

$$\eta = 1 - (1 - \tau)^{n-1}. \tag{2}$$

$$\tau = 1 - (1 - \eta)^{n-1}. \tag{3}$$

Bianchi analyzes the DCF backoff process using Markov chain. Given W = CWmin (minimum contention window), maximum contention window CWmax = 2 m−1, m is the retransmission rate. According to the analysis, The probability of sending a data frame when n vehicles compete the wireless channel is:

$$\tau(\eta) = \frac{2}{1 + W + \eta W \sum_{i=0}^{m-1} (2\eta)^i}. \tag{4}$$

From formula (3) and (4), we can work out the value of and. It is assumed that the probability of at least one frame in a time slot transmitting is P_{tr}, and only one frame transmitted successfully is P_s

$$P_{tr} = 1 - (1 - \tau)^n \tag{5}$$

$$P_s = \frac{n\tau(1 - \tau)^{n-1}}{P_{tr}} = \frac{n\tau(1 - \tau)^{n-1}}{1 - (1 - \tau)^{n-1}} \tag{6}$$

If a vehicle node successfully transmits a frame, the channel is busy for other nodes. The probability of this process is $P_{st} = P_{tr}P_s$, the average time is T_{st}; When the channel is idle, the conflict probability that a node sends data during this time is $P_{co} = P_{tr}(1 - P_s)$, the average time is T_{co}; The idle channel probability during a time slot is $P_{idle} = (1 - P_s)$, the average time is T_σ Among them, $P_{st} = T_{DIFS} + T_{DATA} + T_{SIFS} + T_{ACK}$,
$P_{co} = T_{DIFS} + T_{CODATA} + T_{SIFS} + T_{ACK} \cdot T_{SIFS}$ is minimum frame interval in DCF mechanism; T_{DIFS} is the waiting time between the idle channel confirmation and sending data; T_{ACK} is the acknowledgement frame length; T_{DATA} is a frame data transmission time; T_{CODATA} is the maximum data frame length when conflict occurs. If we assume that all the data frame length is same, then $P_{st} = P_{co}$. The average time of a system time slot is:

$$\begin{aligned} T_{slot} &= P_{idle}T_\sigma + P_{st}T_{st} + P_{co}T_{co} \\ &= (1 - \tau)^n T_\sigma + (1 - (1 - \tau)^n)(T_{DIFS} + T_{DATA} + T_{SIFS} + T_{ACK}) \end{aligned} \tag{7}$$

The transmission efficiency is:

$$\begin{aligned} \Psi(n) &= \frac{P_{tr}P_s T_{DATA}}{P_{idle}T_\sigma + P_{st}T_{st} + P_{co}T_{co}} \\ &= \frac{n\tau(1-\tau)^{n-1}T_{DATA}}{(1-\tau)^n T_\sigma + (1-(1-\tau)^n)(T_{DIFS} + T_{DATA} + T_{SIFS} + T_{ACK})} \end{aligned} \tag{8}$$

According to formula (8), if there is D_{DATA} needed to transmit, the traffic that can successfully transmitted during a frame is $D_{SDATA} = \Psi(n)D_{DATA}$. In 802.11p protocol, the data transmission rate $\omega = \frac{D_{DATA}}{T_{DATA}}$.

It is analyzed in REF. [5], if there are n vehicles in the coverage of the RSU, the total throughput is:

$$E(\Gamma) = E[\sum_{n=0}^{\infty} (np(n)DS_{DATA})\frac{\omega}{n}\frac{1}{D_{DATA}}]$$
$$= E[\sum_{n=0}^{\infty} (n\frac{(\rho 2R_r)^n e^{-\rho 2R_r}}{n!}\psi(n)D_{DATA})\frac{\omega}{n}\frac{1}{D_{DATA}}] \qquad (9)$$
$$= E[\sum_{n=0}^{\infty} (\frac{(\rho 2R_r)^n e^{-\rho 2R_r}}{n!}\psi(n))]\omega$$

Therefore, the probability that there is one vehicle at least in RSU according to the function (1) is $1 - e^{-\rho 2R_r}$. It is also the vehicle i existing probability. And the vehicle i downloading time is: $\Delta t = \frac{2R_r}{v_i}$.

Thus, the total traffic that vehicle i directly downloads (one hop) from RSU is:

$$E[W] = E[\Gamma_{downlink}\Delta t] \approx \frac{(1 - e^{-2\rho R_r})\omega T_{DATA}}{(\frac{2W-1}{2})T_\sigma + (T_{DIFS} + T_{DATA} + T_{SIFS} + T_{ACK})} \cdot \frac{2R_r}{v_i} \qquad (10)$$

If the vehicle i only downloads within the distance d, the downloading traffic is $E(W_d)$:

$$E[W] = E[\Gamma_{downlink}\Delta t] \approx \frac{(1 - e^{-2\rho R_r})\omega T_{DATA}}{(\frac{2W-1}{2})T_\sigma + (T_{DIFS} + T_{DATA} + T_{SIFS} + T_{ACK})} \cdot \frac{d}{v_i} \qquad (11)$$

Assuming the total traffic that vehicle i requested is $E(Q)$, if $E(Q) < E(W_d)$, there is no need to switch RSU completing the download. If $E(Q) > E(W_d)$, it is necessary to switch RSU, it means that we need to cut the download data into different packets. We suppose the traffic downloading from RSU_A is $E(W_{d1})$, if $E(Q) - E(W_{d1}) > E(W)$, we allocate a size of $E(W)$ packet into RSU_B. Otherwise, put the rest of data into RSU_B totally. Using this solution, cut the data sequentially and divide the packet into corresponding RSU. The segmented data is packed as Table 4.

Table 4. Segmented data packet

Name	Original IP	Segments	Destination	Size
Data_1	10.0.0.1.5	Data_1.1	RSU_A	$E(W_{d1})$
		Data_1.2	RSU_B	$E(W)$
		Data_1.3	RSU_C	The rest

3.4 Pre Cache

In order to allow the vehicle to connect with the RSU as soon as possible and reduce the latency maximally, we adopt the pre-cache pattern. The PRE_CACHE packet is shown in Table 5.

We name the time that the vehicle gets to the next RSU as Time to Live (TTL). Flag is a number of Boolean, which 1 represents downloaded already, and 0 is not downloaded yet. Continue Cache represents whether other vehicles requests the data either. When there are multiple vehicles request the same data, we can use the Continue Cache value represents the arrival time of the vehicle requested later. The value of TTL and Continue Cache will decreases over time. If the TTL expires (TTL < 0) and

Table 5. PRE_CACHE packet

Name	Original server IP	TTL	Flag	Continue cache
Data_1.1	{10.0.0.9}	80	1	100
Data_3.2.1	{10.0.0.12}	100	0	0
Data_5.4.1	{10.0.0.20}	−50	1	30

Continue Cache value is not 0, then the TTL is replaced by the value of Continue Cache. For example, the first column of the Table indicates that the vehicle requesting the Data_1.1 will come in 80 s; the original server IP of the data is 10.0.0.9 and the data has already cached in this RSU. At the same time, another vehicle requesting the data ether will come in 100 s. Besides that, the TTL value will be added to the Continue Cache value when the RSU receives the packet and finds that it has been cached already.

3.5 Authentication and Handoff

When RSU detects a vehicle in its coverage, the algorithm below is activated immediately. Given the vehicle ID set in RSU is ϕ, and the ID of vehicle i is ID_k. Then we use the pseudo code in the Table 6 to authenticate the vehicle.

Table 6. Matching algorithm

Matching algorithm
Input: ID_k
1. Switch (ID_k), if case $i == ID_k$, return case i, default.
2. End switch.

Once the vehicle i has been found through the Matching Algorithm, the RSU will send the packets stored in it for vehicle i to it. Thus, the whole dissemination process during the handoff is completed.

4   Performance Evaluation

In this paper, we use OPNET simulator to build the SDN enabled vehicular networks architecture. The simulation architecture and parameters we set are shown in Fig. 4 and Table 7 respectively. Based on this architecture, we verify the advantages of the proposed data dissemination strategy by latency and retransmission ratio.

We first compared the average transmission delay in SDN-based framework with data dissemination strategy against that in traditional framework. In order to verify the strategy performance during the handoff among RSUs we select to transmit the bulk traffic packets trough RSUs to the vehicle, which varies from 0M to 500M. The results are given in Fig. 5. SDN-based framework with the proposed dissemination strategy can reduce the transmission delay by at least 30%. Then we vary the transmission traffic so that the vehicle needs to through more than two RSUs to complete the

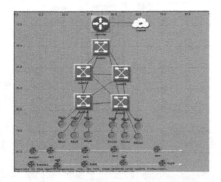

Fig. 4. Simulation model

Table 7. Simulation parameter

Parameter	Value
Mac	802.11p
Wired network bandwidth	20 Mbps
RSU wireless bandwidth	10 Mbps
RSUs spacing and coverage	1000 m
Vehicle speed	20–25 m/s

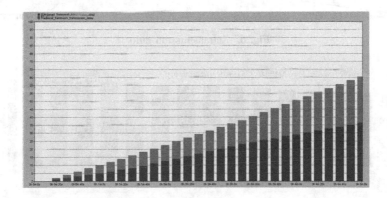

Fig. 5. Transmission delay

transmission, we found that when the offered traffic is low, the improvement is not quite obvious. With the increase of offered traffic, the disparity between SDN-based framework and the traditional framework is more and more obvious. This means that our solution will be more effective when vehicle needs to switch RSU during the transmission.

We further evaluated the retransmission ratio in Fig. 6. As we can see in traditional framework the retransmissions ratio increases rapidly as the increase of packets traffic. On the contrary, the ratio in our solution keeps at about 0.10, The phenomenon indicates that our dissemination strategy can avoid the interruption and reduce the reconnection time, as a result the retransmission ratio can be maintained in a lower level.

At the last, we evaluated the RSU pre cache success ratio. As we known, in traditional VENETs data dissemination mechanism, the bulk data will always be cached totally, which may occupy a lot of memory space in RSU. Thus will cause the cache failure when data is cached to RSU. Our plan will solve this problem perfectly, cause the bulk data will be cut to different segments and then pre cached to corresponding RSUs. In Fig. 7, we can see under traditional data dissemination mechanism, the cache success ratio is about 0.2 to 0.4, while using our solution, the cache success ratio can reach 0.8 to 0.95. It has increased substantially.

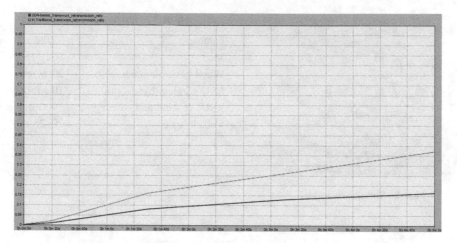

Fig. 6. Retransmission ratio

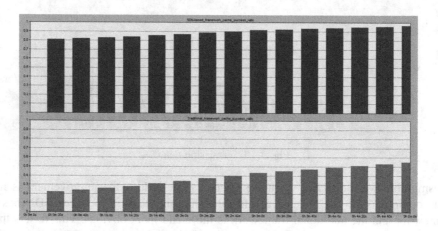

Fig. 7. Cache success ratio

5 Conclusion

The paper based on the traditional traffic distribution theory and classical CSMA/DCF mechanism in 802.11p protocol, constructed a new vehicle network architecture based SDN. More importantly, we propose a data dissemination strategy during the RSU handoff, which is elaborated in detail in the paper. At the last, we simulated the dissemination strategy in OPENET, as expected, the simulation shows that the strategy based the architecture we proposed can reduce the latency and retransmission rate significantly. The following work may carry research on the multi- vehicle competition situation.

Acknowledgments. This work was supported by the National Natural Science Foundation of China (61201133, 61571338 and 61672131), the key research and development plan of Shaanxi province (2017ZDCXL-GY-05-01), the National Key Research and Development Program of China (2016YFE0123000), the National Science and Technology Major Project of the Ministry of Science and Technology of China (2015zx03002006-003, MJ-2014-S-37), the Natural Science Foundation of Shaanxi Province (2014JM2-6089), the National High-tech R&D Program of China (863 Program-2015AA015701), the Ningbo Huimin projects of science and technology (2015C50047), the Research collaboration innovation program of Xi'an (CXY1522-3) and the "111 Project" of China (B08038).

References

1. Toor, Y., Muhlethaler, P., Laouiti, A.: Vehicle ad hoc networks: applications and related technical issues. In: IEEE Communications Surveys and Tutorials, vol. 10, pp. 74–88. IEEE Press (2008)
2. Trullols-Cruces, O., Morillo-Pozo, J., Barcelo, J.M., Garcia-Vidal, J.: A cooperative vehicular network framework. In: IEEE International Conference on Communications, pp. 1–6. IEEE Press (2009)
3. Giuseppe, B.: Performance analysis of the IEEE 802.11 distributed coordination function. IEEE J. Select. Areas Commun. 18, 535–547 (2000)
4. ONF White Paper: Software-Defined Networking: The New Norm for Networks. Open Networking Foundation (ONF) (2012)
5. Bernardos, C.J., de la Oliva, A., Serrano, P.: An architecture for software defined wireless networking. J. IEEE Wirel. Commun. 21(3), 52–61 (2014)
6. Piscataway, N.: IEEE standard for information technology-local and metropolitan area networks-specific requirements—Part 11: wireless LAN medium access control (MAC) and physical layer (PHY) specifications, amendment 6: wireless access in vehicular environments, pp. 1–51 (2010)
7. Labudde, P.: IEEE standard for wireless access in vehicular environments (WAVE). J. Multi-channel Oper. 1609, 4–7 (2005)
8. Truong, N.B., Lee, G.M., Ghamri-Doudane, Y.: Software defined networking-based vehicular ad hoc network with fog computing. In: IEEE International Symposium on Integrated Network Management (2015)
9. Zhao, D., Zhu, M., Xu, M.: Leveraging SDN and OpenFlow to mitigate interference in enterprise WLAN. J. Netw. 9, 1526–1533 (2014)
10. Kaisser, F., Veque, V.: On the scalability problem of high-way ad hoc network. In: IEEE Wireless Communications and Networking Conference, Istanbul (2009)
11. Liu, Y.: The research of RSU downlink traffic in vehicle networks. J. Softw. (2015). (in Chinese)
12. Ku, I., Lu, Y., Cerqueira, E., Gomes, R., Gerla., M.: Towards software-defined VANET: architectures and services. In: Mediterranean Ad Hoc Networking Workshop, pp. 103–110. IEEE Press (2014)
13. OpenFlow Switch. http://openvswitch.org/
14. Floodlight. http://www.projectfloodlight.org/floodlight/
15. Gerlough, D.L.: Poisson and traffic: use of Poisson distribution in highway traffic. Distributions (1990)

RETRACTED CHAPTER: On the Minimum the Sum-of-Squares Indicator of a Balanced Boolean Function

Yu Zhou[1(✉)] and Zepeng Zhuo[2]

[1] Science and Technology on Communication Security Laboratory,
Chengdu 610041, China
zhouyu.zhy@tom.com
[2] School of Mathematical Sciences, Huaibei Normal University,
Huaibei 235000, China
jackchouyu@gmail.com

Abstract. Boolean functions can be used in Cryptography (especially, the global avalanche characteristics of one Boolean function is an important property in symmetric Cipher). In this paper, when an n-variable balanced Boolean function satisfies the minimum the sum-of-squares indicator, we give some new properties of $(n-1)$-variable decomposition Boolean functions. Meanwhile, we derive a new condition on the sum-of-squares indicator, if the sum-of-squares indicator of a balanced Boolean function with n-variable is greater than $2^{2n} + 2^{n+3}$ for $n \geq 3$.

Keywords: Boolean functions · Auto-correlation distribution · The sum-of-squares indicator · Propagation criterion

1 Introduction

Boolean functions can be used in Cryptography (especially, stream ciphers and block ciphers). In theoretical computer and communications security, cryptography is an important tool to ensure data security. How to design some Boolean functions with many good cryptographic properties (including nonlinearity, balanced, algebraic immunity, correlation immunity, etc.) is an important problem in cryptography, if one can find such Boolean functions, then constructed based on this result meets good cryptographic properties of Boolean functions, and then design some cryptographic algorithms, these algorithms will effectively resist the existing types of attacks, these advantages will greatly facilitate computer science, cryptography and machine learning.

In Stream cipher, strict avalanche criteria (SAC) [1,2] and propagation characteristic (PC) [3] of Boolean functions are important properties for studying all kinds of algorithms. But the SAC and PC capture only the local properties of Boolean functions. In order to measure the global properties of Boolean functions, Zhang and Zheng introduced another criterion: the global avalanche

---

The original version of this chapter was retracted: The retraction note to this chapter is available at https://doi.org/10.1007/978-3-319-66628-0_57

© ICST Institute for Computer Sciences, Social Informatics and Telecommunications Engineering 2018, corrected publication 2020
Q. Chen et al. (Eds.): ChinaCom 2016, Part II, LNICST 210, pp. 314–321, 2018
DOI: 10.1007/978-3-319-66628-0_30

characteristics of Boolean functions (GAC) [4], and gave the lower and upper bounds on the two indicators: the sum-of-squares indicator $\sigma_f(2^{2n} \leq \sigma_f \leq 2^{3n})$ and the absolute indicator $\triangle_f(0 \leq \triangle_f \leq 2^n)$. Son et al. [5] derived a lower bound on the sum-of-squares indicator of the balanced functions with n-variable: $\sigma_f \geq 2^{2n} + 2^{n+3}$ and $\triangle_f \geq 8$ for $n(n \geq 3)$. Sung et al. [6] improved Son et al's results, and provide bound on the sum-of-squares indicator for a balanced Boolean function satisfying the propagation criterion with respect to t vectors.

[4] implied that the smaller $\triangle_f$ and σ_f, the better the GAC, thus we must study a balanced Boolean function $f(x)$ with $\sigma_f = 2^{2n} + 2^{n+3}$ for $n \geq 3$ (because this bound is the minimum). The rest of this paper is organized as follows. Some definitions are introduced in Sect. 2. In Sect. 3, some properties of $(n-1)$-variable decomposition Boolean functions are derived if an n-variable balanced Boolean function satisfies the minimum the sum-of-squares indicator. Finally, a condition of which the sum-of-squares indicator of a balanced Boolean function with n-variable is greater than $2^{2n} + 2^{n+3}$ for $n \geq 3$ is obtained.

2   Preliminaries

We denote the set of n variables Boolean functions by B_n. Every Boolean function $f(x) \in B_n$ admits a unique representation called its algebraic normal form (ANF) as a polynomial over F_2 in n binary variables:

$$f(x_1, \cdots, x_n) = a_0 \oplus \sum_{1 \leq i \leq n} a_i x_i \oplus \sum_{i,j \leq n} a_{i,j} x_i x_j \oplus \cdots \oplus a_{1,\ldots,n} x_1 x_2 \cdots x_n$$

where the coefficients $a_0, a_i, a_{i,j}, \cdots, a_{1,\ldots,n} \in F_2$. The algebraic degree, $deg(f)$, is the number of variables in the highest order term with non-zero coefficient. The support of a Boolean function $f(x) \in B_n$ is defined as $Supp(f) = \{(x_1, \cdots, x_n) \in F_2^n \mid f(x_1, \cdots, x_n) = 1\}$. The hamming weight of a Boolean function $f(x) \in B_n$ is $wt(f) = \mid Supp(f) \mid$. A function $f(x) \in B_n$ is balanced if $wt(f) = 2^{n-1}$ holds. The Hamming weight of $a \in F_2^n$, denoted by $wt(a)$, is the number of ones in this vector.

The *Walsh spectrum* of $f(x) \in B_n$ is defined as

$$F(f \oplus \varphi_\alpha) = \sum_{x \in F_2^n} (-1)^{f(x) \oplus \alpha x},$$

where $\varphi_\alpha = \alpha_1 x_1 \oplus \alpha_2 x_2 \oplus \cdots \oplus \alpha_n x_n$, $\alpha = (\alpha_1, \alpha_2, \cdots, \alpha_n) \in F_2^n$. The cross-correlation function $f(x), g(x) \in B_n$ is defined by

$$\triangle_{f,g}(\alpha) = \sum_{x \in F_2^n} (-1)^{f(x) \oplus g(x \oplus \alpha)}, \alpha \in F_2^n.$$

$f(x)$ satisfies the propagation criterion(PC) [3] of degree $p(PC(p))$ for some positive integer p when $\triangle_{f,f}(\alpha) = 0$ for any $\alpha \in F_2^n$ such that $1 \leq wt(\alpha) \leq p$.

Let $f(x), g(x) \in B_n$, the **sum-of-squares** [7] indicator of the cross-correlation between $f(x)$ and $g(x)$ is defined by

$$\sigma_{f,g} = \sum_{\alpha \in F_2^n} \triangle_{f,g}^2(\alpha);$$

the **absolute** indicator of the cross-correlation between $f(x)$ and $g(x)$ is defined by

$$\triangle_{f,g} = \max_{\alpha \in F_2^n} |\triangle_{f,g}(\alpha)|.$$

The above indicators are called the global avalanche characteristics between two Boolean functions. [7] implied $0 \le \triangle_{f,g} \le 2^n$, $(\triangle_{f,g}(\mathbf{0}))^2 \le \sigma_{f,g} \le 2^{3n}$. If $f(x) = g(x)$, then

$$\sigma_f = \sum_{\alpha \in F_2^n} \triangle_f^2(\alpha), \qquad \triangle_f = \max_{\alpha \in F_2^n, wt(\alpha) \ne 0} |\triangle_f(\alpha)|,$$

σ_f and $\triangle_f$ are called the global avalanche characteristics of a Boolean function (GAC [4]), and $0 \le \triangle_f \le 2^n$, $2^{2n} \le \sigma_f \le 2^{3n}$. The smaller $\triangle_f$ and σ_f, the better the GAC.

3   Main Properties and a Condition

[8] derived a result of a balanced Boolean function satisfying the minimum the sum-of-squares indicator. At first, we give this lemma.

Lemma 1. [8] Let $f(x) = f(\overline{x}, x_n) = x_n f_1(\overline{x}) \oplus (x_n \oplus 1) f_2(\overline{x})$, $\overline{x} \in F_2^{n-1}, x_n \in F_2$. Then

$$\sigma_f = \sigma_{f_1} + \sigma_{f_2} + 6\sigma_{f_1,f_2}.$$

Based on Lemma 1, we obtain a necessary condition (Theorem 1) of a balanced Boolean function satisfying the minimum the sum-of-squares indicator in the following.

Theorem 1. Let $f(x) = f(\overline{x}, x_n) = x_n f_1(\overline{x}) \oplus (x_n \oplus 1) f_2(\overline{x})$, $\overline{x} \in F_2^{n-1}, x_n \in F_2$, $wt(f) = 2^{n-1}$. If $\sigma_f = 2^{2n} + 2^{n+3}(n \ge 3)$, then $wt(f_1 f_2) = 2^{n-3}$ or $2^{n-3} - 1$.

Proof. Since $f(x) = f(\overline{x}, x_n) = x_n f_1(\overline{x}) \oplus (x_n \oplus 1) f_2(\overline{x})$, $\overline{x} \in F_2^{n-1}, x_n \in F_2$. For $\overline{\alpha} \in F_2^{n-1}, \alpha_n \in F_2$, we have

$$\triangle_f(\overline{\alpha}, \alpha_n) = \sum_{\substack{\overline{x} \in F_2^{n-1}, \\ x_n \in F_2}} [(-1)^{x_n f_x(\overline{x}) \oplus (x_n \oplus 1) f_2(\overline{x}) \oplus (x_n \oplus \alpha_n) f_1(\overline{x} \oplus \overline{\alpha})} (-1)^{(x_n \oplus \alpha_n \oplus 1) f_2(\overline{x} \oplus \overline{\alpha})}]$$

$$= \sum_{\substack{\overline{x} \in F_2^{n-1}, \\ x_n = 0}} (-1)^{(f_2(\overline{x} \oplus f_2(\overline{x} \oplus \overline{\alpha}))) \oplus [\alpha_n (f_1(\overline{x} \oplus \overline{\alpha}) \oplus f_2(\overline{x}) \oplus \overline{\alpha})]} +$$

$$\sum_{\substack{\overline{x} \in F_2^{n-1}, \\ x_n = 1}} (-1)^{(f_1(\overline{x} \oplus f_1(\overline{x} \oplus \overline{\alpha}))) \oplus [\alpha_n (f_1(\overline{x} \oplus \overline{\alpha}) \oplus f_2(\overline{x}) \oplus \overline{\alpha})]}.$$

Furthermore, for $\overline{\alpha} \in F_2^{n-1}$,

$$\triangle_f(\overline{\alpha}, \alpha_n) = \begin{cases} \triangle_{f_1}(\overline{\alpha}) + \triangle_{f_2}(\overline{\alpha}), & \alpha_n = 0; \\ 2\triangle_{f_1,f_2}(\overline{\alpha}), & \alpha_n = 1. \end{cases}$$

If $\sigma_f = 2^{2n} + 2^{n+3}(n \geq 3)$, we easily prove that $f(x)$ is 3-value auto-correlation: $\{2^n, 0, -8\}$, and $|\{\alpha \in F_2^n \mid \triangle_f(\alpha) = -8\}| = 2^{n-3}$, $|\{\alpha \in F_2^n \mid \triangle_f(\alpha) = 0\}| = 7 \cdot 2^{n-3} - 1$. Thus we have

$$
\begin{cases}
\triangle_{f_1}(\overline{\alpha}) + \triangle_{f_2}(\overline{\alpha}) = 2^n, & \overline{\alpha} = (0, 0, \cdots, 0) \in F_2^{n-1}; \\
\triangle_{f_1}(\overline{\alpha}) + \triangle_{f_2}(\overline{\alpha}) = 0, or, -8, & \overline{\alpha} \neq (0, 0, \cdots, 0) \in F_2^{n-1}; \\
\triangle_{f_1, f_2}(\overline{\alpha}) = 0, or, -4, & \overline{\alpha} \in F_2^{n-1}.
\end{cases}
$$

Thus, $\triangle_{f_1, f_2}(\mathbf{0}) = 0$, or -4. It implies that $wt(f_1 f_2) = 2^{n-3}$ or $2^{n-3} - 1$.

Based on Theorem1, we have the following result.

Denoted $I = \{\overline{\alpha} = (0, 0, \cdots, 0) \in F_2^{n-1} : \triangle_{f_1}(\overline{\alpha}) + \triangle_{f_2}(\overline{\alpha}) = 2^n\}$, $A = \{\overline{\alpha} : \triangle_{f_1}(\overline{\alpha}) + \triangle_{f_2}(\overline{\alpha}) = 0\}$, $B = \{\overline{\alpha} : \triangle_{f_1}(\overline{\alpha}) + \triangle_{f_2}(\overline{\alpha}) = -8\}$, $C = \{\overline{\alpha} : \triangle_{f_1, f_2}(\overline{\alpha}) = 0\}$, $D = \{\overline{\alpha} : \triangle_{f_1, f_2}(\overline{\alpha}) = -4\}$, let

$$|I| = 1; |A| = a; |B| = b; |C| = c; |D| = d \tag{1}$$

then

$$
\begin{cases}
c + d = 2^{n-1}; \\
b + d = 2^{n-3}; \\
a + c = 7 \cdot 2^{n-3} - 1; \\
a + b + c + d + 1 = 2^n.
\end{cases} \tag{2}
$$

(1) Note that $wt(f) = wt(f_1) + wt(f_2) + 2^{n-1}$ and

$$\sum_{\overline{\alpha} \in F_2^{n-1}} \triangle_{f_1, f_2}(\overline{\alpha}) = [2^{n-1} - 2wt(f_1)][2^{n-1} - 2wt(f_1)],$$

so, $d = (2^{n-2} - wt(f_1))^2 + (2^{n-2} - wt(f_2))^2$. It means that a, b, c, d are known.

Furthermore,

$$-4d = \sum_{\overline{\alpha} \in F_2^{n-1}} \triangle_{f_1, f_2}(\overline{\alpha}) = [2^{n-1} - 2wt(f_1)][2^{n-1} - 2wt(f_1)],$$

so, $(2^{n-2} - wt(f_1))(2^{n-2} - wt(f_2)) \leq 0$.

(2) On one hand, note that

$$\sigma_{f_1, f_2} = \sum_{\alpha \in F_2^{n-1}} \triangle_{f_1, f_2}^2(\alpha),$$

so

$$\sigma_{f_1, f_2} = \sum_{\alpha \in F_2^{n-1}} \triangle_{f_1, f_2}^2(\alpha) \geq \triangle_{f_1, f_2}^2(0^{n-1}),$$

where $0^{n-1} \in F_2^{n-1}$ and $wt(0^{n-1}) = 0$. We have

$$16 \cdot d \geq \triangle_{f_1, f_2}^2(0^{n-1}) = [2^{n-1} - 2wt(f_1 \oplus f_2)]^2,$$

that is

$$16wt^2(f_1f_2) - 2^{n+2}wt(f_1f_2) + 2^{2n-2} - 16d \leq 0, \tag{3}$$

thus, if $16wt^2(f_1f_2) - 2^{n+2}wt(f_1f_2) + 2^{2n-2} - 16d = 0$, then

$$wt(f_1f_2) = \frac{2^{n+2} \pm \sqrt{2^{2n+4} - 4 \cdot 16 \cdot (2^{2n-2} - 16d)}}{32}$$

$$= 2^{n-3} \pm \sqrt{d}.$$

So, Eq. (3) imply that

$$2^{n-3} - \sqrt{d} \leq wt(f_1f_2) \leq 2^{n-3} + \sqrt{d}. \tag{4}$$

At the same time,

$$\triangle_{f_1,f_2}(0^{n-1}) = 2^{n-1} - 2wt(f_1 \oplus f_2) = 4wt(f_1f_2) - 2^{n-1},$$

according to Eq. (1), we have $\triangle_{f_1,f_2}(0^{n-1}) = 0$ or -4, so there are two cases:

(i) If $4wt(f_1f_2) - 2^{n-1} = -4$, then $wt(f_1f_2) = 2^{n-3} - 1$, that is $0^{n-1} \in D$. It means $d \geq 1$.

(ii) If $4wt(f_1f_2) - 2^{n-1} = 0$, then $wt(f_1f_2) = 2^{n-3}$, that is $0^{n-1} \in C$.

(3) By $F^2(g \oplus \varphi_\alpha) = \sum_{\omega \in F_2^n}(-1)^{\omega\alpha}\triangle_g(\omega)$ for $g(x) \in B_n$ and $\alpha \in F_2^n$, then for any $\omega \in F_2^{n-1}$, we have

$$F^2(f_1 \oplus \varphi_\omega) + F^2(f_2 \oplus \varphi_\omega) = 2^n - 8\sum_{\alpha \in B}(-1)^{\omega\alpha}. \tag{5}$$

Meanwhile, we have

$$F(f_1 \oplus \varphi_\omega)F(f_2 \oplus \varphi_\omega) = -4\sum_{\alpha \in D}(-1)^{\omega\alpha}. \tag{6}$$

And, according to the relationship between $\triangle_{f_1,f_2}(\alpha)$, $\triangle_{f_1}(\alpha)$ and $\triangle_{f_2}(\alpha)$, we have

$$2^{n-1}d = \sum_{\omega \in F_2^{n-1}}(\sum_{\alpha \in D}(-1)^{\omega\alpha})^2. \tag{7}$$

According to the following relationship:

$$\sum_{\beta \in F_2^{n-1}}\triangle_{f_1}(\beta)\triangle_{f_2}(\beta) = \frac{1}{2}\{\sum_{\beta \in F_2^{n-1}}(\triangle_{f_1}(\beta) + \triangle_{f_2}(\beta))^2 - \sum_{\beta \in F_2^{n-1}}\triangle_{f_1}^2(\beta) - \sum_{\beta \in F_2^{n-1}}\triangle_{f_2}^2(\beta)\}$$

and

$$\sum_{a \in F_2^{n-1}}\triangle_{f_1}(a)\triangle_{f_2}(a) = \sum_{e \in F_2^{n-1}}\triangle_{f_1,f_2}^2(e).$$

so we have

$$\sum_{a \in F_2^{n-1}} \triangle_{f_1}^2(\alpha) + \sum_{a \in F_2^{n-1}} \triangle_{f_2}^2(\alpha) = 2^{2n} + 2^{n+3} - 96(2^{n-2} - wt(f_1))^2,$$

it imply that $\sigma_{f_1} + \sigma_{f_2} \leq \sigma_f = 2^{2n} + 2^{n+3}$.

We have the following theorem:

Theorem 2. *Let* $f(x) = f(\overline{x}, x_n) = x_n f_1(\overline{x}) \oplus (x_n \oplus 1) f_2(\overline{x})$, $\overline{x} \in F_2^{n-1}, x_n \in F_2$, $wt(f) = 2^{n-1}$. *If* $\sigma_f = 2^{2n} + 2^{n+3}$ *for* $n \geq 3$, *then*

(1) For any $\overline{\alpha} \in F_2^{n-1}$,

$$|I| = 1; |A| = 3 \cdot 2^{n-3} - 1 + (2^{n-2} - wt(f_1))^2; |B| = 2^{n-3} - (2^{n-2} - wt(f_1))^2;$$

$$|C| = 2^{n-1} - (2^{n-2} - wt(f_1))^2; |D| = (2^{n-2} - wt(f_1))^2,$$

where $wt(f) = wt(f_1) + wt(f_2) = 2^{n-1}$.
(2) For any $\omega \in F_2^{n-1}$, *we have*

$$F^2(f_1 \oplus \varphi_\omega) + F^2(f_2 \oplus \varphi_\omega) - 2^n = 8 \sum_{\alpha \in B}(-1)^{\omega\alpha};$$

$$2^{n-1}d = \sum_{x \in F_2^{n-1}} (\sum_{\alpha \in D}(-1)^{\omega\alpha})^2;$$

$$F(f_1 \oplus \varphi_\omega)F(f_2 \oplus \varphi_\omega) = \sum_{\alpha \in F_2^{n-1}}(-1)^{\omega\alpha}\triangle_{f_1,f_2}(\alpha);$$

$$\sigma_{f_1} + \sigma_{f_2} = 2^{2n} + 2^{n+3} - 96(2^{n-2} - wt(f_1))^2.$$

Theorem 3. *Let* $f(x) = f(\overline{x}, x_n) = x_n f_1(\overline{x}) \oplus (x_n \oplus 1) f_2(\overline{x})$, $\overline{x}, \in F_2^{n-1}, x_n \in F_2$, $wt(f) = 2^{n-1}$. *If* $wt(f_1)wt(f_2) < 2^{2n-4} - \sqrt{2^{3n-8} + 2^{2n-5}}$, *then* $\sigma_f > 2^{2n} + 2^{n+3}$.

Proof. On one hand, according to Cauchy-Schwarz's inequality, we have

$$\sigma_f = \sigma_{f_1} + \sigma_{f_2} + 6\sigma_{f_1,f_2}$$

$$= \sum_{\alpha \in F_2^{n-1}}\triangle_{f_1}^2(\alpha) + \sum_{\alpha \in F_2^{n-1}}\triangle_{f_2}^2(\alpha) + 6\sum_{\alpha \in F_2^{n-1}}\triangle_{f_1,f_2}^2(\alpha)$$

$$\geq \frac{[\sum_{\alpha \in F_2^{n-1}}\triangle_{f_1}(\alpha)]^2}{2^{n-1}} + \frac{[\sum_{\alpha \in F_2^{n-1}}\triangle_{f_2}(\alpha)]^2}{2^{n-1}} + 6\frac{[\sum_{\alpha \in F_2^{n-1}}\triangle_{f_1,f_2}(\alpha)]^2}{2^{n-1}}$$

with the equality holds if and only if $\triangle_{f_1}(\alpha) = \triangle_{f_2}(\alpha) = 2^{n-1}$ for any $\alpha \in F_2^n$, if and only if $f_1(x) \equiv 0$ or 1, $f_2(x) \equiv 0$ or 1.

On the other hand, since

$$\sum_{\alpha \in F_2^{n-1}} \triangle_{f_1,f_2}(\alpha) = (2^{n-1} - 2wt(f_1))(2^{n-1} - 2wt(f_2)).$$

Thus, we have

$$\sigma_f \geq \frac{[(2^{n-1} - 2wt(f_1))]^4}{2^{n-1}} + \frac{[(2^{n-1} - 2wt(f_2))]^4}{2^{n-1}} + 6\frac{[(2^{n-1} - 2wt(f_1))(2^{n-1} - 2wt(f_2))]^2}{2^{n-1}}$$
$$= 2^{8-n}(2^{2n-4} - wt(f_1)wt(f_2))^2.$$

Suppose $2^{2n} + 2^{n+3} = 2^{8-n}(2^{2n-4} - wt(f_1)wt(f_2))^2$, then

$$wt(f_1)wt(f_2) = 2^{2n-4} \pm \sqrt{2^{3n-8} + 2^{2n-5}}.$$

Thus, if $wt(f_1)wt(f_2) < 2^{2n-4} - \sqrt{2^{3n-8} + 2^{2n-5}}$, then $2^{3n-2} - 2^{2n+2} + 128 + 2^{8-n} \geq 2^{2n} + 2^{n+3}$.

It implies that

$$\sigma_f > 2^{2n} + 2^{n+3}$$

for $wt(f_1)wt(f_2) < 2^{2n-4} - \sqrt{2^{3n-8} + 2^{2n-5}}$.

Remark 1. If $n = 3$, then $wt(f_1)wt(f_2) = 2$ or 5.

Is is because $wt(f_1 f_2) = 2^{n-3}$ or $2^{n-3} - 1$. It implies that $wt(f_1) \geq 2^{n-3} - 1$ and $wt(f_2) \geq 2^{n-3} - 1$. By $2^{n-1} = wt(f_1) + wt(f_2)$ we know

$$wt(f_1)wt(f_2) \geq (2^{n-3} - 1)(2^{n-1} - 2^{n-3} + 1)$$
$$= 3 \cdot 2^{n-6} - 2^{n-2} - 1.$$

Hence,

$$2^{8-n}(2^{2n-4} - wt(f_1)wt(f_2))^2 \leq 2^{8-n}(2^{2n-4} - 3 \cdot 2^{2n-6} + 2^{n-2} + 1)^2$$
$$= 2^{3n-2} - 2^{2n+2} + 128 + 2^{8-n}.$$

It implies that

$$\sigma_f \geq 2^{3n-2} - 2^{2n+2} + 128 + 2^{8-n}.$$

Thus when $n \geq 5$, $2^{3n-2} - 2^{2n+2} + 128 + 2^{8-n} \geq 2^{2n} + 2^{n+3}$, we have

Corollary 1. *Let* $f(x) = f(\overline{x}, x_n) = x_n f_1(\overline{x}) \oplus (x_n \oplus 1)f_2(\overline{x})$, $\overline{x} \in F_2^{n-1}$, $x_n \in F_2$, $wt(f) = 2^{n-1}$. *Then* $\sigma_f > 2^{2n} + 2^{n+3}$ *for* $n \geq 5$.

4   Conclusions

In this paper, we obtain some results on the sum-of-squares indicator of a balanced Boolean function, including some new properties of $(n-1)$-variable decomposition Boolean functions, a condition of the sum-of-squares indicator of a balanced Boolean function with n-variable, and other properties. In the next step, we will study the same autocorrelation distribution of this function by the method in [9,10].

Acknowledgements. This work was supported by the Natural Science Foundations of China (No. 61309034), Sichuan Provincial Youth Science Fund (No. 2014JQ0055), China Electronics Technology Group Corporation innovative technology projects (Nos. JJQN201332) and Anhui Provincial Natural Science Foundation (No. 1608085MF143). Thanks are due to anonymous referees for a series of comment on this paper.

References

1. Adams, C.M., Tavares, S.E.: Generating and counting binary bent sequences. IEEE Trans. Inf. Theory **36**(5), 1170–1173 (1990)
2. Webster, A.F.: Plaintext/ciphertext bit dependencies in cryptograph system. Master's thesis, Department of Electrical Engineering, Queen's University, Ontario, Canada (1985)
3. Preneel, B., Van Leekwijck, W., Van Linden, L., Govaerts, Van Vanwalle, J.: Propagation characteristics of Boolean functions. In: Damgård, I. (ed.) EURO-CRYPT 1990. LNCS, vol. 473, pp. 161–173. Springer, Heidelberg (1991). https://doi.org/10.1007/3-540-46877-3_14
4. Zhang, X.M., Zheng, Y.L.: GAC - the criterion for global avalanche characteristics of cryptographic functions. J. Univers. Comput. Sci. **1**(5), 316–333 (1995)
5. Son, J.J., Lim, J.I., Chee, S., Sung, S.H.: Global avalanche characteristics and nonlinearity of balanced Boolean functions. Inf. Process. Lett. **65**, 139–144 (1998)
6. Sung, S.H., Chee, S., Park, C.: Global avalanche characteristics and propagation criterion of balanced Boolean functions. Inf. Process. Lett. **69**, 21–24 (1999)
7. Zhou, Y., Xie, M., Xiao, G.: On the global avalanche characteristics of two Boolean functions and the higher order nonlinearity. Inf. Sci. **180**(2), 256–265 (2010)
8. Zhou, Y., Dong, X., et al.: New bounds on the sum-of-squares indiactor. In: 7th International ICST Conference on 2012 ChinaCom, Communications and Networking in China (CHINACOM), 8–10 August 2012 (2012)
9. Zhou, Y., Zhang, W., Li, J., Dong, X., Xiao, G.: The autocorrelation distribution of balanced Boolean function. Front. Comput. Sci. **7**(2), 272–278 (2013)
10. Zhou, Y., Wang, Wang, W., Dong, X., Du, X.: One sufficient and necessary condition on balanced Boolean functions with $\sigma_f = 2^{2n} + 2^{n+3} (m \geq 3)$. Int. J. Found. Comput. Sci. **5**(3), 343–354 (2014)

Distributed Framework for Cognitive Radio Based Smart Grid and According Communication/Power Management Strategies

Tigang Jiang[✉]

School of Communication and Information Engineering,
University of Electronic Science and Technology of China, Chengdu, China
jtg@uestc.edu.cn

Abstract. This paper analyses the smart grid's facing challenges and the features of new energy source, then proposes the distributed frameworks for Cognitive Radio based Smart Grid (CRSG) on Home Area Network (HAN), on Neighbour Area Network (NAN), and on distributed power generators respectively. The basic protocols such as the communication protocols of cognitive radio networks, power transmission protocols among different users, and power transmission protocols between users and distributed power plants are presented. Those protocols are evaluated in the proposed distributed CRSG with network simulation platform, and the results show that distributed framework is economic and effective.

Keywords: Smart grid · Cognitive radio networks · Distributed networks · Power grid · Resource allocation

1 Introduction

Smart grid takes advantage of the advancement in communication and control technologies to create an automated, widely distributed delivery network through the use of bidirectional connection of electricity and information flows [1]. Global demand for renewable energy in distribution grids continues to rise and the worldwide installed capacity of PV exceeded 139 GW in 2013 [2,3], a total of approx. 200 GW PV capacity is to be installed by 2050. To reach this amount by 2050, an average of 4–5 GW PV must be installed annually in Germany.

In SG network, because the explosive data transmission demand, the centralized framework face very heavy burden, distributed infrastructure and according communication/power transaction protocol became the most hot research spot recently. Authors in [5] propose a simulation framework for distributed intelligent grid system. [6] describes the overall architecture of a monitoring system for distributed generation infrastructures of the Smart Grid, as well as the developed pieces of hardware and software, in addition, the validation of the system is also outlined. [7] uses two types of scalable distributed communication architectures, communication architecture with distributed meter data management

© ICST Institute for Computer Sciences, Social Informatics and Telecommunications Engineering 2018
Q. Chen et al. (Eds.): ChinaCom 2016, Part II, LNICST 210, pp. 322–331, 2018.
DOI: 10.1007/978-3-319-66628-0_31

system (MDMS) and fully distributed communication architecture to minimize the deployment cost. [8] proposes a distributed, service-oriented control architecture which provides a generic framework that could support numerous smart grid applications. [9] considers an interaction system of the smart grid, which including the cloud computing system and load devices, moreover, the authors propose a nested game-based optimization framework. In [10], the authors investigate the scalability of three communication architectures for advanced metering infrastructure (AMI) in smart grid, formulate an optimization problem and obtain the solutions for minimizing the total cost of the system that considers both the accumulated bandwidth distance product and the deployment cost of the MDMS.

To save the communication cost and avoid the message delivery failure of power line communication (PLC), wireless cognitive radio is a good technology of smart grid. Centralized CRSG infrastructure is easy to create but not suitable for accessing numerous of user-side power generators, Fig. 1 shows the traditional centralized CRSG infrastructure, where HAN is the basic local network connected with different home applications and smart devices, HAN collect the demands/status parameters of home applications and smart devices, each HAN has one gateway named HGW, numbers of HGWs construct the Neighbour Area Network (NAN), each NAN has a gateway named NGW, the collected parameters will be delivered to the control center (CC) through HGW, NGW and CR base station.

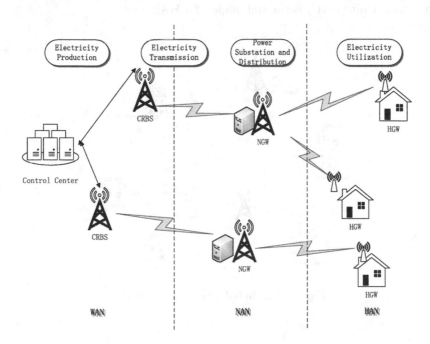

Fig. 1. Centralized CRSG

For the centralized CRSG infrastructure, along the dramatic increasing of data/command communication demand, the burden of CC face big challenge, at the same time, it is not convenience to access user-side distributed power generator, in this paper, we propose a flexible distributed network framework to try to solve those problems, and according communication/power transaction protocols are studied.

2   Distributed CRSG Framework

2.1   Distributed Framework in HAN

In the future of the smart grid, new energy access is the undoubted trend, many countries around the world have the user side new energy access plan, such as Germany's millions of roof plan, solar power systems and smart meters are installed on the user's roof, photovoltaic power generation send power to the grid in the day time and recharge the balance for user's smart meter, in the night, users can buy power from the grid and the balance will be charged.

In the distributed framework in CRSG HAN, the wireless communication and power transmission all are distributed. CR technology allow the CR spectrum can be used by CR based electronic users, and distributed CR network release the heavy burden of control center, the designed distributed network architecture can be seen as Fig. 2. We assume each user has one energy storage, and the Data Aggregation Unit (DAU) is the sink node of a HAN.

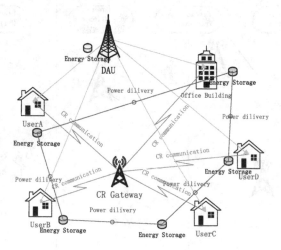

Fig. 2. Distributed framework in HAN

2.2 Distributed Framework in NAN

The distributed infrastructure in NAN can be seen as Fig. 3, different from the centralized infrastructure, we assume each HGW has one DAU and a wireless transmission equipment, HGW can collect the data from user smart meters, communicate with other DAUs/NGWs, and send command for power transmission. NAN support the last mile communication service for smart grid, that is, DAU manage all the data of its covered HAN. In our design, we let different DAU can communicate with each other and translate power with each other, then some times the communication and power interaction between them can be successful without the management of CC.

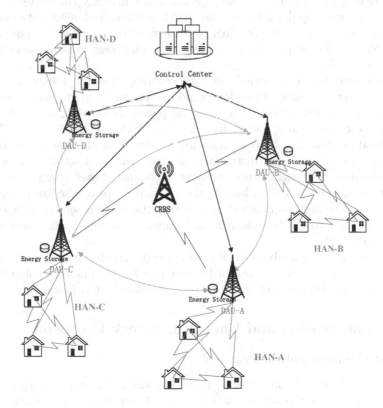

Fig. 3. Distributed framework in NAN

2.3 Framework of Distributed Power Generators

The combination of renewable energy and power grid is an important improvement of the smart grid. Use of renewable energy power generation can be a form of distributed matte or a centralized form. Centralized power generation usually makes unified scheduling directly connected to the transmission grid, for example, large-scale wind field, large-scale photovoltaic power station with MW/GW level. While distributed generation is usually connected to the low voltage distribution network, such as 380 V or 10 kV distribution power network. Distributed generation has the most important features of environmental protection, energy saving and efficient. So the modern smart grid should have good incompatibilities for centralized power, distributed generation, renewable energy access and energy storage device. Distributed generation is the future development direction of power system, the future of the power supply should be the hybrid network of the centralized and distributed grid.

Distributed generation has a key factor of energy storage, this is the bottleneck restricting the distributed power generation. Currently the battery energy storage is the most popular if the storage problem is resolved, electricity two-way flow in the smart grid is possible. Energy storage devices can provide power supply in peak period to reduce the peak lever, and sell power to other users/power company if possible.

As is known to all, renewable energy generally has the following several types, photovoltaic power generation, wind power, small hydropower, geothermal, ocean wave force power, solar thermal power generation, fuel cell power generation, etc. Renewable energy has the biggest characteristic of distributed geographical position, it's hard to uniformly control and manage all the renewable energy, as a result, the distributed management and self-control will be more reasonable, At the same time, because of the distributed energy dispersion and the randomness of the distributed generation, if adopting the fixed frequency allocation in according communication network, the usage of spectrum resources will be inefficient, so CR is a efficient and economy communication technology in such smart grid.

Based on the above analysis, after joining the distributed power, the designed distributed network architecture can be found as Fig. 4. The renewable energy can be saved in energy storage and can be controlled by CR based SG.

3   Communication and Energy Delivery Protocols

3.1   CR Communication Protocol

We adopt the basic CR communication mechanism in this paper, each communication node listens the wireless interference at any time, its communication will fail only if its occupying channel is recycled by a new coming primary user.

3.2   Communication and Power Transmission Protocol Among DAUs

From the distributed NAN architecture, assuming that the area which contains DAU-A has a lot of demand for electricity, the DAU-A will send electricity demand message to other DAUs, by responding message from other DAUs, DAU-A select the DAU-B which is close to DAU-A and has reasonable price as the

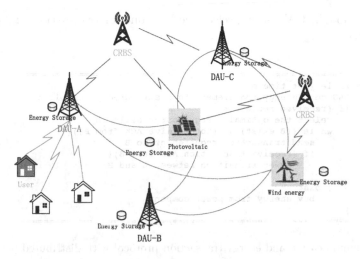

Fig. 4. Framework of distributed power generators

transaction object, so DAU-A sends a purchase request directly to DAU-B. This protocol not only reduces the power transmission distance, transmission costs, but also increases the response speed, this protocol can be seen as Fig. 5.

```
=============================================================
while (not time out)
A broadcasts energy requirement
if (received replay ){
    if (find a energy unit seller B){
       send transaction requirement to B
       if (receive transaction acknowledgement from B){
           power transition between A and B
       }
    } else
       buy energy from power company
}
=============================================================
```

Fig. 5. Communication and power transmission among DAUs

3.3 Communication and Energy Transaction Protocol with Distributed Power Plant

In a HAN, if a user's (say user A) electricity consumption demand increases dramatically during the power consumption peak periods, at this time, if A get power directly from the main power grid, usually the cost is high. For the protocol of considering distributed power plant, DAU-A send power requirement to other DAUs through cognitive radio technology and wait reply, on the other hand, all the DAUs which received DAU-A's power demand will reply if its energy storage is enough, DAU-A will select the best one for transaction, the protocol is illustrated in Fig. 6.

```
===========================================================
while (not time out)
DAU send energy requirement to distributed power plant
if (received replay ){
    select the optimal energy source seller B
    while ((B exist) && (not receive ACK from B)){
        send transaction requirement to B
        if (receive transaction ACK from B){
            power transition between A and B
        }
    } else
        buy energy from power company
}
===========================================================
```

Fig. 6. Communication and energy transaction protocol with distributed power plant

4   Performance Analysis

Under the distributed CRSG framework described before, we create a discrete time driven simulation platform with ns-3 [11] to evaluate the performance of the network with different CR resource allocation and power transaction protocols.

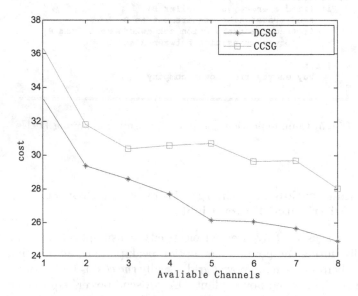

Fig. 7. User cost and available CR spectrum

The simulation parameters are set as follows, there are three NGWs, each NGW has three HGWs, the number of distributed power plant is 10, time-out threshold is in [0.1, 0.8], the number of available spectrum is in [1,8], the price of power grid is set to 0.5/kW, the path loss coefficient is from 0.2 to 0.9, the price of distributed power plant is normally distributed between [0.2, 0.5].

Figure 7 shows that users' cost decreases with the increasing of the number of available spectrum. With the increase of the available spectrum, the probability of a user get CR spectrum for transmission before time out increases, so lager probability users can exchange power from each other, because normally users' transaction price is lower than that of power company, so the users' average electricity cost will be reduced. So under the same number of available CR spectrum, users' cost in distributed cognitive radio smart grid (DCSG) is less than that in centralized cognitive radio smart grid (CCSG).

Figure 8 shows that with the time-out threshold increases, user cost will reduce. because in the spectrum allocation procedure, to avoid the long waiting time for spectrum allocation, if the waiting time exceeds the time-out threshold, the user will purchase power from the power grid. If the threshold is high, the users' waiting time became long, and the probability of users purchase power from distributed other users increases, which leads their cost decrease.

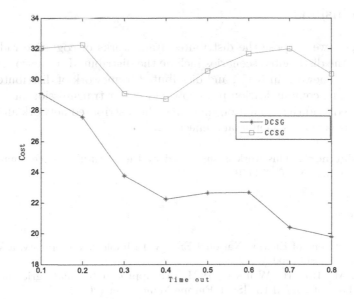

Fig. 8. User cost and time out threshold

Figure 9 shows that with the increase of path loss, user cost will increase, because under the situation, more power will be purchased from the grid company. Compare with the centralized network, distributed infrastructure and according protocols can save users' cost significantly.

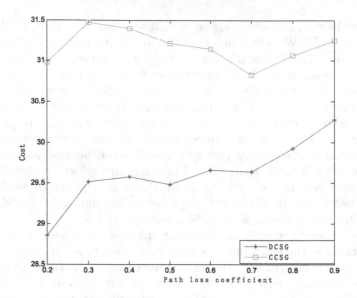

Fig. 9. User cost and path loss coefficient

5   Conclusions

In this paper, we propose the distributed frameworks of cognitive radio based smart grid, the distributed scenarios include the distributed framework in HAN, distributed framework in NAN, and distributed framework of distributed power generators. The communication protocols and power transmission protocols are also presented, and the simulation show that the distributed network and according protocols is very economic and effective.

Acknowledgement. This work is supported by the Natural Science Foundation of China under Grant No. 61271170.

References

1. US Department of Energy, National Energy Technology Laboratory, a Vision for the Modern Grid (2007)
2. Arnold, M., Rui, H., Wellssow, W.H.: An approach to smart grid metrics. In: Proceedings of 2011 IEEE ISGT Europe Manchester (2011)
3. Renewables 2014 Global Status Report, REN21, REN21 Secretariat, 2014, Paris (2014)
4. 50 Hertz Transmission, Amprion, TransnetBW, TenneT, EEG Master Data (2014)
5. Dong, L., Li, Y., Liu, K., Pute, T., Liu, G.: Research on smart grid simulation framework based on distributed intelligent system. In: 2014 International Conference on Power System Technology (POWERCON) (2014)

6. López, G., Moura, P., Moreno, J., de ALMEIDA, A., Perez, M., Blanco, L.: Monitoring system for the local distributed generation infrastructures of the smart grid. In: 22nd International Conference and Exhibition on Electricity Distribution (CIRED 2013) (2013)
7. Barai, G., Raahemifar, K.: Optimization of distributed communication architectures in advanced metering infrastructure of smart grid. In: 2014 IEEE 27th Canadian Conference on Electrical and Computer Engineering (CCECE) (2014)
8. Tariq, M.U., Grijalva, S., Wolf, M.: Towards a distributed, service-oriented control infrastructure for smart grid. In: 2011 IEEE/ACM International Conference on Cyber-Physical Systems (ICCPS) (2011)
9. Wang, Y., Lin, X., Pedram, M.: Coordination of the smart grid, distributed data centers: a nested game-based optimization framework. In: 2014 IEEE PES Innovative Smart Grid Technologies Conference (ISGT) (2014)
10. Zhou, J., Hu, R.Q., Qian, Y.: Scalable distributed communication architectures to support advanced metering infrastructure in smart grid. IEEE Trans. Parallel Distrib. Syst. (2012)
11. https://www.nsnam.org

Hardware Design and Implementation

Design of a Cooperative Vehicular Platoon System Based on Zynq/SoC Architecture

Yi Wang, Yi Zhou$^{(\boxtimes)}$, Wei Li, Gaochao Wang, Lin Ren,
and Ruirui Huang

School of Computer and Information Engineering,
Henan University, Kaifeng 475000, China
zhouyi@henu.edu.cn

Abstract. Different from traditional intelligent transportation systems, vehicular platoon systems pay more attention to interactive communications of vehicle-to-vehicle (V2V) and vehicle-to-road (V2R). Both V2V and V2R communications in platoon have higher demands of real-time and active safety applications, where low-latency transmission and strong perception capability are the fundamental guarantee of platoon cooperation. This paper proposed a cooperative vehicular platoon system based on Zynq-7000 all programmable SoC architecture, in which six miniature vehicles are designed through Zynq modules for evaluating the platooning performance. We use the Vivado development kit to create the system architecture, and evaluate cooperative communication and coordinated control technology of the platoon. The test results show that the Zynq architecture can improve the real-time processing and information interaction performance of cooperative platoon systems.

Keywords: Vehicular platoon · Cooperative control · Zynq/SoC · Programmable architecture

1 Introduction

As a typical application of IoT (Internet of things), Connected vehicles use embedded sensor devices to get vehicular status information, and implement the information interaction through vehicular networks [1], which enables real-time networking and information sharing between vehicles and other traffic elements (e.g. other vehicles, road-side units, infrastructures, and pedestrians) [2, 3].

With the rapid development of vehicular networking technology, the collaborative vehicular platooning networks has become a promising research field of connected vehicles [4]. Vehicular platoons based on cooperative V2 V and V2R communication technology can obtain real-time information through vehicular sensors, which can

Y. Zhou—This work was supported by National Natural Science Foundation of China (No. 61304132) and partly supported by Henan International Cooperative Program of China (No. 134300510049), the Program for Science & Technology Development of Henan Province (No. 162102210022), and CERNET Innovation Project (No. NGII20151005).

© ICST Institute for Computer Sciences, Social Informatics and Telecommunications Engineering 2018
Q. Chen et al. (Eds.): ChinaCom 2016, Part II, LNICST 210, pp. 335–344, 2018.
DOI: 10.1007/978-3-319-66628-0_32

automatically adjust the speed of vehicles, and keep a relatively safe distance among vehicles [5, 6].

The research of Cooperative Vehicular Platoon mainly arises from intelligent vehicle system architecture internationally. The PATH group, from the University of California, Berkeleyin, proposed the 5-tier architecture based on the intelligent vehicle-highway system Architecture in 1991 [7], specifically including the network layer, link layer, coordination layer, control layer, and physical layer. The network layer mainly solves the routing problem while the link layer adjusts the speed of vehicles along with the real-time traffic on the road. The coordination layer selects the corresponding control strategy, and the control layer implements it subsequently. At the same time, the physical layer includes vehicle-mounted controllers and the physical structure of the vehicle [8]. A vehicular collaborative driving system structure was proposed by Tsugawa et al. in 2000. They analyzed the demand of vehicle cooperative driving function and designed a 3-tier system structure, including traffic control layer, vehicle management layer, and vehicle control layer [9]. In this system, the traffic control layer is positioned on the roadside while the vehicle management layer and the control layer are located on the vehicle side, which are used for the implementation of cooperative driving strategy. Hallé and Chaib-draa proposed the collaborative driving systems, which has made a detailed description of data acquisition and processing, platoon coordination control, and platoon communication in the process of cooperative driving [10].

Nowadays, as the emerging embedded applications such as system on a programmable chip (SOPC) and advanced driver assistance systems (ADAS) are developing rapidly, traditional embedded development platforms are hard to satisfy the big data demand, high computation ability and scalable development capability [11]. Xilinx officially launched the first scalable processing platform for Zynq-7000 series embedded in the General Assembly 2010 held in Silicon Valley, where the ARM® Cortex™-A9 MPCore (PS) and 28 nm low-power FPGA logic (PL) are tightly integrated together [12].

Using real cars to carry out the experiment will bring great difficulty to the research and design in real environments, and the complexity of the experiment and maintenance will greatly increase the cost. Therefore, we take smart miniature vehicles as the experimental platform of vehicular platoon and design a cooperative vehicular platoon system based on six Zrobot-III modules, which are built by Zynq-7000 embedded SoC architecture. The remainder of this paper is as follows: Sect. 2 introduces the system model of the cooperative vehicular platoon. Section 3 describes the detailed design of the cooperative vehicular platoon system, followed by a brief of key algorithms in Sect. 4. Section 5 presents the analysis of the experimental results and Sect. 6 concludes this paper.

2 System Model

2.1 Zynq/SoC Architecture

As shown in Fig. 1, The Zynq extensible processing platform (EPP) products consists of a SoC style integrated processing system (PS) and programmable logic (PL), which

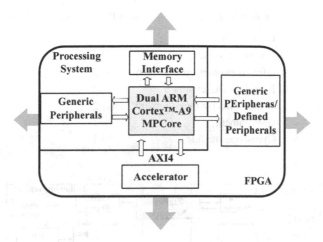

Fig. 1. Zynq/SoC architecture.

provides an extensible and flexible SoC solution on a single chip [13]. On the single chip, the PS includes the dual ARM Cortex-A9 processor, which comes with a dedicated NEON co-processor and a double-precision floating-point arithmetic unit. The PS is connected to the PL resources through multiple AXI (Advanced Extensible Interface) ports.

The PL features Xilinx 7 Series FPGA logic from the Artix and Kintex families which consists of configurable logic blocks (CLBs) and block random-access memories with high performance and ultralow power consumption. AMBA (Advanced Microcontroller Bus Architecture) bus specification is an open standard interconnection specification, which is used for the connection and management of the system function modules on the chip. ARM processor is able to control the design of the function module via AXI bus in accordance with the design of using FPGA to customize function module. Compared to a single ARM Cortex A9 board or a single Xilinx FPGA board, Zynq series products not only integrate different technology characteristic processor and FPAG on a single chip, but also build the high- performance connection between the processors and FPGA.

2.2 Cooperative Vehicular Platooning Model

This vehicle platoon system mainly consists of one miniature leading-vehicle and five miniature following-vehicles, where each vehicle is designed based on the Zynq/SoC architecture. To realize vehicular platooning cooperation, we have added some necessary sensor modules to the miniature vehicles. Table 1 lists all the peripheral devices used in each vehicle of the system.

Figure 2 shows the proposed cooperative vehicular platooning framework. The platoon moves forward in accordance with the safe distance between the vehicles, while the ultrasonic module can ensure the safe distance in real time.

The PL is mainly responsible for processing the received information and collecting the data of the vehicle through sensor modules. Then, the data is processed and

Table 1. Peripheral settings in the system.

Device name	Number
Ultrasonic sensors	3
Infrared photoelectric sensors	3
Brushless DC motors	2
Holzer velocity measurement units	2
USB camera	1
Gyroscope module	1

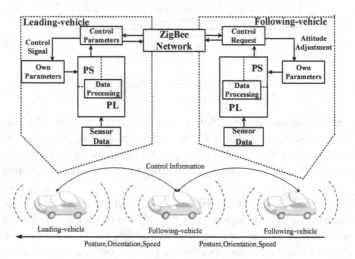

Fig. 2. System architecture.

transmitted to the PS. When the leading-vehicle meets the obstacle, the PS calculates the expected direction and speed through data from the infrared photoelectric sensors and ultrasonic sensors, and sends the signal to the following- vehicles through ZigBee networks. Following-vehicles integrate its self-perception parameters and the received data to extract characteristic and adjust attitude, and then follow the head vehicle to make the corresponding action. Self-perception parameters mainly include the current position, the distance to the vehicle ahead, the direction angle, and the speed. When a vehicle plans to leave the platoon, it will send the request commands to the vehicle platoon through the ZigBee network and perform the corresponding action when receiving the confirmation. After the vehicle leaves the platoon, the following vehicles keep up with the forward vehicle smoothly. If any vehicle intends to join in the platoon, it will send the request parameters to the leading-vehicle, and follow the last vehicle in the platoon with permission.

3   Cooperative Vehicular Platoon System

3.1   Hardware Platform

The proposed system is built on ZedBoard, which is a development board with high performance based on Zynq-7000. ZedBoard provides 512M DDR3, 256M four bit SPI FLASH and 4 GB SD card and contains an OTG USB, a USB serial port and Gigabit Ethernet port. In addition, five Pmod interfaces and a FMC (FPGA Mezzanine Card) extension connection are offered as well. We rebuild ZedBoard through integrating necessary peripheral modules to set up the miniature platooning vehicles.

Figure 3 illustrates the whole underlying hardware architecture of the miniature vehicle. Each miniature vehicle is composed of five components—power module, communication module, display module, attitude acquisition module and obstacle avoidance module.

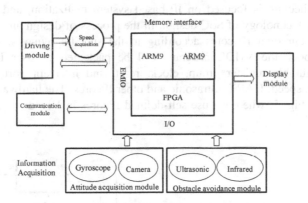

Fig. 3.   Hardware architecture of miniature vehicle.

3.2   Design of PS and PL

We built an embedded Linux operating system on the PS, using Linux to manage all peripheral interfaces of the cooperative vehicular platoon system. The peripheral interfaces include the human-machine interface, acceptance of control signals, and call of IP cores. When the system is powered on, BootROM starts to control the whole initialization process. FSBL (First Stage BootLoader) fulfills the initialization of the PS, and then uses the bitstream file to configure the PL. Finally, FSBL loads U-boot into ARM to complete hardware initialization, and Linux kernel sets up the compile environment. Based on the IP module address (shown in Fig. 4), Linux driver calls the corresponding modules by the address.

Pmod on the ZedBoard has four interfaces: JA, JB, JC, JD. PWM signal is interfaced to the JA port of Pmod to control the motor's speed. Speed signal is connected to the JB port of Pmod to obtain the speed of vehicle, acceleration, and the current direction. Ultrasonic signal is linked with JD port of Pmod, which collects the distance with the front vehicle and identifies the obstacles to maintain the normal inter-vehicle

processing_system7_0					
Data (32 address bits : 4G)					
OLED_0	S00_AXI	S00_AXI_reg	0x43C00000	4K	0x43C00FFF
btns	S_AXI	Reg	0x41230000	64K	0x4123FFFF
leds	S_AXI	Reg	0x41200000	64K	0x4120FFFF
motor_0	S00_AXI	S00_AXI_reg	0x43C01000	4K	0x43C01FFF
opticals	S_AXI	Reg	0x41210000	64K	0x4121FFFF
servo_0	S00_AXI	S00_AXI_reg	0x43C04000	4K	0x43C04FFF
speed_0	S00_AXI	S00_AXI_reg	0x43C02000	4K	0x43C02FFF
sws	S_AXI	Reg	0x41220000	64K	0x4122FFFF
ultrasonic_0	S00_AXI	S00_AXI_reg	0x43C03000	4K	0x43C03FFF
axi_uart16550_0	S_AXI	Reg	0x42A00000	8K	0x42A01FFF
pwm_0	S00_AXI	S00_AXI_reg	0x43C05000	4K	0x43C05FFF
pwm_1	S00_AXI	S00_AXI_reg	0x43C06000	4K	0x43C06FFF

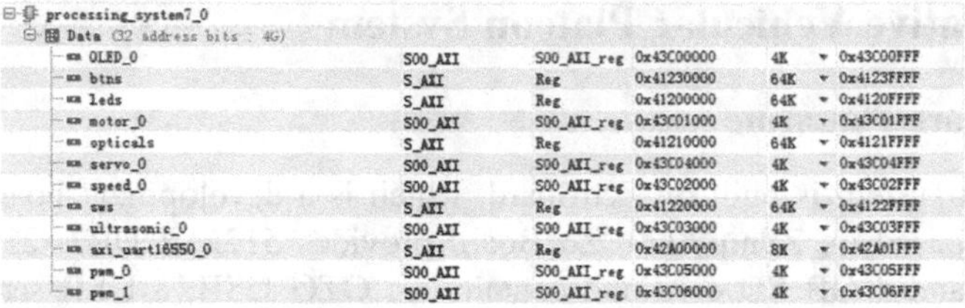

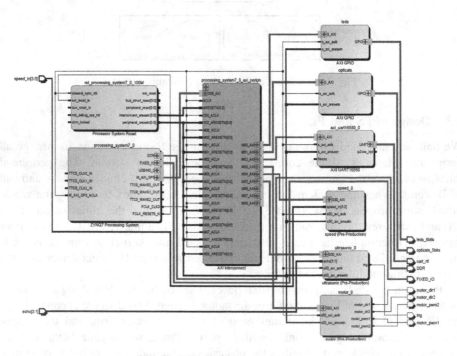

Fig. 4. Module address.

distance. Optical signal and UART signal are jointed with the JC port of Pmod for signal transmission.

3.3 IPcore

Zynq/SoC architecture is focused on IP based system realization, and IPcores have become the key technology of SoC design. In the process of design and development, we can define our own IP cores according to the specific requests. Using vivado development tools, the VHDL program will be packaged as user IPcore, which includes configurable register group, clock, reset, and interrupt port. This system designed motor, speed, UART, ultrasonic and other IPcores. The hardware architecture is illustrated in Fig. 5, where we use self-defined IPcores in Vivado.

Fig. 5. Systems block configuration.

4 Design of Key Algorithms

4.1 Cooperative Sensing

The collaborative sensing requires various sensors to deal with complicated environments. Before making a control decision, we must process the different sensing data in different formats to get effective information, and then transmit to the PS according to the specific format predefined. In the process, the multi-source information fusion is necessary for cooperative sensing. As depicted in Fig. 6, the multi-source information fusion model is divided into two progressive stages. The sensor modules mainly include camera, ultrasonic sensor, gyroscope, and infrared sensor. In the first stage, the raw data obtained from the sensors are processed and transformed to characterize surrounding environments, extracting features transmitted to ARM processors (PS) in Zynq. In the second stage, the system gets the control parameters and evaluates the results after information was processed, and then sends control signals to the platoon.

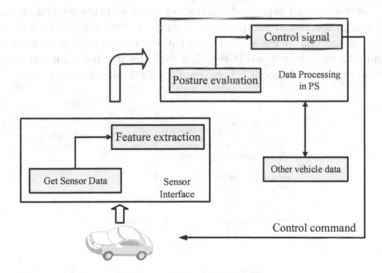

Fig. 6. Multi-source information fusion model.

4.2 Information Interaction

V2V communications play an important role in the vehicle platooning system. ZigBee is mainly used for data transmission between miniature vehicles in short distance and low power consumption, which can be used to transmit periodic data and intermittent data in low reaction time, and also effectively to ensure the transmission of control data. In this system, ZigBee module is connected to the UART port of ZedBoard, which forms a mobile ad-hoc network.

ZigBee on the head-vehicle is served as the coordinate node to supervise the whole network. In that way, ZigBee modules on other vehicles are responsible for communication as routing nodes, Zynq chip calls UART's IPcore, function pthread_create(&tid[0], &attr[0], thread_serial_ttyPS1, NULL) gets ZigBee network data, and packages vehicle information into a data packet in accordance with the custom format, while the packet is sent to other vehicles through the UART. The communication data packet format is defined as follows:

```
StartByte ->1B (represent start byte of packet)
PropertyId->1B (represent PropertyId)
NodeId->1B(represent device node Id)
PacketLength->2B (represent the length of the package)
PrivateData->XB (represent load content)
EndByte->1B (represent end byte of packet)
```

5 Experimental Analysis

The development and design of system algorithms is based on Vivado suite, which provides a new integrated engine, IP and hardware and software integration. After the system is completed, we create the system_wrapper, and add the pins and timing constraints. At the end of the system compilation, Vivado will generate a compile report. From the utilization report in Fig. 7, it indicates that the main consumption of LUT (logical unit table) is about 2/3 and memory LUT only consumes 9%.

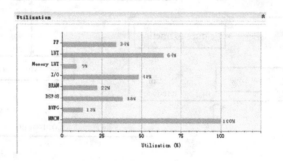

Fig. 7. Utilization report.

After the completion of code writing and simulation debugging, we make the boot. bin image which runs on the miniature vehicle. When the system is powered on, each module on the vehicle operates normally. The camera of leading-vehicle collects surrounding information to confirm and identify the obstacles ahead assisted by ultrasonic distance measuring module. The PL analyzes the underlying dense data stream of image, motion control, and other typical applications in the system, and the data is reported back to the PS, allowing the vehicle make corresponding movements of obstacle avoidance, turning and so on, and also transferring the data to the follow - vehicles behind. As shown in Fig. 8, follow-vehicles travel stably at the back of leading car according to a safety distance at a constant speed.

Fig. 8. Platoon prototype.

Under the normal running of the system, image distortion and dislocation will occur, making it unable to show the processing results, which influences the identification of obstacles. Since the image is displayed completely, after excluding the problem of image transmission width, the problem of unstable IPcore work of image pre-processing is found. During the design of IPcore, in hardware project, the clock of processor, data bus, VDMA transmission channel related to IPcore should be set uniformly, because the reference clock in HLS will influence the compiling results of IPcore, and the PS works normally after the problems are solved. As depicted in Fig. 9, when the front vehicle turns or deviates direction, the system can successfully detect the characteristic points on the vehicle. After that, the PS establishes the coordinate system according to the characteristic points, and calculates the deflection angle of the front vehicle.

Fig. 9. Image processing result.

6   Conclusions

Communication technology is the key support of cooperative vehicular platoon system, which is the future development direction of connected vehicles. Zynq is a high-performance processing platform with low power, and it is a flexible and scalable solution. We designed a cooperative vehicular platoon system based on Zynq-7000 embedded SoC architecture, which can take place of the real car to emulate the scene of vehicular platoon and help to verify the cooperative algorithm as well. It is shown through experiments that the Zynq architecture can improve the real- time processing and information interaction performance of cooperative platoons. In the future, we will mainly focus the cooperative control algorithm embedded into Zynq, and optimize V2V interaction algorithm, which can give full play to the framework advantage of PS + PL of Zynq/SoC.

References

1. Ning, L., Nan, C., Ning, Z., Xuemin, S., Jon, W.M.: Connected vehicles: solutions and challenges. IEEE Internet Things J. **1**(4), 289–299 (2014)
2. Kaiming, R., Jizhou, L., Lingyan, L., Wenying, S.: Development status and tendency of IoV communication technology. J. Commun. Technol. **48**, 507–513 (2015)
3. Jianqiang, W., Chenwen, W., Xiaojun, L.: Research on architecture and key technologies of internet of vehicles. J. Micro Comput. Inf. **27**, 156–158 (2011)
4. Brandon, S., Michael, S.: A survey of public opinion about connected vehicles in the U.S., the U.K., and Australia. In: International Conference on Connected Vehicles and Expo, pp. 687–692 (2014)
5. Shigen, G., Hairong, D., Bin, N., Roberts, C., Lei, C., Xubin, S.: Cooperative adaptive bidirectional control of a train platoon for efficient utility and string stability. Chin. Phys. B **24**, 161–170 (2015)
6. Le, W.Y., Ali, S., George, Y.G., Abhilash, P., Wei, H.Z.: Control of vehicle platoon for highway safety and efficient utility: consensus with communications and vehicle dynamics. J. Syst. Sci. Complex. **27**, 605–631 (2014)
7. Varaja, P., Shladover, S.E.: Sketch of an IVHS systems architecture. In: Vehicle Navigation and Information Systems Conference, vol. 2, pp. 909–922 (1991)
8. Hedrick, J.K., McMahon, D., Narendran, V.K., Swaroop, D.: Longitudinal vehicle controller design for IVHS systems. In: Proceedings of 1991 American Control Conference, vol. 3, pp. 3107–3112 (1991)
9. Tsugawa, S., Kato, S., Matsui, T.: An architecture for cooperative driving of automated vehicles. In: 2000 IEEE Intelligent Transportation Systems Conference Proceedings, Dearborn (MI), pp. 422–427 (2000)
10. Hallé, S., Chaib-Draa, B.: A collaborative driving system based on multiagent modelling and simulations. J. Transp. Res. Part C Emerg. Technol. **13**, 320–345 (2005)
11. Sakaguchi, T., Uno, A., Kato, S.: Cooperative driving of automated vehicles with inter-vehicle communications. In: Proceedings of IEEE Intelligent Vehicles Symposium, Dearborn (MI), USA, pp: 516–521 (2000)
12. Xilinx Inc.: Zynq-7000 all Programmable SoC Technical Reference Manual. Xilinx Inc. (2013)
13. Roland, D., Lukas, S.: Image filter evolution on the Xilinx Zynq platform. In: 2013 NASA/ESA Conference on Adaptive Hardware and Systems (2013)

A Multi-mode Coordinate Rotation Digital Computer (CORDIC)

Lifan Niu, Xiaoling Jia, Jun Wu, and Zhifeng Zhang$^{(\boxtimes)}$

College of Electronics and Information Engineering,
Tongji University, Shanghai 201804, China
{1433332,jia_xiaoling,wujun,zhangzf}@tongji.edu.cn

Abstract. This paper presents a 24-bit fixed-point multi-mode Coordinate Rotation Digital Computer (CORDIC) engine for VLSI implementation of Independent Component Analysis (ICA). Three different modes are integrated for computing sine/cosine, arc tangent and square root to save system resource. We describe the design method for deciding iteration time and fixed-point bits, and present the architecture of a pipelined VLSI implementation. An approximation method is proposed to decrease the data to be pre-stored. The CORDIC engine is designed and implemented with SMIC 65 nm CMOS technology. The performance and computation results of this engine are shown to be very high-accurate and area-efficient.

Keywords: CORDIC · ICA · Sin · Cos · Arctan · Square root

1 Introduction

The Coordinate Rotation Digital Computer (CORDIC) algorithm is an iterative algorithm for computing general vector rotation. It was first brought up by Volder [7], and then it was refined and improved by Walther [8]. CORDIC can compute the trigonometric function, hyperbolic function, logarithm, exponential and square root with only adds and shifts. Therefore, it is suitable for hardware implementation and has applied in many areas including signal processor, communication system and mathematic co-processor.

Independent Component Analysis (ICA) is a widely used algorithm for blind source separation in signal processing. For very large scale integration (VLSI) implementation of ICA, trigonometric and square root functions are necessary [1,4,6], for which CORDIC is a perfect solution. The work in this paper integrates the computation of trigonometric and square root functions in one CORDIC engine, and improves the algorithm specially for hardware implementation. Finally we implement a 24-bit fixed-point multi-mode CORDIC that can compute arc tangent, sine/cosine and square root in one engine with different modes.

The remainder of this paper is organized as follows: Sect. 2 introduces the basic principle of CORDIC. Section 2.1 introduces the improved algorithm

© ICST Institute for Computer Sciences, Social Informatics and Telecommunications Engineering 2018
Q. Chen et al. (Eds.): ChinaCom 2016, Part II, LNICST 210, pp. 345–354, 2018.
DOI: 10.1007/978-3-319-66628-0_33

and design methodology. Section 4 introduces hardware architecture. Section 5 presents the timing and area results of the CORDIC engine implementation. Section 6 is the conclusion.

2 Introduction

2.1 Overview

The basic idea of CORDIC is to approach a rotation angle by swinging a series of fixed angles. CORDIC executes a rotation in each iteration. As shown in Fig. 1, to rotate vector (x_i, y_i) by θ to get the new vector (x_j, y_j):

$$x_j = r\cos(\alpha + \theta) = x_i \cos\theta - y_i \sin\theta \\ y_j = r\sin(\alpha + \theta) = y_i \cos\theta + x_i \sin\theta \tag{1}$$

Split θ into N smaller rotation angles, for the n_{th} rotation:

$$\begin{pmatrix} x_{n+1} \\ y_{n+1} \end{pmatrix} = \cos\theta_n \begin{pmatrix} 1 & -\tan\theta_n \\ \tan\theta_n & 1 \end{pmatrix} \begin{pmatrix} x_n \\ y_n \end{pmatrix} \tag{2}$$

For clarity, a new variable z_n is used to calculate the residue angle to be rotated. Then the final form of the rotation process is shown in (3) and (4):

$$\begin{pmatrix} x_N \\ y_N \end{pmatrix} = \prod_{n=1}^{N} \cos(m^{1/2}\theta_i)$$
$$\begin{pmatrix} 1 & -m^{1/2}d_n \tan(m^{1/2}\theta_i) \\ m^{1/2}d_n \tan(m^{1/2}\theta_i) & 1 \end{pmatrix} \begin{pmatrix} x_0 \\ y_0 \end{pmatrix} \tag{3}$$

$$z_N = z_0 + \sum_{i=1}^{N} d_i\theta_i \tag{4}$$

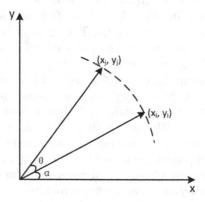

Fig. 1. The coordinate rotation

In rotation mode, z_n is forced to approach zero, while in vector mode y_n is forced to approach zero.

For the convenience of hardware implementation, each rotation angle is chosen to be related with 2^{-n} as (5). With this constraint the complicated computation of arc tangent can be replaced by simple bit-shifting [3].

$$\theta_n = \begin{cases} \arctan(2^{-n}) & m = 1 \\ 2^{-n} & m = 0 \\ \arctan h(2^{-n}) & m = -1 \end{cases} \tag{5}$$

CORDIC executes circular rotation when $m = 1$, hyperbolic rotation when $m = -1$ and linear rotation when $m = 0$.

After times of iteration, $\cos\theta$ in (3) becomes a constant, which is defined as the correction factor K:

$$K = \begin{cases} \prod_{n=0}^{\infty} \sqrt{\frac{1}{1+2^{-2n}}} \approx 0.6072 & m = 1 \\ 1 & m = 0 \\ \prod_{n=1}^{\infty} \sqrt{\frac{1}{1-2^{-2n}}} \approx 1. & m = -1 \end{cases} \tag{6}$$

Correction factor can be multiplied to the final result after the last iteration, so the iteration can be simplified as:

$$\begin{cases} x_{n+1} = x_n - md_n 2^{-n} y_n \\ y_{n+1} = y_n + d_n 2^{-n} x_n \\ z_{n+1} = z_n - d_n \theta_n \end{cases} \tag{7}$$

Different functions are fulfilled with different choices of m and d. This work includes three different calculating modes: sine/cosine, arc tangent and square root. The details of parameter settings, input and output for these three modes are shown in Table 1.

Table 1. Initialization for different modes

Mode	m	d	Input	Output
Sin/cos	1	$sign(z_n)$	$x_0 = 1/k$, $y_0 = 0$, $z_0 = \theta$	$x_n = cos\theta$ $y_n = sin\theta$
Arctan	1	$-sign(y_n)$	$x_0 = 1$, $y_0 = x$, $z_0 = 0$	$z_n = arctan x$
Square root	-1	$sign(z_n)$	$x_0 = x + 1/4$, $y_0 = x - 1/4$, $z_0 = 0$	$x_n = \sqrt{x}$

3 Improvement of Algorithm and Design Methodology

3.1 Algorithm Improvement

As shown in Eq. (6), the value of θ_n is changing in each iteration. These values need to be pre-stored in implementation, which consume more area. To save hardware resource, we optimize the algorithm by an approximate method. We know $\arctan(x_n)$ can be expanded with Taylor series:

$$\arctan(x_n) = x_n - \frac{x_n^3}{3} + \frac{x_n^5}{5} - \frac{x_n^7}{7} + \frac{x_n^9}{9} \cdots \qquad (8)$$

When x_n equals to 2^{-n}, Eq. (8) can be further simplified:

$$\arctan(2^{-n}) = 2^{-n} - \frac{2^{-3n}}{3} + \frac{2^{-5n}}{5} - \frac{2^{-7n}}{7} + \frac{2^{-9n}}{9} \cdots \qquad (9)$$

The value of $\arctan(2^{-n})$ is gradually approaching 2^{-n} as it iterates more times. When the number of iteration time is large enough, we could replace arctan with the first term 2^{-n} only, thus an operation of simply shifting could be used to save area and enhance computing speed as well.

As shown in Table 1, the calculation of square root ($m = -1$) is not required to output z_n, while the other two modes is irrelevant arctanh, thus the calculation of arctanh is not needed, only arctan ($m = 1$) is needed to be implement as above.

3.2 Algorithm Implementation

CORDIC fulfills its function by making a specified parameter approach to zero, z_n is forced to zero for rotation mode, while y_n is forced to zero for vector mode. In VLSI implementation, it is difficult to constantly judge whether the specified parameter has approached to zero during each iteration process, we need to fix the iteration times. An appropriate planning of iteration times could achieve the balance between the consumption of resource and calculation accuracy.

Figure 2 shows the relation between iteration times and absolute error. The result shows that as iteration times increase, the calculation accuracy is higher logarithmically. Square root requires less iteration times than the other two modes. The calculation accuracy of square root reaches around 10^{-6} when iterating 9 times, while the iteration number is required to be 17 for sin/cos and

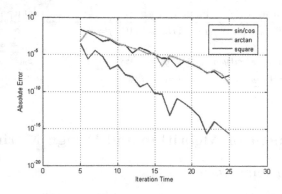

Fig. 2. The relation between iteration time and accuracy

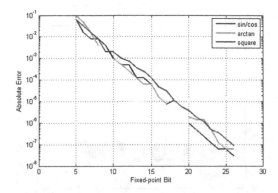

Fig. 3. The relation between fixed-point bit and accuracy

arctan modes. Therefore we choose 17 for sin/cos and arctan modes, and 9 times iteration for square root mode.

The hardware design uses fixed-point instead of floating-point. In the process of converting float-point number to fix-point number, proper bit-width is important. As shown in Fig. 3, the absolute error reaches around 10^{-6} when the fixed-point bit is around 20. Therefore we choose 24 bit fixed points with 20-bit decimal places.

4   Architecture Design

4.1   Pre-processing for Square Root

For arctan mode, the output is in $[-\pi/2, \pi/2]$ [2], and for sin/cos mode, the available interval of input is $[-\pi/2, \pi/2]$ [5], which does not need any initialization. While the simulation results in Fig. 4 show that the input range of square root needs to be $[1.1, 8.1]$, otherwise accuracy gets worse rapidly. So for square root mode, a pre-processing is required before iteration. As shown in Fig. 5, we need to determine whether the input number is in the specified range. If not, shift the input number left or right by $2i$ bit (i for shifting times) until it is in the range. When the calculation is done, shift the output left or right by i bit to eliminate the impact of pre-process. As shown in Fig. 6, when input is out of the range, with pre-process we can still get a result of high accuracy.

As shown in Fig. 7, the system uses a pipelined architecture to implement the core calculation part. According to different input of calculation modes, the rotation direction is decided by a multiplexer, so that addition or subtraction would be executed in each iteration. As mentioned in III-A, value of arc tangent of the rotation angles does not needed to be all saved as a table. As shown in Table 2, only seven values of $\arctan(2^{-n})$ need to be pre-stored. When $n > 6$, value of $\arctan(2^{-n})$ can be easily approximated by 2^{-i}, which is achieved by shifting in hardware implementation.

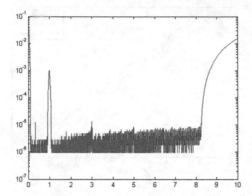

Fig. 4. The available range for the original square root algorithm

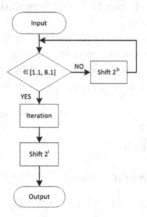

Fig. 5. Flow diagram of initialization for square root mode

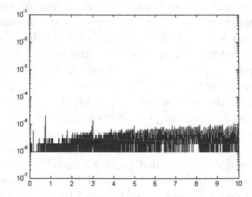

Fig. 6. The available range after the initial operation for square root

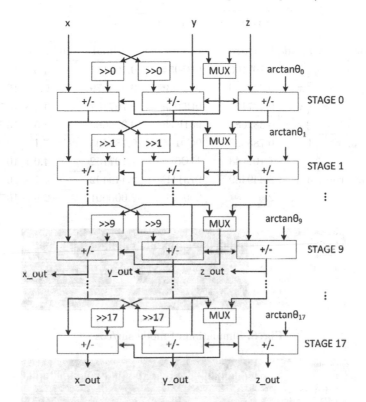

Fig. 7. Structure of the pipelined CORDIC

Table 2. Table of rotation angle

n	Tangent	Value	Hex value
0	arctan	0.78539816	C90FE
1	arctan	0.46364761	76B1A
2	arctan	0.24497866	3EB6F
3	arctan	0.12435499	1FD5C
4	arctan	0.06241881	0FFAB
5	arctan	0.03123983	07FF5
6	arctan	0.01562373	03FFF

5   Results and Dissussion

The CORDIC engine is implemented by Verilog HDL at behavior-level. The simulation is performed in VCS, and its results are shown in Table 3. It can be seen that the CORDIC engine have a high accuracy of about 10^{-6}. For sin/cos and arctan mode, the result is ready after 20 clock cycles as shown in Figs. 8 and 9, respectively. For square root mode, the result is ready after 12 clock cycles when

Table 3. Simulation results

Mode	Input	Exact result	Hex result	Decimal result	Error
Sin	$\frac{1}{4}\pi$	0.707106	0B5054	0.707111	4.6×10^{-6}
	$\frac{3}{8}\pi$	0.923880	0EC836	0.923879	0.1×10^{-6}
Cos	$\frac{1}{4}\pi$	0.707106	0B504a	0.707102	4.2×10^{-6}
	$\frac{3}{8}\pi$	0.382683	061F75	0.382680	3.5×10^{-6}
Arctan	1	0.785398	0C9105	0.785405	7.1×10^{-6}
	2	1.107148	11B6E5	1.107152	4.0×10^{-6}
Square root	6	2.449489	27311F	2.449492	2.7×10^{-6}
	4	2	200001	2.000001	9.5×10^{-7}

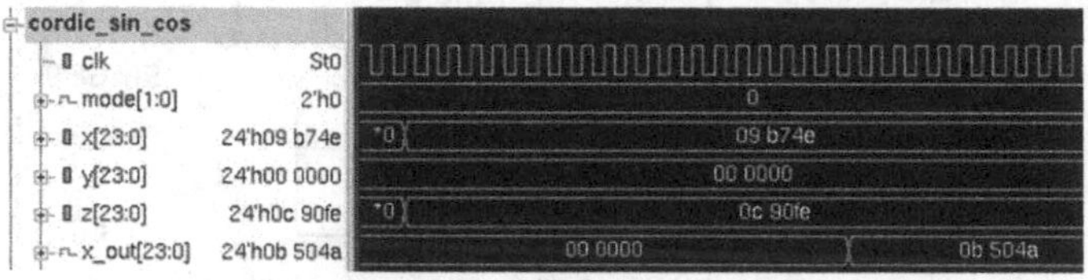

Fig. 8. Simulation of mode sin/cos

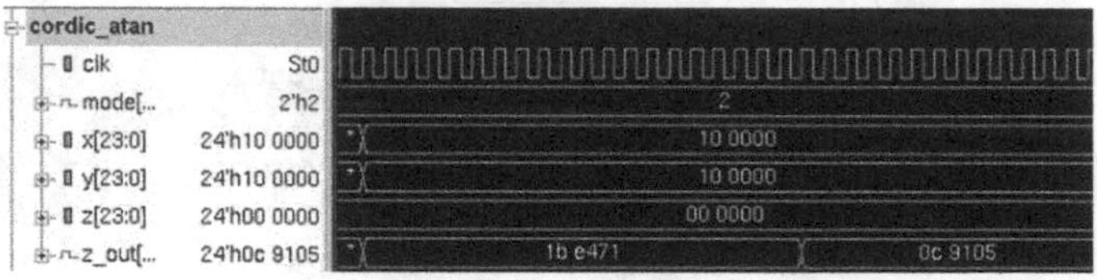

Fig. 9. Simulation of mode arctan

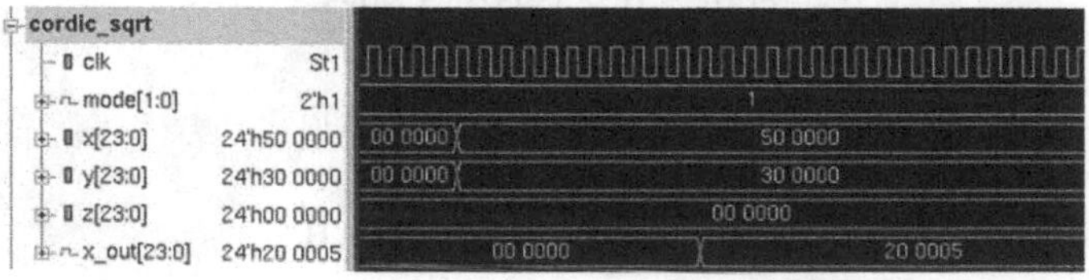

Fig. 10. Simulation of mode square root

input is in the specified range as shown in Fig. 10. Besides the clock cycles for each iteration, there are three more cycles for data input, initialization and choosing output data, respectively.

The design uses 65 nm low power process. Synthesis is carried out by Design Compiler. Placement and route(PR) use IC Compiler. The timing analysis is performed in Primetime. Synthesis and PR is done with the low threshold voltage devices and regular voltage devices under slow corner (1.08v/120°C). The use of low threshold voltage devices can save power consumption. The analysis under slow corner leaves a margin for actual environment. The Table 4 shows the results of synthesis and PR, namely critical path delay and cell area. The size of this CORDIC engine is 600 μm × 350 μm. Design uses 1441 sequential cell to achieve all the three calculation modes which is of high source efficiency. The Fig. 11 indicates the clock tree structure of the design. It has a 7-level clock tree to balance the delay.

Table 4. Synthesis and pr results

	Synthesis	Place & route
Critical path delay	1.03 ns	1.24 ns
Combinational cell	37053	41398
Sequential cell	1441	1441
Cell area	117991.7 μm^2	155176.8 μm^2

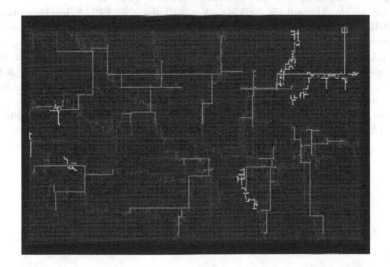

Fig. 11. The clock tree structure of backend place and route

6   Conclusions

In this paper, the design and implementation of an 24-bit efficient multi-mode CORDIC engine are proposed. This CORDIC engine can achieve high-accuracy with appropriate fixed-point design. It is of high-efficiency with fully pipelined architecture. Instead of using various CORDIC units for different modes, it combines the calculation for sine/cosine, arc tangent and square root together. This multi-mode design makes the proposed CORDIC engine very area-efficient. It is suitable for VLSI implementation of high-precision ICA algorithm, as well as other applications in areas such as high-accurate biomedical signal processing, communication system and mathematic co-processor.

References

1. Cavallaro, J.R., Keleher, M.P., Price, R.H., Thomas, G.S.: VLSI implementation of a CORDIC SVD processor. In: Proceedings of Eighth University/Government/Industry Microelectronics Symposium, pp. 256–260 (1989)
2. Gisuthan, B., Srikanthan, T.: Pipelining flat CORDIC based trigonometric function generators. Proc. SPIE - Int. Soc. Opt. Eng. **33**, 77–89 (2002)
3. Maharatna, K., Banerjee, S., Grass, E., Krstic, M., Troya, A.: Modified virtually scaling-free adaptive CORDIC rotator algorithm and architecture. IEEE Trans. Circuits Syst. Video Technol. **5**, 1463–1474 (2005)
4. Ranjith, J., Muniraj, N.: FPGA implementation of optimized independent component analysis processor for biomedical application. In: International Conference on Computer Communication and Informatics, pp. 1–5 (2013)
5. Renardy, A.P., Ahmadi, N., Fadila, A.A., Shidqi, N.: FPGA implementation of CORDIC algorithms for sine and cosine generator. In: International Conference on Electrical Engineering and Informatics (2015)
6. Van, L.D., Wu, D.Y., Chen, C.S.: Energy-efficient FastICA implementation for biomedical signal separation. IEEE Trans. Neural Netw. **22**(11), 1809–1822 (2011)
7. Volder, J.E.: The CORDIC trigonometric computing technique. Electron. Comput. Ire Trans. **EC-8**, 330–334 (1959)
8. Walther, J.S.: A unified algorithm for elementary functions. In: Spring Joint Computer Conference, 18–20 May 1971, pp. 379–385 (1971)

FPGA Design and Implementation of High Secure Channel Coding Based AES

Mostafa Ahmed Mohamed Sayed$^{(\boxtimes)}$, Liu Rongke, and Zhao Ling

School of Electronic and Information Engineering,
Beihang University, Beijing, China
mostafa_adawy@ymail.com, rongke_liu@buaa.edu.cn

Abstract. However applying encryption in physical layer reveals high levels of security, it can increase the system complexity and it can affect the communication reliability. This paper shows how to overcome these problems, where it doesn't only show the design of combined Low Density Parity Check (LDPC) code and Customized Stream Advanced Encryption Standard (CSAES) to increase the security level, but it also introduces a practical implementation for it. The proposed algorithm is designed in order to optimally exploit the hardware resources, and FPGA parallelism to achieve high throughput and to save hardware size. The design method shows how channel coding can be exploited to increase the security and resist attacks without affecting the communication reliability. The proposed algorithm is implemented on (Cyclone-IV4CE115) to achieve variable throughputs. It achieves 604 Mbps and 10^{-6} BER at SNR = 3.25 dB, while it can achieve 2 Gbps for SNR greater than 6 dB. NIST tests are applied to check the ciphered output randomness, and also the resistance of the algorithm against some attacks is discussed.

Keywords: LDPC · AES · McEliece · Combined encryption-channel

1 Introduction and Overview

The methodology of integrating the channel coding algorithm and encryption algorithm is often based on using public generator matrix that gives no information about its parity check matrix such as public key encryption. In 1978, the first channel coding based cryptocodes algorithm was introduced by McEliece Public key (MP) cryptography [1]. It begins with choosing the irreducible t-degree polynomial (Goppa Code) for the parity check matrix H; calculate G from Parity matrix H, then choosing $S_{k \times k}$ scrambling matrix and $P_{n \times n}$ permutation matrix. The next step is to publicly calculate the public key from (1), while keeping the ingredient of the public key secret so only who have the secret key can recover the information from the codeword. In encryption, the sender can encrypt input data $\mathcal{U}$ by multiplying it by the public generator matrix $G^{'}$, then adding random intentional errors to obtain encrypted word C as shown in (2) [1].

This work was supported by the National Natural Science Foundation of China (61401010).

Q. Chen et al. (Eds.): ChinaCom 2016, Part II, LNICST 210, pp. 355–366, 2018.
DOI: 10.1007/978-3-319-66628-0_34

$$G' = S \cdot G \cdot P \tag{1}$$

$$C = \mathcal{U} \cdot G' + e_{\text{int}} \tag{2}$$

The weight of e must be chosen less than the error correction capability of the decoder. Because only the authenticated receiver has the secret key, it can remove the intentional errors and recover the information as shown in the next equation.

$$\widehat{\mathcal{X}} = C \cdot P^{-1} = \mathcal{U} \cdot S \cdot G + e_{\text{int}} \cdot P^{-1} \tag{3}$$

Despite the robustness of MP algorithm, its key length and complexity directed the researchers to try other more lower complexity solutions such as replacing Goppa codes by LDPC codes [2]. However LDPC codes reduce the complexity, it makes the algorithm vulnerable to many attacks that exploit the sparse nature of the LDPC code. Different methods are proposed to solve this problem, such as using of more denser matrices, or QC-LDPC based random differences family code construction [3], using irregular QC-LDPC [4, 5], or selection of better intentional error vectors methods [6]. Other methods of MP based LDPC codes apply the addition of intentional error in modulation function to increase the security [7]. Many researches exploit the MP structure and the AES structure to combine between them. These methods based on exploiting the nature of LDPC code as high diffusion codes to replace the multiplication MixColumns operation of AES and to reduce the number of AES rounds. Because such systems contain both public key encryption algorithm, and also private key encryption, it is called hybrid systems. Some researches show that only six rounds [8] or seven rounds [9] or nine rounds [10] from AES is enough for such combined system.

The evaluation of security level for a certain cryptosystem is defined by the number of operations that are required to break it, which called work factor as described in [4], or cryptanalysis complexity as defined in [11]. This factor represents the capability of the algorithm to resist attacks. For example AES system actually has four parameters in each round. These parameters are the field irreducible polynomial, the affine transformation for Sbox, the offsets for ShiftRows, and the polynomials for MixColumns. Rijndael was designed to have resistance against the majority of known attacks based on its linear and nonlinear function represented in diffusing layer and substitution layer (Sbox) respectively [12]. The Sbox nonlinearity is measured by its differential probability, and output correlation. AES Sbox Differential Probability (DP) is $\delta = 2^{-6}$, and Sbox maximum correlation $\kappa = 2^{-3}$ [13]. As described in [14] the resistance of AES against differential cryptanalysis depends on both the non-linear building blocks and the linear mixing maps interconnecting them (i.e. MixColumns and Shiftrows). Super boxes include both linear and non-linear components. The differential property of the linear mixing map is called the differential branch number which can be calculated from (4). Branch number $\beta(\Phi)$ is used to determine the bound of Expected Differential Probability (EDP) of the Super box as described in (5) based on differential property δ of its nonlinear component (Sbox).

$$\beta(\Phi) \min_{a \neq 0.} (\omega_d(a) + \omega_o(\phi(a))) \tag{4}$$

$$\max_{a \neq 0} \text{EDP} \leq \left(\delta^{\beta(\Phi)} \right) \tag{5}$$

Where ω_d the weight of the input difference and $\omega_o(\phi(a))$ is the weight of the output of the linear mixing mapping. The maximum branch number $\beta(\Phi)$ obtained from EDP/DP as explained in [11, 14] for four rounds of AES is 2^{25}. So the maximum differential probability equals δ^{25}, and the maximum linear probability equals κ^{25}.

To decide the algorithm strength, the maximum differential cryptanalysis must be lower than 2^{-127}, and maximum linear probability must be lower than 2^{-64} to achieve complexity higher than $O(2^{128})$. Customized Sbox has to be tested to check its strength as shown in [15]. The nonlinearity test indicates the minimum hamming distance between its output 2^n binary string and n variable affine transformation. Strict Avalanche Criteria (SAC) test and Propagation Characteristic (PC) test reflect the relationship between the input changes of the Sbox to its output changes, to pass this test, half of the output must change randomly.

The proposed algorithm LDPC-CSAES introduces a practical algorithm that achieves a better level of security compared with previous work. It shows how the integration can increase the system capability to resist attacks, and achieves high throughput, while keeping the error correction performance without effect. It is based on stream AES to encrypt the data before and after LDPC.

Stream ciphers are used in order to not affect the error correction rate, but it requires synchronization, for this reason, a novel idea for synchronization that increases the security and resists attacks is introduced.

The security improvement in the proposed algorithm is based on the following:

- Double AES size, AES parameters customization, and shared shuffling function [16].
- CTR mode of operation combined with LDPC, where CTR mode has better resistance against attacks as described in [17].
- Adding extra data and permutation [18], Parallel processing.
- Using of Sync Word (SW) to prevent modifications as will be discussed later.

The next section discusses the security, the complexity, the reliability degradation problems that are targeted to be solved by LDPC_CSAES. Section 3 explains the proposed algorithm, while Sect. 4 explains its FPGA implementation. Section 5 discusses the results, related work comparison, and LDPC-CSAES resistance to attacks.

2 Problem Formulation

The tradeoff between error correction capability of the algorithm, system complexity, and security level, especially in the presence of side channel attacks, is a serious problem. The problems that face the McEliece like algorithm designers embody in choosing random matrix and method of generating error vector, where adding fixed errors can be removed very easily, while adding variable errors is restricted by the capability of error correction of the decoder, which cannot exceed the minimum hamming distance between codes according to the decoding principles [6], and it resulted in performance degradation. So the tradeoff between error correction rate and security represent a real problem in this situation. The MP secret ingredient can be easily extracted by Power analysis (PA) attacks, the problem that requires adding more complications to the system [19].

Using of joint AES–LDPC, increases the security level of MP like algorithm, but it increases the complexity also, and it is based on ECB mode of operation that resulted in reducing the error capability of the system where one bit error means a frame error because of AES avalanche criteria. The second problem resulted from using ECB mode its vulnerability to attacks [17]. Actually joint AES–LDPC is based on reducing some rounds of conventional AES in order to reduce the complexity, so it is always have low security level compared with conventional systems that contain separate AES and separate LDPC. Increasing the security level of joint AES guided the researchers to increase the no of rounds again from 6 rounds in 2008 [8], to 7 rounds in 2013 [9], to 9 rounds in 2014 [10], ends with 10 rounds again as conventional AES in 2015 [20]. The JASALC method described in [11] based on replacing the MixColumns operation by QC-LDPC parity matrix, and interlace of other AES round's functions with QC-LDPC parity matrix. It is claimed that this method has low complexity, while decoding operation based on Sbox of soft information input, and dual step decoding actually increase the complexity.

3   The Proposed Algorithm and Related Works

Unlike other algorithms, the proposed algorithm is based on CTR mode of operation instead of ECB mode, where CTR mode has better resistance against PA attacks compared with ECB [17]. The problem of CTR mode embodies in its need for synchronization. The LDPC-CSAES introduces a solution for synchronization, where it separately encode the synchronization word with a random constructed LDPC matrix, and repeat it, then concatenate it with the encrypted codeword and send it after permutation operation, this method achieves high error correction rate where it based on repeated codes that is decoded separately and decoded together as will be shown in next subsection. It also increases the security, where the addition of random data to the codeword is recommended to increase the security as described in [18]. The Sync Word (SW) consists of system ID, Counter Value (CV), and Random Vector (RV), where RV is also used to mask the ID and CV, so adding it to encrypted codeword doesn't affect the total frame randomness.

The input data block to the algorithm consists of two frames, each frame input data length is 256 bit which is double size of conventional AES as recommended in [21] to resist side channel attacks. The algorithm begins with input initialization which is executed by XOR of IV and SW. Every round of AES-256 contains customized Sbox, conventional MixColumns for 128 bit input, customized permutation represented in 256 bit permutation, and key 256 bit XOR, as shown in Fig. 1. After 3 rounds of AES-256 the AES output is xored with LDPC input. During LDPC coding operation, the AES-256 is working in parallel to prepare a cipher stream (randomly permuted frame from the AES-256 output after 6 rounds and 9 rounds) to be xored with the 512 bit output of LDPC to obtain the first encrypted codeword W1. The second frame treated like the first frame except for the AES-256 input for the second frame is the output of the AES-256 from the previous frame as represented in Fig. 1 to obtain W2. Repeated SW, W1, and W2, are concatenated together and permuted to obtain the encrypted block. The structure of AES-256 is the same for decryption-decoding process because of using stream cipher. The decryption-decoding process begins with inverse permutation for the received data and then SW decoder is used to decide whether to initialize the operation or not. According to the received data, i.e. if the received data is too noisy or modified the operation is stopped, this method proposes a novel idea to resist fault attacks, and modification attacks, and in the same time not affect the error correction rate in case of noise according to its error correction performance.

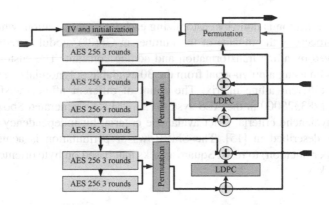

Fig. 1. Data flow for one block of two frames 256 bit length

The LDPC decoding algorithm for the proposed method is consisting of two decoders the first is Scaled Min-Sum (SMS) Algorithm and the second is Weighted Bit Filliping (WBF) algorithm that is used as a post processing decoder to enhance the performance and at higher SNR used as the main decoder to obtain high throughputs. The WBF [22] begins by calculating the hard decision for the received codeword, then calculate syndrome from (6) where Y is the received codeword and H is the parity matrix. If S is null or if the maximum iteration reached, then stop decoding and output X as the decoded data. If S is not null so it uses (7) and (8) to calculate the weight of the error for every variable node and then flip the maximum error e_i bits

$$S = Y \cdot H^T \tag{6}$$

$$w_{ij} = \prod_{i \in 1:n} s_j . H_{ij}, \text{ where } j \in 1 : m \tag{7}$$

$$e_i = \sum_{j \in 1:m} w_{ij} \tag{8}$$

SMS algorithm is a massage passing algorithm that is iteratively calculates the effect of variable/check nodes that share certain check/variable nodes through tanner graph to correct error bits, so the algorithm is based on two main functions which are check node update as shown in (9) and variable node update showed in (10). The algorithm stops decoding if reaches to the right code by the help of syndrome calculator or when reaching to the maximum iteration.

$$E_{i,j}^{new} = \alpha \prod_{i'} sign(L_{i,j}) \times min_{i'} |L_{i,j}| \tag{9}$$

$$L_{i,j}^{new} = u_i^{ch} + \sum_{j'} (L_{i,j}) \tag{10}$$

Sbox customization is done by customizing each internal operation, where the AES substitution process is the inverse of the number in $GF(2^8)$ modulo irreducible polynomial followed by affine transformation and adding constant. The customization for Sbox depends on using a polynomial from the 30 available polynomials, using different constant and different affine matrix. The count of different affine transformation is 194822323021283328000 in the AES system [23, 24]. The generated Sboxs are tested to check its avalanche criteria, strict avalanche criteria, bit independency criteria and correlation as described in [15]. The ShiftRows or permutation is achieved by bit shuffling (bit permutation) to resist Square attacks that based on byte oriented behaviors to extract the key.

4 LDPC-CSAES FPGA Implementation

In this section the hardware implementation and optimization that is achieved in order to reduce the hardware size without affecting the functionality and performance are introduced.

The top-level of decoder-decryption module is shown in Fig. 2. The green modules in Fig. 2 represent the SW/LDPC decoder; the yellow modules represent the AES-256 modules, while the purple modules represent other control modules such as inverse permutation. LDPC-CSAES contains one Round of AES-256 and one LDPC decoder. The AES round has the same structure of conventional AES's round, but the Sbox of the proposed algorithm is customized and a 256 bit permutation is used instead of byte permutation used in conventional AES. The implementation of Sbox is based on Lookup Tables (LUTs), while the MixColumns is implemented by logic functions. The extracted SW is decoded by SMS algorithm through the Variable Node Update (VNU), and Check Node Update (CNU), where CNU, and VNU is generic modules that can process any regular LDPC (column weight = 3, raw weight = 6). So the first hardware reduction is achieved by resources reuse where SW and The other two codewords are

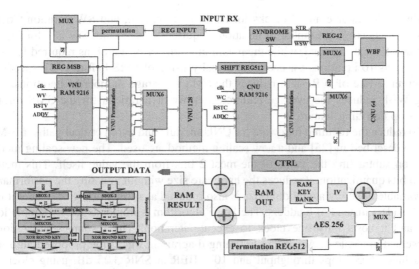

Fig. 2. LDPC-CSAES block diagram

decoded by the same module. The problem is the existence of different mapping according to the Parity matrix H, and this problem is solved by using multiplexers to choose between different mappings according to H.

Figure 3 is simple block diagram of SW decoder to describe the SW decoding operation. It consists of three parallel decoders work in parallel on the repeated SW codeword in the first stage then add the output of the three decoders together and decode it again in the second decoding stage. After decoding if the syndrome gives null it stops decoding and output the SW and initiates the system to start. If the syndrome is not null it saves power and put the system in idle state. The syndrome of WBF decoder is used while SMS iterations execution to allow the decoder to stop decoding early to reduce the computational complexity and reduces hardware size through exploiting WBF Syndrome. If SMS algorithm stops without right decoding the WBF is working on these data as a second decoder until reaching to the maximum number of iteration or reaching to the right code. The SMS one iteration costs 8 clocks 4 clocks for the

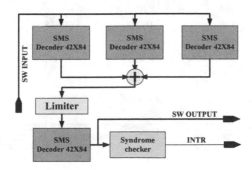

Fig. 3. Sync-word decoder

variable nodes update and 4 clocks for check node update, and SW iteration Costs 2 clocks. The maximum number of iterations required for decoding SW is 5 for the first stage and 5 for the second, while the maximum number of iterations required for SMS and WBF is 10 iterations for each, but actually using of SMS before WBF speeds the convergence rate of WBF and reduces the SMS's average number of iterations. Also using WBF reduces the average required number of iterations for the SMS through early stop decoding feature.

To reduce the required hardware for CNU module and avoid critical paths, a 3-MIN method described in [25] and a new scaling method are used. The new scaling method based on subtracting the value of the most 2 bits from the value itself. This method suits 6 bits quantization; it reduces the hardware size without affecting the performance. The variable node update module size is also reduced as shown in Fig. 4, where it uses only 5 adders instead of 6 adders. The WBF algorithm is implemented by simple logic gats, and it costs only one clock to execute iteration. The resources utilization is represented in Table 1. According to timing diagram in Fig. 5 the proposed algorithm can achieve 603 Mbps throughput and 10^{-6} BER at SNR 3.25 dB, using clock frequency 250 MHz, while it can achieve 2 Gbps and 10^{-6} BER, at SNR > 6 based on using WBF as the main decoder.

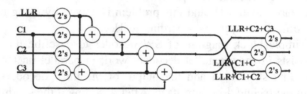

Fig. 4. Variable nodes update circuit diagram

Table 1. Resources utilization for 6 bits quantization for the proposed method

Algorithm		Logic functions	Logic registers	Memory elements
LDPC	CNU	18624	–	13824
	VNU	25216	–	13824
	WBF	4020	512	–
	CTRL	864	810	–
AES		938	1024	69888
Input interface		3840	7424	512
Total (LDPC-CSAES)		53 k (46%)	9 k(8%)	95 k(2%)

Fig. 5. LDPC_SAES timing diagram, (a) encoding, (b) decoding

5 Comparative Results, Testing, and Resistance to Attacks

5.1 Comparative Results, Testing

There are two points for comparison which are the error correction rate, and the security level. The security level can be represented in the maximum deferential probability, maximum correlation, and resistance to attacks. Although the LDPC used is (512, 256) which is short code length it achieves high error correction rates reaches to 10^{-6} at 3.25 dB, and that is because of using the new method of SW decoding that achieves very high block error correction rate as shown in Fig. 6, stream ciphering, and two decoders (SMS and WBF). The proposed method achieves 0.75 dB coding gain compared to JSALC code length 256 [11], and more than 2.5 dB coding gain compared with other joint AES [8, 20]. The customized Sboxs maximum correlation is 2^{-3} and maximum differential probability is 2^{-6}, where they are examined after generation as discussed in Sect. 4, and only the Sboxs that path the test are selected. The proposed method uses MixColumns from conventional AES so the branch number for 4 rounds of the proposed method equals to the conventional AES which equal 2^{25} [11, 14]. So the maximum differential cryptanalysis is (2^{-150}) which is lower than (2^{-127}) and have complexity greater than $O(2^{128})$. The same is the maximum linear probability is (2^{-75}) which is lower than (2^{-64}) and its complexity is greater than $O(2^{128})$. From another point of view, the bit propagation for the 3 rounds of AES is 4^3 and LDPC propagation is 4^2 [11, 14]. For the proposed algorithm we have two frames, every frame is xored before LDPC and after LDPC, where LDPC code rate is 0.5 so we need 256 cipher bit to XOR the LDPC input and 512 bit to XOR the LDPC output for every frame so 6 cipher outputs are required for one block contains 2 frames. Every 3 rounds of the proposed AES, a cipher output with length 256 can be obtained. So the numbers of rounds for the first frame is 3, 6 and 9 rounds of AES, while the second AES input is the previous AES output, so the numbers of rounds for the second frame is 12, 15 and 18 rounds of AES. So the Total Propagation for the first frame is bounded by $4^3 * 4^2 * 4^6 \leq TP \leq 4^3 * 4^2 * 4^9 = 4^{11} \leq TP \leq 4^{14}$, and for the second frame, the TP bounds is $4^{29} \leq TP \leq 4^{32}$, if we consider the least bounds which are 4^{11} for the first frame and 4^{29} for the second frame, the proposed algorithm still achieves higher

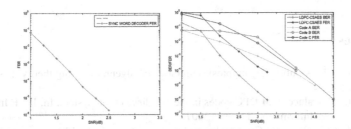

Fig. 6. (a) LDPC-CSAES SW Block error rate against SNR for AWGN channel, BPSK, and (5, 1) Quantization (b) Performance comparison between LDPC-CSAES error correction rate, A: BER 6 round AES-LDPC [8], B: BER 10 round AES-LDPC [20], C FER JSALC code length 256 [11].

propagation than other related works. For more accurate evaluation for the complexity of the proposed algorithm, the NIST tests are used to examine it.

5.2 LDPC-CSAES Resistance to Attacks

If the attacker tries to use brute force to attack the proposed algorithm so, he has to try invisible number of trials (2^{256} key * 2^{256} I_V * 256! internal permutation * 512! intermediate permutation * 1276! final permutation 30 polynomials-Sbox * 20922789888000 affine transformations * (C_6^{256} * C_3^{512}) random LDPC matrix). Which is the highest value compared to others secure channel coding algorithms. The proposed method is also immune against other attacks like differential and linear attacks, where as discussed before it has complexity greater than $O(2^{128})$. Bit shuffling and LDPC make the square attacks which based on byte orientation useless [8]. In side channel attacks the attacker always has a hypothetical model of the encryption algorithm, especially for the last and first round. Unlike other related works the proposed algorithm based on CTR mode integrated with LDPC, and uses customized parameters, so that the attacker has no hypothetical model for it and the attacker cannot attack the last round because of LDPC [17].

The parallel processing of LDPC and AES, beside the double structure make the algorithm very immune for side channel attacks, including fault attacks, especially in the presence of the SW decoding that controls the algorithm and stop it, if modification exist in the received codeword

6 Conclusion

The proposed method introduces a solution that gathers between high level of security, high error correction capability, high throughput, and low complexity for a practical secure channel coding based on the integration between AES and LDPC. In this paper a LDPC is exploited to increasing the security level and resist attacks without any degradation of its performance. The proposed method introduces a solution for stream cipher synchronization that is exploited to make the algorithm immune for modification attacks. It also resists side channel attacks. The throughput achieved at 3.25 dB is 604 Mbps with low hardware size.

References

1. McEliece, R.J.: A public-key cryptosystem based on algebraic coding theory. DSN progress report (1978)
2. Baldi, M., Chiaraluce, F.: LDPC codes in the McEliece cryptosystem. In: IEEE International Symposium on Information Theory (2007)
3. Baldi, M., Chiaraluce, F.: Cryptanalysis of a new instance of McEliece cryptosystem based on QC-LDPC Codes. In: ISIT 2007, pp. 2591–2595 (2007)
4. Shooshtari, M.K., Ahmadian, M.: Improving the security of McEliece-like public key cryptosystem based on LDPC codes. In: ICACT 2009, pp. 1050–1053 (2009)

5. Xu, C., Chang, Y.: Encryption scheme of physical layer based on irregular LDPC codes. In: Proceedings of AIAI 2010 (2010)
6. Stuart, C.M., Deepthi, P.P.: Hardware efficient scheme for generating error vector to enhance the performance of secure channel code. In: IEEE International Conference on Signal Processing, Informatics, Communication and Energy Systems (SPICES), pp. 1–5 (2015)
7. Ayeh, E., Varanasi, M., Adamo, O.: Joint Encryption error correction and modulation (JEEM) scheme. In: 2012 IEEE International Workshop Technical Committee on Communications Quality and Reliability (CQR), pp. 1–7 (2012)
8. Xiao, Y., Su, Q.: Design of LDPC-based error correcting cipher. In: IET 2nd International Conference on Wireless, Mobile and Multimedia Networks (ICWMMN) Proceedings, pp. 470–474 (2008)
9. Gupta, C.P., Gautam, S.: Joint AES encryption and LDPC coding. Int. J. Sci. Eng. Res. (IJSER) 4(7), 603–606 (2013)
10. Lin, K., Lin, W., Deng, Z., Li, N.: A joint encryption and error correction method used in satellite communications. China Commun. J. 11(3), 70–79 (2014)
11. Abu-Surra, S., Taori, R., Pisek, E.: Enhanced cryptcoding: joint security and advanced dual-step quasi-cyclic LDPC coding. In: IEEE Global Communications Conference (GLOBECOM), pp. 1–7 (2015)
12. Federal Information: Announcing the Advanced Encryption Standard (AES), 26 November 2001
13. Lamberger, M., Pramstaller, N., Rijmen, V., Vercauteren, F., Daemen, J.: Computational aspects of the expected differential probability of 4-round AES and AES-like ciphers. IEEE Computing 2009, pp. 85–104 (2009)
14. Rijmen, V., Daemen, J.: New criteria for linear maps in AES-like ciphers. IEEE Cryptogr. Commun. 1(1), 47–69 (2008)
15. Mazumdar, B., Mukhopadhyay, D.: Design for security of block cipher S-Boxes to resist differential power attacks. In: International Conference on VLSI Design, pp. 113–118 (2012)
16. Scripcariu, L.: A study of methods used to improve encryption algorithms robustness. In: 2015 International Symposium on Signals, Circuits and Systems (ISSCS), pp. 1–4 (2015)
17. Ragel, R., Ambrose, J.A., Ignjatovic, A., Parameswaran, S., Jayasinghe, D.: Advanced modes in AES: are they safe from power analysis based side channel attacks? In: 2014 IEEE 32nd International Conference on Computer Design (ICCD), pp. 173–180 (2014)
18. Esmaeili, M., Gulliver, T.A.: A secure code based cryptosystem via random insertions, deletions, and errors. IEEE Commun. Lett. 20(5), 870–873 (2016)
19. Richmond, T., Drutarovsk, M., Petrvalsky, M.: Countermeasure against the SPA attack on an embedded McEliece cryptosystem. In: 2015 25th International Conference Radioelektronika (RADIOELEKTRONIKA), pp. 462–466 (2015)
20. Viswanath, K., Pearlsy, P.V.: Cryptocoding system based on AES and concatenated coding scheme involving BCH and QC-LDPC. In: 2015 International Conference on Applied and Theoretical Computing and Communication Technology (ICATCCT), vol. 15, pp. 189–194 (2015)
21. Khan, A.K., Mahanta, H.J.: Side channel attacks and their mitigation techniques. In: 2014 First International Conference on Automation, Control, Energy and Systems (ACES), pp. 1–4 (2014)
22. Lin, S., Fossorier, M.P.C., Kou, Y.: Low-density parity check codes based on finite geometries: a rediscovery and more. IEEE Trans. Inform. Theory, 2711–2736 (2001)
23. Jing, M.-H., Chen, J.-H., Chen, Z.-H.: Diversified mixcolumn transformation of AES. In: 2007 6th International Conference on Information, Communications & Signal Processing, pp. 1–3 (2007)

24. Chen, Z.-H., Chen, J.-H., Chen, Y.-H., Jing, M.-H.: Reconfigurable system for high-speed and diversified AES using FPGA. Microprocess. Microsyst. **31**(2), 94–102 (2007)
25. Aziz, S.M., Pham, D.M.: An automated design methodology for FPGA-based multi-Gbps LDPC decoders. In: 2012 15th International Conference on Computer and Information Technology (ICCIT), pp. 495–499 (2012)

IoT-Architecture-Based All-in-One Monitoring System Design and Implementation for Data Center

Jinde Zhou, Wenjun Xu$^{(\boxtimes)}$, Fan Yang, and Jiaru Lin

Key Lab of Universal Wireless Communications, Ministry of Education,
Beijing University of Posts and Telecommunications, Beijing, China
wjxu@bupt.edu.cn

Abstract. Modularization and integration are becoming the mainstream trend in the development of data center. However, the integrated monitoring of power and environment has been a challenge in data centers. An All-in-One monitoring system design and implementation has been developed based on Internet of Things (IoT) architecture in this paper. The hardware is composed of two levels: one integrated monitoring gateway and several monitoring modules through the CAN-BUS network. The two-level structure design enables us to achieve module splicing and flexible deployment easily as well as rapid troubleshooting. A series of software applications are developed to establish the sensor network and collect sensor data. In addition, a web interface is provided for users to master the state of data center conveniently. Laboratory tests verify that the proposed system is able to offer automatic and intelligent support for data center management, thus significantly reducing the cost of labor and operation.

Keywords: All-in-One monitoring system · Data center · CAN-BUS · IoT · Integrated management

1 Introduction

Recently, Internet of Things (IoT) has become a future trend of technology in changing humans' life. IoT extends the concept of Internet from the network of computers to the network of all things [1]. In order to meet the needs of users, a new wave of smart IoT services has been set off by massive sensing analysis techniques to integrate more advanced and intelligent applications [2].

With the rapid development of information construction, more and more data centers are widely used around the world. Given the ever increasing role that data center plays in society, business, and science, it is obvious that the construction

This work is supported by the Fundamental Research Funds for the Central Universities (2014ZD03-01), the National Natural Science Foundation of China (61362008), the Special Youth Science Foundation of Jiangxi (20133ACB21007).

© ICST Institute for Computer Sciences, Social Informatics and Telecommunications Engineering 2018
Q. Chen et al. (Eds.): ChinaCom 2016, Part II, LNICST 210, pp. 367–377, 2018.
DOI: 10.1007/978-3-319-66628-0_35

cost and operation management of data center have become a major concern. Managers of data center have been looking for methods to reduce expenses while still ensuring efficient and stable services. All-in-One data center integrates all systems in a standard container, including power supply and distribution, cooling, IT cabinets, cabling, fire extinguishing, surge protection, and monitoring. It has been the mainstream trend nowadays because of its rapid deployment, easy expansion, low operational costs and low energy consumption. Generally speaking, data centers are arranged with complex and expensive equipment which is sensitive to the external environment. Meanwhile, due to the particularity of data center, it does not have the capability to achieve real-time scene monitoring by managers. Therefore, it is difficult to make a timely response under the circumstance of an unexpected danger, resulting in abnormal and inefficient services, or even damaging the expensive server equipment which will lead to serious effects. According to the statistics, companies around the world spend a huge amount of human resources and financial resources to manage servers, but at these high costs, even companies with 99.9% normal time lose hundreds of thousands of dollars every year in unplanned fault time [3]. Nevertheless, power and environment monitoring system provides a possible solution to deal with the aforementioned problems in data centers.

The research in [4] includes monitoring system with the surveillance mainframe and several sensors based on Client/Server (C/S) architecture through the RS-485 network. Studies have been made in fuzzy control theory to reduce the energy consumption and ensure the real-time monitoring of data center using microcontroller in [5]. However, few works are involved in the power and environment monitoring system for All-in-One data center. Current power and environment monitoring systems on the market mostly adopt integrated solution, which combines the management module and the sensor collection module into a block of hardware [6]. Any broken part will lead to the replacement of the entire hardware. Moreover, due to the fixed number of hardware interfaces, the amount and location of mount nodes are subject to certain restrictions.

The architecture and key technologies of IoT offer a new way of rethinking monitoring system for data center [7,8]. Based on IoT architecture, this paper proposes a new All-in-One monitoring system for next generation data center. A two-level structure of one integrated gateway and several sensor monitoring modules through the CAN-BUS network is introduced in the All-in-One monitoring system. Different module splicing schemes support different combinations of monitoring parameters by using various sensors. Thus, the proposed system can achieve rapid and flexible deployment easily within existing Information Technology (IT) infrastructures while bringing a significant reduction in the cost of building a data center. Besides, the distributed structure design makes it convenient for troubleshooting and positioning. Therefore, managers only need to replace the broken parts instead of the whole hardware and the maintenance cost is also reduced.

The rest of this paper is organized as follows. Section 2 introduces the architecture of the All-in-One monitoring system. Section 3 elaborates on the design of hardware boards and their detailed usages. Section 4 describes the software products and applications developed to monitor the data center. Then, the implementation snapshots of the system are shown in Sect. 5. Section 6 provides some results and discussions. The conclusion and future work are given in Sect. 7.

2   All-in-One Monitoring System

The All-in-One monitoring system is deployed in key positions of the All-in-One data center container as depicted in Fig. 1. It consists of five monitoring subsystems and one integrated monitoring gateway. These monitoring subsystems, including IT monitoring system, network monitoring system, precision air-conditioning monitoring system, Uninterruptible Power Supply (UPS) monitoring system and environment monitoring system, almost cover all of the data center's monitoring parameters. Sensor data from different monitoring subsystems is gathered by the gateway in a unified way. The integrated monitoring gateway also offers a dedicated user-friendly web interface to diaplay the device information, the connection status and the sensor values of different sensor nodes.

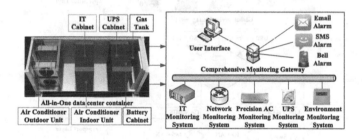

Fig. 1. System architecture of the All-in-One monitoring system

IT equipment can be monitored by IT monitoring system for parameters like Central Processing Unit (CPU) utilization, memory size and process state. Network monitoring system is able to obtain the current network status of data center. Precision air-conditioning monitoring system is mainly responsible for management of the cooling system in data center. UPS parameters such as input and output voltage and current, battery capacity and various powers are monitored by UPS monitoring system. Environment monitoring system provides temperature and humidity monitoring, smoke monitoring, water leakage monitoring, etc.

At present, most monitoring systems in data center are deployed by an integrated block of hardware. This solution actually reduces the flexibility of implementation and management. The architecture of IoT brings us a new idea for monitoring system. Generally, the structure of IoT is divided into five layers, which are the business layer, the application layer, the processing layer, the transport layer and the perception layer [9,10]. The perception layer deals with the identification and collection of sensor information. The transport layer transfers the data from sensors to the data processing system. The processing layer is responsible for storing and processing the information received from the transport layer. The application layer provides global management of diverse applications based on the information processed in the transport layer. The business layer manages the overall IoT system and helps make future decisions and business strategies through some data analysis.

CAN-BUS is becoming a standard bus protocol for embedded industry control network of area because of its good performance and high reliability. CAN-BUS communication can support up to 1 Mbps and upload emergency message in interrupt mode so that data transmission will be very quick. In addition, the number of mount nodes on CAN-BUS is significantly increased compared with the traditional way. This allows users to make the most suitable choice for different scale of data centers.

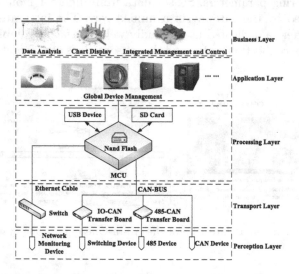

Fig. 2. Hardware collection structure of the All-in-One monitoring system

Based on IoT architecture, the two-level structure design of Micro Control Unit (MCU) and interface converter through CAN-BUS is shown in Fig. 2. It enables us to achieve module splicing and flexible deployment easily, as well as to facilitate the support of a variety of manufacturers, different interface devices and monitoring sensors, etc. The MCU is responsible for the collection and display of data from the CAN-BUS and acts as a gateway for external access, while the two types of interface converter, 485-CAN transfer board and IO-CAN transfer board, collect the data of third-party devices and send to the CAN-BUS. Of course, any CAN device is able to access our bus network directly just following the protocol and any network monitoring device could be reached by means of a switch connected to MCU. Device management and application development in the upper layer are mainly concentrated in the web interface.

3   All-in-One Monitoring System Hardware Design

The All-in-One monitoring system deployment in this work consists of four kinds of hardware which are described in following subsections, respectively. The MCU needs a powerful microprocessor to run an Operating System (OS) and process the data so AT91SAM9X25 is a good choice. As for three interface converters, the cost-effective stm32 singlechip can meet the demand and the hardware overhead can be reduced.

3.1   MCU Board

The MCU board plays the leading role in our All-in-One monitoring system, which just takes on the integrated monitoring gateway in Fig. 1. A series of add-ons modules are developed based on AT91SAM9X25 as shown in Fig. 3 to make the system more user-friendly. The 128 MB Double Data Rate 2 (DDR2) Random Access Memory (RAM) and 256 MB Nand flash enable us to run an embedded linux OS on the board. Two 10/100 M adaptive Ethernet chips are used for network communications to show the web interface and monitor network devices. Usually, the MCU board gets the sensor data through the CAN-BUS and these data can be stored in onboard flash or other external storage devices if needed, such as Universal Serial Bus (USB) and Secure Digital (SD) card. The program can read the different Dual Inline-pin Package (DIP) configurations to set different IP address for identifying each MCU board.

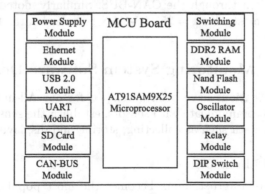

Fig. 3. Hardware components of the MCU Board

3.2   Temperature and Humidity Sensor Board

The temperature and humidity sensor board is applied to monitor environmental data relevant to the cooling processes at a data center. For this purpose, the Sensirion SHT11 temperature and humidity sensor is selected. The principle of this sensor is that the forward voltage of a silicon diode is temperature dependent. The sensor has inbuilt configurable 8/12 bit up to 12/14 bit Analog to

Digital Convertor (ADC) for relative humidity and temperature measurements, offering typical accuracy tolerance of $\pm 3.0\%$ for relative humidity and ± 0.4 °C for temperature. In the stm32 singlechip, the sensor data is obtained by means of Inter-Integrated Circuit (I2C) communication and sent to the CAN-BUS.

3.3   485-CAN Transfer Board

Based on the stm32 singlechip, the 485-CAN transfer board is composed of a series of main elements: one CAN interface, four RS485 ports and one 8-bit DIP switch. The board is used to collect 485 device data and transform them to CAN data. Since a lot of sensors only have 485 interface, our system can be compatible with those third-party 485 devices by this way. By taking full advantage of the stm32 singlechip's CAN and Universal Synchronous/Asynchronous Receiver/Transmitter (USART) Application Programming Interface (API), our transform program becomes easier. Noted that one MCU board can bear at most $2^8 - 1 = 255$ 485-CAN transfer boards by adjusting the 8-bit DIP switch.

3.4   IO-CAN Transfer Board

Similar to the 485-CAN transfer board, the IO-CAN transfer board is composed of such main elements: one CAN interface, eight switching signal ports, four relay output interfaces and one 8-bit DIP switch. The board is used to collect switching signal data and transform them to CAN data. By this way, those switching signal devices, such as smoke sensor and water leakage sensor, also have access to our system. Furthermore, users are able to send command to control a relay switch through the CAN-BUS. Similarly, noted that one MCU board can bear at most $2^8 - 1 = 255$ IO-CAN transfer boards by adjusting the 8-bit DIP switch.

4   All-in-One Monitoring System Software Design

Five software applications have been developed for our All-in-One monitoring system in order to communicate with sensors, establish the sensor network, and manage the sensor data such as collecting, storing and displaying.

4.1   Embedded Linux OS

With the growth of Internet, linux becomes the most popular free operating system because of its powerful kernel and hardware support. Our embedded software is just based on linux 2.6.39 kernel and some modifications are made on the drivers and pins for our specific hardware.

4.2   Embedded Web Server

For the purpose of providing users with a universal interface, transplanting an embedded web server is needed. As a lightweight opensource server, lighttpd has the characteristics of very low memory overhead, low CPU occupancy rate but good performance.

4.3   Singlechip Application

Three different applications have been developed in three different singlechip boards as mentioned in Sect. 3. The Keil integrated development tools and C programming language are adopted. In the 485-CAN transfer board, 485 devices communicate with the controller via Modbus protocol in which the controller acts as a master and the sensor acts as a slave. The sensor data will be read and filled in a generated CAN frame and then sent to the MCU board. Similar to the 485-CAN transfer board, the temperature and humidity sensor board's application and the IO-CAN transfer board's application adopt the similar schema. The only difference is that one reads the data from a temperature and humidity chip, while the other one reads the switch signal data.

4.4   Gateway Application

The gateway connects the CAN-BUS sensor network and the web interface for the bidirectional data movement shown in Fig. 4. Applications in the gateway collect data reported by sensors in order to update the status of real-time monitoring in the web interface. The gathered data will be converted into JavaScript Object Notation (JSON) format and sent to the web interface as a HyperText Transfer Protocol (HTTP) payload. At the same time, applications receive user commands and convert them into CAN command frames and then forward to the desired end board. There are four processes running in the background, dealing with device updating, device lost, data over threshold and commands delivering respectively. For the convenience of users, functions like changing the MCU board's IP, setting the date and time, and recording the system log are also fulfilled. A remote upgrade interface is provided in the web page for users to upgrade their software systems fast and easily.

One month's data is recorded on the gateway for further processing and analysis. Furthermore, four threshold values namely "low warning threshold", "low alarm threshold", "high warning threshold" and "high alarm threshold" can be preset for individual sensor nodes. Once the performance indicators for data center exceed the preset threshold or other abnormal situations appear, alarm information will be sent to the administrators immediately via bell, email or Short Message Service (SMS) and recorded to the system log at the same time.

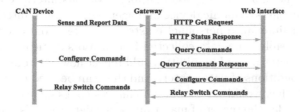

Fig. 4. Data flow of the gateway application

4.5   CAN Communication Protocol

The CAN communication protocol is customized in Table 1 by using the 32 bit
ID of CAN extended frames. In the All-in-One monitoring system, each board,
device and data has its own unique CAN ID. The MCU board identification
depends on the DIP switch state, so does the board number identification. As
for the board type identification, we set 0x01 standing for temperature and
humidity sensor board, 0x02 standing for 485-CAN transfer board and 0x03
standing for IO-CAN transfer board. At last, the device identification relies on
the hardware position of device and the data identification is on the basis of the
user's configuration sequence.

Table 1. CAN communication protocol

ID bits (high→low)	Instructions
1 bit	Reserved
8 bit	MCU board identification
3 bit	Board type identification
8 bit	Board number identification
4 bit	Device identification
5 bit	Data identification

5   Implementation Snapshots

The proposed system will be deployed at banks and Internet companies to provide their data centers with a cost-effective and intelligent monitoring system.
Compared to the integrated solution in [6], our two-level structure reduces the
replacement probability of MCU and the maintenance cost of monitoring system. Besides, the CAN-BUS solution increases the number of mount nodes and
reduces the purchase cost of MCU. Figures 5 and 6 show the physical hardware
connection diagram and the web interface of the implementation respectively.

The All-in-One monitoring system supports various interface devices which
are hot swap and offers dynamic device management. The web interface helps the
operation and maintenance personnel master the state of data center whenever
and wherever possible. The data collected from sensors distributed in every corner, such as temperature and humidity, could reflect how environmental parameters affect the conditions of data center. And they can be used to design dynamic
control systems that would adjust the cooling resources or others according to
the circumstance, for the target of maintaining the data center's normal running.

Fig. 5. Physical hardware connection diagram

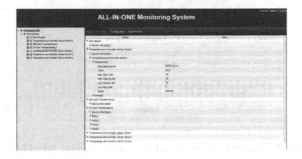

Fig. 6. Web interface of the implementation

6   Results and Discussions

A simple test environment is set up in our 80 square-meter laboratory. More than a dozen temperature and humidity sensors are deployed in each student's seat and the sensor data is collected every three seconds. Figure 7 shows the 24-h monitoring results gathered by the All-in-One monitoring system. The temperature varies from 24 °C to 29 °C, and the humidity fluctuates from 14% to 22%. From a data collection point of view, this experiment demonstrates that the proposed system can be an effective tool for environment monitoring in data center. More scenarios and monitoring parameters will be implemented in the real data center in the next few months.

To validate the performance of device's hot swap as well as the timeliness of detection alarm and commands taking effect in the All-in-One monitoring system, a few measurements are conducted. Figure 8(a) illustrates that a lost device will be detected in no more than 7 s. Figure 8(b) shows that the delay of detecting device plugged mainly concentrates between 1.5 s and 3.5 s. Moreover, Fig. 9(a) verifies that an alarm will be generated within 4 s. Figure 9(b) shows that a user command will take effect between 1 s and 2 s in most cases. In general, above indicators fully meet the needs of data center monitoring.

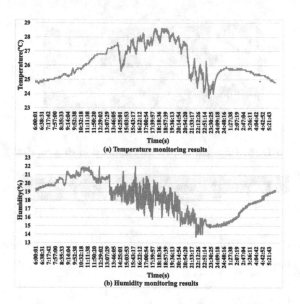

Fig. 7. Monitoring results of temperature and humidity

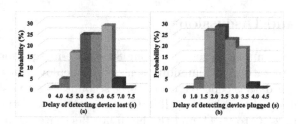

Fig. 8. Performance of device hot swap

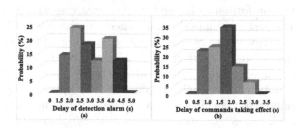

Fig. 9. Timeliness of detection alarm and commands taking effect

7 Conclusions

An All-in-One monitoring system design and implementation is proposed in this paper to solve existing problems in power and environment monitoring of data center. Based on IoT architecture, the two-level structure through CAN-BUS is devised. Then the four hardware components of the distributed sensor network are implemented respectively. Several software applications and a web interface are also developed for the All-in-One monitoring system. Test results in laboratory indicate that the proposed system can be well applied in the micro-module data center. This paper can provide essential foundation for the development of data center monitoring system in the Internet plus age and IoT era.

Data collection in order to understand a data center's environment is the first step to improve the operation and management of a data center. In the future, data analysis methods will be introduced to dynamically change the environmental conditions and energy resource allocation in data centers. Thus, the intelligence of data center could be further enhanced significantly.

References

1. Whitmore, A., Agarwal, A., Da Xu, L.: The internet of things-a survey of topics and trends. Inf. Syst. Front. **17**(2), 261–274 (2015)
2. Gubbi, J., Buyya, R., Marusic, S., Palaniswami, M.: Internet of things (IoT): a vision, architectural elements, and future directions. Future Gener. Comput. Syst. **29**(7), 1645–1660 (2013)
3. Sentilla corporation. http://www.sentilla.com
4. Chen, C., Sun, L., Shao, Y., Hu, Z., Shi, Q.: Iems: an intelligent environment monitoring system of server room. In: 2012 5th International Conference on IEEE Intelligent Computation Technology and Automation (ICICTA), pp. 189–192 (2012)
5. Xianzhe, H.: Room temperature and humidity monitoring and energy-saving system. In: 2011 6th International Conference on IEEE Computer Science & Education (ICCSE), pp. 537–540 (2011)
6. Rle corporation. http://rletech.com
7. Kelly, S.D.T., Suryadevara, N.K., Mukhopadhyay, S.C.: Towards the implementation of IoT for environmental condition monitoring in homes. IEEE Sens. J. **13**(10), 3846–3853 (2013)
8. Chi, Q., Yan, H., Zhang, C., Pang, Z., Da Xu, L.: A reconfigurable smart sensor interface for industrial WSN in IoT environment. IEEE Trans. Industr. Inf. **10**(2), 1417–1425 (2014)
9. Tao, F., Zuo, Y., Da Xu, L., Zhang, L.: IoT-based intelligent perception and access of manufacturing resource toward cloud manufacturing. IEEE Trans. Industr. Inf. **10**(2), 1547–1557 (2014)
10. Khan, R., Khan, S.U., Zaheer, R., Khan, S.: Future internet: the internet of things architecture, possible applications and key challenges. In: 2012 10th International Conference on IEEE Frontiers of Information Technology (FIT), pp. 257–260 (2012)

Research on Receiving Visible Light Signal with Mobile Phone

Qiaozhi Yuan[1], Zhenshan Zhang[1], Yaojun Qiao[1(✉)], Ke Liao[2], and HaiHua Yu[2]

[1] State Key Laboratory of Information Photonics and Optical Communications, School of Information and Communication Engineering, Beijing University of Posts and Telecommunications (BUPT), Beijing 100876, China
qiao@bupt.edu.cn
[2] Ricoh Software Research Center (Beijing) Co., Ltd., Beijing 100044, China

Abstract. In this paper, based on ambient light sensor and camera sensor, two different receiving methods of visible light signal are experimentally studied. For ambient light sensor, its response time and light intensity are analyzed. The results show that it is available to transmit data with 0.2 kbps data rate over 2 m. For camera sensor, the relationship and difference between original data and corresponding image are studied for the first time. Besides, a series of methods are used to process the original data instead of the image, including data adjustment, histogram equalization and polynomial fitting. Using camera sensor, 2 kbps data rate over 0.3 m transmission with real-time processing of data in mobile phone is achieved even if the stripes are not clear enough, which is faster and more robust. The research is beneficial for practical application of visible light communication (VLC).

Keywords: Visible light communication (VLC) · Light sensor · Camera sensor · Signal receiving

1 Introduction

Traditional wireless communication has encountered bottleneck because the spectrum resources are exhausted gradually. The visible light has unregulated spectrum to exploit, which has gained increasing attention [1]. And the development of light emitting diode (LED) technology provides a basis for using the visible light to transmit information [2]. Visible light communication (VLC) is different from the traditional wireless communication and optical fiber communication, it's a kind of new communication technology. It uses LED as transmitter and utilizes the continuous changes in state (on-off) of the light to transmit information. VLC combines lighting with communication together, and it is considered as part of 5G system. However, there are still lots of problems to be solved for practical application, and the signal receiving technology is the key point.

In recent years, smart phone becomes increasing popular and it contains many sensors which can detect the visible light. From the report of Internet

© ICST Institute for Computer Sciences, Social Informatics and Telecommunications Engineering 2018
Q. Chen et al. (Eds.): ChinaCom 2016, Part II, LNICST 210, pp. 378–387, 2018.
DOI: 10.1007/978-3-319-66628-0_36

Data Center (IDC), the shipments of smart phones in the whole year of 2015 reach 1.4329 billion [10]. Therefore it is significant of utilizing the exiting mobile phone resources in VLC system. The rolling shutter effect of camera sensor can be used for receiving the visible light signal [3–9]. However, the problem of blooming effect will affect the decoding of signal seriously. The literatures [3,4] capture the image from a reflected surface to mitigate blooming effect, which wastes lots of energy. The literatures [6–9] process the gray image and solve the blooming problem with the method of digital image processing to a certain extent.

In this paper, we study two different receiving methods of visible light signal using ambient light sensor and camera sensor in mobile phone. The experiments are conducted indoor with sunlight and lamplight, the transmitter is a LED whose output power is 9.8 W, and the receiver is a Samsung Galaxy Nexus mobile phone. For ambient light sensor, its response time and light intensity are analyzed. The minimal response time is about 5 ms and the illumination can still be easily distinguished when the distance is 2 m. The results show that it is available to transmit data with 0.2 kbps data rate over 2 m. This method is simple and it utilizes the existing device in mobile phone instead of additional hardware, which can reduce the cost and be used in low rate demand condition. For camera sensor, the relationship between the original data and corresponding image is studied. In particular, the way of data-represented gray level in mobile phone is different from that in common situation, therefore it is necessary to adjust the data before further processing. The principle of data adjustment is adding 256 to the negative value and remaining the positive value. Moreover, the data matrix of original data is compared to the data matrix of corresponding image in MATLAB, the result shows that the original data is different from the image. The literatures [6–9] process the image to decode the signal, which may loss some information. To solve this problem, processing the original data instead of the image is proposed, which can be more accurate. After adjusting the data, histogram equalization is used to increase the difference between light and dark stripes, and polynomial fitting is used to make decision on the data. We process as much data as possible to avoid random error. After data processing mentioned above, the information sent by LED can be recovered successfully even if the light and dark stripes are not clear enough. Using camera sensor, 2 kbps data rate over 0.3 m transmission with real-time processing of data in the mobile phone is achieved, which is faster and more robust.

2 Principle

2.1 Ambient Light Sensor

The visible light is part of the electromagnetic wave, and its wavelength is from 380 nm to 780 nm. For the receiver, the illumination is often used to represent the strength of the received light signal, and it's measurement unit is lx.

The ambient light sensor is assembled in mobile phone, and it's a hardware device which can detect the visible light signal. The light sensor is a photo-diode, and it can get the value of illumination when the intensity of ambient illumination changes. The light sensor records the data in the perspective of one dimensional. For this reason, it can be used to receive and decode the visible light signal. The illumination of ambient light changes all the time due to the ambient light noise, however, the noise can be ignored when compared to the signal.

2.2 Camera Sensor

The camera sensor is an array of photodiodes, and it is the most important hardware device to detect light signal in mobile phone. We utilize the rolling shutter effect of camera sensor to detect the visible light signal. The detail of rolling shutter effect is in [3–5]. Figure 1 shows the procedure of taking photo with camera, both the data and the image can be got in our program. The relationship and difference between data and image are studied in detail later.

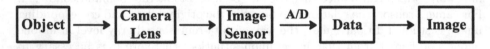

Fig. 1. Procedure of taking photo with camera: the data is YUV format and the image is JPEG format.

3   Experiment, Results, and Discussion

Figures 2 and 3 show our system block diagram and experiment setup respectively. In transmitter (Tx), we use FPGA to generate a certain binary sequence for cycle and drive the LED array light through the LED driver. In receiver (Rx), the light sensor or camera sensor detect the visible light signal, then we process the data and display the results in mobile phone. Because the android system is open source, we do the experiment with a Samsung Galaxy Nexus mobile phone, whose version of android is 4.0.

3.1   Ambient Light Sensor

When the ambient illumination intensity changes, our program can save the intensity of illumination and the time it happens. The sensitivity of ambient light sensor in android has four levels, as shown in Table 1.

We choose the fastest level and conduct the experiment under different conditions. The experiment conditions are shown in Table 2. The data with different rates is analyzed and the result shows that the minimal time interval is about 5 ms, which means the highest sensitivity of light sensor can detect the signal

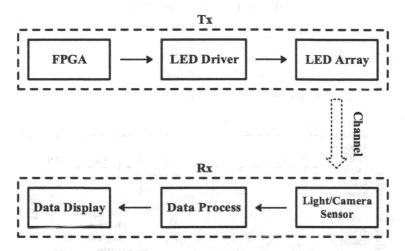

Fig. 2. System block diagram: the upper part shows the Tx (which includes a FPGA, an LED driver and an LED array) and the lower part shows the Rx (mobile phone).

Fig. 3. Experiment setup

Table 1. Sensitivity of ambient light sensor

Sensitivity level	Time delay (μs)
Sensor delay fastest	0
Sensor delay game	20,000
Sensor delay UI	60,000
Sensor delay normal	200,000

Table 2. Experiment condition

Data sent	Binary number
Modulation format	OOK
Frequency (Hz)	0–100
Distance (m)	0–2

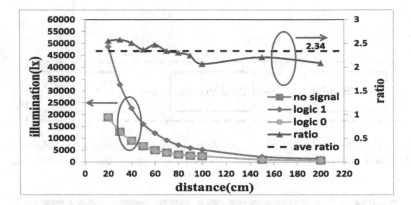

Fig. 4. Illumination with distance: the blue line (continuous) indicates no signal, the red line (continuous) indicates signal logic 1, the green line (continuous) indicates signal logic 0, the purple line (continuous) indicates the ratio of logic 1 and logic 0, the black line (dashed) is the average of the ratio. (Color figure online)

with the rate of 0.2 kbps. Then we choose 100 Hz as an example for further analysis, and the results of illumination (average value) with different distance are shown in Fig. 4.

It particular, the data without signal is the same as the data with signal logic 0 for OOK signal. The blue line coincides with the green line in Fig. 4, which is consistent with the theory. As the distance increases, the illumination decreases accordingly, but the strength of logic 1 signal is always about twice than that of logic 0 signal. Figure 5 shows an example of the illumination data when the distance is 2 m, and the data can be easily distinguished by the threshold. In the example the average of illumination is regarded as the threshold.

3.2 Camera Sensor

Both the data and corresponding image shown in Fig. 1 can be got from our program, then we compare them to find a better source for processing. The relationship between the data and corresponding image is experimented. In our android program some special data is set and corresponding image is generated to verify the relationship between data and image. Figure 6 shows the result of experiment.

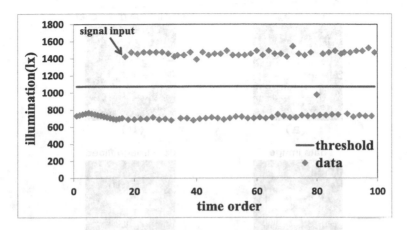

Fig. 5. Illumination of 2 m: the blue spot indicates the illumination and the red line (continuous) indicates the threshold. (Color figure online)

Fig. 6. Relationship between image and data: the gray level of image (left) corresponds to the number (right).

The image is generated according to special data, and the range of byte data is from -128 to 127. Through the experiment we know that in the camera built-in mobile phone the number 0 represents black. When number changes from 0 to 127 the gray level of image changes from black to gray, which is the same as the common method of data representation. In particular, the number -1 represents white. When number changes from -1 to -128 the gray level of image changes from white to gray, which is different from that in common.

Because the way of data-represented gray level in mobile phone is different from that in common situation, it is necessary to adjust the data before further processing. The principle of data adjustment is adding 256 to the negative value and remaining the positive value. After adjusting, the number 0 and 255 represent black and white respectively, and the rest number represent different gray level.

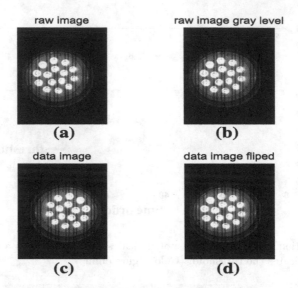

Fig. 7. Data and corresponding image: (a) is the raw image captured by camera, (b) is the gray level of (a), (c) is the image generated in MATLAB with the original data and (d) is the horizonal flipped image of (c).

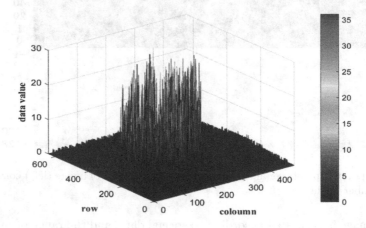

Fig. 8. Difference of data and image: the result of (d)–(b) in Fig. 7

After figuring out the relationship between the data and corresponding image, the data is compared to the image to study the difference between them. We display the data and corresponding image with MATLAB and the result in Fig. 7 shows that the image (b) is the same as the image (d). Then we subtract the data matrix of (b) from the data matrix of (d) and the difference is shown in Fig. 8. It is obvious that most of the data in Fig. 8 is not equal to 0, which means the data is different from the corresponding image. Considering the data is more original than the image, we select the data instead of the image for further processing.

The data captured by camera (in Fig. 9) is not as uniform as the data captured by light sensor (in Fig. 5) due to dimensional factor. The position of LED relative to the mobile phone will affect the value of light and dark stripes. The value of data close to the LED is larger than that far away, which even leads to the value of logic 1 is smaller than that of logic 0. Therefore it is necessary to use polynomial fitting.

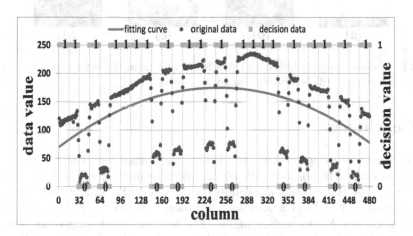

Fig. 9. Polynomial fitting for data decision: the blue spot is the original data, the red curve is the fitting curve, the green spot is the value of decision and the binary number is the data sent by LED. (Color figure online)

Figure 9 shows the approach of data processing, and it is an example for a row of data. We regard the fitting polynomial curve of the original data as the threshold and get the decision data by comparing the original data to fitting curve. Obviously, the data received is same as the data sent.

Fig. 10. Procedure of original data processing

Figure 10 shows the procedure of original data processing. We process the data as much as possible to avoid random error. For the data matrix we get, its size is 640 * 480. It is processed as the example does, then 640 rows of decision data can be got totally. All the 640 rows of data are added together according to column. The number is regarded as logic 1 if it is bigger than 320, otherwise regarded as logic 0. We get the final decision value and recover the data sent by LED. All data processing is done in mobile phone with our android program, and Fig. 11 shows different android program interface.

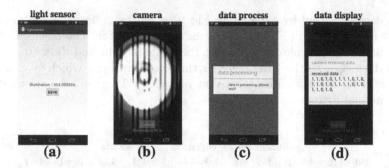

| light sensor | camera | data process | data display |

(a)   **(b)**   **(c)**   **(d)**

Fig. 11. Android program interface: (a) is for light sensor, (b) is for camera, (c) is for data processing and (d) is for data display.

4   Conclusion

Two different receiving methods of visible light signal based on ambient light sensor and camera sensor in mobile phone are experimentally studied in detail in this paper. The experiments are conducted indoor with sunlight and lamplight, the transmitter is a LED whose output power is 9.8 W, and the receiver is a Samsung Galaxy Nexus mobile phone. For ambient light sensor, its response time and light intensity are analyzed. The results show that it is available to transmit data with 0.2 kbps data rate over 2 m. This scheme can be used in low rate demand condition, such as sending the mark of LED beacons for indoor location system, sending the password to access the wireless network and so on. For the camera sensor, the relationship and difference between data and image are studied, and we propose processing the original data instead of the image to avoid loss of information. After data adjustment, histogram equalization and polynomial fitting, the information sent by LED can be recovered successfully even if the light and dark stripes are not clear enough. Using camera sensor, 2 kbps data rate over 0.3 m transmission with the real-time processing of data in mobile phone is achieved, which is significant for practical application of VLC.

Acknowledgments. This work was supported in part by National Natural Science Foundation of China (61271192, 61427813, 61331010); National 863 Program of China (2013AA013401); Research Funded by Ricoh Software Research Center (Beijing) Co., Ltd.

References

1. Wu, S., Wang, H., Youn, C.H.: Visible light communications for 5G wireless networking systems: from fixed to mobile communications. IEEE Netw. **28**, 41–45 (2014)
2. Elgala, H., Mesleh, R., Haas, H.: Indoor broadcasting via white LEDs and OFDM. IEEE Trans. Consum. Electron. **55**(3), 1127–1134 (2009)

3. Danakis, C., Afgani, M., Povey, G., Underwood, I.: Using a CMOS camera sensor for visible light communication. In: GLOBECOM Workshops, vol. 48, pp. 1244–1248 (2012)
4. Rajagopal, N., Lazik, P., Rowe, A.: Demonstration abstract: how many lights do you see? In: Proceedings of the 13th International Symposium on Information Processing in Sensor Networks, pp. 347–348. IEEE Press (2014)
5. Liu, M., Qiu, K., Che, F., Li, S., Hussain, B., Wu, L., et al.: Towards indoor localization using visible light communication for consumer electronic devices. In: 2014 IEEE/RSJ International Conference on Intelligent Robots and Systems, IROS 2014, pp. 143–148 (2014)
6. Ji, P., Tsai, H.M., Wang, C., Liu, F.: Vehicular visible light communications with LED taillight and rolling shutter camera. In: Vehicular Technology Conference, pp. 1–6. IEEE (2015)
7. Chow, C.W., Chen, C.Y., Chen, S.H.: Enhancement of signal performance in LED visible light communications using mobile phone camera. IEEE Photonics J. **7**(5), 1–7 (2015)
8. Liu, Y., Chen, H., Liang, K., Hsu, C.: Visible light communication using receivers of camera image sensor and solar cell. IEEE Photonics J. **8**(1), 1–1 (2015)
9. Chow, C.W., Chen, C.Y., Chen, S.H.: Visible light communication using mobile-phone camera with data rate higher than frame rate. Opt. Express **23**(20), 26080 26085 (2015)
10. IDC report. http://mt.sohu.com/20160218/n437740830.shtml

Mobility Management

STGM: A Spatiotemporally Correlated Group Mobility Model for Flying Ad Hoc Networks

Xianfeng Li and Tao Zhang$^{(\boxtimes)}$

Engineering Lab on Intelligent Perception for Internet of Things (ELIP),
School of Electronic and Computer Engineering, Peking University, Shenzhen, China
lixianfeng@pkusz.edu.cn, taozhang@pku.edu.cn

Abstract. Flying Ad hoc Network (FANET) is a special type of Mobile Ad hoc Network (MANET) consisting of a swarm of Unmanned Aerial Vehicles (UAVs), and simulation is the dominant method for its research. Mobility models that generate the trajectories of UAVs in a flying session are the foundation for constructing a realistic simulation environment. However, existing mobility models targeting general MANETs are not adaptable to FANET, as the mobility patterns of UAVs are fundamentally different from general mobile nodes on the ground. In this paper, we propose a group mobility model called STGM (*S*patio*T*emporally correlated *G*roup *M*obility model) for UAVs in a FANET. The distinct feature of STGM is that both the temporal property on the trajectory of a UAV itself and the spatial correlation across multiple UAVs that fly as a coordinated group are taken into account. In addition, the collision-free distribution of UAVs are maintained in STGM. Built on top of mathematical principles, STGM provides a parameterized framework. By adjusting its parameters, it is able to provide UAV trajectories covering different application scenarios. We validate the effectiveness of STGM with a set of important metrics, and the results show that STGM is a suitable and configurable mobility model, which will facilitate FANET research at upper layers.

Keywords: Mobility model · Flying Ad Hoc Network · Simulation

1 Introduction

Small Unmanned Aerial Vehicles (UAVs) are becoming widely applicable in recent years due to their versatility, flexibility and ease of re-deployment. These small UAVs equipped with various sensors and wireless communication modules can be connected to form Flying Ad hoc Networks (FANETs) [1]. FANETs are increasingly used for civil applications, such as monitoring, surveillance, search and rescue [2].

However, compared to traditional Mobile Ad hoc Networks (MANETs), FANETs are facing some unique challenges caused by their high mobility. For example, the topology of a FANET may change frequently, raising problems for the design and analysis of routing protocols. To overcome these problems,

© ICST Institute for Computer Sciences, Social Informatics and Telecommunications Engineering 2018
Q. Chen et al. (Eds.): ChinaCom 2016, Part II, LNICST 210, pp. 391–400, 2018.
DOI: 10.1007/978-3-319-66628-0_37

we need better understanding on the mobility of FANET nodes. Field testings, although realistic, are very costly, and the observed results are only applicable to the specific settings. In contrast, simulations using mobility models are considered to be a low-cost alternative, and their results can be applicable to more generalized situations [3].

As an abstraction of node movements, a mobility model describes the moving patterns of the node (including the change of its position, velocity, etc.). It can serve as an input to FANET simulation by producing trajectories for UAV nodes in a flying session, or waypoints of UAV nodes at specific times. Therefore, it is the foundation for other FANET research at upper layers, such as network connectivity analysis, network performance evaluation and the design of reliable routing protocols.

Although mobility models have been extensively studied for general mobile ad hoc networks (MANETs), existing models are not very adaptable to the domain of FANETs, as mobility patterns of UAVs are fundamentally different from general mobile nodes on the ground. Thus MANET models may not truthfully emulate FANETs. This limitation suggests an urgent need to comprehensively investigate FANET mobility models for the development of high-quality simulation environments, which will facilitate the research on other FANET problems.

The aim of this paper is to propose a mobility model for FANETs that capture their unique features. The rest of this paper is organized as follows. In Sect. 2, we give a brief description of related works. In Sect. 3, we propose the STGM mobility model. In Sect. 4, we justify the model with experimental results. Finally, we draw conclusions in Sect. 5.

2   Related Work

Mobility models have been extensively studied for MANETs [3], but mobility models targeting FANETs are relatively new and scarce. In [4], a survey on mobility models for airborne networks is presented. The mobility models for aerial vehicles can be classified into two categories: traditional MANET models adapted to aerial ad hoc networks and new models developed for aerial ad hoc networks. The first category includes the pure random models which do not consider any additional constraints. The well-known models among them include Random Way Point (RWP) and Random Direction (RD) model [3]. But the movement of UAV nodes obeys some kinematic and dynamic constraints, e.g., they tend not to make sharp turns or sudden stops. Disregarding these constraints will introduce unrealistic trajectories of UAVs. The very few existing mobility models for aerial vehicles are different from traditional MANET models in that the former capture smooth aerial turns which is caused by kinematic and dynamic constraints. In [5], the Smooth Turn (ST) mobility model is presented. ST perpendicularity ensures the smoothness of the trajectories. It is also an entity model, and it does not take group motion into consideration. The basic Gauss Markov (GM) mobility model [6] and Enhanced Gauss Markov (EGM) mobility model [7] can produce UAV trajectories for more general FANET scenarios, and the waypoints on each trajectory exhibit good temporal correlations that are common in reality. But these Markov models are still entity models, lacking the ability to capture spatial correlations among the UAVs in a group. As for group models, a widely used group model for traditional MANETs is Reference Point Group Mobility Model (RPGM) [3], and a number of its variants have been proposed as well, like Column mobility model, Pursue mobility model, Nomadic mobility model, etc. Up to now, group models targeting FANETs are very scarce. In [8], A pheromone model is proposed for addressing the requirements of ad hoc networks of UAVs cooperating to achieve a common mission. However, this model is not network-friendly, because its pheromone logic pushes the UAVs away from each other, leading to the break of node links.

3   Spatiotemporally Correlated Group Mobility Model

3.1   Overview of the Model

There are three aspects to be considered in our modeling framework. First, a UAV node in the real world cannot move in a random trajectory because of kinematic and dynamic constraints, so the temporal property of the trajectory reflecting these constraints should be considered in our model. Second, the UAVs in a FANET usually form a group or multiple groups, and the UAVs in the same group are moving coordinately. More specifically, there is a logical center in this group, which dictates the motion properties of the entire group, such as location, speed, direction, etc. All UAV nodes in this group should follow the motion of this logical center in a large degree, with some necessary randomness allowed. Third, the UAVs should maintain collision-free distribution during flying session. Hence, this property should also be kept in our model.

Based on above analysis, we propose a **S**patio **T**emporally correlated **G**roup **M**obility model, called STGM. The whole process of STGM can be decomposed into two phases. In the first phase, we propose a *correlated Gauss Markov model* to generate a trajectory (which is a series of waypoints along consecutive time slots) for each UAV in a group. We choose Gauss Markov process for modeling because it is much better at producing a temporally correlated sequence of elements than many other models, e.g., random ones. To capture the spatial correlations among the trajectories of different UAV nodes, we introduce important changes to the basic Gauss Markov model. Besides, since we should avoid collisions among UAVs in the whole flying session, the waypoints in these trajectories should be examined and adjusted to avoid collisions between UAVs when it is necessary. We perform this task in the second phase of the STGM model. Figure 1 illustrates the framework of STGM, and more detailed description about these two phases is given below.

3.2   Phase #1: Generation of Velocities and Waypoints

In UAV simulation, the trajectory of each UAV node can be approximated as a sequence of waypoints at discrete times. If we know the original waypoint and

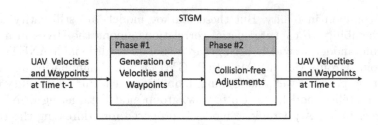

Fig. 1. Overview of STGM process

the velocity of each node at every time slot, we can calculate its waypoints for all time slots. For example, supposing at time t, UAV node i is at waypoint $WP_i(t)$, and its velocity at t is $\mathbf{V}_i(t)$, then its waypoint at time $t + \delta$ can be calculated as $WP_i(t + \delta) = WP_i(t) + \mathbf{V}_i(t) * \delta$. Since the velocity of a UAV consists of its speed and direction, our task is to derive a mathematical formula for each of the two aspects. In our framework, we adopt Gauss Markov process for modeling temporal properties of each trajectory, and take the direction and speed of the logical center as references for modeling spatial correlations between different trajectories. With these considerations, the speed and direction of each node are calculated by the following equations respectively.

$$S_i(t) = (1 - \beta)S_i^{gm}(t) + \beta S_l(t) \tag{1}$$

$$D_i(t) = (1 - \beta)D_i^{gm}(t) + \beta D_l(t) \tag{2}$$

In the equations, $S_i(t)$ and $D_i(t)$ are the speed and direction of a UAV node i at time t respectively. $S_i^{gm}(t)$ and $D_i^{gm}(t)$ is the basic Gauss Markov process for each node itself. $S_l(t)$ and $D_l(t)$ represents the logical center's speed and direction at time t respectively. The parameter $\beta \in [0,1]$ is a coefficient reflecting the correlation of each UAV node with the logical center on their movements. When $\beta = 0$, the UAV nodes have nothing to do with the logical center, indicating that the UAVs are not flying as a group. When $\beta = 1$, the UAV has the strongest correlation with the logical center. In fact, it will follow the moving of the logical center strictly in this case.

The basic Gauss Markov equations for speed $S_i^{gm}(t)$ and direction $D_i^{gm}(t)$ are given as follows:

$$S_i^{gm}(t) = \alpha S_i^{gm}(t - 1) + (1 - \alpha)\overline{S}_i^{gm} + \sqrt{1 - \alpha^2}s(t - 1) \tag{3}$$

$$D_i^{gm}(t) = \alpha D_i^{gm}(t - 1) + (1 - \alpha)\overline{D}_i^{gm} + \sqrt{1 - \alpha^2}d(t - 1) \tag{4}$$

$\overline{S}_i^{gm}$ and $\overline{D}_i^{gm}$ are constants representing the mean value of the speed and direction of node i respectively; $s(t - 1)$ and $d(t - 1)$ are random variables from Gaussian distribution. Parameter α reflects the degree of randomness in the Gauss Markov process, varying in the range $[0,1]$. When $\alpha = 0$, the model is memory-less, and the trajectory for each UAV node will be totally random, without any temporal correlation along its waypoints. In contrast, when $\alpha = 1$, the UAV speed and direction keep unchanged throughout the flying session. In other words, it is flying along a straight line with a constant speed.

In Eq. (1) and (2), the speed $S_l(t)$ and direction $D_l(t)$ of the logical center play their roles in affecting the speed and direction of a UAV node. In this way, the motion of the logical center decides the motion of the entire group. In the context of simulation, $S_l(t)$ and $D_l(t)$ can be provided as input vectors given by the following equations.

$$S_l(t) = \mathbf{VG}(t) \tag{5}$$

$$D_l(t) = \mathbf{DG}(t) \tag{6}$$

$\mathbf{VG}$ and $\mathbf{DG}$ are group motion vectors, which are two sequences of speed and direction values respectively at different times. The values of $\mathbf{VG}$ and $\mathbf{DG}$ are generated by path planning strategy according to specific demands.

It can be seen that by setting the two parameters α and β with different values respectively, we are able to control the degrees of temporal and spatial correlations for the trajectories of the UAV nodes.

3.3 Phase #2: Collision-Free Adjustments

As mentioned in Sect. 3.1, UAVs should avoid collisions in the flying session, which was not taken into account in Phase #1. In this phase, we adjust the original waypoints to ensure that the UAV nodes always keep a safe distance with each other. Note that each waypoint should be moved as little as possible to respect the spatiotemporal properties derived from Phase #1. These adjustments are performed in two steps. The first step is to identify the UAV nodes which are not in safe distance with at least one other UAV in the same group. In case any node violates this condition, the second step is invoked to perform an adjustment algorithm on the waypoint of this node. This algorithm is based on the following assumptions: (1) The global activity space of all UAVs is known. (2) The initial distribution of UAV group is collision-free. (3) Collisions during the interval between t and $t + 1$ is not considered, i.e., collisions are only examined at the start of each time slot. With these assumptions, Algorithm 1 gives the process of the waypoint adjustments.

Note that in Algorithm 1, the *threshold* is the safe distance between UAVs, an empirical value that is set as *ten meters* in this paper. Figure 2 illustrates an instance of the adjustment algorithm. Assuming the node under consideration is i, and its waypoint at time $t - 1$ is $WP_i(t - 1)$, then it will reach the position indicated by $WP_i(t)$ calculated in the first phase at time t. Since i is in danger of collision with another node j, we need to conduct adjustment for i. We start from the current position $WP_i(t)$, and find the nearest safe point around $WP_i(t)$, as indicated by $WP_i'(t)$ in Fig. 2. This point also preserves its spatiotemporal property as much as possible. This procedure will be applied to all the other UAV nodes in this group in a sorted order. Eventually, the adjusted waypoints $WP'(t)$ are obtained.

Algorithm 1. Collision-free Adjustment Algorithm

Input:
Waypoints $WP(t)$ of all nodes calculated in Phase #1.
Output:
Collision-free waypoints $WP'(t)$
1: Sorting UAV nodes in descending order of their distances to the logical center.
2: Picking a node i from the node set in sorted order.
3: If existing a node j, with $Distance(WP_i(t), WP_j(t)) < threshold$, then i is in the unsafe area of j, goto step 4; otherwise goto step 5.
4: Searching the nearest safe waypoint $WP_i'(t)$ around $WP_i(t)$ for i, such that it is not in the unsafe area of j and any other nodes.
5: If all the nodes have been processed then take step 6, otherwise go to step 2.
6: **return** $WP'(t)$.

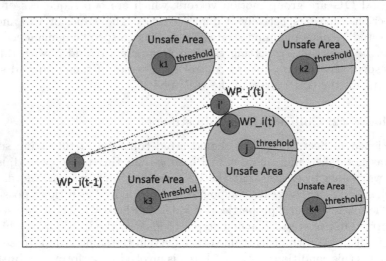

Fig. 2. An instance of collision-free adjustment

4   Simulation Results and Analysis

4.1   Metrics and Experimental Setup

To validate STGM model is flexible and suitable, we use some protocol-independent metrics, such as Spatial Correlation, Temporal Correlation and Path Availability. These metrics are defined in [9]. The BonnMotion [10] is taken to generate mobility scenarios and analyze the performance of the mobility model with above metrics. It has been widely used for studying the characteristics of mobile ad hoc networks. BonnMotion is an open-source software, thus we can implement our proposed STGM model with it and make comparisons with other models. The major simulation parameters set in BonnMotion are described in Table 1.

Table 1. Major simulation parameters

Simulation parameter	Value
Simulation area length	1000 m
Simulation area width	1000 m
Min speed	5 m/s
Max speed	15 m/s
α	[0~1]
β	[0~1]
Number of simulated nodes	30
Simulation Time	600 s

4.2 Results And Analysis

With the above experimental setup, we perform two sets of experiments. The first one is to validate whether STGM can capture the flying characteristics of a FANET across a wide variety of application scenarios. The second one is to compare with a few other mobility models described in the related work to show that STGM outperforms existing mobility models. We perform five independent experiments for each evaluated metric. The illustrated results below are averaged.

As described earlier, STGM should exhibit spatial and temporal correlations for a UAV swarm in the FANET. As the two parameters α and β in the STGM formulas are designed to control the degrees of temporal and spatial correlations for different scenarios, we first evaluate STGM by adjusting the α parameter to reveal the configurable temporal correlation. For this experiment, we set β to 0.5. Figure 3 shows the various values of average temporal correlation by tuning parameter values $\alpha = [0, 0.25, 0.5, 0.75, 1]$. It can be observed that the temporal correlation is low when α is small, and the temporal correlation gets large when α is being increased. Obviously, the temporal correlation is captured, and can be adjusted using the α paramter in STGM. Thus, for application scenarios where the UAVs are required to fly with sharp turnarounds, we will see low temporal correlation among waypoints for individual UAVs. This scenario can be simulated with STGM by setting α with a small value. In contrast, for situations where UAVs are flying in a very predictable trajectory, their high temporal correlation can be satisfied by setting α with a large value. In summary, by adjusting the α parameter, STGM can cover various application scenarios with different requirements on temporal correlation.

Figure 4 shows that the variation of spatial correlation can be controlled by the β parameter (α is set to 0.5 in this experiment). Obviously, the spatial correlation in STGM gets stronger with the increase of β. Therefore, to meet demands on spatial correlation for different application scenarios, we can simply adjusting the β parameter. For example, in search and rescue scenarios, relative low spatial correlation is required to enable larger coverage on scanned areas.

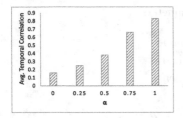
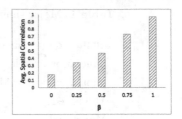

Fig. 3. Temporal correlation   **Fig. 4.** Spatial correlation

In this case, we can set a relative small value for β. On the other hand, in a patrol scenario, where UAV swarms are flying in a more regular path, these UAVs will exhibit strong spatial correlation with each other. In such situation, the requirement can be satisfied by setting a large value for β.

Apart from revealing mobility characteristics of STGM itself using the above metrics, there is still a need to check whether STGM can simulate the dynamic of FANETs. We use path availability metric to make it. Figure 5 shows the path availability over different value pair of α and β. From Fig. 5, the fluctuation of path availability indicates that FANET is a dynamic and unstable network, especially when the value pair of α and β is small. In other words, the smaller value pair of α and β leads to the more randomness of UAV nodes. As a result, FANET is more unsteady in this situation. Another observation is that the dynamic degree of FANET in STGM is controllable. When we want to simulate a relative steady FANET, we can set α and β with relatively large values. In contrast, by setting the α and β with small values, an unsteady FANET scenario can be obtained. It validates that STGM is able to simulate different dynamics of FANETs according to the demands of specific application scenarios. This will enable researchers to construct various simulation environments for evaluating their routing protocols.

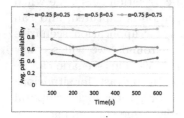
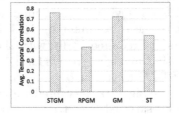

Fig. 5. Path availability   **Fig. 6.** Temporal correlation of different mobility models

From the above experiments and analysis, we can see that STGM model provides a flexible framework to satisfy different requirements of FANETs.

Next, we perform a set of experiments to compare with existing models to show that our model is more suitable for FANET research.

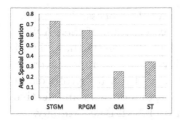

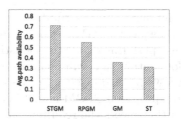

Fig. 7. Spatial correlation of different mobility models

Fig. 8. Path availability of different mobility models

Figure 6 shows STGM and GM model have the higher temporal correlation than RPGM and ST. The reason is that STGM and GM guarantee temporal correlation by Gauss Markov process. The temporal correlation in Gauss Morkov formula is inherent. While RPGM and ST generate their movement by randomly selecting speed and direction, which can not ensure steady temporal correlation. ST has higher temporal correlation than RPGM. This is because ST ensure relative smooth trajectories by adjusting head direction. It is beneficial to obtain temporal correlation.

Figure 7 shows that group mobility models (STGM and RPGM) have higher spatial correlation than the entity models. This is because the entity models do not take spatial correlation into account. For the two group models, the correlation of STGM is higher than RPGM. The reason is that RPGM was proposed for the movement of human populations using the RWP model, where the kinematic and dynamic constraints are not modeled.

Figure 8 presents the average path availability among different mobility models. Obviously, the group mobility model have higher path availability than the entity models. The reason resides in this observation is that the movement of each node in group models is correlated with other nodes. This property is beneficial to obtain higher path availability. Besides, another observation is that STGM is more stable than RPGM. This is because STGM takes both spatial correlation and temporal correlation into account. Whereas, the RPGM generates trajectories by RWP entity model which is a pure random mobility model. In addition, the dynamic of STGM is controllable. Thus, STGM is superior than RPGM for FANETs research.

5   Conclusion

Mobility model serves as the foundation for constructing a realistic simulation environment for FANET research. However, the existing mobility models are mainly developed for MANETs, which may not truthfully emulate FANETs. In this paper, we propose a spatiotemporally correlated group mobility model (STGM) for FANETs. The distinct feature of STGM is that both the temporal correlation on the mobility of a specific UAV itself and the spatial correlation across multiple UAVs that fly as a coordinated group are taken into account.

Moreover, it maintains a safe distribution during the whole process. The experimental results show that STGM not only meets the expectation of the FANET scenarios, but also performs better than existing models. It suggests that STGM can provide a foundation that will facilitate FANET research at upper layers.

In the future, we plan to investigate the performance of routing protocols in FANET using the proposed STGM model in this paper, and develop an effective routing protocol that meets the requirements posed by FANET accordingly.

Acknowledgements. This work is supported by the grant of Shenzhen municipal government for basic research on the basic technology of UAV swarm network (JCYJ20150629144717142).

References

1. Bekmezci, I., Sahingoz, O.K., Temel, Ş.: Flying ad-hoc networks (FANETs): a survey. Ad Hoc Netw. **11**(3), 1254–1270 (2013)
2. Scherer, J., Yahyanejad, S., Hayat, S., Yanmaz, E., Andre, T., Khan, A., Vukadinovic, V., Bettstetter, C., Hellwagner, H., Rinner, B.: An autonomous multi-UAV system for search and rescue. In: ARW 2015, p. 32 (2015)
3. Camp, T., Boleng, J., Davies, V.: A survey of mobility models for ad hoc network research. Wirel. Commun. Mob. Comput. **2**(5), 483–502 (2002)
4. Xie, J., Wan, Y., Kim, J.H., Fu, S., Namuduri, K.: A survey and analysis of mobility models for airborne networks. IEEE Commun. Surv. Tutor. **16**(3), 1221–1238 (2014)
5. Wan, Y., Namuduri, K., Zhou, Y., He, D., Fu, S.: A smooth-turn mobility model for airborne networks. In: Proceedings of the First ACM MobiHoc Workshop on Airborne Networks and Communications, pp. 25–30. ACM (2012)
6. Liang, B., Haas, Z.J.: Predictive distance-based mobility management for PCS networks. In: IEEE Proceedings of the Eighteenth Annual Joint Conference of the IEEE Computer and Communications Societies, INFOCOM 1999, vol. 3, pp. 1377–1384. IEEE (1999)
7. Biomo, J.-D.M.M., Kunz, T., St-Hilaire, M.: An enhanced Gauss-Markov mobility model for simulations of unmanned aerial ad hoc networks. In: 2014 7th IFIP Wireless and Mobile Networking Conference (WMNC), pp. 1–8. IEEE (2014)
8. Kuiper, E., Nadjm-Tehrani, S.: Mobility models for UAV group reconnaissance applications. In: 2006 International Conference on Wireless and Mobile Communications, ICWMC 2006, p. 33. IEEE (2006)
9. Bai, F., Sadagopan, N., Helmy, A.: Important: a framework to systematically analyze the impact of mobility on performance of routing protocols for adhoc networks. In: Twenty-Second Annual Joint Conference of the IEEE Computer and Communications, INFOCOM 2003, IEEE Societies, vol. 2, pp. 825–835. IEEE (2003)
10. Aschenbruck, N., Ernst, R., Gerhards-Padilla, E., Schwamborn, M.: BonnMotion: a mobility scenario generation and analysis tool. In: Proceedings of the 3rd International ICST Conference on Simulation Tools and Techniques, ICST 2010, p. 51 (2010)

Radial Velocity Based CoMP Handover Algorithm in LTE-A System

Danni Xi, Mengting Liu[(✉)], Yinglei Teng, and Mei Song

Electronic Engineering, Beijing University of Posts and Telecommunications,
Beijing 100876, China
{xidanni,liumengting,songm}@bupt.edu.cn,
lilytengtt@gmail.com

Abstract. In the Long Term Evolution-Advanced (LTE-A) systems, coordinated Multi-Point (CoMP) transmission/reception technology is widely used to improve cell-edge throughput and system throughput. With the introduction of CoMP technology, handover scenes have changed and traditional handover algorithms are no longer able to meet the requirements of current handover scenes. Different from traditional CoMP handover trigger mechanism, we adopt the event based handover trigger mechanism to update the CoMP coordinating set (CCS) and transmission points (CTP). Furthermore, under the constraints of the reference signal received power (RSRP) and the load of the base stations (BSs), we propose the cycle selection algorithm to choose CCS and CTP based on the radial velocity and SINR. Simulation results show that the proposed handover algorithm can effectively reduce the total number of handover, system delay and signaling overhead in the practical CoMP system.

Keywords: CoMP · Handover algorithm · Event trigger mechanism · Cycle selection

1 Introduction

In cellular network system, handover mechanism aims at providing seamless service for users during the moving process. Hence, handover is considered as a key issue of mobility management and an important indicator of cellular network performance.

Meanwhile, CoMP technology has been widely applied in the LTE-A network. As a key technique, CoMP technology reduce inter-cell interference and improve cell-edge throughput as well as system throughput effectively by applying cooperation between independent and decentralized transmission points geographically [1]. There are two kinds of CoMP techniques considered in LTE-A systems, i.e., joint processing (JP) and coordinated scheduling/beamforming (CS/CB). JP supports multiple connections between cooperated BSs and a typical UE while CS/CB only supports a single connection between the serving BS and a typical UE using the scheduling/beamforming parameters decided by the coordination among the cooperated BSs [2]. In the case of JP, if multiple BSs transmit data to a UE on the same frequency resource at the same time and turn interference signal into useful signal, it's known as Joint Transmission

© ICST Institute for Computer Sciences, Social Informatics and Telecommunications Engineering 2018
Q. Chen et al. (Eds.): ChinaCom 2016, Part II, LNICST 210, pp. 401–410, 2018.
DOI: 10.1007/978-3-319-66628-0_38

(JT). And if only one BS transmit data to UE at a time, it's known as Dynamic Cell Selection (DCS).

However, handover scenes have changed a lot when CoMP-JT technology is introduced and the traditional handover algorithms can't meet the requirements of current handover scenes any more. On this basis, there are some relevant researches about CoMP handover algorithms. A detailed analysis of information exchange and signaling transmission among multi-cells or between multi-cells and UE is introduced in [3] according to the existing non-CoMP handover mechanism. [4] proposes a RSRP limited CoMP handover algorithm that considers Physical Resource Block (PRB) utilization, system throughput and system delay. In [5] and [6], the authors propose the handover algorithms based on capacity assessment and capacity performance respectively. Although those algorithms improve system throughput, a minimum number of handover can not be guaranteed because they all ignore the necessity of handover. In [7], a handover scheme based on static coordinating set to reduce the number of unnecessary handovers is proposed, but it is only applicable to the environment with fixed BS density. Therefore, we propose a new CoMP handover algorithm based on dynamic coordinating set that considers of the handover overhead and the necessity of handover.

The rest of this paper is organized as follows. In Sect. 2, the system model using CoMP-JT is introduced in detail. In Sect. 3, radial velocity based CoMP handover algorithm in LTE-A system is proposed. Performance evaluation of the simulation results are presented and analyzed in Sect. 4. Finally, we conclude this study in Sect. 5.

2 System Model

In this paper, there are four units involved in CoMP-JT handover algorithm: measurement set, CCS, CTP and serving cell. Among them, serving cell takes the responsibility of making handover decision and each UE can only attach to one serving cell at each time instant. Measurement set is a cluster of cells whose channel state information (CSI) can be received and reported by UE, and then, UE gives serving cell the feedback. CCS is a set of cells selected from the measurement set by serving cell which participates in data transmission to UE directly or indirectly. A CTP is a set of cells chosen from the CCS by serving cell which directly and simultaneously participate in data transmission to UE. Figure 1 demonstrates an example of CoMP system model in LTE-A system. Where, the serving cell of UE is assumed as cell 1, the measurement set is $\chi_i = \{1, 2, 3, 4, 10, 11, 12\}$, the CCS is $C_i = \{1, 2, 3, 4\}$. Moreover, CTP is a subset of CCS with $\psi_i = \{4, 5\}$.

There are two variables involved in CoMP-JT handover algorithm: handover margin (HOM) and time to trigger (TTT). HOM is a constant variable which represents the threshold for the difference of RSRP between the serving BS and the target BS. HOM ensures the target BS is the most appropriate BS which UE switches its connection to. A handover can only be executed after TTT is met on the time. A combination of TTT and HOM can prevent unnecessary handovers, which is also called Ping Pong effect.

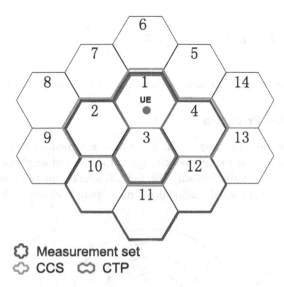

Fig. 1. An illustration of CoMP system model

In CoMP-JT systems, backward compatibility is an important criteria. It means that the emerging handover algorithm can not only be applicable to CoMP handover but also support traditional non-CoMP handover. Based on backward compatibility, this paper no longer distinguishes CoMP UE and non-CoMP UE. Especially, when the size of CTP is one, the UE is represented as non-CoMP UE.

In this paper, we have the following assumptions. The transmit power of each BS is assumed identical and fixed which is expressed by P_0. The channel gains between BS j to UE i can be denoted as $h_{i,j} \cdot r_{i,j}^{-\beta}$ $r_{i,j}^{-\beta}$ is the large-scale fading between BS j and UE i, with, where $r_{i,j}$ denotes the distance and β is the path loss exponent. And $h_{i,j}$ represents the small-scale fading. When the channels follow independent flat Rayleigh fading, the channel power gains are exponentially distributed, i.e., $h_{i,j}$ follows exponential distribution with mean 1. Therefore, the RSRP form BS j to UE i can then be expressed as

$$RSRP_{i,j} = P_0 \cdot h_{i,j} \cdot r_{i,j}^{-\beta} \tag{1}$$

Then the received signal-to-interference and noise ratio (SINR) of UE i in CoMP-JT systems can be given by

$$SINR_i = \frac{\sum_{j \in \psi_i} P_0 \cdot h_{i,j} \cdot r_{i,j}^{-\beta}}{\sum_{m \in \chi, m \notin \psi_i} P_0 \cdot h_{i,m} \cdot r_{i,m}^{-\beta} + \sigma^2} \tag{2}$$

where the noise is additive white Gaussian noise (AWGN) with zero mean and variance σ^2. Therefore, the date rate of UE i is given by

$$R_i = B \cdot \log_2 \left(1 + \frac{\sum_{j \in \psi_i} P_0 \cdot h_{i,j} \cdot r_{i,j}^{-\beta}}{\sum_{m \in \chi, m \notin \psi_i} P_0 \cdot h_{i,m} \cdot r_{i,m}^{-\beta} + \sigma^2} \right) \tag{3}$$

where, B represents the channel bandwidth allocation from each BS of the CTP to UE i.

2.1 User Mobility Prediction

In this section, we propose a user mobility prediction method to improve handover performance. By assessing the relative change in radius from neighboring BSs per unit time which is known as radial velocity [8], the UE selects suitable cooperative cells as CTP set. Figure 2 shows the calculation principle of radial velocity v_r form BS j to UE i.

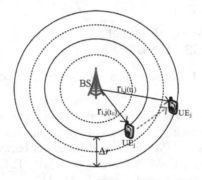

Fig. 2. Calculation principle of radial velocity

Suppose that v_r is constant during the time interval between t_0 and t_1, it can be simply represented by

$$v_r = \frac{r_{i,j}(t_1) - r_{i,j}(t_0)}{t_1 - t_0} \tag{4}$$

From Eq. (4), we can get that UE is moving away from the BS when v_r is positive, and the larger v_r is, the faster UE leaving the BS. UE is closing to the BS when v_r is negative, and the smaller v_r is, and the faster UE closing to the BS.

If we substitute Eq. (1) into Eq. (4), v_r becomes

$$v_r = \frac{1}{P_0^\beta (t_1 - t_0)} \left[\left(\frac{RSRP_{i,j}(t_1)}{h_{i,j}(t_1)} \right)^\beta - \left(\frac{RSRP_{i,j}(t_0)}{h_{i,j}(t_0)} \right)^\beta \right] \tag{5}$$

For the sake of simplicity, $h_{i,j}$ can be considered as a constant variable for the time interval $t_1 - t_0$. We use the mean of $h_{i,j}(t)$, which is represented as $E(h)$, instead of $h_{i,j}(t_1)$ and $h_{i,j}(t_0)$. Then $E(h)$ can be given by

$$E(h) = \int_{t_0}^{t_1} e^{-t}dt = e^{-t_0} - e^{-t_1} \tag{6}$$

Substituting Eq. (6) into Eq. (5), we can get

$$v_r = \frac{RSRP_{i,j}^{\beta}(t_1) - RSRP_{i,j}^{\beta}(t_0)}{P_0^{\beta}(e^{-t_0} - e^{-t_1})^{\beta}(t_1 - t_0)} \tag{7}$$

When choosing the CCS and CTP, UE gives radial velocity a higher priority under the promise of RSRP. During the movement, if the UE has a tendency toward the BS j, i.e., the radial velocity from BS j to the UE is smaller, we give priority to BS j as a candidate BS of CTP. By choosing such a cell as candidate cell, UE can stay connected with that cell for a longer time, which reduces the number of handovers during a call connection.

2.2 Average of RSRP

Caused by the influence of various environmental factors, instantaneous RSRP may cause fluctuation. In this paper, we use the average RSRP to eliminate the influence for convenience. The time interval between t_0 and t_1 is equally divided into N sub-intervals with the length T_m. The average of RSRP form BS j to UE i, which is represented as $E[RSRP_{i,j}]$ and can be obtained as

$$E[RSRP_{i,j}] = \frac{1}{t_1 - t_0} \sum_{n=0}^{N-1} (RSRP_{i,j}(t_1 - n \cdot T_m)) \tag{8}$$

3 CoMP Handover Algorithm

In the mobile terminal, a handover decision process is triggered when the RSRP received from the current network falls below a given threshold or the QoS provided by the networks under a desired threshold of UE [8, 9]. CoMP Handover in LTE-A systems includes not only handover between cells, but also handover of CCS, CTP and the serving cell.

Generally, handover trigger mechanism can be divided into time trigger mechanism and event trigger mechanism. In the existing CoMP handover algorithms, UE gathers measurement reports from the measurement set and feeds the reports back to the serving cell based on time trigger mechanism. Then the serving cell selects a set of cells as CCS from measurement set and selects a set of cells to be CTP from CCS periodically. This allows UE to maintain optimal system throughput but results in a large number of handover and high signaling overhead because handover necessity is not considered.

In this paper, handover process of CCS and CTP is driven by the UE's instantaneous SINR. If the SINR from the current CTP to UE drops below the handover threshold for entire TTT, the election or re-selection of CCS and CTP is executed. The proposed cycle selection algorithm of the CTP set based on radial velocity of UE is shown in Algorithm 1. Where, A PRB is the smallest transmission unit in the downlink LTE-A systems which is the resource of 12 consecutive subcarriers in the frequency-domain and a slot of 0.5 ms in the time-domain. Since handover process is implemented by the serving cell, it sends a cancellation message to the source CTP and interrupts the connection between UE and all cells in the source CTP. Then a new connection is established between UE and the target CTP.

In theory, the more cells participate in cooperating, the better CoMP performance. But in fact, when the number of cooperation cells is large, the throughput gain of CoMP-JT is not necessarily higher as expected after taking the complexity and the overhead into consideration [10]. Therefore, it is not necessary to add cooperation cells when the current cooperation cells is able to meet the QoS requirement of the UE [11]. Specifically, We generally select the size of CTP not larger than four [12].

Algorithm 1

v_j^i : represents radial velocity from BS j to UE i ;

PRB_j : represents RB utilization of BS;

N : represents the maximum size of CTP;

$\gamma_i^{E[RSRP]}, \gamma_i^{RSRP}, \gamma_i^{PRB}$: represent the threshold of $E[RSRP], RSRP, PRB$

1: Input: $RSRP_{i,j}, PRB_j, \gamma_i^{E[RSRP]}, \gamma_i^{RSRP}, \gamma_i^{PRB}$;

2: Output: ψ_i ;

3: measurement set selection of UE i :
   $\chi_i = \{j \mid E[RSRP_{i,j}] < \gamma_i^{E[RSRP]}\}$;

4: CCS selection of UE i : $C_i = \{j \mid RSRP_{i,j} > \gamma_i^{RSRP} and\ PRB_j < \gamma_i^{PRB}\}, j \in \chi$;

5: Calculating the relative radial velocity v_j^i ;

6: Sorting the BSs of the C_i in ascending order
   according to v_r, labeled as $M_i = \{1, 2, \cdots, n\}$, namely,
   n responds to BS with the largest radial velocity.

7: for $k = 1:n, k \leq N$

8:   if $\dfrac{\sum_{j=1}^{k} P_0 \cdot h_{i,j} \cdot r_{i,j}^{-\beta}}{\sum_{j \in \chi} P_0 \cdot h_{i,j} \cdot r_{i,j}^{-\beta} - \sum_{j=1}^{k} P_0 \cdot h_{i,j} \cdot r_{i,j}^{-\beta} + \sigma^2} > \gamma_i^{SINR}$ then

9:       $\psi_i = \{1:k\}$;

10:      break;

11:   else

12:      CCS and CTP will not change.

13:   end if

14: end

After the election or re-selection of CCS and CTP, we need to determine whether the serving cell need to handover. A serving cell handover will be triggered when the triggering condition (9) is satisfied during the entire TTT duration.

$$RSRR_{CTP} > RSRP_S + HOM \qquad (9)$$

where $RSRR_{CTP}$ and $RSRP_S$ are the $RSRP$ received by an UE from the target cell with the maximum RSRP in CTP and the serving cell respectively. Once a handover is triggered, a handover command is sent by the serving cell to instruct the UE to handover to the next serving cell. Otherwise, the current CTP starts transmitting data to the UE and waits for the next measurement period expires.

4 Simulation Results

In this paper, we evaluate the performance of CoMP handover algorithm based on three metrics: total number of handover, handover failure (HOF) rate, and system throughput. In the following part, some numerical results are shown to illustrate the impact of different system characteristics. We assume that UE's direction is randomly between 0 to 2π and stays constant in each time slot. The user's speed is 36 km/h and keeps constant. Other simulation parameters are shown in Table 1.

Table 1. Simulation Parameters

Simulation parameters	Values
Radius	1000 m
System bandwidth	10 MHz
Path loss	$k*r^{\wedge}(-4)$
BS's position	PPP($\lambda = 1e - 5$)
UE's position	Random distribution
Total number of users	20,30,40,50,60,70 and 80
Simulation time	5000 ms
Measurement period	50 ms
TTT	5 ms
System bandwidth	10(Mhz)
The number of subcarriers	600
Size of CCS	no more than 5
Size of CTP	no more than 3

Figure 3 shows the comparison of the total number of handover between the proposed CoMP handover algorithm and capacity based CoMP handover algorithm in LTE-A. As is depicted in Fig. 4, our proposed algorithm has less total number of handover as 20, 51, 81 and 110 times than capacity based CoMP handover algorithm as 38, 85, 129 and 172 times, respectively. That is, the proposed CoMP handover algorithm has a 47.37%, 40%, 37.21% and 36.05% decrease in total number of handover

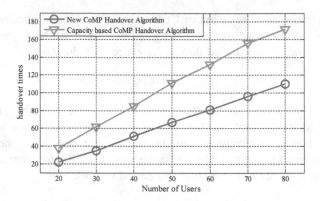

Fig. 3. Total Number of Handover with the change of the number of UE

than existing CoMP handover algorithm in 20, 40, 60 and 80 UE respectively. In conclude, the total number of handovers of the proposed scheme is smaller than that of the existing scheme by analyzing the necessity of handover. this is because the current CTP can meet the service requirements of the UE and the handover of CCS and CTP is not required in the proposed algorithm.

Figure 4 compares the system throughput of new CoMP handover algorithm and capacity based CoMP handover algorithm. We can see that the system throughput is improved with the increase of number of UE. The proposed CoMP handover algorithm provides lower system throughput as 21.60Mbps, 42.08Mbps, 63.25Mbps and 84.29 Mbps, and brings about 8.32%, 6.16%, 6.95% and 6.12% system throughput increase than capacity based CoMP handover algorithm in each scenario of 20, 40, 60 and 80 UE respectively. It is shown that capacity based CoMP handover algorithm has a better throughput because it firstly considers the cells with the best performance to switch periodically, while the proposed algorithm perform doesn't choose the CTP with largest SINR when the current CTP can meet the requirement of UE.

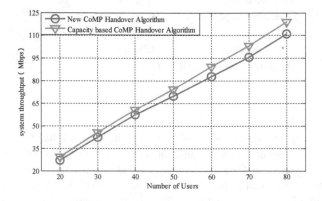

Fig. 4. System throughput with the change of the number of UE

Figure 5 shows the handover fail (HoF) rate comparison between the new CoMP handover algorithm and capacity based CoMP handover algorithm. It is observed that the HoF rate increases as velocity of UE increases, and the increase trend of capacity based CoMP handover algorithm is faster than the new CoMP handover algorithm. In contrast, the new CoMP handover algorithm have less HoF rates, which can be explained that the new CoMP handover algorithm can provide better handover performance, especially in the case of high velocity.

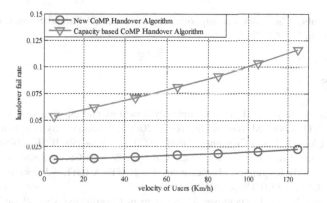

Fig. 5. HoF rates with the change of the velocity of UE

Figure 6 illustrates the comparison of system delay of our proposed CoMP handover algorithm and capacity based CoMP handover algorithm. We can see that the system delay of the proposed algorithm is smaller than that of capacity based CoMP handover algorithm. When number of users is changed from 20 to 80, the proposed handover algorithm results in 9.84%, 8.52%, 10.98%, 9.90%, 9.28%, 7.67% and 8.17% decrease of system delay than capacity based CoMP handover algorithm. This is because we consider a lower loaded cell firstly when making a handover decision.

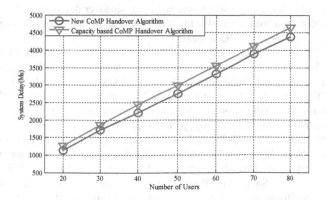

Fig. 6. System Delay with the change of the number of UE

5 Conclusions

In this paper, we propose a radial velocity based CoMP handover algorithm in LTE-A considering the handover necessity and the handover trigger mechanism and the cycle selection of the set of CTP. Simulation results illustrate that radial velocity based CoMP handover algorithm can effectively reduce the total number of handover, the probability of handover failure and the impact of system delay on system performance. Therefore, the proposed mechanism is useful for the practical CoMP-JT system.

Acknowledgments. This work was supported by the National Natural Science Foundation of China under Grant No. 61372117.

References

1. Gao, X., Li, A., Kayama, H.: Low-complexity downlink coordination scheme for multi-user CoMP in LTE-advanced system. In: IEEE 20th International Symposium on Personal, Indoor and Mobile Radio Communications, 2009, pp. 355–359. IEEE (2009)
2. 3rd Generation Partnership Project; Technical Specification Group Radio Access Network, "Feasibility study for further advancements for E-UTRA (LTE-Advanced) (Release 11)," 3GPP TR36.912 V11.0.0,Sept. 2012
3. Xu, X., Chen, X., Li, J.: Handover Mechanism in Coordinated Multi-Point Transmission/Reception System. Zte Commun. **1**, 31–35 (2010)
4. Lin, C.C., Sandrasegaran, K., Zhu, X., et al.: Limited comp handover algorithm for LTE-advanced. J. Eng. **2013**(1), 2314–4912 (2013)
5. Lin, C.C., Sandrasegaran, K., Zhu, X., et al.: Performance evaluation of capacity based CoMP handover algorithm for LTE-Advanced. In: International Symposium on Wireless Personal Multimedia Communications, pp. 236–240. IEEE (2012)
6. Lin, C.C., Sandrasegaran, K., Zhu, X., et al.: On the performance of capacity integrated CoMP handover algorithm in LTE-Advanced. In: 18th Asia-Pacific Conference on Communications (APCC), 2012, pp. 871–876. IEEE (2012)
7. Nakano, A., Saba, T.: A handover scheme based on signal power of coordinated base stations for CoMP joint processing systems. In: 8th International Conference on Signal Processing and Communication Systems (ICSPCS), 2014. IEEE (2014)
8. Gu, J., Bae, S.J., Min, Y.C., et al.: Mobility-based handover decision mechanism to relieve ping-pong effect in cellular networks. In: 16th Asia-Pacific Conference on Communications (APCC), 2010, pp. 487–491. IEEE (2010)
9. Boujelben, M., Ben Rejeb, S., Tabbane, S.: A novel mobility-based COMP handover algorithm for LTE-A/ 5G HetNets. In: 23rd International Conference on Software, Telecommunications and Computer Networks (SoftCOM), 2015. IEEE (2015)
10. Caire, G., Ramprashad, S.A., Papadopoulos, H.C.: Rethinking network MIMO: cost of CSIT, performance analysis, and architecture comparisons. In: Information Theory and Applications Workshop (ITA), 2010, pp. 1–10 (2010)
11. Karam, F.W., Jensen, T.: A QoS based handover decision (Nearest Performance Handover) algorithm for Next Generation Networks. In: 8th International Conference on Computing Technology and Information Management (ICCM), 2012, pp. 554–560. IEEE (2012)
12. Liu, M., Teng, Y., Song, M.: Performance analysis of coordinated multipoint joint transmission in ultra-dense networks with limited backhaul capacity. Electron. Lett. **51**(25), 2111–2113 (2015)

Optimized Traffic Breakout and Mobility Support for WLAN and Cellular Converging Network

Gang Liu[⊠]

School of Statistics and Management,
Shanghai University of Finance and Economics, 200433 Shanghai, China
lgslr@163.com

Abstract. In order to cope with the traffic exploding, operators are looking for offloading solutions which can efficiently offload high-volume Internet traffic from not only mobile access but also mobile core network. WLAN requires no expensive network planning and leverages unlicensed spectrum to add capacity. To expand the reach of revenue-generating services and applications, operators can make use of already-existing WLAN networks. The paper presents a new product concept of Wireless Access Broker (WAB) as well as the innovation solution on how to provide network-based IP flow mobility support and Internet traffic breakout. In contrast with current solutions, this new solution enables the legacy UE to support selective IP flow offloading to the WLAN network. Unlike the IFOM solution defined in 3GPP, our solution does not require the UE to install DSMIPv6 stack and related interacting module. Serving as a breakout point, WAB enables the Internet traffic directly bypass through the fixed access network while bringing no effect on other network elements.

Keywords: WLAN · Convergence · Selective IP flow mobility · Internet breakout

1 Introduction

Due to the ever growing mobile data (including mobile Internet) in the network, the operators are looking for offloading solutions which can efficiently offload high-volume Internet traffic from not only mobile access but also mobile core network.

Wi-Fi has provided tangible data offload benefits to its main proponents, which has helped offload the growth in mobile data traffic from the radio access network at low cost. The technology can also offer an improved user experience, through faster, less congested connectivity and improved indoor coverage [1]. Major operators (AT&T, Verizon, CT, CMCC. etc.) are starting to explore integrated cellular-WLAN solutions. However, the major challenge for operators is how to integrate WLAN into operator's network and maintain the services continuity while the UE moving between the cellular and WLAN network [12].

This paper presents a new product concept of Wireless Access Broker (WAB) as well as the innovation solution on how to construct a telecom WLAN network in operator's network. WAB is designated for the purpose of integrating WLAN into

© ICST Institute for Computer Sciences, Social Informatics and Telecommunications Engineering 2018
Q. Chen et al. (Eds.): ChinaCom 2016, Part II, LNICST 210, pp. 411–420, 2018.
DOI: 10.1007/978-3-319-66628-0_39

operator's network to extend network coverage, add Wi-Fi mobility to the network, and also offload cellular traffic from both mobile access network and mobile core network.

The remainder of this paper is organized as follows. Section 2 introduces some related research and standardization activities in the area of WLAN & 3G/LTE network interworking, especially on the handover and IP flow mobility support. A brief introduction of WAB is presented in Sect. 3. Enhanced IP flow mobility solution and optimized upstream traffic breakout mechanism are provided in Sects. 4 and 5 respectively. Section 6 gives the performance analysis of our approach, followed by the conclusion Sect. 7.

2   Related Work

The 3rd Generation Partnership Project (3GPP) standard is specifying architectures for the WLAN and 3GPP networks interworking [2–4]. The interworking between WLAN and 3GPP systems is provided by connecting WLAN to the EPS through an ePDG (evolved Packet Data Gateway) or directly by connecting the UE through WLAN to the P-GW as depicted in the Fig. 1 below

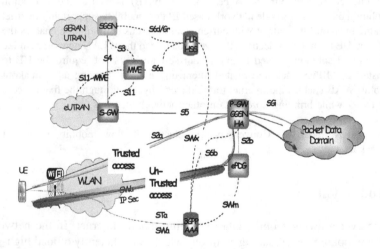

Fig. 1. WLAN/3GPP interworking architecture

Currently, 3GPP is also standardizing support for IP flow mobility and seamless WLAN offload [8] building the solution on Dual-stack Mobile IPv6 [6], multi-homing [7], and flow-based mobility handling [10] using traffic selectors [11]. The goal is to provide mobile data offload support for LTE networks allowing multimode terminals to move certain flows to WLAN hotspots when overlapping coverage is available in the proximity of the terminal.

DSMIPv6 [6] is used to provide mobility between 3GPP and I-WLAN with service continuity e.g. IP address preservation for the UE. The Home Agent may be co-located with GGSN or PDG and terminates the DSMIPv6 signaling within the network. This signaling is transparent to GGSN and PDG. The UE needs to be enhanced by a DSMIPv6 Client to enable the DSMIPv6 based signaling towards the Home Agent. The UE has to initiate DSMIPv6 specific signaling towards the Home Agent to create a binding in the HA and to register its care-of-address. This will, on one side, establish the DSMIPv6 tunnel between the HA and the UE, and on the other side, ensure that mobile terminated traffic is routed by the HA towards the correct access network.

Since the UE registers to the HA and builds DSMIPv6 tunnel to it, all the traffic from UE need to be transported to the HA through this tunnel no matter which access network the UE is connecting. Unlike the MIPv4 protocol [5], there is no other mobility anchor (FA, Foreign Agent) to enable the upstream traffic breakout. For the large amount of Internet or other 3rd party application services, this solution is not efficient enough due to the aggregation point locating at the mobile core network.

IP Flow Mobility (IFOM) defined in 3GPP Rel-10 [4] introduces the concept of treating IP flows individually within a PDN connection. It specifies that the mobility of a PDN connection is handled per IP flow. This means within a PDN connection the following operations can be performed:

(1) Establishment of IP flows over multiple accesses.
(2) Selective removal of IP flows from an access system.
(3) Selective transfer of IP flows between access systems.
(4) Transfer of all IP flows from a certain access system.

This requires some DSMIPv6 extensions to allow the registration of multiple addresses simultaneously [7]. More specifically, the extensions defined for DSMIPv6 have the capability to register multiple local addresses (i.e., CoAs) to a single permanent address (i.e., HoA), and also the capability to bind different IP flows (i.e., HTTP, Video, VoIP, etc.) to different CoA(Care-of address) or directly to HoA (Home-of address) (Fig. 2).

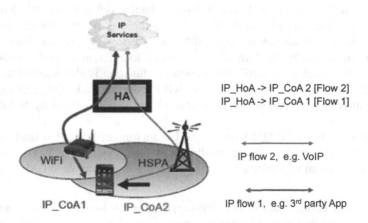

Fig. 2. IFOM solution

3 Wireless Access Broker

The product concept of Wireless Access Broker (WAB, shown in Fig. 3) is proposed to integrate WLAN networks into telecom network and interwork with mobile core network. It relieves cellular network from heavy traffic load while bypassing Internet traffic. In handover scenario, it acts as a mobility anchor and breakout upstream data traffic directly which can efficiently reduce the data flow to the mobile core network.

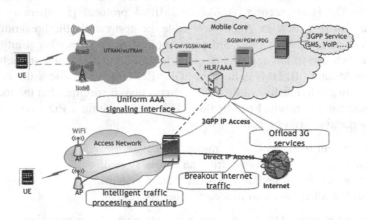

Fig. 3. WAB solution

Providing standard data and signaling interface to cellular network, WAB enables dual mode UE to access 3GPP services through WLAN network. With intelligent traffic processing and routing mechanism, WAB can breakout Internet traffic while bypassing the macro RAN and mobile core. Providing the NAT function, WAB maintains multiple global IP address to setup backhaul to different network domain. UE only obtains a local IP address from WAB, so there is no requirement for UE to maintain different IP address to access different services. WAB can distinguish the different destination of traffic from UE, and routes it to different network domain. Since the traffic is bypassed from WAB, the accounting function is also implemented in the WAB with the signaling interface to the 3GPP core network. Other charging and management functions (e.g. lawful interception) are also supported by WAB for the operation purpose.

Current definition of IFOM requires the UE to support DSMIPv6 stack and other interacting module which may be a hurdle for its deployment. The WAB provides an enhanced mechanism to implement IP flow mobility in cellular & WLAN converging network.

(1) It provides network-based mobility support for IPv4-enabled UE to register its CoAs and routing filter. Through this new mechanism, the legacy UE can support IP flow mobility without any requirements on DSMIPv6 stack and register module.

(2) The mobility anchor in the WAB maintains the CoA address for each UE while the UE only configures one IP on its dual network interfaces.

(3) The mobility anchor in the WAB serves as a pseudo UE to perform HA discovery and binding update. It also interacts with the HA for routing policy transfer.

(4) Serving as a breakout point, WAB enables the Internet traffic breakout through the fixed access network while bringing no effect on other network elements.

In handover scenario, the WAB acts as a mobility anchor and breakout upstream data traffic directly which can efficiently reduce the data flow to the mobile core network. A new routing module in WAB performs package interception and flow control to breakout the upstream Internet traffic. This routing module captures the upstream data package from UE and identifies the real destination address. According to the destination information, WAB decides whether the package is to be encapsulated and transported to mobile core network. If the destination IP address indicates that the package need to be delivered to the Internet or other 3rd party applications domain, this routing module in WAB directly bypasses the package without any tunnel encapsulation through the fixed wireline network.

4 Enhanced Mobility Mechanism for Selective IP Flow

3GPP/WLAN mobility using DSMIP as per 3GPP Rel-8 provides a solution for seamless WLAN offload where all traffic is offloaded to the WLAN. However, it may be desired that in some scenarios only some traffic is moved to the WLAN while other IP flows are maintained over the 3G access. This requires some DSMIPv6 extensions to allow the registration of multiple addresses simultaneously. These protocol extensions, known as IP Flow Mobility (IFOM), are part of 3GPP Rel-10 [4] and introduce the capability to move selective IP traffic – a new dimension in flexibility. This definition of IFOM requires the UE to support a DSMIPv6 stack and related interacting functions which may be a hurdle for its deployment.

To optimize this mobility solution, a mobility anchor is proposed to support the legacy UE with IFOM function. The mobility anchor is located in the WLAN network and help UE to register the CoA and routing filter to the HA/P-GW. The UE only obtains the HoA address from EPS/P-GW when it performs the initial PDN connection establishment through the 3GPP air interface. The conventional UE may configure it on the dual network interfaces. This is called one address on two interfaces. The UE uses the HoA address to access the WLAN network all along since only the HoA address is configured on the Wi-Fi interface of the UE. In contrast with the DSMIPv6 solution defined in Rel.10, our solution does not need to configure one or more CoA addresses for each UE which can significantly save the address resource. Through the WLAN connection procedure, the mobility anchor obtains the HoA/HA address of the UE and performs the HA discovery as well as the DSMIPv6 bootstrapping process substituting for the UE.

When the conventional UE connects to the WLAN and completes the WLAN link establishment with the HoA address obtained cellular network, the mobility anchor serves as a pseudo UE to send BU message which is used to register the CoA and routing filter to the HA/P-GW. The CoA address may be a local address or the IP address of the mobility anchor itself, which can be routed from the HA. The mobility anchor maintains the CoA address for each UE while the UE does not need to configure this IP address. The mobility anchor request the HA to store routing filters so that one or more flows can be associated to a registered CoA. Furthermore, the HA needs to identify individual flows, then it can route a particular flow through a particular access. The work procedure is shown in Fig. 4. The mobility anchor performs the package encapsulate/de-encapsulate function when the traffic arrives.

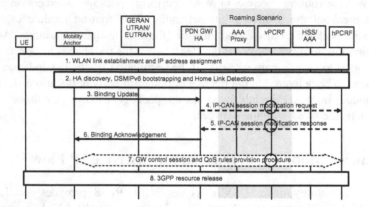

Fig. 4. Work procedure of IFOM support for the legacy UE

This solution can be utilized to enhance the S2c interface in Rel-8 EPS mobility architecture so that it supports this flow level granularity (i.e. flow binding). The IETF extension to DSMIPv6 introduces a new Flow Identification mobility option [9], which is included in the BU message and can be used to distribute routing filters to the recipient of the BU. Using the Flow Identification mobility option, the mobility anchor can bind one or more flows to a CoA while maintaining the reception of other flows on another CoA. Requesting the flow binding can be decided based on local policies within the WLAN network, e.g. link characteristics, types of applications running at the time, etc.

In order to allow the WLAN network elements indicate the HA/P-GW through which access technology PDN connections/IP flows are expected to be routed, inter system routing policies are introduced. Such policies can be defined per APN, per IP flow class under any APN or per IP flow class under a specific APN and can be provided to the UE either through ANDSF [3] or by means of static pre-configuration. The interacting module in the mobility anchor extends DSMIPv6 basic support to allow it to specify policies associated with each binding and even to each flow through individual routing filters. The routing filters are unidirectional and can be different for uplink and downlink traffic. A policy can contain a request for a special treatment of a particular IP flow, e.g. QoS.

We note that there are some concerns about the difference between our method and the Proxy MIP mechanism. We would like to make some clarifications. Firstly, the Proxy MIP is adaptive for the use case that the mobile node makes handover between different access points with one network interface. The PMIP can substitute for the mobile node to de/encapsulate the MIP packets while the mobile node needs to do noting and just keeps the IP address unchanged on the network adapter. In cellular & WLAN converged network, the mobile nodes would have two network interfaces. Basically the mobile nodes would obtain two different IP addresses for accessing the two networks separately. If we use the PMIP mechanism here, the session would be disrupted because the IP address has changed. Secondly, the PMIP is designed for the one interface scenarios. Even with our method that one address is configured on dual interfaces, the PMIP cannot support the selective IP flow mobility. Because the PMIP protocol only supports fully handover between different access points, all the IP flows would be transferred to the destination access point when the handover occurs. Thirdly, the PMIP cannot support the multiple CoAs maintained for one mobile node. So it can not differentiate the service class between multiple IP flows of one mobile node. Our solution help one mobile node to register multiple CoAs which facilitates the differentiation of multiple IP flow classes even these IP flows are over the same the accesses and the same APN manner. The PMIP mechanism cannot support this feature.

5 Optimized Breakout for Upstream Traffic

In current 3GPP defined interworking solution, as dashed line shown in Fig. 5, when the UE accesses to the cellular network and wants to communicate with the correspondent node in the Internet, the destination IP address of the upstream packages is the correspondent node's IP (162.105.203.16). While the UE is roaming to the WLAN network, it obtains a CoA address (172.24.149.166) and notifies the HA of the new binding information. A DSMIPv6 tunnel is built between the UE and the HA and all the upstream packages from the UE are transmitted through the tunnel no matter whether the correspondent node locates in the mobile core network or not. The UE encapsulates the original packages with the destination IP address set as the HA addresses and delivers through the DSMIP tunnel. When the HA receives the upstream packages from the tunnel, it decapsulates the packages and routes the original packages to the correspondent node. For the large amount of Internet or other 3rd party

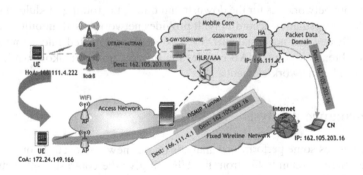

Fig. 5. Current DSMIP mechanism

application services, this solution is not efficient enough due to the aggregation point (HA) locating at the mobile core network.

To optimize this mobility solution, a new routing module is introduced in the WAB which is designated for the purpose of integrating WLAN into operator's network and offloading cellular traffic from cellular network. This routing module performs package interception function and makes en/decapsulation on the packages substituting for the UE. WAB has the capability to identify the destination address of the original data packages transmitted from the legacy UE which does not support DSMIPv6 protocol. It substitutes for the legacy UE to perform MIP signal processing and interworking with HA for the purpose of mobility support. According to the destination information in the upstream package, the WAB decides whether the package is delivered through fixed wireline network directly. If the destination IP address indicates that the correspondent nodes locates in the 3GPP network domain, this routing module will encapsulate the package with DSMIPv6 head and set the HA IP address as the destination address. On the other hand, as the red line shown in Fig. 6, the original package to the correspondent node which locates in the Internet will be offloaded directly by the WAB through the fixed wireline network.

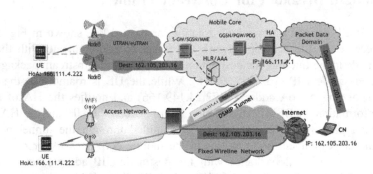

Fig. 6. WAB-based routing mechanism (Color figure online)

With this package interception and traffic processing function, WAB can offload the upstream Internet traffic in mobility scenario which efficiently relieves the traffic load of the mobile core network. As for the downstream traffic, the routing module in the WAB performs the decapsulation accordingly. It provides network-based mobility support for the legacy UE that has not installed DSMIPv6 stack and related interacting modules. Serving as a breakout point, WAB enables the Internet traffic breakout while bringing no effect on other network elements.

6   Performance Analysis

This section gives some performance analysis on our new approach. In our simulation, we estimate the upstream traffic from the UE and give the contrast result between our approach and 3GPP approach.

We assume that there are 1000 APs (Access Points) in the WLAN network and 10 active UEs under each AP on average. In the simulated scenario, each active UE transmits Internet upstream data with the rate of 100 packages per second, and we suppose that there are at least 2 more network entities (e.g. router, switch, gateway) the upstream packets need to be transmitted through when these packages are transported via the mobile core network than they are offloaded through fixed access network directly. In our assumption, each intermediate network entity is equipped with 1Gbps interface which is used to process the traffic.

For a standard IPv6 package, the package head of IP layer is 40-bytes in length. Since the WAB would encapsulate the DSMIP package head with the original package when transmitting it to the mobile core network, there are 40 bytes more data for each package to be transmitted through the mobile core network than the fixed access network. We investigate the total processing time when the upstream Internet packages are transmitted through two different paths and define it as the transportation cost. In our contrast test, we calculate the total transportation cost under two variable quantities. The one variable quantity is the average package length of UE's upstream traffic. The other factor is the intermediate network entities that the packages are transmitted through.

The two charts below give the simulation result of our WAB-based solution and 3GPP solution respectively (Fig. 7).

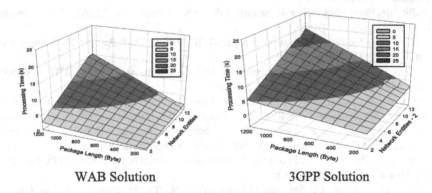

WAB Solution   3GPP Solution

Fig. 7. Transportation cost of two solutions

In the above figure of 3GPP solution, it needs to note that the actual amount of network entities is 2 more than the described value in the X axis. In order to contrast the two mechanisms efficiently, we keep the X-axis value aligned in two figures. As we mentioned before, we assume that there are at least 2 more entities the upstream packages need to be transmitted through in the 3GPP mechanism than our mechanism.

Since the routing module in WAB directly bypasses the upstream Internet traffic through the fixed wireline network, our solution can efficiently relieve the cellular network from heavy traffic load. Due to the less intermediate entities and shorter package length, WAB solution also evidently reduces the processing time and network delay as well. The contrast figures show that the transport cost of 3GPP solution is obviously higher than our WAB solution.

7   Conclusion

This paper introduces an efficient routing mechanism to support mobility between cellular network and WLAN network. In contrast with the DSMIPv6 solution, our solution offloads the upstream Internet traffic through the fixed wireline network which can efficiently relieve the cellular network from heavy traffic load. Serving as a mobility anchor, the network-based mobility support is provided by the WAB in the WLAN network. It helps the UE to send BU message which is used to register the CoA and routing filter to the HA/P-GW. Through this new mechanism, the conventional UE can support selective IP flow offloading to the WLAN network, while maintaining connectivity to the same PDN connection via the 3GPP radio interface.

References

1. Handa, A.: Mobile Data Offload for 3G Network, October 2009. A White Paper from www.intellinet-tech.com/Media/PagePDF/Data%20Offload.pdf
2. 3GPP. 3GPP system to Wireless Local Area Network (WLAN) interworking, System description. TS 23.234, 3rd Generation Partnership Project (3GPP)
3. 3GPP. Architecture enhancements for non-3GPP accesses. TS 23.402, 3rd Generation Partnership Project (3GPP)
4. 3GPP. IP Flow Mobility and Seamless WLAN Offload. TS 23.261, 3rd Generation Partnership Project (3GPP)
5. Perkins, C. (ed.): IP mobility support for IPv4. IETF RFC 3344, August 2002. http://www.ietf.org/rfc/rfc3344.txt
6. Soliman, H. (ed.): Mobile ipv6 support for dual stack hosts and routers. IETF RFC 5555, June 2009. http://www.ietf.org/rfc/rfc5201.txt
7. Wakikawa, R., Devarapalli, V., Tsirtsis, G., Ernst, T., Nagami, K. (eds.): Multiple Care-of Addresses Registration. IETF RFC 5648, October 2009. http://www.ietf.org/rfc/rfc5648.txt
8. Gundavelli, S., Leung, K., Devarapalli, V., Chowdhury, K., Patil, B. (eds.): Proxy mobile ipv6. IETF RFC 5201, August 2008. http://www.ietf.org/rfc/rfc5201.txt
9. Johnson, D., Perkins, C., Arkko, J.: IP mobility support in ipv6. IETF RFC 3775, June 2004. http://www.ietf.org/rfc/rfc3775.txt
10. Tsirtsis, G., Giaretta, G., Soliman, H., Montavont, N.: Traffic selectors for flow bindings. IETF RFC 6088, January 2011. http://www.ietf.org/rfc/rfc6088.txt
11. Tsirtsis, G., Soliman, H., N. Montavont, G. Giaretta, and K. Kuladinithi. Flow bindings in mobile ipv6 and nemo basic support. IETF RFC 5201, January 2011. http://www.ietf.org/rfc/rfc5201.txt
12. Naik, G.I., et al.: LTE WLAN Interworking for Wi-Fi hotspots. In: The Second International Conference on Communication Systems and Networks, January 2011

Application of Mobile IP in the Space-Ground Network Based on GEO Satellites

Feng Liu[1,2,3,4], Han Wu[1,2,3,4(✉)], and Xiaoshen Xu[5]

[1] School of Electronic and Engineering, Beihang University, Beijing, China
liuf@buaa.edu.cn, wuhan19920624@163.com
[2] The Collaborative Innovation Center of Geospatial Technology, Wuhan, China
[3] Beijing Key Laboratory for Network-Based Cooperative Air Traffic
Management (No. BZ0272), Beijing, China
[4] Beijing Laboratory for General Aviation Technology,
Beijing, People's Republic of China
[5] Beijing Space Information Relay and Transmission Research Center,
Beijing, China

Abstract. Current space-ground IP networks cannot achieve real-time signaling interaction between aircraft users and GEO freely in large service ranges, so there is packet drop rate when aircraft users hand off between different GEO satellites. This paper proposes a new scheme to provide seamless handover service for aircraft users. Since the control center can obtain the orbit and position of aircraft can be obtained timely and accurately, during the handover process, it initiates the control signaling in different aspects to fulfill a complete handover process based on standard mobile IP protocol. Compared with other schemes, the proposed scheme can reduce packet drop rate in the handover process. Moreover, the time delay for data transmission is reduced based on mobile IPv6 technique.

Keywords: Space-ground IP network · Mobile IP · Handover management

1 Introduction

With the development of space technology, the demand of real-time and reliable communication between space station and ground become more obvious. Currently, the communication between ground users and aircraft users is achieved with the help of GEO satellites through directional antennas [1]. Since the GEO satellites' directional antennas can only cover a relatively small area in their wide service ranges, it is difficult for aircraft users to initiate the communication with GEO satellites [1]. Besides, the real-time signaling interaction between aircraft users and GEO satellites cannot be achieved freely [3], as a result, standard mobile IP protocol [4] fails to work when aircraft flies through service ranges of different GEO satellites. Therefore, it is difficult to maintain reliable and continuous data transmission from ground users to aircraft users.

Nowadays, several solutions are proposed to solve the above problems. The Centralized Static Routing [5] establishes some possible routing sets for users to choose

© ICST Institute for Computer Sciences, Social Informatics and Telecommunications Engineering 2018
Q. Chen et al. (Eds.): ChinaCom 2016, Part II, LNICST 210, pp. 421–430, 2018.
DOI: 10.1007/978-3-319-66628-0_40

when handover between aircraft users and GEO satellites happens. This scheme is applicable in small scale networks, but causes large calculation pressure in network management. Another solution is mobile router, a software resided in a network. It takes care of handover process in the network, and allows the whole network to roam [6]. However, during handover, the mobile router have to obtain care-of address and register with home agent (ground station1 in this paper) [7], which causes high delay and packets loss, especially in long distance space-ground network.

This paper proposes a new scheme based on mobile IP to present reliable and continuous data transmission in space-ground IP networks. The scheme ensures that aircraft can achieve seamless handover between different satellites. Under the premise that the orbit information and position of aircraft can be obtained timely and accurately by control center during the handover process, the control center can initiate the control signaling, including changing directions of antennas on GEO satellites, assigning new IP addresses for aircraft users and establishing IP address mapping table in ground station, sending multicast data to all of the ground stations. Thus the complete handover process of standard mobile IP protocol can be achieved without real-time signaling interaction between aircraft users and GEO satellites. Moreover, in order to reduce the time delay from ground users to aircraft users after handover, the scheme is improved with techniques in mobile IPv6 [9] to overcome the problem of "triangle routing" [8, 10].

In this paper, Sect. 2 introduces basic scenario of the space-ground IP network. Section 3 describes the operating modes of standard mobile IP and proposes solutions for mobile IP based on the space-ground network. Section 4 presents simulation analysis, including experimental simulation parameters, results and descriptions. Section 5 is the conclusion.

2   Description of Basic Scenario

The space-ground IP network mainly consists of two parts, the ground part and the space part [2].

As shown in Fig. 1, the ground part includes:

(1) Control center: manages the basic information about entire network.
(2) Ground stations: provide service for GEO satellites.
(3) Ground users: terminal users on earth, which are connected with space-ground network through internet.

The space part includes:

(1) GEO satellites: provide transparent forwarding between aircraft and ground stations. The radius of service range of GEO satellites is about 2.5×10^6 m. The radius of cover area of directional antennas is about 1×10^5 m, which is much less than the radius of service range.
(2) Aircraft users: terminal users in space.

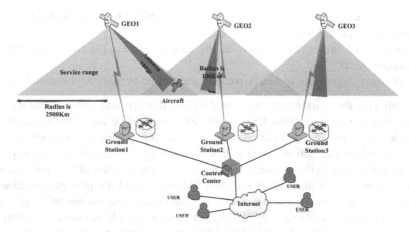

Fig. 1. Basic scenario of the space-ground IP network. It includes space part (GEO satellites and aircraft) and ground part (ground stations, control center and users). The radius of service range of GEO is 2.5×10^6 m, the radius of antenna range is 1×10^5 m. Control center can management the entire network.

2.1   Process of Handover Management

This scenario describes the process that aircraft users cross the network segments made by GEO satellites, using handover management to maintain normal communication with ground users. The specific process is given below:

When the aircraft is in the service range of the GEO1, the business data from ground user is encapsulated into IP packets to be routed to the control center, after processing, packets are forwarded to the ground station 1, and then the ground station1 transmits them to GEO1. Finally packets are delivered to aircraft user. When the aircraft user flies into service range of the GEO2, the connection between aircraft and ground becomes ground station 2. In the ground network, packets are routed according to IP address, ground user does not know the IP address of the aircraft has changed, so the packets are still routed to ground station 1 in accordance with the previous address, which causes communication error. Thus mobile IP is needed to solve the problem.

2.2   Overview of Mobile IP

Mobile IP has three basic elements: mobile node, home agent, foreign agent [4].
Protocol overview is as following:

(1) When mobile node is in the home network, it will be assigned an address, which is called home address. For user, this address is mobile node's permanent address [4].
(2) When mobile node moves to a foreign network, it obtains a care-of address [4] from foreign agent, then mobile node registers its new care-of address with home agent.

(3) Host sends packets to mobile node, via standard IP routing mechanism transmitting the packet to the home agent.
(4) Home agent tunnels the packets to the care-of address [4] (usually address of foreign agent).
(5) The foreign agent decapsulates packets and transmits them to the mobile node.

The above is the working mechanism of mobile IP in ground network, but it cannot be applied in the space-ground IP network. Because mobile node, home agent, and foreign agent are demanded to periodically broadcast their status, so that they can have frequent signaling interaction. Thus it has a very high demand for real-time performance and reliability to the network. However, the characteristics of the space network are long distance, high time delay, complex link status, and the present conditions of GEO satellites can only communicate with directional antenna, the aircraft is unable to detect and connect to GEO actively. So ground-based mobile IP network obviously can not meet the requirements of space-ground IP network, which need to improve existing schemes (Fig. 2).

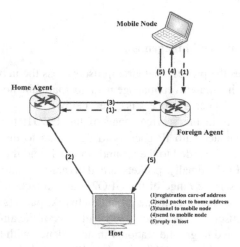

Fig. 2. Overview of mobile IP. The mobile node, home agent and foreign agent periodically broadcast their status, and have frequent signaling interaction.

3   Solution Scheme

This paper proposes revised schemes based on standard mobile IP to solve the problem that the signaling interaction between GEO satellites and aircraft users is not real-time, and the handover process exists packet loss and high time delay. Particularly, the ground station 1 is equivalent to the home agent, the ground station 2 is equivalent to the foreign agent, the aircraft is a mobile node, the control center schedules the entire network.

3.1   Scheme 1

This scheme is proposed on the condition that control center have real-time status information about aircraft (flight obit, position, flight time), and can send signaling to each node and schedule them. It can achieve seamless handover.

(1) Initial condition

When the aircraft is in the service range of GEO1, the transmission path of user data is ground user → control center → station 1 → GEO1 → aircraft.

(2) Set the trigger condition

The trigger condition can be flight time or the position of the aircraft. When the aircraft enters into the overlapping coverage of the two satellites, control center sends signaling to GEO2, which is to let the antenna of GEO2 begin to swing in the direction of GEO1.

(3) Send multicast data to ground stations

When the aircraft enters into the overlapping coverage, the control center sends the data, which is from users, to all of the ground stations. This progress is multicast, which continues to the end of the handover. Using multicast mechanism can guarantee data from users send to all of the ground stations at the same time, including the home agent ground station1 and the foreign agent ground station2. Ground stations store the received data till the aircraft connected with the GEO2, then the data is sent to the aircraft via the GEO2. This progress can result in some data packets are repeatedly received, but can ensure seamless handover.

(4) Establish home agent mapping table

Control center sends the IP address of the ground station 2 to the ground station 1, then the ground station 1 establishes an address mapping table. That is to say, when the aircraft left the service range of GEO1, the data packets via the mapping table are routed from the ground station 1 to the ground station 2.

(5) Assign a new address to aircraft

After establishing the mapping table, control center assign a new IP address to aircraft, which is in the same network segment with the IP address of the GEO2.

(6) Connect GEO2 and aircraft

The antenna of GEO2 is aligned with the aircraft and builds connection, the connection is generally assumed that is instantaneous. Since the ground stations are not connected with each other, they all connect to the control center, the transmission path of the packets is user → control center → ground station 1 → control center → ground station 2 → GEO2 → aircraft.

Since the number of nodes in this scene is small, the connection between aircraft and the next satellite is obvious. Therefore, after the aircraft entered in the overlapping range of the two satellites, the control center can adjust network by sending signaling. It sends the GEO2 instructions, so that the GEO2 has enough time to adjust the antenna, which can improve the probability of successful connection. Besides, it assigns care-of address to aircraft so that aircraft can connect with GEO2. This scheme can achieve seamless handover, on the condition that the connection is instantaneous.

3.2   Scheme 2

The above scheme is proposed based on Mobile IPv4, which can achieve seamless handover between two satellites. However, it still is not good enough because of "triangular routing". Inspired by banding update mechanism of Mobile IPv6 [9], we proposed an optimization routing scheme, called Mobile IPv4-E.

In Mobile IPv4-E, steps of (1), (2), (3), (4), (5) and (6) are the same as the first scheme, additional step is that:

When the handover is completed, the user establishes an address mapping table. Packets should be sent to the ground station 1 are mapped to the ground station 2. Thus, the transmission path of the packets in this scheme is user → control center → ground station 2 → GEO2 → aircraft.

Compared with the first scheme, the transmission path of each packet can decrease by two hops, which can reduce the transmission delay in the ground network. Figure 3 is the Schematic diagram of scheme 1 and scheme 2.

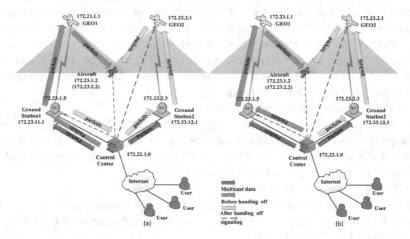

Fig. 3. Schematic diagram of (a) scheme 1 and (b) scheme 2. The green strips are the packet transmission path before the handover, the yellow strips are the transmission path after the handover, the dotted line is signaling, the blue strips are the multicast data sent from control center to all of the ground stations. The difference between scheme 1 and scheme 2 is in the ground network, after the handover, scheme 2 can decrease the transmission path by two hops. (Color figure online)

4   Simulation and Analysis

The simulation was carried out on an discrete-event system simulation platform. The simulation scenario includes two GEO satellites, an aircraft, two ground stations, a control center and several ground users. Basic parameters about network nodes are shown in Table 1. The height is the distance to the center of the earth. The care-of address is 172.23.2.2.

Table 1. Basic parameters of the each node.

Node name	Height\m	Latitude	Longitude	IP address
GEO1	4.2×10^7	0°	16° E	172.23.1.1
GEO2	4.2×10^7	0°	108° E	172.23.2.1
Ground station 1	6.4×10^6	39° N	101° E	172.23.1.5
Ground station 2	6.4×10^6	34° N	116° E	172.23.2.3
Control center	6.4×10^6	34° N	108° E	172.22.1.0
User	6.4×10^6	20° N	105° E	172.23.3.1
Aircraft	6.7×10^6	——	——	172.23.1.2

4.1 Parameters of the Simulation

Besides, the bandwidth of the forward link (ground station → GEO) is 10 M, the backward link (GEO → ground station) is 25 M, the ground link is 100 M, the buffer size of link is 10 M, the sending rate of packets randomly changes between 5 M to 15 M bps, transmission delay in the ground network is 10 ms.

4.2 Result of Simulation

Compared among the mobile router scheme [6], scheme 1 and scheme 2 proposed in this paper, we can get the result:

The mobile router scheme is proposed in [6], which adds a software, called mobile router, into the space-ground network, so device connected with mobile node is unaware of mobility [7]. The mobile router asks for care-of address and then registers it with ground station, this process has delay, which causes packet losing.

Figure 4 shows that the received packet percent of scheme 1 and scheme 2 can achieve 100%, that is to say control center sends signaling to manage GEO and aircraft, cooperated with the multicast data sent from control center to ground stations, can effectively achieve seamless handover.

Another question we concerned is end to end transmission delay. According to the relationship of the distance, time, and the speed of light, the transmission delay

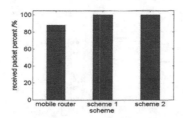

Fig. 4. Received packet percent in different schemes. The received packet percent is defined as the number of received packets divided by the number of sending packets. The received packet percent is statisticsed from the time that the aircraft entries the overlapping service range, to the time that the handover is completed.

between ground station and GEO is about 0.12 s, assume that transmission delay in the ground network is 0.01 s. The simulation result of end to end packet delay in each position can be seen in Table 2.

Table 2. End to end packet delay of the handover process.

Position of the aircraft	Transmission path	End to end delay/s
Before handover	user → control center → ground station 1 → GEO1 → aircraft	0.25
During handover multicast	user → control center → ground station ground station 2 (store the multicast data) → GEO2 → aircraft	0.73
After handover Scheme 1	user → control center → ground station 1 → control center → ground station 2 → GEO2 → aircraft	0.75
After handover Scheme 2	user → control center → ground station 2 → GEO2 → aircraft	0.73

During the handover process, control center sends multicast packet data to all of the ground stations, packets sent to the ground station1 are transmitted directly to the GEO1, but the packets sent to the ground station2 are stored and not transmitted until the aircraft connects with the GEO2. Since the aircraft breaks the connection with the GEO1, and then connects with the GEO2, which needs about 0.48 s. The packets stored in the ground station2 are transmitted to the next hop, which also needs 0.48 s. Since the control center sends multicast packets to all of the ground stations, these packets have been sent by the ground station1. That is to say repeatedly sending packets can ensure a seamless handover process.

In the simulation, the end to end transmission delay of scheme 1 and scheme 2 is different, which is shown in Fig. 5. After the handover, the end to end transmission delay of scheme 1 is about 0.75 s, but the transmission delay of scheme 2 is about 0.73 s.

The end to end transmission delay of two schemes in Fig. 5 both have several segments. In the scheme 1, the first segment is about 0.25 s, which is equal to the transmission time from the control center to the ground station1 via the GEO1 and then to the aircraft. The second segment is about 0.73 s, which is the sum of 0.25 s and

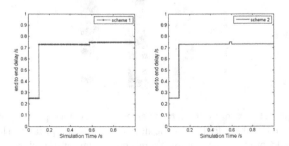

Fig. 5. End to end transmission delay. The delay of scheme 1 and scheme 2 is different.

0.48 s. The meaning of 0.48 s is that multicast packets stored in the ground station2 need about 0.48 s to send to the next hop. The 0.25 s is the same with the first second. The first and the second segments of the scheme 2 is the same with the scheme 1. The comparison of the third segment and the forth segment can be obviously seen in Fig. 6.

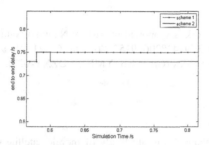

Fig. 6. Comparison of end to end delay of scheme 1 and scheme 2. Note that it is the partial enlarged picture of Fig. 5. Due to the routing optimization, the transmission delay of scheme 2 is less than scheme 1.

Figure 6 partially enlarges the picture, which contains scheme 1 and scheme 2, since scheme 2 has routing optimization in the ground network, the transmission delay is less than scheme 1 after the handover. In the scheme 1, packets sent to the ground station2 (foreign agent) must be via the ground station1 (home agent), that is to say there is a "triangle transmission", which is about 0.02 s in the ground network. So after handover, the end to end delay is about 0.75 s. However, in the scheme 2, there is routing optimization in the ground network, the transmission delay is less than scheme 1 after the handover.

5 Conclusion

In the current space-ground IP network that bases on GEO satellites, when aircraft users with high speed fly through the service range of different GEO satellites, the most important thing is mobility management, i.e., to route packets to the correct destination. However, the standard mobile IP can not be applied, since there is no real-time signaling interaction between aircraft and GEO satellites, they can only communication through directional antenna. A scheme proposed in this paper is that control center uses the flight time and position of the aircraft as a trigger, then sends signaling to GEO satellites, and assigns new IP address, called care-of address, to aircraft users, and sends multicast data to all of the ground stations. This scheme can achieve seamless handover in current condition, which has been verified by simulation. Nevertheless, there is "Triangle Routing" in the scheme, a optimization routing scheme based on the first scheme is further proposed. According to the simulation result, we draw the conclusion that the scheme can reduce transmission delay in the ground network.

The above proposed schemes are based on the current equipment condition. With the development of space technology, high-orbit satellite antenna in the future may be able to support sending signaling and data transmission at the same time. In this case, there will be no need unified scheduling by control center when the aircraft in the overlapping region. The only thing that aircraft in the overlapping region should do will be to send a request to GEO. Then GEO will assign new IP to it and connect with it. It will be similar with mobile IP in the ground network that achieves automatic handover management.

Acknowledgments. This work is supported in part by National Natural Science Foundation of China (Grant Nos. 61231013, 91438206, 91538202 and 61521091) and Fundamental Research Funds for the Central Universities (Grant No. YMF-14-DZXY-027).

References

1. Hu, A.X., Zeng, Y., Wang, Y., et al.: Study of mobile satellite network based on geo/leo satellite constellation. In: Proceedings of SPIE, vol. 5985, pp. 59850F–59850F-11 (2005)
2. Connary, J.A., Donner, P., Johnson, J., et al.: Internet routing in space: architectures for quality of service. In: Aerospace Conference, pp. 1–16. IEEE (2009)
3. Jun, L., Ji-Wei, Z., Nan, X.: Research and simulation on an autonomous routing algorithm for GEO_LEO satellite networks. In: International Conference on Intelligent Computation Technology and Automation, pp. 657–660 (2011)
4. Perkins, C.: RFC 3344IP mobility support for IPv4. Ietf Rfc (2002)
5. Xu, X., Kou, B., Fei, L., Liu, H.: Study on mobility technologies of space-ground integrated IP network toward GEO satellites. In: ICCAIS2015, SanYa (2015)
6. Leung, K., Shell, D., Ivancic, W.D., et al.: Application of mobile-IP to space and aeronautical networks. In: 2001 IEEE Proceedings of Aerospace Conference, pp. 13–18 (2001)
7. Chowdhury, P.K., Atiquzzaman, M., Ivancic, W.: SINEMO: an IP-diversity based approach for network mobility in space. In: IEEE International Conference on Space Mission Challenges for Information Technology, SMC-IT 2006, vol. 7, p. 115 (2006)
8. Woo, W., Leung, V.C.M.: Handoff enhancement in mobile-ip environment. In: 1996 5th IEEE International Conference on Universal Personal Communications, 1996. Record, vol. 2, pp. 760–764. IEEE (1994)
9. Jonhson, D., Perkins, C., Arkko, J., et al.: Mobility support in ipv6. Internet Engineering Task Force Request For Comments (rfc) 3775
10. Perkins, C., Johnson, D.: Route optimization in mobile IP (2001)

Impact of Doppler Shift on LTE System in High Speed Train Scenario

Yu Zhang[1], Lei Xiong[1(✉)], Xuelian Yang[1], and Yuanchun Tan[2]

[1] State Key Laboratory of Rail Traffic Control and Safety,
Beijing Jiaotong University, Beijing 100044, China
lxiong@bjtu.edu.cn
[2] Beijing Xinwei Telecom Technology Group Co., Ltd, Beijing 100094, China

Abstract. Single Frequency Network (SFN) is considered as a vital deployment method in High Speed Train (HST) scenario. HST channel model is of much importance to LTE performance assessment. And SFN channel models are non-stationary. Since the train moves fast, the impact of Doppler rises significantly. The consideration of the effect of Doppler shift in SFN scenario is of much difference from in traditional stationary channels. In this paper, we build a link level simulation system and evaluate the performance of TD-LTE system with single-tap and two-tap SFN High Speed Train (HST) channel models without frequency compensation. The results show that when the Doppler shift exceeds 1000 Hz, the performance degrades much more obviously. Additionally, the absolute value of Doppler shift has great influence on TD-LTE system and the impact of Doppler shift variation on the system performance is not obvious. This paper provides reference for the design of next generation railway mobile communication system and lay a foundation for the LTE high-speed adaptability research.

Keywords: LTE · Doppler shift · Performance evaluation · SFN channel model

1 Introduction

In recent years, the high-speed railway achieves good development, especially in China. Long Term Evolution (LTE) has the characteristics of high spectral efficiency, high peak data rates, as well as flexibility in frequency and bandwidth [1]. So, it is a key problem for LTE to meet the performance requirement of passengers in high speed railway. Many companies have proposed possible high-speed railway scenarios in the 3GPP RAN4 meeting recently, including scenario 1, scenario 2 (scenario 2a to 2g), scenario 3 and scenario 4. And it is explicitly proposed to investigate scenario 1, scenario 2d and the first hop of scenario 2c, namely: open space SFN scenario, SFN scenario in tunnel and leaky cable scenario in tunnel [2].

To avoid frequent handover in HST scenario, multiple Remote Radio Heads (RRHs) are connected with one BBU by fiber, and share the same cell ID. That is to say, one cell contains multiple RRHs, and UE receives the same signal from multiple RRHs, thus forming the open space SFN scenario which is an important solution in

© ICST Institute for Computer Sciences, Social Informatics and Telecommunications Engineering 2018
Q. Chen et al. (Eds.): ChinaCom 2016, Part II, LNICST 210, pp. 431–440, 2018.
DOI: 10.1007/978-3-319-66628-0_41

high-speed railway communication. Many companies have been devoting to evaluate the performance basing on LTE-FDD system. And three candidate solutions are proposed in the RAN 4 #77 meeting, which are respectively UE receiver enhancement, eNodeB frequency pre-compensation and unidirectional SFN arrangement. But for all of the solutions, the Doppler shift caused by high-speed movement will be a key impact factor for system performance [3, 4], especially when the target moving speed is up to 750 km/h which has been put forward in RAN #70 meeting.

Both [3, 4] have investigated the effects of Doppler shift in HST scenario and proposed some methods, including the mean square error (MSE) scheme and the chunk-based resource allocation, to improve the accuracy of the Doppler offset estimation. But the channel models in [3, 4] are traditional Rician or Rayleigh fading model, which are not suitable for the SFN scenario.

So, in this paper, we build an integral system to assess the impact of Doppler shift on TD-LTE system performance with both one-tap and two-tap SFN channel models. This work is useful for the further Doppler frequency offset estimation method research in SFN scenarios. The rest of this paper is organized as follows: Sect. 2 briefly introduces the system models including the channel models and system structure. Section 3 presents and analyzes the simulation results and Sect. 4 gives the conclusions.

2 System Description

Currently, SFN channel models approved in 3GPP RAN 4 meeting include single-tap channel model proposed by Samsung and two-tap SFN channel model proposed by Huawei [5]. We focus on single-tap channel model and two-tap SFN channel model to investigate the impact of Doppler shift. The detailed induction of both of the models are depicted as follows.

2.1 Single-Tap Channel Model

Assume that N RRHs connected to one BBU by optical fiber, and these N RRHs share the same cell ID. Owing to the distance to the receiver are different between RRHs, N paths will be formed [6]. Single-tap SFN channel model is described as Fig. 1. D_s is the

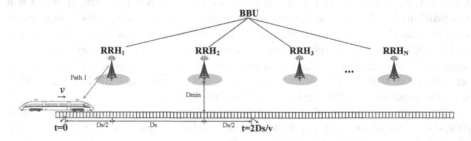

Fig. 1. Sketch map of single-tap SFN channel model. (Color figure online)

distance between two neighbor RRHs; D_{min} is RRH railway track distance in meters; v is the velocity of the train in m/s; t is time in seconds.

When $0 \leq t \leq ND_s/v$, namely the train is in the coverage area of the first cell. The Doppler shift of each path can be denoted as:

$$f_{dn} = f_{d\max} \cos \theta_n(t), \tag{1}$$

where the maximum Doppler shift is calculated as:

$$f_{d\max} = f_c \cdot \frac{v}{c} \cdot \cos \theta_n(t) \tag{2}$$

When $ND_s/v \leq t \leq 2ND_s/v$, that is when the train hands over to the second cell. To maintain the continuity of the frequency offset and avoid the alternation of Doppler shift when handing over, the cosine of angle $\theta_n(t)$ of the nth path can be expressed as [7]:

$$\cos \theta_n(t) = \frac{-\left(n+N-\frac{1}{2}\right)D_s+vt}{\sqrt{\left[-\left(n+N-\frac{1}{2}\right)D_s+v\right]^2+D_{min}^2}}, n \in [1,N] \tag{3}$$

When $t \geq 2ND_s/v$,

$$\cos \theta_n(t) = \cos \theta_n(t \bmod (2ND_s/v)) \tag{4}$$

Obviously, it is very complicated taking N paths into consideration. One tap high speed train channel model is denoted as Eq. (5).

$$\cos \theta(t) = \begin{cases} \dfrac{0.5D_s-vt}{\sqrt{D_{min}^2+(0.5D_s-vt)^2}}, & 0<t\leq \frac{D_s}{v} \\ \dfrac{-1.5D_s+vt}{\sqrt{D_{min}^2+(-1.5D_s+vt)^2}}, & \frac{D_s}{v}<t\leq \frac{2D_s}{v}, \\ \cos \theta(t \bmod (2D_s/v)), & t>2D_s/v \end{cases} \tag{5}$$

Power and delay are not taken into account in one tap HST channel model. The trajectory of the Doppler shift with the condition of $v = 350$ km/h, $D_s = 1000$ m, $D_{min} = 10$ m, and $f_c = 2300$ MHz is shown in Fig. 2.

To evaluate the Doppler shift effect of single-tap SFN channel model, we choose four cases with different variation characteristics of Doppler shift. Case 1 denotes that Doppler shift keeps almost constant positive value, case 2 denotes that Doppler keeps almost constant negative value, case 3 is that Doppler shift ranges from positive to negative and case 4 is that Doppler shift ranges from negative to positive. These four cases are marked in red in Fig. 1. And the simulation time of every case is 1 s. We carry out relative simulations under the condition of no frequency compensation in these 4 cases, and the corresponding results is shown in part 4.

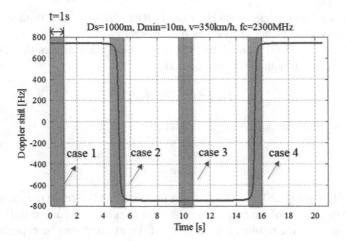

Fig. 2. Doppler shift of single- tap HST channel model. (Color figure online)

2.2 Two-Tap SFN Channel Model

In the two-tap SFN channel model, we assume that RRHs are deployed along the railway in sequential order. Path 1 denotes the path from even RRH and path 2 denotes the path from odd RRH. Doppler shift, tap delay and relative power are all time-variable, as shown in Fig. 3.

Doppler shifts of two paths are given by:

$$f_{d,1}(t) = f_d(t + \frac{1.5D_s}{v}) \tag{6}$$

$$f_{d,2}(t) = f_d(t + \frac{0.5D_s}{v}) \tag{7}$$

Where $f_d(t) = f_{d\max} \cos \theta(t)$, and $f_{d\max}$ is the maximum Doppler frequency. The cosine of angle $\theta(t)$ is given by:

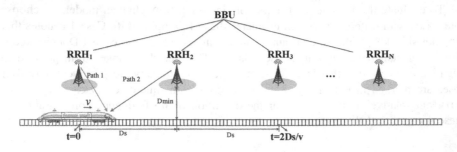

Fig. 3. Sketch map of two-tap channel model.

$$\cos\theta(t) = \begin{cases} \dfrac{0.5D_s - vt}{\sqrt{D_{min}^2 + (0.5D_s - vt)^2}}, 0 < t \le D_s/v \\[4mm] \dfrac{-1.5D_s + vt}{\sqrt{D_{min}^2 + (-1.5D_s + vt)^2}}, D_s/v < t \le 2D_s/v \cdot \\[4mm] \cos\theta(t \bmod (2D_s/v)), t > 2D_s/v \end{cases} \qquad (8)$$

Signal power received by the UE for each path is given by:

$$p_1(t) = \begin{cases} \dfrac{D_{min}^2}{(D_s - vt)^2 + D_{min}^2}, & 0 < t \le 2D_s/v \\[4mm] p_1(t \bmod (2D_s/v)), & t > 2D_s/v \end{cases} \qquad (9)$$

$$p_2(t) = p_1(t + D_s/v) \qquad (10)$$

$p_1(t)$ and $p_2(t)$ are normalized received power to the nearest RRH. Time delay of two taps are given by:

$$d_1(t) = \begin{cases} \dfrac{\sqrt{(D_s - vt)^2 + D_{min}^2}}{c}, & 0 < t \le 2D_s/v \\[4mm] d_1(t \bmod (2D_s/v)), & t > 2D_s/v \end{cases} \qquad (11)$$

$$d_2(t) = d_1(t + D_s/v) \qquad (12)$$

Since the two-tap channel model is featured by three parameters, namely Doppler shift, tap delay and power. In order to investigate the effect of Doppler shift, it is vital to eliminate the influence of other parameters. According to the analysis made on the channel parameters, we can find that only Doppler shift varies while tap delay and power remain unchanged by setting different carrier frequency. As shown in Fig. 2.

To investigate the Doppler shift effect of two-tap SFN channel model, we choose four cases with different variation characteristics of Doppler shift. Case 1 denotes that Doppler shifts of the two taps keep almost constant respectively, case 2 denotes that Doppler shift rapidly changes from positive to negative (tap 1) and changes from negative to positive (tap 2). These two cases are marked in red in Fig. 4. The simulation time of every case is 1 s and the simulation location is right at the first reaching RRH. We carry out relative simulations under the condition of no frequency compensation in these 2 cases of two-tap channel model, and the corresponding results is shown in part 4.

2.3 System Model

The simulation bases on the TD-LTE MATLAB Link simulation platform. The flow chart is shown in Fig. 5.

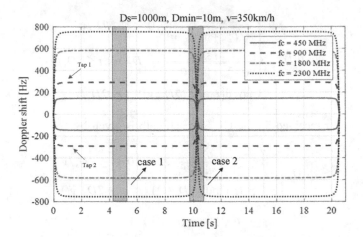

Fig. 4. Doppler shift trajectory of two-tap SFN channel model with different carrier frequencies. (Color figure online)

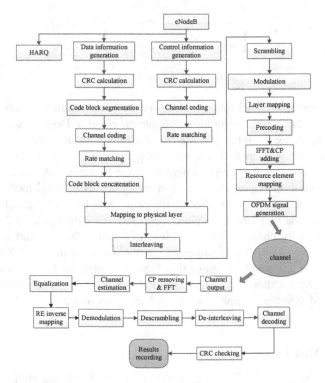

Fig. 5. The flow chart of LTE downlink process.

3 Simulation Results

Then, we carry out simulations to investigate the impact Doppler shift has on system performance under four cases marked in red in Fig. 1. The simulation assumptions are listed in Table 1.

Table 1. Parameters of the simulation for single-tap channel model

Parameters	Value
Carrier frequency [MHz]	450, 900, 1800, 2300
Bandwidth [MHz]	10
D_s [m]	1000
D_{min} [m]	10
MCS	MCS #19
Simulation time [s]	1
Simulation frame	10000
v (Velocity of train) [km/h]	350

In Fig. 6, we get the system BER when Doppler shifts are respectively 250 Hz, 500 Hz, 750 Hz, 1000 Hz and 1500 Hz. From the figure we can see that with the increasing of SNR, all the BERs decrease obviously, especially when SNR is higher than 8 dB. But for different Doppler shifts, the BER variations are not the same, i.e. the smaller the Doppler shift, the faster the BER drops. That is to say, the system performance is obviously influenced by the Doppler shift. Additionally, when the Doppler shift exceeds 1000 Hz, the performance degrades much more obviously.

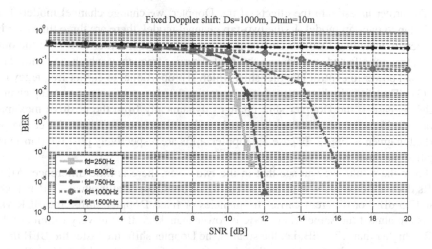

Fig. 6. BER under fixed Doppler shifts.

From the previous analysis, we already know that constant value of Doppler is a major factor affecting performance. Therefore, now we focus on the effect of Doppler shift in single-tap SFN channel model, which is shown in Fig. 7.

Figure 7 shows the simulation results of single-tap channel model. From Fig. 7, we can see that when UE experiences constant value, BER performances are almost the same. So, the absolute value of the Doppler shift is the key factor that affects the system performance. Additional, from case 2 and case 4, we can see that the impact of Doppler shift variation on the system performance is not obvious. However, during the changes of Doppler absolute values, there are some values which are relatively smaller than the values in case 1 and case 3, so the performance becomes better. For example, when SNR = 15 dB, the difference is about 20 dB.

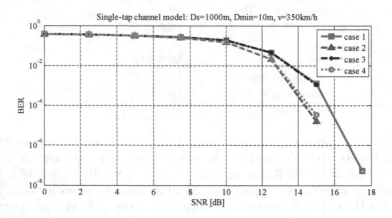

Fig. 7. BER under different Doppler shifts in single-tap SFN channel model.

To further investigate the effects of the Doppler, we change channel models from single-tap to two-tap model. In the two-tap channel model, there are three time-varying parameters, including Doppler shift, tap power and delay. In order to ensure the other parameters not affected, we change the center carrier frequency which does not affect delay and power to control Doppler shift which is proportional to carrier frequency (see Eq. (2)). Therefore, in this part, two cases are simulated respectively in two-tap channel model. In case 1, the Doppler shift changes dynamically from the positive maximum Doppler shift to the negative one for tap 1, and on the contrary for tap 2, see the part marked in green in Fig. 2. In case 2, Doppler shifts are respectively positive (tap 1) and negative maximal value (tap 2).

From the results we can see that in the two cases, there is little difference. All the BERs decrease obviously with the increasing of SNR, especially when SNR is higher than 17.5 dB. For different carrier frequencies or fixed Doppler shifts, the BER variations are almost the same when SNR is lower than 17.5 dB, but very different when SNR is higher than 17.5 dB, i.e. the smaller the Doppler shift, the faster the BER drops. So we can also get the conclusion that the system performance is obviously influenced by the Doppler shift in two-tap SFN channel model (Figs. 8 and 9).

Two-tap channel model (case1): Ds=1000m, Dmin=10m, v=350km/h

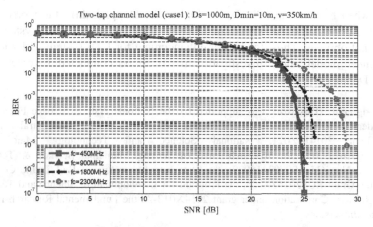

Fig. 8. BER of case 1 in two-tap SFN channel model.

Two-tap channel model (case2): Ds=1000m, Dmin=10m, v=350km/h

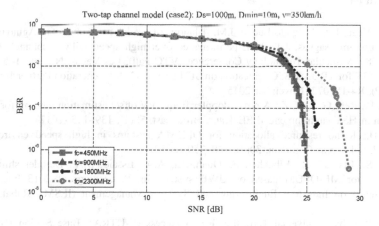

Fig. 9. BER of case 2 in two-tap SFN channel model.

4   Conclusion

The impact of Doppler shift has been an attractive part of research in academia and industry. SFN scenario has been proposed as one of the high speed train scenarios. This paper comprehensively investigates if Doppler shift impacts the performance of LTE system basing on identified SFN channel.

The performance of BER of TD-LTE system has been assessed using single-tap and two-tap high speed train channel model in TR36.878. And we conduct further study on the impact of Doppler shift. The results show that the absolute value of Doppler shift has great influence on TD-LTE system. To be more specific, when the Doppler shift exceeds 1000 Hz, the performance degrades much more obviously in single-tap channel model. And from the results of two-tap channel model, the BER variations are almost the same when the Doppler shift is lower than 300 Hz, but very different when higher than 300 Hz, the higher the Doppler shift, the worse the performance. Additionally, the impact of Doppler shift variation on the system performance is not obvious. Thus, for further enhancement for LTE system under identified SFN channel model, more investigation needs to be conducted to overcome the maximal Doppler shift.

Acknowledgment. This work was supported by the National Natural Science Foundation of China under Grant 61471030, the Fundamental Research Funds for the Central Universities under Grant 2014JBZ021, National Science and Technology Major Project (2015ZX03001027-003), the Research Fund of Beijing Municipal Science & Technology Commission (No. Z151100002415029), the State Key Laboratory of Rail Traffic Control and Safety under Grant RCS2016ZZ004, the Program for Development of Science and Technology of China Railway Corporation under grant 2014X013-A, the Fundamental Research Funds for the Central Universities.

References

1. Martin-Vega, F.J., Delgado-Luque, I.M., Blanquez-Casado, F., Gomez, G., Aguayo-Torres, M.C., Entrambasaguas, J.T.: LTE performance over high speed railway channel. In: 2013 IEEE 78th Vehicular Technology Conference (VTC Fall), Las Vegas, NV, pp. 1–5 (2013)
2. 3GPP, "TP for TR 36.878: Clarification on SFN scenario", 3rd Generation Partnership Project (3GPP), R4-157072, November 2015
3. Yang, L., Ren, G., Qiu, Z.: A novel doppler frequency offset estimation method for DVB-T system in HST environment. IEEE Trans. Broadcast. **58**(1), 139–143 (2012)
4. Zhu, H.: Radio resource allocation for OFDMA systems in high speed environments. IEEE J. Sel. Areas Commun. **30**(4), 748–759 (2012)
5. Kabil, S., Elassali, R., Elbahhar, F., Ouahman, A.A., Essaid, B.A.: Doppler shift impact analyses for MB-OFDM based on UWB system. In: Proceedings of 2013 International Conference on Industrial Engineering and Systems Management (IESM), Rabat, p. 533 (2013)
6. 3GPP, "Evolved Universal Terrestrial Radio Access (E-UTRA); Base Station (BS) radio transmission and reception", 3rd Generation Partnership Project (3GPP), TS 36.104, September 2008
7. 3GPP, "Discussion on High speed train scenarios", 3rd Generation Partnership Project (3GPP), R4-152277, April 2015

SDN and Clouds

Real-Time Fault-Tolerant Scheduling Algorithm in Virtualized Clouds

Pengze Guo$^{(\boxtimes)}$ and Zhi Xue

Department of Electronic Engineering,
Shanghai Jiao Tong University, Shanghai 200240, China
{guopengze,zxue}@sjtu.edu.cn

Abstract. The past decade has witnessed the rapid development of
cloud computing. Virtualization, which is the fundamental technique
in providing Infrastructure as a Service (IaaS), has led to an explosive growth of the cloud computing industry. Fault-tolerance is a significant requirement of cloud computing due to the Service Level Agree-
ments (SLA). In order to achieve high reliability and resilience of real-
time systems in virtualized clouds, a Virtualization-based Fault-Tolerant
Scheduling (VFTS) algorithm is proposed. In this paper, fault tolerance
is implemented by using primary-backup approach. VFTS is designed
for periodic and preemptive tasks in homogeneous environment. Simulation results demonstrate an impressing saving of processing resources
compared with those needed by the dual-system hot backup approach,
which proves the feasibility and effectiveness of the proposed VFTS algorithm.

Keywords: Fault tolerance · Real-time system · Scheduling · Virtualized cloud

1 Introduction

Cloud computing is a new paradigm for providing computing resources to users
on-demand dynamically [1]. The feature of quick deployment relies on virtualization to a large extent. Virtualization is a technology that divides hardware
resources to multiple logical computing units using software method [2]. With
virtualization, dynamic resource allocation, flexible scheduling and cross-regional
sharing can be realized. Virtualization makes it possible to elastically share cloud
resources to multi-users at the same time.

A real-time system is described as one that processes data and returns result
both correctly and timely [3]. In other words, correctness and timeliness are
the main principles of real-time systems. Fault-tolerance plays a significant role
in ensuring the functioning of cloud systems, especially for those with safety-
critical property (e.g. nuclear power system, electronic cruise control system and
medical electronics system). Fault-tolerant scheduling is a superior method which
can combine fault-tolerant technique with many different scheduling methods.

© ICST Institute for Computer Sciences, Social Informatics and Telecommunications Engineering 2018
Q. Chen et al. (Eds.): ChinaCom 2016, Part II, LNICST 210, pp. 443–452, 2018.
DOI: 10.1007/978-3-319-66628-0_42

Among all the fault-tolerant schemes, primary-backup (PB) approach is the most commonly used one. In the PB approach, each task is represented by two copies, i.e., the primary copy and the backup copy. The primary copy executes when the system functions normally, and the backup copy executes depending on its type. If the backup copy is an active one, it always runs just like primary copy. Passive copy executes only in case of system failure.

In this paper, a novel fault-tolerant scheduling algorithm VFTS that combines both virtualization and PB approach is proposed. VFTS assigns tasks to virtual machines (VMs) instead of to hosts directly like [4]. Meanwhile, VFTS provides fault-tolerance for cloud system by scheduling tasks among different VMs. Schedulability and effectiveness are verified by theorems and experiments. It is shown that VFTS can accomplish the purpose of fault-tolerance and saving more precise computing resources.

The remaining part of the paper is organized as follows. Related work in this area is reviewed in Sect. 2. Section 3 gives the notations, assumptions, and detailed descriptions of the scheduling model. Section 4 deals with the scheduling criteria and constrains. Based on the analysis, scheduling algorithm VFTS is then presented. In Sect. 5, simulation results evaluate the performance of VFTS algorithm compared with the simple duplication approach. Finally, Sect. 6 summarizes the major contribution of this paper and discusses future directions of this work.

2   Related Work

Since assigning real-time periodic tasks to processors has been proved to be NP-hard [5], several heuristic algorithms for allocating tasks have been researched. Rate-Monotonic (RM) algorithm for preemptively scheduling periodic tasks on a single processor was proposed by Liu and Layland [6]. In RM scheduling, tasks with smaller periods have higher priorities, and tasks with low priority will be preempted by tasks with high priority if their running time conflicts. Joseph and Pandya [7] proposed the sufficient and necessary condition for testing the schedulability of a bunch of priority driven tasks on a single processor, called the Completion Time Test (CTT). Rate-Monotonic First-Fit (RMFF), which extended RM to multiprocessor systems, was proposed by Dhall and Liu [8].

As for fault-tolerant scheduling algorithms, active duplication approach is simple and commonly used. In order to reduce system overhead, backup overbooking and deallocation were proposed in [9] to tolerate fault in multiprocessor systems. But it is only for nonpreemptive and aperiodic tasks. Fault-Tolerant Rate-Monotonic First-Fit (FTRMFF) was proposed in [4] by extending the RMFF algorithm and combining backup overbooking and deallocation. Active Resource Reclaiming (ARR) was proposed in [10] to extend FTRMFF with the phasing delay technique [11], which reduces the overlapping between a primary and backup copy. Task Partition based Fault Tolerant Rate-Monotonic (TPFTRM) introduces a new type of backup – the overlapping backup, and abandons active backup to utilize the computing resources more efficiently.

However, none of the fault-tolerant scheduling algorithms mentioned above take virtualization, which is the key feature of cloud systems, into account. Wang et al. proposed a fault-tolerant mechanism FESTAL, which extends the primary-backup model to schedule real-time tasks in clouds [12]. Nonetheless, it is a dynamic algorithm for heterogeneous systems.

In this paper, we investigate a novel static scheduling algorithm that assigns tasks to multiple hosts, each of which contains several homogeneous virtual machines. Three objectives are satisfied: (1) tasks are finished before their deadlines, (2) fault-tolerance is guaranteed, and (3) virtualization characteristics are considered.

3   Scheduling Model

This section presents the characteristic descriptions and notations of the model.

3.1   Fault-Tolerance Model

For the fault-tolerance model, some assumptions are made for sake of convenience:

1. Hosts fail in a fail-stop manner, which means a host either functions well or breaks down.
2. Faults are independent. That is to say, a faulty host can not cause incorrect behaviours in a non-faulty host.
3. There exists a failure detection mechanism. The failure of a host is detected as soon as failure happens.
4. A second failure does not occur before the system recovers from the former failure.
5. All VMs in a faulty host would stop working.

3.2   Task Model

A periodic task t_i is characterized by a pair (C_i, T_i) parameter. Each task must complete before its deadline, which is equal to its period in this paper. Each task t_i has a primary copy t_i^P and a backup copy $t_i^B.t_i^P$ and t_i^B execute on different hosts for purpose of fault-tolerance. Periodic tasks $t_1, t_2, ..., t_n$ are independent and preemptive. Backup copy is usually a simplified version of its primary copy. For the purpose of simplicity, it is assumed that primary and backup copy have the same parameter. The backup copy has two status: active and passive. Let W_i be the worst-case completion time (WCRT) of t_i^P. The recovery time of t_i^B is $B_i = T_i - W_i$. If $B_i < C_i$, then set $st(t_i^B)$ to active. Because if t_i^B is a passive backup copy, it would not start execute until failure occurs, and if failure happens just at the WCRT of its primary copy, it would not have enough time to recover from failure. If $B_i \geq C_i$, set $st(t_i^B)$ to passive.

A virtualized host is denoted as h_i. Each host h_i can hold multiple VMs, denoted as $vm_{i1}, vm_{i2}, ..., vm_{im}$. For sake of convenience in comparing between different scheduling algorithms, it is assumed that each host accommodates the same number of identical VMs.

t_i^P and t_i^B are assigned to VMs instead of to hosts directly. $vm(t_i^P)$ and $vm(t_i^B)$ denote the VMs where t_i^P and t_i^B are allocated respectively. $host(t_i^P)$ and $host(t_i^B)$ are their corresponding hosts.

After assigning tasks to VMs, the task copies on the same VM are scheduled by the RM algorithm. Given n periodic tasks $t_1, t_2, ..., t_n$, the goal of the fault-tolerant scheduling algorithm is to minimize the number of VMs.

To facilitate the analysis, we summarize the notations of task model in Table 1.

Table 1. Task model parameters

Symbol	Meaning
t_i	Task i
t_i^P	Primary copy of t_i
t_i^B	Backup copy of t_i
C_i	Computation time of t_i
T_i	Period of t_i
W_i	Worst-case response time (WCRT) of t_i^P
B_i	Recover time of backup copy t_i^B
h_i	Host i
vm_{ij}	jth VM of h_i
$primary(vm_{ij})$	Primary copies on vm_{ij}
$active(vm_{ij})$	Active copies on vm_{ij}
$recover(vm_{ij}, h_f)$	Backup copies on vm_{ij} whose primary copies are on h_f
$st(t_i^B)$	Status of t_i^B
$pri(t_i)$	Priority of t_i
$N_{task}, N_{host}, N_{vm}$	Number of tasks, hosts and VMs per host

4   Virtualization-Based Fault-Tolerant Scheduling Algorithm VFTS

In this section, we leverage the virtualization techniques and scheduling schemes to develop a virtualization-based fault-tolerant scheduling algorithm VFTS. Scheduling strategies of primary, active and passive copies are discussed in detail. The pseudocode of VFTS algorithm is presented. It should be noted that all tasks should be re-indexed with the decreasing order of their priorities which are inversely proportional to their periods. The backup copy is scheduled following its primary. So the actual scheduling order is $t_1^P, t_1^B, t_2^P, t_2^B, t_3^P, t_3^B, \cdots$ with $T_1 \leq T_2 \leq T_3 \leq \cdots$.

4.1 Scheduling Criteria

In the classic paper [6], a critical instant of a task is defined to be a particular time when a task will get the latest finishing time.

Theorem 1. *A critical instant for any task occurs whenever the task is requested simultaneously with requests for all higher priority tasks.*

As a consequence, to check whether a task is schedulable, we just need to check its schedulability when it starts to execute with all higher priority tasks.

Joseph and Pandya proposed the sufficient and necessary condition for verifying the schedulability of a set of fixed-priority tasks on a single processor, called Completion Time Test (CTT) [7].

Theorem 2. *To check whether task t_i is schedulable in a VM, its worst-case response time (WCRT) is:*

$$W(t_i, \tau) = \sum_{\tau_k \in \tau} C_k \lceil W(t_i, \tau)/T_k \rceil \tag{1}$$

where τ is the task set assigned to the VM with priorities equal to or higher than t_i (including t_i). If $W(t_i, \tau) \leq T_i$, then t_i is schedulable in the VM.

To calculate the WCRT, an iterative method was proposed in [10]. The computation time on a processor occupied by tasks in VM during $[0, t]$ is:

$$W(t, \tau) = \sum_{\tau_k \in \tau} C_k \lceil t/T_k \rceil \tag{2}$$

$\lceil t/T_k \rceil$ is the number of periods that t_k experiences during interval $[0, t]$. Owing to t_k's higher priority than t_i, the length of the time interval occupied by t_k is $C_k \lceil t/T_k \rceil$. Let $S_0 = \sum_{\tau_k \in \tau} C_k$, and iterate $S_{l+1} = W(S_l, \tau)$ with $l = 0, 1, 2...$ until $S_n = S_{n+1}$. If $S_n \leq T_i$, then t_i is schedulable and its WCRT in the VM is S_n.

Theorem 3. *If $vm(t_i^P) \in h_j$, then $vm(t_i^B) \notin h_j$.*

Proof. Prove by contradiction. Suppose that t_i^B is assigned to $vm_{jk} \in h_j$, then $host(t_i^P) = host(t_i^B)$. When h_j fails, all the VMs in h_j fail. Thus, both primary and backup copies of t_i cannot execute. Therefore, t_i^P and t_i^B cannot be assigned to VMs in the same host. □

Theorem 4. *If t_i^* is a primary copy or active backup copy, then in case of fault free, the WCRT of t_i^* is*

$$W(t_i^*, \tau) = \sum_{t_k^P, t_k^B \in \tau} C_k \lceil W(t_i^*, \tau)/T_k \rceil \tag{3}$$

where τ is the primary copies or active backup copies on $vm(t_i^*)$ with priorities equal to or higher than t_i^* (including t_i^*). If $W(t_i^*, \tau) \leq T_i$, then t_i^* is schedulable in the VM.

Proof. The primary copies and active backup copies always execute in fault free case, and passive backup copies do not execute. The computation of WCRT is similar to Theorem 2. □

Theorem 5. *If $st(t_i^B)$=passive, then in case of fault free, t_i^B need not execute.*

Theorem 6. *For primary copy t_i^P, in the presence of h_f's failure ($h_f \neq host(t_i^P)$), the WCRT of t_i^P is*

$$W(t_i^P, \tau) = \sum_{t_k^P \in \tau} C_k \lceil W(t_i^P, \tau)/T_k \rceil + \sum_{t_k^B \in \tau} C_k \phi(t_k^B, W(t_i^P, \tau)) \tag{4}$$

where

$$\phi(t_k^B, t) = \begin{cases} \lceil t/T_k \rceil & if\ st(t_k^B) = active \\ 1 & if\ st(t_k^B) = passive\ and\ t \leq B_k \\ 1 + \lceil (t - B_k)/T_k \rceil & if\ st(t_k^B) = passive\ and\ t > B_k \end{cases}$$

$$\tau = \{\tau_k | \tau_k \in primary(vm(t_i^P)) \cup recovery(vm(t_i^P), h_f), pri(\tau_k) \geq pri(t_i^P)\}.$$

If $W(t_i^P, \tau) \leq T_i$, then t_i^P is schedulable in the VM.

Proof. When failure occurs, passive backup copy t_k^B needs to finish C_k during its recovery time. After the recovery interval, t_k^B enters the periodic circulation, and finish C_k in every period. □

Theorem 7. *For backup copy t_i^B, in the presence of $host(t_i^P)$'s failure, the WCRT of t_i^B is*

$$W(t_i^B, \tau) = \sum_{t_k^P \in \tau} C_k \lceil W(t_i^B, \tau)/T_k \rceil + \sum_{t_k^B \in \tau} C_k \phi(t_k^B, W(t_i^B, \tau)) \tag{5}$$

where $\phi(t_k^B, t)$ is the same as that in Theorem 6, and

$$\tau = \{\tau_k | \tau_k \in primary(vm(t_i^B)) \cup recovery(vm(t_i^B), host(t_i^P)), pri(\tau_k) \geq pri(t_i^B)\}.$$

If $W(t_i^B, \tau) \leq T_i$ for active backup copy or $W(t_i^B, \tau) \leq B_i$ for passive backup copy, then t_i^B is schedulable in the VM.

Proof. For passive backup copy t_k^B, the worst case happens when the failure occurs in $host(t_k^P)$ just at the moment when t_k^P is about to finish at its WCRT, which means the time left for t_k^B to recovery is shortest, i.e., B_k. t_k^B must accomplish C_k in its recovery interval with the length of B_k. □

4.2 VFTS Algorithm

Combining the criteria and constraints stated above, the detailed description of the VFTS algorithm is given in Algorithm 1.

Algorithm 1. VFTS Algorithm

```
1   Sort tasks t₁, t₂, ..., tₙ such that T₁ ≤ T₂ ≤ ··· ≤ Tₙ
2   foreach tᵢ in the task set do
3       foreach hⱼ in the host set do                              // loop 1
4           foreach vmₖ in the VMs of hⱼ do
5               (CheckNoFault, Wᵢ) ←NoFaultCTT(tᵢᴾ, vmⱼₖ)
6               if CheckNoFault == True then
7                   for f = 1 → Nₕₒₛₜ do
8                       CheckFault ←FaultCTT(tᵢᴾ, vmⱼₖ, hf)
9                       if CheckFault == False then
10                          break
11                  if CheckFault == False then
12                      continue
13                  Allocate tᵢᴾ → vmⱼₖ
14                  Break out of loop 1
15      if tᵢᴾ fails to be scheduled in any VM then
16          Add a new host with Nₕₒₛₜ ← Nₕₒₛₜ + 1
17          Allocate tᵢᴾ → vm_{Nₕₒₛₜ,1}
18      if Tᵢ − Wᵢ < Cᵢ then
19          Status(tᵢᴮ) ← active
20          foreach hⱼ in the host set do                          // loop 2
21              foreach vmₖ in the VMs of hⱼ do
22                  CheckNoFault ←NoFaultCTT(tᵢᴮ, vmⱼₖ)
23                  CheckFault ←FaultCTT(tᵢᴮ, vmⱼₖ, h_{tᵢᴾ})
24                  if CheckNoFault==True and CheckFault==True then
25                      Allocate tᵢᴮ → vmⱼₖ
26                      Break out of loop 2
27      else
28          Status(tᵢᴮ) ← passive
29          foreach hⱼ in the host set do                          // loop 3
30              foreach vmₖ in the VMs of hⱼ do
31                  CheckFault ←FaultCTT(tᵢᴮ, vmⱼₖ, h_{tᵢᴾ})
32                  if CheckNoFault==True and CheckFault==True then
33                      Allocate tᵢᴮ → vmⱼₖ
34                      Break out of loop 3
35      if tᵢᴮ fails to be scheduled in any VM then
36          Add a new host with Nₕₒₛₜ ← Nₕₒₛₜ + 1
37          Allocate tᵢᴮ → vm_{Nₕₒₛₜ,1}
```

Function NoFaultCTT(t_i^*, vm_{jk}) is used to check schedulability of t_i^* on vm_{jk} in fault free case. For primary copy t_i^P, NoFaultCTT(t_i^P, vm_{jk}) tests the schedulability of $\tau = t_i^P \cup primary(vm_{jk}) \cup active(vm_{jk})$ on vm_{jk} using CTT. The

WCRT W_i of t_i^P is also calculated by this function. For active backup copy t_i^B, NoFaultCTT(t_i^B, vm_{jk}) tests the schedulability of $\tau = t_i^B \cup primary(vm_{jk}) \cup active(vm_{jk})$ on vm_{jk} using CTT. Passive backup copies do not need to perform this test because they do not execute in non-fault case.

FaultCTT(t_i^*, vm_{jk}, h_f) is used to check schedulability of t_i^* on vm_{jk} in case h_f ($f \neq k$) encounters a failure. The analysis is in concert with Theorem 4.

Theorem 8. *The time complexity of VFTS is $O(N_{task}N_{host}^2N_{vm})$.*

Proof. To assign a primary copy, at most $N_{host}N_{vm}$ VMs are tried. Each trial requires in turn one execution of NoFaultCTT and $N_{host} - 1$ executions of FaultCTT, in the worst case. Thus, the time complexity of VFTS is $O(N_{task})O(N_{host}N_{vm})O(N_{host}) = O(N_{task}N_{host}^2N_{vm})$.   □

5   Simulation Experiments

In order to calculate the number of VMs needed by the VFTS algorithm to provide fault-tolerance for virtualized cloud systems, simulation experiments are performed. Simple duplication with RMFF (DRMFF) is used to compare with VFTS. DRMFF schedules tasks with the method of RMFF and provide fault-tolerance by duplicating the hosts. We denote with N the number of VMs required by VFTS algorithm, and with M the number of VMs required by DRMFF algorithm. Since the optimal assignment of tasks to VMs is difficult to figure out, we use the total load $U = U_1 + U_2 + \cdots + U_n$ as the minimum and optimal number of VMs. For simplicity of comparison, each host is assumed to contain 8 identical VMs. Once a new host is added, 8 VMs are created simultaneously. The VFTS and DRMFF algorithms were developed in Matlab and run on a PC with Intel Core i7-2600K CPU and 8 GB RAM.

Task sets with length of $100 \leq n \leq 1000$ are generated. The maximum load $\alpha = max\{U_1, U_2, \cdots, U_n\}$ is chosen to be 0.2, 0.5 and 0.8. Each task period T_i is randomly distributed in the interval [1, 500], and each computation time C_i is uniformly distributed in the interval $[0, \alpha T_i]$. For every chosen n and α, the experiment is repeated for 30 times, and the average result is calculated.

Figure 1 shows the ratios between the number of VMs required by VFTS or DRMFF and the total load. Generally the ratio increases with the increasing of α. The increasing trend of DRMFF is less obvious than VFTS because DRMFF does not take into account the complicated relations and constraints between primary and backup copies, and always tries to fully fill every VM regardless of α. For smaller number of tasks, the ratios are relatively higher because more VMs are not fully utilized due to limited number of tasks.

Figure 2 shows a remarkable saving of VMs compared with those needed by DRMFF. The percentage of VMs saved by VFTS is about 33% for $\alpha = 0.2$, 25% for $\alpha = 0.5$ and 4% for $\alpha = 0.8$ when the number of tasks is large enough.

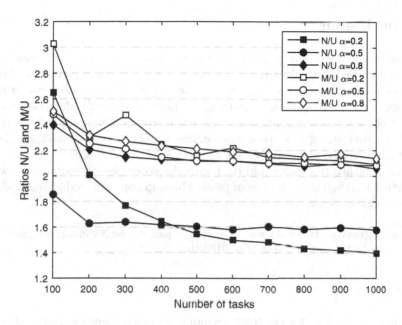

Fig. 1. Ratios between the number of VMs required by VFTS or DRMFF and the total load.

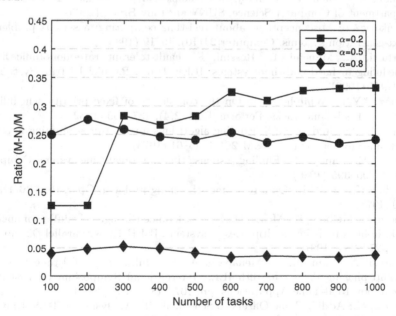

Fig. 2. The percentage of the VMs that VFTS saved compared with DRMFF.

6   Conclusions

This paper considers the problem of providing fault-tolerance for virtualized clouds with scheduling algorithms. VFTS combines the characteristics of cloud and traditional scheduling schemes to provide simple, efficient and low-cost fault-tolerance. VFTS assigns tasks in virtualized clouds instead of isolated computing nodes. Compared with simple duplication fault-tolerant method, VFTS makes use of the computing resources more efficiently. The analysis and simulation results have verified the effectiveness of the VFTS algorithm.

Finally, future research could deal with the strategies of assignment, which can further leverage the idle time of passive backup copy and reduce redundancy of active backup copies.

Acknowledgment. This work was supported in part by the National Natural Science Foundation of China under Grant No. 61332010.

References

1. Mell, P.M., Grance, T.: The NIST definition of cloud computing. Technical report, National Institute of Standards and Technology, Gaithersburg (2011)
2. Nanda, S., Chiueh, T.: A survey on virtualization technologies. Technical report, Department of Computer Science, SUNY at Stony Brook (2005)
3. Stankovic, J.: Misconceptions about real-time computing: a serious problem for next-generation systems. Computer **21**(10), 10–19 (1988)
4. Bertossi, A., Mancini, L., Rossini, F.: Fault-tolerant rate-monotonic first-fit scheduling in hard-real-time systems. IEEE Trans. Parallel Distrib. Syst. **10**(9), 934–945 (1999)
5. Leung, J.Y.T., Whitehead, J.: On the complexity of fixed-priority scheduling of periodic. Real-Time Tasks. Perform. Eval. **2**(4), 237–250 (1982)
6. Liu, C.L., Layland, J.W.: Scheduling algorithms for multiprogramming in a hard-real-time environment. J. ACM **20**(1), 46–61 (1973)
7. Joseph, M., Pandya, P.: Finding response times in a real-time system. Comput. J. **29**(5), 390–395 (1986)
8. Dhall, S.K., Liu, C.L.: On a real-time scheduling problem. Oper. Res. **26**(1), 127–140 (1978)
9. Ghosh, S., Melhem, R., Mosse, D.: Fault-tolerance through scheduling of aperiodic tasks in hard real-time multiprocessor systems. IEEE Trans. Parallel Distrib. Syst. **8**(3), 272–284 (1997)
10. Bertossi, A., Mancini, L., Menapace, A.: Scheduling hard-real-time tasks with backup phasing delay. In: 10th IEEE International Symposium on Distributed Simulation Real-Time Applications, pp. 107–118. IEEE (2006)
11. Tindell, K.: Adding Time-Offsets to Schedulability Analysis, pp. 1–28. University of York, Deparment of Compututer Science (1994)
12. Wang, J., Bao, W., Zhu, X., Yang, L.T., Xiang, Y.: FESTAL: fault-tolerant elastic scheduling algorithm for real-time tasks in virtualized clouds. IEEE Trans. Comput. **64**(9), 2545–2558 (2015)

Resource Allocation with Multiple QoS Constraints in OFDMA-Based Cloud Radio Access Network

Shichao Li[1], Gang Zhu[1], Siyu Lin[1,2(✉)], Qian Gao[1], Shengfeng Xu[1],
Lei Xiong[1], and Zhangdui Zhong[1]

[1] State Key Laboratory of Rail Traffic Control and Safety,
Beijing Jiaotong University, Beijing 100044, China
sylin@bjtu.edu.cn
[2] School of Electronic and Information Engineering,
Beijing Jiaotong University, Beijing 100044, China

Abstract. Due to the spread of mobile Internet and development of many new multimedia applications, there are much different quality-of-service (QoS) requirements of users in fifth generation (5G) communication system. In this paper, we consider two types of users with different QoS requirements in OFDMA based cloud radio access network (C-RAN). One type QoS requirements of users are joint bit error rate (BER) and data rate (type I users), and the other type is the data rate (type II users). We formulate the resource allocation problem in OFDMA-based C-RAN, the problem is maximal weighted sum rate for type II users subject to the QoS requirements of type I users and the fronthaul capacity constraint. Since the formulated problem is a non-convex problem, two subproblems are reformulated firstly, and then based on the CPLEX package, time-sharing and alternating methods, we proposed an iterative algorithm. Simulation results confirm that the proposed algorithm can achieve good performance.

Keywords: Cloud radio access network · Multiple QoS requirements · Subcarrier and power allocation · Time-sharing and alternating methods

1 Introduction

Cloud radio access network (C-RAN) can provide significant enhancement in data rate to support broadband applications [1,2]. It is anticipated that wireless communication systems will support more than 1000 times todays traffic volume by 2020 [2]. Besides, the number of mobile devices with diverse quality-of-service (QoS) requirements is increased. For example, video services need high speed data rate to guarantee with best effort for QoS requirement. However, voice services need low latency and low delay jitter. Therefore, how to satisfy the different QoS requirements of users is a significant problem in C-RAN.

© ICST Institute for Computer Sciences, Social Informatics and Telecommunications Engineering 2018
Q. Chen et al. (Eds.): ChinaCom 2016, Part II, LNICST 210, pp. 453–464, 2018.
DOI: 10.1007/978-3-319-66628-0_43

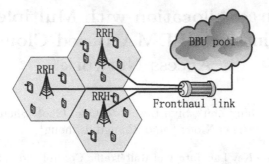

Fig. 1. System model

In wireless communication networks, there are various QoS requirements (such as rate, delay, bit error rate (BER) and energy efficiency) for different users. To meet the multiple QoS requirements of users, resource allocation has attracted considerable attention in recent years. Matalgah et al. proposed a sub-channel and power allocation algorithm to maximize the sum capacity subject to fairness parameters and QoS requirements constraints [3]. Considering the QoS requirements are interference tolerance and data rate, a resource allocation policy was proposed to obtain the maximal sum rate [4]. A resource allocation policy was proposed for different QoS guarantee, fair transmission and high data rate in OFDMA to get maximal sum data rate [5]. An optimal power allocation strategy was investigated maximize effective capacity subject to joint statistical delay and energy efficiency requirements [6].

All the previous works considered the maximal sum rate of all users subject to the different QoS requirements. However, since the resources are limited, we need guarantee the basic services firstly. If the resources are remaining, other services can be guaranteed. For example, voice services are the basic services in wireless networks, and we need guarantee them firstly. But for video services, we can meet their QoS requirements when the resources are remaining. Therefore, how to allocate resources to meet different QoS requirements of users is an urgent problem.

In this paper, we consider two types of users with different QoS requirements to share resources in OFDMA based C-RAN. We focus on the weighted sum rate maximization problem of the users whose QoS requirement is data rate, and the constraints are the other users whose QoS requirements, such as BER and data rate, should be guaranteed. Since the problem is non-convex, two subproblems are reformulated firstly. And then we use CPLEX package, time-sharing and alternating methods to solve these two subproblems. Based the solution of these two subproblems, we proposed an iterative algorithm. Numerical results show that the proposed algorithm can achieve good performance.

2 System Model

In this paper, we consider the downlink transmission in OFDMA-based C-RAN, as shown in Fig. 1. This system consists L remote radio heads (RRHs), which are connected to the baseband unit (BBU) pool via a fronthaul link with capacity of C_f. The transmission power for each RRH is P. Let B denote the bandwidth of each RRH, which is divided into K subcarriers. The set of subcarriers are denoted as $\Omega = \{1, 2 \dots K\}$ and the bandwidth of each subcarrier is B/K. Each RRH can reuse all the subcarriers, we ignore all interference in this system. N_0 is the power spectral density (PSD) of the white Gaussian noise. In this system, there are two types of users with different QoS requirements. One type QoS requirements of users are joint BER and data rate (type I users), the other type is the data rate (type II users). For different QoS requirements users, each RRH divides the available power P and subcarriers Ω into two parts. Let P_I and Ω_I be the power and subcarriers to the type I users; respectively $P_{II} = P - P_I$, $\Omega_{II} = \Omega \setminus \Omega_I$ are the power and subcarriers to the type II users. In each RRH, the set of type I users is $\mathcal{M} = \{1, ..., M\}$, and the set of type II users is $\mathcal{N} = \{1, ..., N\}$. Each user is served by one RRH.

For the type I users, each RRH supports T classes of services, denoted by the set $\mathcal{T} = \{1, ..., T\}$. Let M_t be the number of users belonged to the class t and the 1st user to the M_1^{th} user belong to class 1, the $(M_1 + 1)^{th}$ user to the $(M_1 + M_2)^{th}$ user belong to class 2, and so on [7,8]. To satisfy the QoS requirements, t^{th} class users need a target BER of P_e^t and a constant data rate of D_t bits/OFDM symbol. $c_{m,i}$ denotes the number of bits to be modulated onto one OFDM symbol on the ith subcarrier by the mth user. In this system, we consider M-ary Quadrature Amplitude Modulation (QAM), where $C = 2^{c_{m,i}}$ is the constellation size, as $c_{m,i} = \{2, 4, 6\}$, $C = \{4, 16, 64\}$. $c_{m,i} = 0$ means that no bit is transmitted on the ith subcarrier for the mth user. We denote $p_{m,i}$ and $\tau_{m,i}$ as the power and subcarriers allocated to the type I users by each RRH, where $p_{m,i}$ is the power allocated to user m over the i subcarrier. $\tau_{m,i}$ is a binary indicator, if subcarrier i allocated to user m, $\tau_{m,i} = 1$, otherwise $\tau_{m,i} = 0$. Then $\sum_{m=1}^{M} \sum_{i \in \Omega_I} p_{m,i} \doteq P_I$. And, $\sum_{m=1}^{M} \tau_{m,i} \leq 1$, $i \in \Omega_I$, it means one subcarrier only be allocated to one user. $h_{m,i}$ is the channel gain that user m experiences on subcarrier i.

For the type II users, we denote $p_{n,j}$ and $\tau_{n,j}$ as the power and subcarriers allocated to the type II users by each RRH. $h_{n,j}$ is the channel gain that user n experiences on subcarrier j.

3 Problem Formulation

In this section, we allocate the power and subcarriers to maximize the weighted sum rate of type II users with the constraints of the QoS of type I users and the fronthaul capacity.

For the type II users, the rate R_n achieved by user n in each RRH can be express as

$$R_n = \sum_{j \in \Omega_{II}} \tau_{n,j} \frac{B}{K} \log_2 \left(1 + \frac{p_{n,j}}{N_0 \frac{B}{K}} \right). \tag{1}$$

The fronthaul capacity constraint of RRHs in this system can be expressed as

$$LB \log_2 \left(1 + \frac{P}{N_0 B} \right) \leq C_f. \tag{2}$$

In this paper, we allocate the power and subcarriers to maximize the weighted sum rate of the type II users with the constraints of the QoS requirements of type I users and the fronthaul capacity, the QoS requirements including the BER and data rate for type I users. Then, this problem is formulated as

$$\textbf{(P1)} \quad \max_{\{p_{n,j}, \tau_{n,j}\}} L \sum_{n=1}^{N} \omega_n R_n \tag{3a}$$

$$\text{s.t} \quad \sum_{i \in \Omega_I} \tau_{m,i} c_{m,i} = D_1, \quad m = 1, 2, ..., M_1,$$

$$\sum_{i \in \Omega_I} \tau_{m,i} c_{m,i} = D_2, \quad m = M_1 + 1, \quad M_1 + 2, ...M_1 + M_2,$$

$$\cdots$$

$$\sum_{i \in \Omega_I} \tau_{m,i} c_{m,i} = D_t, \quad m = M_{T-1} + 1, \quad M_{T-1} + 2, ...M_{T-1} + M_T, \tag{3b}$$

$$\sum_{m=1}^{M} \tau_{m,i} \leq 1, \tau_{m,i} \in \{0,1\}, \quad i \in \Omega_I, \sum_{n=1}^{N} \tau_{n,j} \leq 1, \tau_{n,j} \in \{0,1\}, \quad j \in \Omega_{II},$$
$$\tag{3c}$$

$$LB \log_2 \left(1 + \frac{P}{N_0 B} \right) \leq C_f, \tag{3d}$$

$$\sum_{t=1}^{T} \sum_{m=1}^{M} \sum_{i \in \Omega_I} p_{m,i}^t \doteq P_I, \tag{3e}$$

$$P_I + P_{II} \leq P, \quad \Omega_I + \Omega_{II} \subseteq \Omega, \tag{3f}$$

where ω_n is the weight of user n, and it expresses the priority of user n. $p_{m,i}^t$ is the power allocated to user m over the i subcarrier for t class of service. Constraint (3b) guarantees the transmission rate of type I users. Constraint (3c) means one subcarrier only shared by one user. Constraint (3d) is the fronthaul capacity constraint. Constraint (3e) is the power allocated to type I users. Constraint (3f) is the system subcarriers and power constraints. This problem is a mixed-integer nonlinear programming (MINLP) problem, so it can not be solved by classical convex optimization methods [9].

4   Resource Allocation Algorithm

The problem (P1) is to maximize the weighted sum rate of type II users subject to the QoS requirements of type I users and the fronthaul capacity. Because the resources are limited, for the type I users, we only need allocate minimum resources to guarantee their minimum QoS requirements, and the remaining resources are all allocated to type II users. In order to solve this problem, firstly, we use CPLEX package to obtain the minimum resources for type I users. And then, we use time-sharing and alternating methods to allocate resources for type II users.

4.1   Resource Allocation for Type I Users

In this subsection, we formulate a subproblem to minimize the transmission power of type I users while satisfying the QoS requirements of type I users for all classes of services.

For the type I users, according to [10], we denote $f_t(c)$ as the required received power for class t users in a subcarrier for reliable reception of c information bits/symbol

$$f_t(c) = \frac{N_0 B}{3K} \left[Q^{-1}(\frac{P_e^t}{4}) \right]^2 (2^c - 1), \tag{4}$$

where $Q^{-1}(x)$ is inverse function.

In order to satisfy the QoS requirements of each type I user, the allocated power to ith subcarrier by the mth user of class t is

$$p_{m,i}^t = f_t(c_{m,i})/h_{m,i}^2 = \frac{N_0 B}{3K} \left[Q^{-1}(\frac{P_e^t}{4}) \right]^2 (2^{c_{m,i}} - 1)/h_{m,i}^2. \tag{5}$$

Inspired by [7,8], we notice that the term $2^{c_{m,i}}$ can only take discrete values of 2^2, 2^4 and 2^6. Therefore $f_t(c_{m,i})\tau_{m,i}$ can be replaced by

$$q_t(g_{m,i}^s) = 3\rho_t g_{m,i}^1 + 15\rho_t g_{m,i}^2 + 63\rho_t g_{m,i}^3, \tag{6}$$

with additional constraints

$$\sum_{s=1}^{3} g_{m,i}^s \leq 1, m = 1, 2..., M, i \in \Omega_I, \tag{7}$$

where $g_{m,i}^s \in \{0, 1\}$ are the three new binary variables, where $s = 1, 2, 3$. Equation (7) means the selected modulation mode.

$$\rho_t = \frac{N_0 B}{3K} \left[Q^{-1}(\frac{P_e^t}{4}) \right]^2. \tag{8}$$

According to the above analysis, the minimal transmission power of type I users problem can be formulated as

$$\textbf{(P2)} \quad \min_{g_{m,i}^s} L \sum_{t=1}^{T} \sum_{m=1}^{M} \sum_{i \in \Omega_I} \frac{q_t(g_{m,i}^s)}{h_{m,i}^2} \tag{9a}$$

s.t $\quad \displaystyle\sum_{i \in \Omega_I} r_{m,i} = D_1, \quad m = 1, 2, ..., M_1,$

$\qquad \displaystyle\sum_{i \in \Omega_I} r_{m,i} = D_2, \quad m = M_1 + 1, \quad M_1 + 2, ... M_1 + M_2,$

$\qquad ...$

$\qquad \displaystyle\sum_{i \in \Omega_I} r_{m,i} = D_t, \quad m = M_{T-1} + 1, \quad M_{T-1} + 2, ... M_{T-1} + M_T, \qquad$ (9b)

$\qquad r_{m,i} = 2g_{m,i}^1 + 4g_{m,i}^2 + 6g_{m,i}^3, \quad m = 1, ..., M, i \in \Omega_I,$ (9c)

$\qquad q_t(g_{m,i}^s) = 3\rho_t g_{m,i}^1 + 15\rho_t g_{m,i}^2 + 63\rho_t g_{m,i}^3, \quad m = 1, ..., M, i \in \Omega_I,$ (9d)

$\qquad \rho_t = \dfrac{N_0 B}{3K} \left[Q^{-1}(\dfrac{P_e^t}{4}) \right]^2, \quad t = 1, 2..., T,$ (9e)

$\qquad \displaystyle\sum_{s=1}^{3} g_{m,i}^s \leq 1, \quad m = 1, ..., M, i \in \Omega_I,$ (9f)

$\qquad g_{m,i}^s \in \{0, 1\}, \quad s = 1, 2, 3.$ (9g)

Constraint (9b) and (9c) guarantee the transmission rate of type I users. Constraint (9d), (9e), (9f) and (9g) are the relationship between BER and transmission power.

Problem (P2) is a standard binary linear programming (BLP), therefore we can use standard packages such as CPLEX [11] to solve it.

4.2 Resource Allocation for Type II Users

By using CPLEX package, we can obtain the power P_I and subcarriers Ω_I which are allocated to type I users. After that, the remaining resources are all allocated to type II users. The maximal weighted sum rate of type II users problem can be formulated as

$$\textbf{(P3)} \quad \max_{\{p_{n,j}, \tau_{n,j}\}} L \sum_{n=1}^{N} \omega_n R_n \qquad (10a)$$

$$\text{s.t} \sum_{n=1}^{N} \tau_{n,j} \leq 1, \quad \tau_{n,j} \in \{0, 1\}, j \in \Omega_{II}, \qquad (10b)$$

$$\sum_{n=1}^{N} \sum_{j \in \Omega_{II}} \tau_{n,j} p_{n,j} \leq P - P_I, \qquad (10c)$$

$$\Omega_I + \Omega_{II} \subseteq \Omega, \qquad (10d)$$

$$L B_{II} \log_2 \left(1 + \frac{P}{N_0 B_{II}} \right) \leq C_f - C_I, \qquad (10e)$$

where B_{II} is the bandwith allocated to type II users by each RRH. And C_I is the transmission capacity of type I users and it can be get from problem (P2).

Constraint (10b) means one subcarrier only shared by one user. Constraint (10c) and (10d) are the system power and subcarriers constraints. Constraint (10e) is the fronthaul capacity constraint.

4.3   Resource Allocation for Type II Users Without Fronthaul Constraint

For convenience, we denote problem (P3) without fronthaul constraint (2) as problem (P3-1), which is a MINLP problem. In this subsection, we use time-sharing and alternating methods to solve this problem [12].

Problem (P3-1) with Time-Sharing: For constraint (10b), we relax it firstly,

$$\sum_{n=1}^{N} \tau_{n,j} \leq 1, \tau_{n,j} \in [0,1], \quad j \in \Omega_{II}. \tag{11}$$

And then, we use alternating method to solve problem (P3-1) with time-sharing by considering two problems: one for tuning the allocated power for given time-share values and the other for tuning time-share values for given fixed power allocation.

Proposition 1. *For given fixed allocated time-share values, the optimal power allocation is*

$$p_{n,j} = \max \left(\frac{L\omega_n \frac{B}{K}}{\lambda_n \ln 2} - N_0 \frac{B}{K}, 0 \right), \tag{12}$$

where λ_n are the Lagrange multipliers.

Proof. Due to the limited pages, we can easily get (12) by using the dual decomposition method [9].   □

The power allocation $p_{n,j}$ is instantaneous power. The average power used by the user on this subcarrier is $q_{n,j} = p_{n,j}\tau_{n,j}$. Now, we fix the average power $q_{n,j}$ to tune time-share values.

For given fixed allocated average power, the optimal time-share variables are the solutions of the following optimization problem

$$\tau_{n,j} = \arg\max_{\tau_{n,j}} L \sum_{n=1}^{N} \sum_{j \in \Omega_{II}} \omega_n \tau_{n,j} \frac{B}{K} \log_2 \left(1 + \frac{q_{n,j}}{N_0 \frac{B}{K} \tau_{n,j}} \right), \tag{13}$$

subject to the constraints (10d) and (11).

Proposition 2. *For given fixed allocated power, the time-share values of (13) can be found by solving the following equations*

$$u_n(y) = L\omega_n \frac{B}{K} \left(\log_2(1+y) - \frac{y}{\ln 2(1+y)} \right) = \beta_n, \quad y = \frac{q_{n,j}}{N_0 \frac{B}{K} \tau_{n,j}}, \tag{14}$$

where $u_n(y)$ is the utility function of user n and β_n are the Lagrange multipliers.

Proof. Due to the limited pages, we can easily get (14) by using the dual decomposition method [9].   □

Equation(14) means that for any given subcarrier the optimal time-share values should balance the utility function of the users. We propose an iterative algorithm to obtain the optimal time-share values.

For a given subcarrier j, set initial time-share values and calculate the time-share values for the fixed values of $q_{n,j}^{\bar{t}}$

$$\tau_{n,j}^{(\bar{t}+1)} = \frac{u_{n,j}^{\bar{t}}\tau_{n,j}^{\bar{t}}}{\sum_{n=1}^{N}u_{n,j}^{\bar{t}}\tau_{n,j}^{\bar{t}}}, \quad u_{n,j}^{\bar{t}} = u_n\left(\frac{q_{n,j}^{\bar{t}}}{N_0\frac{B}{K}\tau_{n,j}^{\bar{t}}}\right). \tag{15}$$

Proposition 3. *For large enough number of iterations on $\bar{t}$, (15) will converge to the time-share optimal solution.*

Proof. Equation (15) allocates new time-share proportional to the next utility function of users. Therefore, users with larger/smaller utilities will get more/less time-share values. It will make the overall utility increase every step. Moreover, there exists a fixed point corresponding to the balanced utilities. Hence, by increasing the number of iterations Eq. (15) will converge to its fixed point.   □

4.4 Resource Allocation for Type II Users with Fronthaul Constraint

From the previous subsection, we get the resource allocation for type II users without fronthaul constraint. We define the optimal objective value of problem (P3-1) as $R_{IIw/f}$ and define the optimal objective value of problem (P3) as R_{II}^*. Then, R_{II}^* can be found as

$$R_{II}^* = \begin{cases} R_{IIw/f} & if\ R_{IIw/f} \leq C_f - C_I \\ C_f - C_I & if\ R_{IIw/f} \geq C_f - C_I. \end{cases} \tag{16}$$

4.5 Proposed Iterative Algorithm

According to the above analysis, we propose an algorithm to calculate problem (P1). The algorithm is presented as Algorithm 1.

5   Results and Discussions

In this section, simulations are made to confirm our analysis. The number of RRH is 1 and RRH transmission power is 5 w. The fronthaul capacity is 70 Mbps. The bandwidth is set 8 MHz and it is divided into 16 subcarriers. The bandwith of each subcarrier is 512 kHz. There are 2 type I users of two different service classes, i.e. $M_1 = M_2 = 1$, which data rates are $D_1 = 6$, $D_2 = 8$ bits/OFDM symbol and the target BER values are $P_e^1 = 10^{-2}$, $P_e^2 = 10^{-4}$. The PSD level N_0 is 4×10^{-10} W/Hz.

Algorithm 1. Proposed Power and Subcarrier Allocation

1: input $P, B, L, N_0, M, N, K, T, P_e^t, C_f, D_1, D_2, ...D_t$;
2: use CPLEX package to calculate problem (P2), get Ω_I and P_I;
3: use (3f) to get Ω_{II} and P_{II};
4: give a feasible set for $\tau_{n,j}$;
5: give the $\bar{l}$-th iteration $\tau_{n,j}^{\bar{l}}$, use *Proposition* 1 to calculate $\bar{l}$-th iteration $q_{n,j}^{\bar{l}}$;
6: give the $\bar{l}$-th iteration $q_{n,j}^{\bar{l}}$, use (15) to calculate $(\bar{t}+1)$-th iteration $\tau_{n,j}^{(\bar{t}+1)}$;
7: stop if the termination criterion is satisfied, otherwise go to step 5;
8: use (16) to calculate R_{II}^*.

5.1 Resource Allocation for Type I Users

In order to obtain the maximal weighted sum rate of type II users, we only need allocate minimum resources to type I users to guarantee theirs QoS requirements. The problem (P2) is to minimize the transmission power with satisfying the data rate and BER for type I users. To understand subcarrier and bit allocation for type I users. We give one allocated result at one snapshot of channel gain in Table 1. From this table, we can see the subcarrier allocation and constellation selection on each subcarrier for each user with every constraints fulfilled.

Table 1. Subcarrier and bit allocation at minimized transmit power. When $M_1 = M_2 = 1$, $N = 16$, $D_1 = 6$, $D_2 = 8$ bits/OFDM symbol, $P_e^1 = 10^{-2}$, $P_e^2 = 10^{-4}$.

$h_{m,i}^2$	i=1	i=2	i=3	i=4	i=5	i=6	i=7	i=8
m=1	0.7102	0.3216	0.4986	0.4836	0.2572	0.3516	0.4036	0.3317
m=2	0.2006	0.2989	0.3276	0.3062	0.2773	0.6589	0.2274	0.3214
$\tau_{m,i}c_{m,i}$	i=1	i=2	i=3	i=4	i=5	i=6	i=7	i=8
m=1	0	0	0	0	0	0	0	0
m=2	2	0	6	0	0	0	0	0
$h_{m,i}^2$	i=9	i=10	i=11	i=12	i=13	i=14	i=15	i=16
m=1	0.2817	0.3012	0.2417	0.5696	0.3337	0.392	0.6052	0.1373
m=2	0.1254	0.2567	0.4312	0.6865	0.5891	0.1289	0.5698	0.4531
$\tau_{m,i}c_{m,i}$	i=9	i=10	i=11	i=12	i=13	i=14	i=15	i=16
m=1	0	0	0	0	0	0	0	6
m=2	0	0	0	0	0	0	0	0

5.2 Resource Allocation for Type II Users

We compare the following algorithms with our proposed algorithm:

- Average power algorithm: A solution where subcarrier is optimal but power is allocated to each user averagely in each subcarrier at one snapshot.

– Average subcarrier algorithm: A solution where power allocation is optimal but subcarrier is allocated to each user averagely at one snapshot.

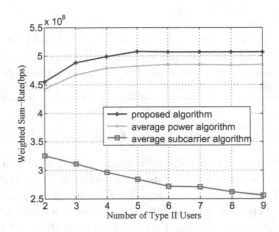

Fig. 2. Weighted sum rate versus number of type II users under different resource allocation policies

Figure 2 illustrates the weighted sum rate versus number of type II users under different resource allocation policies. For the proposed algorithm, it can be seen that with the number of type II users increases, the weighted sum rate increases, which is because of the multiuser diversity. However, when the number of type II users reaches 5, the weighted sum rate can not increase, which is because that the resources are limited. For the average subcarrier algorithm, it can be seen that with the number of type II users increases, the weighted sum rate decreases. We can explain as follows: when the number of type II users increases, the number of deep fading users also increases, and these deep fading users occupy more subcarriers. And the power is allocated to the users who has been allocated subcarriers. Therefore, with the number of type II users increases, the weighted sum rate decreases. The average power algorithm has the same trend with the proposed algorithm, that is because all users are allocated power in these two algorithms.

Figure 3 illustrates weighted sum rate versus number of type II users under different BER of type I users. From this figure we can see that with the BER value of type I users decreases, the weighted sum rate of type II users decreases. This is because when the BER value of type I users decreases, the RRH needs to allocate more power to type I users, so the weighted sum rate of type II users becomes low.

Figure 4 illustrates weighted sum rate versus number of type II users under different data rate of type I users. From this figure we can see that with the data rate of type I users increases, the weighted sum rate of type II users decreases. It is because that as the data rate of type I users increases, the RRH needs to

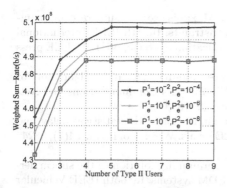

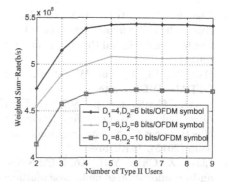

Fig. 3. Weighted sum rate versus number of type II users under different BER of type I users

Fig. 4. Weighted sum rate versus number of type II users under different data rate of type I users

allocate more subcarriers to type I users, so the weighted sum rate of type II users becomes low.

6 Conclusion

In this paper, we investigated the weighted sum rate maximization of type II users with joint QoS requirements of type I users and fronthaul capacity constraints in OFDMA-based C-RAN. To deal with the optimization problem, a MINLP problem was formulated. Because it is a non-convex problem, two subproblems were reformulated firstly. And then based on CPLEX package, time-sharing and alternating methods, an iterative algorithm was proposed. Simulation results have demonstrated that the proposed algorithm can achieve good performance.

Acknowledgments. This work was partly supported by the Fundamental Research Funds for the Central Universities (No. 2015RC032), the State Key Laboratory of Rail Traffic Control and Safety (Nos. RCS2015K011, RCS2015ZT001), the National Natural Science Foundation of China (Nos. 61501023, U1334202, U1534201), the National Science and Technology Major Project (2015ZX03001027), the Project of China Railway Corporation under Grant (No. 2016X009-E).

References

1. Chih-Lin, I., Rowell, C., Han, S., et al.: Toward green and soft: a 5G perspective. IEEE Commun. Mag. **52**(2), 66–73 (2014). IEEE press
2. China Mobile: C-RAN: the road green RAN. In: China Mobile Research Institute (2011)
3. Matalgah, M.M., Hammouri, O.M., Paudel, B.: Cross-layer capacity optimisation in WiMAX orthogonal frequency division multiple access systems with multi-class quality of services and users queue status. IET Commun. **8**(14), 2500–2508 (2014). IET press

4. Che, E., Tuan, H.D., Tam, H.H.M., et al.: Maximisation of sum rate in cognitive multi-cell wireless networks with QoS constraints. In: 8th IEEE International Conference on Signal Processing and Communication Systems, pp. 1–4. IEEE press (2014)
5. Bao, N., Li, J., Xia, W., et al.: QoS-aware resource allocation algorithm for OFDMA-WLAN integrated system. In: IEEE Wireless Communications and Networking Conference, pp. 807–812. IEEE press (2013)
6. Musavian, L., Ni, Q.: Effective capacity maximization with statistical delay and effective energy efficiency requirements. IEEE Trans. Wirel. Commun. 14(7), 3824–3835 (2015). IEEE press
7. Liang, Z., Chew, Y.H., Ko, C.C.: A linear programming solution to the subcarrier-and-bit allocation of multiclass multiuser OFDM systems. In: 65th IEEE Vehicular Technology Conference, pp. 2682–2686. IEEE press (2007)
8. Gong, M., Zhang, C., Lu, J., et al.: Dynamic resource allocation in high speed mobile OFDMA system. In: IEEE International Conference on Communications, pp. 3335–3339. IEEE press (2008)
9. Boyd, S., Vandenberghe, L.: Convex Optimization. Cambridge University Press, Cambridge (2004)
10. Wong, C.Y., Cheng, R.S., Lataief, K.B., et al.: Multiuser OFDM with adaptive subcarrier, bit, and power allocation. J. Sel. Areas Commun. 17, 1747–1758 (1999). IEEE press
11. CPLEX: IBMs Linear Programming Solver. http://www.ilog.com/product/cplex/
12. Hoshyar, R., Shariat, M., Tafazolli, R.: Subcarrier and power allocation with multiple power constraints in OFDMA systems. IEEE Commun. Lett. 14(7), 644–646 (2010). IEEE press

Energy-Efficient and Latency-Aware Data Placement for Geo-Distributed Cloud Data Centers

Yuqi Fan[✉], Jie Chen, Lusheng Wang, and Zongze Cao

School of Computer and Information, Hefei University of Technology, Hefei, China
yuqi.fan@hfut.edu.cn

Abstract. Cloud computing technology achieves enormous scale by routing service requests from users to geographically distributed servers, typically located at different data centers. On one hand, energy consumption of data centers and networks has been receiving increasing attention in recent years. On the other hand, users require low latency during data access from data centers. In this paper, we tackle the problem of energy-efficient data placement in data centers, taking into account access latency, energy consumption of data centers and network transport. We propose two request-routing algorithms to determine the number of copies for each data chunk and the data centers accommodating the data chunk. Our simulation results have shown that the proposed algorithms are effective in terms of the tradeoff among the data access latency, the energy consumed by network transport and data centers.

Keywords: Energy-efficient · Latency · Energy consumption of servers · Energy consumption of network transport · Data placement

1 Introduction

Cloud computing technology achieves enormous scale by routing service requests from end users to a set of geographically distributed servers, typically located at different data centers. In order to reduce data access latency experienced by users, it is quite often to place the data in multiple data centers so that the users can access the data from nearby data centers. However, the data centers are large consumers of electricity, consuming about 1.3% of the worldwide electricity supply [1]. At the same time, a lot of energy needs to power the network equipments, which consume approximately 14.8% of the total ICT energy consumption [2].

There has been some work on reducing the delay, the electricity cost and consumption of the data centers and the networks in recent years. A request-routing scheme to minimize the electricity bill of multi-datacenter systems is proposed in [3]. [4] improves the algorithms in [3] on multi-region electricity markets to better capture the present electricity price situation. [5] proposes an adaptive operational cost optimization framework incorporating time-varying electricity

© ICST Institute for Computer Sciences, Social Informatics and Telecommunications Engineering 2018
Q. Chen et al. (Eds.): ChinaCom 2016, Part II, LNICST 210, pp. 465–474, 2018.
DOI: 10.1007/978-3-319-66628-0_44

prices and dynamic user request rates. [6] considers the joint optimization problem of minimizing carbon emission and electricity cost. [7] adjusts the number of servers running in data centers for a tradeoff between latency and carbon emissions. [8] provides a method to calculate the energy consumption of the network, which can estimate the energy consumption required to transport one bit from a data center to a user through the Internet. [9] jointly considers the electricity cost, service level agreement (SLA) requirement, and emission reduction budget by exploiting the spatial and temporal variabilities of the electricity carbon footprint. [10] proposes a request-routing scheme, FORTE, allowing operators to strive the tradeoff among electricity costs, access latency, and carbon emissions. Assuming each data chunk, i.e. each piece of data, is placed in only one data center, [11] proposes a request-routing scheme to strike the tradeoff among access latency, energy consumption of the data centers and the network transport during data placement.

In this paper, we tackle the data placement problem in geo-distributed cloud data centers, taking into account the access latency, the energy consumption of the servers in the data centers, and the energy consumed by network transport, assuming each data chunk can be placed in more than one data center. The main contribution of this work is two-fold: First, we investigate the data placement problem with the objective to strike the tradeoff among the three factors above. Second, we propose two efficient algorithms to determine the proper number of copies for each data chunk and the data centers accommodating the data chunk.

The rest of the paper is organized as follows. The problem under study is formally defined in Sect. 2. The proposed algorithms are presented in Sect. 3. Section 4 reports the performance evaluation. The paper concludes in Sect. 5.

2   Problem Formulation

The network model that the data centers provide data services to the end users is similar to the one in [8,11], and the energy $e_I(u_i, dc_j)$ required to transport one bit from a data center to a user through the Internet is estimated via Eq. (1).

$$e_I(u_i, dc_j) = 6(3\frac{P_{es}}{C_{es}} + \frac{P_{bg}}{C_{bg}} + \frac{P_g}{C_g} + 2\frac{P_{pe}}{C_{pe}}) \\ +2\frac{P_c}{C_c}h_c(u_i, dc_j) + \frac{P_w}{2C_w}h_c(u_i, dc_j) \tag{1}$$

where P_{es}, P_{bg}, P_g, P_{pe}, P_c and P_w are the power consumed by the Ethernet switches, broadband gateway routers, data center gateway routers, provider edge routers, core routers, and WDM transport equipment, respectively. C_{es}, C_{bg}, C_g, C_{pe}, C_c and C_w are the capacities of the corresponding equipment in bits per second. $h_c(u_i, dc_j)$ is the number of hops during the data transmission in the core network. We assume a server consumes the full-system power when the server is on, because (1) it is an estimator accurate enough to determine the relative rank in energy consumption; (2) no general analytical model of server energy consumption for various kind of servers at different loads is available [12]. The problem is formulated as follows.

Minimize:

$$
\begin{aligned}
&\lambda_1 \sum_{u_i, dc_j, s_m, d_k} rep(dc_j, s_m, d_k) p(u_i \mid d_k) l(u_i, dc_j, d_k) \\
&+\lambda_2 \sum_{dc_j, s_m} rep(dc_j, s_m) e_S(dc_j, s_m) \\
&+\lambda_3 \sum_{u_i, dc_j, s_m, d_k} s(d_k) rep(dc_j, s_m, d_k) p(u_i \mid d_k) e_I(u_i, dc_j)
\end{aligned}
\tag{2}
$$

Subject to:

$$
rep(dc_j, s_m) = min(\sum_{d_k} rep(dc_j, s_m, d_k), 1), \forall dc_j, s_m \tag{3}
$$

$$
\sum_{dc_j, s_m} rep(dc_j, s_m, d_k) \geq 1, \forall d_k \tag{4}
$$

$$
\sum_{u_i} p(u_i \mid d_k) = 1, \forall d_k \tag{5}
$$

$$
e_S(dc_j, s_m) = P_{s_m}^{dc_j} * PUE(dc_j) \tag{6}
$$

$$
\sum_{d_k} rep(dc_j, s_m, d_k) s(d_k) \leq C(s_m, dc_j), \forall dc_j, s_m \tag{7}
$$

where $p(u_i \mid d_k)$ is the probability that a given request coming from user u_i is asking for data d_k, $s(d_k)$ is the size of data d_k, $l(u_i, dc_j, d_k)$ is the average latency between user u_i and data center dc_j for data d_k, $rep(dc_j, s_m, d_k)$ indicates whether data d_k is placed in server s_m in data center dc_j, $rep(dc_j, s_m)$ indicates whether server s_m in data center dc_j has accommodated some data, $e_S(s_m, dc_j)$ is the average energy consumption of server s_m in data center dc_j, $PUE(dc_j)$ is the PUE of data center dc_j, $P_{s_m}^{dc_j}$ is the average processing power of sever s_m in data center dc_j, and $C(s_m, dc_j)$ is the capacity of server s_m in data center dc_j.

λ_1, λ_2, and λ_3 in Eq. (2) are the constant normalized weights of the sub-objectives of the latency, the energy consumption of the servers in the data centers and the energy consumed by the network transport, respectively. Equation (3) mandates the data placement incurs access delay and energy consumption. Equation (4) requires each data chunk to be placed in some data center(s). Equation (5) determines the request for a data chunk comes from one of the users. Equation (6) defines that the energy consumption of the servers should take into account the PUE of the data center. Equation (7) dictates the size of the data stored in a server cannot exceed the capacity of the server.

3   Energy-Efficient Latency-Aware Data Deployment Algorithms

We propose an Energy-efficient Latency-aware Data Deployment algorithm (ELDD) for the problem. The algorithm shown in Algorithm 1 consists of two

---

Algorithm 1. *Algorithm ELDD*

Input: The large data segment set $D^l_{k'}$
Output: The set of working servers
 1: **for all** $d^l_{k'}$ **do**
 2:     Merge.
 3:     Sort the data centers.
 4:     Assume all the data centers have accommodated large data segment $d^l_{k'}$.
 5:     Assign each user to the data center with the least cost that holds $d^l_{k'}$.
 6:     **for all** dc_j **do**
 7:         Evaluate the cost of turning off the server accommodating $d^l_{k'}$ in dc_j.
 8:         Turn off the server if shutting down the server will lead to cost saving.
 9:     **end for**
10: **end for**

---

stages: (1) The data chunks are merged into large data segments so that each data segment consumes nearly the full capacity of a server. (2) The proper servers are found to accommodate each large data segment $d^l_{k'}$.

A data chunk with high access probability is more likely to be placed in more than one data center to reduce the energy consumption of network transport and the access delay. The data chunks are sorted by the non-ascending order of the total access probability from all the users in algorithm ELDD. The algorithm proceeds iteratively using greedy strategy. Within each iteration, the algorithm performs procedure Merge to put multiple data chunks into a large data segment, under the constraint that the large data segment does not exceed the storage size of server. The large data segments are formed one by one. This procedure continues until all data chunks are put merged.

After obtaining the large data segment set with procedure Merge, algorithm ELDD searches for the proper servers to accommodate each large data segment $d^l_{k'}$. The basic rationale of algorithm ELDD is to iteratively turning off the servers. Initially, algorithm ELDD places each large data segment $d^l_{k'}$ in all the data centers. Therefore, all the users can access the required data from the closest data center to reduce the energy consumption of network transport and the access delay. The effect of turning off the server accommodating large data segment $d^l_{k'}$ in each data center is evaluated. The cost of placing data chunk d_k on server s_m in data center dc_j is calculated via Eq. (8). If a server possessing $d^l_{k'}$ is turned off, the users accessing $d^l_{k'}$ from the server have to acquire $d^l_{k'}$ from the next closest data center. The server will be shut down if the inactive server can reduce the placement cost. The procedure repeats for each large data segment set, until all the large data segments are placed into some server(s).

$$cost(d_k, dc_j, s_m) = \lambda_1 \sum_{u_i} l(u_i, dc_j) p(u_i \mid d_k)$$
$$+\lambda_2 e_S(dc_j, s_m) + \lambda_3 \sum_{u_i} s(d_k) e_I(u_i, dc_j) p(u_i \mid d_k) \tag{8}$$

Theorem 1. *Assume the number of data centers and users are $\mathcal{D}$ and $\mathcal{U}$, respectively. The time complexity of algorithm ELDD is $O(\mathcal{D}\mathcal{U} + \mathcal{D}\log\mathcal{D})$.*

Proof: The time complexity of sorting the data centers is $O(\mathcal{D} \log \mathcal{D})$. Assume two arrays $Leastcost$ and $NextLeastcost$, each with the length of $\mathcal{U}$. $Leastcost[\nu] = \omega$ denotes that the working data center with the least cost to accommodate the data required by user u_ν is the data center with the ω-th least cost for user u_ν. $NextLeastcost$ is similar to $Leastcost$, which is to store the level of the working data center with the next to the least placement cost to accommodate the data required by user u_ν. Initially, each user can access the data from the data center with the least cost, since each data chunk has a copy in all the data centers. Therefore, $Leastcost[\nu] = 1$ and $NextLeastcost[\nu] = 2$ for each ν. For each $Leastcost[\nu] = \omega$, we evaluate the cost of turning off server in the data center and assigning user u_ν to the data center with the next to the least placement cost, if possible. If it leads to cost saving by turning off the server in the data center, $Leastcost$ and $NextLeastcost$ will be updated. ν increases from 1 in the range of $[1, \mathcal{D}]$, and the traverse of $Leastcost$ and $NextLeastcost$ runs in $O(\mathcal{D}\mathcal{U})$ time. Therefore, the time complexity of algorithm ELDD is $O(\mathcal{D}\mathcal{U} + \mathcal{D} \log \mathcal{D})$. $\square$

Note that we can deal with the data centers in different orders while placing a data chunk in the data centers. We propose ordering method *ELDD-Standard* which sorts the servers in the data centers in a non-descending order of the average processing power of the servers. Another ordering criteria is defined via Eq. (9).

$$S_j = f_j - \sum_i max\{0, v_i - c_{i,j}\} \tag{9}$$

where f_j denotes the server energy consumption of data center dc_j, v_i is the integrated cost of the data access latency, energy consumption of the network transport and the data centers while placing the data in the closest working data center, and $c_{i,j}$ indicates the cost of the data access latency an energy consumption of network transport by assigning user u_i to data center dc_j. We propose sorting method *ELDD-Fast* which sorts the data centers in the non-descending order of S_j. For Simplicity, we call ELDD-Standard and ELDD-Fast as Standard and Fast, respectively.

4   Simulation

We evaluate the performance of the proposed algorithms Standard and Fast by comparing them with the algorithms FORTE [10] and GLDD [11]. The objective of FORTE indicates that both the electricity costs and carbon emissions increase with the number of the servers used in the data centers. With FORTE, a data chunk may be placed in one or more data centers, while GLDD places each data chunk in a data center. Similar to GLDD, Standard and Fast strike a tradeoff among the factors considered in GLDD. However, a data chunk may be placed in one or more data centers with Standard and Fast, which is similar to FORTE.

We use geographical distance as an approximation for latency similar to [10,11]. The request for a data chunk from a user is random, and any request for a data chunk comes from one of the users. Each data center hosts 200 servers, each with the capacity of $2TB$ and the power of 500 W. The equipments used in the network are the same as [13]. The quantity of data chunks, the average distance between the users and the data centers, the PUE of the data centers, and the number of WDM and core routers are set as the same as [11].

4.1   Impact of Various Number of Data Chunks

In this subsection, we investigate the performance of Standard, Fast, GLDD and FORTE with regard to the distance, the energy consumed by the network transport and the servers in the data centers versus different number of data chunks, assuming the number of users is 1000.

Figure 1 demonstrates that in general the distance increases with the increase of the number of data chunks, which is also shown in Eqs. (2) and (8). FORTE places each data chunk in one or more data centers and each user can access the data from the data center located closest to the user. Each data chunk has only one copy with GLDD, and each user may not be able to access the data from the closest data center. Standard and Fast may place each data chunk in one or more data centers. However, the number of data copies with Standard and Fast may be potentially less than that with FORTE, since Standard and Fast also consider the factors of energy consumed by the network transport and the data centers. Therefore, FORTE leads to the least distance and GLDD results in the largest distance. Standard only considers the energy consumption of the data centers while evaluating the cost of turning off the servers. In contrast, Fast takes into account the energy consumption of the network transport and the data access latency, in addition to the energy consumption of the data centers. Therefore, Fast potentially places more copies of the data than Standard, which leads to less distance than Standard.

Figure 2 illustrates that the energy consumption of the servers in the data centers increases with the increase of number of data chunks, because more servers are needed to accommodate the data. FORTE consumes the most energy, since FORTE places more copies of the data. Each data chunk is placed in only one data center with GLDD, and hence GLDD requires the least energy. Fast potentially places more copies of the data than Standard, which makes Fast consume more energy than Standard.

Figure 3 shows that the energy consumed by network transport increases with the increasing number of data chunks, since more data transfer incurs more energy consumption in the network. FORTE results in the least energy consumed by the network transport. With FORTE, the data go through shorter distances between the data centers and the users than with GLDD, Standard and Fast, which potentially reduces the number of network devices needed for the data transfer as shown in Eq. (1). With GLDD, each data chunk is placed only in one data center. The data access has to experience largest distance, and hence requires the most number of network devices, which makes GLDD consume the most network transport energy consumption. Fast potentially leads to less distance and less network devices than Standard, and hence Standard results in more energy consumed by the networks.

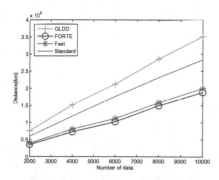

Fig. 1. Distance with the algorithms of Standard, Fast, GLDD and FORTE as the increasing number of data chunks.

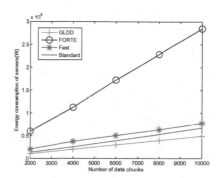

Fig. 2. Energy consumption of servers with the algorithms of Standard, Fast, GLDD and FORTE as the increasing number of data chunks.

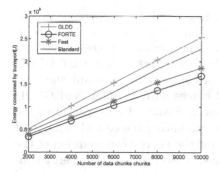

Fig. 3. Energy consumed by transport with the algorithms of Standard, Fast, GLDD and FORTE as the increasing number of data chunks.

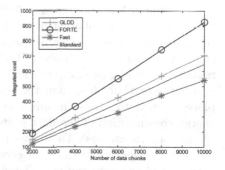

Fig. 4. Integrated cost with the algorithms of Standard, Fast, GLDD and FORTE as the increasing number of data chunks.

The performance in terms of the integrated cost of the distance, the energy consumed by the servers in the data centers and the network transport is depicted in Fig. 4. λ_1, λ_2 and λ_3 are all set as 1, so that all the three factors will have equal impact on the data placement decision. Standard, Fast and GLDD consider all the three factors of the data access latency, and the energy consumption incurred by the network transport and the data centers, while FORTE does not consider the energy consumption of the network transport. Therefore, Standard, Fast and GLDD achieve better results than FORTE.

4.2   Impact of Various Number of Users

In this subsection, we compare Standard and Fast, with GLDD and FORTE versus different number of users, assuming the number of data chunks is 5000.

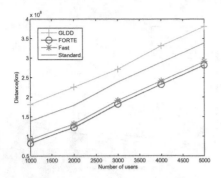
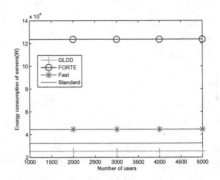

Fig. 5. Latency with the algorithms of Standard, Fast, GLDD and FORTE as the increasing number of users.

Fig. 6. Energy consumption of servers with the algorithms of Standard, Fast, GLDD and FORTE as the increasing number of users.

The simulation results in Fig. 5 show that in general the distance keeps stable with various number of users. When the number of data chunks is fixed, the increase of the number of users decreases the probability that each data chunk is accessed by each user. FORTE leads to the least distance and GLDD results in the largest distance. The number of copies with Standard and Fast may be potentially less than the number of copies with FORTE, and GLDD places each data chunk in only one data center. Standard only considers the energy consumption of the data centers while evaluating the cost of turning off the servers. In contrast, Fast takes into account the energy consumption of the network transport and the data access latency, in addition to the energy consumption of the data centers. Therefore, Fast potentially places more copies of the data than Standard, and results in less distance than Standard.

Figure 6 illustrates the energy consumption of the servers keeps steady because of the fixed number of data. FORTE consumes the most energy, since FORTE potentially creates the most number of data copies. GLDD places each data chunk in only one data center, and hence requires the least number of servers, which leads to the least server energy consumption. Standard achieves better performance than Fast, since Fast places the data in more data centers and thus requires more servers.

Figure 7 shows the energy consumed by the network transport increases with the growth of the number of users, since more users access the data through the network. FORTE achieves the best performance, because users can access the data from the closest data centers. GLDD consumes the most energy, as each data chunk is placed in only one data center so that the users go through largest distance to access the data. Fast outperforms Standard, since the users can access the data from the closer data centers with Fast than Standard.

The performance in terms of the integrated cost of the distance, the energy consumed by the servers in the data centers and the network transport is given in Fig. 8. By considering the three factors of the latency, the energy consumption

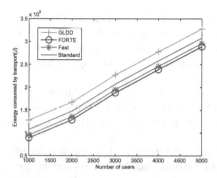

Fig. 7. Energy consumed by transport with the algorithms of Standard, Fast, GLDD and FORTE as the increasing number of users.

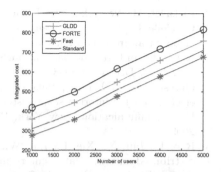

Fig. 8. Integrated cost with the algorithms of Standard, Fast, GLDD and FORTE as the increasing number of users.

of data centers and network transport, Standard and Fast outperforms FORTE and GLDD without the limitation of the number of data copies. Fast performs better than Standard because Fast potentially places the data in more data centers, and the decreased cost of network transport energy consumption can compensate the increased energy consumed by the data centers.

5 Conclusions

Cloud computing technology enables large-scale Internet applications to provide service to end users by routing service requests to geographically distributed data centers. Currently, the data centers and the network transport that power the applications consume significant electricity. At the same time, latency is also an important concern for the end users. In this paper, we tackled the problem of energy-efficient and latency-aware data placement in data centers. The objective was to reduce the energy consumed by network transport and data center servers, while reducing access latency. We proposed two efficient algorithms to determine the proper number of copies for each data chunk and the data centers accommodating the data chunk. Our simulation results have shown that the proposed algorithms are effective in terms of the tradeoff among the data access latency, the energy consumed by network transport and data centers.

Acknowledgments. The work reported in this paper was supported in part by Anhui Provincial Natural Science Foundation (1608085MF142).

References

1. Koomey, J.G.: Growth in data center electricity use 2005 To 2010. In: A Report by Analytics Press, Completed at the Request of The New York Times (2011)

2. Pickavet, M., Vereecken, W., Demeyer, S., Audenaert, P., Vermeulen, B., Develder, C., Colle, D., Dhoedt, B., Demeester, P.: Worldwide energy needs for ICT: the rise of power-aware networking. In: 2008 2nd International Symposium on Advanced Networks and Telecommunication Systems, Piscataway, NJ, Bombay, India, pp. 1–3, 15–17 December 2008

3. Qureshi, A., Weber, R., Balakrishnan, H., Guttag, J., Maggs, B.: Cutting the electric bill for internet-scale systems. In: 2009 ACM SIGCOMM conference on Data communication, New York, Barcelona, Spain, pp. 123–134, 17–21 August 2009

4. Rao, L., Liu, X., Xie, L., Liu, W.: Minimizing electricity cost: optimization of distributed internet data centers in a multi-electricity-market environment. In: 2010 IEEE International Conference on Computer Communications, Piscataway, NJ, San Diego, California, USA, pp. 1–9, 15–19 March 2010

5. Xu, Z., Liang, W.: Operational cost minimization of distributed data centers through the provision of fair request rate allocations while meeting different user SLAs. Comput. Netw. **83**, 59–75 (2015)

6. Le, K.T., Bianchini, R., Nguyen, T.D., Bilgir, O., Martonosi, M.: Capping the brown energy consumption of internet services at low cost. In: 2010 International Green Computing Conference, Piscataway, NJ, Chicago, Illinois, USA, pp. 3–14, 15–18 August 2010

7. Doyle, J., O'Mahony, D., Shorten, R.: Server selection for carbon emission control. In: 2nd ACM SIGCOMM Workshop on Green Networking, New York, Toronto, ON, Canada, pp. 1–6, 5–19 August 2011

8. Baliga, J., Ayre, R.W.A., Hinton, K., Tucker, R.S.: Green cloud computing balancing energy in processing, storage, and transport. Proc. IEEE **99**, 149–167 (2011)

9. Zhou, Z., Liu, F., Zou, R., Liu, J., Xu, H., Jin, H.: Carbon-aware online control of geo-distributed cloud services. IEEE Trans. Parallel Distrip. Syst. **12**(3), 1–14 (2015)

10. Gao, P.X., Curtis, A.R., Wong, B., Keshav, S.: It's not easy being green. In: 2012 ACM SIGCOMM Computer Communication Review, New York, Helsinki, Finland, pp. 211–222, 13–17 August 2012

11. Fan, Y., Ding, H., Hu, D.: Green latency-aware data deployment in data centers: balancing latency, energy in networks and servers. In: 2014 ACM SIGCOMM Workshop on Distributed Cloud Computing, New York, Chicago, USA, pp. 45–46, 18 August 2014

12. Mobius, C., Dargie, W., Schill, A.: Power consumption estimation models for processors, virtual machines, and servers. IEEE Trans. Parallel Distrip. Syst. **25**(6), 1600–1614 (2014)

13. Baliga, J., Ayre, R., Hinton, K., Sorin, W.V., Tucker, R.S.: Energy consumption in optical IP networks. J. Lightwave Technol. **13**(27), 2391–2403 (2009)

Constrained Space Information Flow

Alfred Uwitonze[1], Jiaqing Huang[1(✉)], Yuanqing Ye[2], and Wenqing Cheng[1]

[1] School of Electronic Information and Communications, Huazhong University
of Science and Technology, Wuhan 430074, People's Republic of China
jqhuang@mail.hust.edu.cn
[2] Department of Electrical and Computer Engineering, Carnegie Mellon University,
5000 Forbes Ave, Pittsburgh, PA 15213, USA

Abstract. *Space Information Flow* (SIF), also known as Space Network Coding, is a new research paradigm which studies network coding in Euclidean space, and it is different with *Network Information Flow* proposed by Ahlswede *et al.* This paper focuses on the problem of *Constrained Space Information Flow* (CSIF), which aims to find a min-cost multicast network in 2-D Euclidean space under the constraint on the number of relay nodes to be used. We propose a new *polynomial*-time heuristic algorithm that combines Delaunay triangulation and linear programming techniques to solve the problem. Delaunay triangulation is used to generate several candidate relay nodes, after which linear programming is applied to choose the optimal relay nodes and to compute their connection links with the terminal nodes. The simulation results shows the effectiveness of the proposed algorithm.

Keywords: Network Information Flow · Delaunay triangulation · Network coding in space · Space Information Flow

1 Introduction

Departing from *Network Information Flow* (NIF) proposed by Ahlswede *et al.* [1] in 2000, *Space Information Flow* (SIF) [2,3] is a new concept proposed by Li and Wu in 2011 and it studies *network coding in Euclidean space*. SIF is also different with both Euclidean Steiner Minimal Tree (ESMT) [4] and Minimum Spanning Tree (MST) [5]. ESMT is the optimal routing in space. MST connects together all the terminals of a given set with a shortest network, without any additional relay node, while additional relay nodes are required in SIF [2,3]. The pentagram [6] example illustrated in Fig. 1 demonstrates that SIF can strictly outperforms ESMT, with the *cost advantage* [7] being strictly bigger than 1. The *cost advantage* is defined as the ratio of the minimum network cost without network coding over that with network coding. Consider six multicast terminal nodes in a 2-D Euclidean space depicted in Fig. 1(a). Among the six multicast terminals, five (T_1 to T_5) are equally placed on a circle and form a regular pentagon whose center is node O. The circumscribed circle of the pentagon has a radius of 1. Node O is selected as the multicast source, while the

© ICST Institute for Computer Sciences, Social Informatics and Telecommunications Engineering 2018
Q. Chen et al. (Eds.): ChinaCom 2016, Part II, LNICST 210, pp. 475–485, 2018.
DOI: 10.1007/978-3-319-66628-0_45

remaining five nodes (T_1 to T_5) are the receivers. With ESMT, an optimal solution can be computed [8] and the cost is 4.6400/bit (Fig. 1(b)). Three Steiner nodes (S_1 to S_3) are introduced for connecting the terminal nodes, each adjacent to three links which form three angles of 120°. An optimal solution by SIF is depicted in Fig. 1(c). The total distance is 9.1354, while every sink receives 2 bits. The normalized cost is $9.1354/2 = 4.5677$/bit. Five relay nodes (R_1 to R_5) are introduced for connecting the terminal nodes, each adjacent to three links which form three angles of 120°. The *cost advantage* of the pentagram example is $4.6400/4.5677 \approx 1.0158 > 1$. Despite its small value, we emphasize that the gap between the two optimal costs reveals that multicast with SIF is fundamentally a different problem from geometric ESMT, with a different problem structure, and probably a different computational complexity. The placement of relay nodes in wireless sensor networks is a potential application of SIF [9].

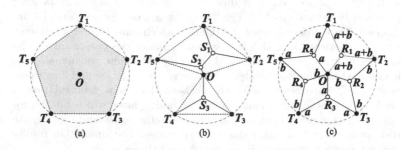

Fig. 1. Illustration example of *pentagram*. (a) Six terminal nodes in 2-D Euclidean space; (b) Optimal solution with ESMT (cost = 4.6400/bit); (c) Optimal solution with SIF (cost = 4.5677/bit).

For SIF, Li and Wu [3] studied the problem of multiple-unicast network coding in space. Yin *et al.* [10] proved a number of properties of optimal multicast network coding in 2-D Euclidean space. Xiahou *et al.* [11] applied SIF as a tool to design a framework for analyzing the network coding conjecture. A heuristic approach based on iterative method has been proposed by Hu *et al.* [12] to address min-cost video multicast problem via Constrained SIF. A polynomial-time heuristic algorithm for computing the optimal SIF solution in multicast network has been proposed by Huang *et al.* [6]. In a subsequent study, Huang and Li [9] presented a polynomial-time heuristic approach based on non-uniform recursive space partitioning for computing SIF. In another subsequent work, Uwitonze *et al.* [13] presented a polynomial-time heuristic approach based on Delaunay triangulation that computes the SIF solutions in multicast networks. In line with routing in space, Gilbert and Pollack [4] studied the properties of optimal ESMT. As for MST, its complexity is polynomial [5].

The objective of SIF is to minimize the cost of constructing a network, allowing network coding to be used and additional relay nodes to be inserted for connecting a given set of terminals in geometric space, while satisfying end-to-end throughput demands among terminals [2]. However, adding more relay nodes may clearly lead to a higher cost in practice, given that each extra relay node may be associated with hardware and deployment cost. Therefore, it is necessary to consider such cost by minimizing the number of additional relay nodes. In this paper, we propose the Constrained SIF (CSIF) problem, which is a new version of SIF that considers the transmission of information flows in a geometric space under the constraint (restriction) on the number of additional relay nodes that can be introduced to connect a set of given terminal nodes. The space we consider in this work is a 2-D Euclidean space. To the best of our knowledge, this is the first work to explore the problem of Constrained SIF (CSIF) and to use Delaunay Triangulation (DT) [14] in CSIF. DT has two properties that are useful to reduce the overall length of the tree, as denoted by Smith et al. [14]. Firstly, since MST of N is contained in the $DT(N)$, a number of edges in ESMT is the same as edges in MST. Secondly, since each Delaunay triangle tends to be equilateral, we achieve the maximum possible reduction in using the ESMT, as compared with using the MST.

The main contribution of our paper can be summarized as follows:

We propose the first heuristic algorithm based on Delaunay Triangulation (DT) and Linear Programming (LP) techniques, with a *polynomial*-time complexity that computes the min-cost in multicast networks and the corresponding network topology (including the way relay nodes are connected with the terminal nodes, as well as the flow rate on the connection links), under the constraint on the number of additional relay nodes to be introduced.

The rest of this paper is organized as follows: Sect. 2 discusses the problem formulation. Section 3 describes the detailed steps of the new heuristic algorithm for CSIF. Section 4 presents the simulation results, while Sect. 5 concludes the paper.

2   Problem Formulation

This work focuses on the problem of min-cost multicast network coding in 2-D Euclidean space. For $N \geq 3$ given terminal nodes $T_1, T_2,\ldots,T_N$ in the Euclidean space and a multicast session from one source to a number of sinks, the objective is to compute a min-cost multicast transmission scheme using SIF, that permits to insert at most M extra relay nodes. The total network cost is defined as $\sum_{uv} w(uv)f(uv)$, where $f(uv)$ denotes the information flow rate on a link uv in space, while $w(uv)$ denotes the weight of the link uv, and it is equal to the Euclidean distance $\|uv\|$ of uv [2,3]. These two variables are called *positions* and *flow assignments*. The connection topology of all nodes will be determined by flow assignments, because a link with a zero rate shows that the link does not exist. Our goal is to achieve the min-cost by tuning these two sets of variables with no more than M relay nodes.

3   The Proposed Heuristic Algorithm for CSIF

3.1   The Main Idea of Heuristic Algorithm

The main idea of our algorithm is to use at most M relay nodes to establish a min-cost multicast network connection from $N \geq 3$ given terminal nodes in space. Before introducing the constraint number of relay nodes M, the algorithm uses two alternative strategies to retain the relay nodes from LP computation: 1DT-2DT strategy and 2DT-1DT strategy. With 1DT-2DT strategy, the algorithm retains the less possible candidate relay nodes first, followed by retaining the most possible candidate relay nodes. With 2DT-1DT strategy, the algorithm retains the most possible candidate relay nodes first, followed by retaining the less possible candidate relay nodes. The less possible candidate relay nodes here refer to the candidate relay nodes generated in triangles, while the most possible candidate relay nodes refer to the candidate relay nodes generated in quadrilaterals. Quadrilaterals are obtained by concatenating two adjacent Delaunay triangles.

3.2   Detailed Description of Heuristic Algorithm

The proposed algorithm is based on DT and LP techniques. DT is used for generating at most $(2N-5)$ Delaunay triangles from $N \geq 3$ given terminal nodes [14]. Subsequently, it helps to compute a number of candidate relay nodes from all Delaunay triangles and quadrilaterals. LP is applied to choose the optimal relay nodes and to compute their connection links with the terminals. The proposed algorithm adopts the following LP model:

Minimize $cost = \sum_{\overrightarrow{uv} \in A} w(\overrightarrow{uv}) f(\overrightarrow{uv})$
Subject to :

$$
\begin{cases}
\sum_{v \in V_\uparrow(u)} f_i(\overrightarrow{vu}) = \sum_{v \in V_\downarrow(u)} f_i(\overrightarrow{uv}) & \forall i, \forall u \\
f_i(\overrightarrow{T_i S}) = r & \forall i \\
f_i(\overrightarrow{uv}) \leq f(\overrightarrow{uv}) & \forall i, \forall \overrightarrow{uv} \\
f(\overrightarrow{uv}) \geq 0, f_i(\overrightarrow{uv}) \geq 0 & \forall i, \forall \overrightarrow{uv}
\end{cases} \tag{1}
$$

The LP model (Eq. (1)) is based on undirected network $G = (V, E)$, where $V = N \cup R$, N denotes the set of terminal nodes and R is the set of extra relay nodes, while E denotes the set of undirected links. There are bi-directed possibilities of transmission in space. Therefore, we make links bi-directed and denote a set of directed links as $A = \{uv, vu | uv \in E\}$. In the objective function, the decision variable $f(\overrightarrow{uv})$ is regarded as the combined effective flow rate on a link $\overrightarrow{uv}$. The coefficient $w(\overrightarrow{uv})$ equals to the Euclidean distance $|\overrightarrow{uv}|(=|\overrightarrow{vu}|=|uv|)$. In the LP constraints, $f_i(uv)$ is regarded as the rate of information flow from the source S to sink T_i on a link $\overrightarrow{uv}$. Such kinds of information flow are *conceptual* because they share instead of competing for available bandwidth on the same link. $f(\overrightarrow{uv})$ of a link uv equals to the maximum among all $f_i(\overrightarrow{uv})$. The constraint $\sum_{v \in V_\uparrow(u)} f_i(\overrightarrow{vu}) = \sum_{v \in V_\downarrow(u)} f_i(\overrightarrow{uv})$ guarantees the conceptional flow equilibrium property for every node and every conceptual flow i. We have both $f_i(\overrightarrow{uv})$ and $f_i(\overrightarrow{vu})$ to indicate the flows in two directions. $V_\uparrow(u)$ and $V_\downarrow(u)$ respectively denote upstream and downstream adjacent set of u in V. The constraint $f_i(\overrightarrow{T_iS}) = r$ characterizes the desired receiving rate at each terminal. The constraints $f(\overrightarrow{uv}) \geq 0$ and $f_i(\overrightarrow{uv}) \geq 0$ give the trivial bound. The detailed steps of the algorithm are shown in Algorithm 1.

Algorithm 1. A Heuristic Algorithm for CSIF

Require: Input: N ($N \geq 3$) terminal nodes, a multicast session
Ensure: Output: a CSIF solution
 1: Initialize the total set of candidate relay nodes $R_{total} = \emptyset$;
 2: Construct all the DT-triangles by Delaunay triangulation;
 3: Initialize the subset of candidate relay nodes $R(x) = \emptyset$, $R'(x) = \emptyset$, MINCOST=$+\infty$;
 4: **for** $x = 1$ to 2, **do**
 5:     Construct polygons P_i of 3 and 4 edges by concatenating x adjacent DT-triangles;
 6:     Construct the MST of each polygon P_i;
 7:     Obtain the candidate relay nodes $R(x)$;
 8:     Construct a complete graph with $(N + \sum_{x=1}^{x} |R(x)|)$ nodes;
 9:     Solve the LP model based on the complete graph and output MINCOST and the corresponding resulting relay nodes $R'(x)$;
10:     **if** There are k ($k \geq 2$) adjacent relay nodes only **then**
11:         Use 2DT-1DT strategy to retain $R'(x)$ from polygon P_i of 4 edges only
12:     **else**
13:         Use 1DT-2DT strategy to retain $R'(x)$ from polygon P_i of 3 edges only
14:     **end if**
15: **end for**
16: Calculate $R_{total} = \overset{2}{\underset{x=1}{\cup}} R'(x)$;
17: **for** $R_{total} = 1$ to M, **do**
18:     Construct a complete graph with $(N + M)$ nodes;
19:     Solve the LP model based on the complete graph and output the CSIF *cost*;
20:     **if** $cost <$ MINCOST **then**
21:         MINCOST=$cost$
22:     **end if**
23:     Compute the ESMTs of each polygon P_i;
24:     Place all ESMTs on a hierarchical priority queue Q based on the value of $\Delta = \frac{MST(P_i)-ESMT(P_i)}{ESMT(P_i)}$;
25:     Construct the network topology by picking ESMTs from Q in the same way as the Kruskal's algorithm;
26: **end for**
27: **if** The flow rates of all constrained relay nodes $== 0$ **then**
28:     Output MINCOST and stop.
29: **end if**

3.3 Complexity Analysis of Our Algorithm

Our heuristic algorithm considers all the possible candidate Steiner nodes generated from all Delaunay triangles concatenations as possible candidate relay nodes. According to [15], the method to obtain the Steiner nodes in a triangle and a quadrilateral is shown in Figs. 2 and 3, respectively.

Triangle: As depicted by Fig. 2, assume $\angle VUW$ is the biggest angle in $\triangle UVW$. If $\angle VUW \geq 120°$, then the Steiner node S is the vertex U. If $\angle VUW < 120°$, draw two equilateral triangles on any of the two edges of $\triangle UVW$, e.g., $\triangle UVX$ and $\triangle UWY$, then the Steiner node S is the intersection of the lines VY and WX. Thus, the time complexity is polynomial.

Quadrilateral: As stated by [15], the process to obtain the Steiner nodes in a convex quadrilateral $UVWX$ consists of three steps, as illustrated in Fig. 3. First, draw two equilateral triangles $\triangle UVY$ and $\triangle WXZ$. Next, draw two circles which pass at the vertices of the two equilateral triangles $\triangle UVY$ and $\triangle WXZ$. Last, draw the line YZ and the two steiner nodes S_1 and S_2 are the intersection of the line YZ with the two circles, as depicted in Fig. 3. Hence, the time complexity is also polynomial.

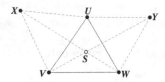

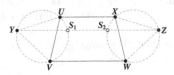

Fig. 2. Computing the candidate Steiner node in a triangle.

Fig. 3. Computing the candidate Steiner nodes in a quadrilateral.

The time complexity of DT is $O(N \log N)$ [16]. The time complexity of computing the candidate Steiner nodes for every Delaunay triangle and quadrilateral formed by concatenating two neighboring Delaunay triangles is polynomial. Given $N \geq 3$ terminal nodes, we can get at most $(2N-5)$ Delaunay triangles and $(3N-6)$ edges by DT. It is possible to concatenate at most $(N-2)$ neighboring triangles and $2N-5$ quadrilaterals, respectively. Hence, $|R_{total}| \leq 6N - 16$, and the time complexity of LP is $O((N+|R_{total}|)^2) = O((7N-16)^2) = O(N^2)$. Thus, the time complexity of our algorithm is $O(N^3 \log N)$, which is polynomial.

4 Simulation Results

We have simulated our heuristic algorithm in 2-D Euclidean space. Our simulations used MATLAB to solve LPs. In multicast networks, the number of relay nodes required for an optimal solution is upper-bounded by $(N-2)$ for $h = 1$

and $(2N - 3)(2N - 2)$ for $h = 2$ [10], where N is the number of the terminals and h is the multicast throughput. Thus, we set $M < (N - 2)$ for $h = 1$ and $M < (2N - 3)(2N - 2)$ for $h = 2$, where M is the constraint on the number of relay nodes. All the tested cases correspond to $h = 1$, except the pentagram network, which corresponds to $h = 2$ [6]. The optimal ESMT is computed by GeoSteiner 3.1 that implements an exact ESMT algorithm [8]. The MST is computed by implementing Prim's algorithm [5] in MATLAB. For each tested case, one node is set as the source, while the remaining nodes are set as the terminals.

4.1   Cases of 10 Nodes Data Sets from OR-Library

We applied our algorithm to 10-points ($N = 10$) data sets from OR-Library [17], which contained 15 cases with different positions. We set $M < 8$ and we evaluated the performance of our algorithm by comparing the results of CSIF with SIF, optimal ESMT and MST. We define the gap between SIF and CSIF as $gap = \frac{SIF}{CSIF}$. Figure 4 shows the MST cost, min-cost for CSIF, SIF cost and optimal ESMT cost for all the 15 cases. Both SIF and optimal ESMT achieve the same results, since SIF degrades into optimal ESMT when $h = 1$ [10]. CSIF outperforms MST for all the cases. Moreover, CSIF cost is very close to both SIF and ESMT costs for all the 15 cases (See Fig. 4). Table 1 shows the gap for all the 15 cases. The gap ≈ 1 for almost all the cases.

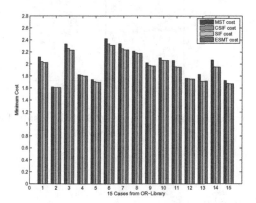

Fig. 4. MST cost, min-cost for CSIF when $M < 8$, SIF cost and ESMT cost.

4.2   The Pentagram Network

We applied our algorithm to the pentagram network, where $N = 6$. We set $M = 5$ and the obtained CSIF topology is shown in Fig. 5. Figure 6 shows the optimal topology with SIF. Both SIF and CSIF achieve the same results (cost $= 4.5677$/bit), because they both use the same number of relay nodes, as

Table 1. Gap $= \frac{SIF}{CSIF}$

Case	Gap	Case	Gap	Case	Gap
1	0.9910367784	6	0.9897108913	11	0.9957873959
2	0.9997107509	7	0.9909349461	12	0.9979368571
3	0.9876711421	8	0.9964208849	13	0.9999795101
4	0.9949909489	9	0.9949003406	14	0.9993935543
5	0.9928556449	10	0.9982077096	15	0.9970678120

it can be seen in Figs. 5 and 6 and the gap $= 1$. Hence, the algorithm achieves the optimal solutions for the pentagram network. Figures 7 and 8 show the MST (cost $= 5.0000$/bit) and ESMT (cost $= 4.6421$/bit) topologies, respectively. CSIF outperforms both MST and ESMT in terms of min-cost.

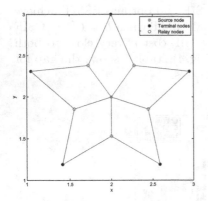

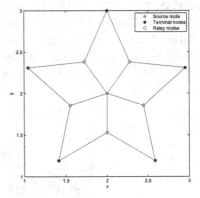

Fig. 5. CSIF result for Pentagram network.

Fig. 6. SIF result for Pentagram network.

4.3 Random Networks

We tested the algorithm in random networks, which are generated by the Waxman model [18]. Throughout our simulations, we observed that in most of the cases for such random networks, gap ≈ 1 when $M < (N - 2)$. Furthermore, CSIF outperforms MST for all tested cases. Figure 9 illustrates the CSIF result (cost $= 1.5776$/bit) for one example of such cases when $N = 8$ and $M = 2$. Figure 10 shows the SIF result (cost $= 1.5771$/bit), Fig. 11 shows the MST result (cost $= 1.6053$/bit), while Fig. 12 shows the optimal ESMT result (cost $= 1.5771$/bit). Both SIF and optimal ESMT achieve the same results, since SIF degrades into optimal ESMT when $h = 1$ [10]. The gap $= 0.9996$.

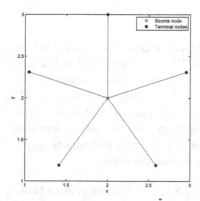

Fig. 7. The MST result for penta gram network.

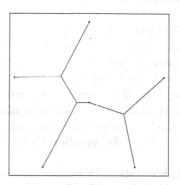

Fig. 8. ESMT by GeoSteiner for pentagram network.

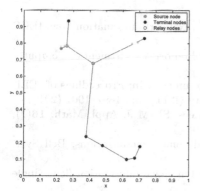

Fig. 9. CSIF result for random network when $N = 8$ and $M = 2$.

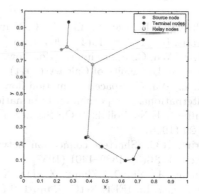

Fig. 10. SIF result for random network when $N = 8$.

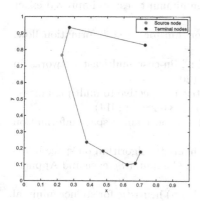

Fig. 11. MST result for random network when $N = 8$.

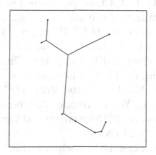

Fig. 12. The optimal ESMT by GeoSteiner for random network.

5   Conclusion

This work proposes a solution to the problem of Constrained Space Information Flow in multicast networks using a new $O(N^3 \log N)$ algorithm which takes into consideration a constraint on the number of relay nodes while computing the min-cost and the topology of the network for $N \geq 3$ terminal nodes in 2-D Euclidean space. The algorithm design is based on DT and LP techniques. The output of the algorithm is a min-cost multicast topology that consists of terminal (original) nodes and relay (additional) nodes. Our future work includes to apply Constrained Space Information Flow to wireless sensor networks.

Acknowledgments. This research was supported by National Natural Science Foundation of China (No. 61271227).

References

1. Ahlswede, R., Cai, N., Li, S.Y.R., Yeung, R.W.: Network information flow. IEEE Trans. Inf. Theory **46**(4), 1204–1216 (2000)
2. Li, Z., Wu, C.: Space information flow. Technical report, Department of Computer Science, University of Calgary (2011)
3. Li, Z., Wu, C.: Space information flow: multiple unicast. In: Proceedings of IEEE International Symposium on Information Theory (ISIT), pp. 1897–1901 (2012)
4. Gilbert, E.N., Pollak, H.O.: Steiner minimal trees. SIAM J. Appl. Math. **16**(1), 1–29 (1968)
5. Prim, R.C.: Shortest connection networks and some generalizations. Bell Syst. Tech. J. **36**(6), 1389–1401 (1957)
6. Huang, J., Yin, X., Zhang, X., Du, X., Li, Z.: On space information flow: single multicast. In: IEEE NetCod, pp. 1–6 (2013)
7. Maheshwar, S., Li, Z., Li, B.: Bounding the coding advantage of combination network coding in undirected networks. IEEE Trans. Inf. Theory **58**(2), 570–584 (2012)
8. Winter, P., Zachariasen, M.: Euclidean steiner minimum trees: an improved exact algorithm. Networks **30**(3), 149–166 (1997)
9. Huang, J., Li, Z.: A recursive partitioning algorithm for space information flow. In: IEEE GLOBECOM, pp. 1460–1465 (2014)
10. Yin, X., Wang, Y., Wang, X., Xue, X., Li, Z.: Min-cost multicast networks in euclidean space. In: IEEE ISIT, pp. 1316–1320 (2012)
11. Xiahou, T., Li, Z., Wu, C., Huang, J.: A geometric perspective to multiple-unicast network coding. IEEE Trans. Inf. Theory **60**(5), 2884–2895 (2014)
12. Hu, Y., Niu, D., Li, Z.: Internet video multicast via constrained space information flow. IEEE MMTC E-letter **9**(2), 17–19 (2014)
13. Uwitonze, A., Ye, Y., Huang, J., Cheng, W.: A heuristic algorithm on space information flow. In: 2015 International Conference on Computer Science and Applications, pp. 20–24 (2015)
14. Smith, J.M., Lee, D.T., Liebman, J.S.: An O (n log n) heuristic for steiner minimal tree problems on the euclidean metric. Networks **11**(1), 23–39 (1981)
15. Yue, M.: Minimum Network: The Steiner Tree Problem. Shanghai Scientific and Technical Publishers, Shanghai (2006)

16. Leach, G.: Improving worst-case optimal Delaunay triangulation algorithms. In: 4th Canadian Conference on Computational Geometry, pp. 340–346 (1992)
17. Beasley, J.E.: OR-Library: distributing test problems by electronic mail. J. Oper. Res. Soc. **41**(11), 1069–1072 (1990)
18. Waxman, B.M.: Routing of multipoint connections. IEEE J. Sel. Areas Commun. **6**(9), 1617–1622 (1988)

Hybrid Roadside Devices Placement for Advertisement Disseminations in Vehicular CPS

Junshan Cui[1,2], Peng Li[1,2(✉)], Dongdong Yue[1,2], Yu Jin[1,2],
Yu Liu[1,2], and Qin Liu[3]

[1] College of Computer Science and Technology,
Wuhan University of Science and Technology, Hubei 430065, China
lipeng@wust.edu.cn
[2] Hubei Province Key Laboratory of Intelligent Information Processing and
Real-time Industrial System, Hubei 430065, China
[3] School of Computer, Wuhan University, Hubei 430074, China

Abstract. There are two types of roadside devices for advertisement dissemination in the Vehicular Cyber-Physical Systems (VCPS), one is roadside units (RSUs) and the other is roadside access points (RAPs). The placement cost of RSUs is lower than RAPs. However, the coverage of RSUs is limited. In this paper, we investigate the hybrid roadside device placement problem in the Vehicular Cyber-Physical Systems (VCPS). Given the budget constraint and the distribution of traffic conditions, our goal is to optimize the deployment of the hybrid roadside device for the merchants to maximize their benefits from advertisement dissemination. With the purpose of all advertisement can be effectively served, we propose a corresponding hybrid greedy placement algorithm. Our algorithm not only obtains the more benefits, but also consider the placement cost. Finally, we evaluate the performance of our proposed algorithm. Extensive simulations show that the performance of our proposed algorithm is superior to the other algorithms.

Keywords: Vehicular Cyber-Physical Systems · Roadside device placement · Advertisement dissemination

1 Introduction

With the development of wireless networks and vehicular ad hoc networks, there are more and more advertisement dissemination applications in Vehicular Cyber-Physical Systems(VCPS). The application of roadside advertisement dissemination in VCPS generally involves three elements: the drivers in the vehicles, roadside units, and merchants. By advertising to drivers in the vehicle, merchant

---

P. Li—This work is partially supported by the NSF of China (61502359, 61572370, 61303117), the National Students' Innovative Entrepreneurship Training Program (201510488016), and the Wuhan University of Science and Technology Innovative Entrepreneurship Training Program (15ZRA093, 15ZRC100).

© ICST Institute for Computer Sciences, Social Informatics and Telecommunications Engineering 2018
Q. Chen et al. (Eds.): ChinaCom 2016, Part II, LNICST 210, pp. 486–495, 2018.
DOI: 10.1007/978-3-319-66628-0_46

attracts so as much as possible customers into the store shopping. However, due to the uneven distribution of merchants geographic location, different types of roadside units may have different profits in different locations. Considering how to ensure that all advertisements can be served timely and effectively, we also need to guarantee the expected merchants benefit. Eventually, it becomes especially important to give a scenario of roadside device placement.

In this paper, we investigate hybrid roadside devices placement, which applies in roadside advertising to maximize the benefit of merchants. The placement problem is correlative to multiple types of roadside device. There are two types of roadside devices for advertisement dissemination in the Vehicular Cyber-Physical Systems (VCPS), one is roadside units (RSUs) and the other is roadside access points (RAPs). As shown in Fig. 1, RAPs have following characteristics: wide coverage, large placement cost and high bandwidth. However, RSUs have features like small coverage range and low placement cost and low bandwidth. Traditional placement strategies only consider using a single type device, such as RAPs or RSUs. Therefore, it will cause the waste of resource inevitably. Thus, the hybrid deployment of multiple types of resource becomes more important. It not only concerns to the maximization of merchants benefits, but also saves the cost of deployment.

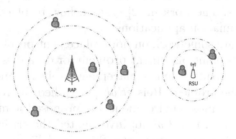

Fig. 1. RAP/RSUs schematic coverage.

Given a budget of deployment and the distribution of traffic flows, our goal is to determine how to deploy hybrid roadside device for the maximization of merchants benefits. In addition to the benefit, all the merchant must be ensure that it can be covered by at least one roadside device. It is a challenging issue in vehicular ad hoc networks. First of all, we consider how to choose an optimal candidate site to place a roadside device, which is proved that the problem is NP-complete. Moreover, we consider different types of roadside devices, that for each candidate site we need to decide which type of roadside devices we should choose, which is more complicated than the placement of the same type roadside devices. Therefore, the main contributions of this paper are summarized as follows:

– We consider the hybrid placement problem for advertising applications. In order to maximize the merchant benefits, we should consider how to place the roadside device efficiently. We conduct the system model and give the formulation of the hybrid placement problem.

- Base on the problem formulation, we propose a hybrid roadside devices placement algorithm, which greedily deploy the roadside device to maximize the potential benefits.
- We conduct an extensive simulations to evaluate the performances of the proposed algorithm. Simulation results show that the performance of our proposed algorithm is superior to the other algorithms.

The remainder of this paper is organized as follows: Sect. 2 is the presentation of related work. Section 3 introduces the system model. In Sect. 4, we describe the proposed algorithm and give concrete solutions for Manhattan grid system. Section 5 includes the experimental results and analysis. Finally, we conclude paper in Sect. 6.

2   Related Work

In recent years, the application of advertisement dissemination becomes a novel and anticipated topic [1,2]. Li *et al.* [1] considered how to allocate bandwidth and schedule advertisement with existing roadside devices. And there are also many other studies about advertisement dissemination application with pre-fixed roadside devices. The work in [2] studied how to place roadside units for advertisement dissemination applications.

Nowadays, there are some work on node placement problem [3–8]. Yan *et al.* [3] investigated access point placement problem for data dissemination. Li *et al.* [4] studied two types roadside units placement problem, and proposed several algorithms to solve the problem. Reis *et al.* [5] studied the roadside units placement problem in the highway environment and propose the method to maximize the network performance. Ke *et al.* [6] investigated the critical-square-grid coverage problem in wireless sensor networks. Silva *et al.* [7] presented an algorithm for deployment of roadside units based on partial mobility information. Zhang *et al.* [8] developed an AP placement algorithm based on theoretical results to deploy the minimal number of roadside APs with QoS guarantees.

In hybrid node placement problem, Li *et al.* [9] considered two types road-side units and studied the delay-bounded minimal cost roadside units placement problem in vehicular ad hoc networks, and Lin and Deng [10] investigated the roadside units and sensors placement problem, and proposed a center particle swarm optimization approach to solve this NP-completed problem. However, none of them considered how to deploy hybrid roadside devices for advertisement dissemination.

3   System Model and Problem Formulation

3.1   System Model

In the system, there are n merchants (denoted by $S = \{s_i | i = 1, 2, ..., n\}$) and each of them contains m advertisements (denoted by $A = \{a_{i,j} | j = 1, 2, ..., m\}$), and each of advertisements has its corresponding size (denoted by $size_{i,j}$). For each advertisement, it has different attractive ratio (denoted by $att_{i,j}$), as well as the potential benefit $utl_{i,j}$. There are two types of roadside device (RAPs and RSUs). We assume that the bandwidth of RAPs is larger than RSUs', the transmission coverage of RAPs is larger than RSUs', and the placement cost of RAPs is larger than RSUs'. We assume that the distribution of traffic flow is known as a priori, vehicular users will take a detour to shopping or back home directly after receiving advertisements from roadside devices. We denote T as the set of traffic flow in the system, and $t_{x,y}$ corresponds to a traffic flow from intersection x to intersection y. Also, $|T|$ denotes the number of traffic flow. We denote the detour distance as $d_{x,y,i}$, which represents the vertical distance from the traffic flow $t_{x,y}$ to the merchant s_i.

We define vehicular users' detour probability as $f(att_{i,j}, d_{x,y,i})$, which means the probability that the vehicular users in traffic follow $t_{x,y}$ would take a detour to go shopping after receiving the j-th advertisement distributed by i-th merchants. Obviously, the vehicular users' detour probability has a positive correlation with advertisements attraction $att_{i,j}$, and it is related with the detour distance $d_{x,y,i}$ negatively. So we use a benefit function to describe the vehicular users' detour probability $f(att_{i,j}, d_{x,y,i})$ as follows:

$$f(att_{i,j}, d_{x,y,i}) = \begin{cases} att_{i,j} \times (1 - \frac{d_{x,y,i}}{D}), & d < D \\ 0, & d \geq D \end{cases} \tag{1}$$

where D is a threshold value which will be detailed later. According to real-world experience, merchants in some places are distributed densely, and they are usually located in relatively prosperous regions where the number of advertisements is large. However, there always exists some suburbs where the merchants distribution is relatively sparse, and the amount of advertisements is also small. So we consider a device (RAP or RSU) only broadcasting advertisements in the nearby area. Because the bandwidth of each roadside device is limited, and the number of advertisements that can be served in a certain period is also limited, so an appropriate device placement strategy can not only ensure adequate coverage range but also the efficiency of receiving advertisement. Therefore, we assume that all the roadside devices are deployed at intersections, and the number of intersections is q. Then, the set of these intersections is defined as $V = \{v_k | k = 0, 1, ..., q-1\}$. We denote $d_{x,y,k}$ as the distance from the intersection v_k to traffic flow $t_{x,y}$, which equals to the minimum distance between the intersection point and any point on the traffic flow. If the coverage range of roadside device is less than the distance of road segment, we also consider that the whole road segment is covered by the deployed roadside device. This assumption is acceptable, because the vehicles eventually go through the whole road segment after receiving the advertisements in the range of deployed roadside device.

We denote R_p and R_u as the transmission range of a RAP and a RSU, respectively. Similarly, we denote C_p and C_u as the cost of a RAP and a RSU for deployment. Then, the traffic flow coverage set of a RAP and a RSU, denoted by $T^{k,p}$ and $T^{k,u}$ can be expressed respectively as:

$$\begin{cases} T^{k,p} = \{t_{x,y} | d_{x,y,k} < R_p\} \\ T^{k,u} = \{t_{x,y} | d_{x,y,k} < R_u\} \end{cases} \quad (2)$$

We take Fig. 2 for example, the graph contains nine intersections, which labeled from #0 to #8. Each grid line represents a known traffic flow $t_{x,y}$. The graph also has 12 traffic flows, such as $t_{0,1}$, $t_{1,2}$, ..., etc. $t_{x,y}$ corresponds to a traffic flow from the intersection v_x to intersection v_y and the number of vehicular users is known. Each traffic flow $t_{x,y} \in T$ denotes a known set of traffic, $|t_{x,y}|$ denotes the number of vehicles on the traffic flow $t_{x,y}$. There is a merchant s_1 in the graph, and the detour distance $d_{4,5,1}$ represents the vertical distance from the traffic flow $t_{4,5}$ to the merchant s_1. If we place a RSU in the intersection v_4, and it's traffic flow cover set is $\{t_{1,4}, t_{3,4}, t_{4,5}, t_{4,7}\}$. Noted that although $t_{4,5}$ is not covered by RSU totally, it is also considered to be in the traffic flow cover set according to our assumption.

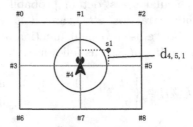

Fig. 2. An example of traffic flow cover set

3.2   Problem Formulation

Our problem can be viewed as : *Given the budget constraint and the distribution of traffic conditions, our goal is to optimize the deployment of the hybrid roadside device for the merchants to maximize their benefit from advertisement dissemination.*

First, we give the definition of merchants' benefit. When a roadside device (like a RAP or RSU) is placed on intersection v_k, we can denote the total benefit obtained by each merchants advertisement as follow:

$$\begin{cases} M_{i,k,p} = \sum_{j=1}^{m} \sum_{t_{x,y} \in T^{k,p}} |t_{x,y}| \times f(att_{i,j}, d_{x,y,i}) \times utl_{i,j} \\ M_{i,k,u} = \sum_{j=1}^{m} \sum_{t_{x,y} \in T^{k,u}} |t_{x,y}| \times f(att_{i,j}, d_{x,y,i}) \times utl_{i,j} \end{cases} \quad (3)$$

If the distance from the merchant to the traffic flow which covered by roadside device does not exceed the predetermined threshold D, this merchant is considered to be served availably. As we consider these merchants are dispersed in the periphery of the main traffic artery, and the roadside device like RAP or RSU is deployed on intersections of these traffic flows. x_i and y_i are used to represent whether this intersection is deployed by a RSU or a RAP:

$$x_k = \begin{cases} 1, & \text{if there is a RAP placed on the intersection } v_k \\ 0, & \text{otherwise} \end{cases} \tag{4}$$

$$y_k = \begin{cases} 1, & \text{if there is a RSU placed on the intersection } v_k \\ 0, & \text{otherwise} \end{cases} \tag{5}$$

According to the above assumption, merchants obtain their benefits mainly by advertisements. So we define the merchants total benefit E as follow:

$$E = \sum_{k=1}^{q} (M_{i,k,p} \cdot x_k + M_{i,k,u} \cdot y_k) \tag{6}$$

Therefore, our problem can be formulated as follows:

$$\max E = \sum_{k=1}^{q} (M_{i,k,p} \cdot x_k + M_{i,k,u} \cdot y_k) \tag{7}$$

subject to:

$$C_p \cdot n_p + C_u \cdot n_u \leq B \tag{8}$$

$$(dev_i.x - dev_j.x)^2 + (dev_i.y - dev_j.y)^2 \geq R^2_{min\{dev_i, dev_j\}} \tag{9}$$

$$x_i + y_i \leq 1 \tag{10}$$

$$x_i, y_i \in [0, 1] \tag{11}$$

Constraint (8) denotes that the total deployment cost should be less than the given budget B, where C_p and C_u represents the placement cost of RAPs and RSUs respectively and n_p and n_u represents the placement number of RAPs and RSUs respectively. Constraint (9) denotes the distance $(dev_i.x - dev_j.x)^2 + (dev_i.y - dev_j.y)^2$ between the i-th roadside device and the j-th roadside device should not be less than the minimum of their transmission range. Constraint(10) ensures only one device can be deployed on each intersection. Constraint (11) guarantees that x_i and y_i only choose 0 or 1.

4   Our Solution

In this section, we give our greedy algorithm, which choose an intersection with high merchants benefit and low placement cost greedily to place a roadside device. Therefore, we define a benefit cost ratio when we install a roadside device in the intersection. As the total benefit E is shown as the Eq.(7). We define the total deployment cost C as follow:

$$C = n_p * C_p + n_u * C_u \tag{12}$$

Therefore, we define the benefit cost ratio Δ as follow:

$$\Delta = \frac{E}{C} \tag{13}$$

The benefit cost ratio is the ratio of merchants benefit and placement cost for roadside device. The higher ratio indicates that the current point has more opportunities to be selected to deploy a roadside device. On the contrary, the lower ratio indicates that it has less benefit and huge cost.

Base on the definition of benefit cost ratio, the main idea of our proposed algorithm are as follows: According to the current commercial distribution and traffic situation, the algorithm calculates the current benefit cost ratio iteratively. Then, it selects an intersection with the maximum benefit cost ratio to place the roadside device. Repeating the above two step until all merchants are covered. Our hybrid greedy algorithm is presented as Algorithm 1.

Algorithm 1. Hybrid Greedy algorithm

Input :
    The set of merchants: $\{S\}$;
    The set of traffic flows: $\{T\}$;
    The set of intersections: $\{V\}$;
    The budget for deployment: B;
Output :
    $\mathcal{R}$: The placement set of RAPs and RSUs
1: Marking all merchants to be uncovered and Initializing:
    $x_i=0, y_i=0, n_p=0, n_u=0$;
2: **while** All the merchants has not been covered **and** current cost less than B **do**
3:    Computing the benefit cost ratio Δ of all the intersection;
4:    Selecting a intersection v_k which has the maximum benefit cost ratio;
5:    Deploying the related device:$\mathcal{R} = \mathcal{R} \bigcup v_k$;
6:    Marking the related intersection:$x_k=1, n_p = n_p+1$ OR $y_k=1, n_u=n_u+1$;
7:    Marking the covered merchants;
8: **end while**;
9: **return** $\mathcal{R}$;

Figure 3 shows an illustrative example of the greedy algorithm and our placement solution. The graph contains 18 intersections, which labeled from #0 to #17. The graph also has 27 traffic flows, such as $t_{0,1}$, $t_{1,2}$, ..., etc. The set of traffic flows covered by RSU is $\{t_{12,13}, t_{13,14}, t_{10,13}, t_{13,16}\}$, and RAP's is $\{t_{3,4}, t_{4,5}, t_{6,7}, t_{7,8}, t_{9,10}, t_{10,11}, t_{1,4}, t_{4,7}, t_{7,10}, t_{10,13}\}$. The traffic flow coverage set refer to the Eq. 2. So RAP's traffic flow coverage set at intersection v_7 is $\{s_1, s_2, s_3, s_5, s_6\}$, and RSU's traffic flow coverage set at intersection v_{13} is $\{s_3, s_4, s_6\}$. The graph have 6 merchants, which should be covered by our algorithm. In the first iteration, we calculate benefit cost ratio of is 0.834 when place a RSU at v_{13}, which has the maximum benefit cost ratio. The merchants s_3, s_4 and s_6 are covered. In the second iteration, we calculate benefit cost ratio of

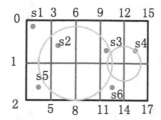

Fig. 3. A example of our solution

is 0.813 when place a RAP at v_7, which has the maximum benefit cost ratio. Then, all the merchants has been covered and the algorithm is ended. So our placement solution is place a RAP at v_7 and place a RSU at v_{13}.

5   Performance Evaluation

In our simulation, four algorithms are used for comparison. (1) All RAPs placement (All RAP), we only deploy RAPs in the simulation. (2) All RSUs placement (All RSU), we only deploy RSUs in the simulation. (3) Hybrid roadside devices placement (Hybrid DEV), our hybrid greedy algorithm, which could choose both RAP and RSU to be placed. (4) Random roadside devices placement (Random DEV), which select the intersection and roadside device randomly.

The parameter setting were given as follows: The grid size is 24 ∗ 20, there is a total of ten merchants dispersed in specified region. Every traffic flow from one intersection to another intersection has different number of passing vehicular users, and here we employed a series of random number (ranges from 40 to 120) to simulate the traffic flow. The radius of RAPs' coverage is set to 6, and 3 for RSUs. And the threshold D for detour distance is set to 10. while advertisements attraction ratio of all merchants are set to 0.5, the potential benefit for each advertisement is set to 1. The budget for placement is set to 1000. Every RSUs' cost for deployment is 120 while RAPs' cost is 300. Finally, we compared four kind of algorithms through the analysis of impacts between the number of placement devices and following parameters: the overall benefits of merchants, the number of merchants, and the coefficient ratio.

Figures 4, 5 and 6 shows the impacts of the merchants' benefits, number of merchants and benefit cost ratio. As shown in Fig. 4, the number of placed devices increases, merchants benefits grows increases too. Due to different roadside device has different transmission coverage, they may contribute to varying degrees of increase on merchants benefits. Especially when some merchants are covered repeatedly, even no extra benefits can be obtained by the placement of these devices.

In Fig. 5, our algorithm has the lowest placement cost than other algorithms. Based on these deployed devices, more and more traffic flows and related merchants are covered. The number of merchant increases up until all merchants in a specified region are covered or no more expenses anymore.

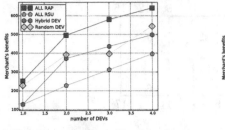
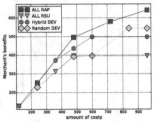

(a) Number of Devices Vs. Benefits   (b) Cost Vs. Benefits

Fig. 4. Impact of the benefits

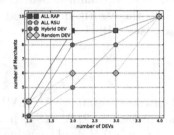
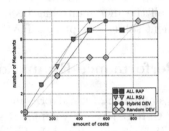

(a) Number of Devices Vs. Mer-   (b) Cost Vs. Merchants
chants

Fig. 5. Impact of merchants

In Fig. 6, it also proves that our algorithm placed the device at the best intersection to have a better gain of each step. With more and more devices are placed, there are fewer merchants who have been not covered by any roadside device. As shown in Fig. 6a and b, the benefit cost ratio declines with the number of placement roadside device. This is because each selection of our algorithm is most valuable.

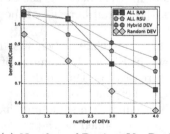
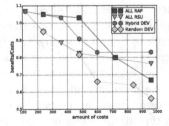

(a) Number of Devices Vs. Ratio   (b) Cost Vs. Ratio

Fig. 6. Impact of the coefficient ratio

6   Conclusions

In this paper, we study hybrid roadside devices placement problem for advertisement dissemination in VCPS. Then, we propose a greedy algorithm which could attract more customers and maximize the merchants benefits. Extensive simulations show that the performance of our proposed algorithm is superior to the other algorithms.

References

1. Li, X., Qiao, C., Hou, Y., Zhao, Y.: On-road ads delivery scheduling and bandwidth allocation in vehicular CPS. In: 2013 Proceedings IEEE, INFOCOM, pp. 2571–2579. IEEE (2013)
2. Zheng, H., Wu, J.: Optimizing roadside advertisement dissemination in vehicular cyber-physical systems. In: 2015 IEEE 35th International Conference on Distributed Computing Systems (ICDCS), pp. 41–50. IEEE (2015)
3. Yan, T., Zhang, W., Wang, G., Zhang, Y.: Access points planning in urban area for data dissemination to drivers IEEE Trans. Veh. Technol. 63(1), 390–402 (2014)
4. Li, P., Huang, C., Liu, Q.: Delay bounded roadside unit placement in vehicular ad hoc networks. Int. J. Distrib. Sens. Netw. 2015, 77 (2015)
5. Reis, A.B., Sargento, S., Neves, F., Tonguz, O.: Deploying roadside units in sparse vehicular networks: what really works and what does not. IEEE Trans. Veh. Technol. 63(6), 2794–2806 (2014)
6. Ke, W.C., Liu, B.H., Tsai, M.J.: The critical-square-grid coverage problem in wireless sensor networks is NP-complete. Comput. Netw. 55(9), 2209–2220 (2011)
7. Silva, C.M., Aquino, A.L., Meira, W.: Deployment of roadside units based on partial mobility information. Comput. Commun. 60, 28–39 (2015)
8. Zhang, B., Jia, X., Yang, K., Xie, R.: Design of analytical model and algorithm for optimal roadside AP placement in VANETs. IEEE Trans. Veh. Technol. PP(99), 1–11 (2015)
9. Li, P., Liu, Q., Huang, C., Wang, J., Jia, X.: Delay-bounded minimal cost placement of roadside units in vehicular ad hoc networks. In: IEEE International Conference on Communications (ICC), pp. 6589–6594. IEEE (2015)
10. Lin, C.C., Deng, D.J.: Optimal two-lane placement for hybrid VANET-sensor networks. IEEE Trans. Industrial Electronics, 62(12), 7883–7891 (2015)

Navigation, Tracking and Localization

A Modified LFF Method for Direct P-Code Acquisition in Satellite Navigation

Xinpeng Guo[✉], Hua Sun, Hongbo Zhao, and Wenquan Feng

Beihang University, Xueyuan Road No. 37, Haidian District, Beijing, China
buaagxp@126.com, bhzhb@126.com,
{sun,buaafwq}@buaa.edu.cn

Abstract. Due to the high dynamic in Satellite Navigation, the vital restriction for P-code Acquisition should be the Doppler frequency offset and large uncertainty of P code. To speed up the P-code acquisition, this paper proposed a novel acquisition method, based on the Local Frequency Folding method (LFF), by folding local frequency cells and generating code with little burden increase. Meanwhile, the coherent integration results storing structure of the method was modified to fit the parallel non-coherent integration, which accelerated the detection process of P-code acquisition. Preliminary result shows that the mean acquisition reduces significantly, with only -2 dB degradation in detection performance. Furthermore, it can be eliminated when the SNR exceed -10 dB.

Keywords: P-code acquisition · Satellite communication · Mean acquisition time

1 Introduction

The direct sequence spread spectrum (DSSS) communication is widely used in Global navigation satellite system. To receive the signal successfully, the Doppler frequency offset and uncertainty of the code phase, which caused by the relative motion between satellites and earth, should be determined by acquisition at a receiver. To achieve the quick acquisition, the downlink information is modulated by C/A code because of its short code period. However, the C/A code could be jammed and spoofed easily. Considering the security, the important link such as the uplink and the military link should take the advantages of precision code (P-code) to modulate the information. The code-searching range of P-code acquisition is much longer than C/A code. Therefore the traditional acquisition method is inapplicable to P-code. Meanwhile the high dynamic phenomenon is existent generally. It is necessary to propose practical direct P-Code acquisition method in high dynamic.

To accelerate the process of P-code searching, some direct P-Code acquisition method were proposed [1, 3]. The Extended Replica Folding Acquisition Search Technique (XFAST) was discussed widely [2], which extended and folded local generated code to achieve parallel code-searching. However because of the coherent combining loss caused by the large Doppler offset, the acquisition performance improvement of the XFAST was still subject to frequency-search. Recently Local Frequency Folding method (LFF) was introduced which folded local frequency cells

© ICST Institute for Computer Sciences, Social Informatics and Telecommunications Engineering 2018
Q. Chen et al. (Eds.): ChinaCom 2016, Part II, LNICST 210, pp. 499–508, 2018.
DOI: 10.1007/978-3-319-66628-0_47

together [4]. The LFF method solved the problem of coherent combining loss without increasing the acquisition time. However, because the LFF method focused on the efficiency of frequency-searching, the acquisition process with linear code-searching became laborious when the P-code period was very long. As solution to this problem, the Two-dimension Folding (TDF) method was presented in this paper which combined the LFF method with XFAST to accelerate the process of code-searching of the LFF method. Meanwhile a novel storing and detection method was proposed for the complex coherent integration, which could accurate the detecting process significantly.

The remaining sections of this paper are organized as follows: Sect. 2 analyzes the improvement of LFF method in parallel Doppler frequency search. Section 3 presents the TDF method. The acquisition performance in terms of detection probability and mean acquisition time is described in Sects. 4 and 5 demonstrates numerical results about some important factors. Finally, the conclusion is given in Sect. 6.

2 Analysis of the LFF Method

The LFF method achieves the parallel Doppler frequency search in high dynamic environment by folding local blocks in frequency domain. However there is lack of research in the LFF method, only the detection probability curve and the mean acquisition time are given. This paper will analyze the improvement of LFF method regarding to the coherent combining loss which is the point of achieving the parallel search.

The radio frequency (RF) signal is processed by the RF module in receiver, and the intermediate frequency (IF) signal down-sampled to twice chip rate are multiplied by local carrier. Than the base-band signal with the Doppler frequency offset is expressed as:

$$S(k) = D_i(k)P(k)e^{[2\pi(f_d/f_s)k + \varphi_i]j} + n_k, \quad k = 1, 2 \ldots \tag{1}$$

where the $D_i(k)$ represents the date in modulated signal. $P(k)$ is the P-code. f_d and f_s represent the Doppler frequency offset and twice chip rate sampling frequency. n_k is the additive White Gaussian Noise (AWGN):

Traditional acquisition method do the coherent integration between the receiving signal and local generated code. Assume that the $D_i(k)$ will not change in the coherent integration process and the code delay is zero. The result is:

$$I_{f_d} = D_i(k_0) \sum_{k=k_0}^{k_0+N-1} \cos(2\pi(f_d/f_s)k + \varphi_i) + \sum_{k=k_0}^{k_0+N-1} n_k P_0(k)$$

$$= \frac{D_i(k_0)\sin(\pi f_d N/f_s)}{\pi f_d N/f_s} \cos(2\pi f_d \frac{k_0+N/2}{f_s} + \varphi_i) + \sum_{k=k_0}^{k_0+N-1} n_k P_0(k) \tag{2}$$

In the Eq. 3, $P_0(k)$ represent the local generated code. N is the integration point. If we designate $\sum_{k=k_0}^{k_0+N-1} n_k P_0(k) = N_k$, then:

$$I_{f_d} = D_i(k_0)\text{sinc}(f_d N/f_s)\cos(2\pi f_d \frac{k_0 + N/2}{f_s} + \varphi_i) + N_k \tag{3}$$

The amplitude of I_{f_d} submits to $\text{sinc}(f_d N/f_s)$. When $f_d N/f_s = K$, $K = 1,2,3\ldots$, $\text{sinc}(f_d N/f_s) = 0$, the gain of coherent integration disappeared. And the peak of the correlation is lower than the noise floor [5]. The situation will happen when the Doppler frequency offset is about 10 kHz. So the Doppler frequency space is divided to cells, which is tested sequentially to avoid the situation happening, but acquisition speed is decelerated.

The LFF method folds the frequency cells to solve the problem. The Doppler frequency lies within $[-f_{d\max}, f_{d\max}]$, then the frequency cell can be expressed as $f_\delta = -f_{d\max} + \delta f_s/2N$, $\delta = 1,2,3\ldots F$ and the folding times $F = 4f_{d\max}N/f_s$. After adding all frequency cells and sampled, the result modulated by local generated P-code is given, where we designate $\theta_k - \frac{2\pi f_{d\max}k}{f_s}$:

$$L(k) = P_0(k)\sum_{\delta=1}^{F} e^{-j\frac{2\pi f_\delta}{f_s}k} = P_0(k)(\cos\theta_k + \sin\theta_k \cot\frac{\theta_k}{F}) = P_0(k)m(k), k = 1,2,3\ldots N \tag{4}$$

The traditional local generated code is replaced by the new sequence $L(k)$, where the $m(k)$ can be generated through two numerically controlled oscillators (NCO). So the coherent integration result between the incoming signal and the new sequence is given, we designate $N_{m,k} = \sum_{k=k_0}^{k_0+N-1} n_k P_0(k)m(k)$:

$$I_{m,fd} = D_i(k_0)\sum_{k=k_0}^{k_0+N-1} e^{[2\pi(f_d/f_s)k + \varphi_i]j}m(k) + N_{m,k} = D_i(k_0)R_{I,k_0} + N_{m,k} \tag{5}$$

The numerical simulation results of R_{I,k_0} is given in Figs. 1 and 2. The results show that the correlation peak of LFF method is more consistent than traditional method in

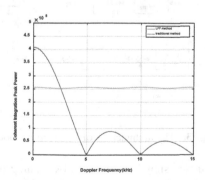

Fig. 1. The correlation peaks of LFF method and traditional method in different Doppler frequency.

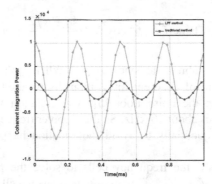

Fig. 2. The waves of coherent integration power of LFF method and traditional method when the Doppler frequency is 4 kHz.

different Doppler frequencies and the amplitude of the correlation peak is sufficient. Meanwhile the Doppler frequency of incoming signal can be detected through the coherent integration result by Fig. 2. The simulation result proves that the LFF method can be used to search the Doppler frequency offset parallelly in high dynamic environments.

3   Two-Dimension Folding Method

3.1   General Method Description

The LFF method can solve the problem of coherent combining loss. However, to achieve the fast P-code acquisition in high dynamic, the code-search process of LFF method should be accelerated. To solve the problem the novel TDF method is presented next. Figure 3 shows the architecture of the novel method and the process of acquisition is put as follows:

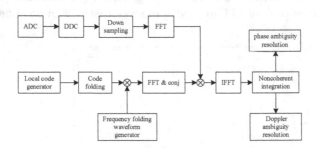

Fig. 3. The architecture of the TDF method

Step 1. Intermediate frequency signal is produced by Analog-digital converter (ADC).
Step 2. Incoming Intermediate frequency signal is shifted to base band by digital down converter (DDC).

Step 3. FFT is performed on the base band signal.

Step 4. The local generated P-code is folded at the same time.

Step 5. Fold Local frequency cells together to produce a waveform, which is then modulated by local folded code.

Step 6. The code-modulated waveform from Step 5 goes through FFT and complex conjunction.

Step 7. Results of step 4 and step 6 are complex-multiplied and IFFT is conducted on the multiplication results.

Step 8. The IFFT result is stored in a deinterleaver and then integrated coherently.

Step 9. Test the power of coherent integration result, and the ambiguity of the code phase is resolved by simple correlation check.

Step 10. The Doppler offset is determined by taking FFT on the stored different temporal IFFT results at the same code phase.

3.2   Storing and Detection Process of Coherent Integration Results

The coherent integration result by FFT will be not sufficient when the SNR of the incoming signal is low. Therefore the non-coherent integration is necessary to amplify the correlation result [6, 7]. Early LFF method proposed to achieve non-coherent integration by FFT. The process of the method is showed in Fig. 4(a). P blocks of coherent integration results are stored in the deinterleaver. Then the results in the same code-phase are processed by P points FFT. The power of the correlation results can be focus on a certain point among the FFT results. To complete the test of N code-phases, there are N times FFT of P points and NP times detection to find the max FFT result. It increased the detecting time substantially.

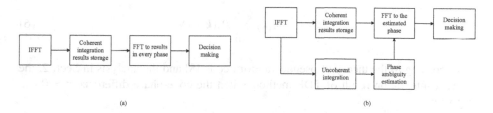

(a)   (b)

Fig. 4. Coherent integration storing and detection process

A novel coherent integration storing and detection process is given in Fig. 4(b), which will accelerate the detecting process and the matched storing architecture is showed in Fig. 5. The process is:

Step1: Write the N points of coherent integration results given by the IFFT module in the rows of deinterleaver. Meanwhile the absolute value of the results are added into the non-coherent integration result memory in the order of code-phase. In the same time, the next block of coherent integration results are being computed.

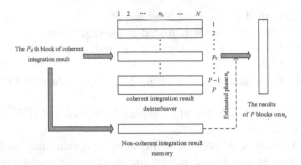

Fig. 5. Coherent integration storing architecture

Step2: After P blocks results added together, test the non-coherent integration results. The index of the max result is considered as the estimated code-phase.

Step3: Read the coherent integration results at the estimated code-phase in every block and do FFT for P point. If the max point of these FFT results exceeds the threshold, the detection is declare and the Doppler frequency can be detected by the index of the max point. Then resolve the ambiguity of code-phase causing by folding local generated code. If the max point does not exceed the threshold, clear all the memories and test next block of signal.

4   Theoretical Performance Analysis

4.1   Coherent Integration Performance

Assuming local generated code are folded X times, the local sequence is:

$$L_x(k) = m(k) \sum_{i=0}^{X-1} P_0(k+iN) \tag{6}$$

According to the theory of pseudo-random code [8] and the analysis in Sect. 2, the coherent integration result of TDF method when the code-phase difference $\tau = 0$ can be given:

$$
\begin{aligned}
I_{m,k_0} &= \sum_{k=k_0}^{k_0+N} (P(k)e^{[2\pi(f_d/f_s)k + \varphi_i]j} + n_k)L_x(k) \\
&= \frac{N+X-1}{N} \sum_{k=k_0}^{k_0+N-1} e^{[2\pi(f_d/f_s)k + \varphi_i]j} m(k) + \sum_{k=k_0}^{k_0+N-1} \sum_{i=0}^{X-1} P_0(k+iN)n_k m(k)
\end{aligned}
\tag{7}
$$

Compare with Eq. 7, we can get:

$$I_{m,k_0} = \frac{N+X-1}{N}R_{I,k_0} + \sum_{k=k_0}^{k_0+N-1} n_k m(k) \sum_{i=0}^{X-1} P_0(k+iN) \tag{8}$$

When the $\tau \neq 0$, the coherent integration result is:

$$I_{m,k_0} = \frac{X}{N}R_{I,k_0} + \sum_{k=k_0}^{k_0+N-1} n_{k+\tau} m(k) \sum_{i=0}^{X-1} P_0(k+iN) \tag{9}$$

Because the local P-code is not correlative with noise, the I_{m,k_0} is decided by R_{I,k_0}. Therefore the characteristic of the coherent integration result is similar as which is described in Sect. 2.

4.2 Detection Probability

To calculate the detection probability, the non-coherent integration result of the signal and noise are necessary. The non-coherent integration result can be expressed:

$$I_u = \sum_{i=1}^{P} \left| I_{m,k_0+(i-1)P} \right| \tag{10}$$

Assume that N is large enough to ensure that $P_0(k)$ is orthogonal with $P_0(k+\tau)$. Then the mean and variance of I_u are:

$$E(I_{u,\tau}) = \begin{cases} \sum_{i=0}^{P-1} \left| R_{m,iN+1} \right|, \tau = 0 \\ 0, \tau \neq 0 \end{cases} = \begin{cases} S_u, \tau = 0 \\ 0, \tau \neq 0 \end{cases} \tag{11}$$

$$D(I_{u,\tau}) = \begin{cases} D(\sum_{i=0}^{P-1} \sum_{k=iN+1}^{(i+1)N} n_k m(k) \sum_{j=0}^{X-1} P_0(k+jN)), \tau = 0 \\ D(\sum_{i=0}^{P-1} \sum_{k=iN+1}^{(i+1)N} n_{k+\tau} m(k) \sum_{j=0}^{X-1} P_0(k+jN)), \tau \neq 0 \end{cases} = \sum_{i=0}^{P-1} \left(\sum_{k=1}^{N} m^2(k) \right) \sigma^2$$

$$= PM\sigma^2 \tag{12}$$

The result of the FFT of P point coherent integration result when $\tau = 0$ is considered next. According to former search the, the max result will appear at $No.Pf_e/2f_c$ point of the FFT result. The mean and variance of the result are:

$$\begin{cases} E(I_{F,\tau,i}) = \begin{cases} P\sum_{k=1}^{N} e^{[2\pi(f_d/f_s)k+\varphi_i]j} m_k, i = Pf_e/2f_c \\ 0, i \neq Pf_e/2f_c \end{cases} = \begin{cases} PS_0, i = Pf_e/2f_c \\ 0, i \neq Pf_e/2f \end{cases} \tag{13} \\ D(I_{F,\tau,i}) = PM\sigma^2 \end{cases}$$

So the peak of the non-coherent integration result $\gamma_u = I_{u,\tau=0}$ and the FFT result $\gamma_F = I_{F,\tau=0,i=Pf_e/2f_c}$ follow the Rician distribution. The noise of non-coherent integration result and the FFT result $\gamma_n = I_{u,\tau\neq0} \cup I_{F,\tau\neq0 \cup i\neq Pf_e/2f_c}$ follows Rayleigh distribution.

The threshold $V_{th} = \sqrt{-2PM\sigma^2 \ln(P_{fa}^{(s)})}$ is set by Constant False Alarm Rate (CFAR) with the designed false alarm probability $P_{fa}^{(s)}$ [9]. Then the Detection Probability can be obtained by referencing the process in Sect. 3.2.

$$P_d^{(c)} = \int_{V_{th}}^{\infty} [F_{\gamma_n}(r_F)]^{P-1} P_{\gamma_F}(r_F) dr_F \int_0^{\infty} [F_{\gamma_n}(r_u)]^{N-1} P_{\gamma_u}(r_u) dr_u \qquad (14)$$

where $P_{\gamma_F}(r_F)$ and $P_{\gamma_u}(r_u)$ are the Probability Density Function the peak of the non-coherent integration result and the FFT result of coherent integration. And the $F_{\gamma_n}(r_F)$ is the Cumulative Distribution Function of the noise of non-coherent integration result.

4.3 Mean Acquisition Time

The incoming signal is processed block by block in the TDF method. So the process unit time is T_d which in Eq. 7. Then the mean acquisition time considering single dwell time is [10, 11]:

$$\overline{T_a} = \frac{(\eta/X - 1)(1 + \kappa P_{fa}^{(s)})(2 - P_d^{(c)})}{2P_d^{(c)}} + \frac{1}{P_d^{(c)}} \qquad (15)$$

where κ is the punishment factor of false alarm and η represents the number of blocks in each code period.

5 Simulation Results

Monte Carlo method and numerical simulation method are used to present the performance of TDF method. The detection probability and mean acquisition time are considered. The number of the coherent integration is set as 1024. The chip rate is 10.23 Mcps. According to practical situation in navigation satellite, the max Doppler offset is 250 kHz and the false alarm probability is set below 10e(−6).

5.1 Detection Probability

Figure 6 shows the detection probability of TDF method on incoming signals with different SNRs. The times of folding local code and frequency cells are $X = 4$ and $F = 256$. The non-coherent integration times P are 1, 10, 20, 50 from right to left. The detection probability is improved evidently by non-coherent integration as the curve of $P = 1$ is far backward as the others. As the non-coherent integration times increase, the

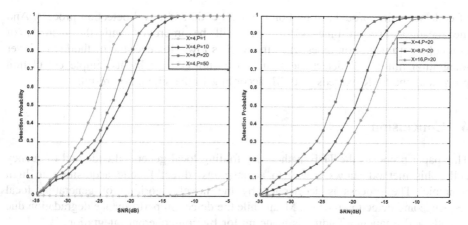

Fig. 6. Detection probability of TDF method as $X = 4$ and $P = 20$

detection performance of the proposed method is improved accordingly. However, when the integration times is larger than 50, the improvement brought in by non-coherent integration is retarded. On the contrary, the cost of storing resource increases rapidly and the mean acquisition time will enlarge, as showed in Fig. 7.

The detection probability of the method with different code folding times is showed in Fig. 6. The non-coherent integration times is set at 20 which is a rational choice by weighing the detection probability and resource cost. It can be seen that the detection probability reduces with the increase of code folding number. However the negative effects on of the cross-correlation diminish in high SNR which exceeds −10 dB. In this situation, the larger folding times will accelerate the acquisition process.

5.2   Mean Acquisition Time

The mean acquisition time of the proposed method with different non-coherent integration is shown in Fig. 7, where the code folding times $X = 4$ and $X = 1$. When $X = 1$, the TDF method degenerates to LFF method. There is a 6 dB difference of mean acquisition time between TDF method and LFF method because of the decreased times

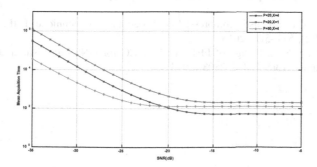

Fig. 7. Mean acquisition time of TDF method

of code-searching brought in by Folding local code and novel detection process. And the mean acquisition time performance will be improved with the increase of non-coherent integration times when the SNR is low. However the method with fewer integration times will detect the signal in a shorter time by its simple calculation process as the SNR exceeds −20 dB, according to the simulation results.

6   Conclusion

This paper proposes the TDF method. By folding local generated code and frequency cells, this method shows a way to achieve fast direct P-code acquisition in high dynamic. The process is accelerated by the novel algorithm of generating local sequence and detection process. Meanwhile the detection performance degradation due to code and frequency folding is made up for by non-coherent integration.

References

1. Pang, J.: Direct global positioning system P-code acquisition field programmable gate array prototyping. Ohio University, Diss (2003)
2. Yang, C., Vasquez, M.J., Chaffee, J.: Fast direct P(Y)-code acquisition using XFAST. In: ION GPS, Nashville, TN, pp. 317–324 (1999)
3. Li, H., Cui, X., Lu, M., et al.: Dual-folding based rapid search method for long PN-code acquisition. J. IEEE Trans. Wirel. Commun. 7(12), 5286–5296 (2008)
4. Zhao, H., Feng, W., Xing, X.: A novel PN-Code acquisition method based on local frequency folding for BeiDou system. In: The 2016 International Technical Meeting of ION, Monterey, California, pp. 940–947 (2015)
5. Xie, G.: Principles of GPS and receiver design. Electron. Ind. Beijing 7, 61–63 (2009)
6. Ping, J., Wu, X., Yan, J.: Modified zero-padding method for fast long PN-code acquisition. In: 2014 IEEE 80th Vehicular Technology Conference (VTC Fall). IEEE (2014)
7. Spangenberg, S.M., Scott, I.: An FFT-based approach for fast acquisition in spread spectrum communication systems. Wireless Pers. Commun. 13(1-2), 27–55 (2000)
8. Peterson, R.L., Ziemer, R.E.: Introduction to Spread Spectrum Communications. Prentice-Hall, Englewood Cliffs (1995)
9. Wu, X.C., Gong, P., Song, H.J.: An FFT-based approach for carrier frequency domain acquisition in spread spectrum TT&C system. J. Appl. Mech. Mater. 135–136, 211–216 (2012)
10. Kong, S.H.: A deterministic compressed GNSS acquisition technique. J. IEEE Trans. Veh. Technol. 62(2), 511–521 (2013)
11. Kim, B., Kong, S.H.: Design of FFT-based TDCC for GNSS acquisition. J. IEEE Trans. Wirel. Commun. 13(5), 2798–2808 (2014)

A Dual-Tone Radio Interferometric Tracking System

Pan Xiao$^{(\boxtimes)}$, Yiyin Wang, Cailian Chen, and Xinping Guan

Department of Automation, School of Electronic Information and Electrical
Engineering, Shanghai Jiao Tong University, Shanghai, China
{novie_pan,yiyinwang,cailianchen,xpguan}@sjtu.edu.cn

Abstract. Localization in wireless sensors networks (WSNs) has been
increasingly significant recently due to the demand of the location
aware services. The low cost and high accuracy requirements make many
positioning systems adopt high-accuracy quasi-synchronization method.
However it remains synchronization errors which lower positioning and
tracking precision within such systems. Hence, we propose a tracking system with low-accuracy quasi-synchronization method based on
dual-tone radio interferometric signals. A mobile target emits dual-tone
signals whose phases contain range information. Several anchors with
known positions receive the dual-tone signals and extract their phase
information. We cancel the synchronization error by differentiating two
phases estimated from two consecutive time instants to increase accuracy.
The tracking accuracy is evaluated by simulations. The tracking system
enjoys low complexity, low cost and obtains a reasonable accuracy.

Keywords: Dual-tone radio interferometric · Quasi-synchronization ·
Tracking · Localization · Positioning

1 Introduction

A wireless sensor network (WSN) is a distributed and self-organizing network
with lots of sensor nodes deployed [1]. They are applied in many fields including
military detection, intelligent traffic, hospital supervision and care [2]. All the
applications are based on the awareness of sensor locations. Therefore, accurate and efficient positioning technology is very important and urgent [3]. For
example, firemen rescue people's life with high risk when fiermen's locations are
unknown in fire disasters. It is safer for them when their positions are located
accurately within the fireplaces.

Localization has been researched for years. The Global Positioning System
(GPS) offers great convenience to people's life. However, the accuracy of traditional GPS is a few meters. Newly developed differential GPS is more accurate

P. Xiao—Part of this work was supported by the National Nature Science Foundation of China (No. 61301223), the Nature Science Foundation of Shanghai (No.
13ZR1421800), and the New Faculty Foundation of Ministry of Education of China
under Grant (No. 13Z102090106).

© ICST Institute for Computer Sciences, Social Informatics and Telecommunications Engineering 2018
Q. Chen et al. (Eds.): ChinaCom 2016, Part II, LNICST 210, pp. 509–518, 2018.
DOI: 10.1007/978-3-319-66628-0_48

but expensive [4]. Additionally, GPS does not work well indoors, in dense forest or cluttered urban environments. So it is not suitable for localization in WSNs. Radio interferometric localization satisfies three of the requirements of wireless localization applications: high precision, low cost and low power. It can achieve centimeter scale accuracy. Hence, We intend to use interferometric technology for tracking. The radio interferometric positioning system (RIPS) [5] has been proposed and developed in WSNs. The RIPS could achieve high accuracy and low cost. Then it is extended in [6,7] for a tracking system, in which Doppler shifts are adopted to estimate the positions and velocities of the motion. Besides, the RIPS is developed in [8] to combat the flat-fading channels. Furthermore, a dual-tone radio interferometric positioning system using undersampling techniques (uDRIPS) avoids amplifying the noise and simplifying the receiver structure simultaneously [9]. However, most of these approaches are in demand of high-accuracy synchronization either among anchors or between the target and anchors.

Time synchronization is still a big obstacle in WSNs, in which the resource and energy are limited. However high-accuracy synchronization system where the synchronization error is less than $10\,\mu s$ consumes additional energy, bandwidth and computational resources [10]. Besides, it is difficult to implemented in practice [11]. Furthermore, it exists synchronization errors which influence the positioning and tracking accuracy. Common synchronization mechanisms have synchronization errors which are around $50\,\mu s$. The average one hop error of the TPSN synchronization method is $21.43\,\mu s$ [12] and DMTS's synchronization error is $30\,\mu s$ [13].

Considering these reasons, we envision an approach based on RIPS to track a mobile target and remove all the synchronization errors in order to increase tracking precision. We adopt the common synchronization method to reduce high resource cost of the high-accuracy synchronization system and lower the system cost. It has the advantage of undersampling which avoids noise amplification. We extract the TOAs accompanied by synchronization error items from the phases of the dual-tone signals in our system. For different anchors, the synchronization errors are different. Each error is fixed once the system starts to work [11]. Here we consider the motion process as a series of uniform linear motions, and each motion is a moving step. We get TDOA to eliminate the offset in two successive moving steps. Then we get the difference of random two TDOAs (DTDOA) and establish relations between DTDOAs and the velocities. And use non-linear least squares method to work out the velocity. With the known initial position of the mobile target, we acquire the position of the target at randomly time. Then we got the motion curve.

The rest of the paper is structured as follows. Section 2 introduces system model. Section 3 describes the algorithm used to estimate the velocity and position of the mobile target. We provide simulation results of this approach in Sect. 4 and evaluate our algorithm. Section 5 contains the conclusions.

2 System Model

Let us assume M anchors with known locations. The moving target moves randomly within the zone, transmitting a dual-tone signal

$$s(t) = \gamma e^{j\varphi} e^{j2\pi(f_c+f_b)t}(1 + e^{j2\pi g_b t}), \tag{1}$$

where γ is the real-valued amplitude of each components, φ is the unknown initial phase offset, f_c is the carrier frequency, and f_b is the frequency difference between the two tones and greater than zero. The frequency g_b is the frequency difference between the two tones and greater than zero as well.

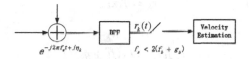

Fig. 1. The receiver structure of the tracking system

Figure 1 shows the receiver structure of the tracking system. The signal $s(t)$ goes through channels, down converted by f_c, and received by the kth anchor. We model the received signal as follows.

$$r_k(t) = \beta_k s\left(t - \tau_k - t_k\right) e^{-2\pi f_c + j\eta_k} + w_k\left(t\right), \tag{2}$$

Combining (1) and (2), we have

$$r_k(t) = \alpha_k \beta_k e^{j2\pi f_b t} e^{j\theta_k}(1 + e^{j2\pi g_b t} e^{j\phi_k}) + w_k(t), \tag{3}$$

where β_k is a complex channel coefficient attributing to the flat-fading channel effects, and can be modeled as a zero-mean complex Gaussian random variable with variance σ_k representing the average power of the flat-fading channel. The $\theta_k = -2\pi(f_c + f_b)(t_k + \tau_k), \phi_k = -2\pi g_b(t_k + \tau_k)$, and $\alpha_k = \gamma e^{j(\varphi+\eta_k)}$ are composite variables. The w_k represents the noise item. The α_k absorbs the effects of the random initial phases between the mobile target and the kth anchor. The unknown time t_k is the remaining time offset of kth anchor plus the transmission instant of the transmitter. The unknown initial phase η_k is due to the randomness of the receiver oscillator. Here ϕ_k includes the range of interest via τ_k which we are interested in. The assumptions as follows are adopted in the entire paper.

Assumption 1: The synchronization problem usually contains two elements which are time offset and skew [14]. Here we use quasi-synchronization [16] which only consider time offset. The synchronization error is t_k due to the low-accuracy synchronization between the mobile target and the kh anchor. Moreover, the synchronization errors are different to anchors according to the reality.

Assumption 2: We assume that the two tones of the dual-tone signal experience the same fading channel because the frequency difference g_b is set to be much smaller than the channel coherence bandwidth [16]. Hence in two centrosymmetric motions we will get the same measured data set and work out the same velocity. For example, when the target moves towards the x-axis positive or negative direction, the estimated velocity directions probably are all the x-axis negative directions or positive directions with the same velocity absolute value.

The received signal $r_k(t)$ is undersampled by a sampling frequency f_s ($f_s < 2(f_b + g_b)$) to lower the requirement of the equipments, at the same time to avoid amplifying the noise. After processing the sample data, we get a parameter $\phi_k = -2\pi g_b(t_k + \tau_k)$. It relates to transmission time and remaining time offset what we are interested. Next we will explain how ϕ_k can be calculated and the integer ambiguity problem. Collecting the kth anchor's samples into a vector r_k, we have

$$r_k = Ax_k,$$

where

$$x_k = [\alpha_k\beta_k e^{j\theta_k}, e^{j(\theta_k+\phi_k)}]^T$$
$$A = [L(f_b/f_s), L((f_b + g_b)/f)]^T$$
$$L(f) = [1, e^{j2\pi f}, \dots, e^{j2\pi(L-1)f}]^T$$

Finally, use the least-squares (LS) estimator to calculate x_k.

$$\hat{x}_k = (A)^\dagger r_k,$$

So the complex parameter ϕ_k can be estimated as

$$\hat{\phi}_k = \arg\{[\hat{x}_k]_1^* [\hat{x}_k]_2\} + 2\pi l,$$

where $[x]_n$ is the nth entry of the vector x. The integer ambiguity means the unknown integer l due to phase wrapping. We assume that the mobile positioning method is applied indoors. The target is moving in a limited space and let's assume as large as $1000\,m \times 1000\,m$. We could get the biggest $\phi_k = 2\pi g_b\left(\frac{1000\sqrt{2}}{3\times10^8} + t_k\right)$ where $g_b = 10\,kHz$ in our system. According to the introduction, $t_k < 50\,\mu s$. Hence, the $\phi_k < 2\pi$. We rewrite the formula above as

$$\hat{\phi}_k = \arg\{[\hat{x}_k]_1^* [\hat{x}_k]_2\} = -2\pi g_b(t_k + \tau_k),$$

This parameter is the key point to our tracking localization algorithm. The t_k here is brought about by the synchronization error between the mobile target and the kth anchor. The propagation time τ_k is the transmission time from mobile target and the k-th anchor and $d_k = \tau_k \nu$. The ν is the transmit speed of the dual-tone signal.

3   The Tracking Method

In this section, we will specifically present the steps to calculate the velocity and location of the mobile target.

3.1   The Movement Model of the Target

As we said, the mobile target moves in the interested zone in which M anchors are distributed to receive signals. Hypothesise the initial location of the mobile target is known as $[x_0, y_0]$. In order to describe conveniently later, we call the location $[x_n, y_n]$ as the nth step and denote as $T^n = [x_n, y_n]$. The ϕ_k^n means the ϕ estimated by the kth anchor when the mobile target in nth step.

$$\phi_k^n = -2\pi g_b(t_k + \tau_k^n), \tag{4}$$

The t_k is the remaining time offset, it varies only from different anchors. It does not change once the system begins to work. Then let us denote $\Delta\phi_k^n$ as the phase difference of the received signal at the kth anchor in the $(n+1)$th step and nth step.

$$\Delta\phi_k^n = \phi_k^{n+1} - \phi_k^n = -2\pi g_b(\tau_k^{n+1} - \tau_k^n), \tag{5}$$

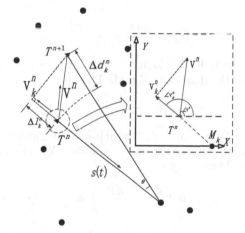

Fig. 2. The movement model of the target

Figure 2 shows the movement of the mobile target and the coordinate system we use. Let the black dots denote anchors and the black triangle indicates the mobile target. The M_k represents the kth anchor. The target moves from the nth step to the $(n+1)$th step (i.e. from T^n to T^{n+1} in Fig. 2). First we have an approximation that

$$\Delta d_k^n \approx \Delta l_k^n, \tag{6}$$

$$\Delta d_k^n = \nu(\tau_k^{n+1} - \tau_k^n), \tag{7}$$

where Δd_k^n is the distance difference of d_k in two adjacent steps (the nth step and the $(n+1)$th step), and Δl_k^n is a component of the distance $\|T^{n+1} - T^n\|$ at the radical direction (i.e. $M_k \rightarrow T^n(x_n, y_n)$). Next we will illustrate this approximate relationship. The tracking frequency can be set according to the reality. In this simulation let us hypothesis the target to be localized about 10 times per second in the tracking system. Usually the movement in such application setting is not very fast. In our movement model, we assume the mobile target moves at 5 m/s, the $\|T^{n+1} - T^n\|$ of two adjacent steps could be 0.5 m which is far less than the distance d_k between the mobile target and anchor. We have the experiment in a 1000 m × 1000 m squares, so the d_k is larger than 10 m. Hence, the $\theta \ll 5/100$ rad, then we have the last approximation. As a result, the radical component of mobile target's speed v, denoted as v_k^n, has relationship as follows:

$$|v_k^n| = \frac{\Delta l_k^n}{t^{n+1} - t^n}, \angle v_k^n = \angle(T^n - M_k), \tag{8}$$

where $\angle v$ is the vector v's direction, defined as the angle with respect to x-axis. The $t^{n+1} - t^n$ means the time difference from nth step to $(n+1)$th step. According to the reality, decrease the positioning frequency will impair the reality of the tracking route. In this paper, we assume $t^{n+1} - t^n = 0.1$ s and we know that to decrease the parameter could increase the positioning accuracy. Combining (6), (7) and (8), we get

$$|v_k^n| = \frac{\nu(\tau_k^{n+1} - \tau_k^n)}{t^{n+1} - t^n}. \tag{9}$$

We know that v_k^n is the radical velocity of v relative to the kth anchor. The ν is the transmit speed of the dual-tone signal. Therefore we get

$$|v_k^n| = |v^n| \cos(\angle v^n - \angle v_k^n). \tag{10}$$

In order to calculate the $|v^n|$ and $\angle v^n$ which are the moving speed and moving angle, we select any two anchors from M anchors. We might as well select the kth and jth anchors. Then we get

$$|v_k^n| - |v_j^n| = -2|v^n| \sin\left(\frac{\angle v_k^n - \angle v_j^n}{2}\right) \sin\left(\frac{\angle v_k^n + \angle v_j^n}{2} - \angle v^n\right). \tag{11}$$

$$\Delta\phi_{kj}^n = \Delta\phi_k^n - \Delta\phi_j^n = -2\pi g_b((\tau_k^{n+1} - \tau_k^n) - (\tau_j^{n+1} - \tau_j^n)),$$

Combining (9) and (11), we arrive at

$$\frac{\nu((\tau_k^{n+1} - \tau_k^n) - (\tau_j^{n+1} - \tau_j^n))}{t^{n+1} - t^n} = -2|v^n| \sin\left(\frac{\angle v_k^n - \angle v_j^n}{2}\right) \sin\left(\frac{\angle v_k^n + \angle v_j^n}{2} - \angle v^n\right),$$

Finally, combining the last two equations above, we obtain

$$\Delta\phi_{k,j}^n = a|v^n| \sin b_{k,j} \sin(c_{k,j} - \angle v^n), \tag{12}$$

where $a = \frac{4\pi g_b}{t^{n+1} - t^n}$ which is composite control variable. The parameter $b_{k,j} = \frac{\angle v_k^n - \angle v_j^n}{2}, c_{k,j} = \frac{\angle v_k^n + \angle v_j^n}{2}$ which need to be calculated by (8). Equation (12) has two parameters, the target's speed magnitude $|v^n|$ and direction $\angle v^n$, which need to be solved.

we rewrite (12) as

$$\Delta\phi_{k,j}^n = f_{k,j}(|v^n|, \angle v^n). \tag{13}$$

The two parameters could be estimated only if we have two equations. As we said above, k, j is chosen arbitrarily. Generally, the system installs $(M \geq 3)$ anchors, and offers $N = C_M^2 > M$ equations. Therefore, we get more information from less anchors which decrease the complexity of the system. Then we denote a matrix equation as

$$\Delta\Phi = a\mathbf{1}_N \, |\mathbf{v}^n| \sin b \sin(c - \angle\mathbf{v}^n). \tag{14}$$

For convenience we denote Eq. 14 as $\Delta\Phi = F(|\mathbf{v}^n|, \angle\mathbf{v}^n)$, where F is the matrix form of functions $\{f_{1,2}, \ldots, f_{M-1,M}\}$. The parameter $\Delta\Phi = [\Delta\phi_{1,2}, \Delta\phi_{1,3}, \cdots, \Delta\phi_{M-1,M}]^T$ which is a measurement vector, $\mathbf{b} = [b_{1,2}, b_{1,3}, \cdots, b_{M-1,M}]^T$. Similarly, $\mathbf{c} = [c_{1,2}, c_{1,3}, \cdots, c_{M-1,M}]^T$. Due to noise influence and machine error, there is no exact $\{|\mathbf{v}^n|, \angle\mathbf{v}^n\}$ to satisfy (14). Instead, we estimate such $\{|\hat{\mathbf{v}}^n|, \angle\hat{\mathbf{v}}^n\}$ so that $\|F(|\mathbf{v}^n|, \angle\mathbf{v}^n) - \Delta\Phi\|$ is minimized.

3.2   The Tracking Algorithm

In this part we will use the theory of the non-linear least squares methods (NLS) [17] to solve the moving velocities and calculate the positions. As we need to minimized the $\|F(|\mathbf{v}^n|, \angle\mathbf{v}^n) - \Delta\Phi\|$, we use least square method to estimate. Then define a new function $\mathscr{F} : R^2 \rightarrow R$, then

$$\mathscr{F}(|\mathbf{v}^n|, \angle\mathbf{v}^n) = \sum_{k=1, j>k}^{M} (\Delta\phi_{k,j} - f(|\mathbf{v}^n|, \angle\mathbf{v}^n))^2, \tag{15}$$

We start with an initial approximation of the estimated augment $\{|\hat{\mathbf{v}}^n|, \angle\hat{\mathbf{v}}^n\}$, linearize $\mathscr{F}$ and update the estimated augment continuously until the object function converges to its local minimum.

We can get the new location as follows

$$\hat{T}^n = HQ,$$

where $\hat{T}^n = [\hat{x}^n, \hat{y}^n]^T$, $Q = [\hat{x}^{n-1}, \hat{y}^{n-1}, \hat{v}_x^n, \hat{v}_y^n]$, $\hat{v}_x^n = |\hat{v}^n| \cos(\angle\hat{v}^n)$, $\hat{v}_y^n = |\hat{v}^n| \sin(\angle\hat{v}^n)$. H is the state transition matrix which is modeled as

$$H = \begin{bmatrix} 1 & 0 & \Delta t & 0 \\ 0 & 1 & 0 & \Delta t \end{bmatrix} \tag{16}$$

where $\Delta t = t_{n+1} - t_n = 1/f$ is the reciprocal of the positioning frequency f. As long as we know the initial position $T^0 = [x^0, y^0]$, then we can get the position $\hat{T}^n$ and velocity $\{|\hat{v}^n|, \angle\hat{v}^n\}$ of any moment.

4   Simulation Results

In this section, we evaluate the performance of our positioning algorithm. We compare the positioning accuracy by changing the undersampling frequency f_s

and the Signal-noise ratio. We set the parameters like this: (1) We set the frequency difference $g_b = 10\,\text{kHz}$. Because the typical channel coherence bandwidth is $100\,\text{kHz}$ which needs to be larger than the frequency difference [18]. (2) The positioning interval is set as $\Delta t = 0.1\,\text{s}$. Actually this constant could influence the simulation graphs of mobile curves. Besides, it relates closely to the energy consumption. When we decrease Δt, it means that increase positioning number per second and add energy consumption. Otherwise, the mobile model does not fit the approximation equation in (6). So we choose $\Delta t = 0.1\,\text{s}$ which is neither long nor short. We also simulated the condition when $\Delta t = 0.01\,\text{s}$. However, the simulation result is similar to this condition except consume more time and energy to over-frequent positioning. It indicates that $\Delta t = 0.01\,\text{s}$ is suitable. (3) The amplitude of the transmitted signal is $\gamma = 1$, and the carrier frequency $f_c = 2.45\,\text{GHz}$ [19]. (4) The average channel power of the flat-fading channel is set to be 1 as usual in simulation for all channels, i.e., $\sigma_k^2 = 1, k = 1, \ldots, M$. (5) The transmission velocity of radio signal is $\nu = 3 \times 10^8\,\text{m/s}$. (6) For each estimation, operate 1000 Monte-Carlo runs to evaluate performance. (7) The positioning accuracy is evaluated with eight anchors and a mobile target. The coordinates for eight anchors are as follows like this $M_1 = [0,0]^T, M_2 = [1000,0]^T, M_3 = [1000,1000]^T, M_4 = [0,1000]^T, M_5 = [700,700]^T, M_6 = [400,800]^T, M_7 = [100,500]^T, M_8 = [600,300]^T$.

Figure 3 shows the variable motion with the speed direction and value change. It consists of three constant motion parts. The direction of arrow represents the speed direction. The dots denote the initial position of mobile target in every step. The inflection points represent the direction change of mobile target. In Fig. 3 velocity range is $2\,\text{m/s} \leq |v| \leq 7\,\text{m/s}$. The direction of speeds change is $\pi/6 \leq \angle v \leq \pi/2$. The maximum direction change is $3/\pi$. The signal-to-noise ratio (SNR) is defined as $1/s2$, and SNR $= 30\,\text{db}$. The $\Delta t = 0.1\,\text{s}$, and $f_s = 30\,\text{kHz}$. Figure 4 shows the CDF of x-axis, y-aixs and average positioning

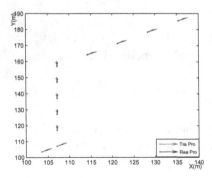

Fig. 3. The variable motion of real process and tracking process

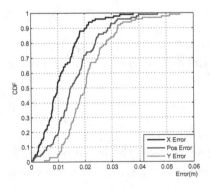

Fig. 4. The CDF of absolute positioning error at x–axis, y–axis and average in variable motion

error of variable motion. The average position error is defined as $\sqrt{\frac{\Delta x^2 + \Delta y^2}{2}}$. We concluded that 90% of the average position errors are less than 3 cm, and the errors in x-axis are less than the error in y-axis. The reason is that the anchors distributed on x-axis direction is more evenly than on y-axis direction.

Furthermore, we simulate the relations among positioning accuracy, the undersampling frequency and SNR. The SNR is defined as $1/\sigma^2$. Figures 5 and 6 show the relations. The location accuracy increases when the sampling frequency increases and SNR increases. Because when the sampling frequency f_s increases, the sample information is more detailed. It helps to estimate the needed parameter exactly. As SNR increases, the dual-tone signal becomes stronger.

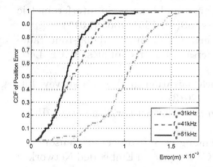

Fig. 5. The variable motion of real process and tracking process

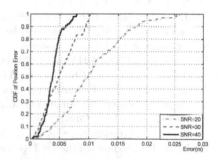

Fig. 6. The CDF position errors at different SNRs

5   Conclusion

In this paper, we propose a tracking system based on dual-tone radio interferometric signals for WSNs. Several anchors with known positions receive the dual-tone signals which are emitted by a mobile target. The key innovation in our tracking system is eliminating the remaining time offsets of the low-accuracy synchronization upon the target and anchors. By differentiating the phase estimation of two consecutive time instants, we can remove the remaining time offsets between the target and anchors. Finally, We concluded that of the average position error are less than 3 cm in viable motion tracking. The low-complexity tracking algorithm is simulated and is proved efficient in tracking.

References

1. Ma, Z., Sun, Y., Mei, T.: Survey on wireless sensors network. China Inst. Commun. **5**(4), 114–124 (2004)
2. Han, G., Xu, H., Duong, T.Q., Jiang, J., Hara, T.: Localization algorithms of wireless sensor networks: a survey. Telecommun. Syst. **52**(4), 2419–2436 (2013)

3. Wang, J., Wang, F., Duan, W.: Application of weighted least square estimates on wireless sensor network node localization. Appl. Res. Comput. **9**, 11 (2006)

4. Hofmann-Wellenhof, B., Lichtenegger, H., Collins, J.: Global Positioning System: Theory and Practice. Springer Science Business Media, Heidelberg (2012)

5. Maróti, M., Völgyesi, P., Dóra, S., Kusý, B., Nádas, A., Lédeczi, Á., Balogh, G., Molnár, K.: Radio interferometric geolocation. In: Proceedings of ACM on Embedded Networked Sensor Systems, pp. 1–12 (2005)

6. Kusy, B., Ledeczi, A., Koutsoukos, X.: Tracking mobile nodes using RF Doppler shifts. In: Proceedings of ACM on Embedded Networked Sensor Systems, pp. 29–42 (2007)

7. Kusy, B., Sallai, J., Balogh, G., Ledeczi, A., Protopopescu, V., Tolliver, J., DeNap, F., Parang, M.: Radio interferometric tracking of mobile wireless nodes. In: Proceedings of the ACM on Mobile Systems, pp. 139–151 (2007)

8. Wang, Y., Ma, X., Chen, C., Guan, X.: Designing dual-tone radio interferometric positioning systems. IEEE Trans. Sign. Process. **63**(6), 1351–1365 (2015)

9. Wang, Y., Li, L., Ma, X., Shinotsuka, M., Chen, C., Guan, X.: Dual-tone radio interferometric positioning systems using undersampling techniques. IEEE Lett. Sig. Process. **21**(11), 1311–1315 (2014)

10. Singh, V., Sharma, S., Sharma, T.: Time synchronization in WSN: a survey. Int. J. Enhanc. Res. Sci. Technol. Eng. **2**(5), 61–67 (2013)

11. Sivrikaya, F., Yener, B.: Time synchronization in sensor networks: a survey. IEEE Network **18**(4), 45–50 (2004)

12. Ganeriwal, S., Kumar, R., Srivastava, M.B.: Timing-sync Protocol for Sensor Networks. In: Proceedings of the 1st International Conference on Embedded Networked Sensor Systems, pp. 138–149. ACM Press (2003)

13. Ping, S.: Delay measurement time synchronization for wireless sensor networks. Intel Research, Berkeley Lab (2003)

14. Noh, K.-L., Chaudhari, Q.M., Serpedin, E., Suter, B.W.: Novel clock phase offset and skew estimation using two-way timing message exchanges for wireless sensor networks. IEEE Trans. Commun. **55**(4), 766–777 (2007)

15. Schaefer, M.: Quasi-synchronization of readers and writers in a multi-level environment. Technical report TM-5407/003, System Development Corporation (1974)

16. Simon, M.K., Alouini, M.S.: Digital Communication Over Fading Channels, vol. 95. Wiley, Hoboken (2005)

17. Madsen, K., Nielsen, H.B., Tingleff, O.: Methods for non-linear least squares problems (2004)

18. Molisch, A.F., Win, M.Z., Winters, J.H.: Space-time-frequency STF coding for MIMIO-OFDM systems. IEEE Commun. Lett. **6**(9), 370372 (2002)

19. Shen, Z., Papasakellariou, A., Montojo, J., Gerstenberger, D., Xu, F.: Overview of 3GPP lte-advanced carrier aggregation for 4G wireless communications. IEEE Commun. Mag. **50**(2), 122–130 (2012)

An Efficient Nonparametric Belief Propagation-Based Cooperative Localization Scheme for Mobile Ad Hoc Networks

Chaojie Xu$^{(\boxtimes)}$, Hui Yu, and Ming Yang

Department of Electronic Engineering, Shanghai Jiao Tong University,
Shanghai, People's Republic of China
{xuchaojie,yuhui}@sjtu.edu.cn, msangel0706@foxmail.com

Abstract. In mobile ad hoc networks, nonparametric belief propagation (NBP) algorithm is a promising cooperative localization scheme because of high accuracy, applicability to non-Gaussian uncertainty. However, the high computational cost limits the application of NBP. To solve the problem, an efficient and practical NBP-based cooperative localization scheme is proposed. In the scheme, the issues of anchor node selection, node mobility and non-Gaussian uncertainty are considered. Firstly, anchor nodes are selected based on a distributively clustered network. Then the cooperative localization process is performed, in which a practical ranging error model is employed. Moreover, to mitigate the influence of node mobility, the re-selection process of anchor nodes is conducted when necessary. The simulation results demonstrate the efficiency of the proposed scheme in improving the positioning accuracy and reducing the computational cost compared with the conventional NBP method.

Keywords: Mobile ad hoc networks · NBP · Anchor node selection · Ranging error model

1 Introduction

In mobile ad hoc networks (MANETs), accurate positioning information is crucial since it enables a wide variety of applications, such as emergency services, first responders operations and factory automation [1,2]. In typical localization schemes, nodes in a MANET can be divided into anchor nodes, which have known positions and account for a small proportion in the nodes, and agent nodes that need to be located by utilizing the information from anchor nodes.

Generally, the existing range-based localization schemes can be classified into non-cooperative schemes and cooperative schemes. In the non-cooperative schemes [1], an agent node is located only depending on the measured distances with neighboring anchor nodes. For the cooperative schemes, by contrast, agent nodes estimate their positions through ranging and exchanging information with neighboring nodes, including anchor nodes and other agent nodes. Cooperation

© ICST Institute for Computer Sciences, Social Informatics and Telecommunications Engineering 2018
Q. Chen et al. (Eds.): ChinaCom 2016, Part II, LNICST 210, pp. 519–528, 2018.
DOI: 10.1007/978-3-319-66628-0_49

among the agent nodes is highly beneficial for improving the performance of localization processes on accuracy and coverage [1]. Lately, extensive works have been focused on cooperative localization [3–7], and most of these schemes are based on belief propagation (BP) algorithm and its extension algorithms [3, 6] for high accuracy and distributed implementation. BP is an efficient message-passing method of estimating the a posterior marginal probability density function (PDF) for the positions of the agent nodes in the network, but the inability in resolving non-Gaussian uncertainty, which is a common occurrence in practical localization scenarios, limits the application of BP. As an extension of BP, nonparametric belief propagation (NBP) algorithm [3] is sample-based and can be applied in the positioning systems with non-Gaussian uncertainties. However, considerable complexity and communication overhead are associated with the employment of NBP in MANETs. Many works have been proposed to reduce the complexity of NBP. In [4], a minimum spanning tree approach is proposed to mitigate the influence of loops in message passing process. In [5], the communication overhead and the computational cost are reduced by passing approximate beliefs represented by Gaussian distributions. In addition, a space-time hierarchical-graph model is proposed in [6] that messages propagates by layers to achieve decrease in computational complexity.

However, many of the proposed NBP-based schemes are validated with simplified assumptions such as static network [4] and Gaussian uncertainty [7]. In MANETs, where nodes are all mobile and randomly deployed, achieving a reasonable distribution of anchor nodes is advantageous in enhancing the performance of localization processes [8] and should be performed in distributed way. Moreover, considering a practical ranging error model is necessary and of great importance when designing an efficient and practical localization scheme [5].

To address the problems mentioned, an efficient and practical NBP-based cooperative localization scheme is proposed. In the scheme, anchor node selection is considered firstly, nodes in the network are aggregated into clusters in a distributed manner and anchor nodes are selected based on the established clusters. Then the cooperative localization process is performed. Considering the influence of node mobility, the re-selection process of anchor nodes is conducted when needed. Furthermore, a practical ranging error model is employed in the scheme with the propose of enhancing the performance of the localization process. The results of the simulations verify that the proposed scheme can significantly improve the positioning accuracy and evidently reduce the computational cost of the localization process in comparison with the conventional NBP algorithm.

2 Preliminaries

2.1 Ranging Error Model

In range-based positioning systems, ranging errors usually obey some kind of distribution. Reasonable modeling of the ranging errors can be beneficial in mitigating the influence of ranging noises. However, many existing localization schemes are validated using simulations based on simplified ranging error models such as the Gaussian ranging error model. In [5], based on the collected ranging data from a real positioning system, a range-dependent asymmetric double exponential model is proposed. And in our previous experimental work, we observed a kind of similar distribution, which is strictly non-Gaussian and long tailed on the right hand side, when using an ultra-wideband based positioning system. In this paper, the ranging error model proposed in [5] is adopted.

2.2 Network Model

We consider a two-dimensional MANET composing of N mobile nodes (N_a anchor nodes and N_t agent nodes), which are randomly deployed. Initial position of each node is known and the position of node n_u is denoted as $\mathbf{x}_u=[x_u, y_u]^T$.

Considering the transmission radius R of each node and the actual distance between nodes, $P_o(\mathbf{x}_u, \mathbf{x}_{u'})$ can be achieved to denote the probability of whether n_u and $n_{u'}$ can detect each other or not

$$P_o(\mathbf{x}_u, \mathbf{x}_{u'}) = \exp\left(-||\mathbf{x}_u - \mathbf{x}_{u'}||^2/2R^2\right), \tag{1}$$

where $||\mathbf{x}_u - \mathbf{x}_{u'}||$ is the Euclidean distance between n_u and $n_{u'}$. We use a binary variable $o_{uu'} = 1$ to denote the situation that n_u and $n_{u'}$ can detect each other and are neighbor nodes, then a noisy distance measurement can be obtained

$$d_{uu'} = ||\mathbf{x}_u - \mathbf{x}_{u'}|| + v_{uu'}, \tag{2}$$

where $v_{uu'}$ is the range error. Following [3], potential functions are used to represent the joint posterior PDF for the locations of all the nodes. For n_u, the single potential function $\psi_u(\mathbf{x}_u)$ is defined as corresponding a prior distribution $p(\mathbf{x}_u)$. If $o_{uu'} = 1$, the pairwise potential function defined over n_u and $n_{u'}$ is given by

$$\psi_{uu'}(\mathbf{x}_u, \mathbf{x}_{u'})=P_o(\mathbf{x}_u, \mathbf{x}_{u'})p_v(d_{uu'}, d_{uu'}-||\mathbf{x}_u-\mathbf{x}_{u'}||), \tag{3}$$

where p_v is the ranging error model. Only the single-hop neighbor nodes are considered in localization process. Therefore, when $o_{uu'} = 0$, corresponding $\psi_{uu'}(\mathbf{x}_u, \mathbf{x}_{u'}) = 0$. Then the joint posterior PDF for the locations of all the nodes is denoted as

$$p(\mathbf{x}_1, ..., \mathbf{x}_N|\{o_{uu'}, d_{uu'}\}) \propto \prod_{u=1}^{N} \psi_u(\mathbf{x}_u) \prod_{u' \in \Gamma_u, u} \psi_{uu'}(\mathbf{x}_u, \mathbf{x}_{u'}), \tag{4}$$

where Γ_u denotes the neighbor node set of node n_u. For each node n_u, by marginalizing this PDF, we can obtain the corresponding position which is characterized by the posterior marginal PDF $p(\mathbf{x}_u|\{d_{uu'}\})$, where $\{d_{uu'}\}$ is the set of the distances between node n_u and its neighbor nodes.

3 Proposed Scheme

3.1 Anchor Node Selection Phase

In the network, the distribution of anchor nodes influences the performance of localization process [1]. For the previously mentioned MANETs, the issue of selecting anchor nodes with reasonable distribution is quite challenging, especially without a central controller of the whole network.

Cluster Formation Process. To achieve a reasonable distribution of anchor nodes, firstly, all the nodes in the network are clustered distributively. Affinity propagation clustering algorithm [9] is a distributed clustering scheme and only relies on the similarity $s(u, u')$ between node $n_{u'}$ and node n_u. The negative value of the distance between n_u and $n_{u'}$ is used as $s(u, u')$. After the clustering process, all the nodes are aggregated into several clusters, and the cluster header node (CH) of each cluster is responsible for anchor node selection process.

Anchor Node Selection Process. In [8], an optimal anchor node selection algorithm is proposed to select three existing anchor nodes for each agent node. Inspired by this work, based on the clustered network, we consider selecting three nodes implementing an approximate regular triangle in each cluster to act as anchor nodes. The selection process is conducted by CH of each cluster and bases on the gathered positions of the nodes in the cluster.

In cluster C, the number of nodes is N_C, C_i $(i = 1, ..., N_C)$ represents the i-th node, the centroid is represented as o and d_{io} denotes the distance between C_i and o. In addition, the set of the distance between o and each node in C is denoted as S_d, the median value and the maximum value in S_d are d_m and d_{max}.

In each cluster C, if the distance between o and node C_i is between d_m and $(d_m + d_{max})/2$, node C_i is selected. Any three selected nodes C_{i_1}, C_{i_2}, C_{i_3} can form a triangle, whose area can be calculated with Heron's formula

$$Area_{tri} = \sqrt{p(p - d_{i_1 i_2})(p - d_{i_2 i_3})(p - d_{i_3 i_1})}, \tag{5}$$

where $p = (d_{i_1 i_2} + d_{i_2 i_3} + d_{i_3 i_1})/2$; $d_{i_j i_k}$ $(j, k = 1, 2, 3, j \neq k)$ denotes the distance between node C_{i_j} and C_{i_k}. Suppose a triangle, the distances between o and its vertexes are assigned as $d_{i_1 o}$, $d_{i_2 o}$, $d_{i_3 o}$, keeping o inside the triangle, the maximum area of the triangle can be achieved when it is a regular triangle

$$Area_{max} = \frac{3\sqrt{3}}{4} \times \left(\frac{d_{i_1 o} + d_{i_2 o} + d_{i_3 o}}{3}\right)^2. \tag{6}$$

To evaluate how approximate the triangle composed of C_{i_1}, C_{i_2}, C_{i_3} is to the equilateral triangle, approximation ratio λ is introduced and denoted as

$$\lambda = Area_{tri}/Area_{max}, \tag{7}$$

the three nodes with the largest λ are selected as anchor nodes.

Anchor Node Re-selection Process. Since nodes in the network keep moving, the topology of the network is influenced dynamically and randomly. From the perspective of positioning accuracy, anchor nodes may not be suitable for the localization process all the time, the anchor node re-selection process should be introduced to mitigate the influence of node mobility. When the number of agent nodes, which are not well located in the localization process, reaches a predefined threshold, the re-selection process of anchor nodes begins. In the process, based on the estimated locations of agent nodes and the real positions of anchor nodes, clustering process is performed again and new anchor nodes are selected using the anchor node selection algorithm.

3.2 NBP-Based Cooperative Localization Scheme

NBP Implementation. With the defined statistical framework in Section II and the selected anchor nodes, NBP is utilized to estimate the locations of the agent nodes with two updating rules, namely the belief updating rule and the message updating rule. The belief (or the estimated posterior distribution of the position) of agent node n_t in the l-th iteration is computed by taking a product of the local potential $\psi_t(\mathbf{x}_t)$ with the messages from the neighbor nodes participating the localization process of n_t

$$b_t^{(l)}(\mathbf{x}_t) \propto \psi_t(\mathbf{x}_t) \prod_{n_u \in \Gamma_t} m_{ut}^{(l)}(\mathbf{x}_t), \tag{8}$$

where Γ_t denotes the neighbor nodes participating the localization process of n_t; $m_{ut}^{(l)}(\mathbf{x}_t)$ is the message from neighbor node n_u, which can be anchor node or agent node, to n_t. In the l-th iteration, the message sent from agent node $n_{t'}$ is

$$m_{t't}^{(l)}(\mathbf{x}_t) \propto \sum_{\mathbf{x}_{t'}} \psi_{tt'}(\mathbf{x}_t, \mathbf{x}_{t'}) \frac{b_{t'}^{(l-1)}(\mathbf{x}_{t'})}{m_{tt'}^{(l-1)}(\mathbf{x}_{t'})}, \tag{9}$$

and the message from anchor node n_a is given by $m_{at}^{(l)}(\mathbf{x}_t) \propto \psi_{at}(\mathbf{x}_a, \mathbf{x}_t)$.

In NBP, stochastic approximations are used when computing the belief and the message: for node n_u ($n_u \in \Gamma_t$), firstly, samples are drawn from the belief $b_u^{(l-1)}(\mathbf{x}_u)$, and these samples are used to approximate the message $m_{ut}^{(l)}(\mathbf{x}_t)$ sent to agent node n_t. In the l-th iteration, weighted samples $\{\mathbf{x}_u^{(lj)}, \omega_u^{(lj)}\}_{j=1}^M$ are drawn from the belief $b_u^{(l-1)}(\mathbf{x}_u)$, each sample $\mathbf{x}_u^{(lj)}$ is moved in a random direction $\theta_{ut}^{(lj)}$ by a noisy measurement $d_{ut}^{(lj)}$ of the distance between n_u and n_t

$$\mathbf{x}_{ut}^{(lj)} = \mathbf{x}_u^{(lj)} + d_{ut}^{(lj)} \cdot [sin(\theta_{ut}^{(lj)}), cos(\theta_{ut}^{(lj)})]^T, \tag{10}$$

where $d_{ut}^{(lj)} = \|\mathbf{x}_u - \mathbf{x}_t\| + v_{ut}^{(lj)}$, $v_{ut}^{(lj)} \sim p_v$; $\theta_{ut}^{(lj)} \sim U[0, 2\pi]$. The weight of $\mathbf{x}_{ut}^{(lj)}$ is

$$\omega_{ut}^{(lj)} = \frac{\omega_u^{(lj)} P_o(\mathbf{x}_u^{(lj)}, \mathbf{x}_t)}{m_{tu}^{(l-1)}(\mathbf{x}_u^{(lj)})}. \tag{11}$$

Modifications Based on NBP. To decrease the complexity of NBP, modifications are considered. In the localization process of agent node n_t, only when there are no less than three reference nodes (anchor nodes or located agent nodes),

---

Algorithm 1. NBP-based cooperative localization scheme for agent nodes

Input: Γ_r: the reference node set of n_t;
$\{d'_{r_it}\}_{i=1}^{|\Gamma_r|}$: range measurements between n_t and reference nodes.
Output: $\hat{\mathbf{x}}_t$: the final estimated position of n_t.

1 **Initialization:** Set $[\theta_{min}^{r_i,1}, \theta_{max}^{r_i,1}]$ for reference node n_{r_i} $(i = 1, ..., |\Gamma_r|)$ as $[0, 2\pi]$;
2 **for** *iteration $l = 1$ to L* **do**
3 **Message computing in each reference node n_{r_i}:**
4 Draw random values $\{v_{r_it}^{(lj)}, \theta_{r_it}^{(lj)}\}_{j=1}^M$: $v_{r_it}^{(lj)} \sim p_v$, $\theta_{r_it}^{(lj)} \sim U[\theta_{min}^{r_i,l}, \theta_{max}^{r_i,l}]$;
5 Calculate $\mathbf{x}_{r_it}^{(lj)}$ with (12), and set corresponding weight $\omega_{r_it}^{(lj)}$ as $1/M$;
6 Broadcast message $\{\mathbf{x}_{r_it}^{(lj)}, \theta_{r_it}^{(lj)}, \omega_{r_it}^{(lj)}\}_{j=1}^M$ to n_t;
7 **Belief computing in n_t:**
8 **for** *each sample $\{\mathbf{x}_{r_it}^{(lj)}, \theta_{r_it}^{(lj)}, \omega_{r_it}^{(lj)}\}$ received by n_t* **do**
9   Update the weight $\omega_{r_it}^{(lj)}$ with (13);
10 **for** *$i = 1$ to $|\Gamma_r|$* **do**
11   Filter $M/|\Gamma_r|$ samples with maximum weights from samples from n_{r_i};
12   Get the range $[\theta_{min}, \theta_{max}]$ of the directions in reserved samples;
13   Update $[\theta_{min}^{r_i,l+1}, \theta_{max}^{r_i,l+1}]$ of n_{r_i} as $[\theta_{min}, \theta_{max}]$;
14 Normalize the weights of remaining samples with $\omega_t^{(lk)} = \omega_t^{(lk)}/\sum_{k=1}^M \omega_t^{(lk)}$;
15 Update the belief $b_t^{(l)}$ of n_t using (8);
16 Calculate the estimated position $\widehat{\mathbf{x}_t^{(l)}}$ of n_t with (15);
17 **if** *$l > 1$* **then**
18   Check the convergence condition using (16);
19   **if** *converged or $l == L$* **then**
20   Set $\widehat{\mathbf{x}_t^{(l)}}$ as the final estimated position $\hat{\mathbf{x}}_t$;
21   Terminate the iteration process.

---

in the neighboring node set Γ_t of n_t, can n_t locate itself by ranging with the reference nodes, and it will become a reference node for other agent nodes when well located. In this way, all the agent nodes are located incrementally.

Specifically, the generation principle (10) of samples is changed as

$$\mathbf{x}_{rt}^{(lj)} = \mathbf{x}_r + d_{rt}^{(lj)} \cdot [sin(\theta_{rt}^{(lj)}), cos(\theta_{rt}^{(lj)})]^T, \qquad (12)$$

where if reference node n_r is an anchor node, $\mathbf{x}_r$ is the real position of n_r, and otherwise $\mathbf{x}_r$ is the estimated position. Through storing the random direction $\theta_{rt}^{(lj)}$ with $\mathbf{x}_{rt}^{(lj)}$ and initialising the weight $\omega_{rt}^{(lj)}$ of $\mathbf{x}_{rt}^{(lj)}$ as $1/M$, samples $\{\mathbf{x}_{rt}^{(lj)}, \theta_{rt}^{(lj)}, \omega_{rt}^{(lj)}\}_{j=1}^M$ can be achieved.

For each weighted sample $\{\mathbf{x}_{rt}^{(lj)}, \theta_{rt}^{(lj)}, \omega_{rt}^{(lj)}\}$ generated by n_r, the weight $\omega_{rt}^{(lj)}$ is updated by the deviation degrees between $\mathbf{x}_{rt}^{(lj)}$ and the real position of n_t evaluated by other reference nodes of n_t. The update principle is

$$\omega_{rt}^{(lj)} = \omega_{rt}^{(lj)} \prod_{n_{r'} \in \Gamma_r \setminus n_r} p_v(r't), \qquad (13)$$

where Γ_r is the reference node set of n_t; $p_v(r't)$ is given by

$$p_v(r't) = p_v(d'_{r't}, d'_{r't} - d''_{r't}), \tag{14}$$

where $d'_{r't} = \|\mathbf{x}^{(lj)}_{rt} - \mathbf{x}_{r'}\|$ and $d''_{r't}$ is a noisy measurement of the distance between n_t and reference node $n_{r'}$, and regarded as the real distance between them for further evaluation. To evaluate the deviation degree between $\mathbf{x}^{(lj)}_{rt}$ and the real position $\mathbf{x}_t$ of n_t, firstly, $\mathbf{x}^{(lj)}_{rt}$ is assumed as $\mathbf{x}_t$, then $d'_{r't}$ can be considered as a distance measurement between $n_{r'}$ and n_t, thus $d'_{r't} - d''_{r't}$ is ranging error of $d'_{r't}$ and $p_v(r't)$ denotes the deviation degree between $\mathbf{x}^{(lj)}_{rt}$ and $\mathbf{x}_t$ evaluated by $n_{r'}$.

With all the samples received by n_t, sample filtering process is conducted. For the M samples generated by n_r in this iteration, $M/|\Gamma_r|$ samples with the maximum weights are reserved, where $|\Gamma_r|$ is the number of nodes in Γ_r. Through recording the random directions of the reserved samples generated by n_r in this iteration, a direction range S_θ can be achieved, which will be the random direction range for n_r to generate samples of n_t in the next iteration. For n_t, through normalizing the weights of the remaining samples $\{\mathbf{x}^{(lk)}_t, \theta^{(lk)}_t, \omega^{(lk)}_t\}^M_{k=1}$, the estimated position in this iteration is calculated with

$$\widehat{\mathbf{x}^{(l)}_t} = \sum_{k=1}^{M} \omega^{(lk)}_t \mathbf{x}^{(lk)}_t. \tag{15}$$

The iteration process terminates when convergence condition is met or maximum number L of the iterations is reached, and the convergence condition is

$$\|\widehat{\mathbf{x}^{(l)}_t} - \widehat{\mathbf{x}^{(l-1)}_t}\| \leq \varepsilon, \tag{16}$$

where ε is a predefined threshold. In the iteration process of agent node n_t, if the convergence condition is met, which indicates that n_t is well located and it will become a reference node for other unlocated agent nodes. And the final estimated position of n_t is assigned as the estimation of current iteration. Otherwise, n_t is unlocated in the localization process of current time slot and the estimation of the last iteration will be the final estimated position of n_t. The detailed NBP-based cooperative localization process is summarized in Algorithm 1.

4   Simulation Results

4.1   Simulation Setup

In the simulations, we consider a $100 \times 100 \, \mathrm{m^2}$ area with 150 nodes, including 18 anchor nodes (i.e., 6 clusters are established). And we assume that the movement of each node follows the Gaussian-Markov mobility model [10]. Table 1 lists the key parameters used in the simulations.

Results of the simulations are obtained from the localization process of the agent nodes in 500 continuous time slots.

Table 1. The key parameters in simulations

Parameter	Value
R: transmission radius	30 m
L: maximum number of iteration	10
ε: convergence threshold	0.1 m
Condition of anchor node re-selection	5 unlocated agent nodes

4.2 Performance Evaluation

Influence of Anchor Node Distribution. Three kinds of anchor node distribution are considered. The uniform distribution means that we choose the nodes that distributing in approximately uniform way in the network as anchor nodes, and the random distribution denotes that anchor nodes are randomly selected.

The performance on the positioning error of all the agent nodes in the network is valued by the root mean square error (RMSE)

$$\text{RMSE} = \sqrt{\frac{1}{N_t} \sum\nolimits_{n_t \in S_t} \|\mathbf{x}_t - \widehat{\mathbf{x}}_t\|^2}, \tag{17}$$

where N_t is the number of agent nodes in the network; S_t represents the agent node set; $\widehat{\mathbf{x}}_t$ denotes the final estimated position of agent node n_t. Figure 1 shows the cumulative distribution functions (CDFs) of the RMSE performance of NBP with 200 samples based on the three kinds of anchor node distribution, we can see that compared with the random distribution case, the performance of NBP based on the proposed distribution is very close to the performance of the uniform distribution case, which can be regarded as the optimal distribution. The result indicates that the proposed anchor node selection algorithm can achieve a reasonable distribution of anchor nodes for the NBP-based localization schemes.

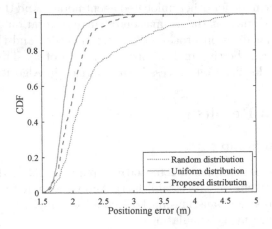

Fig. 1. Performance comparison on positioning error (RMSE) of NBP with different kinds of anchor node distribution.

Positioning Performance. Figure 2 shows the CDFs of the positioning error in the proposed scheme and NBP with different numbers of samples. The result reveals that more samples can improve the RMSE performance of both the proposed scheme and NBP. With same number of samples, the performance on positioning accuracy of the proposed scheme outperforms that of NBP. Compared with NBP, the change of sample number has less impact on the performance on positioning accuracy of the proposed scheme, and the proposed scheme with less samples can achieve a better performance on positioning accuracy.

Complexity Comparison. The performance on time complexity of the proposed scheme and NBP is evaluated by the normalized CPU running time. Figure 3 shows the comparison of the computational cost of the proposed scheme

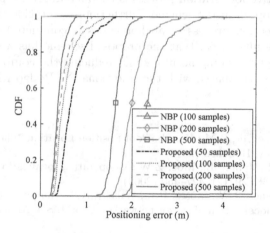

Fig. 2. Performance comparison on positioning error (RMSE) of the proposed scheme and NBP with different numbers of samples.

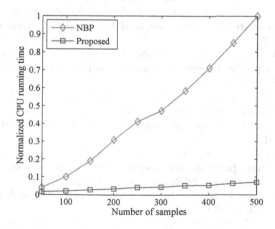

Fig. 3. Performance comparison on computational cost of the proposed scheme and NBP with different numbers of samples.

and NBP with different numbers of samples. Compared with NBP, improved performance on the computational cost of the proposed scheme can be clearly observed, which demonstrates the low computational cost of the proposed scheme.

5 Conclusions

This paper focuses on solving the problems of applying NBP in MANETs, where nodes are randomly deployed and keep moving, and proposes an efficient and practical NBP-based scheme. The proposed scheme considers the issues of anchor node selection, node mobility and non-Gaussian uncertainty to obtain a better performance of the localization process. Specially, anchor nodes are firstly selected based on the clustered network, which is established in a distributed way, then the cooperative localization process is conducted. And a practical ranging error model is adopted in the scheme. Furthermore, to tackle the issue of node mobility, a re-selection process of anchor nodes is conducted when necessary. The simulation results reveal that the proposed scheme has a significant effect on improving the positioning accuracy and reducing the computational cost of localization process compared with the traditional NBP algorithm.

References

1. Zekavat, R., Buehrer, R.M.: Handbook of Position Location: Theory, Practice and Advances. Wiley, Hoboken (2012)
2. Wymeersch, H., Jaime, L., Moe, Z.W.: Cooperative localization in wireless networks. Proc. IEEE **97**(2), 427–450 (2009)
3. Ihler, A.T., Fisher, J.W., Moses, R.L., Willsky, A.S.: Nonparametric belief propagation for self-localization of sensor networks. IEEE J. Sel. Areas Commun. **23**(4), 809–819 (2005)
4. Li, X., Gao, H., Cai, H., Lv, T.: Nonparametric belief propagation based cooperative localization: a minimum spanning tree approach. In: IEEE Wireless Communications and Networking Conference (WCNC), pp. 1775–1780. IEEE Press (2015)
5. Li, S., Hedley, M., Collings, I.B.: New efficient indoor cooperative localization algorithm with empirical ranging error model. IEEE J. Sel. Areas Commun. **33**(7), 1407–1417 (2015)
6. Lv, T., Gao, H., Li, X., Yang, S., Hanzo, L.: Space-time hierarchical-graph based cooperative localization in wireless sensor networks. IEEE Trans. Signal Process. **64**(2), 322–334 (2016)
7. Van de Velde, S., Arora, G., Vallozzi, L., Rogier, H., Steendam, H.: Cooperative hybrid localization using Gaussian processes and belief propagation. In: IEEE International Conference on Communication Workshop (ICCW), pp. 785–790. IEEE Press (2015)
8. Wang, X., Qiu, J., Fan, J., Dai, G.: MDS-based localization scheme for large-scale WSNs within sparse anchor nodes. In: IEEE International Conference on Communications (ICC), pp. 6609–6614. IEEE Press (2015)
9. Frey, B.J., Dueck, D.: Clustering by passing messages between data points. science **315**(5814), 972–976 (2007)
10. Liang, B., Haas, Z.J.: Predictive distance-based mobility management for multidimensional PCS networks. IEEE/ACM Trans. Netw. **11**(5), 718–732 (2003)

Mutual Coupling Calibration in Super-Resolution Direction Finding for Wideband Signals

Jiaqi Zhen[(⊠)], Danyang Qin, and Bing Zhao

College of Electronic Engineering, Heilongjiang University,
Harbin 150080, China
zhenjiaqi2011@163.com

Abstract. Most super-resolution direction finding methods need to know the array manifold exactly, but there is usually mutual coupling error in application, which directly leads to the performance degradation, and even failure. The paper proposed a novel calibration method in super-resolution direction finding for wideband signals based on spatial domain sparse optimization when mutual coupling exists in the array. First, the optimization functions are founded by the signals of every frequency bin, then the functions are optimized iteratively, after that the information of all frequencies is integrated for the calibration, finally, the actual directions of arrival (DOA) can be acquired, the performance of the method has been proved by simulations.

Keywords: Super-resolution direction finding · Array calibration · Mutual coupling · Wideband signals

1 Introduction

Super-resolution direction finding is one of the major research contents in array signal processing, it is widely used in radio monitoring [1–3], internet of things [4, 5] and electronic countermeasure [6, 7]. At present, most direction finding methods are based on knowing the accurate array manifold, but there are often high frequency oscillation and amplifiers in practical systems, which lead to the mutual coupling in the array, it causes the performance of the direction finding methods deteriorated, and even failure, so they are necessary to be calibrated.

For the presence of mutual coupling, the early methods are usually based on the electromagnetic measurement [8], or calculating the mutual coupling coefficient by matrix measure, then compensate and calibrate the corresponding parameters [9–11]. These methods can often not meet the calibration accuracy in the actual projects,

J. Zhen—This work was supported by the National Natural Science Foundation of China under Grant Nos. 61501176 and 61302074, University Nursing Program for Young Scholars with Creative Talents in Heilongjiang Province No. UNPYSCT-2016017, Specialized Research Fund for the Doctoral Program of Higher Education under Grant No. 20122301120004, Natural Science Foundation of Heilongjiang Province under Grant No. QC2013C061.

© ICST Institute for Computer Sciences, Social Informatics and Telecommunications Engineering 2018
Q. Chen et al. (Eds.): ChinaCom 2016, Part II, LNICST 210, pp. 529–538, 2018.
DOI: 10.1007/978-3-319-66628-0_50

especially for the radar, sonar and other fields of array signal processing, their electromagnetic environments are very complex, whether measure or electromagnetic computation are not suitable for the array calibration. With the development of the research, more and more scholars are keen to parameterize the coefficient by special structure of the mutual coupling matrix, this kind of methods not only have a high precision but also adapt to the various circumstances and electromagnetic parameters. Some classic algorithms are proposed successively: Wang et al. proposed a calibration method for mutual coupling in 2003 [12], it only needs one dimensional searching and is easy to be implemented; Dai et al. [13] eliminated the unknown mutual coupling in the uniform array by inherent mechanism; Xie et al. [14] achieved localization of mixed far-field and near-field sources under unknown mutual coupling. Liu et al. [15] proposed a DOA estimation method based on fourth-order cumulants along with mutual coupling, it can be applied when non-Gaussian signals coexist with unknown colored Gaussian noise. Elbir and Tuncer [16] estimated DOA and mutual coupling coefficient for arbitrary array structures with single and multiple snapshots. But all of these methods are just appropriate for narrowband signals, so far there are few public literatures about mutual coupling among sensors in super-resolution direction finding for wideband signals.

The paper proposed a novel mutual coupling calibration method in super-resolution direction finding for wideband signals based on spatial domain sparse optimization, when mutual coupling exists in the array, the corresponding optimization functions are founded by the signals of every frequency bin, then the functions are optimized iteratively, at last, the information of all frequencies is integrated for the calibration, consequently the actual DOA can be obtained.

2 Signal Model

2.1 Ideal Signal Model

It is seen from Fig. 1, suppose there are K far-field wideband signals $s_k(t)$ $(k = 1, 2, \cdots, K)$ impinging on the uniform linear array composed of M omnidirectional sensors, the space of them is d, it is equal to half of the wavelength of the center frequency, DOAs of them are $\boldsymbol{\alpha} = [\alpha_1, \cdots, \alpha_k, \cdots, \alpha_K]$, the first sensor is defined as the reference, then output of the mth sensor can be written as

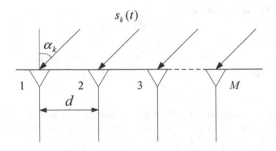

Fig. 1. Array signal model

$$x_m(t) = \sum_{k=1}^{K} s_k(t - \tau_m(\alpha_k)) + n_m(t), m = 1, 2, \cdots, M \tag{1}$$

Where $\tau_m(\alpha_k) = (m-1)\frac{d}{c}\sin\alpha_k$ is the propagation delay for the kth signal arriving at the mth sensor with respect to the reference of the array, c is the propagating speed of the signal, $n_m(t)$ is the Gaussian white noise on the mth sensor.

Assume that the range of the frequency band of all signals is $[f_{\text{Low}}, f_{\text{High}}]$, before the processing, we divide the output vector into J nonoverlapping components, Discrete Fourier Transform (DFT) is performed on (1) and the array outputs of J frequencies can be represented as

$$X(f_i) = A(f_i, \boldsymbol{\alpha})S(f_i) + N(f_i) \quad i = 1, 2, \cdots, J \tag{2}$$

Where $f_{\text{Low}} \leq f_i \leq f_{\text{High}}$ $(i = 1, 2, \cdots, J)$, KP snapshots are collected at every frequency, then we have

$$X(f_i) = [X_1(f_i), \cdots, X_m(f_i), \cdots, X_M(f_i)]^{\text{T}} \tag{3}$$

Where

$$X_m(f_i) = [X_m(f_i, 1), \cdots, X_m(f_i, kp), \cdots, X_m(f_i, KP)] \tag{4}$$

$A(f_i, \boldsymbol{\alpha})$ is a $M \times K$ dimensional steering vector

$$A(f_i, \boldsymbol{\alpha}) = [a(f_i, \alpha_1), \cdots, a(f_i, \alpha_k), \cdots, a(f_i, \alpha_K)] \tag{5}$$

$$a(f_i, \alpha_k) = \left[1, \exp(-j2\pi f_i\frac{d}{c}\sin\alpha_k), \cdots, \exp\left(-j(M-1)2\pi f_i\frac{d}{c}\sin\alpha_k\right)\right]^{\text{T}} \tag{6}$$

And

$$S(f_i) = [S_1(f_i), \cdots, S_k(f_i), \cdots, S_K(f_i)]^{\text{T}} \tag{7}$$

is the signal vector matrix after DFT to $s_k(t)$ $(k = 1, 2, \cdots, K)$, where

$$S_k(f_i) = [S_k(f_i, 1), \cdots S_k(f_i, kp), \cdots, S_k(f_i, KP)] \tag{8}$$

Here, $S_k(f_i, kp)$ is the kpth snapshots of the kth signal at f_i, then

$$N(f_i) = [N_1(f_i), \cdots, N_m(f_i), \cdots, N_M(f_i)]^{\text{T}} \tag{9}$$

$$N_m(f_i) = [N_m(f_i, 1), \cdots, N_m(f_i, kp), \cdots, N_m(f_i, KP)] \tag{10}$$

is the noise vector after performing DFT on $n_m(t)$ $(m = 1, 2, \cdots, M)$ with mean 0 and variance $\mu^2(f_i)$.

2.2   Array Error Model

For convenience, we only discuss the information at frequency f_i for the moment, the degree of mutual coupling is closely related to signal frequency, when there is only mutual coupling among sensors, perturbation matrix can be expressed by $W(f_i)$, we itemize Q corresponding the freedom degree of the array, according to the property of uniform linear array, we know $W(f_i)$ can be expressed as:

$$W(f_i) = \begin{bmatrix} 1 & c_1(f_i) & \cdots & c_Q(f_i) & & \\ c_1(f_i) & 1 & c_1(f_i) & & \ddots & \\ & c_1(f_i) & & & & c_Q(f_i) \\ \vdots & & \ddots & \ddots & \ddots & \\ c_Q(f_i) & & & & & \\ & \ddots & & & 1 & c_1(f_i) \\ & & c_Q(f_i) & & c_1(f_i) & 1 \end{bmatrix} \tag{11}$$

Where $c_q(f_i)$ $(q = 1, 2, \cdots, Q)$ is the mutual coupling coefficient, when the distance between two sensor is q, signal frequency is f_i, the steering vector of the array can be revised to

$$a'(f_i, \alpha_k) = W(f_i)a(f_i, \alpha_k) \quad (k = 1, 2, \cdots, K) \tag{12}$$

Corresponding array manifold is

$$A'(f_i, \alpha) = [a'(f_i, \alpha_1), \cdots, a'(f_i, \alpha_k), \cdots, a'(f_i, \alpha_K)] = W(f_i)A(f_i, \alpha) \tag{13}$$

For the sake of simplicity, we define the mutual coupling perturbation vector between sensors as $w(f_i) = [c_1(f_i), \cdots, c_Q(f_i)]^T$. So the output of the array at frequency f_i can be expressed as

$$\begin{aligned} X'(f_i) &= A'(f_i, \alpha)S(f_i) + N(f_i) = W(f_i)A(f_i, \alpha)S(f_i) + N(f_i) \\ &= A(f_i, \alpha)N(f_i) + \Lambda(f_i)w(f_i) + N(f_i) \end{aligned} \tag{14}$$

Where $\Lambda(f_i)$ is the coefficient vector related to the mutual coupling.

3   Estimation Theory

The searching space can be divided into several discrete angle grids $\Omega = [\bar{\alpha}_1, \cdots, \bar{\alpha}_l, \cdots, \bar{\alpha}_L]$, and $K \ll L$, take it into (2), we have

$$\bar{X}'(f_i) = A'(f_i, \Omega)\bar{S}(f_i) + N(f_i) \quad (i = 1, 2, \cdots, J) \tag{15}$$

Then corresponding covariance matrix of $\bar{X}'(f_i)$ is

$$\bar{R}'(f_i) = E\left\{\bar{X}'(f_i)(\bar{X}'(f_i))^{\mathrm{H}}\right\} \quad i = (1, 2, \cdots, J) \tag{16}$$

In (15), $\bar{S}(f_i) = [\bar{S}(f_i, 1), \cdots, \bar{S}(f_i, kp), \cdots, \bar{S}(f_i, KP)]$, where $\bar{S}(f_i, kp) = [\bar{S}_1(f_i, kp), \cdots \bar{S}_l(f_i, kp), \cdots, \bar{S}_L(f_i, kp)]^{\mathrm{T}}$ is a sparse matrix, it only contains K non-zero elements, they are non-zero if and only if $\bar{\alpha}_l = \alpha_k$ and $\bar{S}_l(f_i, kp) = S_k(f_i, kp)$, ($l = 1, 2, \cdots, L;\ k = 1, 2, \cdots, K$). Define $\delta(f_i) = [\delta_1(f_i), \cdots, \delta_l(f_i), \cdots, \delta_L(f_i)]^{\mathrm{T}}$ as the vector formed by variances of the elements in $\bar{S}(f_i)$, it reflects the energy of the signal, that is

$$\bar{S}(f_i) \sim N(0, \Sigma(f_i)) \tag{17}$$

Where $\Sigma(f_i) = \mathrm{diag}(\delta(f_i))$, as $\bar{S}(f_i)$ is $S(f_i)$ jointed many zero elements, $\delta(f_i)$ contains K non-zero elements too.

It can be seen from (15) and (17), probability density of the output signal at f_i along with the error simultaneously is

$$\begin{aligned}
P(\bar{X}'(f_i)|\bar{S}(f_i); w(f_i), \mu^2(f_i)) &= \left|\pi\mu^2(f_i)I_M\right|^{-KP}\exp\left\{-\mu^2(f_i)\|\bar{X}'(f_i) - A'(f_i, \Omega)\bar{S}(f_i)\|_2^2\right\} \\
&= \left|\pi\mu^2(f_i)I_M\right|^{-KP}\exp\left\{-\mu^2(f_i)\times\|\bar{X}'(f_i) - W(f_i)A(f_i, \Omega)\bar{S}(f_i)\|_2^2\right\}
\end{aligned} \tag{18}$$

Combining (15), (17) and (18), probability density of $\bar{X}'(f_i)$ is

$$\begin{aligned}
P(\bar{X}'(f_i); \delta(f_i), w(f_i), \mu^2(f_i)) &= \int P(\bar{X}'(f_i)|\bar{S}(f_i); w(f_i), \mu^2(f_i))P(\bar{S}(f_i); \delta(f_i))\mathrm{d}\bar{S}(f_i) \\
&= \left|\pi\left(\mu^2(f_i)I_M + A'(f_i, \Omega)\Sigma(f_i)(A'(f_i, \Omega))^{\mathrm{H}}\right)\right|^{-KP} \\
&\quad \times \exp\left\{-KP \times \mathrm{tr}\left(\left(\mu^2(f_i)I_M + A'(f_i, \Omega)\Sigma(f_i)(A'(f_i, \Omega))^{\mathrm{H}}\right)^{-1}\bar{R}'(f_i)\right)\right\}
\end{aligned} \tag{19}$$

Then we can employ Expectation Maximization (EM) method [17] to iteratively estimate each unknown parameters, compute distribution function of $P(\bar{X}'(f_i), \bar{S}(f_i); \delta(f_i), w(f_i), \mu^2(f_i))$, in the E-step:

$$\begin{aligned}
&F(\bar{X}'(f_i), \bar{S}(f_i); \delta(f_i), w(f_i), \mu^2(f_i)) \\
&= \langle \mathrm{In}P(\bar{X}'(f_i), \bar{S}(f_i); \delta(f_i), w(f_i), \mu^2(f_i)) \rangle \\
&= \langle \mathrm{In}P(\bar{X}'(f_i)|\bar{S}(f_i); w(f_i), \mu^2(f_i)) + \mathrm{In}P(\bar{S}(f_i); \delta(f_i)) \rangle \\
&= \left\langle -M \times KP \times \mathrm{In}\mu^2(f_i) - \mu^{-2}(f_i)\|\bar{X}'(f_i) - A'(f_i, \Omega)\bar{S}(f_i)\|_2^2 - \sum_{l=1}^{L}\left(KP \times \mathrm{In}\delta_l(f_i) + \frac{\left(\sum_{kp=1}^{KP}|\bar{S}_l(f_i, kp)|^2\right)}{\delta_l(f_i)}\right) \right\rangle \\
&= \left\langle -M \times KP \times \mathrm{In}\mu^2(f_i) - \mu^{-2}(f_i)\|\bar{X}'(f_i) - W(f_i)A(f_i, \Omega)\bar{S}(f_i)\|_2^2 - \sum_{l=1}^{L}\left(KP \times \mathrm{In}\delta_l(f_i) + \frac{\left(\sum_{kp=1}^{KP}|\bar{S}_l(f_i, kp)|^2\right)}{\delta_l(f_i)}\right) \right\rangle
\end{aligned} \tag{20}$$

In the M-step, solve derivatives of $F(\bar{X}'(f_i), \bar{S}(f_i); \delta(f_i), w(f_i), \mu^2(f_i))$ for each parameter, that is

$$
\frac{\partial F\left(\bar{X}'(f_i), \bar{S}(f_i); \delta(f_i), w(f_i), \mu^2(f_i)\right)}{\partial w(f_i)}
$$
$$
= -2\mu^{-2}(f_i)\left[\left\langle \Lambda^H(f_i)\Lambda(f_i)\right\rangle w(f_i) - \left\langle \Lambda^H(f_i)(\bar{X}'(f_i) - A(f_i, \Omega)\bar{S}(f_i))\right\rangle\right] \tag{21}
$$

$$
\frac{\partial F(\bar{X}'(f_i), \bar{S}(f_i); \delta(f_i), w(f_i), \mu^2(f_i))}{\partial \mu^2(f_i)} = -\frac{M \times KP}{\mu^2(f_i)} + \frac{1}{(\mu^2(f_i))^2}\left\langle \left\|\bar{X}'(f_i) - A'(f_i, \Omega)\bar{S}(f_i)\right\|_2^2\right\rangle \tag{22}
$$

$$
\frac{\partial F(\bar{X}'(f_i), \bar{S}(f_i); \delta(f_i), w(f_i), \mu^2(f_i))}{\partial \delta_l(f_i)} = -\frac{KP}{\delta_l(f_i)} + \frac{1}{\delta_l^2(f_i)}\left\langle \sum_{kp=1}^{KP} |\bar{S}_l(f_i, kp)|^2\right\rangle \tag{23}
$$

Set them to be 0 respectively, then estimation values of every parameter of the pth iteration can be solved

$$
w^{(p)}(f_i) = \left\langle \Lambda^H(f_i)\Lambda(f_i)\right\rangle^{-1}\left\langle \Lambda^H(f_i)(\bar{X}'(f_i) - A(f_i, \Omega)\bar{S}(f_i))\right\rangle \tag{24}
$$

$$
(\mu^2(f_i))^{(p)} = \frac{1}{M \times KP}\left\langle \left\|\bar{X}'(f_i) - (A'(f_i, \Omega))^{(p)}\bar{S}(f_i)\right\|_2^2\right\rangle \tag{25}
$$

$$
\delta_l^{(p)}(f_i) = \frac{1}{KP}\left\langle \sum_{kp=1}^{KP} |\bar{S}_l(f_i, kp)|^2\right\rangle \tag{26}
$$

Where (p) denotes number of iterations, after several times, the variations of $w(f_i)$, $\mu^2(f_i)$ and $\delta_l(f_i)$ tend to be zero, then they are deemed to be convergent, we can acquire their final estimation results: $\hat{w}(f_i)$, $\hat{\mu}^2(f_i)$ and $\hat{\delta}_l(f_i)$, combining $\hat{\delta}(f_i) = [\hat{\delta}_1(f_i), \cdots, \hat{\delta}_l(f_i), \cdots, \hat{\delta}_L(f_i)]^T$ and $\hat{\Sigma}(f_i) = \text{diag}\left(\hat{\delta}(f_i)\right)$. They can be used for array calibration, define X as the vector composed by sum of signal of all frequencies, as the signal of every frequency is independent of one another, the joint probability density of X is

$$
P(X) = \prod_{i=1}^{J} P\left(\bar{X}'(f_i); \hat{\delta}(f_i), \hat{w}(f_i), \hat{\mu}^2(f_i)\right)
$$
$$
= |\pi|^{-J \times KP}\prod_{i=1}^{J}\left|\left(\hat{\mu}^2(f_i)I_M + A'(f_i, \Omega)\hat{\Sigma}(f_i)(A'(f_i, \Omega))^H\right)\right|^{-KP} \tag{27}
$$
$$
\times \exp\left\{-KP \times \sum_{i=1}^{J}\text{tr}\left(\left(\begin{matrix}\hat{\mu}^2(f_i)I_M + A'(f_i, \Omega)\times \\ \hat{\Sigma}(f_i)(A'(f_i, \Omega))^H\end{matrix}\right)^{-1}\bar{R}'(f_i)\right)\right\}
$$

Perform logarithm operation on both sides of the (27), we have

$$\ln(P(X)) = -J \times KP \times \ln\pi - KP \times \left(\sum_{i=1}^{J} \ln \left| \hat{\mu}^2(f_i)\mathbf{I}_M + \mathbf{A}'(f_i, \mathbf{\Omega})\hat{\boldsymbol{\Sigma}}(f_i)(\mathbf{A}'(f_i, \mathbf{\Omega}))^{\mathrm{H}} \right| \right)$$

$$-KP \times \sum_{i=1}^{J} \mathrm{tr}\left(\left(\begin{array}{c} \hat{\mu}^2(f_i)\mathbf{I}_M + \mathbf{A}'(f_i, \mathbf{\Omega}) \times \\ \hat{\boldsymbol{\Sigma}}(f_i)(\mathbf{A}'(f_i, \mathbf{\Omega}))^{\mathrm{H}} \end{array} \right)^{-1} \bar{\mathbf{R}}'(f_i) \right) \tag{28}$$

Maximize (28), that is

$$\frac{\partial \ln(P(X))}{\partial \boldsymbol{\alpha}} = 0 \tag{29}$$

Take (28) into (29) and we can infer

$$\hat{\alpha}_k = \arg\max_{\alpha_k} \left| \mathrm{Re} \left| \times \left| \begin{array}{c} \left[\sum_{i=1}^{J} \left[(\mathbf{a}'(f_i, \alpha_k))^{\mathrm{H}} \times \left(\begin{array}{c} \hat{\mu}^2(f_i)\mathbf{I}_M + \mathbf{A}'(f_i, \mathbf{\Omega}_{-k}) \times \\ \hat{\boldsymbol{\Sigma}}_{-k}(f_i)(\mathbf{A}'(f_i, \mathbf{\Omega}_{-k}))^{\mathrm{H}} \end{array} \right)^{-1} \right) \right] \\ \times \left[\sum_{i=1}^{J} \left(\begin{array}{c} \mathbf{a}'(f_i, \alpha_k)(\mathbf{a}'(f_i, \alpha_k))^{\mathrm{H}} \times \\ \left(\left(\begin{array}{c} \hat{\mu}^2(f_i)\mathbf{I}_M + \mathbf{A}'(f_i, \mathbf{\Omega}_{-k}) \times \\ \hat{\boldsymbol{\Sigma}}_{-k}(f_i)(\mathbf{A}'(f_i, \mathbf{\Omega}_{-k}))^{\mathrm{H}} \end{array} \right)^{-1} \bar{\mathbf{R}}'(f_i) \right) \end{array} \right) - \sum_{i=1}^{J} \left(\bar{\mathbf{R}}'(f_i) \left(\begin{array}{c} \hat{\mu}^2(f_i)\mathbf{I}_M + \\ \mathbf{A}'(f_i, \mathbf{\Omega}_{-k})\hat{\boldsymbol{\Sigma}}_{-k}(f_i) \times \\ (\mathbf{A}'(f_i, \mathbf{\Omega}_{-k}))^{\mathrm{H}} \end{array} \right)^{-1} \times \mathbf{a}'(f_i, \alpha_k)(\mathbf{a}'(f_i, \alpha_k))^{\mathrm{H}} \right) \right] \\ \times \sum_{i=1}^{J} \left[\left(\begin{array}{c} \hat{\mu}^2(f_i)\mathbf{I}_M + \mathbf{A}'(f_i, \mathbf{\Omega}_{-k}) \times \\ \hat{\boldsymbol{\Sigma}}_{-k}(f_i)(\mathbf{A}'(f_i, \mathbf{\Omega}_{-k}))^{\mathrm{H}} \end{array} \right)^{-1} \times \frac{\partial \mathbf{a}'(f_i, \alpha_k)}{\partial \alpha_k} \right] \end{array} \right| \right|^{1} \tag{30}$$

Then final result of DOA can be estimated.

We can get $c_1(f_i), \cdots, c_Q(f_i)$ according to $\hat{w}(f_i)$, then $W(f_i)$ can be acquired by (11), then $\mathbf{a}'(f_i, \alpha_k)$ and $\mathbf{A}'(f_i, \mathbf{\Omega}_{-k})$ can be acquired, we will get the accurate estimation of the DOA based on (30) and the parameters above.

The method adapts to wideband signal, and has employed spatial domain sparse optimization for mutual coupling, so we can call it WSM for short.

4 Simulations

In order to verify the effective of the method, some simulations are presented with matlab below, consider some wideband chirp signals impinge on a uniform linear array with 8 omnidirectional sensors from directions $(5°, 15°, 25°)$, the center frequency of the signals is 3 GHz, width of the band is 20% of the center frequency, the band is divided into 10 frequencies, and spacing d between adjacent sensors is equal to half of the wavelength of the center frequency, the array errors are related to the signal frequency and very complicated, it is difficult to establish accurate function, therefore we will simplify the process in the simulations, suppose there is mutual coupling error in the array, and it is subject to zero mean Gaussian distribution, the freedom degree among sensors $Q = 2$, mutual coupling perturbation vector $w(f_i) = [a+bj, c+dj]^T$, a, b is selected between $-1 - +1$ randomly and c, d is selected between $-0.5 - +0.5$ randomly.

4.1 Mutual Coupling Estimation

Suppose SNR is 16 dB, the number of snapshots at every frequency is 40, WSM is employed for estimating the error, 300 Monte-Carlo simulations are repeated, their average values are deemed as the final results, the mutual coupling estimation is shown in Table 1.

Table 1. Mutual coupling estimation

	c_1	c_2
Actual value of f_1	0.726 + j0.527	0.213 + j0.132
Estimated value of f_1	0.702 + j0.509	0.187 + j0.151
Actual value of f_2	0.647−j0.234	0.286 + j0.172
Estimated value of f_2	0.667−j0.255	0.309 + j0.193
Actual value of f_3	0.645 + j0.257	0.288 + j0.176
Estimated value of f_3	0.617 + j0.240	0.271 + j0.194
Actual value of f_4	0.742 + j0.218	0.385−j0.183
Estimated value of f_4	0.727 + j0.202	0.401−j0.199
Actual value of f_5	0.969 + j0.316	0.380 + j0.188
Estimated value of f_5	0.977 + j0.322	0.374 + j0.197
Actual value of f_6	0.916 + j0.792	0.495 + j0.257
Estimated value of f_6	0.920 + j0.801	0.488 + j0.264
Actual value of f_7	0.836 + j0.491	0.434 + j0.279
Estimated value of f_7	0.850 + j0.506	0.417 + j0.288
Actual value of f_8	0.758 + j0.343	0.392 + j0.156
Estimated value of f_8	0.777 + j0.331	0.408 + j0.140
Actual value of f_9	0.772 + j0.306	−0.318−j0.277
Estimated value of f_9	0.791 + j0.323	−0.302−j0.299
Actual value of f_{10}	0.562 + j0.297	0.235 + j0.148
Estimated value of f_{10}	0.540 + j0.321	0.252 + j0.175

It can be seen from Table 1, the method can effectively estimate the mutual coupling vectors, especially when the frequency is near to the center point, we can use these results to calibrate the array and acquire the actual DOA of the wideband signal.

4.2 DOA Estimation

First, traditional two-sided correlation transformation (TCT) [18] and WSM are employed for estimating DOA of wideband signals along with the mutual coupling, here, TCT is performed without correction, 300 Monte-Carlo simulations are repeated, their average values are deemed as the final results. Suppose snapshots is 40, other conditions are the same with 4.1, the root mean square error (RMSE) versus SNR are shown in Fig. 2; then suppose SNR is 12 dB, the RMSE versus number of snapshots are shown in Fig. 3.

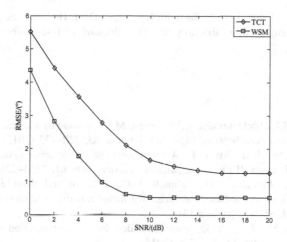

Fig. 2. Calibration accuracy versus SNR

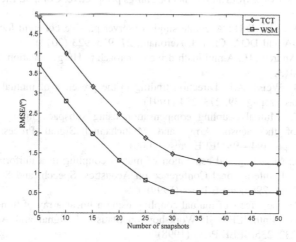

Fig. 3. Calibration accuracy versus number of snapshots

It can be seen from Figs. 2 and 3, WSM method can effectively estimate the DOA of wideband signals along with the mutual coupling existing in the array, when the SNR or number of snapshots increase to some threshold, the estimation error approximately converges to 0.52°, but that of the traditional TCT method without correction converges to 1.2° under the same condition.

5 Conclusion

The paper proposed a novel array calibration method in super-resolution direction finding for wideband signals based on spatial domain sparse optimization to the mutual coupling existing in the array, it can calibrate the array and estimate the DOA relatively accurately.

Acknowledgments. I would like to thank Professor Qun Ding, Heilongjiang province ordinary college electronic engineering laboratory and post doctoral mobile stations of Heilongjiang University.

References

1. Muhammad, M.R., Iftekharuddin, K.M., Ernest, M.: Autonomous wireless radar sensor mote for target material classification. Digit. Sig. Process. **23**, 722–735 (2013)
2. Soh, P.J., Vanden, B.B., Xu, H.T.: A smart wearable textile array system for biomedical telemetry applications. IEEE Trans. Microw. Theory Tech. **61**, 2253–2261 (2013)
3. William, R.O., Aniruddha, G., Schmidt, D.C.: Efficient and deterministic application deployment in component-based enterprise distributed real-time and embedded systems. Inf. Softw. Technol. **55**, 475–488 (2013)
4. Luis, S., Luis, M., Jose, A.G.: SmartSantander: IoT experimentation over a smart city testbed. Comput. Netw. **61**, 217–238 (2014)
5. Verdouw, C.N., Beulens, A.J., van der Vorst, M.J.G.A.J.: Virtualisation of floricultural supply chains: a review from an Internet of Things perspective. Comput. Electron. Agric. **99**, 160–175 (2013)
6. Li, J., Zhao, Y.J., Li, D.H.: Accurate single-observer passive coherent location estimation based on TDOA and DOA. Chin. J. Aeronaut. **27**, 913–923 (2014)
7. Giuseppe, F., Andrew, H.: A multipath-driven approach to HF geolocation. Sig. Process. **93**, 3487–3503 (2013)
8. Friedlander, B., Weiss, A.J.: Direction finding in the presence of mutual coupling. IEEE Trans. Antennas Propag. **39**, 273–284 (1991)
9. Svantesson, T.: Mutual coupling compensation using subspace fitting. In: 2000 IEEE Proceedings of the Sensor Array and Multichannel Signal Processing Workshop, Massachusetts, pp. 494–498. IEEE Press (2000)
10. Svantesson, T.: Modeling and estimation of mutual coupling in a uniform linear array of dipoles. In: IEEE International Conference on Acoustics, Speech, and Signal Processing, Phoenix, pp. 2961–2964. IEEE Press (1999)
11. Svantesson, T.: The effects of mutual coupling using a linear array of thin dipoles of finite length. In: The Ninth IEEE SP Workshop on Statistical Signal and Array Processing, Portland, pp. 232–235. IEEE Press (1998)
12. Wang, B.H., Wang, Y.L, Chen, H.: A robust DOA estimation algorithm for uniform linear array in the presence of mutual coupling. In: IEEE Antennas and Propagation Society International Symposium, vol. 3, pp. 924–927 (2003)
13. Dai, J.S., Xu, W.C., Zhao, D.: Real-valued DOA estimation for uniform linear array with unknown mutual coupling. Sig. Process. **92**, 2056–2065 (2012)
14. Xie, J., Tao, H.H., Rao, X.: Localization of mixed far-field and near-field sources under unknown mutual coupling. Digit. Sig. Process. **50**, 229–239 (2016)
15. Liu, C., Ye, Z.F., Zhang, Y.F.: Autocalibration algorithm for mutual coupling of planar array. Sig. Process. **90**, 784–794 (2010)
16. Elbir, A.M., Tuncer, T.E.: 2-D DOA and mutual coupling coefficient estimation for arbitrary array structures with single and multiple snapshots. Digit. Sig. Process. **54**, 75–86 (2016)
17. Tipping, M.E.: Sparse Bayesian learning and the relevance vector machine. J. Mach. Learn. Res. **1**, 211–244 (2001)
18. Valaee, S., Kabal, P.: Wideband array processing using a two-sided correlation transformation. IEEE Trans. Signal Process. **43**, 160–172 (1995)

Walking Detection Using the Gyroscope of an Unconstrained Smartphone

Guodong Qi and Baoqi Huang[✉]

Inner Mongolia University, Hohhot 010021, China
cshbq@imu.edu.cn

Abstract. In recent years, mobile devices (e.g., smartphones, tablets and etc.) equipped with various inertial sensors have been increasingly popular in daily life, and a large number of mobile applications have been developed based on such built-in inertial sensors. In particular, many of these applications, such as healthcare, navigation, and etc., rely on the knowledge of whether a user is walking or not, so that walking detection thus has attained much attention. This paper deals with walking detection by using the gyroscope of any commercial off the-shelf (COTS) smartphone, which can be placed at different positions of the user. Inspired by the fact that the walking activity often results in notable features in the frequency domain, we propose a novel algorithm based on fast Fourier transformation (FFT) to identify the walking activity of a user who may perform various activities and may hold the smartphone in different manners. A thorough experiment involving three testers and multiple activities is carried out and confirms that the proposed algorithm is superior to the existing well-known counterparts.

Keywords: Smartphone · Walking detection · Unconstrained · Fast Fourier transformation(FFT) · Angular velocities

1   Introduction

Nowadays, with the development of Micro-electromechanical Systems (MEMS) technologies, various low-cost inertial sensors have been integrated in almost every commercial off-the-shelf (COTS) smartphone, and are playing a vital role in a multitude of applications like gaming, navigation, augmented reality, and etc. [1–5]. Therein, gait recognition through the built-in sensors of any smartphone, involving the estimation of the step count and step length, is receiving increasing attention and has become a hot research topic. For instance, in the fields of pedestrian navigation and tracking [6–9], pedestrian dead reckoning (PDR) can be implemented on smartphones to improve positioning accuracy by providing pedestrian displacement and orientation. Evidently, successfully identifying the phase of walking during consecutive activities is prerequisite to these applications.

Therefore, many efforts have been invested on walking detection, but most of existing studies were focused on either dedicated devices, e.g. foot-mounted

© ICST Institute for Computer Sciences, Social Informatics and Telecommunications Engineering 2018
Q. Chen et al. (Eds.): ChinaCom 2016, Part II, LNICST 210, pp. 539–548, 2018.
DOI: 10.1007/978-3-319-66628-0_51

inertial sensors, or smartphones with fixed placements. As a result, it is still challenging to identify the walking activity by using unconstrained smartphones, in the sense that the smartphone's placement can be arbitrary to some extent.

In this paper, we deal with the problem of walking detection with unconstrained smartphones, and propose a robust and efficient walking detection algorithm inspired by the fact that the gyroscope data obtained by a smartphone shows notable cyclic features in most cases when its user is walking. Specifically, the optimal axis is firstly selected from the three dimensional axes in the device frame according to their respective amplitudes, the fast Fourier transformation (FFT) technique is then adopted to derive the frequency-domain gyroscope data in the optimal axis, and a sliding time window is applied to evaluate the amplitudes of multiple frequencies within the current time window, so as to judge whether the smartphone user is walking. A thorough experiment is carried out by taking into account various activities of three testers. It is shown that the overall performance of the proposed algorithm is superior to the existing best walk detection algorithms.

The remainder of this paper is organised as follows. A brief review on related works is presented in Sect. 2. Section 3 introduces the proposed algorithm in details and Sect. 4 reports the experimental results. Section 5 finally concludes this paper and sheds lights on future works.

2   Related Works

There is a wealth of studies on walk detection and step counting for smartphone users in the literature, which can be categorized into time domain approaches, frequency-domain approaches and feature clustering approaches. A thorough survey can be found in [10].

The time domain approaches include thresholding [11], autocorrelation [12], and etc. The thresholding method is simplest, but the difficulty lies in selecting optimal thresholds, especially for unconstrained smartphones. The autocorrelation method detects the period directly in the time domain through evaluating auto-correlation, and is able to obtain good performance at relatively low costs in comparison with frequency-domain approaches.

The frequency-domain approaches focus on the frequency content of successive windows of measurements based on short-term Fourier transform (STFT)[13] and continuous/discrete wavelet transforms (CWT/DWT) can generally achieve high accuracy, but suffer from either resolution issues or computational overheads.

The feature clustering approaches employ machine learning algorithms (e.g. Hidden Markov models (HMMs) [14], KMeans clustering [15], and etc.) to classify activities based on both time-domain and frequency-domain features extracted from the measurements of inertial sensors [16].

3   Method

Commonly, positions and attitudes of a smartphone often experience continuous and dramatic changes when its user is conducting a series of activities, such as walking, texting, calling, playing games and etc. Since different activities result in different inertial measurements, activity recognition can be realized to some extent by extracting unique features of different activities from such measurements.

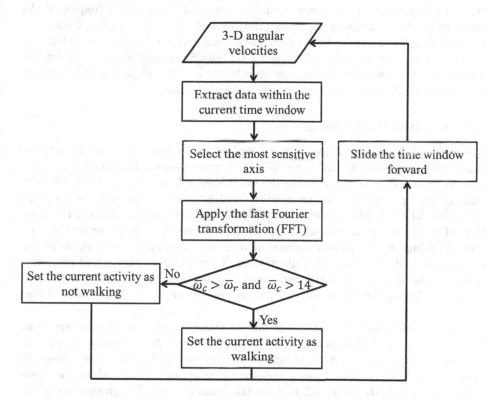

Fig. 1. The flow diagram of the walk detection

Considering the fact that gyroscope is more sensitive and accurate than accelerometer, and for cyclic activities like walking, the angular velocities sensed by gyroscope often swing around zero, though most existing studies on walk detection were carried out based on accelerations as mentioned previously, gyroscope is adopted in the proposed algorithm, the flow diagram of which is illustrated in Fig. 1.

As can be seen, the algorithm mainly involves three components, namely a sliding time window, sensitive axis selection and a spectrum analysis, which will be described in detail in what follows.

3.1 Sliding Time Window

In order to continuously detect walking activities, the algorithm is designed based on a sliding time window. As suggested in [17], the typical walking frequency of human ranges between 0.6 Hz and 2 Hz; that is to say, the duration of the walking activity approximately ranges between 0.5 s and 1.6 s. Therefore, the time window should contain a sequence of data longer than 1.6 s and the sliding step is around the duration of one stride.

Moreover, according to the Shannon sampling theorem, it is sufficient that the sampling frequency is more than two times of the walking frequency. As such, by trading off the energy consumption and minimal sampling frequency, the sampling frequency of the sensors in the smartphone is set to be 20 Hz.

On these grounds, since the base-2 FFT algorithm will be adopted, let the sizes of the time window and sliding step be 64 and 25, respectively, which are equivalently 3.2 s and 1.25 s in the terminology of time.

3.2 Sensitive Axis Selection

Imagining that a smartphone user is required to perform an identical activity repeatedly, it is true that the three axes of inertial measurements derived by the gyroscope of the smartphone in the device reference frame demonstrate different characteristics according to the position and attitude of the smartphone, and thus play different roles in successfully identifying the user's activity. Therefore, it is of great importance to select the most sensitive axis in the sense that the corresponding data is closely correlated with the activity, so as to improve the performance of the recognition algorithms. Currently, an alternative approach is to use the magnitude of the corresponding 3-dimensional (3D) inertial measurements instead of the sensitive axis, but inevitably suffers from information loss.

On the one hand, the measurements of the gyroscope incur constant bias, thermo-mechanical white noise, flicker noise or bias stability, temperature effects, and calibration errors (e.g. scale factors, alignments and output linearities). In general, the measurement noises appear to be quite obvious when the measurements are relatively small, and on the contrary, can be ignored when the measurements are huge. Therefore, it is advisable to select the axis whose data has the maximum magnitude. On the other hand, regarding the walking activity, no matter where the smartphone is placed, certain cyclic features are involved in all the three axes of measurements; that is to say.

Inspired by the above analysis, we come up with the following simple method based on the absolute values of the 3-D angular velocities to select the sensitive axis for the proposed walking detection

$$\text{The most sensitive axis} = \max_{a=x,y,z} \sum_{i=1}^{n} |\omega_a(i)| , \tag{1}$$

where $\omega_a(i)$ denotes the angular velocity of the axis a with $a = x, y, z$ at time i within the current time window, and n is the size of the time window.

3.3 Walking Detection

Based on the above step, the most sensitive axis is determined and the corresponding measurements are fed into the process in this step.

In the first step, FFT is applied to transform the time-domain angular velocities in the most sensitive axis into the following frequency-domain data

$$X(k) = \sum_{n=0}^{N-1} \omega(n)(e^{-j\frac{2\pi}{N}})^{nk}, \tag{2}$$

where $k = 0, 1, \ldots, N-1$, $\omega(\cdot)$ is the angular velocity in the most sensitive axis, N denotes the number of the sampling points and equals to 64 in this case. The frequencies can be calculated as follows

$$F_n = (n-1) * \frac{F_s}{N}, \tag{3}$$

where F_n represents the frequency of the n-th point, and F_s is the sampling frequency and equals to 20 Hz in our case.

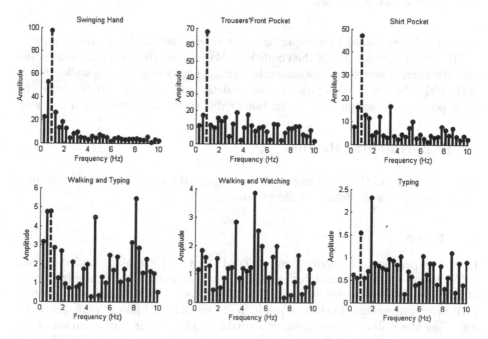

Fig. 2. Frequency-domain data obtained by FFT with respect to various daily activities. The dashed line denotes the amplitude at the frequency 0.9375 Hz.

In the second step, the frequency-domain data obtained through (2) is plotted with respect to various activities performed by Tester1 (see Table. 1) in Fig. 2.

As can be seen, the amplitudes at the frequencies in the vicinity of 0.9375 Hz are obviously greater than the counterparts at the other frequencies provided that the tester is walking with the smartphone placed at different positions (e.g. hand, shirt pocket, and etc.), except that the smartphone is being operated regardless of walking or not. Inspired by the observation, we propose to identify the walking activity by comparing the amplitudes of different frequencies. To be specific, the average amplitude within the typical walking frequencies (i.e. between 0.6 Hz and 2 Hz), denoted by ω_c, and that at the frequencies which fall outside of the typical frequencies, denoted by ω_r, are evaluated respectively, and then, walking is identified if the following condition is satisfied

$$\bar{\omega}_c > \bar{\omega}_r. \tag{4}$$

As illustrated in Fig. 2, when the holder is operating the smartphone (e.g. walking and typing, walking and watching, and typing), the resulting amplitudes are relatively small, reflecting that the smartphone is experiencing some mild motions which might involve walking or not; however, in this situation, it always happens that the condition in (4) is satisfied such that incorrect detection results are returned. Therefore, another condition is imposed by thresholding the average amplitude as follows

$$\bar{\omega}_c > 14, \tag{5}$$

where the lower bound 14 is experimentally determined and does not change.

To sum up, if and only if the conditions (4) and (5) are simultaneously satisfied, the current activity of the smartphone holder is identified to be walking. It is noticeable, the proposed algorithm cannot detect the walking activity when the smartphone is being operated by its holder due to the aforementioned analysis.

4   Experimental Results

In this section, an thorough experiment is reported to confirm the effectiveness of the proposed walk detection algorithm.

4.1   Setup

In the experiment, a smartphone (RedMi Note 2) running Android 5.0.2 LRX22G was adopted to collect measurements of gyroscope at the frequency of 20 Hz, and three testers with different heights, step lengths and genders were invited to continuously perform a predefined sequence of different daily activities including the walking activity along a corridor. The detailed information of the three testers is shown in Table 1. Specifically, the daily activities included in the experiment are shown in Table 2. In order to better distinguish all these activities during each trial, a video camera is used to record the whole procedure.

In order to verify the performance of the proposed algorithm (denoted by FFT), another two walking detection algorithms are performed in the experiment. The first one, denoted by STD_TH, belongs to the time-domain

Table 1. Subjects and their characters in the experiment

	Gender	Height(cm)	Step length(cm)
Tester1	Male	176	130
Tester2	Male	184	151
Tester3	Female	159	88

Table 2. The symbols and the corresponding daily activities

Symbol	Daily activities
A	Standing with the smartphone in the trousers' front pocket
B	Picking up the smartphone
C	Standing with the smartphone in the palm
D	Walking with the smartphone in the swinging hand
E	Standing and typing
F	Walking with the smartphone in the trousers' front pocket
G	Walking with the smartphone in the shirt pocket
H	Standing with the smartphone in the shirt pocket

approaches, and is implemented by thresholding the standard deviation of accelerations [11]. The other one, denoted by STFT, belongs to the frequency-domain approaches, and relies on STFT and accelerations [13]. Both of the algorithms were validated to be best among many existing algorithm for detecting the walking activity with an unconstrained smartphone [10].

The parameter values of all the three algorithms for comparison are listed in Table 3. As can be seen, f represents the length of FFT, w is the length of the apodization window (Hanning), dft_{win} and std_{win} are the size of the sliding step, dft_{th} is the threshold of spectral energy and std_{th} is the threshold of the standard deviation for the acceleration magnitudes.

Table 3. Parameter values

Algorithm	Frequency/time	Window size (s)	Step size (s)	Threshold
FFT	Frequency	3.2	1.25	14
STFT	Frequency	3	0.7	20
STD_TH	Time	1.25	1.25	0.74

4.2 Performance Evaluation

In the first place, the results of the three walking detection algorithms associated with the three testers are illustrated in Figs. 3, 4 and 5, respectively, where

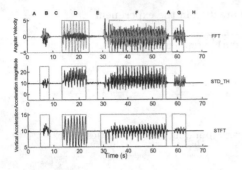

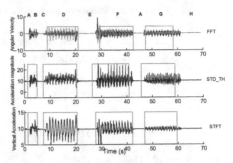

Fig. 3. The results of walking detection associated with tester1

Fig. 4. The results of walking detection associated with tester2

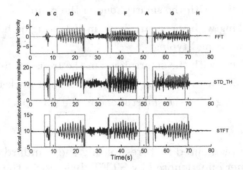

Fig. 5. The results of walking detection associated with tester3

symbols A–H define the corresponding activities listed in Table 2, the blue solid lines reflect the detection results and the other curves denote the measurements adopted by the corresponding algorithms. Specifically, if one tester is identified to be walking during a period of time, the corresponding blue solid line will be drawn in the upper side; otherwise, it is drawn in the lower side.

As can be seen, unlike the algorithms of STD_TH and STFT, the propose algorithm (i.e. FFT) seldom identify other activities into the walking activity, revealing that the proposed algorithm is more robust than the other two algorithms.

In the second place, in order to have a more clear knowledge about the performance of the proposed algorithm, precision (P) and recall (R) are calculated as follows:

$$\text{Precision} = \frac{TP}{TP+FP} \times 100\% \tag{6}$$

$$\text{Recall} = \frac{TP}{TP+FN} \times 100\% \tag{7}$$

where TP is the true positive duration of walking, FP is the false positive duration of walking and FN is the false negative duration of walking. The precision

Table 4. Experimental results for different testers

Tester	FFT		STD_TH		STFT	
	P(%)	R(%)	P(%)	R(%)	P(%)	R(%)
User1	94.79	92.15	75.99	87.72	84.04	95.94
User2	89.44	90.7	73.31	91.69	77.56	95.92
User3	95.83	99.11	68.06	93.16	85.23	98.73
Total	93.49	94.1	72.19	90.83	82.33	96.90

and recall are listed in Table 4. As can be seen, the proposed algorithm outperforms STD_TH in both precision and recall, and is slightly worse than STFT in precision but is significantly better in recall. To sum up, the proposed algorithm is able to achieve superior overall performance in comparison with the other two algorithms which were shown to be best.

5 Conclusion

In this paper, we proposed an efficient and robust walking detection algorithm for users with unconstrained smartphones. Unlike most existing solutions relying on accelerometer, gyroscope is adopted for walking detection. The algorithm was developed based on the sliding time window. At any time window, one most sensitive axis among the 3-D measurements are selected according to their absolute values, the corresponding measurements are then quickly transformed into frequency domain through FFT, and a spectrum analysis is conducted to judge whether the user is walking within the time window. Finally, a thorough experiment was carried out and confirmed the superiority of the proposed algorithm in comparison with the other two algorithms which had been verified to be best.

Regarding future works, we would like to take into account the following problems. First, we plan to continue studying on improving the accuracy of the walking detection algorithm. Second, besides walking detection, we would like to work on movement detection which is contributable to localization and navigation via smartphones.

Acknowledgments. This work is supported by the National Natural Science Foundation of China under Grants 61461037 and 41401519, the Natural Science Foundation of Inner Mongolia Autonomous Region of China under Grant 2014MS0604, and the "Grassland Elite" Project of the Inner Mongolia Autonomous Region under Grant CYYC5016.

References

1. Bahl, P., Padmanabhan, V.N.: RADAR: an in-building RF-based user location and tracking system. In: Proceedings of Nineteenth Annual Joint Conference of the IEEE Computer and Communications Societies, INFOCOM 2000, pp. 775–784. IEEE (2000)

2. Das, S., Green, L.T., Perez, B.: Detecting user activities using the accelerometer on Android smartphones, the team for research in ubiquitous secure technology, TRUSTREU Carnefie Mellon University, pp. 1–10 (2010)
3. Zou, H., Huang, B., Lu, X., Jiang, H., Xie, L.: Standardizing location fingerprints across heterogeneous mobile devices for indoor localization. In: IEEE Wireless Communications and Networking Conference (WCNC), Doha, Qatar, pp. 503–508 (2016)
4. Zhao, H., Huang, B., Jia, B.: Applying kriging interpolation for WiFi fingerprinting based indoor positioning systems. In: IEEE Wireless Communications and Networking Conference (WCNC), Doha, Qatar, pp. 1822–1827 (2016)
5. Zou, H., Huang, B., Lu, X., Jiang, H., Xie, L.: A robust indoor positioning system based on the procrustes analysis and weighted extreme learning machine. In: IEEE Transactions on Wireless Communications, vol. 15, no. 2, pp. 1252–1266 (2016)
6. Foxlin, E.: Pedestrian tracking with shoe-mounted inertial sensors. Comput. Graph. Appl. **25**(6), 38–46 (2005). IEEE
7. Huang, B., Qi, G., Yang, X., Zhao, L., Zou, H.: Exploiting cyclic features of walking for pedestrian dead reckoning with unconstrained smartphones. In: 2016 ACM International Joint Conference on Pervasive and Ubiquitous Computing, UbiComp 2016, Heidelberg, Germany, pp. 374–385 (2016)
8. Yang, X., Huang, B., Miao, Q.: A step-wise algorithm for heading estimation via a smartphone. In: 28th Chinese Control and Decision Conference (CCDC), China, pp. 4711–4715 (2016)
9. Yang, X., Huang, B.: An accurate step detection algorithm using unconstrained smartphones. In: 27th Chinese Control and Decision Conference (CCDC), Qingdao, China, pp. 5702–5707 (2015)
10. Brajdic, A., Harle, R.: Walk detection and step counting on unconstrained smartphones. In: Proceedings of the 2013 ACM International Joint Conference on Pervasive and Ubiquitous Computing, pp. 225–234. ACM (2013)
11. Goyal, P., Ribeiro, V.J., Saran, H.: Strap-down pedestrian dead-reckoning system. In: Indoor Positioning and Indoor Navigation (IPIN), pp. 1–7. IEEE (2011)
12. Rai, A., Chintalapudi, K.K., Padmanabhan, V.N.: Zee: zero-effort crowdsourcing for indoor localization. In: Proceedings of the 18th Annual International Conference on Mobile Computing and Networking. ACM (2012)
13. Barralon, P., Vuillerme, N., Noury, N.: Walk detection with a kinematic sensor: frequency and wavelet comparison. In: 28th Annual International Conference of the IEEE Engineering in Medicine and Biology Society, EMBS 2006, pp. 1711–1714. IEEE (2006)
14. Nickel, C., Brandt, H., Busch, C.: Benchmarking the performance of SVMs and HMMs for accelerometer-based biometric gait recognition. In: 2011 IEEE International Symposium on Signal Processing and Information Technology (ISSPIT), pp. 281–286. IEEE (2011)
15. Choe, B.W., Min, J.-K., Cho, S.-B.: Online gesture recognition for user interface on accelerometer built-in mobile phones. In: Wong, K.W., Mendis, B.S.U., Bouzerdoum, A. (eds.) ICONIP 2010. LNCS, vol. 6444, pp. 650–657. Springer, Heidelberg (2010). doi:10.1007/978-3-642-17534-3_80
16. Dargie, W.: Analysis of time and frequency domain features of accelerometer measurements. In: Proceedings of 18th Internatonal Conference on Computer Communications and Networks, ICCCN 2009, pp. 1–6. IEEE (2009)
17. Henriksen, M., Lund, H., Moe-Nilssen, R.: Test-retest reliability of trunk accelerometric gait analysis. Gait posture **19**(3), 288–297 (2004)

FMN

Spectrum Access Based on Energy Harvesting with Optimal Power Allocation

Jiaying Wu[1], Weidang Lu[1(✉)], Hong Peng[1], and Xin Liu[2]

[1] College of Information Engineering, Zhejiang University of Technology,
Hangzhou, China
luweid@zjut.edu.cn
[2] School of Information and Communication Engineering,
Dalian University of Technology, Dalian 116024, China

Abstract. In this paper, we propose a spectrum access method based on energy harvesting with optimal power allocation. Specifically, in the first phase, the primary user broadcasts its signal. The cognitive user receives the primary signal, and splits the power into two parts, one is to decode information, another is to harvest energy. In the second phase, the cognitive user forwards the primary signal by using the power harvested in the first phase, which assists the primary user to achieve the target rate. The cognitive user can access the primary spectrum to transmit its own signal by using its own power as a reward. We study the optimal power allocation to maximize the cognitive achievable rate, meanwhile the target rate of the primary user is achieved. Simulation results indicate that the proposed method can improve the performances of both the primary and cognitive users.

Keywords: Energy harvesting · Power allocation · Spectrum access

1 Introduction

With the dramatic demand increase of wireless communications, the requirement of the data transmission rate of wireless communication is becoming so large that more spectrum resource is needed. However, the spectrum resource is limited, and there are different degrees of wastes in time and space of the spectrum resource allocated by the existing wireless systems, which restricts the development of wireless communications. Cognitive radio technology can utilize the idle spectrum resources, which is capable of effectively improving the spectrum utilization under the premise of not affecting the primary user's performance [1]. The power allocation optimization to obtain the maximal cognitive rate is researched in [2, 3], which the primary rate can be guaranteed with the constraint of the primary power.

Recently, cooperative diversity technology has been broadly applied in cognitive radio for spectrum access, since it enlarges the system coverage and increases the link reliability [4, 5] proposed a centralized cooperative spectrum leasing protocol, in which the primary user leased a part of its transmission time to the cognitive user transmitting its signal, and the cognitive user allocated a portion of the acquired transmission time to help transmit the primary signal. Distributed spectrum sharing protocols with

© ICST Institute for Computer Sciences, Social Informatics and Telecommunications Engineering 2018
Q. Chen et al. (Eds.): ChinaCom 2016, Part II, LNICST 210, pp. 551–559, 2018.
DOI: 10.1007/978-3-319-66628-0_52

cooperative relay were proposed in [6, 7], where the cognitive user used parts of power to help transmit the primary signal to guarantee the primary target rate no worse than direct transmission, and the remaining power is used to transmit its own signal. We proposed spectrum access protocols based on OFDM relaying in [8, 9], the cognitive user plays a relay role to assist the primary user to achieve the target rate by using a portion of subcarriers to forward the primary signal, while the remaining are used to transmit its own signal.

However in these spectrum access methods, for the purpose of gaining the spectrum access, the cognitive user is required to contribute a part of its power to help forward the primary signal. The more power of the cognitive is split to forward the primary signal, the less power will be left for the cognitive user to transmit signal itself that may results in poor performance of the cognitive user. Then, the cognitive user will be unwilling to gain the spectrum access.

Wireless energy harvesting technology has drawn significant attention in wireless signal and power transmission. Different forms of energy harvesting are studied in [10–12]. In [10], a dynamic power splitting method based on energy harvesting was proposed, where the receiver allocates a part of the transmission power to decode information, and the remaining to harvest energy. In [11] a time switching method was presented, in which the receiver needs to select the different phases to decode information or harvest energy to maximize the system performance.

In this paper, we propose a spectrum access method based on energy harvesting with optimal power allocation, where the cognitive user allocates a part of the power obtained from the received primary signal to harvest energy in the first phase, and uses the remaining power for information decoding. Then, in the second phase, the cognitive user utilizes the power harvested in the first phase to assist transmitting the primary signal to ensure the target rate. As a reward, the cognitive user can transmit its own signal by its own power by gaining the primary spectrum access. We study the optimal power allocation to obtain the maximal cognitive rate, given that the target rate of the primary user is achieved.

2 System Model

The system model is showed in Fig. 1. We can see that the primary system is composed of a primary transmitter (PT) and a primary receiver (PR) which supplies relay function and operates with a licensed spectrum W. The cognitive system consists of a cognitive transmitter (CT) and cognitive receiver (CR), which is seeking opportunity to gain the primary spectrum access to send its own signal.

We use the Rayleigh flat fading to model the channel coefficients of links $PT \rightarrow PR$, $PT \rightarrow CT$, $CT \rightarrow PR$ and $CT \rightarrow CR$, which are denoted as h_1, h_2, h_3 and h_4, respectively. We have $h_i \sim CN(0, d_i^{-v})$, $i = 1, 2, 3, 4$, where v denotes the path loss exponent, d_i denotes the normalized distance between PT and PR. $\gamma_i = |h_{i,k}|^2$ denotes the instantaneous channel gain of h_i. We further assume that all the channel coefficients are constant in the two phases.

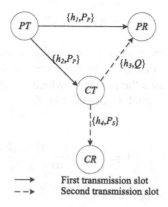

$\longrightarrow$ First transmission slot
$--\blacktriangleright$ Second transmission slot

Fig. 1. System model.

3 Achievable Rates of Primary and Cognitive Users

Firstly, to consider the direct transmission, the primary user sends its signal to *PR* without cognitive user access. The primary user can achieve the rate that can be expressed as

$$R_D = W \log_2 \left(1 + \frac{\gamma_1 P_P}{\sigma^2} \right) \tag{1}$$

where P_P is the transmit power of *PT* and σ^2 is additive Gaussian noise variance.

When R_D falls below the target rate R_T, as $PT \rightarrow PR$ is highly attenuated, e.g., due to strong shadow fading, *PR* will search for cooperation from the nearby cognitive users for the sake of improving the performance. Only the cognitive user who can assist guaranteeing the primary target rate will have the chance to access the spectrum of primary user. The cognitive user determines whether it can provide assistance for the primary user to reach the target rate within two phases.

In the first phase, *PT* broadcasts signal to *PR* and *CT*. *CT* allocates a part of the power obtained from the received primary signal to harvest energy, and utilizes the remaining to decode information. Thus, the achievable rates of $PT \rightarrow PR$ and $PT \rightarrow CT$ links can be written as

$$R_d = \frac{1}{2} W \log_2 (1 + \frac{\gamma_1 P_P}{\sigma^2}) \tag{2}$$

$$R_1 = \frac{1}{2} W \log_2 (1 + \frac{\alpha \gamma_2 P_P}{\sigma^2}) \tag{3}$$

And the energy harvested at *CT* can be written as

$$Q = \varepsilon(1 - \alpha)\gamma_2 P_P \tag{4}$$

where ε is a constant which represents the loss coefficient of transforming the energy to electric energy. It is assumed that $\varepsilon = 1$ in this paper for convenience.

In the second phase, CT uses the power Q, which is harvested in the first phase, to assist forwarding the primary signal. Consequently, $CT \rightarrow PR$ link can achieve the rate that can be shown as

$$R_2 = \frac{1}{2} W \log_2 \left(1 + \frac{(1 - \alpha)\gamma_2\gamma_3 P_P}{\sigma^2 + \gamma_3 P_S} \right) \tag{5}$$

where P_S is the total transmit power of CT.

After two phases, the achievable rate of the primary user is

$$R_P = \min\{R_1, R_2\} \tag{6}$$

Meanwhile, CT uses its own power P_S to transmit its own signal to CR. Therefore, the rate the cognitive user achieves is expressed as

$$R_S = \frac{1}{2} W \log_2 \left(1 + \frac{\gamma_4 P_S}{(1 - \alpha)\gamma_2\gamma_4 P_P + \sigma^2} \right) \tag{7}$$

4   Optimal Power Allocation

We study the optimization of power α for the purposes of not only maximizing the cognitive user's rate R_S, but also ensuring the primary target rate R_T. Consequently, the optimization problem is written as

$$\max_{\alpha} R_S \tag{8}$$

Subject to

$$\begin{cases} R_P \geq R_T \\ 0 < \alpha < 1 \end{cases} \tag{9}$$

Substituting (3), (5), (6), (7) and (8) into (9), we can obtain

$$\max_{\alpha} \frac{1}{2} W \log_2 \left(1 + \frac{\gamma_4 P_S}{(1 - \alpha)\gamma_2\gamma_4 P_P + \sigma^2} \right) \tag{10}$$

Subject to

$$\begin{cases} \frac{1}{2} W \log_2 \left(1 + \frac{\alpha \gamma_2 P_P}{\sigma^2}\right) \geq R_T \\ \frac{1}{2} W \log_2 \left(1 + \frac{(1-\alpha)\gamma_2 \gamma_3 P_P}{\sigma^2 + \gamma_3 P_S}\right) \geq R_T \\ 0 < \alpha < 1 \end{cases} \tag{11}$$

We convert the first condition of (11) and obtain

$$\alpha \geq \frac{\sigma^2 M}{\gamma_2 P_P} \tag{12}$$

where $M = 2^{2R_T/W} - 1$. Then we convert the second condition of (11) and finally obtain

$$\alpha \leq 1 - \frac{M(\sigma^2 + \gamma_3 P_S)}{\gamma_2 \gamma_3 P_P} \tag{13}$$

Thus, we can obtain

$$\frac{\sigma^2 M}{\gamma_2 P_P} \leq \alpha \leq 1 - \frac{M(\gamma_3 P_S + \sigma^2)}{\gamma_2 \gamma_3 P_P} \tag{14}$$

From (7), we can find that R_S monotonically increases with α. Therefore, the optimal power allocation of the optimization problem can be written as

$$\alpha^* = 1 - \frac{M(\sigma^2 + \gamma_3 P_S)}{\gamma_2 \gamma_3 P_P} \tag{15}$$

Substituting α^* into (7), we can obtain

$$R_S^* = \frac{1}{2} \log_2 \left(1 + \frac{\gamma_3 \gamma_4 P_S}{\gamma_4 M(\sigma^2 + \gamma_3 P_S) + \sigma^2 \gamma_3}\right) \tag{16}$$

5   Simulation and Analysis of Power Allocation

We consider PT, PR, CT and CR are in a two-dimensional X-Y plane, where PT and PR are located are points $(0,0)$ and $(1,0)$, respectively, thus $d_1 = 1$. CT moves on the positive X axis, its coordinate is $(d_2, 0)$. CR is in the middle of PR and CT. Thus, $d_3 = 1 - d_2$, and $d_4 = 0.5d_3$. The path loss exponent denotes $v = 3$, $R_T = 1.5$ bps/Hz, $P_S/\sigma^2 = 10$, $W = 1$, unless otherwise specified.

The optimal power allocation with our proposed spectrum access method is showed in Fig. 2. With CT gradually becomes far away from PT, the power allocated to decode the primary signal will be smaller. This is because, when d_2 becomes larger, the $CT \rightarrow PR$ link obtains better SNR, from (5) we can find that the interference to primary user by reason of cognitive user will be larger. In the meantime the SNR of $PT \rightarrow CT$ link will be worse. Hence to guarantee the target rate of primary user, more power is needed of cognitive user to assist forwarding the primary signal, so that less power is obtained to decode the signal at CT.

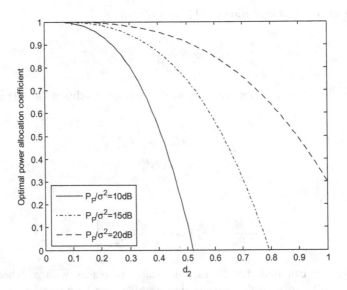

Fig. 2. Optimal power allocation versus different locations of CT

Figure 3 shows the cognitive achievable rate with our proposed spectrum access method. We can conclude that when the primary user gets larger power, the cognitive user will have larger region to gain the primary spectrum access. It is because the cognitive user can harvest more power from the primary user with larger power of the primary user. We can also observe from Fig. 3 that the cognitive user will achieve the same rate with different power of primary user within the access region for the reason that with the same target rate of the primary user, the cognitive user will harvest the same power to forward the primary signal. Thus, the interference to the cognitive user by reason of the primary user is the same. Then, with the same power of the cognitive user, the achievable rate will be same.

Figure 4 shows the optimal power allocation versus different power of CT. We can find that with larger target rate of the primary user, more power is needed to harvest at CT to help forward the primary signal. What's more, with smaller target rate of the primary user, the cognitive user will gain larger region to gain the primary spectrum access. Because the cognitive user will give more contribution to assist the primary user to achieve smaller target rate.

In Fig. 5, we can observe that the cognitive user will achieve larger rate with smaller target rate of the primary user. This is because, with smaller primary target rate, CT will harvest smaller power to assist forwarding the primary signal. Then, the interference caused to forward the primary signal to the cognitive user will be smaller. Thus, the cognitive user will achieve larger rate.

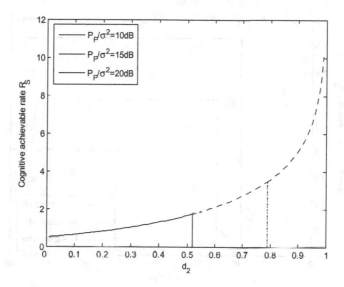

Fig. 3. Cognitive achievable rate versus different locations of CT

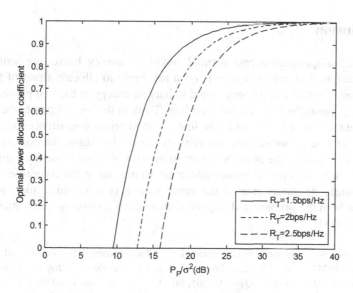

Fig. 4. Optimal power allocation versus different power of *PT*

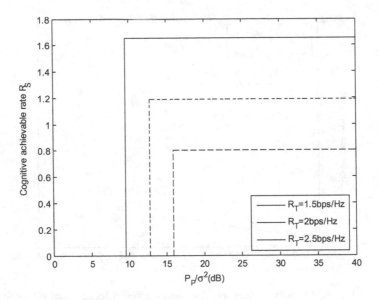

Fig. 5. Cognitive achievable rate versus different power of *PT*

6 Conclusion

We proposed a spectrum access method based on energy harvesting with optimal power allocation. The cognitive user plays a relay role to allocate a part of the power obtained from the received primary signal to harvest energy in the first phase, and uses the remaining power for information decoding. Then, in the second phase, the cognitive user can use the power harvested in the first phase to provide assistance to achieve the primary target rate by forwarding the primary signal. In return, the cognitive user is capable of accessing to the primary spectrum transmit its own signal by using its own power. We study the optimal power allocation to maximize the cognitive achievable rate, meanwhile the target rate of the primary user is achieved. Simulation results confirm that both the primary and cognitive users can improve the performance in our proposed method.

Acknowledgments. This work was supported by China National Science Foundation under Grant Nos. 61402416 and 61303235, Natural Science Foundation of Zhejiang Province under Grant Nos. LQ14F010003 and LQ14F020005, NSFC-Zhejiang Joint Fund for the Integration of Industrialization of Jiangsu Province under Grant No. BK20140828, the Fundamental Research Funds for the Central Universities under Grant No. DUT16RC(3)045 and the Scientific Foundation for the Returned Overseas Chinese Scholars of State Education Ministry.

References

1. Haykin, S.: Cognitive radio: brain-empowered wireless communications. IEEE J. Sel. Areas Commun. **23**(2), 201–220 (2005)

2. Kang, X., Garg, H.K., Liang, Y.-C., Zhang, R.: Optimal power allocation for OFDM-based cognitive radio with new primary transmission protection criteria. IEEE Trans. Wireless Commun. **9**, 2066–2075 (2010)
3. Ghasemi, A., Sousa, E.S.: Fundamental limits of spectrum-sharing in fading environments. IEEE Trans. Wireless Commun. **6**(2), 649–658 (2007)
4. Sendonaris, A., Erkip, E., Aazhang, B.: User cooperation diversity part I and part II. IEEE Trans. Wireless Commun. **51**(11), 1927–1948 (2003)
5. Asaduzzaman, Kong, H.Y.: Multi-relay cooperative diversity protocol with improved spectral efficiency. J. Commun. Netw. **13**, 240–249 (2011)
6. Han, Y., Pandharipande, A., Ting, S.H.: Cooperative decode-and-forward relaying for secondary spectrum access. IEEE Trans. Wireless Commun. **8**(10), 4945–4950 (2009)
7. Han, Y., Pandharipande, A., Ting, S.H.: Cooperative spectrum sharing via controlled amplify-and-forward relaying. In: PIMRC 2008 IEEE 19th International Symposium on Personal, Indoor and Mobile Radio Communications, pp. 1–5. IEEE (2008)
8. Lu, W.D., Gong, Y., Ting, S.H., Wu, X.L., Zhang, N.T.: Cooperative OFDM relaying for opportunistic spectrum sharing: protocol design and resource allocation. IEEE Trans. Wireless Commun. **11**(6), 2126–2135 (2012)
9. Lu, W.D., Wang, J.: Opportunistic spectrum sharing based on full-duplex cooperative OFDM relaying. IEEE Commun. Lett. **18**(2), 241–244 (2014)
10. Liu, L., Zhang, R., Chua, K.C.: Wireless information and power transfer: a dynamic power splitting approach. IEEE Trans. Wireless Commun. **61**(9), 3990–4001 (2013)
11. Liu, L., Zhang, R., Chua, K.C.: Wireless information transfer with opportunistic energy harvesting. IEEE Trans. Wireless Commun. **212**(1), 288–300 (2013)
12. Shi, Q.J., Liu, L., Xu, W.Q., Zhang, R.: Joint transmit beamforming and receive power splitting for MISO SWIPT systems. IEEE J. Sel. Areas Commun. **13**(6), 3269–3280 (2014)

The CEEFQPSK Scheme for Two-Way Relay Communication Systems with Physical-Layer Network Coding

Hongjuan Yang, Jinxiang Song, Bo Li[(✉)], and Xiyuan Peng

School of Information and Electrical Engineering,
Harbin Institute of Technology (Weihai), 264209 Weihai, China
{hjyang, songjinxiang, libol983, pxy}@hit.edu.cn

Abstract. A physical-layer network coding (PNC) scheme based on CEEFQPSK (constant envelope enhanced FQPSK) is established for satellite communications. The scheme is implemented for uplink and downlink. In the uplink, the two signals to be sent are modulated into electromagnetic wave signal by CEEFQPSK in two channels (I, Q) and broadcasted to the relay node. At the same time, the electromagnetic wave signal is superimposed on the relay node and mapped into a binary bit, and then it will be modulated and broadcasted to the two terminals. In the downlink, soft information is received according to the maximum posterior probability criterion, and the required information is de-mapped with its own information. The bit-error rate (BER) and throughput of the entire system are analyzed by simulation. Theoretical analysis and simulation results show that the BER of the physical-layer network coding scheme using this method is close to that of the traditional scheme and network coding scheme, but the throughput is higher than the other two.

Keywords: Physical-layer network coding (PNC) · FQPSK modulation · Two-way relay communication · Relay mapping

1 Introduction

With the continuous development of global network information, communications on the ground can no longer satisfy the people's growing demands for information acquisition and transmission, to extend the space resources for communications has been increasingly focused on by more and more people. Therefore, the theory of transmitting information via satellite becomes the focus of people's attention. As with other types of networks, network capacity is one of the important performance parameters for satellite communication networks. Based on Shannon's maximum flow minimum cut theory [1]: "the minimum cut of network determines its maximum end-to-end information flow." finding a way to get close to or reach the upper bound of network capacity has become a heated research. In 2000, researchers like Ahlswede [2] brought up the theory of network coding (NC) and theoretically proved that the top capacity determined by maximum flow minimum cut theorem can be reached through coding information on each code of the network, and NC is a break-through in communication field. Different from traditional information transmission scheme, NC

© ICST Institute for Computer Sciences, Social Informatics and Telecommunications Engineering 2018
Q. Chen et al. (Eds.): ChinaCom 2016, Part II, LNICST 210, pp. 560–568, 2018.
DOI: 10.1007/978-3-319-66628-0_53

technology is no longer just store-and-forward, its core idea is to allow the relay nodes to process the received packets by combining or coding, thus immensely increase the network's transmission capacity.

As the research on NC gets deeper and deeper, people find that NC technology has good compatibility and ability of information extraction when applied to wireless communication network, but it still can't get rid of the problem of interference, especially the interference caused by electromagnetic wave of the same frequency, like traditional coding scheme, TDMA is applied in NC. As data transmitted in the form of electromagnetic waves are all transmitted in the physical layer of wireless link, people naturally get the idea of applying NC in physical layer. In 2006, researchers like Zhang put forward physical-layer network coding (PNC) theorem [3], whose principle is: the transmitted electromagnetic waves are superposed in the airspace, map the superposed signal on the relay node, and make the interference part of the encoding algorithm, then broadcast the mapped signal to both sides, and demodulate the mapped signal at the terminals. Once this theory is brought up, great attention was drawn to it. PNC theory dramatically increases the throughput of the network system, and it help to reach the maximum of spectrum efficiency. For the three-node two-way relay communication system, the throughput of physical-layer network coding is improved a lot, which increased 100% than that of traditional scheme and 50% than that of NC scheme [4].

The idea of PNC is to process the electromagnetic wave signals superposed in wireless channel, and the modulation technology adapted is its key point when applied to satellite communications. Different rules of modulation have different mapping mechanism on the relay nodes. [3] introduced such modulation mapping rules like QPSK and QAM. [5] firstly explored a PNC system suitable for deep-space communications, which applies FQPSK modulation, and its relay mapping uses waveform classification criteria. [6] was the improvement of FQPSK and then brought up CEEFQPSK. This paper will focus on analyzing the performance of PNC based on CEEFQPSK.

2 The Modulation Model of CEEFQPSK

CEEFQPSK is an improvement of IJF-OQPSK, which adds a cross correlation after IJF coding to decrease the envelop fluctuation, its modulation diagram is shown in Fig. 1.

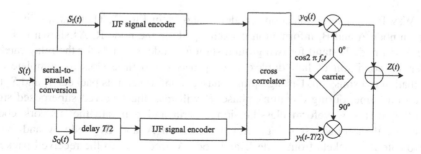

Fig. 1. The modulation diagram of CEEFQPSK

16 kinds of waveform, $s_i(t)$, $i = 0, 1, 2, \ldots, 15$ are defined, whose interval is $-TS/2 \le t \le TS/2$. They form the signal set of channel I and Q. For arbitrary interval T_s on each channel, the selection of waveform on channel I and Q depends on its data jump and two continuous data jumps on another channel. Therefore, FQPSK is a modulation type with memory. As the slope of basic waveform is not continuous in the midpoint in FQPSK, which only achieves quasi constant envelope, we make an improvement on FQPSK and then propose CEEFQPSK, and its basic waveform is defined as follow [6]:

$$
\begin{aligned}
&s_0(t) = A, && -\tfrac{Ts}{2} \le t \le \tfrac{Ts}{2} && s_8(t) = -s0(t) \\
&s_1(t) = \{ \begin{array}{l} A, \\ \sqrt{1 - (\sin\frac{\pi(t+Ts/2)}{Ts} - (1-A)\sin^2\frac{\pi(t+Ts/2)}{Ts})^2}, \end{array} && \begin{array}{l} -\tfrac{Ts}{2} \le t \le 0 \\ 0 \le t \le \tfrac{Ts}{2} \end{array} && s_9(t) = -s1(t) \\
&s_2(t) = \{ \begin{array}{l} \sqrt{1 - (\sin\frac{\pi(t+Ts/2)}{Ts} - (1-A)\sin^2\frac{\pi(t+Ts/2)}{Ts})^2}, \\ A, \end{array} && \begin{array}{l} -\tfrac{Ts}{2} \le t \le 0 \\ 0 \le t \le \tfrac{Ts}{2} \end{array} && s_{10}(t) = -s2(t) \\
&s_3(t) = \sqrt{1 - (\sin\frac{\pi(t+Ts/2)}{Ts} - (1-A)\sin^2\frac{\pi(t+Ts/2)}{Ts})^2}, && -\tfrac{Ts}{2} \le t \le \tfrac{Ts}{2} && s_{11}(t) = -s3(t) \\
&s_4(t) = \{ \begin{array}{l} \sin\frac{\pi t}{Ts} + (1-A)\sin^2\frac{\pi t}{Ts}, \\ \sin\frac{\pi t}{Ts} - (1-A)\sin^2\frac{\pi t}{Ts}, \end{array} && \begin{array}{l} -\tfrac{Ts}{2} \le t \le 0 \\ 0 \le t \le \tfrac{Ts}{2} \end{array} && s_{12}(t) = -s4(t) \\
&s_5(t) = \{ \begin{array}{l} \sin\frac{\pi t}{Ts} + (1-A)\sin^2\frac{\pi t}{Ts}, \\ \sin\frac{\pi t}{Ts}, \end{array} && \begin{array}{l} -\tfrac{Ts}{2} \le t \le 0 \\ 0 \le t \le \tfrac{Ts}{2} \end{array} && s_{13}(t) = -s5(t) \\
&s_6(t) = \{ \begin{array}{l} \sin\frac{\pi t}{Ts}, \\ \sin\frac{\pi t}{Ts} - (1-A)\sin^2\frac{\pi t}{Ts}, \end{array} && \begin{array}{l} -\tfrac{Ts}{2} \le t \le 0 \\ 0 \le t \le \tfrac{Ts}{2} \end{array} && s_{14}(t) = -s6(t) \\
&s_7(t) = \sin\frac{\pi t}{Ts}, && -\tfrac{Ts}{2} \le t \le \tfrac{Ts}{2} && s_{15}(t) = -s7(t)
\end{aligned}
\tag{1}
$$

After this improvement, the slope is now continuous on the midpoint. So, the slope of the signal is continuous between intervals, and keeps zero-slope at the border, which promises the signal continuous whenever. Meanwhile, as the roll-off speed of signal frequency spectrum is relevant to its smoothness, the frequency spectrum roll-off speed of the modified signal outstanding increases, this tremendously enhances the spectrum efficiency. And this makes FQPSK into constant envelop modulation.

3   System Model for Two-Way Relay Communications

Two-Way Relay Communications model is shown in Fig. 2. There is no direct link between node A and B, information is exchanged via the node R. As shown in Fig. 2, node A and node B stand for two ground stations, node R stands for the relay satellite. Under the condition of half duplex, it only needs two time slots to complete once information transmission. During uplink phase, A and B send its packets S_1 and S_2 to R at the same time; during downlink phase, R will map the received superposed signal according to the waveform classification criteria and generate the network coding packet S_3, then broadcast the generated packet to A and B. Node A and B will demodulate the packets from node B and node A according to the received packet S_3 and the original data they have. Then, a data transmission cycle is completed.

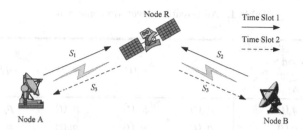

Fig. 2. System model for two-way relay communications

4 The Schemes of Relay Mapping and Terminal De-mapping

4.1 The Mapping Scheme

As the phase constellation points of FQPSK are irregular distributed on the unit circle, the traditional constellation classification criteria is no longer suitable for this system. The scheme of relay mapping adapted in this system is the mapping scheme based on waveform cluster classification criteria, which introduced in [5]. The superposed signal received at the relay node can be described as:

$$y_R(t) = z_A(t) + z_B(t) + n(t) \tag{2}$$

$n(t)$ stands for Gaussian noise with zero mean and variance σ^2, the variance is relevant to the average power of each signal. $z_A(t)$ and $z_B(t)$ stand for the signal from node A and B. Assuming that in the nth time slot, $x_I(t)$ and $x_Q(t)$, the envelope of baseband signal of channel I and Q, are formed by $s_i(t)$ and $s_j(t)$, i and j are decided by the modulation rule. Set $x_I(t) = s_i(t - nT_s)$ and $x_Q(t) = s_j(t - nT_s + T_s/2)$, then the transmitted signal envelop can be expressed as:

$$
\begin{aligned}
z_A(t) &= x_I(t) + jx_Q(t) = \sum_n s_i(t - nT_s) + j\sum_n s_j(t - nT_s + T_s/2) \\
z_B(t) &= x_I'(t) + jx_Q'(t) = \sum_n s_i'(t - nT_s) + j\sum_n s_j'(t - nT_s + T_s/2)
\end{aligned}
\tag{3}
$$

For convenience, the superposed signal can be expressed as:

$$
\begin{aligned}
S_I &= \sum_n s_i(t - nT_s) + \sum_n s_i'(t - nT_s) \\
S_Q &= \sum_n s_j(t - nT_s + T_s/2) + \sum_n s_j'(t - nT_s + T_s/2)
\end{aligned}
\tag{4}
$$

The idea of classifying the 16 kinds of basic waveform into 4 categories in FQPSK receiver is applied to the received signal on relay nodes. We separate the two channels and then detect the signal S_I and S_Q of channel I and Q according to energy offset theorem. According to the principle brought up above, all possible waveform combination of the superposed signal S_I received at the relay node, interfered by no noise in channel I, is displayed in Table 1.

Table 1. All possible waveform combination

superposed signal	station B $q_0(t)$	$q_1(t)$	$q_2(t)$	$q_3(t)$
station A				
$q_0(t)$	$P_{00}(t)$	$P_{01}(t)$	$P_{02}(t)$	$P_{03}(t)$
$q_1(t)$	$P_{10}(t)$	$P_{11}(t)$	$P_{12}(t)$	$P_{13}(t)$
$q_2(t)$	$P_{20}(t)$	$P_{21}(t)$	$P_{22}(t)$	$P_{23}(t)$
$q_3(t)$	$P_{30}(t)$	$P_{31}(t)$	$P_{32}(t)$	$P_{33}(t)$

During each symbol period, energy offset is carried out on baseband signal $S_k(t)$:

$$V'_{ii}(t) = \int_{-\frac{T_s}{2}}^{\frac{T_s}{2}} p'_{ii}(t) \cdot S_k(t) dt - \frac{1}{2} \int_{-\frac{T_s}{2}}^{\frac{T_s}{2}} p'_{ii}(t) \cdot p'_{ii}(t) dt \ k \in \{I, Q\} \tag{5}$$

Then the maximum offset energy $V_{max}(t)$ is picked up, which is also the biggest value of $V'_{ii}(t)$. A new standard symbol $\Gamma_k(\bullet)$ for mapping is now defined, and the mapping rule is as follow:

$$\Gamma_k(V_{max}(t)) = \begin{cases} 0, V_{max}(t) = \left\{ \begin{array}{l} V_{00}(t), V_{01}(t), V_{10}(t), V_{11}(t) \\ V_{22}(t), V_{23}(t), V_{32}(t), V_{33}(t) \end{array} \right\} \\ 1, V_{max}(t) = \left\{ \begin{array}{l} V_{02}(t), V_{20}(t), V_{03}(t), V_{30}(t) \\ V_{12}(t), V_{21}(t), V_{13}(t), V_{31}(t) \end{array} \right\} \end{cases} \tag{6}$$

Then, we get a new code word sequence $x_r(t) = \Gamma_k(V_{max}(t)) \in \{0,1\}$.

After mapping, $x_r(t)$ is modulated by CEEFQPSK, and then broadcasted to the two ground receiving stations.

4.2 The De-mapping Scheme

According to the symmetry of the system, we take ground station A as an example for information recovery, and it's also appropriate for ground station B. Assuming that the downlink signal received by station A is $y_r(t) = \{r_1, r_2, \ldots, r_L\}$, the soft information carried by the signal is estimated by MAP algorithm. While this information is not what we expect from station B, but the codon formed by the superposed signal which is mapped on the relay node, it only carries the relationship between the two signals form station A and B.

Station A will obtain the information from station B according to its own information and the information demodulated from the codon. The de-mapping algorithm is just like an inversed process of the mapping process. Therefore, we can decide the scope of the superposed signal $p'_{ii}(t)$ according to the Eq. (6), then get the scope of information from station B according to its own information and Table 1.

However, the operation above can neither certainly make sure that, q_0 and q_1, which one is the electromagnetic wave envelop from station B, nor distinguish q_2 and q_3. But according to the interweave chart of simplified CEEFQPSK, we can see that when adapting Viterbi demodulation to the signal from station B, the demodulation output is always 0, whatever the signal is q_0 or q_1. Besides, the output is always 1 whatever the signal is q_2 or q_3. In conclusion, there is no need to distinguish between q_0 and q_1 or q_2 and q_3.

Therefore, Table 2 shows the resumed information at station A (which is also adaptable to station B).

Table 2. The resumed information at station A

If $\Gamma(V_{\max}(t)) = 0$ and $q_i \in \{q_0, q_1\}$, the output is $y_b = 0$;
If $\Gamma(V_{\max}(t)) = 0$ and $q_i \in \{q_2, q_3\}$, the output is $y_b = 1$;
If $\Gamma(V_{\max}(t)) = 1$ and $q_i \in \{q_0, q_1\}$, the output is $y_b = 1$;
if $\Gamma(V_{\max}(t)) = 1$ and $q_i \in \{q_2, q_3\}$, the output is $y_b = 0$;

In conclusion, we can make it easier to de-mapping and demodulate the information from station B by applying intertwined de-mapping and demodulation mechanism. It not only reduces the complexity of the system, but also effectively enhances the fault-tolerance of the whole system, which make the operability of whole system stronger.

5   Simulation Results and Analysis

In this section, we study the performances of the PNC based on CEEFQPSK modulation, as discussed above, by using computer simulation in terms of BER and system throughput.

5.1   BER Performance of the Two-Way Relay System

Figure 3 shows the BER comparison between the traditional scheme, network coding scheme and physical-layer network coding scheme. Because of the integral of BER formula of CEEFQPSK is too complex, its BER performance can be understand through the curve in the Fig. 3.

Form Fig. 3, it can be seen that the changing tendency along with SNR is in consistence between the 3 schemes, all improve with SNR, and the BERs of the 3 schemes are quite similar. Besides, we can see that the traditional scheme has better performance. However, it only needs 2 time slots for physical-layer network coding scheme to accomplish once two-way relay communication, while 4 time slots for traditional scheme and 3 time slots for network coding scheme. So, we can see that physical-layer network coding scheme can help to increase the system throughput.

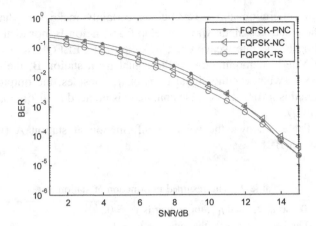

Fig. 3. BER performance comparison

5.2 Throughput Performance of the Two-Way Relay System

In this paper, the system throughput for the two-way relay system is defined as:

$$T = \frac{(1 - BER)^L \cdot 2LR \log_2 M}{n\frac{d}{c}} \tag{7}$$

where BER stands for the bit-error rate of a given scheme; L stands for the length of the data frame transmitted, and we assume that L to be 1024 bits; R stands for the bit rate of the encoded channel, here we assume that the end-to-end channel coding is adapted, and R equals 1/2; M is the modulation order; n stands for the number of time slots required for once two-way relay communication, and the n is to be 4, 3, 2 in traditional scheme, network coding scheme and physical-layer networking scheme, respectively. d stands for the distance between the two communicating stations, here we set $d = 30$ km; c stands for the travelling speed of the electromagnetic wave, which is close to the speed of light, and d/c equals one time slot. To normalize formula (7), we get:

$$T = \frac{(1 - BER)^L}{n} \tag{8}$$

The throughputs of these three schemes are shown in Fig. 4.

Figure 4 shows that the throughput of physical-layer network coding scheme is much better than that of traditional scheme and network coding scheme. With the SNR increasing, once the system works in stable condition, the throughput of PNC is increased by 100% and 50% than that of traditional scheme and network coding scheme, respectively. This improvement is mainly own to the decreasing of the transmission time slot. As these three schemes have similar BER, the decreasing of the transmission time slot will tremendously increase the throughput performance.

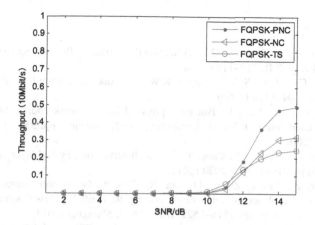

Fig. 4. Throughputs for different schemes

6 Conclusions

This article mainly focuses on researching the performances of physical-layer network coding scheme based on CEEQPSK when applied to satellite communication. During the research process of the PNC system based on CEEFQPSK modulation, signals from the two channels are modulated by CEEFQPSK and then transmitted to the relay node. The signals are superposed on the relay node, and then being processed according to the relay-mapping scheme based on waveform classification criteria before being broadcast. Then, the required information is recovered on the terminal by demodulation and de-mapping. Finally, the system is verified by software simulation.

According to the comparison among traditional scheme, network coding scheme and physical-layer network coding scheme, it can be seen that the BER performances of the three systems are quite close when using CEEFQPSK and the traditional scheme has better performance.

A method for calculating the throughput of the two-way relay communication system is brought up. The simulation results show that when the system works in stable condition, PNC can provide up to 100% and 50% throughput gains compared with traditional scheme and network coding scheme, respectively.

Acknowledgments. This work is partly supported by National Natural Science Foundation of China under Grant Nos. 61401118, 61371100 and 61671184, Natural Science Foundation of Shandong Province under Grant No. ZR2014FP016, the Research Funds for the Central Universities under Grant Nos. HIT.NSRIF.2016100 and HIT.NSRIF.201720, Subject Guide Foundation under Grant No. 201509, and the Scientific Research Foundation of Harbin Institute of Technology at Weihai under Grant Nos. HIT(WH)201409 and HIT(WH)201410.

The author would like to be grateful to the Editor and anonymous reviewers for their invaluable comments and suggestions, which have improved the quality of the paper significantly.

References

1. Elias, P., Feinstein, A., Shannon, C.E.: A note on the maximum flow through a network. IEEE Trans. Inf. Theory **2**(4), 117–119 (1956)
2. Ahlswede, R., Cai, N., Li, S.-Y.R., Yeung, R.W.: Network information flow. IEEE Trans. Inf. Theory **46**(4), 1204–1216 (2000)
3. Zhang, S., Liew, S.C., Lam, P.: Hot topic physical layer network coding. In: 12th Annual International Conference on Mobile Computing and Networking, pp. 358–365. IEEE Press, Los Angeles (2006)
4. Zhao, M., Zhou, Y., Yuan, Q., Yang, Y.: Research survey on physical layer network coding. J. Comput. Appl. **31**(8), 2015–2020 (2011)
5. Qin, J., Yang, Z., Jiao, J., Zhang, Q., Lin, X., Cao, B.: On symbol mapping for FQPSK modulation enabled physical-layer network coding. In: IEEE Wireless Communications and Networking Conference, pp. 1516–1521. IEEE Press, Shanghai (2013)
6. Xie, Z., Zhang, G.: A constant envelope enhanced FQPSK modulation for deep space communication. J. Astronaut. **30**(3), 1095–1100+1158 (2009)

A Brief Review of Several Multi-carrier Transmission Techniques for 5G and Future Mobile Networks

Zhen-yu Na[1($\boxtimes$)], Xiao-tong Li[1], Xin Liu[2], Zhi-an Deng[1], and Xiao-ming Liu[1]

[1] School of Information Science and Technology,
Dalian Maritime University, Dalian 116026, China
{nazhenyu, dengzhian, lxmdmu}@dlmu.edu.cn,
xtongli@yeah.net
[2] School of Information and Communication Engineering,
Dalian University of Technology, Dalian 116024, China
liuxinstar1984@dlut.edu.cn

Abstract. In 5G and future mobile networks, multi-carrier techniques will greatly multiply data rate to meet people's requirements of high-speed mobile services. Traditionally, Orthogonal Frequency Division Multiplexing (OFDM) got a wide application for past decade. While OFDM has many nice aspects, it also has some disadvantages making it less attractive in the fifth generation (5G). Based on this, several advanced techniques supposed in latest literature were expected to replace OFDM because of their respective technical advantages in spectrum efficiency, complexity, compatibility and some aspects. Filter Bank Multi Carrier (FBMC), Generalized Frequency Division Multiplexing (GFDM) and Filter Bank OFDM (FB-OFDM) were reviewed in this paper. Also, their characteristics were compared with each other briefly.

Keywords: Mobile network · Multi-carrier transmission · OFDM · FBMC · FB-OFDM

1 Introduction

As the most popular signal transmission technique, Orthogonal Frequency Division Multiplexing (OFDM) has enjoyed its dominance on broadband wired and wireless channels, which was listed in the technical specifications, such as LTE-A of 3GPP. It is obvious that OFDM has high spectrum efficiency, low complexity and easy

This paper was supported by the National Natural Science Foundation of China (Grant Nos. 61301131 and 61601221), the Scientific Research General Project of Liaoning Province Education Commission (Grant No. L2014204), the Natural Science Foundation of Jiangsu Province (Grant No. BK20140828), the Chinese Postdoctoral Science Foundation (Grant No. 2015M580425) and the Fundamental Research Funds for the Central Universities (Grant No. DUT16RC(3)045).

© ICST Institute for Computer Sciences, Social Informatics and Telecommunications Engineering 2018
Q. Chen et al. (Eds.): ChinaCom 2016, Part II, LNICST 210, pp. 569–576, 2018.
DOI: 10.1007/978-3-319-66628-0_54

combination with Multiple Input Multiple Output (MIMO). However, its deficiencies also apparent: high Peak-to-Average Power Ratio (PAPR), sensitive to frequency offset and low out-of-band power decay [1]. The long-term vision of the fifth generation (5G) and future mobile network includes providing higher spectrum efficiency, supporting massive MIMO and distributed low-power terminal. In view of these requirements, OFDM may not be the optimal solution to the physical layer of 5G and future mobile network partially due to the rectangular pulse shaping adopted in OFDM. With strict specifications, innovative multi-carrier modulation techniques with different pulse shaping filters are proposed as alternative solutions.

As the typical representatives, three multi-carrier techniques proposed lately were addressed in this paper: Generalized Frequency Division Multiplexing (GFDM), Filter Bank Multi-Carrier (FBMC) and Filter Bank OFDM (FB-OFDM). GFDM adopts flexible pulse shaping so that have lower out-of-band radiation. Compared with OFDM, it is featured by lower complexity. FBMC havs higher spectral efficiency and avoids inter-symbol interference (ISI) effectively. On the basis of FBMC, FB-OFDM well deals with two aspects: complexity and compatibility. Thus, the technique is easier to realize. Each technique has its merits, which will be analyzed in the following sections.

The remainder of the paper is organized as follows: Sects. 2, 3 and 4 introduce the design principles and characters of GFDM, FBMC and FB-OFDM respectively. Then, In Sect. 5, comparison and analysis, the compatibility and complexity of each multi-carrier technique are presented and analyzed. Finally, the conclusions of this paper are drawn.

2 GFDM

GFDM is a kind of alternative solution on physical layer in the future 5G mobile communications which incorporates with tail-biting technique [2]. Since OFDM uses rectangular pulse shaping causing extensive spectral leakage, GFDM system adopts flexible pulse shaping (generally Root Raised Cosine or Raised Cosine) aiming to lower out-of-band radiation.

The transmitter part of GFDM technique is shown in Fig. 1. First, binary data is modulated and then divided into several sequences. Next, by applying circular convolution the transmitted signal implements filtering function. Then, sub-carrier up-conversion is performed. Similar to OFDM, GFDM also needs to add cyclic prefix (CP) in transmitter to transmit the signal flow. Further, the modulated signal is concerted to analog signal from digital signal by D/A converter and sent to the channel. The receiver part of GFDM multi-carrier system is shown in Fig. 2. After analog-to-digital (A/D) conversion, CP is removed from the receiver. Then, after channel equalization, sub-carrier down-conversion is realized [3]. Next, the signal goes through the matched received filter, the signal finally obtained after sampling and detection process.

In GFDM, due to the flexibility of shaping pulse, orthogonality is lost between sub-carries leading to the increase of Inter-Carrier Interference (ICI). So compared with

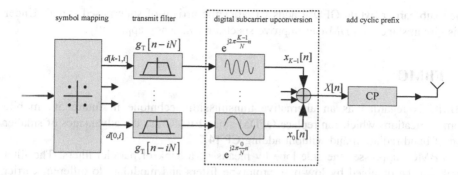

Fig. 1. The transmitter part of GFDM system

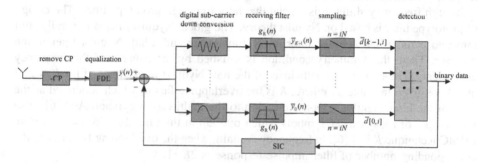

Fig. 2. The receiver part of GFDM system

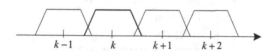

Fig. 3. The adjacent sub-carries interference in frequency domain

OFDM, GFDM has worse BER performance. As shown in Fig. 3, in frequency domain, the adjacent sub-carries interference causes ICI.

To solve the problem, Serial Interference Cancellation (SIC) is adopted in GFDM system [3]. Once a sub-carrier is detected, it is modulated once again and pulse shaping is done before up-conversion to generate the approximate transmitted signal. Then, the estimated signal is subtracted from the received signal. The same procedure is executed when the next sub-carrier comes.

There exist three differences between OFDM and GFDM: (1) GFDM does not apply rectangular pulse while OFDM does. This results in not only faster out-of-band decay but also decreased ICI for GFDM. (2) GFDM applies circular convolution in filtering process which makes GFDM less in time delay and lower computation complexity. (3) The different ways to add CP: OFDM adds CP after the modulation of each sub-carrier, while GFDM adds CP after the arrival of superposed signal. Under this circumstance, GFDM can improve spectrum efficiency apparently.

3   FBMC

FBMC is regarded as an alternative transmission technique in future 5G mobile communications which can replace OFDM since FBMC has the advantages of smaller out-of-band radiation and without adding CP [4].

FBMC suppresses the side lobe by means of a bank of parallel filters. The filter bank can be obtained by low-pass prototype filters and modulate to different carrier frequency respectively [5]. The first filter in the bank, the filter associated with the zero frequency carriers, is called prototype filter, because the other filters are deduced from it through frequency shifts. It is crucial that how to design prototype filter. The design of prototype filter is based on Nyquist theory. The global Nyquist filter is generally split into two parts, a half-Nyquist filter in the transmitter and a half-Nyquist filter in the receiver. Then, the symmetry condition is satisfied by the squares of the frequency coefficients. The frequency coefficients of the half-Nyquist filter obtained for $K = 2, 3$ and 4 are given in Table 1. Where, K is the overlapping factor, which is defined as the ratio of the filter impulse response duration to the multi-carrier symbol. And it is also the number of multi-carrier symbols which overlap in the time domain. Generally, in FBMC technique K is 4 [6]. In frequency domain, when the overlapping factor is K, the corresponding number of filter impulse response is $2K-1$.

Table 1. Frequency domain prototype filter coefficients

K	H_0	H_1	H_2	H_3
2	1	0.707106		
3	1	0.911438	0.411438	
4	1	0.971960	0.707106	0.235174

A particular realization structure of FBMC is called poly-phase network (PPN). PPN realizes the filtering function at time domain which can reduce calculation amount notably. The implementation of FBMC using PPN is shown in Fig. 4. In the transmitter, first of all, IFFT is applied to the input signals. And then, filtering is achieved by PPN. Finally, the output of the transmitter is the total of sub-channel filtering output.

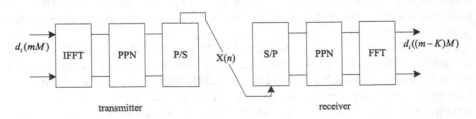

Fig. 4. The construction of PPN-FBMC

Because of the overlapping of adjacent sub-channels in frequency domain, FBMC uses a special modulation called Offset Quadrature Amplitude Modulation (OQAM) [7]. OQAM separates the input into real part and imaginary part, but the imaginary part is delayed by half the symbol duration, so that the real part and the imaginary part can output separately. OQAM makes sure all the sub-channels are exploited.

The most obvious distinction between OFDM and FBMC is that FBMC abandons CP to gain higher spectral efficiency. OFDM suffers from significant spectral leakage, while FBMC overcomes this shortcoming.

4 FB-OFDM

FBMC is a huge step forward to the technical level with good spectrum containment and relaxing synchronization condition. However, there exist two problems suspended, i.e. compatibility and complexity. The complexity is related to modulation and demodulation for a multi-carrier system, channel estimation, equalization, MIMO pre/decoding, etc. The compatibility means that FBMC should be able to reuse the existing Long Term Evolution (LTE) techniques in a straightforward manner. To solve these two problems, a new solution called FB-OFDM has been put forward.

The steps of signal processing of FB-OFDM are shown in Fig. 5. The modulation is consists of four parts: (1) symbol extension; (2) filtering process; (3) mapping and the last (4) MK-point IFFT, where M refers to sub-carries number and K is the extension factor [8].

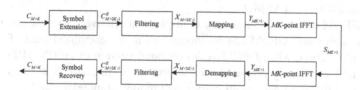

Fig. 5. The signal processing of FB-OFDM

Since OQAM processes the real part and imaginary part symbols separately to achieve high spectral efficiency, which leads to double complexity, in the first part of FB-OFDM, QAM symbol extension is used instead of OQAM compared with FBMC by some specific algorithms. The QAM symbols need to be extended according to some pre-defined pattern. Once the extension is accomplished, it then goes to the filtering part. Next, it goes to the mapping process by some overlap-sum operation which is later fed to the IFFT entries. The last step is using an MK-point IFFT to transform the combinational symbols from frequency domain to time domain. In theory, FB-OFDM also keeps full Nyquist rate as the classical FBMC. The difference between them is that FB-OFDM transmits QAM symbols instead of OQAM.

The FB-OFDM demodulation process is completely dual to the modulation process. The received signal uses MK-point FFT to transform to frequency domain at first. Then, each sub-carrier goes to the de-mapping part. Next, the filtering process is identical to the modulation part [9]. At last, the dual operation is taken to the extension process to recover the transmitted QAM symbol.

In a practical multi-carrier system, only some parts of sub-carriers are used. Moreover, these sub-carriers are separated into several chunks so that the chunks can be allocated to multiple users. In FB-OFDM, overlapping at the extended symbol layer will cause inter-user interference when adjacent chunks are allocated to different users. To solve the problem, null symbols are inserted to the first or the last sub-carrier of the extended symbols. However, transmitting null symbols leads to the decrease of spectral efficiency. Fortunately, the loss is not significant when the chunk number is equal or greater than two.

FB-OFDM has two advantages over FBMC: complexity and compatibility. FB-OFDM does not process the real parts and the imaginary separately which makes the system more concise. Moreover, FB-OFDM does not overlap in time domain which makes system more flexible.

5 Brief Analysis

The technical implementation processes of FBMC, GFDM and FB-OFDM were expounded in previous sections. Their technical features were also mentioned. As a summary, the following technical comparisons were presented.

In general, FBMC is an asynchronous transmission technique with high spectral efficiency. The outstanding feature of FBMC is without CP. However, to keep the high spectral efficiency, FBMC has to adopt OQAM modulation. It causes the highly difficult compatibility with MIMO.

Since GFDM reserves CP, it is easy to implement relatively because complex filter design is unnecessary. GFDM can be thought of as a generalized case of frequency division multiplexing, while OFDM is degenerated version of GFDM [10–12].

FB-OFDM is a newly proposed modulation mode in 2015. It relieves two difficulties in traditional FBMC multi-carrier technique: complexity and compatibility. Actually, OFDM can be seen as one special case of FB-OFDM. Thereby, the techniques already suitable for OFDM, such as channel estimation, equalization can be easily applied to FB-OFDM system.

When it is comes to implementation complexity, we suppose the total number of the carriers is N, and M sub-carriers are used in practice. The evaluation criterion of complexity is the multiplication times when SM signal flows are transmitted. The expressions of complexity of OFDM, PPN-FBMC, GFDM and FB-OFDM are given below, respectively [8]:

$$SN \log_2 N$$
$$SK(N \log_2 N + 2M + N \log_2 K)$$
$$S(N \log_2 N + (N + M) \log_2 M)$$
$$(2N(K - 1) - K + 1)/2 \tag{1}$$

where K is overlapping factor. It is apparent that FB-OFDM is easiest to be implemented, while PPN-FBMC and GFDM are relatively difficult because their complexity depends on parameters setting.

6 Conclusion

In 5G and future mobile networks, high-speed multimedia applications will dominate the majority of services. It requires that new multi-carrier techniques keep pace with the trend. In view of this situation, several multi-carrier transmission techniques proposed in recent years were reviewed. In contrast to traditional OFDM, FBMC, GFDM and FB-OFDM are now attracting more and more attention. These techniques overcome drawbacks of OFDM in this aspect or another, in the meantime, focus on the easy implementation.

From the perspective of computation complexity, FB-OFDM is the simplest. FBMC and GFDM can suppress the side lobe leakage effectively. The sub-band filters of FBMC are allowed to overlap each other, so it has high spectrum efficiency compared with GFDM and FB-OFDM. On the other hand, FBMC is restricted in the combination with MIMO due to OQAM modulation. But, GFDM and FB-OFDM have simplified and flexible structure.

Concentrating on three typical cases, the developmental trend of multi-carrier techniques was reviewed in this paper. So far, multi-carrier transmission technique has still been the hot focus for 5G and future mobile networks and more suspended issues have been under investigations.

References

1. Farhang-Boroujeny, B.: OFDM versus filter bank multicarrier. IEEE Signal Process. Mag. **28**(3), 92–112 (2011)
2. Vilaipornsawai, U., Jia, M.: Scattered-pilot channel estimation for GFDM. In: IEEE Wireless Communications and Networking Conference (WCNC), New York, pp. 1053–1058. IEEE Press (2014)
3. Datta, R., Fettweis, G., Koll´r, Z., Horv´th, P.S., Foster, I.: FBMC and GFDM interference cancellation schemes for flexible digital radio PHY design. In: 14th Euromicro Conference on Digital System Design (DSD), pp. 335–339 (2011)
4. Qu, S.L., Jiang, T.: Multi-block joint optimization for the peak-to-average power ratio reduction of FBMC-OQAM signals. IEEE Trans. Signal Process. **61**(7), 1605–1613 (2013)
5. Berg, J.B.D., Noguet, D.: A flexible FS-FBMC receiver for dynamic access in the TVWS. In: 9th International Conference on Cognitive Radio Oriented Wireless Networks and Communications (CROWNCOM), New York, pp. 285–290. IEEE Press (2014)
6. Bellanger, M.: FBMC: physical layer: a primer. In: ICT-PHYDYAS Project, pp. 131–133 (2010)
7. Lu, S., Qu, D., He, Y.: Sliding window tone reservation technique for the peak-to-average power ratio reduction of FBMC-OQAM signals. Wirel. Commun. Lett. **1**(4), 268–271 (2012)

8. Lin, H.: Filter bank OFDM: a new way of looking at FBMC. In: IEEE International Conference on Communication Workshop (ICCW), New York, pp. 1077–1082. IEEE Press (2015)

9. Gutiérrez, F.A., Martin, E.P., Perry, P.: 100 Gbit/s real-time all-analogue filter bank OFDM based on a gain-switched optical comb. In: European Conference on Optical Communication (ECOC), New York, pp. 1–3. IEEE Press (2015)

10. RezazadehReyhani, A., Farhang, A., Farhang-Boroujeny, B.: Circularly pulse-shaped waveforms for 5G: options and comparisons. In: IEEE Global Communications Conference (GLOBECOM), New York, pp. 1–7. IEEE Press (2015)

11. Matthe, M., Gaspar, I., Zhang, D., Fettweis, G.: Near-ML detection for MIMO-GFDM. In: 82nd IEEE Vehicular Technology Conference (VTC), New York, pp. 1–2. IEEE Press (2015)

12. Datta, R., Panaitopol, D., Fettweis, G.: Cyclostationary detection of 5G GFDM waveform in cognitive radio transmission. In: IEEE International Conference on Ultra-WideBand, New York, pp. 108–112. IEEE Press (2014)

RSSI Based Positioning Fusion Algorithm in Wireless Sensor Network Using Factor Graph

Wanlong Zhao[1(✉)], Shuai Han[1], Weixiao Meng[1], and Zijun Gong[2]

[1] Communication Research Center, Harbin Institute of Technology, Harbin, China
zhaowanlong001@sina.cn, {hanshuai,wxmeng}@hit.edu.cn
[2] Memorial University of Newfoundland, St. John's, Canada
zg7454@mun.ca

Abstract. Various positioning techniques have been widely developed based on received signal strength indicator (RSSI) in Wireless Sensor Network (WSN) positioning systems. Multilateration-based positioning technique is simple and easy to realize, but it can not provide very high positioning accuracy caused by fluctuation of range measurement. Fingerprinting technique is a promising method benefitting from its high precision. However, the process of building radio map cost too much time and labor. In this paper, a fusion algorithm based on both multilateration and fingerprinting is proposed to reduce cost and maintain high accuracy at the same time. An adaptive radio propagation mode is presented in this algorithm as well as a multilateration approaches based on sparse fingerprint. Factor graph is adopted to fuse the results of these two positioning techniques. Simulation experiments demonstrate that the proposed positioning fusion algorithm performs much better than any of the original algorithms participated in the fusion process.

Keywords: Wireless Sensor Network (WSN) · Received Signal Strength Indicator (RSSI) · Fingerprinting · Multilateration · Fusion algorithm · Factor graph

1 Introduction

Location Based Services (LBS) are attracting more and more attentions. Although Global Navigation Satellite System (GNSS) performs very well in outdoor environment, it can work scarcely in indoor environment causing of the insufficient satellite coverage. In indoor localization, Wireless Sensor Network (WSN) positioning system is a good choice befitting from its low cost, easy implementation and high positioning accuracy. In WSN positioning systems, the location of unknown nodes is determined by anchor nodes [1].

There are two elementary kinds of positioning approaches frequently used in WSN positioning which are range based approaches and range free approaches [2]. In the range based approaches, multilateration technique is a key method to position the unknown node based on estimated distances between unknown nodes and anchor nodes. The distances are estimated by using some

© ICST Institute for Computer Sciences, Social Informatics and Telecommunications Engineering 2018
Q. Chen et al. (Eds.): ChinaCom 2016, Part II, LNICST 210, pp. 577–586, 2018.
DOI: 10.1007/978-3-319-66628-0_55

physical properties of communication signals, such as time-of-arrival (TOA), time-difference-of-arrival (TDOA), angle-of-arrival (AOA) and received signal strength indicator (RSSI) [3]. Precise synchronized clocks are required in TOA and TDOA, which is difficult to implement in practical applications. As AOA is easily influenced by the external environment and needs complex hardware devices, it is not only to increase the cost but also unsuitable for large-scale sensor networks. The radio propagation model is adopted in RSSI technique. The range between anchor node and unknown node is achieved by calculating signal propagation loss. Although it owns advantages of low cost and easy to realize, the positioning accuracy is worse than other approaches. The typical technique in range free approaches is fingerprinting which is also based on RSSI. There are two phases in fingerprinting. In the offline phase, the RSSI is collected at reference points (RPs) and then stored in a database named radio map. In the online phase, the target location is determined by comparing the rear-time collected RSSI with radio map using match algorithms such as KNN. Higher accuracy can be obtained by fingerprinting technique, however, the process of building radio map is a big challenge in terms of labor and time.

In this paper, a fusion positioning algorithm based on RSSI in WSN is proposed. The motivation is to deliver stable and precise position information in WSN by manipulating erratic and unstable RSSI signals [4]. The proposed algorithm is a combination of fingerprinting technique and radio propagation model based multilateration technique. A factor graph framework is used to achieve the final location information by fusing the positioning results from two positioning techniques. [5] proposed a kalman filter-based bybrid fusion approaches based on integration of fingerprinting and trilateration techniques, in which the radio propagation model is replaced by Euclidian distance formula to estimate distance. However, a radio map with high density is needed to achieve high positioning accuracy. In the proposed algorithm, only a sparse radio map is needed which reduces the workload of building radio map greatly. Under a factor graph framework, the proposed algorithm attempts to exploit the complementary advantages of these two algorithms to achieve a better positioning accuracy.

The remainder of this paper is organized as follows. Section 2 describes the proposed algorithms which include an adaptive radio propagation model, multilateration approaches based on sparse fingerprint and factor graph based fusion algorithm. In Sect. 2, several simulation experiments are conducted to verify performance of the proposed algorithms. Conclusions are given in the last section.

2 Proposed Algorithm

2.1 An Adaptive Radio Propagation Model

In the process of signal propagation, the overall effect results in lognormal distribution of received power at receiver. A general radio propagation model can be expressed as Eq. 1.

$$P(d) = P(d_0) - 10 \times \alpha \times \log_{10}(\frac{d}{d_0}) + \varepsilon \tag{1}$$

where $P(d)$ and $P(d_0)$ indicate the mean power received at reference distance d and d_0, respectively. $d_0 = 1\,\mathrm{m}$ is adopted in usual situations. The path loss exponent α is determined by environment. In free space, this exponent is selected as $\alpha = 2$. ε presents the noise caused by shadow fading and fast fading.

Based on the model, the distance d can be expressed as Eq. 2.

$$d = d_0 \times 10^{\frac{P(d_0)-P(d)+\varepsilon}{10\alpha}} \tag{2}$$

where ε is Gaussian distributed random variable with zero mean and variance σ_ω^2, $\varepsilon \sim N(0, \sigma_\omega^2)$.

In view of the system model, literature [6] proposed an unbiased estimator, in which the distance in the model is estimated as Eq. 3.

$$\hat{d} = d_0 \times 10^{\left(\frac{P(d_0)-P(d)}{10\alpha} - \frac{\sigma_\omega^2 ln 10}{2(10\alpha)^2}\right)} \tag{3}$$

At the same time, the author presented a method to take multi-time ranging to restrain the fluctuation of RSSI. However, when the RSSI fluctuates very widely, it will lead to big deviation especially when the number of measuring times is not enough. To resolve this problem, an adaptive iterative algorithm is designed. During which, the σ_ω in Eq. 3 is self-updated through iteration step by step.

Algorithm 1. Adaptive Iterative Algorithm

Input
   The set of measurement RSSI, $\{\varepsilon \sim N(0, \sigma_i^2)\}$;
Output
   The estimated RSSI, $\{\varepsilon \sim N(0, \sigma_\Omega^2)\}$;
Initial
   $\sigma_\Omega^2 = \sigma_0^2$;
while $\| \sigma_i^2 \| \neq 0$ **do**
   $\sigma_i^2 = \frac{\sigma_i^2 \sigma_{i-1}^2}{\sigma_i^2 + \sigma_{i-1}^2}$;
end while
   $\sigma_\Omega^2 = \sigma_i^2$;
Return σ_Ω^2;

Using the adaptive iterative algorithm, the fluctuation of RSSI is more gentle. The σ_ω^2 in Eq. 3 is replaced by σ_Ω^2. Then the estimate of $\hat{d}$ will be much more precision. The algorithm will be verified by the simulations in Sect. 3.1.

2.2 Multilateration Approaches Based on Sparse Fingerprint

Fingerprinting positioning technique is a combination of offline building radio map and online matching positioning. The offline phase is a training phase where RSSI fingerprints are collected to build radio map. In the WSN fingerprinting system, the network is usually divided into grids with the same size. The reference points (RPs) is located in the grids. The radio map is built jointly by the location coordinates and RSSI of all RPs. In a general way, the bigger the density of the radio map is, the higher the positioning accuracy will be. In online phase, the location of positioning target is determined by using matching algorithm. K-Nearest Neighbors (KNN) is the most popular matching algorithm in fingerprinting. The parameter K indicates the number of the nearest RPs to target point (TP). Supposing there are n RPs totally, the signal distance between TP and the ith RP is calculated as:

$$D_p = (\sum_{i=1}^{n} | TP - RP_i |^p)^{1/p} \qquad (4)$$

when $p = 1$ and $p = 2$, the distance is named Manhattan distance and Euclidean distance, respectively. And the Euclidean distance is the most commonly used.

During fingerprinting process, the building of radio map with high density will cost too much time and labor. To overcome this problem, in this paper, a sparse fingerprint is proposed as shown in Fig. 1. RPs are presented by blue circles in the grids. From this figure, it can be seen that all of the grids are collected to be RPs in usual radio map. However, lots of the grids will be given up to be RPs in the radio map of sparse fingerprint. Taken the Fig. 1(b) and (c) as examples, the density of radio map is reduced greatly. The number of RPs is cut down more than half in the level-1 sparse radio map, further more, the level-2 sparse radio map is only one-sixteenth than usual radio map. Concurrently, the work load of building radio map is decreased with the same ratio.

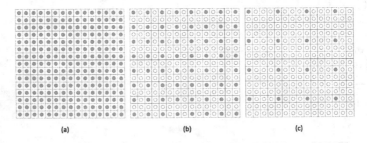

Fig. 1. (a) An usual radio map, (b) A level-1 sparse radio map, (c) A level-2 sparse radio map. (Color figure online)

Obviously, by using KNN algorithm, the positioning accuracy is worse when the density of radio map decreases. It is cased that the final positioning result is achieved by the average of RPs in KNN. In order to improve the positioning precision, a multilateration approaches based on sparse fingerprint (MASF) is proposed as followed.

The diagram of multilateration approaches is shown in Fig. 2(a). During multilateration in WSN, the location of unknown node is estimated only if not less than three anchor nodes can be used. The anchor nodes are arranged in fixed position in WSN.

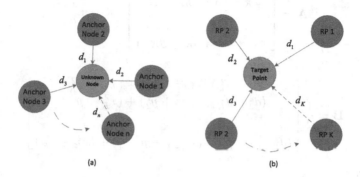

(a)   (b)

Fig. 2. (a) Diagram of multilateration approaches, (b) Multilateration in sparse fingerprint.

Based on KNN, we can get K nearest RPs with their location coordinates and RSSI. In MASF, as shown in Fig. 2(b), the selected RPs are considered as the anchor nodes. And the target point is considered to be unknown node. As the anchor nodes are replaced by RPs, there is no need to know the location information of anchor nodes any more, which is different with general WSN positioning. The distance between anchor nodes and unknown node is estimated by the adaptive radio propagation model which is shown in Sect. 2.1. Supposing that the coordinates of nearest RPs are $(x_j, y_j), j = 1, 2, ... K$, the distance between unknown node and the jth anchor node is indicated as $d_j, j = 1, 2, ... K$. The location coordinate of unknown node is assumed to be (x, y). Then we can get the formula as shown in Eq. 5.

$$\begin{cases} (x - x_1)^2 + (y - y_1)^2 = d_1^2 \\ (x - x_2)^2 + (y - y_2)^2 = d_2^2 \\ \vdots \\ (x - x_K)^2 + (y - y_K)^2 = d_K^2 \end{cases} \tag{5}$$

After a series of mathematical transformations, the Eq. 5 can be transformed to be Eq. 6.

$$\begin{bmatrix} x_K - x_1 & y_K - y_1 \\ x_K - x_1 & y_K - y_2 \\ \vdots & \vdots \\ x_K - x_{K-1} & y_K - y_{K-1} \end{bmatrix} \begin{bmatrix} x \\ y \end{bmatrix} = \frac{1}{2} \begin{bmatrix} (d_1^2 - d_K^2) - (x_1^2 + y_1^2) + (x_K^2 + y_K^2) \\ (d_2^2 - d_K^2) - (x_2^2 + y_2^2) + (x_K^2 + y_K^2) \\ \vdots \\ (d_{K-1}^2 - d_K^2) - (x_{K-1}^2 + y_{K-1}^2) + (x_K^2 + y_K^2) \end{bmatrix} \tag{6}$$

Let

$$\mathbf{A} = \begin{bmatrix} x_K - x_1 & y_K - y_1 \\ x_K - x_1 & y_K - y_2 \\ \vdots & \vdots \\ x_K - x_{K-1} & y_K - y_{K-1} \end{bmatrix}, \mathbf{X} = \begin{bmatrix} x \\ y \end{bmatrix}$$

$$\mathbf{B} = \frac{1}{2} \begin{bmatrix} (d_1^2 - d_K^2) - (x_1^2 + y_1^2) + (x_K^2 + y_K^2) \\ (d_2^2 - d_K^2) - (x_2^2 + y_2^2) + (x_K^2 + y_K^2) \\ \vdots \\ (d_{K-1}^2 - d_K^2) - (x_{K-1}^2 + y_{K-1}^2) + (x_K^2 + y_K^2) \end{bmatrix} \tag{7}$$

then we can get:

$$\mathbf{AX} = \mathbf{B} \tag{8}$$

or

$$\mathbf{X} = (\mathbf{A}^T \mathbf{A})^{-1} \mathbf{A}^T \mathbf{B} \tag{9}$$

The unknown node lies at the intersection of all the circles. However, not only one point is intersected by all the circles caused by noise. To minimize the location error, the minimum mean square error (MMSE) technique is adopted to estimate the coordinate of unknown node.

Although only a sparse radio map is used in the proposed multilateration approaches based on sparse fingerprint (MASF), the positioning accuracy still maintains at a high level benefitting adopt the adaptive radio propagation model and multilateration technique. At the same time, the workload of fingerprinting positioning is reduced greatly. The performance of MASF will be verified in the simulation experiments.

2.3   Fusion Algorithm Based on Factor Graph

Factor graph is a relatively new modeling framework which has been used in a wide variety of applications. It is used for multi-source data fusion in wireless localization in [7]. In this paper, the KNN and MASF are considered to be two different fusion sources in WSN positioning. A better positioning result will be achieved by fusing these two positioning algorithm using factor graph. The core of factor graph is sun-product algorithm, which is shown in Fig. 3 in detail.

There are two kinds of nodes in factor graph named variable nodes and function nodes. The soft-information transmitted in factor graph can be expressed as:

$$\begin{cases} \mu_{x \to f}(x) = \prod_{\mathbf{H}/x} \mu_{h \to x}(x), \\ \mu_{f \to x}(x) = \sum_{\sim x} \{ f(\mathbf{Y}) \prod_{\mathbf{Y}/x} \mu_{y \to f}(y) \} \end{cases} \tag{10}$$

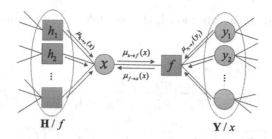

Fig. 3. Soft-information transmission rules in sum-product algorithm.

where x indicates variable nodes, f presents function nodes in factor graph. $\mathbf{H}/f$ denotes all the nodes connected to x other than f and $\mathbf{Y}/x$ means all the nodes connected to f other than x. $\mu_{x \to f}(x)$ and $\mu_{f \to x}(x)$ stand for the soft-information transmitted from x to f and from f to x, respectively.

Supposing that soft-information measurements satisfy Gaussian distribution with mean being m and variance being σ. The soft information is defined to be I. Noted that the product of any Gaussian Probability Distribution Functions (PDF) is still a Gaussian PDF, the soft-information can be expressed as:

$$\begin{cases} I = \{m_I, \sigma_I\} \\ \prod_{i=1}^{k} N(x, m_i, \sigma_i^2) \propto N(x, m_I, \sigma_I^2) \end{cases} \tag{11}$$

where

$$\begin{cases} \dfrac{1}{\sigma_I^2} = \sum_{i=1}^{k} \dfrac{1}{\sigma_i^2} \\ m_I = \sigma_I^2 \sum_{i=1}^{k} \dfrac{m_i}{\sigma_i^2} \end{cases} \tag{12}$$

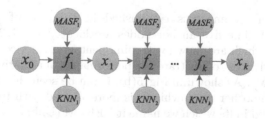

Fig. 4. Fusion structure model based on factor graph.

A fusion structure model is designed based on factor graph shown in Fig. 4. The KNN variable node and MASF variable node is fused in function node.

Based on the fusion structure model, the soft-information is obtained as shown in Eq. 13.

$$
\begin{cases}
I_{x_0} = \{m_0, \sigma_o^2\} \\
I_{x_1^0} = \{\dfrac{1}{1/\sigma_{K_1}^2 + 1/\sigma_{M_1}^2}(\dfrac{m_{K_1}}{\sigma_{K_1}^2} + \dfrac{m_{M_1}}{\sigma_{M_1}^2}), \dfrac{1}{1/\sigma_{K_1}^2 + 1/\sigma_{M_1}^2}\} \\
I_{x_1} = \{\dfrac{1}{1/\sigma_{x_0}^2 + 1/\sigma_{x_1^0}^2}(\dfrac{m_{x_0}}{\sigma_{x_0}^2} + \dfrac{m_{x_1^0}}{\sigma_{x_1^0}^2}), \dfrac{1}{1/\sigma_{x_0}^2 + 1/\sigma_{x_1^0}^2}\} \\
\qquad\qquad \vdots \\
I_{x_k^0} = \{\dfrac{1}{1/\sigma_{K_k}^2 + 1/\sigma_{M_k}^2}(\dfrac{m_{K_k}}{\sigma_{K_k}^2} + \dfrac{m_{M_k}}{\sigma_{M_k}^2}), \dfrac{1}{1/\sigma_{K_k}^2 + 1/\sigma_{M_k}^2}\} \\
I_{x_k} = \{\dfrac{1}{1/\sigma_{x_{k-1}}^2 + 1/\sigma_{x_k^0}^2}(\dfrac{m_{x_{k-1}}}{\sigma_{x_{k-1}}^2} + \dfrac{m_{x_k^0}}{\sigma_{x_k^0}^2}), \dfrac{1}{1/\sigma_{x_{k-1}}^2 + 1/\sigma_{x_k^0}^2}\},
\end{cases}
\tag{13}
$$

where $\{m_0, \sigma_o^2\}$ indicites initial input of fusion process. $\{m_K, \sigma_K^2\}$ and $\{m_M, \sigma_M^2\}$ present the positioning result of KNN and MASF, respectively. The fusion result is m_{x_k} as shown in Eq. 14.

$$
m_{x_k} = \frac{1}{1/\sigma_{x_{k-1}}^2 + 1/\sigma_{x_k^0}^2}(\frac{m_{x_{k-1}}}{\sigma_{x_{k-1}}^2} + \frac{m_{x_k^0}}{\sigma_{x_k^0}^2})
\tag{14}
$$

The location information of KNN and MASF are utilized adequately in the factor graph framework, which can improve positioning accuracy effectively.

3   Simulation Experiments

To verify the performance of the proposed algorithms, some simulation experiments are taken as follows.

3.1   Performance of Adaptive Radio Propagation Model

The simulation environment is established in a space of 25 m × 20 m as shown in Fig. 5(a). The five anchor nodes are located at $(7, 2), (18, 2), (3, 12),$ $(22, 12), (12.5, 8)$, which are shown with pink pentagrams. A contrast simulation experiment is conducted to illustrate the performance of adaptive radio propagation model (ARPM). As shown in Fig. 5(b), it can be seen that the trajectory of ARPM is much smoother, meanwhile it is more aligned with the real trajectory than the model used in [6] which we name it UERPM (Unbiased Estimator based radio propagation model). Figure 5(c) shows the cumulative distribution function (CDF) of the positioning error which is the root-mean-square error (RMSE) between the positioning results and the true coordinates. From the figure, it is clearly seen that both the ARPM and UERPM perform better than the general radio propagation model, meanwhile ARPM is more outstanding.

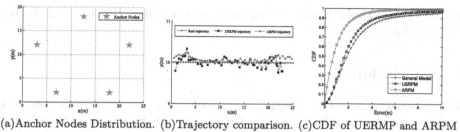

(a)Anchor Nodes Distribution. (b)Trajectory comparison. (c)CDF of UERMP and ARPM

Fig. 5. Performance simulation of adaptive radio propagation model

3.2 Performance of MAFS

The second simulation experiment is taken based on an actually measured radio map. The experiment is taken in $12th$ floor, 2A Building, Harbin Institute of Technology. Four CISCO AIR 1242 Access Points (AP) are adopted to build two kinds of radio map with grids size of $2 * 2\,m^2$ and $4 * 4\,m^2$, respectively. Compared to $2 * 2\,m^2$ radio map, the $4 * 4\,m^2$ radio map is considered to be sparse fingerprint. CDF of positioning error is used to demonstrate the performance of KNN and MASF. In the experiment, the parameter K is set to be 4. As shown in Fig. 6 (a), the proposed algorithm MASF performs much better than KNN obviously. Using the sparse radio map, the positioning accuracy within 1 m of MASF achieves 75%, while KNN is only 48%. The MASF using $4 * 4\,m^2$ radio map performs basically the same as KNN using $2 * 2\,m^2$ radio map. The fact that positioning accuracy can be improved by MASF is verified in this experiment.

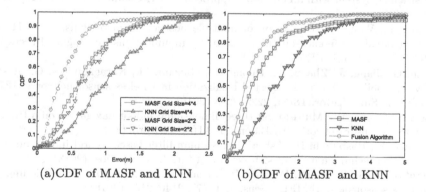

(a)CDF of MASF and KNN   (b)CDF of MASF and KNN

Fig. 6. Performance simulation of MASF and fusion algorithm

3.3 Performance of Fusion Algorithm Based on Factor Graph

In this simulation, the CDF is chosen to be evaluation criteria similarly. As shown in Fig. 6(b), taken positioning error within 2 meters as an example, the CDF of KNN, MASF and factor graph based fusion algorithm are 72%, 87%, and 95%, respectively. It can be seen that the fusion algorithm performs better than any fusion source.

4   Conclusion

A RSSI measurement based positioning fusion algorithm in WSN is proposed in this paper. An adaptive radio propagation model is presented to restrain the fluctuation of RSSI based range measurement. In addition, to improve the positioning performance more deeply, a multilateration approaches based on sparse fingerprint is proposed to reduce the cost of building radio map in fingerprinting technique. A fusion algorithm based on factor graph is proposed to fuse two different positioning algorithms of MASF and KNN. The fusion algorithm takes full advantages of both multilateration and fingerprinting techniques and outperforms conventional methods. Some simulation experiments are conducted to confirm performance of all the proposed algorithms.

Acknowledgments. This work was supported by the National Natural Science Foundation of China (No. 61401119), the National Science and Technology Major Project (No. 2015ZX03004002-004), the Distinguished Academic Leadership Foundation of Harbin (No. 2014RFXXJ002) and the Science and Technology Project of Ministry of Public Security China (No. 2015GABJC37).

References

1. Fang, S.H., Wang, C.H., Huang, T.Y., Yang, C.H.: An enhanced ZigBee indoor positioning system with an ensemble approach. IEEE Commun. Lett. **16**(16), 564–567 (2012)
2. Wang, L., Wong, W.-C.: Fusion of multiple positioning algorithms. In: 2011 8th International Conference on Information, Communications and Signal Processing (ICICS), pp. 1–5. IEEE Press (2011)
3. Han, G., Jiang, J., Zhang, C., Duong, T., Guizani, M., Karagiannidis, G.: A survey on mobile anchor node assisted localization in wireless sensor networks. IEEE Commun. Surv. Tutor. **18**(3), 2220–2243 (2016)
4. Lee, B., Chung, W.: Multi-target three-dimensional indoor navigation on a PDA in a wireless sensor network. IEEE Sens. J. **11**(3), 799–807 (2011)
5. Subhan, F., Hasbullah, H., Ashraf, K.: Kalman filter-based hybrid indoor position estimation technique in bluetooth networks. Int. J. Navig. Obs. (2013)
6. Han, S., Gong, Z., Meng, W., Li, C.: Automatic precision control positioning for wireless sensor network. IEEE Sens. J. **16**(7), 2140–2150 (2016)
7. Zhao, W., Meng, W., Chi, Y., Han, S.: Factor graph based multi-source data fusion for wireless localization. In: IEEE Wireless Communications and Networking Conference, Doha, pp. 592–597. IEEE Press (2016)

Crowdsourcing-Based Indoor Propagation Model Localization Using Wi-Fi

Yongliang Sun[1,2(✉)], Jian Wang[2], Wenfeng Li[2],
Rui Jiang[1], and Naitong Zhang[2,3]

[1] School of Computer Science and Technology,
Nanjing Tech University, Nanjing, China
`syl_peter@163.com`
[2] School of Electronic Science and Engineering, Nanjing University, Nanjing, China
[3] Communication Research Center, Harbin Institute of Technology, Harbin, China

Abstract. To save labor and time costs, crowdsourcing has been used to collect received signal strength (RSS) for building radio-map of Wi-Fi fingerprinting localization with common users' mobile devices. However, usually a great number of crowdsourcing data should be collected to calculate a satisfactory localization result. Therefore, we proposed a crowdsourcing-based indoor propagation model (PM) localization system in this paper. Our system only needs to collect crowdsourcing data at a few locations called crowdsourcing points, which can be easily finished in a short time. The system first eliminates RSS outliers in crowdsourcing data and then optimizes PM parameters using the processed data. Furthermore, the processed data is also used to estimate a distance between a user and the nearest crowdsourcing point for coordinate correction. Experimental results show that our system is able to achieve a comparable performance and the mean error of PM localization method is reduced from 7.12 m to 3.78 m.

Keywords: Crowdsourcing · Wi-Fi localization · Outlier processing · Propagation model · Coordinate correction

1 Introduction

With the development and popularization of mobile devices, demand for location-based services (LBS) has been increasing rapidly. Owing to limitations of satellite and cellular network-based localization systems in indoor environments, various indoor localization systems based on different techniques, such as Wi-Fi, infrared and ultrasound, have been developed [1]. Among them, the localization systems using Wi-Fi are favored because Wi-Fi has been widely deployed for communications and its received signal strength (RSS) can be easily measured by commonly available mobile devices [2]. Several localization methods using Wi-Fi have been proposed like fingerprinting, propagation model (PM), time of arrival (TOA), time difference of arrival (TDOA), and angle of arrival (AOA) [2–4].

© ICST Institute for Computer Sciences, Social Informatics and Telecommunications Engineering 2018
Q. Chen et al. (Eds.): ChinaCom 2016, Part II, LNICST 210, pp. 587–596, 2018.
DOI: 10.1007/978-3-319-66628-0_56

Compared with TOA, TDOA and AOA, fingerprinting method has been extensively researched because it only needs software update and outperforms the other methods under non-line-of-sight (NLOS) environments. However, it requires a process of building a database called radio-map with location-labeled RSS samples. Real-time RSS samples are matched with the samples in the radio-map for coordinate estimation using fingerprinting algorithms like K-nearest neighbors (KNN), weighted KNN (WKNN) and artificial neural network (ANN) [3]. Usually the radio-map is established by professionals and the process involves intensive labor and time costs, so the application of fingerprinting method is limited to some degree. Regarding PM method, it needs no radio-map, but its performance heavily relies on the PM that is employed to calculate distances between a user and different access points (APs) for trilateration localization. So the performance of PM method is usually far from satisfactory.

Since crowdsourcing offers a new solution to data collection at low cost, it is very suitable for constructing the radio-map of fingerprinting method. Instead of professionals, crowdsourcing employs common users, namely crowdsourcing participants, to collect RSS and location information [5]. So far, several crowdsourcing-based fingerprinting localization systems have been proposed. Some of them labeled RSS samples with location information using indoor electronic maps [5,6]. Mirowski et al. deployed a number of two-dimensional code labels in their experimental environment, with which crowdsourcing participants are able to obtain location information of collected RSS samples [7]. Wu et al. recorded numerous trajectories of crowdsourcing participants with smartphone sensors and then matched the trajectories with RSS samples using multidimensional scaling (MDS) [8].

However, one problem of radio-map establishment through crowdsourcing is nearly no reliable localization coordinates can be obtained until enough crowdsourcing data are collected. To solve this problem, we apply crowdsourcing to PM method that requires no radio-map and propose a crowdsourcing-based indoor PM localization system using Wi-Fi. The proposed system only needs location-labeled RSS samples collected at a few crowdsourcing points (CPs). These RSS data can be easily collected in a short time and usually are not enough for fingerprinting method.

To improve the quality of crowdsourcing data, we eliminate RSS outliers with quartile method that does not involve RSS data distribution. Then the processed crowdsourcing data are used to optimize PM parameters for estimating more accurate distances between a user and APs, which improves the performance of trilateration localization. Because RSS data and location coordinates of CPs are known, the distance between a user and CP can be estimated and then used to correct coordinates calculated by trilateration localization. Before the collected crowdsourcing data are enough for building the radio-map of fingerprinting method, our proposed PM localization system is able to achieve a comparable performance. To the best of our knowledge, so far no localization system that employs crowdsourcing data to optimize PM parameters and also to correct trilateration localization results has been proposed.

The rest of this paper is organized as follows: Sect. 2 introduces the related works of our proposed crowdsourcing-based indoor PM localization system. In Sect. 3, a general frame of the proposed system is given and every part of it is described in details. The experimental setup, results and analyses are presented in Sect. 4. Finally, Sect. 5 concludes the paper.

2   Related Works

2.1   RSS Outlier Processing

Usually a certain amount of RSS samples should be collected by crowdsourcing participants. However, it will be boring for crowdsourcing participants to collect RSS data for a long time. Some researchers stated that the time for data collection at each CP should be less than one minute [9]. Thus, we collect RSS samples at every CP for one minute with a sampling rate of 2 RSS samples per second. Most statistical outlier detection methods, such as Grubbs, Chauvenet and three-sigma criterions, are based on the assumption that is data should follow Gaussian distribution. Because the RSS data of such amount from each AP are difficult to fit Gaussian distribution as shown in Fig. 1, we detect RSS outliers with quartile method that has no requirement for data distribution.

Assume that a total of K APs are deployed in an indoor environment and L RSS data from AP k denoted as $[r_1^{(k)}, r_2^{(k)}, \cdots, r_L^{(k)}]$, $k \in (1, 2, \cdots, K)$ are collected, then these collected RSS data are sorted in a non-descending order as $[r_{(1)}^{(k)} \leq r_{(2)}^{(k)} \leq \cdots \leq r_{(L)}^{(k)}]$, $k \in (1, 2, \cdots, K)$. We find the upper-quartile Q_{Up} and lower-quartile Q_{Low} of the sequence that split off the highest 25% and lowest 25% of data from the other ones, respectively. Then the inter-quartile range Q_{IQR} can be calculated by:

$$Q_{\mathrm{IQR}} = Q_{\mathrm{Up}} - Q_{\mathrm{Low}}. \tag{1}$$

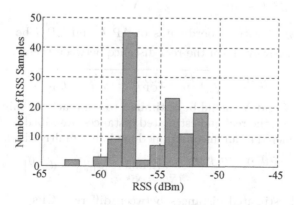

Fig. 1. Distribution of 120 RSS data at a crowdsourcing point.

With the inter-quartile range Q_{IQR} computed by (1), the boundaries for defining RSS outliers can be determined. If an RSS value $r_{(i)}^{(k)}$, $i \in (1, 2, \cdots, L)$ from AP k satisfies: $r_{(i)}^{(k)} < Q_{\mathrm{Low}} - 1.5 Q_{\mathrm{IQR}}$ or $r_{(i)}^{(k)} > Q_{\mathrm{Up}} + 1.5 Q_{\mathrm{IQR}}$, then it is recognized as an RSS outlier.

Compared with other RSS outlier detection methods, this quartile method does not require RSS data distribution information and has a low computation complexity. Also, RSS outliers have less influence on quartile calculation.

2.2 Propagation Model Optimization with Crowdsourcing Data

In our indoor office environment, we model the radio path loss between a user and AP with site-general model [10], which is given by:

$$P_{\mathrm{L}} = 20 \log_{10} f + N \log_{10} d + P_f(n) - 28, \tag{2}$$

where P_{L} is the path loss in dB; f is the frequency in MHz; d is the distance between a user and AP in meters ($d > 1$ m); $P_f(n)$ is the floor penetration loss factor in dB; n is the number of floors between a user and AP; N is the distance power loss coefficient, which equals 30 at 2.4 GHz in office environments.

Because all the APs we utilize are deployed on the same floor as our experimental area, we remove $P_f(n)$ from (2). Let $P_{\mathrm{T}}^{(k,j)}$ and $P_{\mathrm{R}}^{(k,j)}$ be transmission power of AP k and received power measured by a crowdsourcing participant's mobile device at CP j, respectively. Then we rewrite (2) as:

$$P_{\mathrm{T}}^{(k,j)} - P_{\mathrm{R}}^{(k,j)} = 20 \log_{10} f + N^{(k,j)} \log_{10} d^{(k,j)} - X^{(k,j)}, \tag{3}$$

where $X^{(k,j)}$ and $N^{(k,j)}$ are the PM parameters we need to optimize. $P_{\mathrm{T}}^{(k,j)}$ and $P_{\mathrm{R}}^{(k,j)}$ in dBm can be derived from AP configuration and RSS data, respectively. The distance between the crowdsourcing participant at CP j and AP k can be calculated by:

$$d^{(k,j)} = 10^{\dfrac{P_{\mathrm{T}}^{(k,j)} - P_{\mathrm{R}}^{(k,j)} - 20 \log_{10} f + X^{(k,j)}}{N^{(k,j)}}}. \tag{4}$$

Let the known location coordinates of AP k and CP j be $(x_{\mathrm{AP}}^{(k)}, y_{\mathrm{AP}}^{(k)})$ and $(x_{\mathrm{CP}}^{(j)}, y_{\mathrm{CP}}^{(j)})$, respectively. Then the real distance between them is calculated by:

$$d_{\mathrm{Real}}^{(k,j)} = \sqrt{(x_{\mathrm{AP}}^{(k)} - x_{\mathrm{CP}}^{(j)})^2 + (y_{\mathrm{AP}}^{(k)} - y_{\mathrm{CP}}^{(j)})^2}. \tag{5}$$

Parameters X and N should be optimized to approach the minimum value of differences between the real and estimated distances described by (6). The problem can be considered as an unconstrained nonlinear multivariable optimization.

$$(\widehat{X}^{(k,j)}, \widehat{N}^{(k,j)}) = \operatorname*{arg\,min}_{(\widehat{X}^{(k,j)}, \widehat{N}^{(k,j)})} \left| d_{\mathrm{Real}}^{(k,j)} - d^{(k,j)} \right|. \tag{6}$$

All real and estimated distances between different CPs and APs are used for optimizing the two PM parameters. Then mean values $\widehat{X}$ and $\widehat{N}$ of the two optimized parameters are calculated, respectively.

2.3   Coordinate Correction with Crowdsourcing Data

Because location coordinates of CPs are known, if a distance between a user and the nearest CP is estimated, then the distance can be used to correct the user's localization coordinates. Assume that J CPs are selected and CP j is the nearest to a user who is at location i, as shown in Fig. 2. Let $P_R^{(1,i)}$ and $P_R^{(1,j)}$ be the received powers from AP 1 measured at location i and CP j, respectively. Then the received power $P_R^{(1,i)}$ can be written as:

$$P_R^{(1,i)} = P_T^{(1,i)} - 20\log_{10}f - \bar{\hat{N}}\log_{10}d^{(1,i)} + \bar{\hat{X}}. \tag{7}$$

Using the similar equation for $P_R^{(1,j)}$, we can have:

$$P_R^{(1,j)} - P_R^{(1,i)} = \bar{\hat{N}}\log_{10}\frac{d^{(1,i)}}{d^{(1,j)}}. \tag{8}$$

As shown in Fig. 2, the distance $d^{(i,j)}$ between location i and CP j should not be less than $|d^{(1,i)} - d^{(1,j)}|$ given by:

$$d^{(i,j)} \geq |d^{(1,i)} - d^{(1,j)}| = \left|10^{\frac{P_R^{(1,j)} - P_R^{(1,i)}}{\bar{\hat{N}}}} - 1\right|d^{(1,j)}. \tag{9}$$

When RSS samples from K APs are measured, (9) is applicable to all the K APs and the real distance $d_{\text{Real}}^{(k,j)}$ between AP k and CP j is calculated with their coordinates, so we conclude that:

$$d^{(i,j)} \simeq \max_{k\in(1,2,\cdots,K)}\left|10^{\frac{P_R^{(k,j)} - P_R^{(k,i)}}{\bar{\hat{N}}}} - 1\right|d_{\text{Real}}^{(k,j)}. \tag{10}$$

Even though the PM is optimized, due to variations of radio propagation environment, sometimes a localization result calculated by trilateration localization may deviate from its real location greatly. The estimated distance $d^{(i,j)}$ can be used as a restrictive condition to correct the localization result.

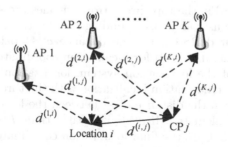

Fig. 2. Distance estimation between a user and crowdsourcing point.

3   Proposed Localization System

As shown in Fig. 3, our proposed crowdsourcing-based PM localization system is divided into three parts: data preparation, distance estimation and localization.

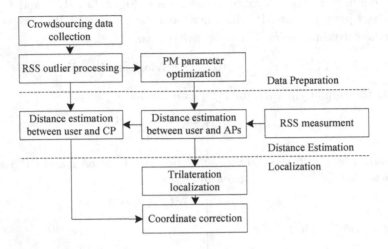

Fig. 3. Frame of the proposed localization system.

In the data preparation part, after L RSS samples from K APs are collected by a crowdsourcing participant at CP j. With the location coordinates of CP j that can be labeled on the ground, the collected RSS samples are merged with the coordinates of CP j as $\left[r_1^{(j)}, r_2^{(j)}, \cdots, r_L^{(j)}, x_{\mathrm{CP}}^{(j)}, y_{\mathrm{CP}}^{(j)} \right]$, $j \in (1, 2, \cdots, J)$. Then L RSS data from AP k, $k \in (1, 2, \cdots, K)$ are examined with quartile method in order to eliminate RSS outliers. The recognized outliers are replaced by the mean values of normal data that have already been examined. Due to RSS data from only three APs are used by trilateration localization, we select the top three strongest crowdsourcing RSS data for optimizing the PM parameters. Then mean values $\widehat{X}$ and $\widehat{N}$ of the two optimized parameters are calculated.

Regarding distance estimation, when a user at location i measures K RSS data from all the K APs, the top three strongest ones are selected to estimate distances between the user and corresponding APs for trilateration localization. Also with the measured RSS data, the distance $d^{(i,j)}$ between the user and nearest CP j is estimated by (10) for localization coordinate correction.

In the last part of the localization system, localization coordinates $(\widehat{x}_i, \widehat{y}_i)$ are first calculated by trilateration localization with the three distances between the user and APs. Then the distance $\widehat{d}^{(i,j)}$ between the localization coordinates $(\widehat{x}_i, \widehat{y}_i)$ and CP j is calculated. If $\widehat{d}^{(i,j)}$ is greater than $d^{(i,j)}$, then $(\widehat{x}_i, \widehat{y}_i)$ are corrected to $(\widehat{x}_i', \widehat{y}_i')$ that are the final localization coordinates by:

$$\begin{cases} \hat{x}_i' = \left(\hat{x}_i - x_{CP}^{(j)}\right) d^{(k,j)} \Big/ \hat{d}^{(k,j)} + x_{CP}^{(j)} \\ \hat{y}_i' = \left(\hat{y}_i - y_{CP}^{(j)}\right) d^{(k,j)} \Big/ \hat{d}^{(k,j)} + y_{CP}^{(j)} \end{cases}. \tag{11}$$

4   Experimental Results and Analyses

4.1   Experimental Setup

Our experimental area is on an office floor with 9 Linksys WAP54G APs deployed. As shown in Fig. 4, the experimental area is a rectangular area of $24.9\,\text{m} \times 28.0\,\text{m}$ and 4 APs are in the area. The area contains office rooms and a corridor that are two kinds of typical experimental environments for indoor localization. Because office rooms were not free to enter sometimes, we only selected 7 CPs in the corridor marked with blue points in Fig. 4. We selected CPs near the entrances of the floor, where it was convenient for crowdsourcing participants to collect data when they entered, and also at the corners of the corridor where radio propagation was more complicate due to multipath effect. We used a laptop to collect RSS samples for one minute at each CP with a sampling rate of 2 RSS samples per second. A total of 6500 RSS samples were collected in the shadow area for testing the proposed PM system. For performance comparison, a fingerprinting localization system was also performed in the experimental area. A total of 91 specific locations were selected and 300 RSS samples were measured at each selected location for radio-map establishment. The fingerprinting localization system was tested with the same 6500 RSS samples as PM localization.

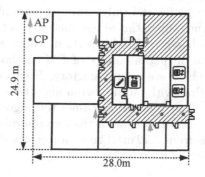

Fig. 4. Experimental area plan.

4.2   Results of RSS Outlier Processing

When we examine crowdsourcing RSS data with quartile method, the RSS outliers that are very different from the other data of the same AP are replaced by the mean values of the examined normal RSS data. Figure 5 shows the differences between original crowdsourcing RSS data and the processed ones from the

same AP at one CP. The processed RSS data vary more smoothly after eliminating the RSS outliers. Meanwhile, RSS data from some APs may quite weak
and these APs even cannot be sensed sometimes. Although our system exploits
the top three strongest RSS data for trilateration localization and these APs
have no influence on our system performance, the quartile method is also able
to recognize these weak RSS data and eliminate them.

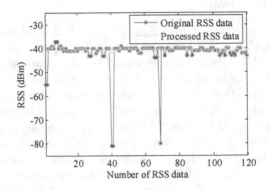

Fig. 5. Original and processed RSS data.

4.3   Localization Results with Optimized Propagation Models

We optimize PM parameters with processed crowdsourcing data and then compare performances of PM method with different optimized parameters. At first,
we set parameter X to be 28 and only optimize parameter N as well as set
parameter N to be 30 and only optimize parameter X both using single-variable
optimization algorithm based on golden section search and parabolic interpolation. But the localization performances of PM method with the optimized
parameters mentioned above are not satisfactory. Then we optimize parameters
X and N at the same time with quasi-newton algorithm [11]. The starting values of the parameters X and N for quasi-newton algorithm are set equal to
28 and 30, respectively. Mean error with the two optimized parameters X and
N is reduced to 5.05 m from 7.12 m. The mean errors and corresponding PM
parameters X and N are listed in Table 1.

Table 1. Mean errors of propagation model localization with different parameters

X	N	Mean error (m)
28	30	7.12
28	30.46	6.58
27.67	30	6.85
25.86	30.91	5.05

4.4   Coordinate Correction with Estimated Distance Between a User and Crowdsourcing Point

To improve localization performance, we take advantage of CP data to correct localization results of optimized PM. In theory, the distance $d^{(i,j)}$ in (9) should be equal to the maximum one among all the distances $\left| d^{(k,i)} - d^{(k,j)} \right|$, $k \in (1, 2, \cdots, K)$. However, in practical application, radio propagation may vary significantly, so the maximum distance may be too large to correct localization coordinates. Thus, we eliminate distance outliers also with quartile method and take the median distance as $d^{(i,j)}$ to correct coordinates [12]. The mean error of optimized PM localization with coordinate correction are 3.78 m and its cumulative probabilities within 2 m and 3 m localization errors are 38.12% and 60.43%, respectively. As shown in Fig. 6, after correcting coordinates, the proposed system outperforms the others that also use PM method. By contrast, mean errors of fingerprinting algorithms KNN, WKNN and ANN are 2.77 mm, 2.74 mm and 2.55 mm, respectively. Although the performances of these fingerprinting algorithms are a little better than our proposed system, a total of $91 \times 300 = 27300$ RSS samples are collected to establish the radio-map, which is difficult in practical application. Our proposed system is able to achieve a comparable performance with the crowdsourcing data collected at only 7 CPs. Furthermore, 120 RSS samples at each CP can be easily collected in one minute.

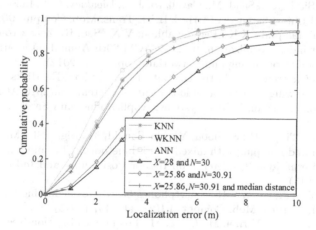

Fig. 6. Cumulative probability of localization errors.

5   Conclusion

In this paper, a crowdsourcing-based indoor PM localization system using Wi-Fi is proposed. Compared with traditional PM and fingerprinting localization systems, the proposed system has a greatly improved localization performance without intensive labor for data collection. The system makes use of RSS samples and location information of only a few CPs, which can be easily collected by crowdsourcing participants. RSS outliers in crowdsourcing data are first eliminated and the processed data are used for optimizing PM parameters. So the performance of trilateration localization for a user is improved. Then an estimated distance between the user and nearest CP is calculated and the localization results of trilateration localization can be corrected with the estimated distance. Experimental results confirm the effectiveness of our proposed crowdsourcing-based indoor PM localization system and that the system is able to achieve a comparable performance with easily collected crowdsourcing data.

Acknowledgment. The authors gratefully thank the referees for the constructive and insightful comments. This work was supported by the Natural Science Foundation of the Jiangsu Higher Education Institutions of China under Grant No. 16KJB510014 and partially by the Cooperative Innovation Foundation of Jiangsu Province Prospective Joint Research Project under Grant No. BY2014126-02.

References

1. Liu, H., Darabi, H., Banerjee, P., Liu, J.: Survey of wireless indoor positioning techniques and systems. IEEE Trans. Syst. Man Cybern. **37**(6), 1067–1080 (2007)
2. He, S.N., Chan, S.H.: Wi-Fi fingerprint-based indoor positioning: recent advances and comparisons. IEEE Commun. Surv. Tutor. **18**(1), 466–490 (2016)
3. Sun, Y.L., Xu, Y.B.: Error estimation method for matrix correlation-based Wi-Fi indoor localization. KSII Trans. Internet Inf. Syst. **7**(11), 2657–2675 (2013)
4. Makki, A., Siddig, A., Saad, M., Cavallaro, J.R., Bleakley, C.J.: Indoor localization using 802.11 time differences of arrival. IEEE Trans. Mob. Comput. **99**, 1–10 (2015)
5. Rai, A., Chintalapudi, K.K., Padmanabhan, V.N., Sen, R.: Zee: zero-effort crowdsourcing for indoor localization. In: 2012 ACM 20th Annual International Conference on Mobile Computing and Networking, pp. 1–12 (2012)
6. Park, J.G., Charrow, B., Curtis, D., Battat, J., Minkov, E., Hicks, J., Teller, S., Ledlie, J.: Growing an organic indoor location system. In: 2010 ACM 8th International Conference on Mobile Systems, Applications, and Services, pp. 271–284 (2010)
7. Mirowski, P., Tin, K.H., Saehoon, Y., Macdonald, M.: SignalSLAM: simultaneous localization and mapping with mixed WiFi, bluetooth, LTE and magnetic signals. In: 2013 International Conference on Indoor Positioning and Indoor Navigation, pp. 1–10 (2013)
8. Wu, C.S., Yang, Z., Liu, Y.H.: Smartphones based crowdsourcing for indoor localization. IEEE Trans. Mob. Comput. **14**(2), 444–457 (2015)
9. Yang, S., Dessai, P., Verma, M., Gerla, M.: FreeLoc: calibration-free crowdsourced indoor localization. In: 2013 IEEE International Conference on Computer Communications, pp. 2481–2489 (2013)
10. Rao, T.R., Balachander, D.: RF propagation investigations at 915/2400 MHz in indoor corridor environments for wireless sensor communications. Prog. Electromagnet. Res. B **47**, 359–381 (2013)
11. Aderibigbe, F.M., Adebayo, K.J., Dele-Rotimi, A.O.: On quasi-newton method for solving unconstrained optimization problems. Am. J. Appl. Math. **3**(2), 47–50 (2015)
12. Pourahmadi, V., Valaee, S.: Indoor positioning and distance-aware graph-based semi-supervised learning method. In: IEEE 2012 Global Telecommunications Conference, pp. 315–320 (2012)

Retraction Note to: On the Minimum the Sum-of-Squares Indicator of a Balanced Boolean Function

Yu Zhou and Zepeng Zhuo

Retraction Note to:
Chapter "On the Minimum the Sum-of-Squares Indicator of a Balanced Boolean Function" in: Q. Chen et al. (Eds.): *Communications and Networking*, LNICST 210, https://doi.org/10.1007/978-3-319-66628-0_30

The authors are retracting this article [1] because following its publication a number of errors affecting the validity of the results have come to light. Specifically

1) The result of **Theorem 1** is error. See Page 317.

2) The analysis of **Remark 1** is not correct, we cannot obtain the following fact: See Page 320 in Remark 1.

"It is because $wt(f_1 f_2) = 2^{n-3}$ or $2^{n-3} - 1$. It implies that $wt(f_1) > = 2^{n-3} - 1$ and $wt(f_2) > = 2^{n-3} - 1$". This fact is error, Thus Corollary 1 is not correct.

3) The result of **Corollary 1** is error. See Page 320.

[1] https://doi.org/10.1007/978-3-319-66628-0_30

All authors agree to this retraction.

The retracted version of this chapter can be found at
https://doi.org/10.1007/978-3-319-66628-0_30

© ICST Institute for Computer Sciences, Social Informatics and Telecommunications Engineering 2020
Q. Chen et al. (Eds.): ChinaCom 2016, Part II, LNICST 210, p. C1, 2020.
https://doi.org/10.1007/978-3-319-66628-0_57

Author Index